VIETNAM

An American Ordeal

FIFTH EDITION

George Donelson Moss

PEARSON

Prentice
Hall

Upper Saddle River, New Jersey 07458

Library of Congress Cataloging-in-Publication Data

Moss, George, 1935-
   Vietnam, an American ordeal / George Donelson Moss.-- 5th ed.
      p. cm.
   Includes bibliographical references and index.
   ISBN 0-13-192588-1 (alk. paper)
   1. Vietnamese Conflict, 1961-1975.   2. Vietnam--History--1945-1975.
3. Vietnam--Relations--United States. 4. United States--Relations--United States.
I. Title.
   DS557.7.M66 2005
   959.704'3373--dc22

                                       2005013266

VP, Editorial Director: Charlyce Jones Owen
Editorial Assistant: Maureen Diana
Director of Marketing: Heather Shelstad
Marketing Assistant: Cherron Gardner
Managing Editor: Joanne Riker
Production Liaison: Randy Pettit
Manufacturing Buyer: Ben Smith
Art Director and Cover Design: Jayne Conte
Cover Illustration/Photo: U.S. troops engaged in combat. Firefights between small units
   erupted suddenly and were fierce while they lasted. Photo courtesy of U.S. Army.
Director, Image Resource Center: Melinda Reo
Manager, Rights and Permissions: Zina Arabia
Manager, Visual Research: Beth Brenzel
Manager, Cover Visual Research & Permissions: Karen Sanatar
Composition/Full-Service Project Management: Pine Tree Composition, Linda Duarte
Printer/Binder: R. R. Donnelley & Sons

Pearson Prentice Hall™ is a trademark of Pearson Education, Inc.
Pearson® is a registered trademark of Pearson plc
Prentice Hall® is a registered trademark of Pearson Education, Inc.

Pearson Education LTD.   Pearson Education Australia PTY, Limited
Pearson Education Singapore, Pte. Ltd   Pearson Education North Asia Ltd
Pearson Education, Canada, Ltd   Pearson Educación de Mexico, S.A. de C.V.
Pearson Education–Japan   Pearson Education Malaysia, Pte. Ltd

10 9 8 7 6 5 4 3
0-13-192588-1

*For the young Americans who fought the
Vietnam War and for those who opposed it.
They are heroes and victims all.*

Contents

BIBLIOGRAPHY   469

INDEX   503

Preface: The War That Won't Go Away

It was more than thirty years ago that the fall of Saigon brutally terminated America's mission to create a democratic nation state in southern Vietnam that could block the further expansion of Communism into Southeast Asia. But the U.S. Vietnam War will not retreat into the misty realms of forgotten or only dimly remembered history. Vivid memories of that long-ago war continue to preoccupy millions of Americans.

At times the 2004 presidential election appeared to be more about Vietnam than about the ongoing war in Iraq and the global war against terror. Senator John Kerry, the Democratic Party's candidate for the presidency, validated his bid to unseat a wartime president by parading his heroic military service performed during the Vietnam War. Navy Lieutenant Kerry was awarded a Bronze Star and a Silver Star for his valorous actions. Additionally, he was awarded three purple hearts for wounds suffered in combat.

His supporters contrasted Kerry's military service record with President George W. Bush's actions during the Vietnam War. They charged that Bush took advantage of his family's political connections to land a coveted billet in the Texas Air National Guard, thereby avoiding a possible tour of duty in Vietnam. Investigative journalists found documentary evidence indicating that Lieutenant Bush did not meet all of his obligations while serving in the National Guard.

Critics of the U.S. war in Iraq have revived painful memories from the Vietnam War era. Senator Ted Kennedy exclaimed, "Iraq is George Bush's Vietnam!" His senate colleague, John McCain, another decorated Vietnam War hero, who spent five and one-half years as a prisoner of war (POW), rebutted Kennedy's accusation by pointing out, "Iraq is no Vietnam," adding, "And I know something about Vietnam."

The most powerful way memories of Vietnam have influenced American attitudes about the Iraq war and the troubled occupation that followed the war has been the fear that Iraq might become another Vietnam-like quagmire. The United States-led coalition will not provide enough troops to suppress the insurgents, stabilize the country under a democratic government, and devise an exit strategy that will allow all the soldiers to return to their homelands.

In our time, Vietnam remains a metaphor haunting the American imagination. It serves as a cautionary tale of the catastrophe that awaits a nation, however rich and powerful, that ever again allows its crusading idealism to override its realistic sense of limits. Indeed, the lingering resentments, regrets, bitterness, rage, and grief, may, as historian Robert Schulzinger has suggested, not disappear until the last public official involved with setting Vietnam policy, the last Vietnam combat veteran, and the last antiwar protester have died.

When the combined North Vietnamese and VietCong forces overthrew the last South Vietnamese government at the end of April 1975 and one year later unified the country under the control of the Vietnamese Communist Party, it was undeniably obvious that the American mission to build a democratic nation state in southern Vietnam had failed. Within the United States, a curious calm set in. No one wanted to think about or talk about Vietnam for years, much less argue about it. Then, as the seventies were ending, there began a revival of interest in all issues connected to the Vietnam War. Journalists who had covered the Vietnam beat, civilian and military officials involved with making and implementing policy during the Vietnam era, and concerned scholars from various disciplines began meeting in conferences held around the country to examine the Vietnam War. Books about Vietnam poured from the academic and mainstream presses. Hollywood discovered Vietnam and a rash of generally excellent films made their appearance in movie theaters around the country. The major television networks, led by CBS, produced fine documentaries about the Vietnam War. Popular TV programs flourished. *M*A*S*H**, ostensibly about the Korean War, was a long-running implicit indictment of the brutality of the Vietnam War.

Remembering and reliving the Vietnam War became something of a national obsession during the early and mid-1980s. It was within the context of this intense revived concern with Vietnam that I, a former naval aviator who had become a historian, and one of those engaged scholars caught up in the ongoing 1980s national conversation about Vietnam, conceived the project that eventuated in the publication of *Vietnam: An American Ordeal* in 1989.

I wanted to write a book that answered the two big questions everyone who has ever thought about the Vietnam War, even for a moment, inevitably asks:

1. Why? Why Vietnam? Why did the United States ever become involved in the affairs of this small, comparatively insignificant nation with which Americans had no history of relations? Why did the United States fight the longest war in its national history in a country that, prior to 1950, most Americans had never heard of nor could they find on a map?

2. Why did the United States and its allies in Southeast Asia lose America's longest war? How was it possible that the United States, the world's richest and most powerful nation state, which fielded the best-educated, best-trained, best-supported, and best-armed military forces any nation has ever sent to war, could lose a war to a small, poor Third World country?

While doing research for the book, I gradually came to understand that before I could fully answer question 2, another question had to be addressed. Why did the surprise Communist Tet-68 offensive, which was a strategic disaster for the VietCong (it left their main force units decimated and their infrastructure in tatters) become the turning point of the war? Why was Tet-68 such a psychological, and thus a crushing, political defeat for the United States, after which a U.S. victory in Vietnam was not a realistic possibility? I have done extensive research in all the available sources, thought hard about this matter, and I believe that I have provided a solid, admittedly somewhat complex answer to the great paradox of the U.S. Vietnam War. How could the decisive military victory that the United States and its South Vietnamese allies gained during Tet-68, which resulted in a virtual wipeout of the VietCong armies, turn out to be a decisive political victory for the North Vietnamese and the VietCong revolutionaries? This victory pointed toward their ultimately winning the war.

Chapter 3, *An Experiment in Nation Building,* Chapter 4, *Raising the Stakes,* and Chapter 5, *America Goes to War,* together provide an answer to the first big question: Why did the United States go to war in Vietnam? Chapter 5 is the key chapter. During the summer of 1965, President Lyndon Johnson had to confront a crisis in South Vietnam: the impending defeat of South Vietnam's military forces and the probable collapse of its government. Johnson, after consultations with his senior civilian and military advisers, made a series of fateful decisions, which Americanized what had previously been a civil war between Vietnamese factions. In August and September 1965, thousands of American ground combat forces found themselves fighting in the jungles and rice paddies of South Vietnam, while simultaneously U.S. Naval and Air Force bombers waged an air war against North Vietnam.

Chapter 7, *Year of the Monkey,* tells the paradoxical story of Tet-68; that is, how the most decisive U.S. military victory of the entire war turned out to be the beginning of the end of the American mission in Vietnam. It makes for fascinating history. If the story proves anything, it proves only that powerful historical forces often outstrip human capacities to control them or even understand them. It also provides a classic example of the law of unintended consequences on full display.

Chapter 8, *A War to End a War,* and Chapter 9, *End of the Tunnel,* provide an answer to the hardest question: Why did the United States lose its longest war? At its outset, the war looked like an obvious mismatch—a mighty superpower taking on a nation that President Johnson characterized as a "4th-rate raggedy-ass" power. U.S. military commanders confidently expected it be a short war that would end relatively quickly with the inevitable American victory.

Seven and one-half years later, Americans sorrowfully acknowledged that they had fought a war that they could not win. See the section in Chapter 9, *Why We Lost and Why They Won,* in which I address those issues. I also suggest that a more useful perspective involves not merely focusing on why the United States and its allies lost, but also focusing on why the North Vietnamese and the VietCong ultimately prevailed. We need to look at their strategies, their political operations, their diplomacy, and, above all, their vision and determination in order to fully understand the outcome of that long, desperate conflict.

I, of course, was delighted when Prentice Hall thought enough of the book to publish it, and I was also quite pleased to discover that there was a receptive audience. But it did not occur to me at the time that the book might still be in print 15 years later, still be finding an audience, and that I would be asked to do a fourth revision. But I am happy to have the opportunity to prepare this fifth edition. Each chapter has been carefully reworked, and in many instances extensively revised.

Chapter 9, *End of the Tunnel,* has been rewritten and restructured. In previous editions of the book, I traced U.S.-Vietnam relations in the post-1975 period. I focused on the issues that divided the two nations and prevented them from normalizing relations. For this edition, I have ended the story in 1975, with the overthrow of the last South Vietnamese government and the disappearance of South Vietnam from history. I have expanded and deepened my analysis of *Why We Lost and Why They Won.* In the section of Chapter 9 entitled *The Wounds Within,* I have expanded my treatment of the myriad of mostly negative impacts the Vietnam War had on American institutions, on American culture, and on the American people.

Because the United States is at war at this writing (fall, 2004), I have added a new concluding section to Chapter 9, *Vietnam and Iraq: Analogies At War.* Most historians are wary of analogies—they are generally superficial, incomplete, and reductive. Analogies are as likely to distort historical events as they are to illuminate them. Political leaders and partisan writers often use historical analogies either to support or to attack contemporary diplomatic and strategic policies.

In the case of the Iraq War and the occupation that succeeded it, critics of the Bush administration's war policies and unilateralist diplomacy have raised the specter of Vietnam in an effort to discredit them and drive away popular support. But I show that if used carefully and with restraint, analogies can be helpful and can provide perspective and detachment that is often lacking in the sound and fury of contemporary debates over crucial issues.

Acknowledgments

The greatest satisfactions of scholarship derive from the collective nature of the enterprise. As an industrious member of that small army of scholars working assiduously to discover, write, and disseminate the history of the American Vietnam intervention, I want to thank all of you who have helped with this fourth revision.

Many scholars have read all or part of the book at one time or another. They have been both generous in their praise and helpful with their constructive criticisms. To mention a few: Jesse J. Hodges, Montgomery County Community College; Xiao-Bing Li, University of Central Oklahoma; Ken La Fountaine, Shoreline Community College; Jeffrey Kimball, Miami University, Oxford, Ohio; Jack Colldeweih, Fairleigh Dickinson University; the late Stephen Ambrose, formerly at New Orleans University; the late Robin Winks, formerly at Yale University; the late George Mct. Kahin, formerly at Cornell University; Michael Schudson, University of California, San Diego; Daniel Hallin, University of California, San Diego; Diane Shaver Clemens, University of California, Berkeley; David Hollinger, University of California, Berkeley; the late Douglas Pike, formerly Director of the Vietnam Archive; Ronald Walters, The Johns Hopkins University; Lawrence Lichty, Northwestern University; and Larry Berman, University of California, Davis. To all of you, I once again say many thanks for your invaluable help.

I also want to express my deep gratitude to so many other people whose efforts made this book much better than it otherwise would be—former colleagues from VAW-11 and VAW-13 with whom it was my great honor and privilege to serve, former students and research assistants whose hard work contributed much to the project, and all of the Vietnam veterans with whom I spent many evenings listening to their war stories

I also want to express my heartfelt gratitude and deep appreciation to Charles Cavaliere, my principal editor at Prentice Hall who decided to bring out another edition of the book. Charles, I appreciate the phone calls, the e-mails, the sound advice, the support, and the encouragement.

Thanks to the production editor, Linda Duarte, and Teri Stratford, the photo researcher extraordinaire. Thanks to the readers who subjected the entire book to searching critiques and made many suggestions for revising. It is a far better book as a result of their Herculean labors, and I am immensely grateful for their help.

And my last and best thanks to the lovely Linda, who, failing to read the fine print inserted into our marriage vows, has nevertheless adapted graciously to life with an obsessive scribbler. Please remember, dear heart: They also serve who only sit in front of the great white bull of a word processor and type, type, type.

CHAPTER 1

A Place and a People

We must weaken [the enemy] by drawing him into protracted campaigns. When the enemy is away from home for a long time and produces no victories and families learn of their dead, then the enemy population becomes dissatisfied and considers it a Mandate from Heaven that their armies be recalled. Time is always in our favor. Our climate, mountains, and jungles discourage the enemy; but for us they offer sanctuary and a place from which to attack.

Tran Hung Dao, 1284

THE LAND

The Vietnamese say that their country resembles two baskets borne on the ends of a peasant's bamboo carrying pole. The baskets constitute two of the world's most densely populated rice-growing regions: to the north, the Red River Delta, and to the south, the Mekong River Delta. The pole represents the narrow and curving central part of the country composed of jungle-covered mountains and a fertile coastal strip. Vietnam's geographic area of 127,000 square miles makes it about the size of the state of New Mexico. When separated from northern Vietnam from 1954 to 1975, South Vietnam formed an elongated and sinuous country with a coastline as long as California's.

Most of Vietnam's 85 million (2005 estimate) people cluster in the two alluvial deltas formed by the Red and Mekong rivers and in small coastal enclaves lying between them. The people inhabiting these regions make up the 85 percent of the country's inhabitants who are ethnically Vietnamese. The sparsely populated mountainous regions north and west of the Red River delta and those of central Vietnam are home to a melange of ethnic minorities, representing about 15 percent of the country's people.

1

They comprise the people the French called *Montagnards* (mountain people), who inhabit the mountainous terrain that constitutes three-quarters of the country's landmass. In addition to the *Montagnards,* about 800,000 Cambodians reside in the Ca Mau peninsula region and 1 million ethnic Chinese live in Vietnam. In southern Vietnam, about 80 percent of the people live on one-fourth of the land; over 40 percent of the terrain is uninhabited. These unpopulated regions of South Vietnam, covered with jungle, elephant grass, and swamps, provided sanctuaries for the VietCong guerrillas and avenues for invading North Vietnamese forces during the war against the Americans.

Vietnam lies entirely within the tropical zone. Its northernmost point is the same latitude as Key West, Florida; its southernmost extremity is the same latitude as the Panama Canal. Its climate is determined by monsoon cycles. From November to April, the winter monsoon, coming off the cold, dry steppes of Central Asia, dominates. During these months, it does not rain much in Vietnam, and the climate is moderate throughout the northern half of the country. Between May and October, the summer monsoon blows in from the southwest, coming off the Indian Ocean and bringing with it high winds, heavy rains, and stifling heat and humidity. Vietnam's average annual rainfall is about six feet. The effects of the monsoons vary with the terrain. The Red River Delta enjoys a mild winter, and summertime temperatures rarely exceed 100 degrees. It is hot year-round in the Mekong River Delta. During the winter monsoon, it never rains in the south, but the summer monsoon brings torrential downpours. Some years it rains much more than the normal six feet, causing floods. Other years, far less than normal rainfall occurs, bringing droughts. Cycles of floods, drought, and famine have afflicted the Vietnamese people throughout their long history.

French troops, and later Americans fighting in Vietnam, encountered serious obstacles posed by the summer monsoon. The heat, humidity, rain, and mud exhausted and discouraged the young soldiers carrying 60-pound packs and struggling through elephant grass, jungle vines, and up mountainous terrain. The French and the Americans also discovered that they could not operate some of their sophisticated military equipment during the summer monsoon season. Highly mobile guerrilla forces often took advantage of the weather conditions to outmaneuver their Western enemies. Summer monsoons also meant special hazards for aviators. Pounding rains, dense ground fog, and treacherous winds caused many fatal aircraft accidents. French and American aviators faced some of the most hazardous weather conditions in the history of aerial warfare. Weather also determined the cycle of fighting for both the French and U.S. forces. The heaviest fighting in southern Vietnam occurred during the dry season, from February to June, with combat intensity usually falling off from October to January.

THE FORGE OF HISTORY

The origins of the Vietnamese people are shrouded in the misty realms of prehistory. Thousands of years ago, people from China to the north, Thailand to the west, and Indonesia to the south settled in the Red River valley. Over the centuries, they intermin-

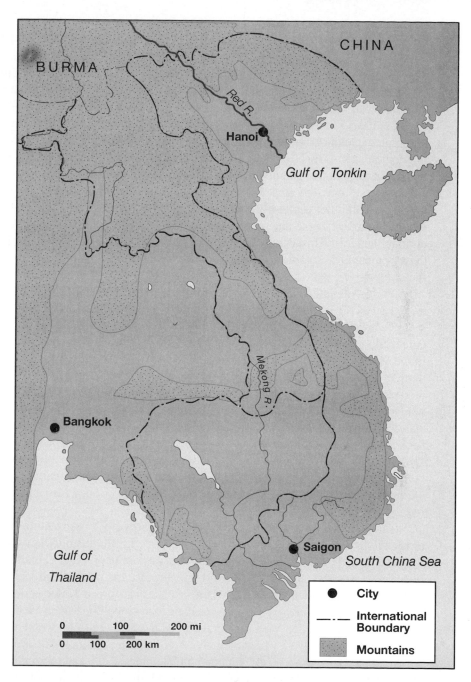

Figure 1.1 Physical geography of Vietnam and other countries of Southeast Asia.
Source: Public domain.

gled. From their ethnological and biological fusion emerged an ethnically and racially distinct population, the Viets. A Viet culture based on rice cultivation and feudal principles of social organization was well established by the second century BCE, when the Viets came into contact with their powerful neighbors to the north, the Chinese.[1]

Vietnamese history began in 208 BCE. On that date, recorded in Chinese annals, a Chinese war lord, Trieu Da, declared himself ruler of a large area encompassing southern China and Vietnam as far south as present-day Danang. This new addition was incorporated into the Chinese Empire as the province of Giao Chi. The informal name for this region was "Nam Viet," meaning "the land of the southern Viets." Trieu Da ruled his Vietnamese domains indirectly, content to leave Viet feudal lords in charge of local affairs. In 111 BCE, the great Han emperor, Wu-ti, conquered Nam Viet.[2] It became a province within the Chinese Empire and Chinese officials took over its governance. Wu-ti's conquest began an era of Chinese colonial domination of Vietnam that would last a millennium. This lengthy period of Chinese domination powerfully influenced the development of Vietnamese culture and the formation of a distinctive Vietnamese national identity.

For the next thousand years, the northern half of present-day Vietnam was controlled by the Chinese. During this long period of colonial rule, the Vietnamese adopted many features of Chinese culture. They incorporated Chinese technology into their socioeconomic system. The elite Vietnamese classes embraced Confucian social and political values. Chinese became the official language of Vietnam, and all writing was done in Chinese characters. The Vietnamese also adopted the Chinese mandarinate, a hierarchical administrative system based on mastery of Chinese literary and philosophic works. To become a mandarin, candidates had to devote years of study to the Chinese classics, then pass a series of rigorous examinations. Most mandarins came from elite backgrounds, because only the wealthy could afford to allow their sons the years of study and training required to pass the demanding tests. The Vietnamese mandarins incorporated many Chinese institutions into their evolving administrative system, including a centralized tax system and judicial hierarchy. They also adopted Chinese royal palace architectural styles.

Although the Vietnamese admired many features of Chinese culture and benefited in many ways from their long, close association with the magnificent Chinese civilization, they fiercely resented Chinese political domination and economic exploitation. They also resented Chinese efforts to Sinicize them and steadfastly refused to embrace a Chinese identity. In fact, Chinese efforts at forced Sinicization of the Vietnamese elite classes provoked the first of their many rebellions against Chinese rule. A rising, long-celebrated in Vietnamese history and led by two noblewomen, Trung Trac and her sister, Trung Nhi, occurred in 39 CE. The Trung sisters led an army that overwhelmed the Chinese garrisons stationed on Vietnamese soil and promptly proclaimed themselves queens of an independent Viet kingdom. Their rule was short-lived, however, for the emperor sent a strong army that restored Chinese rule in 42 CE.[3]

Over the subsequent centuries of Chinese overlordship, the Vietnamese upper classes embraced much of the Chinese culture based on Confucian principles. But the vast majority of Vietnamese, the 90 percent of the population constituting the peasantry, remained relatively unaffected by this process of Sinicization. They retained many of their traditional customs, a testament to the strength of their indigenous culture nurtured during their long pre-Chinese ethnic past as inhabitants of the Red River valley, the cradle of Vietnamese civilization.

There was one important Chinese cultural import enthusiastically embraced by the Vietnamese peasantry: the Buddhist religion. Originally founded by an Indian prince in the sixth century BCE, Buddhism reached the Vietnamese during the second century CE when Chinese Buddhist monks sought political asylum in the land of the Viets. Within a few centuries, Buddhism, particularly its Mahayana sect, had become a pervasive influence in the lives of the Vietnamese peasants. Mahayana Buddhism was a form of religion that stressed moral redemption through salvation and community spirit. Buddhist monks, living among the villagers, played prominent roles in community life.

Even though the Vietnamese elite were thoroughly Sinicized, they retained a strong sense of their Vietnamese identity and remained restive under Chinese rule. Between the sixth and tenth centuries, these Sino-Vietnamese notables led numerous rebellions against their Chinese masters. The Chinese suppressed them all. During most of this era of Chinese dominance, the empire was ruled by a mighty dynasty, the T'angs. Try as they might, Vietnamese nationalists could not rid themselves of Chinese control.

After the T'ang Dynasty fell in 907, a series of uprisings in Vietnam eventually ended Chinese dominion. The crucial battle occurred in 939. During that year, a Vietnamese army, led by Ngo Quyen, confronted a far larger Chinese invasion force, led by the heir to the Chinese throne, along a stretch of the Bach Dang River, a tidal waterway in the vicinity of present-day Haiphong. Knowing his troops were overmatched, Ngo resorted to a clever stratagem to defeat the more powerful Chinese. He had his troops drive pilings into the riverbed so at high tide the stakes would lie just below the water's surface, hidden from sight. Ngo then engaged the Chinese in battle and ordered his boats to feign retreat. The Chinese, sensing victory, pressed after Ngo's retreating ships, passing over the undetected pilings. He waited until the tide began to ebb. Timing the maneuver perfectly, Ngo ordered his ships to wheel about, and they drove the Chinese boats against the now-exposed pilings. With their ships impaled, the immobilized Chinese troops were slaughtered by Ngo's warriors. The imperial heir was taken prisoner and later beheaded.[4] The Battle of Bach Dang, which destroyed Chinese colonialism in Vietnam, is commemorated by all Vietnamese as the beginning of Vietnamese national independence.

After gaining their independence in 939, the Vietnamese endured a precarious national existence. They were threatened externally by powerful foes, particularly China, the colossus to the north. Internally, Vietnam was frequently ruled by inept leaders and riven by civil wars. But the Vietnamese managed to maintain their independence for over

900 years. They twice fought off Chinese invading armies in the thirteenth century and thereafter stayed free of foreign rule, except for a brief period during the fifteenth century when the Chinese, taking advantage of Vietnamese disunity, reestablished a colonial regime of brief duration.

For centuries, it remained a constant of Vietnamese statecraft to be aware of the colossus to the north, to guard against Chinese intrusions upon their sovereign independence.[5] In modern times, this theme of Vietnamese independence from foreign conquerors reasserted itself following the defeat of the French in 1954 and again following the withdrawal of the Americans in 1973. In Hanoi's Historical Museum today, a large room is devoted to celebrating the struggles of the Vietnamese people against Chinese invaders.[6]

Until the fifteenth century, Vietnamese expansion south of the 16th Parallel was blocked by the kingdom of the Chams, a people of Indonesian origin. The Vietnamese eventually destroyed the Champa kingdom, and under the leadership of Emperor Le Loi, whose reign began in 1427, they began to march south. Advancing colonies of Vietnamese peasant-warriors reached the Mekong Delta region in the early seventeenth century, about the same time that British colonists established settlements along the Atlantic seaboard of the United States.

By 1757, Vietnam had attained its current geographic size. As the Vietnamese consolidated their geographic gains in the Mekong Delta, they either slaughtered or pushed the indigenous population they encountered, the Khmer, who were ethnic Cambodians, up the river into present-day Cambodia. Vietnamese peasants made formidable warriors. The hard life of rice farming prepared them for the physical rigors of military combat. The group discipline of communal rice farming prepared them for the discipline and esprit de corps of battle. Peasant warriors were tenacious and resourceful in combat, and they were motivated by the high value that traditional Vietnamese culture placed on bravery and victory in war.

History, geography, and economics combined to ensure that the two major regions of Vietnam evolved differently. Life was typically easier and slower paced in southern Vietnam than in the north. The Mekong River flowed gently and predictably. It flooded in July and again in September, providing rich alluvial soil for abundant rice crops. Ample amounts of arable land were available for enterprising farmers, many of whom became large landholders and established prosperous families. The relative recency of settlement in southern Vietnam created a more rural society, with more individualistic and materialistic personality types than could be found in the older, poorer, and more densely populated region of northern Vietnam. Crop yields were lower in Tonkin, and rice had to be imported from the South, the breadbasket of Vietnam. The land was generally less fertile in northern Vietnam and landholdings tended to be smaller. There was also a more sophisticated level of political and economic organization and a much stronger sense of community among the inhabitants of Tonkin. Northerners tended to be more aggressive, sophisticated, and urbane than their country cousins to the south.

Political disunity hampered Vietnamese expansionism during the seventeenth and eighteenth centuries. During this period, Vietnam was ruled by separate, hostile governments, one located in the traditional capital of Hanoi, the other in a new city lying 400 miles to its south, Hue. Their armies clashed repeatedly, but neither was able to prevail over the other. With much of its energy absorbed in fighting the Hanoi regime, the Hue government was still developing the relatively underpopulated southern frontier region of the Mekong Delta in the late eighteenth century.

From 1771 until 1802, peasant rebellions led by three brothers named Tay-son convulsed Vietnam. Taking advantage of the internal disarray, Chinese armies once again invaded the land of the Viets. The Tay-sons rallied the Vietnamese people to drive the invaders out of their country in 1789. But the Tay-sons, their resources depleted by their battles against the Chinese, were overthrown as the eighteenth century ended.

Nguyen Anh emerged in 1802 as the ruler of all Vietnamese. For the first time in its history, a single ruler governed the region extending from the Chinese border in the north to the Gulf of Siam in the south, the boundaries of the modern Vietnamese state. Nguyen Anh proclaimed himself emperor, made Hue his imperial capital, and called his politically unified nation Vietnam.[7] He took the name Gia Long, founding the last Vietnamese imperial dynasty, the Nguyen. Nguyen emperors were reduced to ruling in name only after 1883 because of the French conquest of Vietnam.

The advent of the Nguyen Dynasty ushered in an era of political stability and national unity that lasted until the French colonial conquest. It also signaled the attainment of a unique Vietnamese identity. Centuries-long struggles to resist foreign conquerors and internal divisions "had created in Vietnam a distinctly 'national' ethnic spirit, more self-conscious, and more passionate than that found virtually anywhere in Southeast Asia."[8]

Vietnam's turbulent history, characterized by the use of military force to fend off foreign aggression, overcome internal factionalism, and extend the boundaries of the nation ensured that a warrior tradition formed an integral part of the Vietnamese national identity. Vietnamese history celebrated military heroes and glorified martial qualities. Eternal war was the primal theme of Vietnamese history, but there was also the corollary theme as well—the myth of indomitability. It became a staple of Vietnamese belief that they themselves were unconquerable. If they were prudent, if they were patient, if they used the natural advantages provided by geography and climate, and if they avoided a direct confrontation with more powerful foes, they could wear their invading enemies down. When the time was ripe and the enemy was confused and demoralized, when the enemy's fighting spirit was sapped and he was vulnerable, strike! Attack and either destroy or drive out the hated foe!

Famous Vietnamese generals used protracted warfare strategy successfully against the Mongols and Chinese invaders over the centuries. Tran Hung Dao used it to destroy the Mongols during the 1280s and wrote a manual on the art of protracted warfare that became a classic of Vietnamese military science. Le Loi used Dao's strategy to beat the Chinese during the early fourteenth century. General Nguyen Hue, the warrior most admired by North Vietnamese Generals Vo Nguyen Giap and Van Tien Dung, used the strategy to drive the last Chinese invasion out of Vietnam in 1789. To gain his victory, Hue violated the sanctity of Tet, the lunar New Year holiday, observed by both sides. He surprised a much larger Chinese army encamped on the outskirts of Hanoi. He attacked at midnight, when the Chinese soldiers were sleeping off the effects of the food and wine consumed in daylong celebrations, and destroyed their army. Nguyen Hue's great triumph is the most celebrated military victory in Vietnam's long history. The strategy of protracted warfare worked well over the centuries against the Chinese. It would also work against the French from 1946 to 1954, and against the Americans from 1965 to 1973.

The reign of Gia Long lasted until 1820. During his years of power, he reestablished a traditionalist Vietnamese state administered by the Confucian mandarinate that had prevailed for centuries. According to Confucian theory and practice, Gia Long was an absolute monarch whose powers derived from a Mandate of Heaven (the Vietnamese metaphor for political legitimacy). He was the supreme lawmaker, head of all civil and military institutions, and chief justice. The mandarins derived their authority solely from him. The despotism of the regime was modified in two ways. The emperor respected the authority of the head of a family, the most important Vietnamese social institution. Traditionally, submission to the head of one's family was the most important moral obligation facing every Vietnamese. Second, Gia Long partially observed the ancient Vietnamese proverb, "The law of the emperor ends at the village gate." He and his mandarins permitted a certain amount of village self-government. Local officials enforced village laws and customs, dealt with local problems, and collected taxes. Loyalty to one's village was a deeply rooted sentiment and a profound civic obligation for all Vietnamese.[9]

The Vietnamese economy under Gia Long and his successors remained what it had been for ages: a static agrarian system based on the cultivation of rice. The great mass of the Vietnamese people remained peasants, tending their own fields or working as tenants and residing in villages and hamlets concentrated in the great rice-growing regions of the Red River and Mekong River deltas. True to their Confucian principles, Gia Long and his mandarins discouraged all new economic developments and all modernizing trends. There was little industry, little commerce, and almost no foreign trade. No middle class of manufacturers and tradesmen emerged in nineteenth-century Vietnam. Modern science and technology were forbidden. Few Vietnamese traveled beyond the confines of their native land or studied abroad.

Gia Long was succeeded in 1820 by his son Ming Mang, who embraced a Confucian orthodoxy in all matters of governance. He believed Vietnam's national interest was best served by maintaining traditional institutions and ways of life based on the ancient Confucian way. He tried to isolate his country from all Western influences. He resisted all European efforts to open trade, and he tried to suppress the activities of French Catholic missionaries who had been active in Vietnam since the seventeenth century. Because he and his mandarin advisers rejected all Western contacts, all efforts at mod-

Figure 1.2   Tran Hung Dao, a great Vietnamese military hero. In 1284, Dao defeated a powerful invading Mongol army in 1284 to preserve Vietnamese national independence. Dao's guerrilla warfare strategies were adopted by Vo Nguyen Giap, a history professor turned military commander, in order to defeat both the French and American invaders. Photographer: John R. Jones. *Source:* Maurice Durand Collection, L'Ecole Francaise d'Extreme–Orient.

ernization, Vietnamese officials found themselves virtually powerless to defend themselves against aggressive European imperialists. When the French came to conquer them in the 1860s, about all the Nguyens could muster to resist the intruders was a deep reservoir of nationalist feeling that had been nurtured through centuries of Vietnamese struggles to retain their independence from foreign conquerors. But fierce patriotism and national pride proved to be no match against modern French organizational skills and their powerful military technology.

MISSION CIVILISATRICE

The French came to Vietnam in two major waves, first during the seventeenth century and later in the nineteenth. A Jesuit priest, Alexandre de Rhodes, first arrived in Hanoi in 1627. While there, he not only converted thousands of Vietnamese to Roman Catholicism, but also created a Latin alphabet for the Vietnamese language. The Vietnamese twice expelled de Rhodes, but he succeeded in planting the seeds of empire in Vietnamese soil. During their long involvement in Vietnam, French missionaries converted approximately 8 percent of the population to Catholicism. Converts were most likely to come from elite land-holding families. Numerous converts joined the local French civil service.

The period of Vietnamese political unity achieved under the Nguyens ended with the French conquest of the 1860s. Fearing the political meddling of French missionaries working in his country, Ming Mang and his successors, Thieu Tri and Tu Duc, took strong measures to suppress them. These actions gave French officials a pretext to intervene in Vietnam. French officials, in the service of Emperor Napoleon III, had additional motives for intervention in Southeast Asia. Napoleon III, activated by expansionist dreams of imperial glory, wanted to acquire a colony in the region the French called *Indochina* to obtain markets for French manufactures, to provide raw materials for their factories, and to expand their trade within their sphere of influence in China. The French also sought a foothold in Southeast Asia to compete with the British, who had conquered a vast colonial empire in the region stretching from India to the eastern half of New Guinea.[10]

Napoleon III sent a French naval expedition, under Admiral Rigault de Genouilly, to establish a French military base at Tourane (Danang) in 1858. De Genouilly's forces occupied the port city but could not reach the Vietnamese leaders residing in the imperial capitol at Hue, 75 miles to the north. Stalled at Tourane, the French were drenched by monsoon rains and stricken by disease. Realizing his efforts to establish a French base at Tourane were failing, de Genouilly sailed south. His troops occupied Saigon in early 1859. At first, the Vietnamese drove the French out of Saigon. A year later, however, the French, with reinforcements, returned to stay. In 1861, they added three provinces to their empire in southern Vietnam.

Vietnamese officials repeatedly tried to drive the French out of their country, but obsolete military technologies fatally handicapped their efforts to resist French imperialism. Military deficiencies, not a lack of fighting spirit, forced the imperial court at Hue to sign a treaty formally ceding Saigon and the three southernmost provinces of Vietnam to the French in 1862. Even as they lost their lands, the proud Vietnamese told their French conquerors that while "disorder will be long . . . our cause will triumph in the end."[11] By 1867, growing military strength enabled France to conquer all of southern Vietnam, which they organized politically as a colony they called Cochin China.[12] The French required another 16 years of political maneuvering and military action to complete the conquest of all of Vietnam. The imperial court at Hue was forced to sign a treaty with their conquerors in 1883 that extended French authority over the entire country. But the Vietnamese did not submit to French imperialism easily; it was not until the end of the nineteenth century that the French finally crushed all opposition and secured their hold on Vietnam.[13]

During the years they were conquering Vietnam, the French also imposed protectorates over neighboring Cambodia (1863) and Laos (1893). All these acquisitions were formally organized into the French Indochinese Union. After 1893, French Indochina consisted of five administrative departments: Cochin China, a colony in southern Vietnam, and the four protectorates of Cambodia, Laos, Annam (central Vietnam), and Tonkin (northern Vietnam). The French ruled their colony directly, initially using military personnel as administrators. In Annam and Tonkin, the French initially ruled through the Nguyen administrative apparatus, which they controlled. But as the years passed, French control over all of its Vietnamese departments became more centralized and more pervasive. The imperial court at Hue and its mandarins were reduced in time to largely ceremonial functions. Hanoi served as the capital of the entire Union. The French governor-general resided in that city and served directly under the Ministry of Colonies in Paris. Residents-superiors governed each of the five administrative departments. Most French nationals who emigrated to Vietnam settled in Cochin China. Saigon, its capital and commercial center, became known as the "Paris of the Orient." French economic and financial interests were concentrated in southern Vietnam. There they invested most of their capital, and their administrative apparatus penetrated most deeply. Cochin China was the most important department of the French Southeast Asian empire.

The French conquest of Indochina was part of a larger pattern of European imperialism that imposed Western institutions and values upon much of Africa and Asia during the latter decades of the nineteenth century. Western penetration usually began with missionaries and traders, gradually expanding to include military conquest, political control, and economic exploitation. Europeans rationalized these often brutal and exploitative imperialistic enterprises as benign undertakings—the spreading of "civilization" to "backward" or "savage" peoples.

As was typical of European imperialists of this era, the French ruled solely by force, or the imminent threat of force, in Indochina. The Vietnamese never accepted French control as legitimate nor ceased resisting it whenever they could. Although French officials paid lip service to the goals of modernizing and civilizing the

Vietnamese (what they called their *mission civilisatrice*), in practice, French colonialism remained brutally exploitative. The French viewed Vietnam, its land, natural resources, and people, as existing for the benefit of France, specifically for the enrichment of French economic interests that had invested in that country. They expected Vietnam to generate valuable raw materials to feed into the French industrial economy and furnish a tariff-protected market for French manufactures. Many of the French regarded the Vietnamese as an inferior, childlike race, ideally suited for a life of hard work for low wages.

The French invested mainly in Vietnamese rice, rubber, and coal, which became the three leading Indochinese export commodities. The rich Mekong River Delta become one of the world's leading rice-exporting regions. Rice growing in this region was dominated by a class of wealthy landowners, many of them French, joined by a small class of Vietnamese landlords who cooperated with their colonial masters and enriched themselves in the process. During the 1920s and 1930s, rubber became the second most important Vietnamese export. Hundreds of rubber plantations, concentrated in southern Vietnam, and all owned by the French, made Vietnam one of the world's leading sources of raw rubber. Vietnamese coal production was centered in Tonkin, where two large French-owned mining companies accounted for more than 92 percent of the country's total coal output.[14]

Under French colonialism, the Vietnamese economy remained what it had always been, predominantly agricultural. The peasantry comprised about 90 percent of the national population, a vast labor force that paid relatively high taxes and bought cheap French imports if they could afford them. Industrial development of Vietnam was discouraged, as it was contrary to French neomercantilist policies. During the first three decades of the twentieth century, however, the French improved Vietnamese infrastructures—building railroads, highways, bridges, and harbors—and some local light industries evolved.[15]

As a result of French colonial rule, aggravated by the worldwide depression of the 1930s, living standards were lower for most of the Vietnamese people on the eve of World War II than they had been a century earlier under the Nguyens. The concentration of land owning under the French brought the pauperization of millions of Vietnamese peasants, who lost ancestral lands formerly in their possession.[16] These landless families dropped into the ranks of tenants and day laborers, entrapped in a vicious cycle of hard labor, low income, debt, usurious interest rates, and high taxes.

Before the arrival of the French, the Vietnamese prized a highly developed educational system. Literacy was widespread, and learning, according to the Confucian way, was revered. The French closed the Vietnamese schools, replacing them with schools modeled after the French system of education. The Chinese classics were abolished and the Chinese ideographic language was replaced with the Romanized *quoc ngu*.[17] After 1878, the French declared that only *quoc ngu* and French could serve as the official languages. But most Vietnamese children were excluded from the new schools. On the eve of World War II, only about 15 percent of Vietnamese school-age children

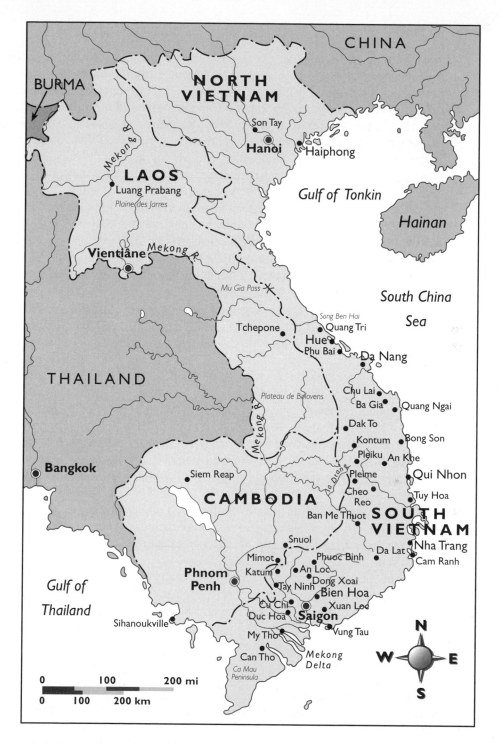

Figure 1.3   Map of Indochina.

were attending schools of any kind. In 1939, Vietnam had only fourteen secondary schools and one university, serving a population of 20 million people. "About 80 percent of the population was illiterate after sixty years of French rule, in contrast to precolonial Vietnam where 80 percent of the people possessed some degree of literacy."[18]

In addition to creating a society made up mainly of landless, illiterate peasants, ruled by a colonial bureaucracy, and a small class of privileged Vietnamese, who joined in the exploitation of their countrymen, French colonialism also disrupted the traditional Vietnamese way of life based on the extended family and the village. French and Vietnamese bureaucrats violated the traditions of village autonomy. Traditional leaders, who neither understood the legal and political systems imposed by the French nor collected enough taxes, were replaced by Vietnamese middlemen. These brokers, who were chosen by French officials, were often without roots or kin in the villages under their control and were an alien force against which there was no recourse or appeal.

French colonial rule imposed many changes on Vietnam, and most changes brought by the French worked to the grave disadvantage of Vietnamese peasants and workers who comprised most of the Vietnamese population. The profits earned by the French-owned enterprises—the banks, factories, mines, and plantations of Vietnam—benefited a relatively small group of investors. Neither the French government nor most French earned a franc from Indochina. Under harsh French governance, the Vietnamese were accorded no political rights. Political parties were proscribed. A combination of neomercantilist economic policies and political repression prevented the rise of a substantial middle class and precluded "the development of a liberal, Western-oriented political movement."[19]

For the large majority of Vietnamese families, mass immiseration was the chief consequence of three generations of French colonial rule. The people were enmeshed in a socioeconomic system controlled by French officials and an elite class of Gallicized Vietnamese that allowed almost no opportunity for improvement or escape. The Vietnamese peasantry understood that French colonialism was responsible for their oppression, but they also understood that they had two enemies: the French who ruled them and the privileged Vietnamese elite who exploited them. In time, the struggle to achieve independence after World War II, common throughout Asia and Africa, throughout what would become known during the 1950s as the Third World, became for the Vietnamese a social revolution as well. This intertwining of nationalistic and revolutionary goals made the postwar history of Vietnam unique to Southeast Asia. Only in Vietnam did the struggle for home rule also become a struggle for who should rule at home. Only in Vietnam did the revolutionaries seek to smash French imperialism and dispossess the wealthy Francophilic Asian elite class.

EMERGENT VIETNAMESE NATIONALISM

Vietnamese resistance to French rule began as the French were establishing their colony of Cochin China in the 1860s and continued, whenever possible, for as long as the French controlled Indochina. The earliest rebellions were led by local mandarins, scholars, and officials from the emperor's court at Hue, who detested the European intruders and whose own powers were threatened by the advent of the French. Resistance took the forms of refusals to work, sabotage, and, most commonly, guerrilla warfare. Rebel mandarins appealed to the peasantry, in the name of the emperor and Confucian ideals drawn from Vietnam's precolonial heritage, to join them in efforts to regain their country's independence. A teenage emperor himself, Ham Nghi, joined one of these rebellions in Annam in 1885. He was later captured by the French and was exiled to Algeria.

For decades, periodic revolts challenged the growing French colonial power. They all failed because of French military superiority and because the mandarin rebels could offer the people only a return to the imperial past in place of French rule. But for many Vietnamese, the Nguyen Dynasty had been discredited. The court's shortsighted efforts to forestall all progress and isolate Vietnam from Western forces in the first half of the nineteenth century had been responsible for the inability of the Vietnamese to keep the French out. Further, the catastrophe of the loss of political independence was proof to many patriots that the House of Nguyen had lost its moral sanction, the Mandate of Heaven, and thus its right to rule.

Other factors contributed to the defeat of the rebellions. They were local, isolated insurrections, district uprisings, with no chance to inflict permanent defeat on the French or drive them out of Vietnam. The French also were able to call up some segments of the Vietnamese population for assistance in suppressing the rebellions. Catholic Vietnamese often sided with the French, remembering their persecution under the Nguyens. Various *Montagnard* tribes, for centuries neglected and despised by the lowland Vietnamese who regarded them as uncivilized, often joined French expeditions against the rebels.[20]

Vietnamese people paid a severe price for these uprisings; local economies were disrupted, taxes were increased to pay for the police forces required to suppress the insurrections, and thousands of Vietnamese were killed by the French. As the nineteenth century ended, all of the rebels were dead, imprisoned, or exhausted. For a time, social peace settled on the land, although it was an imposed peace of the dead.

A new generation of Vietnamese nationalists came of age during the first decade of the twentieth century. Their leader was the scholar Phan Boi Chau, who had received a modern education. Chau embraced Western philosophical rationalism, science, and constitutionalism. Detesting French suzerainty over his countrymen, he called for independence from France and for Vietnam to develop a constitutional monarchy. He hoped to place Prince Coung De, a descendant of Gia Long, on a restored, modernized throne.

An energetic propagandist and organizer, Chau, working with the prince, formed the Association for the Modernization of Vietnam while both were living in Japan. For a time, Chau and the Prince hoped Japanese liberals would support and finance their cause. In 1908, nationalistic followers of Chau, protesting high taxes, staged mass demonstrations in cities throughout Vietnam. The French responded by jailing thousands of demonstrators.[21] In the aftermath of the failed protests, and disillusioned by lukewarm Japanese support, Chau moved to China where he became an enthusiastic follower of Chinese revolutionary leader Dr. Sun Yat-sen.

After World War I, Chau's movement declined. Kidnapped by French agents, he returned to Vietnam and was condemned to death. But the governor-general commuted his sentence to confinement for life at his home in Hue. Chau's movement had always lacked mass support, and further suffered from a lack of discipline and the absence of a coherent program; but Chau had been the first Vietnamese national leader to espouse modern political ideas and to call for the use of more sophisticated resistance tactics against French colonialism than the hopeless rebellions led by mandarin traditionalists.

French repression hindered the political activities of Vietnamese nationalists. Even moderates who tried to work for independence through legal political activity often found themselves in jail, under house arrest, or forced into exile. Nationalist organizations were forced to go underground to have any chance of political effectiveness. During the 1920s, the Vietnam Quoc Dan Dang (VNQDD), the Vietnamese Nationalist Party, was the major underground organization. The VNQDD's goals were political independence and the creation of a Vietnamese republic. In early 1930, a garrison of Vietnamese soldiers stationed in northern Tonkin, influenced by VNQDD ideas, rebelled against French rule. They hoped their revolt would create similar uprisings everywhere in Vietnam, starting a revolution. They were disappointed when French forces, moving quickly, suppressed their rebellion before it could generate any momentum. Afterward, French authorities destroyed the VNQDD organization, although some of its leaders were able to escape to exile in China.

Following the destruction of the VNQDD, Marxist organizations took over the revolutionary nationalist cause in Vietnam. In 1930, the Indochinese Communist Party was organized by a professional revolutionary and Vietnamese patriot who called himself Nguyen Ai Quoc (Nguyen the Patriot). The world would later know him as Ho Chi Minh.[22] He was born Nguyen Sinh Cung on May 19, 1890, in Kim Lien, a small village in Nghe An province located in central Vietnam, a site of many rebellions against French colonial rule over the years. Most of Nghe An consists of low coastal plains bordered on the west by the rugged Annamese Mountains. Because of its dense population, poor soil, and bad climate, most inhabitants of Nghe An endured harsh lives. Despite its poverty, or perhaps because of it, Nghe An has produced many poets and scholars. Much of the artistic and intellectual talent of Vietnam has come from this hard, poor place.

Ho Chi Minh was the son of Nguyen Sinh Sac, a minor mandarin who had been a supporter of Phan Boi Chau and was later dismissed from government service because of his fiercely anti-French nationalistic activities. As a boy, Ho Chi Minh had been inspired by Chau's and his father's visions of a modern Vietnam freed from French imperialism. Since his youth, Ho Chi Minh held a passionate hatred of French imperialism, and he would devote most of his life to the great task of reclaiming Vietnam for the Vietnamese people. Ho Chi Minh attended Quoc Hoc lycée in Hue to prepare for a career in government service, but left the school in 1911 without graduating. He shipped out on a French steamer determined to see the world, and he would not set foot on Vietnamese soil again for almost thirty years. For the next several years, Ho Chi Minh traveled widely and worked at a variety of jobs. He made a voyage to the United States, visiting Boston and New York.[23]

Ending up in France during World War I, Ho Chi Minh quickly immersed himself in the political activities of Vietnamese nationalists living in Paris. Within the Vietnamese expatriate community, he soon became a leader. In 1919, while the victorious Allies were meeting at the Versailles Conference, Ho Chi Minh presented a petition to the Big Four demanding that the principle of self-determination embodied in Woodrow Wilson's Fourteen Points be applied to French Indochina. The leaders of the victorious great powers ignored the demands of this obscure Vietnamese patriot. He also sought, unsuccessfully, to meet with President Wilson. Even had Wilson met with Ho, it is doubtful that the future course of U.S. relations with Vietnam could have evolved differently. Wilson believed that self-determination applied only to European nationalists and would doubtless have spurned Ho's request. The meeting that never took place between Ho and Wilson set a precedent for U.S.-Vietnamese relations that would endure for the next 45 years, which would last until 1965 when the Americans took over the expanding war in Vietnam. Until that fateful summer of 1965, Washington always considered its relations with European nations to be more important than anything that happened in Vietnam. As a consequence, U.S. officials knew next to nothing about Vietnamese history, culture, or politics. Even as the United States became more deeply involved in Vietnamese affairs after 1965, issues other than what was happening in Vietnam were always more important to U.S. officials. As a result, the Americans consistently underestimated the difficulties that they would encounter in Vietnam. In time, this pernicious reality, the underestimation by official Washington of the complexities of its involvement in Vietnam, would contribute to the eventual defeat of the American cause.[24]

At about the same time, Ho Chi Minh also joined the French Socialist Party, and he belonged to the radical faction that broke off to found the French Communist Party in 1920. He was drawn to Lenin's ideology, especially his *Imperialism, the Highest Stage of Capitalism* and *Theses on the National and Colonial Questions.* From his reading of Lenin's works, Ho derived his understanding of the dynamics of French colonial rule of his homeland. The French, aided by a small class of privileged Vietnamese collaborators who staffed the local bureaucracies and security forces, had grown rich by depriving the mass of peasants and workers of the fruits of their labor. They would never leave Vietnam voluntarily. Only revolution involving the mass of Vietnamese peasants could liberate Vietnam and drive out the French. Lenin also argued that there were two enemies to be overthrown: Western capitalist imperialists and their elite Asian collaborators. Following his conversion to Marxist-Leninism, Ho Chi Minh was to remain a passionately committed Communist revolutionary leader for the rest of his life.

But he also was a bone-deep Vietnamese patriot steeped in Confucian culture, practicing the traditional virtues of wisdom, benevolence, sincerity, righteousness, moderation, and harmony. He would prove to be a charismatic leader who inspired both the intellectuals and the peasants who constituted most of the population of his native land.

Ho Chi Minh journeyed to Russia in 1923. He lived and studied in Moscow, becoming a specialist on colonial questions and a professional revolutionary organizer. He went to China in 1925 as an assistant to the Comintern's adviser to the *Koumintang* during the years of cooperation between Moscow and the Chinese Nationalists. In Canton, Ho Chi Minh organized Vietnamese political exiles into the Vietnamese Revolutionary Youth Movement, a precursor of the Indochinese Communist Party (ICP). He also edited a political journal called *Thanh Nien* (Youth) and wrote his only book, *The Road of Revolution.* Ho Chi Minh insisted that a revolution would succeed only when it organized the mass of Vietnamese workers and peasants. In China, he met a brilliant Vietnamese nationalist, Pham Van Dong, whose father had been a high-ranking mandarin involved in anti-French resistance activities. Thirty years later, Dong would become prime minister of the People's Republic of Vietnam.[25] After the Sino-Soviet split of 1927, Ho Chi Minh returned to Moscow for a time. In 1929, he traveled to Hong Kong, where he joined with other Vietnamese nationalists, including Le Duc Tho, Pham Van Dong, and Vo Nguyen Giap, to organize the ICP. "Together, these men formed the nucleus of the movement that fought first the French, then the Japanese, then the French again, and finally Americans until 1975" before achieving a unified, independent Vietnamese nation.[26] Ho and his band of dedicated organizers formed underground cells in Vietnam, and Haiphong became the center for Communist activities in the country. They eagerly worked to organize peasant associations and trade unions.

The modern Vietnamese revolution began in 1930 and 1931 when peasant rebellions, provoked by hard times and high taxes, erupted in several districts of central Vietnam. The fledgling ICP moved in to furnish leadership for the peasants in those regions. Party leaders included Pham Van Dong and Vo Nguyen Giap. The Communists managed to set up people's *soviets* in two provinces of central Vietnam, in Ha Tinh and in the troublesome Nghe An, Ho Chi Minh's ancestral home. They moved against large landlords and redistributed land to hard-pressed peasant farmers.[27]

But French forces quickly moved into these regions. Police and Legionnaires instituted a reign of terror and crushed the peasant insurrections. Suspected agitators were given summary trials en masse and condemned. Giap's wife and daughter died in a French prison, and Giap had to go into exile to survive. French authorities tried Ho Chi Minh in absentia, convicted him of treason, and sentenced him to death. Pham Van Dong spent eight bitter years in one of the worst French penal colonies on Con Son Island. An estimated 10,000 Vietnamese were killed, and another 50,000 were deported.[28] In the 1930s, French prisons and penal colonies in Indochina bulged with thousands of political prisoners. French authorities believed they had eliminated the Vietnamese Communist movement while it was in its infancy. They were mistaken.

Despite their savage losses, the Communists survived, and within a decade they had organized a broad-based revolutionary nationalist movement. After the French suppressions of 1931, the Communists smuggled most of their best cadres into China. The ICP remained the best-organized, strongest, and most popular of the underground nationalist groups operating in Vietnam. Its key leaders also survived all French efforts to eliminate them.[29] From 1936 to 1939, pressure on the Communists in Vietnam eased as a Popular Front government in France allowed the parties both in France and Indochina an increased freedom for peaceful political activity. Both the French and Vietnamese Communists, following orders from Moscow, moderated their revolutionary programs and sought alliances with liberals and socialists. Many non-Communist Vietnamese nationalists were attracted to the Communist program, which emphasized democratic reform rather than revolution during the Popular Front years. During the Popular Front era, the ICP assumed unrivaled leadership of the Vietnamese drive for national independence.[30]

THE JAPANESE OCCUPATION

When World War II began in Europe with the German invasion of Poland on September 1, 1939, the Vietnamese Communists opposed the French war effort and resumed their revolutionary activity. Within Indochina, the French were still in firm control. The secret police suppressed the Communists and other radicals, but the events of war would break France's hold on its Southeast Asian Empire and bring the liberation of the Vietnamese people from colonialism. The unique fusion of nationalism and Communism in Vietnam also imparted a social revolutionary thrust to the Vietnamese drive for self-determination. The war would also propel the United States into Southeast Asian affairs, inaugurating an entanglement in that region that would persist for 30 years.

In the late spring of 1940, Nazi armor rolled to an easy victory over French armies in a stunningly successful campaign, forcing France's surrender after only six weeks of fighting. Their German conquerors chose to occupy only northern France and turned over the government of the rest of the country to a collaborationist regime in Vichy. The Vichy government retained nominal control of French overseas territories, including Indochina. German victories over France and other European powers, British preoccupation with European threats to its interests, and U.S. neutrality at the outset of war all created opportunities for Japanese expansionists to take over weakly defended European colonial possessions in Southeast Asia.

The Japanese, who had been waging war against China since 1937, exploited France's weakened defenses. They quickly moved into Indochina after Germany defeated France. Indochina was an important component of the expanding Japanese East Asian Empire for several reasons. The Japanese wanted to stop the French from sending supplies to the Chinese via a route that wound through the mountains, separating southern China from Tonkin. They also wanted to acquire airfields in Vietnam for launching attacks against Chinese targets. Further, Vietnam would serve Japan well as a rich source of raw materials such as rice and rubber. Vietnam's strategic location also provided the Japanese with a staging area for their expansion into the Dutch East Indies and British Malaya. Finally, Vietnam served as a basing area for Japanese troops, and its harbors served as transshipment points for the resources the Japanese would be extracting from the Southeast Asian territories they planned to conquer.

In August 1940, Japanese troops poured out of China into northern Vietnam. The governor-general of Indochina, Admiral Jean Decoux, offered little resistance to the Japanese presence. By the end of 1941, the Japanese had acquired a free hand in Vietnam. Admiral Decoux granted them permission to station troops anywhere in the country and to use all of the French naval and air bases. He also signed agreements guaranteeing that Japan would receive all of Vietnam's exports. In return, the Japanese acknowledged French sovereignty over Indochina and permitted the French to maintain their administrative apparatus. Technically, the Japanese did not occupy Vietnam; Japan and Vichy France agreed to joint control, a de facto dual sovereignty. The French were saddled with the costs of administering territories whose riches were now going to Japan.[31]

The coming of the Japanese gave some Vietnamese nationalist groups unprecedented opportunities to achieve a greater role in political affairs, because now both the French and the Japanese had to compete for the allegiance of the people. French administrators granted the Vietnamese additional political freedoms, upgraded the status of Vietnamese officials, and sought to organize young people into various groupings.[32] Some Vietnamese nationalists sought to work with the Japanese in the hopes of achieving independence from the French, including the adherents of two religious sects whose members mostly resided in southern Vietnam, the Cao Dai and the Hoa Hao. The Japanese encouraged these religious groups, playing on their Pan-Asian nationalistic and anti-French sentiments, but they had no intention of granting the Vietnamese their independence.[33] In time, Vietnamese enthusiasm for Japanese assistance in seeking liberation from the Vichy French cooled.

The new French-Japanese arrangement in Vietnam did not favor the Vietnamese Communists or other radical nationalistic groups. They suffered severe repression and were forced to seek sanctuary in southern China to survive. Here, they benefited from the truce in China arranged between the Nationalists and the Maoists, who agreed to curtail their civil war in order to fight the Japanese invaders of their homeland. The Vietnamese Communists operated freely in southern China during the war. The Chinese government also worked with Vietnamese nationalists, both Communist and non-Communist, to hinder the Japanese war effort being mounted against China from Vietnam. The Chinese tried to unite all Vietnamese nationalists living in China within a front organization dedicated to carrying on sabotage and espionage activities against the Japanese in Vietnam.[34] But only the Vietnamese Communists proved capable of carrying out these dangerous tasks, and the Chinese turned to them.

Ho Chi Minh, still known as Nguyen Ai Quoc to his followers, the leader of the Vietnamese Communist remnant, resided in southern China in 1941. He understood that the French defeat in the European war and its forced acceptance of the Japanese presence in Vietnam offered his cause a great opportunity if he could exploit it. Japanese dominance in Southeast Asia had destroyed whatever lingering notions of white superiority had survived in the region. Ho Chi Minh knew that these revelations of French weakness had encouraged many Vietnamese, including businessmen, landowners, and urban workers, to join the peasants in supporting independence. He also knew that these groups needed leadership; they had to be organized and given direction. Further, he knew that he had to establish a political base in Vietnam. Independence from both Japan and France could not be achieved by emigres living in China.

Ho Chi Minh set out to achieve both objectives. Vietnamese Communist leaders met on May 10, 1941, on Vietnamese soil in the village of Pac Bo in the Cao Bang province, with Ho Chi Minh chairing the meeting. It was the first time in 30 years that he had set foot in his native land. The participants agreed that the party's main goal was to organize all Vietnamese—peasants, workers, middle-class elements, and landlords—to achieve independence. The social revolution would have to wait. The Communist leaders played down their revolutionary goals of land redistribution and the nationalization of industries. To organize all these groups, a new organization was created: the *Viet Nam Doc Lap Dong Minh* (Vietnamese League for Independence). The French and the Americans would come to know this group as the Vietminh.

Organizations of peasants, workers, students, intellectuals, women, and landlords all gathered under the Vietminh umbrella. These associations organized at the village level. Pyramids of associations paralleled the political jurisdictions of the country, including district and provincial associations. At the top stood the Central Committee, controlled by Ho Chi Minh and his senior colleagues, all of whom were Communists. Party members also controlled the associations, but many non-Communist participants joined them because the Vietminh represented the most effective anticolonial movement in Indochina. At the time the Vietminh were forming, Ho Chi Minh wrote a public letter in which he appealed to the nationalistic and anti-imperialist traditions of the Vietnamese people:

> National salvation is the common cause of our entire people. Every Vietnamese must take part in it. . . . The hour has struck. Raise aloft the banner of insurrection and lead the people throughout the country to overthrow the Japanese and the French. The sacred call of the fatherland is resounding in our ears, the ardent blood of our heroic predecessors is seething in our hearts.[35]

Ho Chi Minh and his associates created the Vietminh as a national-front organization controlled by the Indochinese Communist Party to attract Vietnamese patriots of all political persuasions to rid their country of Japanese and French rule. Ho Chi Minh and his Vietminh colleagues also viewed their struggle against Japanese and French imperialism as part of the worldwide struggle against fascism. When the mighty United States entered the war against the Axis powers, Ho Chi Minh associated the Vietnamese nationalist cause with the American war aims embodied in the Atlantic Charter. When Japan suddenly attacked Pearl Harbor on December 7, 1941, the Vietminh allied its cause with the United States.[36]

In addition to forming the Vietminh front organizations, Ho Chi Minh and his associates established a revolutionary base in Cao Bang. Following Maoist strategies, the Vietminh's goal was to liberate this remote mountainous northern province and replace the colonial administration with their own party apparatus. Within six months, they had succeeded. A training site for guerrillas was established near Pac Bo to transform peasant recruits into revolutionary warriors.

When Chinese officials selected the Vietminh to take charge of anti-Japanese espionage and guerrilla campaigns in Vietnam, a Chinese general, Chang Fa-K'uei, upon learning of Nguyen Ai Quoc's Communist past, urged him to change his name, lest the Chinese Nationalist leaders reject him. To oblige his Chinese sponsors, Nguyen selected the name Ho Chi Minh ("he who enlightens") sometime in early 1943.[37] With Chinese sponsorship, the Vietminh automatically qualified for funding from the U.S. Mission in China, which was bankrolling the entire Chinese war effort against the Japanese.

ROOTS OF AMERICAN INVOLVEMENT

World War II marked a rapid expansion of the power of the United States everywhere in the world, including Southeast Asia. Long before the 1940s, the United States had acquired major economic, political, and strategic interests in Southeast Asia. The United States became an imperial power with important colonial possessions in that region when it wrested the Philippine archipelago and the island of Guam from the Spanish following the Spanish-American War. During the first few decades of the twentieth century, the United States developed a thriving trade with the Southeast Asian colonies of Great Britain, France, and the Netherlands. From Malaysia came tin and rubber, from the Dutch East Indies came rubber and oil, and from Vietnam came rubber. During the early 1940s, the exigencies of world war thrust America into more prominent roles in the political affairs of this vital region. These wartime experiences confirmed the American sense of Vietnam's significance as a source of foodstuffs and raw materials and as a strategic location astride major shipping lanes linking India, the islands of the southeast Pacific, China, and Japan.

The fall of France in June 1940 created serious diplomatic problems for the United States. President Franklin Roosevelt despised and distrusted the collaborationist Vichyites, but granted them diplomatic recognition to forestall German occupation of their colonies in North Africa and to try to prevent, unsuccessfully, the Japanese occupation of Indochina. U.S. officials were angered by French acquiescence in the Japanese penetration of Vietnam. From their perspective, it appeared that French officials made little effort to resist Japanese demands and settled rather comfortably into a joint occupation with them. U.S. officials also perceived that possession of Indochina gave the Japanese strategic leverage in Southeast Asia for its continuing war with China. They later attributed many of the Japanese successes in conquering Southeast Asian territories, including the Philippines during 1941 to 1942, to their ability to use Indochina as a base of operations.

It was the Japanese move into all of Indochina in the summer of 1941 that probably made war between the United States and Japan inevitable. Roosevelt viewed Japanese entry into that strategic region as a clear sign that the Japanese planned further imperialistic moves into the southeast Pacific region. The U.S. response to Japan's takeover of all of Indochina was to cut off Japan's supply of oil. The oil cutoff created a crisis for the Japanese leaders. With only six weeks of oil reserves on hand, the Japanese would have to get the oil embargo rescinded quickly or find a new source of supply to prevent their war machine and industrial economy from grinding to a halt. U.S. and Japanese negotiators met through the summer and fall of 1941 to try to resolve their conflicts. As the price for restoring Japan's oil supplies and other trade goods that had been embargoed, Washington demanded that the Japanese get out of China and Indochina. These terms proved unacceptable to Japan, who would not consider abandoning their expansionist ambitions. They preferred war with the United States rather than surrender their dreams of empire. The Japanese response came on December 7, 1941, at Pearl Harbor, which brought the United States into the Asian war. Soon afterward, the Japanese, using Vietnam as a staging area, occupied the East Indies and began extracting oil from this former Dutch colony. The Japanese also made use of Vietnamese ports as depots for the oil and other resources they were getting from their newly conquered empire in Southeast Asia.

The Japanese move into Indochina brought the first U.S. military intervention into Vietnam in early 1942, about a month after America had entered the war. Cutting the Japanese lifeline from Southeast Asia and denying the Japanese use of air bases in Vietnam for continuing attacks on China became major tactical objectives of the American Volunteer Group, famed as the "Flying Tigers," under the command of General Claire L. Chennault. The Flying Tigers operated under the control of the Chinese Nationalist Army. Flying out of bases in southern China, the Flying Tigers, in early 1942, began attacking Japanese airfields in northern Vietnam.[38]

As the war progressed, the future political status of Indochina became a diplomatic problem among the wartime allies. It was tied to a larger issue, the postwar fate of the European Asian empires. On the one hand, U.S. officials, faithful to Atlantic Charter war aims, firmly opposed the restoration of colonial imperialism in Asia. Liberation from Japanese occupation was to be followed by independence. The end of colonialism in Asia would liberate subject peoples, open markets to U.S. exports, and bring stability to turbulent regions. On the other hand, President Roosevelt had an understanding with British prime minister Winston Churchill that the Atlantic Charter did not apply to British colonial possessions, particularly India. But in a private conversation with Secretary of State Cordell Hull, Roosevelt made clear early in 1944 the kind of future he envisioned for Indochina:

> France has had the country—30 million inhabitants—for nearly one hundred years, and the people are worse off than they were at the beginning. . . . France has milked it for one hundred years. The people of Indochina are entitled to something better than that.[39]

Charles De Gaulle, the leader of the Free French government-in-exile, whom Roosevelt disliked intensely, joined with Churchill in an effort to thwart Roosevelt and forestall the loss of Indochina after the war. Churchill, linking De Gaulle's attempts to retain France's Asian colonies with his own efforts to cling to empire, supported De Gaulle. The colonial issue created fissures in the wartime alliance's conduct of the war in Southeast Asia. The British tried to claim wartime jurisdiction of Indochina, which the Americans had assigned to the China theater, in order to restore the colony to France at the conclusion of the war. Roosevelt, perceiving Churchill's strategy, blocked the British efforts by ordering that no U.S. aid would go to French forces in Indochina and forbidding the British to conduct military operations in the region without clearance from the U.S.-China command.[40]

Pursuing efforts to prevent a return of French colonialism in Vietnam, Roosevelt asked Jiang Jieshi, the nationalist leader of China, if he wanted to govern Indochina. The answer he received was an emphatic no! Jiang, aware of Vietnam's long history of resistance to Chinese colonialism, told Roosevelt that the Vietnamese were "not Chinese. They would not assimilate into the Chinese people."[41] Following Jiang's rejection, Roosevelt proposed the creation of an international trusteeship for Indochina until the people were ready for independence.[42]

Roosevelt understood that the collapse of European colonial authority in Southeast Asia had created a power vacuum, and he was openly hostile to British, Dutch, and French colonialism in those regions. He was anticolonialist to the core, an anti-imperialist ideologue. He especially wanted to see Vietnam freed of the burden of French colonialism. He was motivated in part by spite, the desire to punish the French for their wartime capitulation to the Axis, and he wished to shear off one of their prized imperial possessions. He also sensed that the days of Western imperialism in Asia were ending and that colonialism promoted imperial rivalries that led to war. He wanted to make use of a historic opportunity to liquidate French imperialism in Southeast Asia and align U.S. foreign policy with the forces of Asian nationalism. At various international conferences among the Allied leaders during World War II, Roosevelt pursued his idea of an international trusteeship for Vietnam that would prevent the return of French colonialism and provide for the eventual restoration of sovereignty to the Vietnamese.

AUGUST REVOLUTION

While world leaders quarreled over the political future of Indochina, Vietminh guerrillas carried out espionage missions and raids on Japanese forces occupying northern Vietnam. The Vietminh also used their wartime guerrilla activities and the prestige gained from their American connections to strengthen their leadership of the Vietnamese nationalist movement. In December 1944, in the Cao Bang province, Ho Chi Minh ordered the creation of a military division of the Vietminh, the Vietnamese Liberation Army. During the winter of 1944 to 1945, under the leadership of Vo Nguyen Giap, Vietminh guerrillas gained control of three northern provinces and engaged Japanese forces in sporadic combat.[43]

Beginning in the spring of 1945, the Vietminh received support from an Office of Strategic Services (OSS) contingent operating out of the U.S. China Mission at Kunming. The Vietminh and OSS units collaborated to hasten the defeat of the Japanese. The Vietminh helped OSS commandos rescue downed U.S. pilots and escaped prisoners, accompanied them on sabotage missions, and provided them with information on Japanese troop movements in Vietnam. The OSS in return provided the Vietminh with radios, small arms, and ammunition. The OSS officers served with the Vietminh at Ho Chi Minh's headquarters at Pac Bo. The Americans came to know many of the Vietminh leaders and assisted them in their struggle for national independence. Ho energetically cultivated the American OSS officers. Like other Asian nationalists, he assumed that the United States would support the Vietminh drive for independence. The OSS officers who knew him viewed Ho Chi Minh as a Vietnamese patriot who would subordinate his Leninist revolutionary principles to the larger cause of national liberation. For their part, the Vietminh leaders viewed this small group of American OSS officers working with them to defeat the Japanese as a symbol of liberation, not only from the Japanese occupation but also from 80 years of French colonial rule.[44]

By early 1945, U.S. and British forces had reclaimed many of Japan's wartime Southeast Asian conquests. They had liberated important territories, including the Dutch East Indies, Malaya, and the Philippine archipelago. Confronted with their rapidly shrinking assets in Southeast Asia, Japan made a determined effort to hold its vital Indochina positions. Aircraft operating from carriers of the U.S. Third Fleet in the Gulf of Tonkin began attacking Japanese shipping in Saigon harbor. Army Air Corps bombers from Clark Field in the Philippines carried out raids on Saigon and Danang, destroying Japanese warships and freighters. Within a few months, American planes had closed Japanese supply lines from Vietnam to China and their home islands. U.S. strategic bombers knocked out all railway linkages between Vietnam and China. Indochina was cut off from the remaining Japanese theaters of war.

These U.S. air raids signaled that the end of the Japanese presence in Indochina was fast approaching. Many of the French in Vietnam, who had collaborated with the Axis for years, prepared to join the fight for Vietnam's liberation from Japan. Sensing the changed French attitudes, the Japanese moved to prevent French action against them. On March 9, 1945, the Japanese abruptly brought the 80-year-old French rule over the Indochinese people to an end. In a series of lightning raids that took the French by surprise, Admiral Decoux and many French officials were arrested, and most French soldiers were disarmed and interned. Thousands of French nationals were also interned. Only a few hundred managed to escape to the hills. Some joined the Vietminh guerrillas; others fled to China. Japanese officials seized control of the Indochina government.[45]

In their efforts to retain control of Vietnam, the Japanese also installed a Vietnamese government headed by Emperor Bao Dai, who, prior to the war, had been the French-controlled ruler of Annam for 10 years from his palace in Hue.[46] Japanese officials informed Bao Dai that he was the ruler of an "independent" nation that had been "liberated" from the French imperialists. In reality, the Japanese were going through a desperate charade. The new government had neither the resources nor the power to command. Japanese Army officers remained in control of Vietnamese affairs. Bao Dai also understood that Japan would soon be defeated, and his shadow government would be discredited because of its association with the Japanese, who were no more loved by the Vietnamese people than the French.

Ho Chi Minh understood that the Japanese coup d'état created a political vacuum in Indochina, and he intended to exploit this development. He also understood that the Japanese defeat of the French, as well as their conquest of former British and Dutch colonies in Southeast Asia, had destroyed the lingering myth of European invincibility that had previously restrained Asian nationalists.

With the French removed from power and the Japanese on the verge of defeat, the Vietminh moved quickly to position themselves to take control of their country. General Giap took command of the Vietnam Liberation Army. Vietminh forces now controlled much of Tonkin, and their influence was spreading rapidly over the country, reaching from the villages into the cities.[47] Within the provinces they controlled, the Vietminh installed revolutionary regimes, recruited guerrillas, abolished taxes, reduced land rents, and redistributed land taken from French landlords to poor peasants.[48] The Vietminh were rapidly harnessing the vast energies of a people who were sensing that their moment of liberation from both Japanese and French dominion was fast approaching. Where positive appeals to patriotism and economic self-interest failed, the Vietminh relied on terror to intimidate opponents. Known collaborators with the French or Japanese were liquidated.

The Vietminh also gained followers during the summer of 1945, because they responded effectively to a famine that was especially acute in the northern provinces. The famine had been caused by the Japanese, who, in 1943, had ordered French soldiers to seize the rice harvest for shipment to Japan. Peasants went bankrupt in 1943 and starved in 1944. Severe drought aggravated the famine, during which an estimated 500,000 to 1 million Vietnamese perished. French and Japanese officials were not concerned about the plight of the starving Vietnamese, but the Vietminh confiscated rice from landlords and raided granaries containing rice stored for export. The Vietminh turned these precious rice stores over to the people to alleviate some of the misery.

The Vietminh got their opportunity to seize power when the Japanese forces in Vietnam surrendered to Vietminh forces in mid-August 1945, a few days after U.S. planes had dropped atomic bombs on the Japanese cities of Hiroshima and Nagasaki, abruptly ending World War II. Immediately, the Vietminh called for a national revolution. Its political cadres and military forces sprang into action. In August 1945, Vietnam rapidly underwent a nationalist revolution.[49] Everywhere, Vietminh associations took control of local, district, and provincial governments.[50] A provisional council in Saigon, comprising religious sectarians, various Communist splinter groups, and several non-Communist nationalist groups, declared their support for the Vietminh. Within 10 days, from August 18 to 28, the revolutionaries took over virtually the entire country.

The Vietminh supplanted the deposed French and the beaten Japanese and took power without any significant opposition.[51] On August 19, the Vietminh took Hanoi. On August 23, they claimed Hue, the seat of government of the Nguyen dynasty. Between August 18 and 28, Vietminh supporters took control of some 60 district and provincial capitals. On August 29, the Vietminh formed a national government called the Provisional Government of the Democratic Republic of Vietnam, with its capital in Hanoi. On September 2, 1945, Ho Chi Minh publicly declared Vietnamese independence before 500,000 people assembled in Hanoi's Ba Dinh Square.[52] Ho admired the United States because it had defeated the Japanese and because of its official commitment to

Figure 1.4   Vietnamese nationalist leader Ho Chi Minh (1892–1969), born Nguyen Sinh Cung. *Source:* Getty Images, Inc. – Liaison.

self-determination for Asian peoples following the war. Ho, who also hoped that Vietminh cooperation with the United States in the war against the Japanese would bring American support of Vietnamese independence, began his speech with words taken from the American Declaration of Independence: "We hold truths that all men are created equal, that they are endowed by their Creator with certain unalienable Rights, among these are Life, Liberty, and the pursuit of Happiness."[53]

Later in the day, Americans joined the festivities that celebrated Vietnam's independence. A flight of U.S. aircraft flew over the city. U.S. Army officers stood with Giap and other Vietminh leaders on the reviewing stand as Vietminh forces passed in review. A Vietnamese band played "The Star Spangled Banner."[54] Later a Vietnam-American Friendship Association was formed in Hanoi. Ho Chi Minh, hoping for U.S. support for Vietnam's independence and for economic development, cultivated the friendship of the small American contingent in Hanoi and repeatedly appealed to the U.S. government for diplomatic recognition. U.S. officials in Washington did not respond to Ho's requests. No other nation in the world, including China and the Soviet Union, officially recognized Ho's government.

The Vietnamese people had reclaimed their national identity that had been submerged for 80 years under French and Japanese colonialism. For the first time in 80 years, Vietnam was united and independent under a government controlled by the Communist-led Vietminh. Its revolution represented a remarkable merging of a people and a movement that gave expression to the deep yearning of nearly all Vietnamese citizens to be rid of foreign control. In the rush to achieve national independence, factional conflicts and ideological differences among Vietnamese political parties, which were sharpest in southern cities, were temporarily submerged. On August 30, Emperor Bao Dai presented the imperial seal and sword, the twin symbols of Vietnamese sovereignty, to the Vietminh leaders and then abdicated.[55] Bao Dai promised to support the new provisional government, conferring legitimacy upon it and linking it to Vietnamese political traditions. In return, Ho named him "Supreme Adviser" to the new government. Most Vietnamese, Communist and non-Communist alike, accepted Ho Chi Minh as the leader of the revolution that had retrieved Vietnamese independence.

But the August revolution was not destined to endure peacefully. As U.S. Army officers joined with Vietminh leaders in Hanoi to celebrate the rebirth of Vietnamese independence, American leaders in Washington were clearing the way for the return of the French to Vietnam. The U.S. military personnel serving in Vietnam who supported Ho's revolutionary nationalism had no political clout in Washington. Roosevelt may have been an anticolonialist ideologue, but he was also a pragmatist and certainly a Europeanist first. He did not believe that the provisions of the Atlantic Charter extended to Asians. He never developed a consistent or concrete program for dealing with the Vietnam issue, and the policy had not been clearly defined at the time of his death on April 12, 1945. Even before he died, Roosevelt had retreated from his support of Vietnamese nationalism. His top priority always was an orderly and stable world controlled by a concert of the great powers. Asian national liberation remained a distant goal. Had he lived and continued to push for an end to French colonialism in Indochina, he would have provoked a crisis in relations between the United States and France. Concerned with maintaining good relations with important European allies at Yalta, FDR did not actively oppose France's announced intention to return to Indochina.[56] Secretary of State Edward Stettinius told the French foreign minister that the United States had never questioned, "French sovereignty over Indochina."[57]

Roosevelt's successor, Harry Truman, was initially overwhelmed by the vast economic, political, and strategic problems resulting from the upheavals of World War II and the emerging Cold War with the Soviet Union. From Truman's vantage point in August 1945, Vietnam was a diplomatic backwater, and Ho Chi Minh was an obscure leader for whom he had no time.

If ever there was a time when Washington could have aligned itself with the forces of Vietnamese nationalism, it failed to grasp it. Truman and other senior U.S. officials, struggling with the vast array of postwar issues cascading down upon them, knew very little about the political realities of Vietnam, and they were not listening to the experts and officials on the ground in China and Southeast Asia who did. Washington was content to allow the French to resume their control of Indochina if that would make France a stronger and more compliant ally in the emerging Cold War with the Soviet Union.[58] Truman, a more parochial nationalist than the cosmopolitan statesman he replaced, supported the French goal of reimposing colonialism on the Vietnamese people.[59] State Department officials had urged Truman to placate the French, who were still seething over Roosevelt's modest efforts to remove Vietnam from their empire. Truman made a point of telling Charles de Gaulle that the United States would not try to undermine the French position in Indochina.

Truman and other Allied leaders, meeting at Potsdam a few weeks before Ho Chi Minh made his declaration of independence, had determined that Vietnam would be divided temporarily at the 16th Parallel of North Latitude at the war's end. North of that boundary, Chinese Nationalist troops were to handle the surrender of Japanese forces, arrange for their repatriation to Japan, and obtain the release of all prisoners of war and Allied internees. South of that line, British troops would take charge of these matters. As the Potsdam conferees made these secret agreements, they did not specify the shape that the political future of Vietnam would take, but, in effect, they granted the French a free hand to return to Indochina and reimpose colonialism on the Vietnamese people.[60]

At the historic moment that the Vietnamese nation made its reappearance, French forces were planning their re-entry into Vietnam. For Ho Chi Minh and his Vietnamese compatriots, a moment of celebration would be followed by decades of turmoil. No one could foresee it during that fateful summer of 1945, but consolidating the Vietnamese national revolution would take 30 years and exact a horrific toll in blood and treasure from those who made the revolution and from those who tried and failed to defeat it.

NOTES

1. Duiker, William J., *Vietnam: Nation in Revolution* (Boulder, CO: Westview Press, 1983), 13.
2. Le Thanh Khoi, *Le Viet-nam: Histoire et Civilization* (Paris: Editions du Minuit, 1955), 88–97.
3. Duiker, *Vietnam: Nation in Revolution,* 15.
4. Hall, Daniel G. E., *A History of Southeast Asia,* 2d ed. (New York: St. Martin's Press, 1955), 199–200.
5. Cady, John F., *Southeast Asia: Its Historical Development* (New York: McGraw-Hill, 1964), 103–6; Duiker, *Vietnam: Nation in Revolution,* 18–19.
6. Kahin, George M., and Lewis, John, *The United States in Vietnam: An Analysis in Depth of the History of America's Involvement in Vietnam* (New York: Delta, 1967), 5.
7. Duiker, *Vietnam: Nation in Revolution,* 22–23. Although during the war Americans often referred to Hue as the "ancient imperial capital" of Vietnam, it only became the capital in the early nineteenth century, and its eminence lasted for less than a century. Hanoi is the ancient capital of Vietnamese civilization; it has been the seat of government in Vietnam for most of its 2,000-year history and is today the capital of Cong Hoa Xa Hoi Chu Nghia Viet Nam (The Socialist Republic of Vietnam).
8. Duiker, William, *The Rise of Nationalism in Vietnam, 1900–1941* (Ithaca: Cornell University Press, 1976), 16.
9. Buttinger, Joseph, *The Smaller Dragon: A Political History of Vietnam* (New York: Praeger, 1958), 283–94.
10. Cady, John F., *The Roots of French Imperialism in Eastern Asia* (Ithaca: Cornell University Press, 1954), 97–102, 136–59, 178–80, 186–91.
11. Buttinger, Joseph, *A Dragon Defiant: A Short History of Vietnam* (New York: Praeger, 1972), 60; also his *Vietnam: A Dragon Embattled,* vol. 1 (New York: Praeger, 1967), 495.
12. Hall, Daniel G. E., *The History of Southeast Asia,* 560–70. Cochin China, Annam, and Tonkin are the Western names given to the three regions of Vietnam. The French also called Vietnam "Annam" and referred to the Vietnamese people as "Annamites" or the "Annamite people," names the Vietnamese despised and rejected. The Vietnamese have never thought of their country as being divided into autonomous regions. They think of their country as one nation, at the same time recognizing its distinctive regional characteristics. During the colonial period, they called the aforementioned three regions Nam Viet, Trung Viet, and Bac Viet, that is, South Vietnam, Central Vietnam, and North Vietnam.
13. Buttinger, *Vietnam: A Dragon Embattled,* vol. 1, 138–44; Duiker, *Vietnam: Nation in Revolution,* 23–26.
14. Doyle, Edward; Lipsman, Samuel; and the editors of Boston Publishing, *Setting the Stage* (Boston: Boston Publishing, 1981), 119–20.
15. Thompson, Virginia, *French Indochina* (London: Allen & Unwin, 1937), 228–34; Cady, John F., *Southeast Asia: Its Historical Development* (New York: McGraw-Hill, 1964), 406–34.
16. Lancaster, Donald, *The Emancipation of French Indochina* (London: Oxford University Press, 1961), 65–66.
17. The Vietnamese language is monosyllabic. Words are invariable. Verbs are not conjugated, and nouns are not declined. Different meanings of the same word are expressed by different levels of pitch. For most of Vietnamese history, Chinese ideographs were used in writing the language. In the seventeenth century, Portuguese and French missionaries invented a system of writing Vietnamese in the Latin alphabet called *quoc ngu.* In *quoc ngu,* syllabic tone is indicated by diacritical marks above, below, or through a letter. During their colonial tenure, the French made

quoc ngu an official language along with French. Currently, *quoc ngu* is in general use throughout Vietnam.

18. Buttinger, *A Dragon Defiant,* 68.

19. Hess, Gary R., *Vietnam and the United States* (Boston: Twayne, 1990), 11.

20. Buttinger, *A Dragon Defiant,* 111–44.

21. Ibid., 151–56.

22. The man the world knows as Ho Chi Minh employed numerous pseudonyms until 1943 when he adopted his final, famous name.

23. Lacouture, Jean, *Ho Chi Minh: A Political Biography,* translated from the French by Peter Wiles, translation edited by Jane Clark Seitz. (New York: Random House, 1968), 13–21; Fall, Bernard B., ed., *Ho Chi Minh on Revolution, Selected Writings, 1920–1966* (Boulder, CO: Westview Press, 1984), 43–51.

24. Doyle et al., *Setting the Stage,* 156 57. Ho Chi Minh's petition is entitled Revendications du Peuple Annamite. It begins, "Depuis la victoire des Allies, tous le peuples assujettis fremissent d'espoir devant la perspective d'lere de droit et du justice qui doit s'ouvrir pour eux en vertu des engagements formeis et solennels, pris devant le monde entier par les differentes puissance de L'Entente dans la lutte de la Civilisation contre la Barbarie." Schulzinger, Robert D., *A Time for War: The United States and Vietnam, 1941–1975* (New York: Oxford University Press, 1997), 9.

25. Duiker, William J., *The Communist Road to Power in Vietnam* (Boulder, CO: Westview Press, 1981), 17–18.

26. Schulzinger, *A Time for War,* 11; Duiker, *The Communist Road,* 32–33.

27. Hammer, Ellen J., *The Struggle for Indochina* (Stanford, CA: Stanford University Press, 1954), 84–86; Duiker, *Communist Road,* 33–40.

28. Duiker, *Communist Road,* 40–43.

29. Duiker, *Vietnam: Nation in Revolt,* 37–38.

30. In 1935, Stalin became alarmed at the growing power of fascist states in Europe, concluding that they posed a grave threat to Soviet interests. He instructed Communist parties in Western democracies to abandon their revolutionary tactics and form coalitions, "popular fronts," with liberal and socialist parties to combat the Fascist menace. A popular Front coalition governed France from 1936 to 1939. The Indochinese Communist Party, under Ho Chi Minh's leadership, responded to Comintern directives. It moderated its revolutionary program and formed alliances with liberal and socialist groups within Vietnam. The Popular Front strategy ended in August 1939 with the signing of the Nazi-Soviet Non-Aggression Pact. Communist parties in France, Vietnam, and elsewhere resumed their revolutionary postures as war began in Europe and intensified in Asia.

31. Lancaster, Donald, *The Emancipation of French Indochina* (London: Oxford University Press, 1961), 98–104.

32. Buttinger, *Dragon Embattled,* vol. 1, 244–50; Hammer, *Struggle,* 31.

33. Buttinger, *Dragon Embattled,* vol. 1, 250–53.

34. Chen, King C., *Vietnam and China, 1938–1954* (Princeton, NJ: Princeton University Press, 1969), 44–48.

35. Ho Chi Minh, *Selected Writings, 1920–1969* (Hanoi: People's Publishing House, 1973), 46.

36. Devillers, Philippe, *Histoire du Vietnam de 1940 à 1952* (Paris: Editions du Seuil, 1952), 96–113; Duiker, *The Communist Road,* 64–72; Chen, *Vietnam and China,* 51–55; Pike, Douglas, *History of Vietnamese Communism, 1925–1976* (Stanford, CA: Hoover Institution Press, 1978), 30–51.

37. Lacouture, *Ho Chi Minh,* 78–79.

38. Doyle et al., *Setting the Stage,* 176.

39. Quoted in ibid., 177.

40. LaFeber, Walter, "Roosevelt, Churchill, and Indochina, 1942–1945," *American Historical Review* (December 1975): 1277–95.

41. Quoted in Pettit, Clyde Edwin, *The Experts* (Secaucus, NJ: Lyle Stuart, 1975), 13.

42. Hess, Gary R., "Franklin D. Roosevelt and Indochina," *Journal of American History* (September 1972): 353–68.

43. Patti, Archimedes L., *Why Vietnam? Prelude to America's Albatross* (Berkeley: University of California Press, 1980), 55–56. The Office of Strategic Services was a wartime intelligence agency whose agents also engaged in commando operations behind enemy lines. They committed sabotage and aided resistance forces, which often included Communists within their ranks, in both the European and Asian theaters of war. See "Instructions by Ho Chi Minh for Setting Up of the Armed Propaganda Brigade for the Liberation of Vietnam, December 1944," printed in Porter, Gareth, ed., *Vietnam: The Definitive Documentation of Human Decisions* (Stanfordville, NY: Earl M. Coleman Enterprises, 1979), vol. 1, 14.

44. Devillers, *Histoire,* 152; Chen, *Vietnam and China,* 113–14. Chen points out that the Chinese Nationalists only helped the Vietnamese Nationalists, particularly the VNQDD and Dong Minh Hoi. He finds no evidence that the Vietminh received any help from the Chinese Communists. The Soviets displayed no interest in the Vietminh revolution. The Vietminh were on their own except for some help from their American friends in the OSS. Hess, Gary, *Vietnam and the United States,* rev. ed. (New York: Twayne, 1998), 31.

45. Hammer, *Struggle,* 36–45.

46. Ibid., 46–47; Schulzinger, *A Time for War,* 17. When Bao Dai formed his government, he wanted Ngo Dinh Diem to become prime minister. Diem, a devout Catholic, had refused collaboration with the Japanese and retained impressive credentials as a non-Communist Vietnamese nationalist. But the Japanese rejected Diem, and Bao Dai then chose Tran Trong Kim for the post.

47. Buttinger, *Dragon,* vol. 1, 292–95; Duiker, *The Communist Road,* 94–100.

48. Woodside, Alexander B., *Community and Revolution in Modern Vietnam* (Boston: Houghton Mifflin, 1976), 225–40.

49. Hess, *Vietnam,* 20.

50. Buttinger, *Dragon,* 296–98; Duiker, *The Communist Road,* 94–100; Porter, Gareth, & Emerson, Gloria, eds., *Vietnam: A History in Documents,* vol. 1, New York: New American Library, 1981; (ed.), *Resolutions of the Vietminh Conference to Establish a Free Zone, June 4, 1945,* 47–49.

51. Duiker, *The Communist Road,* 98–99; Chen, *Vietnam and China,* 102–114 is a good brief account of the Vietminh August Revolution; Porter, *Vietnam Documents,* vol. 1, *Appeal by Ho Chi Minh for General Insurrection, August 1945,* 60–61.

52. Chen, *Vietnam and China,* 111–12.

53. Smith, R. Harris, *OSS: The Secret History of America's First Central Intelligence Agency* (New York: Delta Books, 1973), 351–55; Ho's Declaration is printed in Porter, *Vietnam Documents,* vol. 1, 64–66.

54. Herring, George C., *America's Longest War: The United States and Vietnam, 1950–1975,* rev. ed. (New York: Knopf, 1986), 3; quoted in Kahin, George McT., *Intervention: How America Became Involved in Vietnam* (New York: Knopf, 1986), 14–15.

55. Young, Marilyn B., *The Vietnam Wars* (New York: Harper Collins, 1991), 10.

56. Gaddis, John Lewis, *We Now Know: Rethinking Cold War History* (New York: Oxford, 1997), 58; Bills, Scott L., *Empire and Cold War: The Roots of U.S.-Third World Antagonism, 1945–1947* (New York: St. Martin's Press, 1990), 204; Hess, *Vietnam,* 29–30; Kahin, *Intervention,* 5.

57. Gardner, Lloyd C., *Approaching Vietnam: From World War II through Dienbienphu* (New York: W. W. Norton, 1988), 46–63; Lafeber, *Roosevelt, Churchill, and Indochina,* 1289.

58. Schulzinger, *A Time for War,* 21–22.

59. Kahin, *Intervention,* 19–20; Arnold A. Offner, "The Truman Myth Revealed: From Parochial Nationalist to Cold Warrior," March 1988. Unpublished paper presented at the Organization of American Historians Convention; Herring, George, *The Truman Administration and the Restoration of French Sovereignty in Indochina, Diplomatic History,* vol. 1 (spring 1977), 97–117.

60. Kahin, *Intervention,* 15–16; Tuchman, Barbara, *The March of Folly: From Troy to Vietnam* (New York: Ballantine, 1984), 239–40.

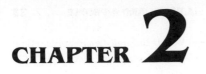

The Elephant and the Tiger

It will be a war between an elephant and a tiger. If the tiger ever stands still, the elephant will crush him with his mighty tusks. But the tiger will not stand still. He will leap upon the back of the elephant, tearing huge chunks from his side, and then he will leap back into the dark jungle. And slowly the elephant will bleed to death. That will be the war of Indochina.

Ho Chi Minh

RETURN OF THE FRENCH

The end of World War II presaged the end of Western imperialism in Southeast Asia. Emergent nationalist leaders took advantage of the sudden surrender of the Japanese and the evident strategic weakness of the European powers to demand independence. The August Revolution of the Vietminh paralleled nationalist revolutions in the Dutch East Indies, Burma, and India.[1] In the Philippines, nationalists urged the United States to fulfill its prewar pledge to grant their country independence. In China, the defeat of the Japanese ended the wartime collaboration of the Koumingtang and the Maoists, and they resumed their civil war.

The French dismissed the Vietnamese claim of independence and maneuvered to reestablish their Indochina colony. They did not take seriously the claims of a fragile government struggling to feed its starving people, lacking a powerful army, with limited financial resources, and having no standing or support in the international community. British and Chinese troops entered Vietnam in September 1945 to carry out the Potsdam directives issued the previous month by the victorious Allied powers. In the train of the British troops entering southern Vietnam came French forces. Insertion of these outside military forces triggered a series of conflicts that engulfed Vietnam for decades, delaying the emergence of an independent, unified Vietnamese state for more than 30 years.

In the aftermath of World War II, the French instinct was to hang on to all of their overseas possessions and privileges, and they were willing to use military force if necessary to preserve them in the Middle East, North Africa, and Southeast Asia. Because they were determined to cling to their empire, the French fought a series of disastrous colonial wars from the 1940s to the 1960s and still lost their colonies. The first of these colonial wars occurred in Indochina. The French were driven by a mix of motives to try to reimpose their rule on the Vietnamese, Cambodian, and Laotian peoples. Economic considerations were important, especially in Cochin China, where French financial and commercial interests were concentrated. The French also had a politico-psychological motive for returning to Indochina. The quick Nazi conquest of France in 1940, followed by the rigors and humiliations of the German occupation, had dealt French national esteem serious blows, as had Japanese occupation of Indochina and other French possessions in the South Pacific.

The most important reason for the French drive to regain control of their former Southeast Asian possessions transcended Indochina and concerned the political cohesion of France's entire overseas empire. French officials had a view of colonialism resembling the subsequent American domino theory: If one colony won its independence, others would then be tempted to stage similar breakaways from French control. If the Vietnam domino fell, not only would the Cambodian and Laotian dominoes follow quickly, but also, far worse in the French view, their more valuable North African possessions, Morocco, Tunisia, and the most valuable of all French overseas territories, Algeria, would rise in rebellion against French colonialism. To safeguard the interests of their 1 million Algerian *colons,* the French prepared to reconquer 24 million Vietnamese.[2]

The advance wave of 2,000 British and Indian troops, most of them famed *Gurkhas,* marched into Saigon on September 13, 1945, under the command of General Douglas D. Gracey. Eighteen thousand additional troops soon joined them. General Gracey did not acknowledge the Democratic Republic of Vietnam's claim of sovereignty. He favored the French returning to Indochina, and he reacted to the political disorder he encountered within a country in the throes of revolution after a disruptive war by declaring martial law. He also gave orders to disarm all Vietnamese forces, but he released and rearmed about 5,000 French troops that the Japanese had interned. These French forces, armed with U.S. weapons, and joined by newly arriving French troops carried to Indochina in U.S. and British ships, overthrew the Vietminh government in Saigon on September 23, 1945. The French had forced their way back into Vietnam. The Tricolor once again flew over public buildings in the "Paris of the Orient." The French return was supported by the British and the Americans. At the time of the French reentry into Vietnam, Acting Secretary of State Dean Acheson wrote the

American chargé d'affaires in China that the "U.S. has no thought of opposing the re-establishment of French control in Indochina."[3]

The Vietminh leader in Saigon, Tran Van Giau, ordered a general strike and also ordered counterattacks against the French. Nearly all Vietnamese, determined to prevent a return of the French, joined the resistance, including the religious sectarians and a criminal organization, the Binh Xuyen, the Cochin China "Mafia." General Gracey responded to these actions by releasing and rearming Japanese soldiers! Multinational British, Indian, French, and Japanese forces, many armed with American weapons, undertook the pacification of southern Vietnam in the fall of 1945. For the British, what has been called the First Indochina War, from 1945 to 1946,[4] proved to be short. As more French troops arrived and as the British completed their assigned task of supervising the repatriation of Japanese troops, their troops were withdrawn. As spring came to southern Vietnam in 1946, the British soldiers were gone.

Most Americans knew nothing of the complex political developments taking place in a remote corner of the world at the end of World War II. American media gave little attention to these events or to the major role Americans played in helping the French return to Vietnam. Americans would have been astounded to learn that Allied political maneuvering in Vietnam in the fall of 1945 was preparing the ground for a long U.S. entanglement in that country. But one famous American who was following events in Vietnam did not like what he saw. General Douglas MacArthur, the preeminent hero of the Pacific war and newly appointed American proconsul in Japan, passionately denounced the Allied intervention in southern Vietnam: "If there is anything that makes my blood boil, it is to see our allies in Indochina deploying Japanese troops to reconquer the little people we promised to liberate."[5]

By February 1, 1946, French forces, under the command of General Jacques Phillipe LeClerc,[6] had brought Cochin China under their control. But Leclerc's troops controlled only the cities, towns, and main roads. Vietminh forces effectively contested French authority in the countryside, where most Vietnamese lived. Ho Chi Minh and his Vietminh associates in Hanoi supported these resistance efforts, but they could not control events in the south. While concerned about the French presence in southern Vietnam, Ho Chi Minh remained focused on the Tonkin region because once again Chinese forces had invaded northern Vietnam.[7]

To carry out his part of the Potsdam bargain, Chiang Kai-shek sent an army of 180,000 troops, commanded by General Lu Han, into Tonkin. The Chinese generals, like the British, did not recognize Ho Chi Minh's government. The Chinese brought along some non-Communist Vietnamese nationalist politicians, remnants of the VNQDD, the Dong Minh Hoi, and other groups who had been living in exile in China since the 1930s. As the Chinese troops marched through hamlets and villages, they replaced Vietminh officials with the Vietnamese political leaders that they had brought with them. Chiang appeared to be using Chinese troops to destroy the Vietminh revolution in the northern half of Vietnam and to install a government headed by Vietnamese nationalists who would look to China for guidance and protection. By the end of September, Dong Minh Hoi and VNQDD officials, backed by Chinese troops, controlled the countryside.[8] Posing a further problem for the Vietminh, the Chinese troops behaved more like bandits than soldiers, systematically looting the Vietnamese villagers as they marched through the countryside. The Vietminh, powerless to stem the invasion of the huge Chinese army, remained in power only in Hanoi. Facing a French takeover in the south and Chinese occupation in the north, Ho Chi Minh and his colleagues maneuvered desperately to save their imperiled revolution.

The Vietminh resorted to bribery to keep themselves in power. Requisitioning gold and currency from the Vietnamese people, Ho Chi Minh made General Lu Han and his friends rich men. In return, the Chinese were content to leave his fledgling government in power and to avoid conflict with the Vietminh leaders. Ho Chi Minh also appointed VNQDD leaders to positions in the Vietnamese Provisional Government. Soon afterward, the VNQDD split, with half joining the Vietminh coalition. In addition, Ho Chi Minh dismantled the ICP apparatus and introduced a range of democratic reforms that brought Vietnamese Catholic and other non-Communist groups over to his government. Most important, he called for elections to select delegates to the National Assembly to draft a constitution and establish a permanent government for Vietnam. To save his social revolution, Ho Chi Minh was forced to softpedal it.

The first national elections in Vietnamese history took place on January 6, 1946. Voter turnouts were massive. Over 90 percent of eligible voters participated, and Vietminh candidates scored an overwhelming victory, winning 206 of the 254 seats.[9] But Ho Chi Minh allowed nationalist delegates 70 slots to guarantee them an important role in his new government. His deft maneuvering had bought off the Chinese generals, co-opted the political threat posed by the Vietnamese nationalists that the Chinese had brought with them, and broadened the popular base of support for his Vietminh-controlled government among non-Communist elements who made up the large majority of the Vietnamese population.

The Chinese Nationalists, resuming their civil war with the Maoists in the aftermath of the Japanese defeat, were less interested in taking control of northern Vietnam or in restoring Vietnamese nationalist political groups to power than in using their temporary occupation of the country to wrest concessions from the French. U.S. officials, committed to the restoration of French sovereignty in Indochina, also pressured the Chinese to "facilitate the recovery of power by the French."[10] But the Chinese refused to permit French troops to enter northern Vietnam until they had extracted major concessions from France.

French and Chinese negotiators concluded a series of important agreements in February and March 1946. The French agreed to give up all of their prewar trading rights and concessions in China in exchange for China's acquiescence in French reentry into northern Vietnam. Under the terms of the Sino-French accord, French forces could start landing at Haiphong on March 6, 1946. But the return of French troops to the north would require Vietminh permission in the spring of 1946 because the French were not strong enough at the time to simply walk in and overpower Ho Chi Minh's forces without absorbing considerable casualties if the Vietminh chose to resist them.

There also was the possibility of the Chinese backing the Vietminh to keep the French out if Ho Chi Minh refused to accept the return of the French.

For his part, Ho Chi Minh was willing to seek a compromise with the French in order to rid his country of the rapacious Chinese whom he believed posed a greater long-range threat to Vietnamese sovereignty than the French.[11] Delicate negotiations between the French and Vietminh officials took place at the same time as the French-Chinese talks. Ho Chi Minh headed the Vietminh team of negotiators dealing with the French. Jean Sainteny, the commissioner-delegate for Tonkin and an old friend of Ho Chi Minh, headed the French delegation. Sainteny offered many concessions to obtain Vietminh acceptance of their reoccupation of northern Vietnam. The two sides reached a preliminary understanding signed on March 6, 1946. By its terms, France appeared to be taking its first steps toward decolonizing Indochina. Ho Chi Minh's government was declared to be "a free state within the French Union," with its own government and army. France also agreed to hold a national referendum to determine whether the colony of Cochin China would rejoin Annam and Tonkin in a reunited Vietnam or would remain a separate French territory. In return, the Vietminh agreed that 25,000 French troops would replace Chinese forces north of the 16th Parallel, and they could remain there until 1951. Both sides also agreed that a Vietminh delegation would travel to Paris later in the year to work out the details of the agreement that had been deliberately left vague. The Chinese accepted these arrangements, agreeing to withdraw all of their troops by June 16, 1946. For a hopeful moment it appeared that moderation and statesmanship had averted both a war and a reversion to colonialism in Vietnam.[12]

But the Ho-Sainteny agreement of March 6 soon proved a sham. French officials refused to hold the promised plebiscite in Cochin China and construed the new status of Vietnam as a "free state within the French Union" as being only a facade for continuing French domination of the country. Meanwhile, 15,000 French troops reentered Tonkin, with Chinese and U.S. acceptance.

While these crucial events that set the stage for the subsequent French and U.S. involvements in Vietnam were taking place, the Soviet Union ignored Vietnam. In the early postwar period, the Soviet Union was not a major player in Southeast Asia. It confined its actions to anti-imperialist propaganda, meanwhile conceding Western hegemony in the Third World. The Soviets had no choice. At the time, their reach was limited, and they were preoccupied with consolidating their sphere of influence in Eastern Europe and rebuilding their shattered economy in the aftermath of World War II. Even though the Communist revolutionaries in Vietnam were fighting for their survival in 1945 and 1946, Soviet aid to the Vietminh did not begin until the 1950s.

Ironically, in 1946 Stalin favored French Communist officials over a minor Communist leader in Southeast Asia, who appeared from Moscow's perspective to be a Vietnamese nationalist first and a Communist second. Stalin had hopes that the French Communist Party, the largest political party in France, might win the 1946 elections and legally take control of the French government. Although they did not win that election, the Communists came out of it with several cabinet positions, and their leader, Maurice

Thorez, became deputy premier. Fearful that they would lose electoral appeal if they supported anticolonialism, Communist leaders serving in the government supported the French drive to reimpose colonialism on Indochina, a popular cause in France in 1946 and 1947. Stalin backed the French Communists, leaving Ho Chi Minh and the Vietminh to fend for themselves!

From his vantage point in Hanoi in the spring of 1946, Ho Chi Minh felt isolated and vulnerable. He headed a struggling revolutionary regime within a small country that had almost no financial resources and a poorly equipped army. The major powers were either backing or accepting French efforts to reimpose colonialism in Indochina. The Vietminh had no allies in either the Communist or Western camps as they prepared to face the powerful French alone.[13]

Ho Chi Minh and his associates tried hard to negotiate agreements with the French to avoid a war and to preserve a measure of autonomy. French and Vietminh officials met at Dalat, a mountain resort in the Central Highlands, to try to define the Ho-Sainteny agreement. The French representatives made clear that their interpretation of the phrase "free state within the French Union" meant continuing French colonial domination of Vietnam. Ho Chi Minh refused to accept the outcome of the Dalat conference as final, and he prepared for further negotiations to be held later in France.

In the summer of 1946, French and Vietnamese delegates met for a series of talks at Fontainebleau Palace near Paris. Ho Chi Minh journeyed to France to head the Vietminh contingent. For eight weeks, he tried desperately to achieve the substance of independence for his country and to avoid war. But these talks were also doomed to fail because the French refused to budge from their Dalat interpretation of the Ho-Sainteny agreement. At the same time that they refused all of Ho's overtures, the French also reestablished their control over Laos and Cambodia. These developments ensured that the fledgling DRV would henceforth face three hostile French-controlled governments within the Indochina Federation.

Trying to obtain help from any quarter, Ho Chi Minh contacted the American embassy in Paris. He promised the Americans that he would open up Vietnam to U.S. investment, and he offered to lease Cam Ranh Bay to the U.S. Navy in exchange for help in keeping the French out. Ho was rebuffed by a low-level State Department functionary. He then met with French Prime Minister Georges Bidault and other top French officials. He pleaded with them to make some concessions that he could take back to his people. On September 14, 1946, Ho Chi Minh warned Bidault: "If we must fight, we will fight. You will kill ten of our men and we will kill one of yours. Yet, in the end, it is you who will tire."[14]

Despite all his of pleading and threats, all Ho Chi Minh could extract from the determined French was a promise to hold the Cochin China referendum and agree to more negotiations at a later date. They never made good on either commitment. Sick at heart, Ho Chi Minh had to return to Hanoi in October 1946, bringing only a flimsy modus vivendi to show for his efforts.[15]

The fragile peace in Tonkin was shattered the following month. On November 20, French and Vietminh customs collectors quarreled over who had the right to collect customs duties at the port of Haiphong. That night, squads of French and Vietminh soldiers exchanged fire in the city's streets. "These were the opening shots in the eight-year war between the French and the Vietminh."[16]

In the aftermath of these skirmishes, French officials decided to teach a hard lesson to the Vietnamese. On November 23, after giving the Vietminh only two hours to vacate the Chinese Quarter of Haiphong, the French attacked guerrilla hideouts in that sector. French infantry and armored units swept through the city. French aircraft provided tactical air support for the ground forces. The French cruiser *Suffren* bombarded the city for hours. When the day ended, much of Haiphong lay in rubble; 6,000 people were dead and another 25,000 were wounded, mostly civilians. On November 28, the French commander General Morliere issued an ultimatum demanding that the Vietminh yield control of the city, its suburbs, and the main highway between Haiphong and Hanoi to the French military forces. The Vietminh refused General Morliere's demands. On December 18, the French moved troops into Hanoi and occupied several government buildings. On December 19, General Morliere ordered General Giap to disarm his forces.[17] Giap refused to obey his command.

That night the Vietminh leaders held a plenary meeting. General Giap ordered that a war of national resistance begin. Later that same evening, Vietminh guerrillas destroyed the Hanoi power plant, plunging the city into darkness. Other guerrilla units attacked the homes of French officials, assassinating several, and planted mines in the streets of Hanoi. All over northern Vietnam, French installations were attacked by guerrilla raiders. As the attacks were taking place, Ho Chi Minh removed himself from Hanoi and set up a temporary government at Ha Dong, six miles to the south.[18]

By the end of 1946, the war that had begun in Saigon in September 1945 had spread north, engulfing all of Vietnam. In retrospect, the conflict that Ho Chi Minh had tried hard to avoid appears inevitable because the French were determined to reimpose colonialism on a people who absolutely refused to accept it and who were ready to fight to preserve their revolution if they must. The Vietnamese nationalists had a charismatic leader in iron-willed Ho Chi Minh, part Communist revolutionary and part Confucian philosopher, who was absolutely devoted to the cause of Vietnamese independence.

As the war began that was destined to last eight years and end in France's humiliation, confident French officials predicted that the conflict would last three months at most. Their modern army faced a native militia force that was both poorly armed and poorly trained. French officials, assuming a quick, easy victory over the forces they contemptuously called "the barefoot army," regretted only that their soldiers would not be home for Christmas.

THE FRANCO-VIETMINH WAR

When the war began in December 1946, the Vietminh could field about 60,000 troops. In addition to these main force units, the Vietnamese had large peasant and youth militia forces. Altogether, there were about 150,000 soldiers available to the Vietminh. But only one-third of these troops were equipped with even small arms. The Vietminh possessed neither a navy nor an air force. The poorly prepared Vietminh soldiers could not hope to defeat "a serious French effort to restore colonial rule in Vietnam."[19] In 1946, the French could field a modern well-equipped and well-trained army of 150,000 fighters, including French soldiers, Legionnaires, and colonial troops. At the outset French forces quickly took control of the cities and large towns. The early phase of the Franco-Vietminh War severely tested Ho Chi Minh's claim that the Vietnamese tiger could survive the French elephant's efforts to crush it.

Ho Chi Minh, who had continued to seek a negotiated settlement until French military actions forced him to accept war rather than capitulate to French colonialism, now called his people to arms:

> Those who have rifles will use their rifles; those who have swords will use their swords; those who have no swords will use spades, hoes or sticks. Long live an independent and unified Vietnam! Long live the resistance![20]

The Vietminh looked to Maoist doctrines of guerrilla warfare for strategic guidance as they planned their campaigns against the French forces. On December 22, 1946, the revolutionary government announced that the struggle against the French imperialists would advance through three stages. The revolutionaries stated that the first stage of the war would be defensive, during which the Vietminh guerrillas would abandon the urban areas if they had to and retreat into the countryside and to the mountains of northern Vietnam. During this stage, they would avoid major battles with the French forces, concentrate on building up their own main force units, and continue political organization in the villages. The second stage would be one of equilibrium, in which the revolutionary forces would be growing in strength and the imperialist forces would be declining. The third stage would feature a general offensive by the revolutionary forces, stronger than their enemies, that would defeat the imperialist armies and drive them from the country.[21] No specific time frames were mentioned in the December 22 announcement; there were no indications how long they expected each phase to last. But it was clear that the Vietminh planned for a protracted war against the French, a war that could go on for years, and one that they were confident they would ultimately win. Protracted warfare had defeated Chinese invaders over the centuries. The Vietminh, serenely patient, believed it would also beat the French.

Already controlling Cochin China, the French forces in the early months of 1947 occupied the major cities and towns of Annam and Tonkin. The outgunned Vietminh main force units avoided combat with the more powerful invaders, and what resistance the French encountered in these early campaigns came mostly from local guerrillas. The Vietminh put up their stiffest resistance in Hanoi, and it took the French forces three months to take the city. Beyond the cities, the Vietminh remained in control of much of the countryside, where they retained the loyalty of most of the population.

Viet Bac, the mountainous northern provinces, remained a revolutionary stronghold and haven. Near the remote mountain village of Bac Can, 50 miles from the Chinese border, Ho Chi Minh established his headquarters.[22]

In October 1947, the French launched a major offensive designed to destroy the Vietminh main forces and capture the revolutionary leaders in their Viet Bac sanctuaries. The French sent a powerful force of 12 infantry battalions, reinforced by armored units and air support, deep into the northern countryside. French paratroopers staged a surprise raid on Vietminh headquarters in a cave near Bac Can. They missed capturing Ho Chi Minh and other Vietminh leaders by less than one hour![23] Although they failed to capture the revolutionary leadership, the French military campaign scored major successes. They killed an estimated 10,000 Vietminh main force personnel and forced the rebels to abandon large areas of Viet Bac.

At the same time they launched their military offensive in the north, the French, convinced that they could not defeat the Vietminh by force alone, moved to undercut the Vietminh politically by forming alliances with Vietnamese groups that would cooperate with them against the revolutionaries. The heart of the French political strategy involved forming a Vietnamese government in Saigon and persuading former emperor Bao Dai to head it. The French plan was to create a non-Communist Vietnamese state that would offer a political alternative to the Vietminh revolutionary regime and provide a rallying point for non-Communist Vietnamese nationalists. If Bao Dai succeeded in uniting the various non-Communist political factions into a cohesive force, he could create "a serious alternative to the Vietminh Front for the loyalty of the Vietnamese people."[24]

The French political strategy in 1947 failed for two main reasons. The first, a perennial problem of Vietnamese politics, especially southern urban Vietnamese politics, was the inability of various non-Communist nationalist factions to overcome chronic political fragmentation and form a stable coalition government. The second was the French refusal to grant the proposed government anything resembling sovereignty. The French would promise only a puppet regime that most Vietnamese regarded as a cover for French colonialism, and the people of Vietnam made a point of shunning it.

Although the French had seized both the military and political initiative in the fall of 1947, they had failed to either destroy the Vietminh army or to create a viable political alternative to Ho Chi Minh's revolutionary nationalism. French leaders did not realize it at the time, but their effort to reimpose colonialism on the Vietnamese had reached its high water mark. Given Vietminh control of most of the countryside and the fact that it had the support of most of the people, a French military victory was never a realistic possibility.

Vietminh prospects improved markedly in 1948. In China, the Communists were fast gaining the upper hand against Chiang Kai-shek's deteriorating nationalist armies. Mao's victory, which now appeared to Ho Chi Minh and his associates to be only a matter of time, offered the promise of significant economic and military assistance, as well as political support for the struggling Vietnamese revolutionaries.

Emboldened by developments in China and by a sense that the French campaign to destroy their revolution had already reached its limits, General Giap announced that the Vietnamese struggle against the French had progressed to its second stage, the stage of equilibrium. No longer would the rebels be content to remain on the defensive; they would henceforth move to expand both the geographic area under their control and to wear down the French main forces. During the second phase of their struggle, they relied mostly upon guerrilla tactics, but occasionally deployed main force units in swift mobile assaults on French forces when they knew they could win.[25] During 1948, both the Vietminh military forces and their political apparatus doubled in size. They regained most of the territory they had lost the previous year and expanded the area in Cochin China under their control. As the year ended, the Vietminh controlled about 55 percent of all Vietnamese villages, north and south. The French found themselves bogged down in what one writer called a quicksand war.[26]

French officials in Vietnam, having failed to defeat the rebels militarily, tried again to outmaneuver them politically. The French also sought to attract direct U.S. military support for their increasingly expensive efforts in Indochina that were quickly losing favor with the French public. After a series of negotiations, the French finally persuaded Bao Dai to head a new government that was given the status of "an associated state within the French Union." According to the Elysee Agreement, signed March 8, 1949, the French granted "independence" to the "State of Vietnam," Laos, and Cambodia, all of which became "associated states" within the French Union. The French now claimed, disingenuously, that they were not fighting a colonial war at all. Vietnamese nationalists and Communists were fighting a civil war for control of Indochina, and the French were fighting for the nationalist cause.

But all the new states were to be incorporated into the French Union without most of the attributes of sovereignty. The French retained control over the new Vietnamese government's foreign affairs, defense forces, and taxes levied on French properties. The new political order was merely a facade for continuing French domination, and it failed to attract the support of most prominent Vietnamese nationalists.[27] For most Vietnamese, there were only two political choices available in 1949: One could either support the French effort to reimpose colonialism on Indochina, or one could support the revolutionary nationalists resisting the French efforts to reimpose colonialism. The vast majority of the Vietnamese people, whatever their politics, opted for the Vietminh cause.

Perceiving that Bao Dai's government lacked legitimacy, had little real power, and had only a narrow base of support, the Vietminh forces located in the south escalated their revolutionary activity in Saigon and its vicinity. They also infiltrated the new government's police force and its civil service bureaucracies. Vietminh military forces launched a series of assaults on provincial capitals in the Mekong River Delta. But French troops routed the guerrillas in the delta, and they were forced to seek refuge in the Plain of Reeds, a huge area of swamps, waterways, and rice paddies 50 miles southwest of Saigon.[28]

By far the most important political event of 1949 influencing the course of the Franco-Vietminh War and the growing U.S. involvement in Vietnam was the Maoist victory in China. The People's Republic of China (PRC) was established in October 1949, as Chiang Kai-Shek, accompanied by remnants of his bureaucracy and army, fled the Chinese mainland for the island of Formosa (Taiwan). One month later, Chinese Communist military forces appeared at the Vietnamese border. In January 1950, the new Chinese government extended both military assistance and diplomatic recognition to Ho Chi Minh's government, the Democratic Republic of Vietnam (DRV). Moscow soon followed suit, formally recognizing the DRV.[29]

The new relation between China and the Vietminh transformed the Franco-Vietminh conflict both politically and militarily. Until now, Ho Chi Minh had waged his battles with France alone. Now he had a powerful friend and ideological soul brother next door. Responding to the more favorable political situation they found themselves inhabiting, Ho's government also threw off its Patriotic Front trappings. It became openly Communist, and many non-Communist elements were purged from the ranks of the Vietminh. The ICP, which had been dissolved in 1945, reappeared in 1950 as the Dang Lao Dong Viet Nam (the Vietnamese Worker's Party, or VWP, aka the Lao Dong).

For the first time since the formation of the Vietminh in 1941, the Vietnamese revolution was cast within a Marxist-Leninist framework.[30] Henceforth, the Vietnamese revolution would be led openly by the Lao Dong. The revolutionaries also made it clear that the socialist revolution, which they had played down for so long for the sake of national unity, would begin as soon as the French were driven out of Vietnam. In fact, the social revolution began before the French were expelled. In 1951, Lao Dong cadres began land reform in various districts in the countryside. Land rents were reduced, and rice lands were confiscated from landlords and given to poor peasants who owned no land. Land reform both restructured rural class relations and strengthened popular support in the countryside for the ongoing war against the French.[31]

Although the political consequences of the new alliance with China were significant, the most important immediate result of the new relationship was to strengthen the Vietminh military forces tremendously and give them the option of moving to the general counteroffensive, the projected third stage of their protracted struggle against the French.[32] In April 1950, Ho Chi Minh journeyed to Beijing, where he concluded a lend-lease arrangement with the Chinese and much more.[33] The Chinese loaned the Vietminh artillery, mortars, and modern rifles. In addition, Chinese instructors and technicians arrived in Viet Bac to train the Vietnamese in the use of more effective weapons and tactics. By the fall of 1950, General Giap had 60,000 regulars organized into five infantry divisions. All his soldiers were indoctrinated, disciplined, well trained, and armed with modern weapons. The Vietminh Army had been transformed. The army that French professionals had once dismissed as the "barefoot army" had become a formidable modern fighting force.

While the Vietnamese revolutionaries were being strengthened immensely by their Chinese friends, the French effort in Vietnam was sagging, hampered by declining popular support at home. In the eyes of many of the French back home, the Indochina War had become too expensive. They did not like it or want it. Responding to the war's growing unpopularity, the French government refused to send conscripts to fight in the war and also reduced the number of French troops in Vietnam by nearly 10,000. When Giap took the offensive in 1950, the French forces found themselves having to face the newly enhanced Vietminh units with fewer troops.

Giap's objectives were to clear out a string of French garrisons that reached into the northern countryside along the Chinese frontier. The principal garrison was at Dong Khe, which fell to the aggressive assaults of the Vietminh on September 16, 1950.[34] The loss of Dong Khe was a military disaster for the French. It exposed all their other outposts to attack. They were either overrun or evacuated, and the retreating troops were often hammered by the mobile, aggressive Vietminh units using artillery, mortars, grenades, and machine-gun fire. French losses were heavy, and they also abandoned huge stockpiles of valuable weapons, ammunition, medical supplies, and foodstuffs.[35] Giap's forces drove the French out of northern Tonkin and pushed them back into the coastal enclaves.

Giap's border offensive during the fall of 1950 represented a major turning point in the Franco-Vietminh War. For the first time, the Vietminh had attacked and defeated sizable units of a modern European army. Giap's troops were now positioned to invade the strategic Red River Delta with its large population and rich rice harvests. They also had unrestricted access to China and its resources and growing prospects for aid from the USSR and Eastern bloc countries. Most of all, the Vietminh could now seize the tactical initiative in the war.[36] French morale sank, and, for the first time, worried French officials had to confront the unthinkable possibility that they could be beaten militarily by their former colonial subjects.

A Franco-American Partnership

Although President Truman appeared less committed than his late predecessor to fostering Asian nationalism at the expense of fading European colonial powers after the war, Washington nevertheless pressured the British to grant India independence and leaned even harder on the Dutch to get out of Indonesia. However, Cold War imperatives increasingly drove Truman's approach to Southeast Asia. Whatever remained of Washington's enthusiasm for self-determination in Indochina quickly evaporated in the wake of the emergence of an avowed Communist revolutionary leading the Vietnamese effort to restore its national independence. When the French rejected Ho Chi Minh's efforts to achieve a settlement that would permit his government to retain at least some autonomy and war erupted, it was the Franco-Vietminh conflict that impelled the United States toward its initial political commitments in Indochina. Subsequent major U.S. political and military involvement in Vietnam and the other countries of Indochina derived from the American response to the Franco-Vietminh War.

Although the Truman administration had supported the return of the French to Indochina following the defeat of the Japanese, Washington was nevertheless alarmed by the outbreak of the Franco-Vietminh War in 1946. Although pro-French, Washington sent representatives to Vietnam who met with Ho Chi Minh and French officials in an effort to avert an all-out war. The Americans made at best a halfhearted effort because Ho's Communist credentials and U.S. concern for French sensibilities precluded a genuine effort at mediation. But their failed efforts to avert a war in Vietnam more deeply involved the Americans in that turbulent region.

Because the Indochina conflict was only one of several national revolutions occurring simultaneously in Southeast Asia, that economically and strategically significant region, from Washington's vantage point, appeared to be one of the globe's most volatile areas.[37] The State Department was leery of the United States overtly aligning itself with French colonialism. Further, by the end of 1947, Washington officials were skeptical that the French could ever defeat the Vietminh militarily or that Vietnamese nationalism could be subdued by force. They believed the French would have to make some accommodation to satisfy the nationalist aspirations of the Vietnamese people.

But if U.S. officials were skeptical of French efforts to retrieve their Indochinese empire, acting and later Secretary of State Dean Acheson was appalled at the prospect of an independent Vietnamese nation under the control of Communist revolutionary Ho Chi Minh. Acheson's problem was that U.S. State Department officials serving in Vietnam and those who traveled to that country on official business in the late 1940s could find no credible evidence linking Ho Chi Minh to Moscow, nor any sign that he was carrying out Soviet policies in Indochina. In fact, the Soviet Union did not appear to have an Indochina policy, and Stalin had no interest in promoting revolution in Southeast Asia during the late 1940s. U.S. officials also knew that Ho Chi Minh led and personified the Vietnamese drive for self-determination. Further, they were aware that he and other Vietminh leaders had repeatedly appealed to the Americans for support and protection from the French imperialists.

Acheson finally resolved the question of how Communist Ho Chi Minh and his Vietminh colleagues might be in 1949 by asserting what the secretary of state no doubt regarded as a self-evident proposition: Ho Chi Minh is a Communist and if Vietnam achieves its independence, he will show his true Stalinist colors. Acheson operated on the assumption that Communism and nationalism were incompatible ideological forces. He refused to consider the possibility that the Vietminh leaders, although surely committed Communist ideologues, also represented the nationalistic aspirations of most Vietnamese, whatever their politics or class interests. Acheson knew little of Vietnamese history, culture, or politics, and he had no understanding of Ho Chi Minh's fierce determination not only to rid Vietnam of French imperialism, but also to remain free of Soviet or Chinese domination. While the Vietminh willingly accepted help from the major Communist powers, they had no intention of exchanging French colonialism for any form of Communist subordination. But Washington assumed that Ho Chi Minh and his chief associates were Stalinist agents and therefore believed it was in the best interest of the United States to prevent a Communist revolution from occurring in Indochina, which they equated with advancing the imperial interests of the Soviets and Chinese.[38] Truman's and Acheson's flawed Indochina policies laid the groundwork for the American ordeal in Vietnam.

In short, U.S. policy makers confronted a dilemma in Indochina in the late 1940s. On the one hand, they rejected reimposing colonialism as neither desirable nor possible; on the other hand, they rejected a French military withdrawal that would leave chaos and terroristic activities in its wake and open the way to a Communist takeover in Vietnam. Not wanting the French either to win or get out, State Department officials began an elusive search to find a third force in Vietnam politics: leaders possessing authentic nationalist credentials, who were neither Communist stooges nor French puppets.[39]

America's Indochina policy at the outset of the Cold War with the Soviet Union in 1946 and 1947 was distinctly secondary to U.S. interests in Europe. The Truman administration pursued a Euro-centered foreign policy premised on the view that Soviet expansionism across war-torn Europe represented the principal threat to American national interests in the postwar world. In March 1947, the president had proclaimed the Truman Doctrine, which committed the United States to a policy of containing Communism in Europe. Within Western Europe, France was the focus of U.S. concerns in the late 1940s because it had a war-shattered economy, an unstable government, and a popular Communist Party. U.S. officials feared the Communists could legally come to power in France.

Committed to keeping France within the Free World orbit, the United States provided France with political, economic, and moral support during the late 1940s. Part of this support took the form of leaving the French a free hand in Indochina. Between 1946 and 1949, the official U.S. position on the Franco-Vietminh War was one of neutrality. Covertly, the United States furnished the French with substantial amounts of financial and military assistance.[40] In late 1946, Washington made $160 million available to the French for use in Vietnam. In September 1948, the U.S. ambassador to France privately told French officials that Washington would consider it appropriate for the French to spend a portion of their Marshall Plan funds on military operations in Indochina.[41] American Indochina policy during the late 1940s was hostage to the much more important commitment of building up postwar France to prevent a possible Communist takeover in that crucial European country.

Just as it profoundly altered the political and strategic situation in Indochina, the Chinese revolution induced major changes in America's Indochina policy that, in turn, were components of a general reorientation of U.S. global policy during 1949 and 1950. The French, facing both a much more formidable foe armed and trained with Chinese assistance and the loss back home of popular support for their colonial war, began requesting direct assistance from the United States. France warned U.S. officials that without greater amounts of American military and economic assistance they could lose the war and would have to leave Indochina. They found a receptive audience in

Washington, where President Truman and his advisers were reappraising American foreign policy in the light of two disasters that had occurred in the fall of 1949: the Soviet's successful testing of an atomic device and the fall of China to the Communists.

In the aftermath of these two major blows to American prestige and power, President Truman and his advisers, convinced that the recent Chinese revolution accorded with Stalinist ambitions for imposing Communism worldwide, looked at a world divided into two hostile camps. In his public utterances, Truman interpreted this political bipolarity in highly charged moralistic terms. In Truman's Manichaean view, the complex conflicts of interest between the Western powers and the Communist nations pitted the forces of light against the forces of darkness in a mortal struggle for control of the political future of the planet.[42] Fearing a shift in the balance of power in favor of the Communists and dreading the prospect of global war, the Truman administration initiated plans to increase American military capabilities, shore up the defense of Western Europe, and extend the containment policy to the Far East.[43]

Convinced that Europe faced grave danger from an expansionist Soviet Union now empowered with nuclear weapons, the United States moved to shore up French defenses and to propose rearming West Germany. Fearful lest the French not approve the creation of a European Defense Community (EDC), a plan for integrating French and West German forces into a multinational army, the United States met French demands for direct American support for their Indochina campaign. The Truman administration implemented a program of direct military and economic assistance for the French colonial war in Indochina in the hopes that such support would induce the French to cooperate with U.S. strategic designs for Europe and would also free up French resources for the newly created North Atlantic Treaty Organization (NATO).

At the same time the United States was committing itself to underwriting the security of Western Europe, Washington came to the conclusion that, in the aftermath of the Chinese revolution, the strategic security of Southeast Asia itself had become an important U.S. national interest. From the American perspective, it appeared that Southeast Asia, with its explosive mix of declining European imperial powers and unstable newly independent states, was vulnerable to pressure from both China and the USSR. Loss of these rich former European colonies to the Communists would close Western Europe out of major markets. Cutting off sources of vital raw materials such as rubber, tin, and oil would retard Europe's postwar recovery. Loss of the region would also set back the economic recovery of Japan, the nation that had become America's principal Far Eastern ally following the fall of China. Japan had quickly metamorphosed from vanquished foe to strategic and economic anchor of America's expanded containment policy. America also needed prosperous trading partners in Europe and the Pacific Rim that could earn the foreign exchange convertible to dollars needed to buy the exports that would sustain its economic growth and prosperity in the postwar era.

According to the new American Southeast Asian policy calculus, U.S. officials regarded Indochina, particularly Vietnam, as the key to the security of the entire region. If Ho Chi Minh's revolution, now backed by both the Chinese and the Soviets, succeeded in driving the French out of Vietnam, it would open the rest of Southeast Asia to Communist penetration.[44] It was this application of the domino theory to the Franco-Vietminh War following the Maoist triumph in China that greatly raised the American stake in Indochina. It transformed what had been a comparatively minor appendage of the U.S. Euro-centered goal of shoring up France after World War II into a major foreign policy commitment. The domino theory reflected the American ignorance of the profound differences among Asian nations and societies. It also reflected a failure to appreciate the power of Asian nationalisms, and simultaneously it revealed a tendency to exaggerate the appeal of European ideologies to Asian populations that possessed rich histories and highly evolved cultures. U.S. officials assumed that as Vietnam went, so went the rest of the Third World. The conviction that "any single state could dominate so vast a region or that its diverse inhabitants might embrace a single ideology now seems one of the strangest artifacts of Cold War thinking."[45] It also highlights the misconceptions and ahistorical underpinnings of America's flawed Vietnam policies.

Washington feared that if Vietnam fell to the Communists, so would Laos, Cambodia, Thailand, Burma, and Malaysia. Japan, Indonesia, even the Philippines and the Indian subcontinent, would be vulnerable. In time, possibly Australia and New Zealand could fall to the Communist juggernaut. Americans feared that severe economic problems and political instability in many of these Asian countries in the aftermath of war and decolonization made Communism appealing to people and undermined their ability to resist aggression. Linking its security to the security of these weak Asian nations, Washington appeared to believe that the United States itself could one day be threatened by the expansionist Communist monolith.

What Washington perceived to be at stake in Vietnam by 1950 was no longer merely the outcome of a regional colonial war. Indochina had become one of the front lines in the global Cold War between Communism and freedom, one of the key links in the security chain. In American eyes, the French were no longer merely fighting to reimpose colonialism on the Vietnamese, they were part of the Western world's concerted effort to contain Chinese and Soviet Communism in Europe and Asia. The United States had to "draw the line" in Southeast Asia by providing economic assistance to friendly governments and helping to reconstruct the Japanese economy. Southeast Asia would be crucial for the Japanese future, as a source of raw materials and as a market for manufactures, now that China had been removed from the capitalist orbit.

In addition to developments in Europe and Asia, another factor drove Washington to invest the outcome of the Franco-Vietminh War with enhanced strategic significance in 1950. Internal political considerations, particularly the growth of domestic anti-Communism, exerted a strong influence on the Truman administration's new foreign policy design. Republicans accused Truman's administration of being "soft on Communism"; that is, they accused these officials of not taking the tough, effective measures that they insisted were needed to contain the spread of Communism abroad and to squelch "Red" subversion at home.[46]

The Maoist triumph in China gave domestic anti-Communists an enormous boost. Many Republicans, and some Democrats, charged President Truman, Secretary of State Dean Acheson, and other high administration officials, with the "loss of China." Jiang fell, these critics asserted, because the Truman administration did not provide the Chinese Nationalists with enough military and economic support. Senator Robert Taft of Ohio led the Republican onslaught against the Truman administration for losing China.

Truman feared that if his administration did not energetically back the French in Vietnam and they subsequently lost their war, the senatorial wolf pack would be after him again, this time for the "loss of Indochina." Such an outcome would cost both him and the Democrats popular support and probably the next election. This domestic political factor that bedeviled Truman and Acheson became "one of the most powerful and enduring factors shaping American policy toward Vietnam."[47] During the early and mid-1960s, the domestic politics of anti-Communism strongly influenced the foreign-policy decisions of the Kennedy and Johnson administrations that gradually committed the United States to its longest war.[48]

The French made it easier for the United States to support directly its Indochina War by creating the Bao Dai puppet regime in 1949. It enabled the French to claim that they were fighting to preserve a non-Communist Vietnamese nation from the forces of international Communism. Although Bao Dai remained a weak and unpopular ruler, U.S. officials claimed publicly that the French were offering the Vietnamese people a genuine nationalistic alternative to the revolutionary cohorts of Ho Chi Minh. Privately, they doubted that the French would either grant Bao Dai any real power or win the war against the Vietminh.

During the first few months of 1950, U.S. State Department planners began putting together a program of direct economic and military aid for Indochina. In April, Washington officially adopted National Security Council Document Number 64 (NSC-64). NSC-64 expressed official thinking at the highest levels and demonstrated how Cold War considerations crucially shaped the way Truman and his senior advisers responded to the ongoing war in Indochina. Washington's primary objective was to promote national leaders who could rally non-Communist Vietnamese nationalists and nullify the appeal of the Vietminh. It was Washington's understanding that Ho Chi Minh's band of Communist revolutionaries simultaneously advanced the imperial goals of Chinese and Soviet leaders. NSC-64 also revealed doubts about the ability of the French, even with American help, to defeat the Vietminh. The authors of NSC-64 worried that Chinese Communist troops or Communist-supplied arms from outside Vietnam would strengthen the Vietminh cause. Summing up a portentous situation, the report urged Washington to take "all practical measures to prevent further Communist expansion in Southeast Asia." U.S. envoys in Vietnam were even more skeptical of the viability of the Bao Dai government and the struggling French war effort. But Washington took these "fateful steps toward involvement because officials considered alternative courses of action even more perilous." The Americans feared that if they did not lend assistance, the French would surely lose and that outcome would be ruinous to U.S. interests in Southeast Asia and ruinous to the Truman adminstration's domestic political interests.[49] In February 1950, the United States formally took sides in the Franco-Vietminh War when it extended diplomatic recognition to Bao Dai's "Associated States of Vietnam."

The American decision to aid openly the anti-Communist forces fighting in Indochina not only drew Americans more directly into Vietnam affairs, but it also brought Washington face-to-face with what would prove to be the central dilemma of its long, tragic involvement with Vietnam: "How to foster an independent Vietnamese government while providing the sort of aid likely to make it more dependent on American charity."[50] Repeatedly over the next 25 years Vietnam would require infusions of military and economic assistance to stave off an imminent Communist victory. But every time the United States came to their rescue, the non-Communist Vietnamese nationalists that we saved became ever more dependent on the patronage of the United States.

By backing the French and their Vietnamese puppets, the United States had aligned itself with the losing side in the Franco-Vietminh War. By the time America had committed itself to directly supporting the French military effort, the Vietminh armed forces had gained the strategic initiative and had taken the offensive. The revolutionary nationalists controlled two-thirds of the land and the people of Vietnam. The Chinese were providing Vietminh forces with substantial amounts of modern weaponry, and Chinese staff officers were helping General Giap plan his campaigns. The French were on the defensive, clinging to the cities and coastal enclaves. The war had become unpopular in France, and the French government was wavering in its support of the war.

The unanticipated outbreak of the Korean War in late June 1950, when North Korean armies suddenly invaded South Korea to try to unify Korea under Communist control, confirmed the Truman administration's belief that the Soviet Union was an expansionist power intent on dominating all of Asia. Although they had no intelligence data to confirm it, Truman and his senior advisers assumed that the North Korean troops were Soviet proxies and that Beijing also marched to Stalin's orders. Chinese intervention in the Korean War in late November 1950 raised the specter in Washington and Paris that Chinese troops could also invade Vietnam. These developments reinforced President Truman's and Secretary of State Acheson's sense of the strategic importance of Vietnam and of the vital need for the French to continue their war to prevent Communist expansion into Southeast Asia. Washington linked the French war against the Vietnamese Communists with the U.S. war against the North Korean and Chinese Communists; they were twin fronts in a larger campaign to save Asia from Communist conquest.

Initially, American support for the French in the Indochina War derived from American efforts to shore up France after the devastation and humiliation of World War II. With the success of the Chinese Communist revolution and the outbreak of war in Korea, support for the French in the war now took on a far larger purpose: stopping the spread of Communism in Asia. U.S. officials may have had little faith in the ability of Bao Dai to attract the support of non-Communist Vietnamese nationalists, and Washington did not expect the French to grant the Vietnamese government any real authority, but U.S. officials simply could not see any acceptable alternatives. Supporting the French side and Bao Dai was the least bad choice out of only bad options.

In the summer of 1950, the first U.S. aid package for the French Indochina War was implemented, and a unit of U.S. military advisers, designated the Military Assistance and Advisory Group (MAAG), was sent to Vietnam. The MAAG officials were to coordinate the aid program and instruct the French, and, later, the Vietnamese, in the use of American weapons and tactics. At the same time, U.S. officials inaugurated a program of economic and technical assistance for the Bao Dai government. During 1951 and 1952, the United States provided increasing amounts of military and economic aid to sustain the French war effort.[51] Washington supplied aircraft, tanks, artillery, automatic weapons, small arms, and ammunition. By the end of Truman's presidency, U.S. aid to the French war effort had cost nearly $1 billion. With the United States backing the French and China backing the Vietminh, the Franco-Vietminh War had become an international affair. It was conjoined with the Korean War, and both were perceived as major Cold War ideological contests—the defense of freedom against an encroaching Communism.

The French also feared a Chinese invasion of northern Vietnam akin to the Chinese intervention in Korea. Knowing their forces could not cope with the Chinese should they come in, the French sought Washington's assurance that American troops would be sent to Indochina to fight the Chinese if they entered Vietnam. Truman, wary of getting into another land war in Asia after Korea, made it clear to French officials that under no circumstances would U.S. ground troops be sent to Indochina. Although Truman firmly resisted French entreaties to send U.S. ground combat forces to Vietnam, he apparently considered sending Nationalist Chinese troops from Taiwan to Vietnam to fight alongside the French in the event of a Chinese invasion.[52]

The Americans found themselves repeatedly frustrated by their French partners. Despite receiving large amounts of U.S. military aid, the French forces could never reverse the course of the war. To defeat a guerrilla army, an invader force must have overwhelming military superiority and strong popular support. The French never had either. French forces never seriously considered fighting for a truly independent Vietnam. They paid lip service to the cause of Vietnamese nationalism, but they kept the Bao Dai regime tightly under their control, thus preventing it from ever becoming a credible alternative to the revolutionary nationalists. The French also hampered the U.S. aid programs that furnished economic and technical assistance to the Vietnamese people, because they did not want the Vietnamese people to know that the Americans were helping them.

Any efforts by Americans to pressure a series of weak French governments to fight harder or consider a grant of independence to the Vietnamese were met by French arguments that they could not approve the EDC, or that they might have to leave Vietnam and let the United States confront the results of a Communist takeover. The French could always play their trump card against the Americans: They could threaten to pull out of Vietnam and allow the Communists to take over. Viewing such an outcome as intolerable and having no comparable leverage with the French, Washington, rather than risk such possibilities, acquiesced in the face of these threats. The United States continued to provide ever increasing amounts of aid and let the French call the shots.[53] Consequently, in the eyes of most Vietnamese, the Americans appeared to be supporters of French colonialism, not Asian nationalism, and the French position in Indochina continued to deteriorate.

The new U.S. Southeast Asian foreign policy forged from 1949 to 1950 rested on a series of misunderstandings. The Vietminh revolution was not inspired or directed by Moscow or Beijing. Washington failed to understand that Vietnamese revolutionary nationalism had indigenous roots and causes. The United States did not comprehend the powerful and widespread appeal that the drive for independence from European colonialism had with a large majority of the Vietnamese people regardless of their politics. Washington could not see that Ho Chi Minh was not a Stalinist or Maoist stooge.

It was the U.S. decision to support the French war in Vietnam that drew the Americans into their "initial political commitments in Indochina."[54] Here lay the roots of the subsequent long American involvement in Southeast Asia that culminated in the American Vietnam war. Gradually, by stages, the American commitment in Indochina escalated under a succession of presidencies. President Truman made the initial decision to support the French war effort. President Eisenhower made the decision to intervene in southern Vietnam to replace the French and support the efforts of Ngo Dinh Diem to establish a non-Communist state in order to prevent the further spread of Communism in Indochina. President Kennedy escalated the American effort and inaugurated a small-scale secret U.S. war in South Vietnam. President Johnson made the fateful decision in July 1965 to fight a major U.S. war in Vietnam.

A fatal pattern appears to have been established early. Decisions to increase American involvement in Vietnam, including eventually taking over and fighting a major war in that tortured land, were always made as responses to immediate crises. They were made to stave off imminent disaster, that is, a Communist victory, which was always viewed within the larger context of the ongoing Cold War. To U.S. officials, Vietnam was always about more than Vietnam. A Communist victory in Vietnam was always understood to be a significant victory for international Communism and a major defeat for the United States and the Free World that would threaten vital U.S. national interests. Domestic political considerations also were an integral part of the Vietnam calculus. Presidents viewed a Communist victory in Vietnam as likely to cause fatal damage to their and their party's cause in the next elections, and they always had the next elections to worry about.

These presidents did not often seek advice from Congress, nor was there extensive public debate about Vietnam at any stage of the gradually expanding U.S. involvement. Most Americans were not informed about the Vietnam foreign policy process over the long interval during which an initial commitment to support the French Indochina War grew incrementally into a major American war in Southeast Asia. Vietnam did not become an important political issue in this country until 1965, and did not become a source of major controversy until 1967, nearly twenty years after American involvement in that region had begun. When Americans awakened one day in the summer of 1965 to find their country fighting a major war in a remote part of the world that most citizens could not find on a map, they had no inkling of the two-decades-long preparation time or the policies or events that had drawn the United States into its longest war.

THE ROAD TO DIEN BIEN PHU

As the Truman administration, responding to the Soviet possession of nuclear weapons, the Chinese revolution, the Korean War, and the Franco-Vietminh War, devised its expanded foreign policy based on containing Communism around the world, the war in Indochina also expanded. The Vietminh offensive during the fall of 1950 forced the French to confront a hard choice. They could either increase their military forces substantially and seek a military victory over the Vietminh, or they could try for a negotiated settlement with their stubborn foes. Neither choice appealed to French officials, and they tried to avoid the dilemma by calling on the United States for military aid and by creating a Vietnamese national army to supplement the French forces. American aid was soon forthcoming, and "the new Army of the Republic of Vietnam began to take shape."[55] In addition, the French brought in their best field commander to take charge of the war, General de Lattre de Tassigny, who soon infused the French forces with new determination and confidence. He viewed controlling the Red River Delta as the key to winning the war, and he built up French defenses in that region by stringing a series of concrete forts along the boundaries of the delta to prevent infiltration of this strategic region by Vietminh forces.

General Giap, having concluded that the time had come to launch the third stage of the protracted war against the French imperialists, opened a general offensive in January 1951 in the western end of the delta. Two Vietminh infantry divisions, 22,000 troops altogether, attacked the provincial capital of Vinh Yeh, which was defended by a force of 10,000 French. In two days of hard fighting in which Giap employed a series of human wave attacks, the outnumbered French beat back the Vietminh and inflicted heavy casualties on them by using artillery and air attacks. During the ensuing months, the Vietminh attacked other towns at the edges of the delta, and the outnumbered French fought them off every time. Giap called off the failed offensive in June after having lost about 15,000 troops either killed or wounded.[56]

Clearly, Giap's decision to go on the offensive had been premature, and his soldiers paid dearly for his strategic blunder. The campaigns against de Lattre's soldiers showed that the French were still full of fight and that there were serious weaknesses in the DRV Army's ability to conduct large-scale conventional warfare. But the failed Vietminh offensive in 1951 did not alter the basic military situation. The DRV forces significantly outnumbered the French; they could marshal 225,000 troops against approximately 150,000 French main forces deployed throughout Indochina.[57] The Vietminh controlled the countryside while the French forces remained in defensive positions. Substantial amounts of U.S. military aid; the creation of the Vietnamese National Army, the forerunner of the Army of the Republic of Vietnam (ARVN); the presence of General de Lattre; and the bloody losses inflicted on the Vietminh troops could not turn the tide of war in favor of the French.

Between 1951 and 1953, the Vietminh launched several attacks primarily in northern Vietnam. There was correspondingly little fighting in central and southern Vietnam. French pacification efforts were relatively successful in Cochin China, and, consequently, the Vietminh forces had a much thinner base of popular support in Saigon and its vicinity. In the north, the DRV forces retained the strategic initiative; the French remained in defensive positions, although occasionally de Lattre would send out a strike force to hit the Vietminh. The normal pattern was for the Vietminh to choose the time and place for an assault. They probed for weak spots, attacked in force, inflicted as many casualties as they could, and then broke off the engagement and retreated to their mountain sanctuaries in Viet Bac. Their objective was to wear the French down by keeping pressure on them, undermining their morale, and weakening their political support in France.

One of the major campaigns fought during this phase of the war took place at Hoa Binh in November 1951. Hoa Binh was a town about 50 miles west of Hanoi, outside the de Lattre line of defense. It sat astride a major communications route of the Vietminh in the hills to the west of the Red River Delta. If the French could hold Hoa Binh, they would seriously hamper the ability of Vietminh main forces to mount attacks in the delta regions, and they would extend the French defense perimeter 25 miles west. The French occupied the town without initially meeting much resistance from the Vietminh.

But Giap, determined to drive the French out of the strategic site, committed several divisions to the battle. The Hoa Binh campaign lasted three months and included many intense battles. Both sides deployed modern U.S. weapons. The weapons had been furnished to the French under the U.S. aid program; the Vietminh had acquired them from the Chinese and through theft and capture. Giap sent wave after wave of attackers against the French positions. The DRV attacks gradually wore the French down, and they were forced to withdraw from Hoa Binh in mid-February.[58] Meanwhile, General de Lattre, who had become seriously ill during the battles for Hoa Binh, returned to France, where he died of prostate cancer on February 11, 1952. Hoa Binh was a major victory for the Vietminh. Six months after their victory, Vietminh political cadres had organized most of the villages of the western delta. More important, the victory at Hoa Binh gave Ho Chi Minh, General Giap, and the other DRV leaders a growing confidence that defeating the French was within their grasp.

During the years 1951 to 1953, as the war raged on, the Vietminh political cadres continued their efforts to organize the Vietnamese people in the cities and coastal enclaves still under French control. The DRV leaders had always emphasized the crucial role that political organization played in their revolution to rid Vietnam of the French presence and implement their socialist program. They hoped to foment popular uprisings in the cities that would further weaken the declining French grip on Indochina. But Vietminh organizers found little support for their cause among the urban populations.[59] Among the urban classes that they assumed might share an affinity for their movement—students, workers, and intellectuals—they often encountered either opposition or indifference. Disappointed, Vietminh leaders concluded that the major political base of the Vietnamese revolution would have to remain the peasants in the countryside.

To solidify their support among the poorer classes of peasants and to strike against landlords who opposed their program, the Vietminh implemented land reform in areas under their control, modeling it after the Maoist program implemented during the Chinese civil war. In Tonkin and Cochin China, thousands of peasants received land.[60] Land reform strengthened the Vietminh political base in the countryside, weakened the landlord classes, advanced the Vietminh social revolution, and foreshadowed the large-scale land reform programs undertaken in North Vietnam during the mid-1950s, following the defeat of the French and their American backers.

In April 1953, General Henri Navarre assumed command of the French forces in Indochina with orders to win the war. Given the assets available to him, he knew he had been assigned an impossible mission. The DRV forces now totaled 350,000 armed troops, organized into eight infantry and one armored division, and the size of the Vietminh army increased daily as new troops arrived from China where they had been undergoing military training and political indoctrination.[61] French force levels, deployed over the whole of Vietnam, were not sufficient to counter this large and growing DRV army. The new Vietnamese National Army had not developed as expected; its troops had little incentive to fight for the Bao Dai government. There was wholesale avoidance of military service and the quality of its recruits was low. Navarre knew that this inept army could not effectively supplement the French expeditionary forces. In France, by the spring of 1953, public opposition to the war was widespread; many politicians were openly calling for negotiations to end the conflict that its critics called *la guerre sale* (the dirty war). Washington, fearing the French might falter and that Indochina would be lost to the Communists, was putting intense pressure on the French government to step up its war effort and to grant the Bao Dai government more control over its own affairs.

Feeling the pressure both from his government and the Americans, General Navarre developed a plan to try to improve the French military position in Indochina before any negotiations began. The first phase involved regaining control of the Red River Delta. Navarre attacked Vietminh strongholds in the western delta. Following a strategy that had been worked out the previous January, Giap did not challenge the French forces; his troops retreated in the face of Navarre's assaults. French troops regained delta provinces that had fallen under Vietminh control. Washington, although skeptical that the Navarre Plan could succeed, felt no choice but to support it. U.S. officials feared that the French might give up and pull out of Indochina, thus forcing the Americans to deal with the Vietminh insurgency. By the summer of 1953, it appeared that the maintenance of the French war in Vietnam was becoming more important to the Americans than it was to the French.

While French forces reoccupied parts of the delta, Giap's forces ranged widely over northwest Vietnam and into Laos where his forces threatened a French-supported regime in that lightly defended landlocked country. The Vietminh foray into Laos was launched from the remote village of Dien Bien Phu, located in a mountainous region in northwestern Vietnam just 10 miles from the Laotian border. Giap sent units of the Vietminh army into Laos because he knew that the French would be forced to protect that part of Indochina. He also understood that to defend Laos the French would have to extend their supply lines across a lengthy stretch of Vietminh-controlled territory.[62]

General Navarre, concerned for the safety of Laos and wanting to disrupt the Vietminh offensive in northwest Tonkin, decided to take a strategic gamble. In mid-November 1953, he sent his paratroopers to occupy strong points, thereby blocking a major Vietminh invasion route into Laos and cutting off one of their supply routes from China. He also intended to tie down a sizable number of Giap's forces to keep them out of the Red River Delta. He chose a site by the village of Dien Bien Phu that lay 170 miles northwest of Hanoi. Nearby were two airstrips located in a broad valley surrounded by hills and mountains.

Navarre assumed Giap would be forced to attack the new fortress. Knowing that he would have control of the air over the valley and that he would install artillery at various strong points, Navarre anticipated that his forces would annihilate the attacking Vietminh soldiers. He intended to force the Vietminh to fight at a place of his own choosing and then inflict a significant defeat on them that would improve the French military position in Indochina and rekindle domestic French support for the war. The site he chose, Dien Bien Phu, would soon pass into history as a symbol of French futility and defeat in Indochina.

Giap had a different view of the strategic situation at Dien Bien Phu. He did not respond immediately to the French thrust into the valley. Having learned the hard way about premature human wave attacks against entrenched opponents who retained superior firepower, he postponed massive frontal assaults until after French defenses and morale had been weakened. Meanwhile, he encircled the fortress and kept the French forces tied down in what he perceived to be a trap that they had set for themselves.

Navarre, while building up his defenses at Dien Bien Phu, also launched the second phase of his plan to regain the military initiative in Indochina, a series of operations in northern Annam called *Operation Atlante*.[63] These attacks were designed to clear the Vietminh forces out of north-central Vietnam in order to permit the pacification of this major rice-growing region. Giap chose not to commit any main force units to challenge *Operation Atlante*, relying instead on local guerrillas to disrupt French efforts to pacify these key coastal provinces.

While the DRV and French forces battled each other throughout northern and central Vietnam during the fall of 1953, both sides also moved toward negotiating a settlement. Premier Joseph Laniel indicated his interest in finding a compromise solution to the conflict.[64] Ho Chi Minh said that he would like to hear the French proposals. In February 1954, the foreign ministers of the major powers scheduled an international peace conference to convene in Geneva in April to consider proposals for the unification of Korea in the aftermath of the armistice agreement that had ended the Korean War the previous August. Over American objections, the foreign ministers added the settlement of the Indochina War to the proposed conference agenda. News of an impending political settlement to the long war energized both sides. Generals Giap and Navarre intensified their preparations for what they both understood would be the decisive battle of the Franco-Vietminh War.

Shortly after the announcement that a peace conference would be meeting in May to settle the war, General Giap decided that the moment had come to attack Dien Bien Phu. He had several reasons for doing so: He wanted to inflict a major military defeat on the French that would coincide with the opening of the Geneva Conference in order to maximize the DRV's leverage at the bargaining table. If the French garrison at Dien Bien Phu were taken, Navarre's strategy would fail, and the Vietminh would retain the military initiative. A defeat at Dien Bien Phu could destroy the remaining French will to continue the war.[65] In the aftermath of a decisive Vietminh victory, they believed that the war-weary French might abandon Vietnam.

Giap was confident that he and his staff had devised a strategy that would bring the Vietminh forces victory at Dien Bien Phu. He planned a siege of the French positions. He also planned to destroy the airstrips, thereby cutting off French supply sources and preventing them from bringing in reinforcements. He would place artillery and mortars in the hills overlooking Dien Bien Phu, and the Vietminh gunners would bombard the French and wear them down. Infantry assaults would seize their strong points one by one until their center was taken. Giap calculated that control of the heights surrounding the valley gave the Vietminh a decisive advantage.[66]

For the battle, Giap deployed over 50,000 main force troops, another 50,000 support forces, and 200,000 workers to man his supply lines. The Vietnamese were also joined by an estimated 20,000 to 30,000 Chinese workers, technicians, mechanics, truck drivers, advisers, and artillerymen. In addition to personnel, the Chinese supplied ammunition, weapons, gasoline, and foodstuffs. Chinese staff officers also helped Giap plan and implement his tactics. The Soviets also provided aid to the Vietminh forces as they prepared for the most important battle of the long war. The Soviets furnished trucks and artillery, and they also established an Eastern Bloc aid pool to support the DRV war effort.[67] Giap and his staff took three months to prepare the battlefield in meticulous detail. Their patient, careful planning, in which the soldiers spent many weeks rehearsing their roles in the impending operations, reflected Giap's approach to fighting wars.

The French had a scant 12,000 troops under Colonel Christian de Castries dug in at Dien Bien Phu to face Giap's carefully prepared forces. They had arrayed themselves in a coordinated series of strongly defended areas. The main ones were clustered around the larger airstrip; away from these main points there were four other defended areas, each guarding an approach to their center.[68]

The Battle of Dien Bien Phu began on March 13, 1954, at sunset, when Vietminh artillery placed in the surrounding mountainsides opened fire on the French positions below. Vietminh infantry also assaulted one of the outlying strong points that first night. Fighting was fierce, and the Vietminh sustained heavy losses. Within two days, Vietminh artillery and mortars had shut down both airstrips. Thereafter, the French defenders could only be reinforced and supplied by parachute drop. Vietminh artillery continually shelled the French positions. Within a few days, Giap's rain of fire had silenced most of the French big guns. Navarre had not anticipated that the Vietminh could bring in the firepower that they did. He had counted on his air force silencing the enemy's artillery. But the French planes could not destroy the Vietminh guns, because they had been placed in camouflaged tunnels dug deep into the mountains and they were moved around constantly. French flyers were also hampered by dense clouds and fog that continually enshrouded the Vietminh mountain redoubts.[69]

In early April, Giap launched a series of infantry assaults in an effort to overrun the outer defenses. The French fought them off and inflicted heavy losses on the attacking Vietnamese. Following the failure of his assault tactics, Giap resorted to tunneling. Vietminh sappers tunneled their way toward the French positions. They dug night and day. The French perimeter steadily shrank in the face of the steady advances of the Vietminh sappers. French artillery, mortars, explosive charges, and counterattacks delayed, but could never halt, the tunneling process.

As Giap's sappers slowly tightened the noose, Navarre realized Dien Bien Phu was doomed. With the airstrips closed down, he could not extract his soldiers from what had become a trap that he had inadvertently set for them. Neither could he adequately reinforce and supply his beleaguered force or evacuate his wounded. He concluded that only massive air strikes by U.S. bombers could save the defenders. High French officials urged the Americans to intervene and save them. After a series of discussions among themselves and consultations with NATO allies, the United States refused the French desperate pleas for salvation.

The end came quickly. Giap ordered a series of assaults beginning May 1. Night and day the Vietminh soldiers attacked the French positions. They came in waves, unrelentingly. The valiant French defenders fought hard and inflicted heavy casualties on the attackers. On May 7, the Vietminh 308th broke through into the center of the French defenses. The next day the French surrendered. They had lost about 7,500 men, killed or wounded. About 10,000 French soldiers were marched off into captivity, over half of whom perished while they were prisoners of war. During the 55-day battle, the Vietminh sustained an estimated 25,000 casualties.[70]

But the Vietminh had won the decisive battle of the long war. Bernard Fall, the foremost historian of the Franco-Vietminh war, has called Dien Bien Phu one of the most decisive military campaigns of the twentieth century. Whatever lingering popular

Figure 2.1   French soldiers during a lull in the fighting at Dien Bien Phu. Three weeks after this photo was taken, the Vietminh overran the battered fortress, forcing the French to surrender. *Source:* CORBIS.

support for the war still existing in France collapsed, as did any remaining resolve on the part of the French government to continue the bloody, expensive, and futile campaign. The victorious general, Vo Nguyen Giap, defined the historic significance of Dien Bien Phu:

> A colonized people once it has risen up and is united in the struggle and determined to fight for its independence and peace, has the full power to defeat the strong aggressive army of an imperialist country.[71]

The day after the French surrendered at Dien Bien Phu, the Indochina phase of the Geneva Peace Conference began. As the delegates began negotiations at Geneva, the war raged on in Indochina. Pumped up by its great victory at Dien Bien Phu, the Vietminh tiger, with teeth bared and looking for the kill, closed in on the weary French elephant. The French withdrew to a restricted area around Hanoi and Haiphong. About 80 percent of the country was now under Vietminh control. They held nearly all of Tonkin, most of Annam, and about half of Cochin China, including much of the rich Mekong River Delta. While the politicians talked at Geneva, the French army battled for its life in Vietnam.

THE BRINK OF WAR

President Eisenhower and his energetic Secretary of State John Foster Dulles assumed office in January 1953, committed to continuing the Truman-Acheson policies in Indochina. They shared their predecessors' assumptions and goals, believing that the fall of Indochina to the Communists would cause the loss of all Southeast Asia with disastrous political, economic, and strategic consequences for the United States and its allies in Europe and Asia.[72]

Eisenhower initially tried to infuse the sagging French war effort in Indochina with new energy to prod the French to fight the Vietminh more aggressively. He tried to persuade them to grant the Bao Dai government greater powers so it could become a genuine nationalistic alternative to Ho Chi Minh's movement. Washington substantially increased the amount of military and economic aid to the French and Bao Dai nationalists. Ironically, Vietnam had become more important to Washington than it was to France.[73] General Navarre's ill-fated strategy derived from Eisenhower's exerting increased pressure on the French government to make another effort to win the war. Ike was disappointed to see that despite the large increase in U.S. miltary and economic assistance and his pep talks, the French military situation continued to deteriorate, and the French efforts to strengthen Bao Dai's regime continued to founder. The Vietminh retained the military initiative in Indochina and continued to add territory to its domain and increase its popular base of support in Vietnam and eastern Laos.

Weary of a seemingly interminable war it no longer had any realistic chance of winning despite the huge step-up in U.S. aid, the French government sought a compromise solution. Premier Laniel, over American objections, got the Foreign Ministers' Council to place the Indochina War on the agenda of the upcoming Geneva Peace Conference. Reluctantly, the Eisenhower administration acquiesced in the French decision to seek a political solution to the war. Like the Truman administration that preceded them, Eisenhower and Dulles discovered that they had little leverage with the French, who still had not committed their forces to the EDC. Too much pressure from Washington to fight harder in Vietnam and the French might then refuse to join the EDC, undermining European unity and playing into the hands of the Soviet Union. U.S. officials also understood that French manpower commitments to the Indochina War significantly reduced the number of soldiers available for NATO assignments or the hoped for EDC.[74]

French Chief of Staff General Paul Ely journeyed to Washington to request additional U.S. military assistance. Fearful that Dien Bien Phu would soon fall unless the

United States intervened militarily, Chairman of the Joint Chiefs of Staff Admiral Arthur Radford proposed a series of U.S. air strikes to save the beleaguered fortress. Code-named Operation VULTURE, the plan included possible use of tactical nuclear weapons. Neither Eisenhower nor Dulles supported Operation VULTURE or any other use of U.S. air and naval forces to try to save the French. Dulles preferred a diplomatic response to the crisis, the formation of a coalition of powers, including the United States, Great Britain, France, Australia, New Zealand, the Philippines, and Thailand, to guarantee the security of Southeast Asia.

Among the joint chiefs, only Air Force General Nathan F. Twining supported the proposed Operation VULTURE. The other chiefs warned that air intervention entailed many risks and could not save the French cause in Vietnam. Army Chief of Staff General Matthew Ridgway emphatically rejected Operation VULTURE, and he warned his old army buddy, President Eisenhower, that air power could not win the Franco-Vietminh War and that U.S. ground forces would have to be sent to fight. He also told Eisenhower that if U.S. ground troops were sent into that war, they "would have to fight under the most difficult logistic circumstances and in a uniquely inhospitable terrain."[75] Influenced by Ridgway's caveats, Eisenhower ruled out the use of U.S. ground forces. With the bitter experiences of the stalemated Korean War, which had ended only the previous year, still fresh in his mind, Eisenhower was not about to send ground troops to Vietnam and risk another unpopular quagmire. There was also no support for fighting another land war in Asia coming from Congress, the influential media, or the American people.

Eisenhower would not consider intervening in Vietnam unilaterally. He insisted that any intervention would have to be an international affair joined by America's European allies, mainly the British. He also sought a bipartisan congressional resolution of support for any action America might undertake in Vietnam. On April 3, 1954, Dulles and Radford met with the congressional leadership. Both Democratic and Republican leaders told him that without firm commitments from U.S. allies, especially the British, to join any proposed intervention, they would not support it. Since no international support had been forthcoming by this date, Congress, in effect, killed any possibility of a U.S. air attack to save Dien Bien Phu. These views probably accorded with Eisenhower's views. Two days later, he formally rejected the French request for air strikes.[76]

For the next three weeks, while the battle for Dien Bien Phu raged on and disaster crept ever closer to the French cause, the United States tried to enlist Allied support for some form of united action in Vietnam. President Eisenhower wrote a long personal letter to his friend Prime Minister Winston Churchill, urging him to join an allied coalition to block Communist expansion in Southeast Asia. Eisenhower also held a much publicized press conference on April 7, during which he tried to rally public support for a possible U.S. military intervention in Vietnam. He emphasized the crucial geopolitical stakes that the United States and the Free World had in the outcome of the Indochina War. He made two major arguments on behalf of Allied interests: First, he stressed that Indochina was a major source of raw materials, such as tin and rubber.

Second, he stated that if Indochina fell to the Communists, the rest of Southeast Asia would fall very quickly, like a "row of dominoes." Japan, our most important ally in the Far East, would be threatened; American strategic interests would be undermined: "So the possible consequences of the loss are just incalculable to the free world."[77]

Despite the pleas and pressures emanating from Washington, British Foreign Secretary Anthony Eden, speaking for Churchill, rebuffed the U.S. request to join its crusade to prevent a Communist victory in Vietnam. The British did not share the American faith in the domino theory nor did they share Washington's belief that the loss of Indochina would threaten other members of the international community of nations. They also had no desire to become involved in what they saw as a lost cause. The British also believed that outside military intervention on the eve of the Geneva conference would wreck any prospect for a negotiated settlement of the war and might provoke a Chinese intervention into Indochina. They looked to improving relations with China and the Soviet Union and to the prospects of negotiating with the major Communist powers.[78]

Even if some agreement for intervention could have been worked out between the British and the Americans, the terms on which Washington would consider intervening in April 1954 were unacceptable to the French. The United States was willing to try to save the French at Dien Bien Phu, but only if they would reject a negotiated settlement and agree to continue fighting the Indochina War. The French would also have to grant the Americans a greater role in formulating strategy and training indigenous forces. Further, the French would have to agree to Vietnamese demands for complete independence. The exigencies of French domestic politics required that they reject all the strings attached to the U.S. aid proposal.[79] They would risk losing at Dien Bien Phu and take their chances on obtaining an acceptable negotiated settlement at Geneva, rather than accede to the American demands. To the end of the Franco-Vietminh War the two allies sought incompatible goals: The French fought to restore their empire; "the Americans wanted them to liquidate that empire in order to build an anti-Communist nationalist base."[80]

In late April, as the end neared at Dien Bien Phu, French Foreign Minister Georges Bidault made a desperate eleventh-hour plea for a U.S. air strike to save the French. Unable to count on British or congressional support and unhappy with France's continuing unwillingness to accept the U.S. conditions for intervention, Eisenhower once again refused to go to war for the French cause in Indochina. Final refusal of the United States sealed the French fate. Having lost the war in northern Vietnam, France prepared to abandon Hanoi-Haiphong and salvage what it could in southern Vietnam. The day after the French surrendered at Dien Bien Phu, diplomats from nine nations gathered around a horseshoe-shaped table inside the old League of Nations building in Geneva to hold open discussions on the "Indochina problem."[81]

As U.S. efforts to organize an eleventh-hour multilateral rescue effort failed and the French debacle in Vietnam played out at Dien Bien Phu, Washington feared that the French government might accede to a settlement that would force their withdrawal from Vietnam and result in Communist control of the entire country. Far from curtailing U.S.

involvement in Southeast Asia, the looming French disaster prompted Washington to look for ways to become more directly engaged in Vietnam without committing its own military forces. Eisenhower saw that the United States would have to take control of Indochina's future. In his view, only the United States could prevent a complete Communist victory in Vietnam that would threaten the stability of non-Communist governments throughout Southeast Asia.

The Geneva Solution

U.S. officials reluctantly participated in the Geneva conference; they would have much preferred that there be no political solution to the Indochina War. They wanted the French, with U.S. support, to continue fighting and ultimately defeat the DRV forces. Washington also feared that the French, given the war-weariness of the French people and the military and political momentum the Vietminh had gained in Indochina, would accept a negotiated settlement that would lead to a Communist takeover of Vietnam, Laos, and Cambodia. Most of all, U.S. officials feared that a Communist takeover of Indochina would open the floodgate of Communist expansion in Southeast Asia.

Even though the Western allies, especially the French, were negotiating from a weak position, U.S. officials at Geneva bargained shrewdly and eventually achieved a settlement that forced the Vietminh to accept much less than complete control of a unified Vietnam. For weeks, Washington also kept alive the option of a possible U.S. military action in Vietnam in the event the conference failed to produce an acceptable diplomatic solution to the war.

Nine delegations attended the Geneva Conference. There were representatives from Laos, Cambodia, and two delegations from Vietnam, one representing Bao Dai's government and the other representing Ho Chi Minh's. Ngo Dinh Diem, Bao Dai's newly appointed prime minister, represented his government; Pham Van Dong headed the delegation from the DRV. France, of course, attended, as did the Americans, the Soviets, the British, and the Chinese. Soviet Foreign Minister Vyacheslav Molotov and British Foreign Secretary Anthony Eden served as cochairs of the conference. In the awkward position of having to attend a conference they did not support and whose outcome they feared, the Americans played a relatively minor public role in the negotiations. Dulles instructed the American delegation to participate in the proceedings only as an interested party, not as a principal or belligerent power. The secretary of state rarely attended the sessions; the U.S. delegation was headed by Dulles's assistant, Undersecretary Walter Bedell Smith. At one point, Zhou En-lai, the head of the Chinese delegation, offered his hand to Dulles. Dulles, not wishing to recognize a regime he loathed, refused to shake Zhou's hand and turned away.

Negotiations at Geneva were dominated by the foreign policy concerns of the major powers who negotiated over the heads of the Vietnamese and imposed an agreement on them. Since they were winning the war and controlled most of the land and population of Vietnam, the DRV expected to emerge from Geneva with agreements reflecting their strategic superiority. The Vietminh did not achieve political gains at the conference table commensurate with their military triumphs. The Vietminh failure occurred because of U.S. diplomatic efforts and because such a resolution of the Franco-Vietminh War did not conform to the national interests of the major powers dominating the conference.[82]

While the conference was in session, the United States used the threat of military intervention to strengthen France in relation to the DRV and to lessen Chinese and Soviet support for the Vietminh. Washington was opposed to any agreement that took away territory from Cambodia, Laos, or Vietnam. Dulles got the British to back the American position and tried to persuade the French to avoid making any settlement that would transfer territory to the Communists. But the French negotiated skillfully at Geneva, playing the Soviets and Americans against each other. French officials threatened Washington with rejection of the proposed EDC, the top U.S. priority in Europe, if the United States insisted on making unrealistic demands at the bargaining table that might prevent a political resolution of the conflict. On the other hand, the French held out to the Soviets the prospect of French rejection of the EDC, which the Soviets desired, if the Soviets could persuade the Vietminh to moderate their demands and offer the French terms that they could accept. The Soviet leaders, in the aftermath of Stalin's death, were also interested in moderating Cold War tensions, and since they did not have major interests in Southeast Asia, Soviet diplomats played a role in restraining DRV demands.

Fearful of U.S. intervention in the war if it went on much longer, China joined the Soviets in putting pressure on the Vietminh to reach an agreement that was acceptable to the French. China, exhausted after years of civil war and fighting in the Korean War, where its armies sustained a million casualties, wanted to devote its resources to internal development. The Chinese leaders were also seeking international recognition and reasoned that if they were seen as playing a responsible role at the conference, their standing in the eyes of European leaders would be enhanced. The Chinese did not care whether the Communist state on its southern periphery controlled all or part of the territory of Vietnam as long as it protected China's southern flank.

The Soviets and the Chinese made it clear to Ho Chi Minh that the repeated U.S. threats to intervene necessitated compromise: Soviet and Chinese pressure forced the Vietminh to moderate their demands and played a crucial role in arranging the final settlements. "The political reality of Vietminh power in Vietnam must yield to the larger reality of its powerlessness in the world at large."[83]

Over the next two months, the outlines of a settlement gradually emerged, based on the temporary partitioning of Vietnam to allow the regrouping of military forces following a cease-fire. Elections to unify the country would be held in two years, in July 1956. Before an agreement could be fully worked out, Laniel's government fell. His place at Geneva was taken by the radical socialist leader Pierre Mendes-France, who had assumed office pledging to achieve a settlement by July 21, or resign. Mendes-France came to

Geneva committed to disengaging France from the war as quickly and gracefully as possible.[84] Movement toward a settlement based on partition accelerated. With an agreement in sight, the conference recessed for a few days.

While the delegates rested from their labors, the United States "made the most fundamental decision of its thirty-year involvement" in Vietnam.[85] Washington realized that military intervention was not possible and that the French would not continue fighting. Despite their concerted efforts to prevent its occurrence, U.S. leaders could also see that a political resolution to the Franco-Vietminh War was imminent and that the Communists were going to gain control of the northern half of Vietnam. Eisenhower and Dulles decided to intervene directly in Vietnam's internal affairs. Washington planned to replace the French in Vietnam and to assume responsibility for the defense of Cambodia, Laos, and southern Vietnam in the aftermath of the French defeat. America would pick up the sword that the French were dropping. They would hold the line against further Communist expansion in that region. There would be no more Dien Bien Phus on their watch. It was Eisenhower's fateful decision to intervene in southern Vietnam that directly involved the United States in the Vietnam conflicts that culminated in the American Vietnam War.

The conference resumed, and agreements were reached on the details of the settlement that would end the Franco-Vietminh War on July 19, 1954. A cease-fire was declared, and Vietnam was partitioned at the 17th Parallel of north latitude. Chinese Premier Zhou En-lai had to put enormous pressure on Ho Chi Minh to get him to accept the 17th Parallel as a temporary boundary between the two regroupment zones. Ho Chi Minh had wanted the 13th Parallel as the boundary. It would have given the French Cochin China, the southern third of Vietnam and the only region where the French and Bao Dai government could claim to have control.

The agreements specified that the partition line was to be a provisional military demarcation "on either side of which the forces of the two parties shall be regrouped after their withdrawal."[86] The DRV forces were to regroup north of the line; Bao Dai's and the French forces were to regroup south of the line. The conferees made clear that they never intended the line to become a permanent political or territorial boundary. The Geneva Accords did not create two states; they only created a temporary military division within a single state. To prevent further fighting, both sides were to have 300 days from the date the document was signed to make all personnel transfers to either regroupment zone. People were encouraged to move if they wished. There were to be no reprisals against people for the side they had chosen or anything they had done during the war. Both regroupment zones of Vietnam were prohibited from entering into any military alliances, bringing in any new military forces or weapons, or developing additional military bases.

As neither government would tolerate the permanent division of Vietnam's territory, the agreements provided for consultations between representatives of the two zones to begin July 20, 1955. These consultations were to lead to free elections to be held in July 1956, supervised by an International Control Commission made up of inspectors from Poland, India, and Canada. Whichever government won the elections would govern a reunified Vietnam beginning in 1956. The agreements also established cease-fires for Cambodia and Laos and declared these countries to be independent nations under their current governments.[87] The accords also acknowledged that the two new nations had the right of self-defense, but they were prohibited from entering military alliances or permitting foreign bases on their soil unless their security was clearly threatened. Most of the Geneva participants assumed that the French would remain in Vietnam to supervise the implementation of the settlement that had been worked out at the conference. During the subsequent two years, Vietnam would constitute two military zones administered north of the 17th Parallel by the Democratic Government of Vietnam and south of the 17th Parallel by Bao Dai's Associated States, also called the State of Vietnam.

Washington was unhappy with the loss of northern Vietnam to the Communists and refused to be associated formally with the Geneva agreements. Walter Bedell Smith did not assent to them, explaining that the U.S. policy of nonrecognition of the Communist government in China precluded any official agreements with Chinese officials. Instead, he issued a separate protocol stating that the United States acknowledged the agreements and would "refrain from the threat or use of force to disturb them."[88] President Eisenhower added to the ambiguity of American policy toward the Geneva Accords by announcing that since the U.S. government had not signed them, Washington did not consider itself bound by them.[89] Ngo Dinh Diem denounced the accords and also refused his assent.

The war that had ended in defeat for the French was, by extension, also perceived as a serious setback for the United States. But Eisenhower and Dulles were not entirely displeased with the outcome of the Geneva conference. In their view, it could have been much worse. They knew that their power politics, adroit French diplomacy, and Soviet and Chinese pressure had forced Ho Chi Minh to accept half a country at Geneva, even though his armies controlled most of the entire country. They also saw that the provisions of the Geneva agreements partitioning Vietnam, permitting a temporary regroupment of forces and people, and calling for nationwide elections within two years to reunify the country, amounted to a face-saving formula permitting the defeated French to make a gradual exit from Indochina. Eisenhower and Dulles saw a window of opportunity for achieving a greater role in determining the Vietnamese future in these provisions designed to give the French a delayed exit.

Washington believed that within the two years allotted to them under the Geneva agreements, they could supersede the French. They would use that two-year interim to turn Bao Dai's government into a nation-state that would provide the people of Vietnam with a genuine nationalistic alternative to Communism. They held out the possibility that Bao Dai could even win the elections two years hence and emerge as the leader of a united Vietnam. U.S. officials also believed they could effect arrangements that would protect the strategic security of Southeast Asia in the aftermath of the partial Communist victory in Vietnam and that those arrangements would confine the

Figure 2.2 The Geneva Accords (July 1954) ended French colonial domination of Indochina. Cambodia and Laos emerged as sovereign nations. Vietnam was temporarily partitioned at the 17th Parallel of north latitude. *Source:* Public domain.

spread of Communism to northern Vietnam. They would hold the line at the 17th Parallel and save the rest of Indochina and Southeast Asia from Communist expansion.

Even before the Geneva conference had officially ended, the United States was pledging its support to the Bao Dai government and preparing to subvert the accords.[90] Because of U.S. intervention in southern Vietnam, the Geneva Accords did not produce a permanent political solution to the Indochina conflict, only a temporary military truce. The "conference was merely an interlude between two wars—or rather, a lull in the same war."[91]

LESSONS

There is a kind of symmetry between the reactions of the Americans and the Vietminh to the outcome of the Geneva Conference. Both came away disappointed, but at the same time both perceived opportunities to exploit in the settlement and both expected the future to go their way.

Ho Chi Minh had been willing to bow to Soviet and Chinese pressure and to settle for half of Vietnam because he feared the United States would intervene militarily if a reasonable settlement were not arranged. U.S. forces in Vietnam would seriously impede the Vietminh's planned scenario for Vietnam, so Ho Chi Minh did what he had to do to keep them out. From his vantage point at Geneva in July 1954, the DRV had gained more than it had lost at the conference. The international community had acknowledged the legitimacy of his government. Despite partition and the continuing presence of French troops on its soil, Vietnam had officially regained its sovereignty after over 80 years of colonial subjugation. The accords kept the Americans out and also prepared the ground for the departure of the French. Only the discredited Bao Dai regime remained as Ho Chi Minh's political competition. Ho was confident that he could win the upcoming unification elections, and he looked ahead to governing a reunified Vietnam under Lao Dong control.[92] Within two years, the Vietminh expected to acquire control of all of Vietnam through democratic political processes. Ho Chi Minh did not anticipate that the Americans would soon supplant the French in southern Vietnam and block his plans.

For its part, the Eisenhower administration thought the French had lost for two reasons: They had not fought hard enough or long enough. They had lacked the determination and firepower to defeat the DRV forces, even with substantial U.S. help. They were also an anachronistic colonial power, trying to cling to the remnants of empire in Indochina. They could not bring themselves to offer the Vietnamese a genuine nationalistic alternative to the Vietminh. Eisenhower and Dulles both believed that American intervention in southern Vietnam could succeed, because the United States was a vastly richer and more powerful nation than France, and it was coming to help Bao Dai build a modern nation-state. American technology, know-how, and good intentions would work where French efforts had failed.

Washington's diagnosis of the French defeat was simplistic. It was the case that the French were losing in Indochina in part because they had never sent enough troops to give themselves a realistic chance to win the war, and because most Vietnamese perceived the Bao Dai government as only a cover for continuing French domination. However, there were other, more important, factors that were determining the outcome of that war. The proper question to ask was not why were the French losing, but why were the Vietminh winning? What the Vietnamese accomplished in their country determined the outcome of the Franco-Vietminh War. The French, backed by the United States, were fighting a war that they could not realistically expect to win, even if they had been willing to send more troops and offer Bao Dai's government independence. Local conditions and historical circumstances brought about the Vietminh victory over the French, which is to say that Vietnam realities determined the outcome of the Franco-Vietminh War.

During the years of the Franco-Vietminh War, Vietnam still possessed a colonial society with many serious social and economic problems, all of which contributed to popular support for the revolutionaries. Inflation, high taxes, and usurious interest rates all bore heavily on the people of Vietnam, especially on the rural poor. Government corruption and incompetence coupled with official indifference to the welfare of the rural population strengthened popular discontent and played into Vietminh hands.[93]

In addition to the indigenous social and economic conditions, the organizational strength of the revolutionaries played a crucial role in bringing them their ultimate success. The revolutionary political organization of the Vietminh and the extraordinary leadership of Ho Chi Minh were the decisive determinants. Until the war's end, the party apparatus continued its organizing efforts both in the urban areas and in the villages of Vietnam. Most important, the party succeeded in channeling the nationalistic aspirations of most of the Vietnamese people regardless of their politics. Ho Chi Minh had a rare combination of talents: he was a skilled revolutionary organizer and a charismatic figure, a visionary who gave expression to the nationalistic aspirations of most Vietnamese. The revolution's prime strength was always politics, not war.

Ho Chi Minh and his associates also perceived that in the long run the chief weakness of the French war effort in Vietnam was not that their soldiers could not fight effectively or that they were pursuing a colonial agenda, but that it was undermined by declining public support in France for the Indochina War. The loss of popular support for the war eroded the political will of a succession of French governments to conduct it vigorously, and eventually forced them to the conference table where they negotiated agreements that provided for their phased withdrawl from Indochina. Vietminh party leaders developed a sophisticated military, political, and diplomatic strategy to undermine their enemy's will to fight.[94]

Years later, when the North Vietnamese and the National Liberation Front (NLF) forces fought another war, this time against the American successors to the French and the Vietnamese successors to Bao Dai, they remembered the lessons that they had learned during the war with France: What the Vietnamese do and what happens in Vietnam are crucial to the outcome of the war. Be patient, they learned, and fight a protracted war. It had taken a thousand years to rid Vietnam of Chinese dominion. It had taken 80 years to get rid of the French colonialists. Be prepared to fight the Americans until they too lose their political will and abandon Vietnam, however long that takes. Exploit the social and economic conditions created by a series of corrupt, ineffective, and elite-based governments. Rely on party organization and political discipline. Retain the voice of Vietnamese nationalism. Fight a people's war. These strategies enabled the Communists to defeat a more powerful foe, the French. Twenty years later they used the same strategies to defeat a much more powerful foe, the Americans.

The American war in Vietnam, fought from 1965 through 1972, largely replicated the French war. There were, of course, important differences between the two conflicts; there was no American equivalent of Dien Bien Phu. U.S. troops were never defeated in any major battles or ever suffered any decisive military setbacks. Americans made much greater use of helicopters and employed vastly greater air power. The Americans also used military force on a much larger scale than the French. But the similarities between the two wars were quite remarkable and significant. Their duration and outcomes were similar. Both began with high hopes and ended in disaster for the Western powers and in victories for the Asian Communists. Both the Americans and the French tried to use their technological superiority, which gave them greater firepower, mobility, and control of the sea and air to win this war of attrition. They found that these advantages were not sufficient to defeat the complex and sophisticated diplomatic-political-military strategies employed by their enemies. Political maneuver defeated military firepower and tactics defeated technology in both wars.

Neither the French nor their American successors ever managed to create stable governments that offered the Vietnamese people a viable nationalistic alternative to the Communists. Both failed to develop pacification strategies that effectively neutralized the efforts of insurgent political cadres to maintain support among the rural population. Neither nation ever developed ARVN forces strong enough to defend themselves against the Communist forces that were receiving support from China, the Soviet Union, and the Eastern Bloc. Both only used Vietnamese forces extensively after domestic public support for the wars had seriously eroded. "The areas that caused the most problems for the French in South Vietnam were also the worst trouble spots for the Americans."[95]

The French and the Americans were eventually forced to negotiate agreements that provided for their withdrawal from Vietnam, mainly because the long-running wars had become unpopular among their home populations and their governments no longer had enough political support to continue them. During both wars, the Vietnamese revolutionaries, sensing that the loss of popular support was the fatal weakness that would eventually undermine both the French and the American war efforts, patiently and skillfully employed a variety of political, military, and diplomatic strategies that promoted war weariness on the Western home fronts.

Many French and American war veterans felt they had made sacrifices in vain. They had fought well in a losing war and had returned home to civilian populations

Figure 2.3 Editorial cartoonist Daniel Fitzgerald's prophetic cartoon anticipating the outcome of the American Vietnam intervention. Uncle Sam marches into the heart of darkness to replicate the French disaster. *Source: St. Louis Post Dispatch.*

that did not appear to care about, understand, or appreciate what they had done. They returned to encounter civilian populations that had lost faith in the war and ignored them, or worse, condemned them. The long, losing wars also had devastating impacts on national morale and national self-esteem in both countries, draining both nations of significant amounts of their wealth.

Eisenhower and Dulles and their successors, enmeshed in the ideology of containment and its domino correlatives and responding to the political imperatives of domestic anti-Communism, neither understood nor heeded the lessons of the Franco-Vietminh War. American leaders, ignorant of Vietnam's history, culture, and politics, and contemptuously indifferent to the French analogue, would in time replicate their disaster.

Notes

1. Hess, *Vietnam,* 33.
2. Kahin, *Intervention,* 9.
3. Doyle, Edward; Lipsman, Samuel; and the editors of Boston Publishing, *Passing the Torch* (Boston: Boston Publishing, 1981), 16–17; Isaacs, Harold, *No Peace or Asia* (New York:

Macmillan, 1947), 152–75. Isaacs was an American journalist in Saigon who wrote a firsthand account of Anglo-French cooperation in the South from 1945–1946 to suppress the Vietnamese nationalist revolution. He also documented the Anglo-French use of Japanese troops against the Vietnamese. Acheson is quoted in Young, *Vietnam Wars,* 12.

4. Dunn, Peter M., *The First Vietnam War* (New York: St. Martin's Press, 1985). Dunn has written a history of the complex political and military conflict in Vietnam during the first year after World War II, which he states made up a "First Vietnam War." According to Dunn, the French-Vietnamese conflict, 1946–1954, was the "Second Vietnam War," and the war waged between U.S./ARVN forces and the NLF/PAVN forces, 1965–1975, was the "Third Vietnam War."

5. Quoted in Pettit, *The Experts,* 11.

6. "Jacques Phillipe Leclerc," second only to De Gaulle himself as a war hero in France, was the assumed name of Jean de Hautecloque.

7. Buttinger, *A Dragon Defiant,* 81; O'Ballance, Edgar, *The Indo-China War, 1945–1954* (London: Faber and Faber, 1964), 59–60.

8. Hammer, *Struggle,* 135–40; Chen, *Vietnam and China,* 120–29; McAlister, John T., Jr., *Vietnam: The Origins of Revolution* (New York: Knopf, 1969).

9. Doyle, *Passing the Torch,* 18–20; Duiker, *The Communist Road to Power,* 114–18.

10. Quoted in Kahin, *Intervention,* 19.

11. In defense of his strategy of accepting the return of the French for a few years to get the Chinese out of Vietnam, Ho Chi Minh berated a group of VNQDD leaders who wanted to keep the Chinese in Vietnam in order to keep the French out: "You fools! Don't you realize what it means if the Chinese stay? Don't you remember your history? The last time the Chinese came, they stayed one thousand years! As for me, I prefer to smell French shit for five years rather than Chinese shit for the rest of my life." Quoted in Doyle, *Passing the Torch,* 21.

12. A copy of the Preliminary Franco-Vietnamese Convention of March 6, 1946, is printed in Porter (ed.), *Vietnam Documents,* vol. 1, 95–97, Document 59; Sainteny, Jean, *Histoire d'une Paix Manquee* (Paris: Amoit Dumont, 1953) is an insider's account of French Indochina policy in 1945–1946; and Chen, *Vietnam and China,* 146–50. The most comprehensive account of the negotiations leading to the March 6 agreement is found in Devillers, *Histoire du Vietnam,* chaps. 11–13.

13. Between August and October 1945, Ho Chi Minh wrote seven letters to U.S. leaders appealing for support for Vietnamese independence. In one letter, Ho proposed that Vietnam be placed on the same status as the Philippines and that Vietnam be allowed to become an American territory. Because the United States did not recognize Ho Chi Minh as the head of a legitimate government, all the letters were ignored. Copies of several of his letters are printed in Porter, *Vietnam Documents,* vol. 1, 83–86, 95.

14. Quoted in Doyle, *Passing the Torch,* 23.

15. Hammer, *Struggle,* 159–74.

16. O'Ballance, *The Indo-China War,* 75.

17. Kahin, *Intervention,* 23–24; Hammer, *Struggle,* 181–91.

18. Doyle, *Passing the Torch,* 26.

19. Duiker, *The Communist Road,* 127.

20. Quoted in Young, *Vietnam Wars,* 19.

21. Duiker, *The Communist Road,* 128–31; O'Ballance, *The Indo-China War,* 74–85. The Vietminh military treatise was written by Troung Chinh, the leading Vietminh theoretician and ideologist. Chinh borrowed much of his doctrine from Mao's book, *On Protracted War.*

22. O'Ballance, *The Indo-China War,* 79–80.

23. Duiker, *The Communist Road,* 131–32.

24. Ibid., 133.

25. Vo Nguyen Giap, *"Activate Guerrilla Warfare,"* a directive issued by Giap November 17, 1947, printed in Porter (ed.), *Vietnam Documents,* vol. 1, Document 113, 169–71.

26. Duiker, *The Communist Road,* 136.

27. Hammer, *Struggle,* 224–28; Kahin, *Intervention,* 25–26.

28. Kahin, *Intervention,* 28–33.

29. Duiker, *The Communist Road,* 139–40. The Soviets, not involved in Southeast Asia, still inclined to concede Western hegemony in that region, felt compelled to recognize the DRV so as not to lose influence in the Communist camp to the more militant Chinese.

30. Shaplen, Robert, *The Lost Revolution: The U.S. in Vietnam, 1946–1966,* rev. ed. (New York: Harper & Row, 1966), 69–75; see the *Platform of the Vietnam Worker's Party,* February 19, 1951: "The primordial task of the Vietnam revolution, therefore, is to drive out the imperialist aggressors to gain complete independence and unity for the people, . . . and root up the vestiges of feudalism and semifeudalism so that there is land for those who till it, to develop the People's Democratic Regime, and to lay the foundations for socialism." A copy of the platform is printed in Porter (ed.), *Vietnam Documents,* vol. 1, Document 212, 337–44.

31. Kolko, Gabriel, *Anatomy of a War: Vietnam, the United States, and the Modern Historical Experience* (New York: Pantheon Books, 1985), 57–61.

32. O'Ballance, *The Indo-China War,* 104–5.

33. Ibid., 106–7. Zhia, Quang, *China and the Vietnam Wars, 1950–1975* (Chapel Hill: University of North Carolina Press, 2000), 18–19.

34. Ibid., 114–15.

35. Ibid., 116–17. Bodard, Lucien, *The Quicksand War: Prelude to Vietnam* (Boston: Little, Brown, 1967), translated from the French, *La Guerre d'Indochine: L'enlisement* (Paris: Gallimard, 1963) and *La Guerre d'Indochine: L'humiliation* (Paris, Gallimard, 1965) has an account of the battle.

36. Duiker, *The Communist Road,* 144–45.

37. Schulzinger, *A Time for War,* 28–29. National revolutions were occurring in Burma, Malaya, and Indonesia at the same time the Vietnamese were fighting the French.

38. Young, *Vietnam Wars,* 21–24. Telegram from Secretary of State Acheson to the U.S. Consulate in Hanoi, May 20, 1949. A copy is printed in Porter (ed.), *Vietnam Documents,* vol. 1, Document 131, 198–99. Acheson commented on Soviet recognition of the DRV in a State Department bulletin issued February 13, 1950, in which he said, "The recognition by the Kremlin of Ho Chi Minh's Communist movement in Indochina . . . should remove any illusions as to the 'nationalist nature' of Ho Chi Minh's aims and reveals Ho in his true colors as the mortal enemy of native independence in Indochina." The U.S. Department of State *Bulletin,* 22 (February 13, 1950) is also printed in Porter (ed.), *Vietnam Documents,* vol. 1, Document 156, 225.

39. Schulzinger, *A Time for War,* 31–32. Department of State Policy Statement, September 27, 1948. A copy of this policy statement is found in Porter (ed.), *Vietnam Documents,* vol. 1, Document 121, 178–181.

40. Kahin, *Intervention,* 36–37. Between 1946 and 1949, the United States provided indirect, covert, and extensive financial and military assistance via metropolitan France for the French colonial war in Indochina. This aid remained hidden to avoid public criticism of both its purpose and cost.

41. Ibid., 37–38. Kahin has found evidence suggesting that of the $525 million in U.S. aid to support the French budget in fiscal 1953, almost half came from ECA counterpart funds released for the use of the French military in Indochina. Vadney, T. E., *World,* 133; Young, *Vietnam Wars,* 22.

42. On March 12, 1947, President Truman appeared before Congress to give his famed speech, calling for enactment of an aid package for Greece and Turkey. The substance of his address has become known as the Truman Doctrine, and it announced the first application of the developing U.S. policy of containment of Communism in southern Europe and the rationale for such a policy.

43. Herring, *America's Longest War,* 12. In April 1950, at Truman's request, the State Department and Defense Department jointly prepared a top-secret report for the National Security Council, known as *NSC-68,* which outlined an enlarged U.S. Cold War foreign policy.

44. Kahin, *Intervention,* 29; Hess, Gary, *The United States' Emergence as a Southeast Asia Power, 1940–1950* (New York: Columbia University Press, 1987), 40.

45. Gaddis, *We Now Know,* 190.

46. Kahin, *Intervention,* 40–41.

47. Ibid., 29–30.

48. Gardner, *Approaching Vietnam,* 80–86.

49. My summary of the contents of *NSC-64* is taken from Schulzinger, *A Time for War,* 43, 46–47.

50. Ibid., 48.

51. Morrocco, John, and the editors of Boston Publishing, *Thunder from Above: Air War, 1941–1968* (Boston: Boston Publishing, 1984), a volume in The Vietnam Experience series. In the summer of 1950, Congress authorized $164 million for arms, ammunition, planes, ships, trucks, jeeps, and tanks for the French war effort in Indochina. At about the same time, the U.S. economic and technical assistance program for the Bao Dai government committed $50 million over a two-year period. The first U.S. military advisers arrived in Vietnam in August 1950.

52. Ibid., 21–22.

53. Shaplen, *Lost Revolution,* 87–91.

54. Duiker, *The Communist Road,* 146; Hess, *Vietnam,* 34.

55. O'Ballance, *The Indo-China War,* 120–39.

56. The two DRV divisions that fought in the Battle of Vinh Yeh were the 308th and the 324th. Both were infantry divisions equipped with Chinese weapons.

57. Duiker, *The Communist Road,* 355.

58. The account of the Battle of Hoa Binh is taken from O'Ballance, *The Indo-China War,* 159–68.

59. Duiker, *Communist Road,* 152–53.

60. Ibid., 154.

61. Duiker, *The Communist Road,* 154–55; Kahin, *Intervention,* 39. At the time of the Battle of Dien Bien Phu, total French forces in Indochina numbered about 500,000. Only about 80,000 of them were ethnic French, over half of whom were noncommissioned and commissioned officers. The French did not send conscripts to fight in their Indochina colonial war for political reasons. The rest of the French Indochina Expeditionary Force was made of French Foreign Legion forces, French North African troops, Indochinese, predominantly Vietnamese troops, and Bao Dai's inchoate Vietnamese National Army (ARVN).

62. Hess, *Vietnam,* rev. ed., 43.

63. O'Ballance, *The Indo-China War,* 208–9.

64. Porter, *Vietnam Documents,* vol. 1, Document 292, 495–97, "Speech by Premier Laniel Before the National Assembly," March 5, 1954 (extracts).

65. Ibid., vol. 1, Document 292, 493–94, "Report by Giap to Senior Field Commanders on the Dienbienphu Campaign," January 14, 1954 (extract).

66. Ibid. vol. 1, Document 295, 497–98, "Appeal by Vo Nguyen Giap to All Cadres and Fighters, Units and Services, on Beginning the Dienbienphu Campaign," March 1954.

67. O'Ballance, *The Indo-China War*, 218, 225, and 230; Fall, Bernard, *Hell in a Very Small Place: The Siege of Dien Bien Phu* (New York: Lippincott, 1967), 177–80.

68. O'Ballance, *Indo-China War*, 213–17. Another 4,000 to 5,000 troops parachuted into Dien Bien Phu during the battle to join the defenders.

69. Ibid., 224.

70. Duiker, *The Communist Road*, 162. Of the 18,000 defenders of Dien Bien Phu, fewer than half were French. The others included Legionnaires, mainly Germans, Africans, and over 6,000 Vietnamese loyal to the French.

71. Giap, Vo Nguyen, *People's War, People's Army*, 187. Giap is also quoted in Young, *Vietnam Wars*, 36.

72. Herring, *America's Longest War*, 29.

73. Kahin, *Intervention*, 42. In fiscal 1953, the Eisenhower administration spent $1.3 billion, 61 percent of the total cost of the war for that year. For 1954, America financed 78 percent of the total cost. The total cost to Americans for supporting the French colonial war in Indochina from 1950 to 1954 came to over $2.8 billion. Tuchman, *March of Folly*, 257, states that most of the U.S. aid money "trickled away into the pockets of profiteering officials."

74. Herring, George C., and Immerman, Richard H., "Eisenhower, Dulles, and Dienbienphu: 'The Day We Didn't Go to War' Revisited," *Journal of American History* 71 (September 1984), 343–63.

75. Kahin, *Intervention*, 45–46; Herring and Immerman, "The Day We Didn't Go to War," 343–63; and Herring, George C., *America's Longest War: The United States and Vietnam, 1950–1975*, 3d ed. (New York: McGraw Hill, 1996), 33–34. Ridgway quote is cited in Herring, 34.

76. Kahin, *Intervention*, 48; Herring, *America's Longest War*, 3d ed., 35.

77. Herring, *America's Longest War*, 3d ed., 34–35.

78. Porter, *Vietnam Documents*, vol. 1, Document 315, 542–43, "Telegram from Dulles in Geneva to the State Department," April 25, 1954.

79. Herring, *America's Longest War*, 35. It is not true, as has sometimes been written, that the United States offered the beleaguered French the use of two nuclear weapons in the spring of 1954 in order to save Dien Bien Phu.

80. Hess, *Vietnam*, 47; Herring, *America's Longest War*, 3d ed., 34.

81. Kahin, *Intervention*, 52–53; Karnow, Stanley, *Vietnam: A History* (New York: Viking Press, 1983), 198. Arnold, James R., *The First Domino: Eisenhower, the Military, and America's Intervention in Vietnam* (New York: Morrow, 1991) says Ike wanted to help the French and only reluctantly bowed to domestic political pressures to keep U.S. forces out of Indochina. Herring, *America's Longest War*, 3d. ed., states that it is difficult to tell what Eisenhower and Dulles wanted to do because they maneuvered so craftily during this crisis. Ike probably did not want to intervene militarily in Vietnam because he did not believe that air power could do the job, and he did not want to get the United States bogged down in another land war in Asia.

82. Kahin and Lewis, *The United States in Vietnam*, 43.

83. Quote is from Young, *Vietnam Wars*, 38–39; Herring, *America's Longest War*, 3d. ed., 41–42.

84. Kahin, *Intervention*, 63–65.

85. Ibid., 66.

86. Porter, *Vietnam Documents*, vol. 1, Document 378, 642, "Agreement on the Cessation of Hostilities in Vietnam," July 20, 1954.

87. The armistice agreements, the Final Declaration, the protocol issued by Bedell Smith, and the statement by Eisenhower are found in U.S. Department of State, *American Foreign Policy, 1950–1955: Basic Documents* (Washington, DC: U.S. Government Printing Office, 1957), vol. 1, 750–88. The Geneva Accords consist of two distinct, related agreements: (1) A bilateral

armistice agreement signed on July 20, 1954, by Brigadier General Henri Delteil on behalf of the French forces fighting in Indochina and by Ta Quang Buu on behalf of the People's Army of Vietnam that partitioned the country into two temporary regroupment zones; and (2) A Final Declaration issued on July 21. It was endorsed by oral assent by all but Walter Bedell Smith representing the United States and Ngo Dinh Diem, who both refused to give their approval. Its key provisions include chapter 6, which states that "the military demarcation line is provisional and should not in any way be interpreted as constituting a political or territorial boundary," and chapter 7, which spells out the terms for preparing for and holding elections in order to reunify Vietnam in July 1956.

88. Porter (ed.), *Documents,* vol. 1, Document 381, 656, "Declaration by Walter Bedell Smith, Representing the U.S. Delegation to the Geneva Conference," July 21, 1954.

89. Kahin and Lewis, *The United States in Vietnam,* 59–62.

90. Moss, George Donelson, ed., *A Vietnam Reader: Sources and Essays* (Englewood Cliffs, NJ: Prentice-Hall, 1991). See essay by the editor, "An American Entanglement: U.S. Involvement in Indochina, 1942–1975," 5.

91. Karnow, *Vietnam,* 199.

92. Duiker, *The Communist Road,* 163–64; Kahin and Lewis, *The United States in Vietnam,* 47. The Vietminh would never have accepted partition if guarantees of elections within two years to reunify Vietnam had not been written into the agreements.

93. Duiker, *The Communist Road,* 166–67.

94. Ibid., 168.

95. Thayer, Thomas C., *War without Fronts: The American Experience in Vietnam* (Boulder, CO: Westview Press, 1985); also see Dunn, Peter M., "The American Army: The Vietnam War, 1965–1973" in Beckett, Ian F. W., and Pimlott, John (eds.), *Armed Forces and Modern Counter-Insurgency* (London: Croom Helm, 1985), 80–81, 85. Dunn faults the Americans for not seeking the advice of the French and for not absorbing "their bitterly-learned lessons." The U.S. Army "became, in effect, a large French Expeditionary Corps—and met the same frustrations."

An Experiment in Nation Building

There are profound differences between the Vietnamese and American people, in customs, outlook, political training, and philosophy. I hope we can find a bridge between Eastern and Western cultures.

Ngo Dinh Diem

NGO DINH DIEM TAKES CHARGE

During the summer of 1954, the Eisenhower administration firmly committed itself to creating a new nation in the southern half of Vietnam in order to block further Communist expansion in Southeast Asia. The National Security Council (NSC), meeting a month after the Geneva Conference, interpreted the accords as a major victory for the Communists, which gave them a salient for applying pressure to the nations of Southeast Asia. The NSC report called for the United States to negotiate new international agreements in order to provide strategic security for the new country it was going to create in southern Vietnam, and to protect Laos, Cambodia, Thailand, Burma, and the other nations of Southeast Asia from possible Communist inroads.[1]

To fulfill the policy recommendations of the NSC review, Secretary of State Dulles journeyed to Manila to orchestrate the Southeast Asia Treaty Organization (SEATO). Dulles had been promoting an alliance of Asian powers since the Dien Bien Phu crisis. Washington intended the alliance to evolve into "a regional multilateral defense system."[2] The creation of SEATO was part of a dual U.S. strategy developed during the summer of 1954 to block the further spread of Communism in Indochina in the aftermath of the Geneva settlement. U.S. officials sought simultaneously to create a viable non-Communist nation-state out of the temporary regroupment zone south of the 17th Parallel and to broaden international involvement in Southeast Asia by joining partners in Europe and Asia.

The new security arrangements were embodied in the Pact of Manila, signed on September 8, 1954. SEATO was a loosely constructed alliance including the United States, Great Britain, France, Australia, New Zealand, and the three Southeast Asian nations of the Philippines, Thailand, and Pakistan. The major neutral nations of the region—Burma, India, and Indonesia—declined to join. Because of restrictions imposed by the Geneva agreements, Laos, Cambodia, and southern Vietnam could not join. But Dulles arranged for a protocol to be attached to the SEATO agreement that projected an "umbrella of protection" over Laos, Cambodia, and southern Vietnam. This protocol circumvented the provisions of the Geneva Accords, which had tried to neutralize Indochina.[3] Cambodia promptly repudiated the SEATO protocol, and Laos was later excluded by treaty. But the French and Bao Dai accepted the protection offered by SEATO for the temporary military regroupment zone south of the 17th Parallel created at Geneva, which the protocol referred to as "the free territory under the jurisdiction of the State of Vietnam."[4]

Unlike NATO, SEATO carried no military obligations. It called only for members to consult with one another in the event of an attack on a signatory or one of the Indochina countries covered by the protocol. SEATO allowed the United States a freedom to maneuver and to decide if military intervention was warranted to suppress an insurrection or to thwart aggression. Washington viewed SEATO as a defensive alliance erected to block Chinese expansion in Southeast Asia and to prevent a possible invasion of southern Vietnam across the 17th Parallel by the Hanoi regime. SEATO helped promote the diplomatic fictions that the United States was proclaiming, that the southern half of Vietnam had quickly evolved from a temporary administrative zone into a free and independent state, and that the 17th Parallel had just as quickly metamorphosed from a transient demarcation line into a permanent political boundary. Thus, SEATO was part of a U.S. instigated process of defining a new state at a time when there was legally only one Vietnam, which was prohibited from joining any alliances or entering into any military agreements and whose political future would be determined by free elections scheduled for July 1956. SEATO later proved useful by furnishing a legal justification for American intervention into Vietnam to deter North Vietnamese "aggression" against South Vietnam when the United States moved to subvert both the letter and the spirit of the Geneva Accords.[5]

The man Washington selected in the summer of 1954 to head the new state that they planned to create in southern Vietnam was a staunch Vietnamese nationalist, Ngo Dinh Diem. The new leader was born near the imperial city of Hue on January 3, 1901, one of nine children of Ngo Dinh Kha. Kha was a wealthy man who had served as court chamberlain to Emperor Thanh Thai. The Ngo Dinhs were Catholics, and even as a boy Diem stood out for his unusual piety and devotion to religious duties. For a time he considered becoming a priest. He attended Quoc Hoc lycée in Hue, the same school that Ho Chi Minh, another mandarin's son, had attended ten years earlier. Graduating at sixteen, Diem enrolled in the French-run School for Law and Administration in Hanoi, where he performed brilliantly, graduating at the top of his class. Following graduation, Diem moved immediately into government service. Within a few years, he had reached mandarinic rank and was the provincial chief of a district containing 300 villages.[6]

An ardent Vietnamese patriot, Diem early demonstrated an abiding hatred of the French for their domination of his country, and of the Communists, whom he regarded as enemies of Vietnamese nationalism. In 1932, the young emperor Bao Dai, aware of Diem's energy and administrative talents, appointed him minister of the interior. Diem eagerly threw himself into his new job. He proposed a long list of reforms to modernize the ministry and to give it real authority. Neither Bao Dai nor his French masters would accept the reforms, and Diem, angry and disillusioned, resigned.[7] He retreated from public life and never held another government position until he became premier under American auspices in 1954.

Scholarly and reclusive by nature, Diem lived in his father's village near Hue from 1933 until 1945. He refused all offers from the Japanese, the Vietminh, and Bao Dai to participate in various governments that were formed after World War II. At one time he was captured by Vietminh guerrillas, who took him to Ho Chi Minh. Ho Chi Minh offered Diem a position in his government, which he declined with the explanation that a Vietminh guerrilla had murdered his older brother. During the Franco-Vietminh War, Diem was one of the few Vietnamese nationalists who did not join the Vietminh. He appears to have hoped that the French would accept a political settlement that would grant the Vietnamese autonomy within a French Union. When the French set up Bao Dai's puppet government in 1949, Diem urged the emperor to ask the French for greater autonomy; Diem was disappointed when Bao Dai declined to do so.[8]

In 1951, Diem came to the United States and lived for two years at a Maryknoll seminary in Lakehurst, New Jersey. From that base, he traveled around the country campaigning for Vietnam's independence. He attracted the support of Francis Cardinal Spellman, the leading spokesman for American Catholics. Through Spellman, he met several prominent Catholic laymen, including Democratic Senators John Kennedy and Mike Mansfield, and Supreme Court Associate Justice William O. Douglas.[9]

In the summer of 1954, when it appeared that France would lose the Indochina War and the Communists might take over Vietnam, Washington decided to intervene to replace the French and to try to save the South. U.S. officials looked for a leader of southern Vietnam whom they could back. They wanted no part of Bao Dai, the titular head of the French-backed regime in Saigon, who preferred living on the Riviera with his mistress to residing in Saigon. Dulles had become aware of Diem, thanks to the efforts of Diem's lobby of prominent supporters. Diem's administrative experience, staunch patriotism, and anti-Communism appealed to the Americans. Since the Americans were planning to replace the French in southern Vietnam, Diem's lifelong hatred and mistrust of the French increased his attractiveness to U.S. officials. Even so, U.S. officials had misgivings about Diem. They knew that he lacked popular support, he lacked political experience, and he had rather odd personality traits. They viewed him as the least bad choice. Bao Dai appointed him premier in June.[10]

Upon arriving in Saigon, June 25, 1954, Diem discovered that the government he had inherited from the French rested on an inefficient and a corrupt bureaucracy, a demoralized army whose fighting prowess and loyalty to him were both questionable, and a capital city seething with a bizarre amalgam of fierce political rivalries. Local military and political leaders conspired with the French and Bao Dai to ensure an early demise to Diem's fledgling government. Compounding Diem's troubles, the Geneva agreements, promulgated on July 21, called for nationwide elections to unify the country within two years. Ho Chi Minh and the Lao Dong were odds-on favorites to win these forthcoming elections and to take over the whole country. Diem had arrived in southern Vietnam only to find that he had no money, no power, no bureaucracy, no army, and no popular base of support.

Throughout the fall and winter of 1954–1955, Diem was caught in the midst of a fierce conflict between the French and the Americans for influence in southern Vietnam. The French bitterly observed that the United States was trying to supplant them in southern Vietnam. Their charges were confirmed when Eisenhower wrote Diem a letter on October 23, 1954, pledging U.S. economic and military assistance.[11] At the time, according to the Geneva Accords, Bao Dai, although residing in the south of France, was still the head of state of Vietnam, and the French were still nominally in charge of Vietnamese affairs. General Paul Ely, who commanded an army of 90,000 French troops, served as both high commissioner, the highest civilian authority, and commander-in-chief of all military forces in southern Vietnam.

Henceforth, U.S. aid money went directly to Diem rather than through the French legation, which had previously been the recipient of all aid. When the French delayed turning over full powers of governance to Diem until December 1954, U.S. officials suspected that the French were trying to hang on in the South and also build bridges to the Hanoi regime to protect extensive French investments in that region. U.S. officials also knew that the French were encouraging Diem's political rivals and trying to undermine Diem because he was strongly pro-American and anti-French. The French supported Prince Buu Hoi, a royal cohort of Bao Dai; they wanted him to supplant Diem as premier of the emergent state. Franco-American Vietnamese disputes were exacerbated by the French rejection of the U.S. plan for a European Defense Community a month after Geneva.[12]

Support from key U.S. officials enabled Diem to eventually overcome all of his political foes. Support came from an American Central Intelligence Agency (CIA) group headed by Air Force Colonel Edward G. Landsdale. An experienced anti-Communist nation-builder, Landsdale had previously helped Philippine President Ramon Magsaysay defeat the Huk rebellion on the island of Luzon. Colonel Landsdale quickly became a close friend and trusted adviser to Ngo Dinh Diem. Landsdale and General J. Lawton

"Lightning Joe" Collins, Eisenhower's special envoy to Vietnam, foiled a military coup headed by dissident Army Chief of Staff General Nguyen Van Hinh. Hinh, a French citizen with a French wife, plotted to overthrow Diem in the fall of 1954. Landsdale and Collins saved Diem by informing Hinh's backers that if the coup went forward, the United States would cut off all funding for the Vietnamese army. The plot collapsed when Hinh was dismissed from his command and forced to exit Vietnam.[13]

U.S. support also helped Diem cope with a massive influx of refugees who fled northern Vietnam during the last six months of 1954 following the Communist takeover. About 1 million civilians, some 700,000 of them Catholics, moved south of the 17th Parallel under the provisions of the Geneva Accords, which permitted free movement between regroupment zones. The Catholic emigrants who went south were mostly peasants who fled their villages in the districts of Phat Diem and Bui Chi in the Red River Delta south of Haiphong. The refugees also included former soldiers in the Vietnamese National Army, colonial administrators, wealthy landlords, and businessmen who feared reprisals at the hands of the victorious Vietminh. Whole parishes under the leadership of parish priests left the North. Diem's officials settled many of them in 203 villages in southern Vietnam in a cordon around Saigon. They sent others into areas of the central highlands, inhabited by *Montagnards,* which were regarded as strategically significant areas.[14]

Even though many of these Catholic peasants were uncertain and fearful about life under the Communists and voted with their feet, the mass migration south was not an entirely spontaneous folk movement. The Catholic Church, U.S. and French officials, and the Diem administration all promoted the migration. The Catholic migrants were urged to come south, both to form a base of support for the Diem government and to serve as compelling symbols of the Cold War. The mass migration of northern Catholics received extensive media coverage in America. U.S. officials and journalists depicted the migrants as pitiable refugees fleeing Communist tyranny for the freedom and religious tolerance they would find in southern Vietnam. Tom Dooley, a young Navy doctor and devout Catholic involved in transporting the refugees, wrote powerfully of a people fleeing from the godless cruelties of Communism. Anyone reading Dooley's best-selling book or seeing a popular movie based on it would respond positively to his emotional appeal for Americans to support South Vietnam. Vivid images of a flight to freedom became ingrained in the American public consciousness. To spur the migration along, Landsdale's CIA agents used propaganda and psychological warfare operations to induce reluctant villagers to flee North Vietnam. U.S. naval ships hauled over 310,000 of these northerners, and private American religious and charitable agencies helped the migrants resettle in southern Vietnam.[15]

The migrants more than doubled the South Vietnamese Catholic population, which, augmented by the newcomers, totaled about 10 percent of the southern population by 1955. These Catholics from the north became an important part of Diem's political base. In return, they held "a disproportionate share of high military and government positions in the Diem government."[16] More than 400,000 of the newcomers settled in the Mekong Delta, often on land previously worked by the Khmer. The Khmer villagers resented these newcomers from North Vietnam, regarding them in much the same manner as native white southerners had regarded the northern carpet-baggers who had come south after the American Civil War to live and work.

Diem's government nearly fell in the spring of 1955, when he challenged two powerful religious sects and also confronted the Binh Xuyen, the crime lords of Saigon and Cholon, the Chinese suburb of Saigon. Led by a godfather-type crime boss named Bay Vien, the Binh Xuyen controlled a huge underworld empire. In downtown Saigon, the Binh Xuyen operated the Grande Monde, a huge and opulent casino. Down the block from the casino was the world's largest brothel, the Hall of Mirrors. Another block down was an opium factory that supplied all of Indochina with high-grade products. By the early 1950s, the Binh Xuyen had become a powerful political faction in southern Vietnam. They also maintained their own private army of 25,000 thugs and enforcers. Bao Dai sustained his lavish lifestyle at his Riviera villa on payoffs from Bay Vien. In return, with French approval, Bao Dai appointed Vien a general in the Vietnamese National Army. He also placed Vien in charge of the national police, with authority over gambling, prostitution, and opium traffic!

Two powerful Buddhist sects, the Cao Dai and the Hoa Hao, claimed millions of followers; both had their own private armies and exercised political control over large areas of southern Vietnam. The Cao Dai sect, founded by Ngo Van Chieu in the late nineteenth century, fused traditional Buddhist and Christian beliefs with a worship of films. Believers prayed to Buddha, Confucius, Jesus Christ, and Charlie Chaplin. The Cao Dai strongholds were in the northern Mekong Delta region, centered around Tay Ninh, about 60 miles northwest of Saigon. By the 1950s, the Cao Dai claimed 2 million adherents and could field a private army of 25,000 troops.

The Hoa Hao had been founded by Huynh Phu So during World War II. Hoa Hao theology blended religious and nationalistic themes. So's followers worshipped heroic figures from Vietnam's past, such as the Trung sisters, Tran Hung Dao, Le Loi, and Nguyen Hue. Vietminh assassins, concerned with the growing power of the Hoa Hao, murdered Huyhn Phu So in 1947. The new leader who stepped forward was Ba Cut. By the early 1950s, the Hoa Hao claimed 1.5 million followers, mostly living in the Mekong Delta, and it had raised an army of 15,000 men.

The two sects, along with the Binh Xuyen, were strongly anti-Communist. All had enjoyed symbiotic relations with the French and all had opposed the Vietminh during the Franco-Vietminh War. Long accustomed to autonomy under the French, they refused to submit to the authority of Diem's new national government. After all parties failed to negotiate an acceptable political compromise, the sects, with French support, joined forces with the Binh Xuyen in March 1955. Together, they prepared to destroy Diem's struggling government.[17] Diem appeared to be finished before he had really gotten started.

But Diem moved first. He ordered the Binh Xuyen to close down their opium dens and brothels and to lay down their arms. Bay Vien refused. Diem's army invaded

Cholon and opened fire. Civil war raged in the streets. Thousands of people, mostly Chinese civilians, were killed. But Diem crushed the Binh Xuyen forces, and Bay Vien, with the remnants of his army, fled into the Mekong Delta.

Prior to Diem's assault on Cholon, General Collins, who had grown skeptical of Diem's ability to govern and defeat his various enemies, had flown to Washington to tell Eisenhower that Diem lacked the requisite qualities of leadership to prevent a Communist takeover of southern Vietnam. He told Eisenhower that Diem had been beaten by a cabal of religious sectarians, gangsters, and French officials. Eisenhower accepted Collins's judgment and prepared to withdraw U.S. backing for Diem. Shortly after 6:00 P.M. on April 27, 1955, the State Department sent a cable to the U.S. envoy in Saigon directing him to withdraw U.S. support from Diem and replace him with Phan Huy Quat and Tran Van Do, two officials with popular followings among the predominantly Buddhist population.

Scarcely six hours later, Secretary of State Dulles sent a telegram instructing the U.S. envoy in Saigon to wait for further orders. Dulles had reversed the order to dump Diem upon hearing of his army's successful assault on the Binh Xuyen. Diem, with Landsdale's support, at the last possible moment, had taken the decisive actions that saved his government and retained U.S. backing. Landsdale's actions had been critical to Diem's success. He had provided the assurances and moral support that gave Diem the confidence to take military action. Landsdale had also bribed the leaders of the Cao Dai to join Diem, and most of their forces were integrated into Diem's army. Further, Landsdale had used bribe money to induce most of the Hoa Hao soldiers to either join Diem or to remain neutral. The sects did not bribe cheaply; CIA officials stated that it cost about $12 million to buy off the sects' leaders and save Diem.

By the end of May 1955, Diem had overcome his political enemies and had outmaneuvered the French. He was master of Saigon and now controlled his army, which had been augmented by the addition of thousands of sectarian troops. In less than a year after his arrival in South Vietnam, Diem, with major help from Landsdale and other U.S. officials, had acquired considerable power.[18]

Eisenhower and Dulles reembraced Diem as the only man who could create the new U.S. sponsored state in southern Vietnam. Collins, good soldier that he was, went along with Washington's decision to reclaim Diem. But Collins's conviction that Diem lacked the requisite qualities to be an effective leader remained. His final report portrayed the bleak future awaiting South Vietnam under Diem's inept leadership:

> I still feel that even if Diem manages to suppress the Binh Xuyen, this will not change his own basic incapacity to manage the affairs of government. . . . I am still convinced Diem does not have the knack for handling men nor the executive capacity truly to unify the country and establish an effective government. If this should be evident, we should either withdraw from Vietnam because our money will be wasted, or we should take steps as can be legitimately taken to secure an effective new premier.[19]

Eisenhower and Dulles chose to ignore Collins's prescient advice because they could see no alternative to Diem. Over the ensuing five years, Washington became more committed to Diem and more involved in the affairs of southern Vietnam. No one in Washington or Vietnam seriously considered either a U.S. withdrawal from that region or abandoning Diem.

Following Diem's consolidating his regime with U.S. help, the French abandoned whatever remained of their hopes to retain influence in the South and made preparations to leave Vietnam. By March 1956, the last French soldiers and civilian officials would depart Saigon, ending nearly 100 years of French colonial rule.

Diem had vanquished his foes and shaken free of lingering French influence. Confident of the strong backing of U.S. officials, Diem now moved to eliminate Bao Dai, who was still the nominal head of the South Vietnamese state. Bao Dai posed no threat to Diem, but he resented Bao Dai's monarchial pretensions and decadent lifestyle. While the emperor remained in France, Diem arranged a referendum in which people could vote either for Bao Dai or himself as head of state. Even though Diem would surely have beaten Bao Dai in a fair election, he took no chances. His henchmen rigged the election to ensure an overwhelming mandate for Diem. Before the vote was held, he mounted a propaganda campaign against Bao Dai through the government-controlled press and radio. The referendum was held on October 23, 1955. Diem's soldiers supervised the polling places and Diem's officials counted the ballots. Diem was urged by his U.S. advisers to settle for a 60 percent majority. But Diem wanted more, and his enthusiastic election managers obliged him. Some districts tallied more votes for Diem than there were resident voters. The Saigon-Cholon area, with 450,000 registered voters, cast 605,025 votes for Diem. At the end of the day, Diem announced that he had won, with 98.2 percent of the vote.[20] He proclaimed the establishment of the Republic of Vietnam with himself as head of state. The political career of Bao Dai, Vietnam's last emperor, had reached its end. He never returned to the land his ancestors had ruled since 1802.

As he consolidated his authority, Diem could rely on the political support of four main groups: (1) the sizable Catholic population, now more than doubled in size by the addition of the northern exiles; (2) a small but influential class of wealthy planters; (3) the Vietnamese serving in the government bureaucracies, the police, and the armed forces; and (4) a new urban middle class created by the massive flow of U.S. funds to South Vietnam. For 20 years, U.S. economic assistance would maintain Diem's government and all its successor regimes.

U.S. economic aid allowed a generation of enterprising southerners to enjoy a lifestyle that could not be supported by the indigenous economy and one that quickly collapsed in 1975 when the great American money spigot was shut off. The members of this new class fully understood that their affluence was absolutely dependent on the American pipeline, which would continue to pump money into South Vietnam only as long as the United States backed whatever government happened to be in power in Saigon.[21]

The major component of the American economic aid program to South Vietnam was embodied in the Commodity Import Program (CIP). The CIP began in January 1955. Originally designed to absorb purchasing power to hold down inflation that would have been ignited by the rapid injection of large sums of money into the relatively small Vietnamese economy, the CIP also enabled the United States to fund the cost of Diem's army, police, and civil service. Diem was relieved of the need to tax the Vietnamese people because, in effect, the American taxpayers were underwriting the costs of his government.

The most important part of the CIP was a method of subsidizing imports, whereby the United States furnished dollars to Diem's officials who, in turn, sold them to licensed local importers who bought them with Vietnamese piasters at about one-half the official exchange rate. The importers then purchased American imports with their cut-rate dollars. They imported mostly consumer goods. The piasters government officials collected from the sale of the dollars that had been given to them by American CIP officials were put into a fund used for paying South Vietnam's police, soldiers, and officials, and for meeting other government expenses. Any additional revenues required by the government were raised by taxing the imports subsidized by the CIP. The commodity-import system generated the consumer goods that the new middle class wanted at prices they could afford. It kept taxes down, inflation rates low, and paid for most of the costs of Diem's and his successors' governments.[22] It also purchased the loyalty of the new urban middle classes to Diem, and to whomever might come after him in Saigon, and to their American sponsors.

The CIP did have some adverse long-run impacts on the economy and on many of the people of South Vietnam. While the CIP greatly expanded the size of the urban middle classes and made some Vietnamese wealthy, it created a narrowly based prosperity that never reached into the countryside or benefited the rural masses, who made up 85 percent of the southern Vietnamese population. The villagers could never afford to participate in the new consumer economy that American aid dollars sustained. The gap between city affluence and rural poverty widened. Saigon prospered, while poverty persisted in the countryside.

The CIP, in effect, created an artificial economy that could last only as long as U.S. officials were willing to pump hundreds of millions of dollars of American tax money into South Vietnam each year. The CIP also brought wholesale corruption and graft. Importers eagerly paid huge bribes to government officials to obtain licenses that practically guaranteed their becoming rich. Sizable black markets flourished. Some counterpart funds were simply stolen. The CIP, which brought in mostly consumer goods, also retarded South Vietnamese industrial development. There were no incentives for Vietnamese entrepreneurs to import capital goods and set up factories to produce items that could be imported easily and cheaply from America and then sold for windfall profits.

The South Vietnamese economy never industrialized or moved toward self-sufficiency. South Vietnam remained an economic dependency of the U.S. capitalist juggernaut. In the long run, two of the chief reasons for the failure of Diem and his successors to achieve stable and popular governments in South Vietnam were their failures to promote economic development and establish a popular base of support among the rural masses. The seductive lure of the CIP is partly to blame for both failings.

As the time approached for holding nationwide elections in Vietnam, as called for in the Geneva agreements, Diem made it known that he had no intention of permitting them to be held in the half of Vietnam that he controlled. The United States backed Diem's actions even though it was inconsistent with Washington's calls for free elections in other divided countries such as Germany and Korea.[23] Diem justified his refusal to hold the elections by stating that his government did not "consider itself bound in any respects by the Geneva Agreements which it did not sign."[24] He contended that the Vietnamese Communists were responsible for the partition of his country. He also insisted that only his government stood for the fulfillment of the nationalist aspirations of all Vietnamese people to live within a unified, independent Vietnam. Until the Hanoi government permitted genuine freedom and democracy in its territory, there could be no election. Diem also stated that the Communists would never permit a free election to be held in those parts of Vietnam under their control.[25] Diem failed to mention another important reason for his refusal to hold elections. President Eisenhower acknowledged that if elections had been held during that summer of 1956 to reunite Vietnam in accordance with the provisions of the Geneva Accords, Ho Chi Minh would have received 80 percent of the votes.[26]

During the mid-1950s, the major arena of Cold War competition between the United States and the Soviet Union shifted to the Third World, that is, to the emerging nations of Africa, Asia, and the Middle East. This shift in focus occurred primarily because the Soviet Union launched its first important programs of military and economic assistance designed to win friends and influence people in the Third World. The Soviets moved into the Third World arena during the mid-1950s for a mix of motives. They needed to find sources of strategic raw materials, and they were looking for trade opportunities. Favorable trade balances with Third World countries would provide the Soviets with opportunities to accumulate hard currencies (dollars or currencies convertible to dollars) with which to offset their trade deficits with the developed nations of the West.

The fact that a Soviet balance of payment problem had risen testified to the dynamic power of Western capitalism, as well as to the intrinsic weakness of the Soviet monetary system. The Soviets were forced to play the game of international trade by capitalist rules. Although Soviet penetration of Third World countries during the mid-1950s had powerful economic wellsprings, the most important reasons were geopolitical and ideological. As the Soviets recovered from the devastation of World War II and consolidated their sphere of influence in Eastern Europe, it became possible for them to challenge Western dominance in the Third World. As its capacity to function as a global power increased, the Soviet Union was no longer willing to concede Western hegemony in the Third World. Many of these Third World nations into which the

Soviets ventured were similar to Vietnam—newly independent former colonies and protectorates of European imperial powers such as India, Indonesia, and Egypt.[27]

For Washington, this shifting context of the Cold War rivalry brought about by Soviet penetration of the Third World significantly enhanced the American sense of what was at stake in Vietnam. It confirmed Washington's essentially defensive mentality. It reinforced the U.S. notion of global mission—the urgent need to deflect an aggressive international conspiracy reaching into regions of vital interest to America and her allies. It also reinforced the U.S. tendency to view all diplomatic developments within a zero-sum framework, to calculate any shift in the political fortunes of contending Vietnamese factions as a gain or loss for either Communism or freedom.

By mid-1956, U.S. officials had made fundamental commitments to Vietnam. After Eisenhower had settled in with Diem following his refusal to hold the elections called for in the Geneva protocol, none of Eisenhower's successors found themselves able to get out of Vietnam until America had fought its longest war.

SOCIAL REVOLUTION IN THE NORTH

While Diem was taking charge in the south, Ho Chi Minh directed a Communist version of nation-building in the half of Vietnam that lay north of the 17th Parallel. Although the Communists did not have to confront the political challenges to their rule in North Vietnam that Diem had to face in South Vietnam, the serious economic challenges facing the Communist leaders were much more daunting than those facing Diem. Most of the fighting during the Franco-Vietminh War had occurred in northern Vietnam; consequently, the damage to the war-torn economy of Tonkin was far greater than any damage done to the southern half of the country.

When the French and non-Communist Vietnamese pulled out in the fall of 1954, they "gutted basic services, and sabotaged or dismantled industries as they withdrew from the North."[28] Much of the technical and skilled manpower in northern Vietnam also left with the French. North Vietnam had fewer resources and more people than South Vietnam. Agricultural productivity was low. The division of the country deprived North Vietnam of its traditional source of rice. Historically, the North had imported much of the rice its people consumed from the south, and Diem refused to meet with Hanoi's emissaries to discuss economic integration or trade. Only an emergency loan from the Soviets enabled North Vietnam to import rice from Burma in 1955 and avoid a famine.[29]

The requirements of reconstructing northern Vietnam in the wake of a destructive war and the urgent need for food forced Hanoi to seek assistance from China and the Soviet Union. External aid was crucial, not only to meet immediate needs, but also to realize North Vietnam's long-term objective of building a modern socialist political economy.[30] Although China and the Soviet Union provided significant economic and technical assistance for Ho Chi Minh's reconstruction of that portion of Vietnam under Communist control, that aid amounted to only a fraction of the assistance that the United States lavished on South Vietnam during the same period.

The new government that the revolutionaries established in Hanoi in the fall of 1954 was cast in the Marxist-Leninist mold. All power was concentrated within the executive directorate (Politburo) of the Lao Dong, headed by Ho and his senior colleagues. Opposition parties were forbidden on the grounds that non-Communists could not possibly be Vietnamese patriots. This Communist rationale for repression of all opposition represented an inversion of the logic used by Diem and American Cold Warriors, which held that Communists could not possibly be national patriots because their primary loyalties lay with an external power. The Vietnamese Communists permitted a national legislature to exist and regularly scheduled elections were held, but the legislature had no power independent of the Politburo, which ignored its laws whenever it wanted to and routinely presented it with programs to approve. "People's democracy" in practice meant that the masses were free to obey the edicts of the party directorate who decided all policy. The people of North Vietnam came under the control of a Communist ruling elite whose authority flowed from its monopoly of state power.

Political authority at all levels, down through the levels of urban neighborhoods, rural villages and hamlets, workplaces, schools, and occupations, was wielded by party members organized into blocs called cadres. These cadres also monopolized local government offices. Through the cadres, both party doctrine and government policy, often one and the same, reached every citizen. When fully articulated, the party apparatus was the mechanism for collectivizing the entire society.[31] The cadres, using a combination of positive incentives and coercion, worked especially hard to impose collectivist discipline on the rural masses.

While Diem, with American help, was maneuvering to overcome his many political rivals in Saigon, Ho Chi Minh announced on January 1, 1955, that the time had come to implement his long-held Communist principles of economic and social organization. He launched a two-point program for rebuilding the northern economy and restructuring it along socialist lines:

> We shall endeavor to restore our economy, agriculture, commerce, industry, and transport, gradually to raise our living standards. We shall continue our work of mobilizing the masses for land rent reduction and land reform.[32]

It was through rebuilding and restructuring the northern economy that the Communist leaders sought to achieve their major objective: a self-sufficient industrializing economy within five years. Socialist reconstruction would be based upon the twin pillars of agricultural reform and industrial development.

When the government turned to the difficult task of rebuilding the war-shattered economy of northern Vietnam, its first priority was rebuilding the infrastructure. Transportation and communication systems lay in shambles. One of the first projects the government undertook was the rebuilding of the railroad that linked Hanoi with Lang Son at the Chinese border. Under relentless pressure from party officials, 80,000 workers rebuilt the lines in six months. Most of the workers were "volunteers," who were not paid for their hard labor. The human costs of this forced labor were high, resulting in deaths, injuries, illness, malnutrition, and exhaustion.[33] Rebuilding the railroad was crucial to the development of the northern economy because it linked Vietnam not only with China but also with the Soviet Union and the East European Communist countries. Over North Vietnam's Hanoi-Lang Son railroad would come over $2 billion of industrial and military equipment that "fueled its recovery and later its war against South Vietnam."[34]

China, the traditional overlord of Vietnam, furnished extensive economic assistance to the North Vietnamese. Ho Chi Minh journeyed to Beijing in 1955 where he was met personally at the airport by Mao Zedong himself.[35] Between 1955 and 1960, Chinese aid to North Vietnam totaled about $225 million, and thousands of Chinese technicians worked in various projects all over the country. The Chinese interest in helping Ho Chi Minh modernize his country was to ensure that a friendly regime protected China's southern flank; the Chinese did not want either the United States or the Soviet Union to dominate Indochina. Ho Chi Minh, for his part, was quite willing to accept the Chinese aid on behalf of his desperately poor, war-battered economy; but he also recalled the long history of Chinese domination of his country and took care not to become dependent on China.

Ho Chi Minh also traveled to Moscow in 1955, where he was warmly received by the Soviet leaders. He had lived and worked in the Soviet Union for many years and had derived his political ideology from Marxist-Leninist doctrines. His goal was for North Vietnam to industrialize along Soviet lines. The Soviets granted the North Vietnamese a wide array of aid programs. Soon, northern Vietnam was swarming with Soviet technicians, engineers, agricultural experts, and managers to help the North Vietnamese industrialize their predominantly rural and agrarian economy.

But Ho was no more likely to become a Soviet puppet than a dependent of China. He rather skillfully extracted much aid and technical assistance from both countries, retained his freedom of maneuver, and played one Communist power against the other, the entire time moving his country in the direction of economic self-sufficiency. By contrast, the Diem government in southern Vietnam, between 1955 and 1960, became ever more dependent on U.S. economic and military aid to finance its operations, to keep its consumer economy going, and to protect its security. Contrary to official U.S. views, Diem's regime was much more an instrument of U.S. foreign policy than Ho Chi Minh's was ever a pawn of Chinese and Soviet diplomacy.

Ho Chi Minh and his colleagues on the Politburo proceeded to restructure the North Vietnamese economy during the mid-1950s. They moved gradually, permitting a mixed economy to evolve. French-owned coal mines, steel factories, and textile plants were taken over by the government, as were banks and utilities. The former owners were not compensated for their lost properties. The commissars permitted some capitalist enterprises to survive; they retained a private sector of commerce and small-scale manufacturing. While a private sector and profits were permitted, wages and prices were subject to government regulation. The Politburo did not allow free-wheeling entrepreneurial capitalism to develop in North Vietnam.

Politburo economic planners regarded the creation of a more efficient agricultural system as the key to economic development. Industrialization would be retarded until they could make their rural economy more productive. Party officials also wanted to drive a sizable part of the rural population, which made up about 85 percent of the total population, off the land in order to ease population pressures in the countryside and to furnish workers for developing industries. Party planners believed the ultimate solution to the problem of low farm productivity would be the collectivization of agriculture à la the Soviet Union and China. Large-scale, mechanized collective farms would raise productivity and eliminate surplus rural populations. But to placate the land-hungry peasantry for whom socialism held no attractions, the Communists "preceded collectivization with a program of land reform."[36] Lands belonging to wealthy landlords were seized and turned over to the poor. Since there were not enough rich landowners to satisfy the massive land hunger of North Vietnam's rural poor, roving political cadres of land reformers classified some of the wealthier peasants as landlords. Their lands were confiscated, they were imprisoned, and sometimes killed.[37]

Land reform accomplished both its political and economic objectives. About 2 million peasants received land. The old landlord class was destroyed, and a new class of landowners composed of newly middle-class peasants strongly supportive of the Hanoi regime took control of the villages. But many abuses accompanied the North Vietnamese land reform. Thousands of people were dispossessed, imprisoned, beaten, and murdered.

The excessive brutality of the land reformers provoked a rebellion among Catholic farmers in Nghe An Province in November 1956. The farmers protested to the International Control Commission, which had been created at Geneva to monitor the armistice. Militia forcibly dispersed the peasants who fought back. To halt the spreading violence, Ho Chi Minh sent a division of regular army troops to suppress the rebellion. Thousands of people were killed, injured, or deported.[38] Conditions got so bad in some regions that Ho Chi Minh had to call a halt to the land reform program, order the release of prisoners, and apologize publicly for the abuses and mistakes that party cadres had committed. Officials responsible for the excesses and atrocities were dismissed. The harsh land reform program and the methods used to implement it left a residue of bitterness and distrust, as well as deep divisions in the countryside between the beneficiaries and the victims of land reform.

Although preoccupied with rebuilding the northern economy and implementing socialism, Ho Chi Minh expected the reunification elections to be held in the summer of 1956 as scheduled. He also expected to win the elections and shortly thereafter to assume leadership of a unified, independent Communist-controlled Vietnam, which had been his lifelong goal. Hanoi assumed that the French, who had pledged to hold the elections, would still be in control of affairs in southern Vietnam when it came time to hold them. But by the spring of 1956, the American-backed regime of Ngo Dinh Diem ruled South Vietnam. Bao Dai had been deposed, all French troops had been withdrawn, and French influence in Vietnam was at its end.

During 1955 and 1956, North Vietnamese officials repeatedly tried to establish communications with Diem and start consultations in preparation for the elections. Diem ignored them. They also tried to persuade the members of the International Control Commission to get the electoral process underway. Its members were not responsive to Hanoi's requests. Neither the Chinese nor the Soviets showed much interest in seeing that the electoral provisions of the Geneva Accords were carried out. As 1956 ended, it was evident that none of the members of the International Control Commission and none of the major powers were going to back North Vietnamese efforts to hold the elections.

Diem was able to subvert the provisions of the Geneva Accords that called for the national unification of Vietnam via the political mechanism of free elections in July 1956 largely because the major powers supported the division of Vietnam. The French had departed and were no longer involved in Vietnamese political affairs. The United States backed Diem, but neither the Soviet Union or China considered it to be in their national interest to back Hanoi's efforts to fulfill the terms of the Geneva settlement and to unify their country.[39] As far as the international community was concerned, Vietnam had been permanently partitioned at the 17th Parallel, and two de facto states, North Vietnam and South Vietnam, had been created.

Although disappointed, Hanoi officials, preoccupied as they were with implementing their socialist revolution in northern Vietnam and lacking support from the major Communist powers, were not prepared to resort to force to unify their country in 1956. Ho Chi Minh also feared that he might provoke a U.S. military intervention if he sent his troops south of the 17th Parallel. Ho could also be patient because he believed the Saigon regime would soon collapse from its own failures and lack of popular support.

BUILDING A NATION IN THE SOUTH

The ambitious American effort to create a non-Communist nation-state in southern Vietnam in the middle and late 1950s took on the aspects of a crusade in Southeast Asia. By 1958, over 1,500 Americans representing both government and private agencies were at work in South Vietnam on various projects. South Vietnam received the largest single share of the American foreign aid budget, and the U.S. mission headquartered in Saigon was the largest in the world. The mission, under the nominal direction of the U.S. ambassador to Saigon, comprised a myriad of agencies, each with its own personnel, budget, and programs. In addition to the regular embassy staff, these agencies included the Central Intelligence Agency (CIA), the United States Information Agency (USIA), the United States Operations Mission (USOM), and the Military Assistance-Advisory Group (MAAG). The MAAG was undoubtedly the most important of these agencies, because building up the South Vietnamese Army (ARVN) was the top U.S. priority; about 80 percent of the total U.S. assistance program for South Vietnam went to building up its military forces.[40] Washington officials believed that before South Vietnam could have a chance to survive and develop its economy, it had to be able to defend itself.

The MAAG had been assigned primary responsibility for training the ARVN. The 342 members of the American advisory group inherited a challenging assignment. They found the South Vietnamese military forces that they were to try to whip into fighting shape to be in a sorry state. The ARVN soldiers were poorly trained and poorly equipped. The ARVN was short in officers, certainly in qualified officers. "Diem tended to value political reliability in senior officers far more than military expertise."[41] Consequently, the officer corps, especially at the senior level, was riven with political intrigue. Diem, who functioned as his own minister of defense, frequently bypassed the military chain of command to give orders directly to unit commanders.

The MAAG advisers also discovered that the South Vietnamese commanders lacked any national feeling for their country. Most of its senior officers had fought with the French Expeditionary Force during the Franco-Vietminh War. Most spoke French better than they did Vietnamese, and many were French citizens. None of Diem's senior commanders had ever been associated with the resistance to French colonialism, the supposed foundation of Diemist nationalism and South Vietnamese patriotism. Insubordination was rampant, and senior officers were reluctant to discipline subordinates who had political connections. Army Chief of Staff General Le Van Ty bluntly told General Samuel T. Williams, the MAAG commander, that "many of our units would disappear into the countryside at the very start of the reopening of hostilities."[42]

Corruption in the ARVN was rampant. Many South Vietnamese officers saw their military careers as an opportunity to enrich themselves and their families. Senior officers often developed nonmilitary enterprises on the side that included black marketeering, drug dealing, and prostitution. Some regional commanders set themselves up as warlords in outlying districts, and their soldiers collected "taxes" from the villagers.[43]

General Williams and his advisory teams went to work to try to turn a thoroughly politicized, thoroughly corrupt South Vietnamese army that was incapable of fighting into an effective military organization. American-style training schools and methods were implemented. Thousands of Vietnamese officers were sent overseas to attend U.S. military schools. The ARVN was trimmed from a bloated 250,000-man force to a leaner, more efficient 150,000 troops. Soldiers were equipped with modern weapons and taught modern tactics. The "heart of the American advisory effort was the Combat Arms Training Organization (CATO),"[44] an operations staff that controlled all the MAAG field detachments assigned to the various Vietnamese commands from the corps level down to the infantry, artillery, or armored battalions in the field. Advisers played key roles in determining the effectiveness of the training and discipline that the ARVN units acquired.

The effectiveness of the American advisers was sometimes hindered by language and cultural barriers. Few Americans could speak Vietnamese (or French) or knew anything about Vietnamese culture, and they sometimes displayed racist attitudes, calling the Vietnamese "natives." Some American advisers vented anti-Asian stereotypes, viewing their Vietnamese charges as passive, cunning, and incapable of understanding modern technology. For their part, some Vietnamese were slow to learn English, often resented their brusque American advisers, and did not always train conscientiously. Many remained suspicious that the Americans had come to replace the French as their new colonial masters. U.S. advisers had to spend much time reassuring their South Vietnamese counterparts that they had not come as conquerors; they had come to help South Vietnam achieve independence and to be able to defend itself against aggression.

By the late 1950s, U.S. efforts to turn the ARVN into a modern and disciplined fighting force had only partially succeeded. Diem still insisted on selecting senior commanders on the basis of their politics rather than on their professional competence. Corruption continued to pose problems. But the chief shortcoming of the new model ARVN was that the MAAG had trained it for the wrong mission.[45] The MAAG advisers, perceiving that Diem appeared to have eliminated all internal political opposition, concluded that an invasion across the 17th Parallel posed the chief threat to the security of South Vietnam. The U.S. advisers were also influenced by their Korean experiences; many of them had helped the South Koreans build up their defenses against invasion from the North Koreans during the Korean War. The U.S. advisers therefore created a South Vietnamese army with the capability of fighting a conventional main force war that could defeat an external invader, and they were dismayed to discover that the ARVN could not cope with the guerrilla insurgencies that arose in the South Vietnam to challenge Diem's rule.[46] By training the ARVN forces for the wrong mission, the Americans also revealed that they had failed to assimilate the lessons learned so painfully by the French in the Indochina War.

Along with military assistance, Washington pumped over $1 billion in foreign aid into the South Vietnamese economy during the late 1950s, most of it into the aforementioned CIP that sustained the South Vietnamese government and created a new class loyal to Diem and his American sponsors. The United States also provided over $150 million in direct economic and technical aid. U.S. money repaired war-damaged roads and railroads, enhanced agricultural productivity, improved schools, and raised public health standards. A group of advisers from Michigan State University improved the performance of South Vietnamese police and public administrators.[47]

By 1957, the American experiment in nation building in southern Vietnam appeared to be a stunning success. Starting with almost nothing in the summer of 1954, Ngo Dinh Diem had risen to preside over a stable government protected by a modern army and sustained by a flourishing consumer economy. To confirm South Vietnam's nationhood and to celebrate Diem's political achievements, America's mandarin was flown to Washington in the American presidential jet for a triumphant two-week tour of the United States. President Eisenhower himself met Diem at the airport: "You have exemplified in your corner of the world patriotism of the highest order. You have brought to your great task of organizing your country the greatest of courage, the greatest of statesmanship."[48]

Diem's American tour was the high point of his presidency among his American benefactors. He enjoyed far greater popularity within the United States than he did in his own country. Diem was invited to address a joint session of Congress. The *New York Times* profiled him as "An Asian Liberator," who had saved his country from disintegration and who was a strong, popular leader.[49] Diem enjoyed a tickertape parade in his honor down Broadway and attended a private Mass celebrated by Cardinal Spellman. He was feted at public gatherings as a miracle worker, who, with American help, had done the impossible: the gutsy little leader had overcome the inveterate political fragmentation of Saigon to create a strong, stable government, a showcase of freedom. South Vietnam was offered to the world as a model of enlightened U.S. foreign policy in action. A thriving South Vietnam proved that foreign aid worked. The South Vietnamese had established a free society and were holding the line against the further spread of Communism in Indochina. Diem was the leader of his people fighting on the front lines of freedom, stemming the Communist tide.

But beneath the brightly shining surface of public celebration all was not going well in Vietnam south of the 17th Parallel, even during 1957, Diem's *annus mirabilis*. Diem did not believe in nor did he implement a democratic political system in South Vietnam. He clearly stated his political philosophy: "Our political system has been based not on the concept of management of the public affairs by the people or their representatives, but rather by an enlightened sovereign."[50]

To please his American sponsors, Diem established a constitutional system in 1956 modeled on the U.S. Constitution, with executive, judicial, and legislative branches. Formally his creation, the Republican Government of Vietnam (GVN or RVN) was a constitutional democracy. But Diem was observing the forms, not practicing the substance of democracy. Diem's constitution lodged almost all powers of government in the executive branch. Diem's powers resembled those of the Vietnamese emperors or the French governors-general, not the limited powers exercised by American presidents. The South Vietnamese judiciary never established its independence from the all-powerful executive, and Diem controlled all judicial appointments. Diem also had considerable legislative authority; the National Assembly could only initiate legislation covering comparatively minor matters.

Diem also moved to assert his authority over all of South Vietnam. He extinguished the regional autonomy of Cochin China and southern Annam. He appointed province chiefs for South Vietnam's 41 provinces and all administrators for the nation's 246 districts. Diem also extended his rule to the villages themselves. By decree, he abolished elective village councils and then appointed officials to supervise the affairs of the country's 2,500 villages and 16,000 hamlets, the local levels of government with which the peasants identified.[51]

As a result of Diem's centralizing thrust, South Vietnam had the most authoritarian governmental system in its history. Neither the imperial Confucian administrators nor

Figure 3.1   President Eisenhower shakes hands with Ngo Dinh Diem, President of Vietnam, as the visiting chief of state arrives (May 1957) at National Airport for a two-week visit. Looking on at center is Secretary of State John Foster Dulles. *Source:* AP/Wide World Photos. I.D.#: RB0412105TF

the French colonial administrators had ever completely abolished the tradition and practices of village autonomy. There was also a symmetry between what Diem was doing in South Vietnam and the centralization that Ho Chi Minh's government implemented in North Vietnam through the agency of the Lao Dong. One ironic consequence of ridding Vietnam of French colonialism and the remnants of the old monarchy was that Ngo Dinh Diem and Ho Chi Minh saddled the Vietnamese people with the most ruthlessly authoritarian governments in their history.

Diem also filled government positions with mostly northern and central Vietnamese. The highest-ranking positions contained the highest proportions of northerners and people from central Vietnam. Diem and his family were from Hue and were Catholics. Many of the northern Catholics who had migrated south in the fall of 1954 filled civilian and military positions in his government. Southerners resented these outsiders who enjoyed special privileges, did not speak their dialects, and did not understand their particular problems. This regional imbalance caused special problems for the

Diem government's relations with many southern peasants and prevented the national government from ever winning their trust or loyalty. Southern Buddhist peasants especially resented having northern Catholics, who looked down on them and were indifferent to their welfare, administering their affairs.[52]

Trusting no one, Diem relied heavily on his family to govern South Vietnam. Behind a democratic facade, nearly total power "remained lodged with Diem and his immediate family,"[53] the Ngo Dinhs. The most powerful members, after Diem, included Diem's youngest brother Ngo Dinh Nhu and Nhu's wife Tran Le Xuan, who functioned as South Vietnam's First Lady. (Diem, because he took a vow of celibacy, never married.) Two of Diem's brothers, Ngo Dinh Thuc, the archbishop of Hue and Catholic primate of Vietnam, and Ngo Dinh Can, ruled central Vietnam. Another brother, Ngo Dinh Luyen, bright and well educated, served as the international spokesman for the family, roaming the world as a kind of all-purpose envoy. Several other relatives and in-laws held important offices, including Madame Nhu's father, who was South Vietnam's ambassador to the United States for many years.

The Can Lao, a secret political party directed by Nhu, was the chief instrument of family rule. It was the only political party permitted in South Vietnam. Cells of the Can Lao reached into every agency of the government, infiltrated the South Vietnamese army, controlled the National Assembly, the police, the militia, the schools and colleges, the media, and entered into every level of the administrative apparatus of the Diem government.[54] The Can Lao cells provided the sinews that connected all the parts of Diem's authoritarian political system in much the same fashion as the Communist party operated north of the 17th Parallel.

Having consolidated its power in Saigon and the other cities in South Vietnam, Diem's family regime moved to suppress all remaining opposition in South Vietnam. They set out to exterminate Vietminh supporters, who had remained in the South following the armistice and who controlled many of the southern villages. In the course of fighting and defeating the French, the Vietminh had established itself in many regions of southern Vietnam. It controlled perhaps one-fourth of the villages within South Vietnam, with a total estimated 2 to 3 million people. The Vietminh was strongest in the Mekong Delta and in coastal enclaves. Nhu spearheaded the drive to eliminate the Vietminh presence in South Vietnam. During 1955 and 1956, thousands of Vietminh cadres rallied to the Diem government, or were imprisoned or killed. Perhaps as many as 50,000 were imprisoned and 12,000 killed. Diem issued ordinances in 1956 and 1959 that gave government officials virtually a free hand to root out any opposition to his regime.[55] Diemist repression fell most heavily on the countryside. In theory, Nhu's campaign aimed only to root out the Communists, but it also included anyone opposed to or suspected of opposing Diem: religious sectarians, intellectuals, journalists, socialists, and liberals.

The shortcomings of Ngo Dinh family rule were reflected above all in its failure to achieve its most important objective: building support in the countryside. Eighty-five percent of all South Vietnamese lived in rural areas. It was the persistent failure of

Diem's government, and of all subsequent governments of South Vietnam during its turbulent 20-year history, to gain the support of the rural populations that doomed these governments to failure. The Diem government's approach to land reform alienated many peasants. Landlords loyal to Diem were allowed to repossess rice lands that Vietminh cadres had confiscated during the Franco-Vietminh War and had given to poor peasants. The special courts established to adjudicate landlord-tenant disputes were dominated by landlords and officials responsive to landlord interests. Programs designed to hold land rents to no more than 25 percent of the value of the annual crop often were inefficiently administered.[56] A program to settle villagers on abandoned lands in the Mekong Delta promised to be popular, but Diem's insistence that the people buy the land from the government angered many peasants. Another program to distribute rice-growing lands to tenants succeeded in providing some tenants with land. But only about 10 percent of the eligible poor peasantry in southern Vietnam were able to get the land, which came from expropriated French estates that Diem's government had purchased from their former owners, with funds provided by the United States. Under Diem's program, landlords were allowed to retain sizable landholdings, up to 100 hectares, for their own use.[57]

Starting in 1957, the Diem government initiated a resettlement program for some of the Catholic refugees from North Vietnam and for peasants from overpopulated coastal enclaves. They were resettled on lands in areas within the sparsely populated central highlands. The new settlers were placed in fortified villages on lands claimed by *Montagnard* tribes. In addition to seizing their lands, Diem also attempted to impose his rule on the *Montagnards* and to Vietnamize them. Long accustomed to autonomy and allowed to retain their cultural identities under French rule, the *Montagnards* fiercely resented the intrusive Diemist policies. By 1958, some of the *Montagnards* were rebelling against the government's policy of forced assimilation.[58] Subsequently, the Communists were able to win the support of some of the *Montagnard* tribes by exploiting their many grievances against the GVN.

During the years when U.S. government officials and journalists were extolling Diem's triumphs in the South, his policies were alienating much of the rural population. The United States in South Vietnam "devoted little attention to political matters and despite its massive foreign aid program, exerted little influence."[59] Even though Diem's government was entirely dependent on American aid for its survival, U.S. officials had very little leverage against the strong-willed ruler. Diem was convinced that only he knew what needed to be done and that only he knew how to do it. Democracy in South Vietnam would be nice, but it could always be implemented later. Besides, the Americans reasoned, Vietnam lacked an indigenous democratic tradition; the people were accustomed to authoritarian rulers. Diem and Nhu also believed the Americans would be forced to go along with them no matter what they did as long as the family oligarchy maintained a tough anti-Communist stance in South Vietnam. They were correct, because it was not until the early 1960s, when Diem's government was engulfed by revolution, that worried U.S. officials began pressing him to make reforms.

Diem's political ideology, an unwieldy mix of doctrines called "personalism" developed by his brother Nhu to provide an ideological alternative to Communism, blended Confucian, Catholic, and Marxist principles. It added up to a rationale for a species of paternalistic despotism: As the leader-father of his people, Diem knew what was best for his country, and it was his duty to implement the policies that would achieve the Diemist conception of the general good. The people's duties were to respect and obey their leader. Personalist theory called for a government for the people, but not of the people or by the people. In fact, Diem viewed his people, if by the people one referred to the rural masses who constituted 85 percent of the South Vietnamese population, as potential enemies who must be kept under surveillance and tight administrative control. The Ngo Dinh family oligarchy was indifferent to the needs of most of its people and violated their sensibilities. It promulgated policies that alienated much of the rural population. Worst of all, it repeatedly attacked and tried to suppress all of its opponents. Inevitably, its actions provoked resistance. In time, that resistance evolved into armed rebellion. Hanoi took over and directed that rebellion, which evolved into revolution.

ROOTS OF REVOLUTION

According to the provisions of the Geneva agreements that arranged an armistice and proposed a political settlement for the Franco-Vietminh War in 1954, the armed forces and supporters of both sides were allowed 300 days in which to withdraw to one of the two regroupment zones, with the French and their supporters retiring to the zone south of the 17th Parallel and the Vietminh and their supporters moving north of that line. During the 300-day interim, about 800,000 people moved south. An estimated "50,000 to 90,000 Vietminh sympathizers went to the North, while approximately 10,000 to 15,000 remained in the South."[60] The Vietminh cadres remaining in South Vietnam were under instructions to protect the remaining revolutionary forces in that region, maintain the party apparatus, and retain their influence in the villages sympathetic to the Vietminh program. Neither these "stay-behinds" nor their leaders in Hanoi anticipated the rapid decline of French influence in South Vietnam or the emergence of the Diem government backed by a strong U.S. presence. They also did not anticipate that the elections to unify the country would be aborted. These Vietminh stay-behinds formed the nucleus of the armed rebellion that would erupt within a few years in South Vietnam.

During the first few years of Diem's administration, opposition had come mainly from the sects and the Binh Xuyen. During these years, the Vietminh stay-behinds, following their instructions, involved themselves mostly in political activity, preparing for the upcoming unification elections that they expected to win. They were shocked and angry when the promised elections were never held. They also were disappointed that the major powers, including their Communist allies, accepted the cancellation of the elections and that Hanoi was not prepared to force the issue. Some left the ranks of the Vietminh, but most remained loyal to Hanoi and to its goal of a unified and an independent Vietnamese nation under a Communist government.

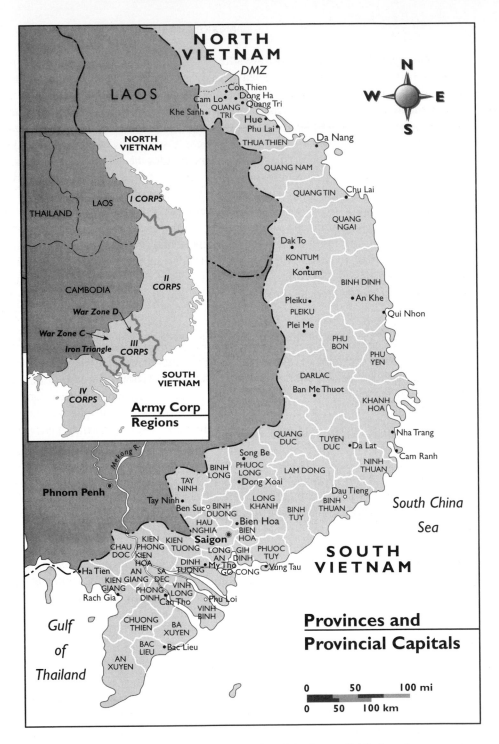

Figure 3.2 Provinces and provincial capitals. *Source:* Public Domain

Nearly all Vietnamese, northerners and southerners, whatever their political beliefs and affiliations, held to a concept of a single all-embracing nation. These nationalistic sentiments were either not perceived or were ignored by U.S. officials who had embarked on a crusade to create a new nation south of the 17th Parallel. Disregarding the strong sense of national identity held by most Vietnamese citizens, a succession of American administrations advanced the notion that those Vietnamese who happened to live south of the 17th Parallel under a "free" government had developed their own sense of nationhood and patriotism that was distinct from the sentiments held by the Vietnamese living north of that line under a Communist regime.

But the idea of a permanently divided Vietnam was no more acceptable to Diem, his successors, or their followers than it was to Ho Chi Minh, his successors, or their followers. Nor was it any more acceptable to that broad spectrum who did not support either the Communists or the Diemists. "Adherence to the principle of a unified Vietnam was common to almost all Vietnamese; where they differed was under what authority it should be reunited."[61] Both Diem and Ho Chi Minh believed that there could be only one Vietnamese nation, as did their fellow citizens. For nearly all Vietnamese, there was only one homeland; the conflict was over who should rule that homeland. The rebellion that became a revolution, which in time involved the United States in a major war in Vietnam, was always a struggle for control of one country.

These nationalistic aspirations to live within a unified country, embraced by nearly all Vietnamese, explain why no "South Vietnamese" national consciousness ever evolved. There existed only a region cut off from the rest of Vietnam by an arbitrary line drawn by diplomats who never intended for it to become a permanent political boundary. The 17th Parallel never did become permanent. What did evolve in the southern part of Vietnam by the late 1950s were three political groupings. One was loyal to Diem and his successors and supported their American patrons; a second group supported the Vietminh and looked to national reunification under the leadership of Ho Chi Minh. But a third force evolved, composed of those who held to a goal of wanting to live in a Vietnamese nation governed neither by Saigon nor Hanoi.[62]

In 1956, the head of the southern branch of the Vietnamese Communist Party, Le Duan, a veteran revolutionary leader and member of the Politburo, recommended rebuilding military forces in South Vietnam and reviving guerrilla activities to protect the political cadres. A southerner himself, Duan was concerned for the survival of the Lao Dong political apparatus in South Vietnam because of defections, attrition, and the depredations of Nhu's campaigns to root out Vietminh influences in southern Vietnam.[63]

Hanoi was not responsive to Duan's request. The Communist leadership in North Vietnam was fully engaged in nation-building enterprises of its own and had no desire to provoke U.S. military intervention in South Vietnam, especially given the lack of support for Vietnam's reunification from the USSR and China. The Soviets, under Khrushchev's leadership, were promoting peaceful coexistence with the Western powers; China, absorbed with its own national development, had no stomach for any more

Korean-style military conflicts with the United States. The Soviets even went so far as to propose that the United Nations admit both North Vietnam and South Vietnam in 1957, apparently acknowledging a permanent partition of the country, a position surely at odds with the desires of Hanoi's leaders.

Hanoi's leaders also told Duan that before there could be military action in South Vietnam, the southern Communist Party apparatus would have to be rebuilt. Consequently, the political directorate reaffirmed its policy of calling for peaceful political activity in South Vietnam. Duan wrote a pamphlet to the southern cadres outlining Hanoi's policies.[64] While affirming Hanoi's contention that the revolution in South Vietnam would develop peacefully and Diem's government would inevitably fall because of its inherent political weaknesses, Duan also advocated a more militant policy that would actively promote reunification and prepare the southern cadres for possible revolutionary activity. Some southerners read into Duan's ambiguous tract a call for more militant actions, including armed struggle. Duan's paper served as Hanoi's policy in South Vietnam until 1959 when fast-developing events in that region forced the political directorate to change it.

The southern Vietminh cadres did have some successes in 1957 and 1958. They exploited popular dissatisfaction with Diem's methods and policies in some districts. But Diem's drive to root out the Lao Dong was effective in many areas. Cadre members were arrested, imprisoned, and killed. In many districts, the party apparatus disappeared or was reduced to a harried rump scrambling to elude Nhu's "hound dogs."[65] Some cadre members resorted to violence in some districts. They murdered Diemist police and village officials. The rebellion in South Vietnam began a death at a time when some cadres took violent reprisals against the GVN minions.[66] But Nhu kept the pressure on and continued to eradicate Communist cells in the South. They were reduced to pockets of resistance in a few regions, struggling to survive, without any help from Hanoi, and under tremendous pressure applied by Nhu's Can Lao operatives, the police, and ARVN units.

"In desperation, local leaders in many areas began to act on their own initiative."[67] They resorted to violent reprisals to keep themselves and their cause alive. Armed units were formed in response to attacks by Diem's forces, even though these actions violated Hanoi's official policy. Guerrilla units were formed in the Quang Ngai province, in the U Minh forest, in the Mekong Delta, and in what U.S. soliders would come to know as War Zone D, a region northwest of Saigon. War Zone D would become a key basing area during the revolution, because it was near the Cambodian border and also allowed access to the Mekong Delta and central highlands. By the end of 1958, the insurgents "had clearly reopened the deferred war of national liberation."[68]

Hanoi began developing a new policy in March 1959 in response to the growing militancy among their southern cadres and fears that Diem's repression would permanently cripple the revolutionary organization in South Vietnam. The Communist leadership also perceived the growing popular discontent in the south with Diem's policies and methods of governance, and they wanted to exploit it. But they had also concluded that Diem could not be overthrown by political means. His overthrow would require military activity. Among the Communist leaders, debates turned on how high a priority to assign the growing southern insurgency and on what combination of political and military strategies should be used in South Vietnam to overthrow Diem and reunify the country. They hoped to continue developing the northern economy and to avoid an overt military strategy that would provoke the United States into armed intervention. If that happened, there would be a full-scale, protracted war, which would surely engulf them. Such a prospect Hanoi devoutly wished to avoid.[69]

A Politburo directive issued in May 1959 authorized the formation of a base in the central highlands for political organizing leading to limited guerrilla warfare. A few months later, the Central Committee widened the scope of permissible politico-military activity to include other regions as opportunities developed and circumstances required. It also instructed the North Vietnamese army to establish a special transportation unit with the capability of moving weapons, ammunition, people, and supplies overland from North Vietnam to South Vietnam along an infiltration route that ran through the Laotian panhandle. This infiltration route would become famous during the American Vietnam War as the Ho Chi Minh Trail.

Hanoi also began sending southern cadres that had regrouped in North Vietnam following the 1954 armistice down the Ho Chi Minh Trail to join the southern insurgency. Some of these infiltrators entered the South by crossing the Demilitarized Zone (DMZ) that divided the two countries near the 17th Parallel.[70] Many of these "regroupees" had received special training in revolutionary tactics while in North Vietnam, and once they returned to South Vietnam, they assumed leadership positions in the developing insurgency.

In 1959 and 1960, the level of conflict between Diem's forces and the revolutionaries intensified throughout South Vietnam. Guerrillas raided ARVN outposts and assassinated thousands of Diemist village officials. The Communists staged significant uprisings in three areas that had been long-time insurgent strongholds: in the Ben Tre province in the lower Mekong Delta; in the Tay Ninh province, northwest of Saigon near the Cambodian border; and in the Tra Bong district of Quang Ngai province near the northern coast of South Vietnam. In January 1960, in the Ben Tre province, Madame Nguyen Thi Dinh led 160 soldiers armed with only a few homemade weapons. The insurgents acquired a large popular following, gained control of several districts within the province, and overran government outposts. These attacks forced the Saigon government to withdraw its troops from enough areas to allow the Vietminh to distribute thousands of hectares of land to poor peasants. In the Tay Ninh province, a Vietminh main force unit overran a government outpost. In the Tra Bong district, the insurgents were able to fight off Diem's troops and establish "liberated zones" incorporating dozens of villages and thousands of people.[71]

Diem struck back hard at his enemies in an effort to suppress the rising insurgency. Nhu continued his efforts to break the back of the Communist organizations. The ARVN troops raided guerrilla strongholds. Diem, with strong U.S. backing, implemented a program to isolate villages from the guerrilla forces by relocating the people in areas where the ARVN forces could protect them. A series of fortified villages, called "agrovilles," were constructed in strategic areas, and the peasants were relocated.

The agroville program demonstrated how far out of touch Diem was with the rural population of South Vietnam. The peasants deeply resented being forcibly removed from their ancestral lands. They were not adequately compensated for their losses, and they were forced to work on community projects without pay. Originally, Diem's officials planned to construct 80 agrovilles. But peasant resistance and insurgent attacks led to the abandonment of the program at the end of 1960, after only 22 agrovilles had been built. After the war, it was discovered that the architect of the agroville scheme, Colonel Pham Ngoc Thao, was a Communist agent. He had sold the plan to Diem, then designed it in such a way as to ensure that the peasants were alienated from Diem's government.[72]

As the southern insurgency escalated, the Third Party Congress of the Lao Dong, meeting in Hanoi in September 1960, formally endorsed the revolutionary uprising in southern Vietnam. It adopted a resolution stating that the Vietnamese revolution now had two primary goals: completing the socialist revolution in North Vietnam and liberating South Vietnam from the Diemist puppet regime in order to complete reunification of the country. The resolution stated that the two goals were of equal importance and integrally related.[73]

To achieve its revolutionary goal in South Vietnam, the Party Congress also approved plans to reorganize the developing revolutionary forces in the South and form a new united front. Following the Congress, the military cadres in the South gathered to form a united military command. On February 15, 1961, the People's Liberation Armed Force (PLAF) was created. Tran Luong, a southerner, was chosen to head the PLAF command, but soon after his appointment several generals arrived in South Vietnam from the People's Army of Vietnam (PAVN) to reactivate the southern command that had directed Vietminh forces during the Franco-Vietminh War. It was known as the Central Committee Directorate for the South (*Truong Uong Cuc Mien Nam*). The Americans referred to the southern command as COSVN (Central Office for South Vietnam). The southern command, which had direct ties to the Lao Dong Politburo, in early 1962 took control of the PLAF with its 17,000 main force troops. In addition to its main force units, the PLAF also included regional forces, guerrillas who operated at district levels, and local irregulars who were farmers by day, indistinguishable from other villagers, and terrorists by night.

It was these PLAF forces that American soldiers called the "VietCong." No revolutionary organization in South Vietnam ever called itself the VietCong. Ngo Dinh Diem coined the term, VietCong, a contraction of the phrase, "Viet-nam Cong-san," meaning "Vietnamese who are Communists." Diem had coined the term to disparage all of his political opponents, both Communist and non-Communist alike, by calling all of them VietCong.[74] Not to be outdone by Diem in the coining of propagandistic epithets, the insurgents promised to liberate the country from "My-Diem," which can be translated as "American-Diem." My-Diem reminded the villagers that Diem's government was so dependent on the intrusive Americans as to be inseparable from them. While Diem and Nhu vowed to rid the land of VietCong, the rebels promised to rid the land of My-Diem.[75]

As the PLAF was forming, at a secret meeting place near Saigon on December 20, 1960, delegates, responding to the September Party Congress plans, created the National Liberation Front for the Liberation of South Vietnam (NLF or *Mat Tran Dan Toc Giai Phong Mien Nam Viet Nam*). The NLF was a reincarnation of the Vietminh Front tactic adapted to southern Vietnamese politics. Its Central Committee included representatives of the sects, Catholic and Buddhist organizations, labor, intellectuals, women, nationalists, socialists, and *Montagnards*. Below the Central Committee, the NLF had various administrative levels paralleling the various levels of government. Its basic units of organization were the village-level associations.[76] The overall structure of the NLF resembled a pyramid, with the Central Committee forming the apex and the village associations forming the base.

At their founding conference, the NLF organizers adopted a 10-point program, which, like its Vietminh predecessor, stressed nationalistic rather than revolutionary goals.[77] Most of its leadership was not recruited from Communist ranks, although some, like Chairman Nguyen Huu Tho, had close links with the Vietminh. In fact, at all levels, the number of Communist Party members who were permitted to assume leadership roles within the NLF was strictly limited. The Hanoi leadership had taken care to disguise its relationship with the National Liberation Front, which had the appearance of an autonomous organization composed of a broad spectrum of southern nationalists whose main political goals were expelling the Americans, replacing Diem's government with a democratic coalition government, and seeking peaceful reunification with North Vietnam.[78] The NLF represented itself as a democratic political alternative to the authoritarian Diem regime. Hanoi hoped its exercise in political camouflage would enable it to avoid an armed confrontation with the United States. The political composition of the NLF, its program, indeed its very existence, proved to many observers that the rebellion was an indigenous southern uprising.

For many critics of American policy in Vietnam, the NLF was a standing contradiction to Washington's oft-proclaimed charge that the southern insurgency was in reality an invasion from North Vietnam. Was the rebellion in South Vietnam in fact a spontaneous insurgency provoked by Diemist repression? It was true that by 1960 there was throughout South Vietnam a hostility to Diem's government that stretched across a broad political spectrum. This popular antagonism fueled the rising level of insurgency. A potent list of grievances had accumulated from the Diemist terror, the failed land-reform program, the loss of village autonomy, and governmental policies that usually favored Catholics and the landlord class at the expense of the poorer rural classes. But it also is true that Hanoi organized and directed the rebellion in South Vietnam from its inception. Party cadres provided the organizational structure and leadership that gave the southern insurgency the focus and dynamism it needed to mount a serious challenge to the GVN. "The insurgency was a genuine revolt based in the South, but it was organized and directed from the North."[79] The Lao Dong Central Committee's southern branch (COSVN) commanded the revolutionary struggle in southern Vietnam.

The NLF was not a spontaneous formation of dissident southern nationalists. It was linked to Hanoi and represented the southern wing of the Vietnamese revolutionary nationalist movement. It was formed in response to and in accordance with directives issued by Hanoi. The Lao Dong political directorate meeting in Hanoi determined the NLF's program, and its strategy. But the decentralized structure of the NLF and its communitarian basis gave the southern movement a degree of autonomy and flexibility. It often solved its problems its own way, punished enemies, and promoted land reform, without directives from Hanoi or even at odds with the Politburo.[80]

Hanoi exercised general control of the NLF through the instrumentality of the People's Revolutionary Party (PRP), created in January 1962. The PRP formed the inner core of the NLF pyramid. The PRP, formerly the southern branch of the Lao Dong, was directed by the COSVN and thus connected to the Hanoi political directorate. The PRP cadres operated within all departments and at all levels of the NLF, providing education, administration, coordination, and leadership. The PRP was the hidden government of the NLF.[81] From the Politburo through the COSVN and PRP, the NLF and PLAF were guided by Hanoi, which viewed the developing revolutionary situation in southern Vietnam as a continuation of the national revolution that had been going on in Vietnam since August 1945.

Hanoi did not set out to overthrow the Saigon government in 1956 after the scheduled elections that would have given the Communists control of all Vietnam were aborted. It only gradually and reluctantly embraced revolutionary goals. Initially, party leaders hoped to achieve reunification by peaceful political means. By 1959, they perceived that Diem's government, although repressive and unpopular, was too strong to be toppled by political means because of its American backing. By 1960, after years of delay and internal debate, the political directorate in Hanoi, whose hand was forced by the developing revolutionary situation in southern Vietnam and by the demands of the militant southern cadres, decided to support a revolution in South Vietnam as a necessary means to achieve its long-standing goal of a unified Vietnam under its control. But even at that late date, Hanoi still hoped to avoid a war with the U.S. backers of Diem's government. The ever-rising level of conflict between Saigon and the insurgents had forced Hanoi to embrace a revolutionary struggle that they would have preferred to avoid if they could have found an alternative political route to reunification.[82]

While Hanoi directed the formation of the PLAF and the NLF, the insurgency in the southern countryside continued to spread, and the level of violence steadily escalated. The number of districts and villages under rebel control increased rapidly. Hanoi's policy change had removed the restraints on the insurgents' use of violence in the South. The Diem government's response to the expanding revolt in the countryside was to remove its troops from exposed outposts, conceding control of districts and villages to the rebels.[83]

Diem and Nhu had nearly succeeded in eradicating the Vietminh in 1958. At one low point, the despairing rebels, scrambling to survive, verged on extinction. In 1959 and 1960, they managed a remarkable comeback. They had forced Hanoi's hand. The Politburo had to support the insurgents and allow the hard-pressed survivors to take military action. Otherwise, Hanoi risked losing control of the movement and perhaps its failure. What saved the insurgents in the South was their own developing militancy, eventual backing from Hanoi, and, most important, Diem's lack of support among the villagers in the countryside.[84]

In November 1960, Diem narrowly averted a military coup. It was led by Colonel Nguyen Chanh Thi, commander of an elite paratroop brigade, and by Colonel Doung Van Dong. The coup may have had the backing of a few U.S. officials who had lost confidence in Diem and had pledged to support the coup leaders if they were successful. The coup attempt, and the fact that it almost succeeded, highlighted the growing vulnerability of Diem's government.[85]

U.S. military advisers, worried about the survival of the GVN, finally began to shift the emphasis of their military training of the ARVN units from conventional warfare to counterinsurgency tactics. Three U.S. Special Forces arrived in South Vietnam to train elite units of the ARVN for counterinsurgency warfare.[86] The American ambassador to South Vietnam, Elbridge Durbrow, tried to persuade Diem to reform his government and mobilize public support. He suggested that Diem allow greater civil liberties and freedom of the media, restore village elections, and offer more economic assistance to the peasants.[87]

Diem ignored Durbrow's advice and tightened his control of the South Vietnamese government. The MAAG officials, concerned with developing an effective military response to the insurgency, opposed Durbrow's efforts to reform Diem. These military officers felt that such pressures to push Diem toward democracy at a time when his government was under stress, both from the rebels and disloyal army elements, could only undermine him and endanger the whole nation-building enterprise. As 1960 ended, even though the American experiment in nation building in South Vietnam was clearly imperiled, Washington did not make any major moves to salvage Diem. Eisenhower was preoccupied with crises elsewhere in the world and was preparing to turn the reins of government over to his successor, elected in November, John Fitzgerald Kennedy.[88]

LAND OF A MILLION ELEPHANTS

Even as Diem struggled to control his army and fight the rebels at the end of 1960, Washington was more concerned about developments in Laos than it was about what was happening in South Vietnam. Even though Laos had not received nearly as much attention in the U.S. media as had Vietnam, Washington considered it a strategically important country and had become increasingly involved in its affairs at the same time that U.S. officials were pouring funds and people into South Vietnam in support of Ngo Dinh Diem's government.

In July 1954, when the Geneva Accords were promulgated and Laos had received its independence, the Royal Lao government had a mildly pro-Western tilt. The United States, replacing the French, in the name of anti-Communism, lavished economic and military aid on that country. It made Laos its first test of strength in Southeast Asia, the first country in which the line against further Communist expansion in the post-Geneva era would be clearly drawn. By the early 1960s, the United States had invested nearly a half billion dollars in Laos, mostly in military aid, in support of a series of leaders.[89]

In the mid-1950s, Laos, a mountainous, landlocked feudal kingdom, was hardly a nation at all. Until the Americans intervened and pulled it into the Cold War, it was a quiet political backwater—a poor, underdeveloped, sparsely populated region. It had been colonized by the French at the end of the nineteenth century as a sort of afterthought to their conquest of Vietnam, with whom it shares a long border. About half of the 3 million inhabitants of Laos consisted of ethnic Lao, who lived on fertile plains near the Mekong River and its tributaries. The remainder of the population constituted a melange of hill tribes who inhabited the mountainous interior. At the time of the American intervention in the mid-1950s, perhaps 2 million people lived in areas nominally controlled by the Royal Lao government. The other million inhabitants lived in areas nominally controlled by a Communist movement that called itself the *Neo Lao Hak Sat* (Lao Patriotic Front). Americans knew the Laotian Communists as the *Pathet Lao,* which translates "land of the Lao."[90]

In accordance with the provisions of the Geneva Accords, the *Pathet Lao,* led by Prince Souphanouvong and backed by the North Vietnamese, had regrouped in the two easternmost provinces of the country. Prince Souvanna Phouma, the leader of the royalist forces, had negotiated an agreement with Prince Souphanouvong, establishing a neutralist Laos under a coalition government. Washington opposed Phouma's effort to form a coalition government with the Communists and pursue a neutralist foreign policy.[91] In its efforts to nudge the Royalist government away from its concert with the Communists, U.S. officials provided Phouma with about two-thirds of his budget during the years 1956–1958.

In 1959, the Eisenhower administration, using the CIA, installed a pro-Western government in Laos under the rule of General Phoui Sananikone. Embracing a strident anti-Communism, he ousted Prince Souvanna and had Prince Souphanouvong imprisoned. Washington backed General Sananikone, significantly increasing the amount of U.S. aid going to Laos, which reached $55 million in 1960, and sending a military mission. The Sananikone government proved to be inept, unpopular, and corrupt. Much of the money for U.S. assistance programs went into the pockets of officials.[92] The *Pathet Lao,* now excluded from power and with the support of the Soviet Union and Hanoi, resumed its guerrilla war against the Laotian government. The North Vietnamese sent cadres to train and equip the *Pathet Lao* who consolidated their control over the eastern provinces of Laos.

One day, in August 1960, while General Sananikone was out of town, a military coup led by paratroop Captain Kong Le seized power. Captain Le invited Prince Souvanna to return to power and form a neutralist government. General Sananikone, reacting to the coup, proclaimed his own government and marched on the capital, Vientiane. Prince Souvanna fled to Cambodia, and Captain Le joined the *Pathet Lao* forces. The United States continued to back General Sananikone. The CIA recruited tribes from the mountainous regions who supported General Sananikone's forces. The most important of these tribal forces came from the Hmong (Meo), led by General Vang Pao.[93] In December 1960, General Sananikone overthrew the neutralist government and returned to power. Washington's unrelenting hostility toward Laotian neutrality drove Souvanna Phouma into the arms of the *Pathet Lao* and the Soviet Union. He also sought support from China and North Vietnam. Responding to the U.S.backed coup, the Soviets airlifted supplies to the *Pathet Lao* neutralist forces.[94]

As 1960 ended, the crisis in Laos was intensifying. A dirt-poor, largely passive population was caught amidst political chaos and a fitful, low-intensity civil war. U.S. efforts to prevent Laotians from forming a neutralist government in coalition with the Communists had destabilized Laotian politics and provoked Soviet intervention. American efforts, paralleling their endeavors in Vietnam, to create a strong anti-Communist government in Laos, had failed. U.S. intervention had created an ominous possibility: a civil war that could bring about a Cold War confrontation between the United States and the Soviet Union. When Eisenhower, on his last day in office (January 19, 1961), briefed Kennedy on Southeast Asian problems, he talked mostly about "the mess in Laos" and the possibility of U.S. military intervention there, never once mentioning Vietnam.[95] When Kennedy assumed office, he had to confront two serious problems in Indochina. In South Vietnam and Laos, the governments of Ngo Dinh Diem and Phoui Sananikone, both dependent on the United States for their survival, were faltering.

A Failed Experiment

When Washington intervened in Indochina at the time of the Geneva agreements to create a new nation in the southern half of Vietnam and to prevent the further spread of Communism in Southeast Asia in the aftermath of the French military defeat, U.S. officials confidently believed that they could succeed where the French had failed. Ignorant of Vietnamese history and culture, and not understanding the breadth and depth of Vietnamese nationalistic feelings, Eisenhower and his advisers did not fully realize the perils and the low potential of the enterprise they had so eagerly embraced. It is hard to imagine their choosing a less promising place than southern Vietnam to try their experiment in nation building. Sixty percent of the Vietnamese population resided in northern Vietnam. Ho Chi Minh was by far the best known Vietnamese leader. His leadership of the struggle to liberate Vietnam from French colonialism had earned him enormous prestige and a popular following among the rural masses. He and the other Vietminh leaders were committed to unifying Vietnam under their rule. The Vietminh had left between 10,000 and 15,000 of their forces in the South to work for unification. At the time of the American intervention, Bao Dai's government was virtually nonexistent. He remained in France and his new premier, Ngo Dinh Diem, arrived in Saigon only to discover that he had no popular following. The bureaucracies and army existed mostly on paper. Diem had no money and no real power. The French, still in charge in Saigon, wanted to get rid of him. The political culture of Saigon and its environs was riven with factionalism. The economy, based on exporting rice and rubber, had been devastated by years of warfare.[96]

U.S. officials did not grasp the fundamental political reality of Vietnam: That there was scant basis for erecting a viable nation-state in the southern half of a country whose inhabitants had a strong sense of national identity and a proud tradition of national independence stretching back over 900 years before the coming of the French. The Vietnamese people may have quarreled violently among themselves for years over what kind of government should rule their country, but nearly all Vietnamese agreed that there was only one Vietnam to rule. In addition, conditioned by their history and culture to be wary of outsiders, many Vietnamese resented the American presence, viewing U.S. officials as colonial surrogates for the French. Even if Diem had established a more democratic and popular government than his family-run despotism, he and his American backers would eventually have been challenged by Ho Chi Minh and his followers, who would not have tolerated forever partition of their country, an alien foreign presence, or a Diemist government. Ho Chi Minh would have sought and received assistance from the Chinese and Soviets. Vietnam was fated for either reunification or perpetual turmoil.

Neither Diem nor any of his successors, the vast panoply of American aid programs, or U.S. military power were able to create a durable new nation out of a political fragment. The U.S. effort in southern Vietnam always was a long-odds gamble without realistic prospects of success. Although U.S. officials could not see it that fateful summer of 1954, they had undertaken an impossible mission that would eventuate in a war America could only lose. The fundamental flaw in the U.S. strategy of nation building lay in the Americans' attempt to create a separate state and society in the southern half of a unitary nation.

Ngo Dinh Diem was a man of considerable intelligence and courage; he was hardworking, conscientious, and patriotic. His nationalistic commitments gave him some claim to the loyalty of his countrymen even though he had not joined the fight against the French. He could not be corrupted by money. He was probably the best available man for Americans to support in 1954, and he was the most honest and ablest of a succession of leaders that the United States backed during the tortured twenty-year existence of South Vietnam.

But Diem also had numerous flaws and shortcomings. His obsolete political philosophy and authoritarian methods of governance prevented him from ever achieving a broad base of popular support. Diem's favoritism toward his Catholic coreligionists, the shortcomings of his land reform programs, his failure to promote industrialization, his assault on village autonomy, and his repressive attacks on all his critics and opponents had alienated the large majority of Vietnamese from his regime by the late 1950s. Diem was especially unpopular among the rural populations, whom he distrusted and disliked. He never found the programs or the policies to win the trust and loyalty of much of the peasantry nor to wean them away from the appeals of the Vietminh and their successors, the NLF. The failure of Diem's land reform program doomed his efforts to win a popular base of support among the rural populace and possibly undermine Vietminh support.[97] By 1960, he faced a powerful and expanding revolutionary opposition that his military forces could not suppress.

South Vietnam remained a political contrivance, a figment of American anti-Communist diplomatic and strategic imperatives in Southeast Asia.[98] In effect, the United States had created South Vietnam and its leaders. What U.S. officials had labored mightily to produce was not an independent nation-state. They had brought forth an autocratic family oligarchy that could only be sustained by immense infusions of American economic aid and military power.[99]

Only the caprice of the American electoral calendar saved President Eisenhower from having to confront the failure of the U.S. nation-building experiment in southern Vietnam and the failure of the U.S. effort to shore up anti-Communist forces in Laos as well. It would be the fate of his successor to have to choose between abandoning South Vietnam and Laos to the Communists or significantly raising the American stakes in Indochina. A major part of the developing American ordeal came from President Kennedy, who felt compelled to raise the American stakes in Vietnam.

Notes

1. Porter, *Vietnam Documents,* vol. 1, Document 386, 666–68, NCS 5492/2, "Review of U.S. Policy in the Far East," August 20, 1954.
2. Hess, *Vietnam,* 49.
3. Porter, *Vietnam Documents,* vol. 1, Document 389, 672–75, South East Asia Collective Defense Treaty, September 8, 1954; Herring, *America's Longest War,* 3d ed., 48–49.
4. Ibid., 675.
5. Tuchman, *March of Folly,* 270–72; Herring, *America's Longest War,* 45; Young, *Vietnam Wars,* 46–47.
6. Bouscaren, Anthony T., *The Last of the Mandarins: Diem of Vietnam* (Pittsburgh, PA: Duquesne University Press, 1965), 11–17; Fitzgerald, Frances, *Fire in the Lake: The Vietnamese and the Americans in Vietnam* (New York: Vintage Press, 1973), 107–8.
7. Bouscaren, *The Last of the Mandarins,* 17; Shaplen, *Lost Revolution,* 107–8.
8. Shaplen, *Lost Revolution,* 111–12.
9. Ibid., 112–13; Scheer, Robert, *How the United States Got Involved in Vietnam* (Santa Barbara, CA: Center for the Study of Democratic Institutions, 1965), 13–16.
10. No one appears to know precisely why Bao Dai was persuaded to appoint Diem to be his prime minister. Cooper, Chester L., *The Lost Crusade: America in Vietnam* (New York: Dodd, Mead,

1970), 120–28, believes that Dulles persuaded Bao Dai to appoint him in the hopes that Diem could ease out the French and defeat the Communists. If Diem succeeded in these endeavors, Bao Dai could then return to Vietnam as the ruler of a reunited, independent nation. Also see Karnow, *Vietnam,* 217–18. The most logical explanation is that Bao Dai, feeling abandoned by the French, appointed Diem in the hopes that Diem's American connections might make U.S. officials more helpful. Schulzinger, *A Time for War,* 78; Hess, *Vietnam,* rev. ed., 54–55.

11. Porter, *Vietnam Documents,* vol. 1, Document 395, 681–82. "Letter from Eisenhower to President Ngo Dinh Diem," October 23, 1954. Eisenhower clearly hedged U.S. aid commitments to Diem. The key sentence reads, "The Government of the United States expects that this aid will be met by performance on the part of the Government of Viet-Nam [*sic*] in undertaking needed reforms."

12. Gardner, *Approaching Vietnam,* 327–38; Herring, *America's Longest War,* 49–50.

13. Landsdale, Edward Geary, *In the Midst of Wars: An American's Mission to Southeast Asia* (New York: Harper & Row, 1972), 170–76; Scigliano, Robert, *South Vietnam: Nation under Stress* (Boston: Houghton Mifflin, 1964), 18; Young, *Vietnam Wars,* 43–46. Eisenhower and Dulles's decision to back Diem was influenced by the U.S. experience in the Philippines during the late 1940s and early 1950s. In the Philippines, U.S. military forces suppressed the Hukbalahap, a Communist insurgency strongest on Luzon. The Americans later backed the rise to power of Ramon Magsaysay, a popular reform leader who established a stable, pro-American government in the former U.S. colony, which had achieved its independence on July 4, 1946. In 1954, Washington saw the challenge it faced in southern Vietnam as finding a Vietnamese Magsaysay.

14. Kahin, *Intervention,* 75–77; Scigliano, *South Vietnam,* 52–55. According to Scigliano, in 1960 there were 1,014,000 Catholics in South Vietnam, more than half of whom were recent migrants from northern Vietnam. For that same year, Catholic officials estimated the total Catholic population of Vietnam at 1,807,784, of whom 793,000 resided in the north. In 1960, Catholics represented 9 percent of South Vietnam's population, 6 percent of North Vietnam's population, and about 7 percent of the total population.

15. Landsdale, *In the Midst of Wars,* 165–70; Kahin, *Intervention,* 76–77.

16. Doyle and others, *Passing the Torch,* 141–42; Brush, Peter, "Personality," (a feature article about Tom Dooley) in *Vietnam* 17 no. 2 (August 2004): 16.

17. There are several accounts of Diem's struggles to defeat his political opponents and to establish his government in the south. See Landsdale, *In the Midst of Wars,* 154–227 and 244–312; and Shaplen, *Lost Revolution,* 100–28. Also see James S. Olson and Randy Roberts, *Where the Domino Fell: America and Vietnam,* 1945–1995, 2d ed., 52–57, for brief, colorful accounts of the various political factions that composed the exotic stew that was South Vietnamese political life in the mid-1950s.

18. Landsdale, *In the Midst of Wars,* 260–312; Neil Sheehan, *A Bright Shining Lie: John Paul Vann and America in Vietnam* (New York: Random House, 1988), 138.

19. The quote from Collins's report is taken from Schulzinger, *A Time for War,* 86.

20. Kahin, *Intervention,* 95.

21. Ibid., 84–85.

22. Ibid., 84–88; Scigliano, *South Vietnam,* 125–37. Kahin states that of the $322.4 million in economic aid for South Vietnam spent in 1955, 87 percent of those funds, $280 million, were channeled through the CIP. The flow of CIP funds was large enough to allow Diem to accumulate a dollar reserve of $216.4 million by 1960.

23. Herring, *America's Longest War,* 55.

24. Eisenhower, Dwight David, *The White House Years: Mandate for Change, 1953–1956* (New York: Doubleday, 1963), 372.

25. Porter, *Vietnam Documents,* vol. 2, Document 1, 1–2, Declaration of the Government of Vietnam on Reunification, August 9, 1955.

26. Ibid.

27. Vadney, *World,* 215–17; Herring, *America's Longest War,* 56.

28. Turley, William S., *The Second Indochina War: A Short Political and Military History, 1954–1975* (New York: New American Library, 1986), 18.

29. Karnow, *Vietnam,* 225.

30. Hess, *Vietnam,* 64.

31. Doyle et al., *Passing the Torch,* 102–3.

32. Quoted in Doyle et al., *Passing the Torch,* 102.

33. Ibid., 103–4. Thousands of workers gladly worked on the project without pay for patriotic reasons. Thousands, however, were pressed into unpaid labor by squads of soldiers who swept through villages and forcibly recruited workers for the project.

34. Ibid., 104.

35. Neither the Russian premier Nikita Khrushchev nor the American president Richard Nixon were met personally upon their arrival in Beijing by Mao. When he greeted Ho Chi Minh at the airport, Mao was acknowledging the visit of an Asian revolutionary nationalist of a stature equivalent to his own.

36. Duiker, William, *Vietnam: A Nation in Revolution* (Boulder, CO: Westview Press, 1983), 107.

37. Karnow, *Vietnam,* 225–26; Hess, *Vietnam,* 64.

38. Turley, *The Second Indochina War,* 19; Karnow, *Vietnam,* 225–26; also see Moise, Edwin E., *Land Reform in China and North Vietnam* (Chapel Hill: University of North Carolina Press, 1983), 178–240; and his article "Land Reform and Land Reform Errors in North Vietnam," *Pacific Affairs* 49 (spring 1976): 70–92. Moise says about 5,000 peasants were executed. Porter, Gareth, *The Myth of the Bloodbath: North Vietnam's Land Reform Reconsidered* (Ithaca, NY: Cornell University Press, 1972). Porter found that about 2,500 people lost their lives.

39. Note from Pham Van Dong to the Geneva Co-Chairs, April 9, 1956, insisting that the Geneva agreements required both the French and Diem's government to hold elections, in Porter, *Vietnam Documents,* vol. 2, Document 8, 15–16; also see Note from the British Embassy in Moscow to the Soviet Foreign Ministry, April 9, 1956, informing the Soviets that the British government did not agree that South Vietnam was required to hold the elections, in ibid., 17–18; see also Message from the Two Co-chairs of the Geneva Conference to the Governments of the Democratic Republic of Vietnam and the Republic of Vietnam, May 8, 1956, in which the Soviets, in effect, conceded that they would not push for reconvening the Geneva Conference or the holding of elections, in ibid., 19–20.

40. Herring, *America's Longest War,* 57; Hess, *Vietnam,* 60. Between 1954 and 1959, $1.2 billion in American assistance poured into South Vietnam. The top priority was always military security, and most of the U.S. aid went into military programs.

41. Spector, Ronald H., *Advice and Support: The Early Years, 1941–1960* (Washington, DC: Center of Military History, U.S. Army, 1985), 278.

42. Ibid., 280.

43. Ibid., 281.

44. Ibid., 289.

45. Ibid., 268–74; Herring, *America's Longest War,* 58–60.

46. Herring, *America's Longest War,* 61.

47. Scigliano, *South Vietnam,* 102–29.

48. Video clip from "America's Mandarin," part three of the television documentary series "Vietnam: A Television Series," produced by Boston WGBH and the Public Broadcasting System (PBS), first shown in October 1983.

49. Young, *Vietnam Wars,* 58.

50. Diem's quote is found in Olson and Roberts, *Where the Domino Fell,* 6.

51. Shaplen, *The Lost Revolution,* 132–34.

52. Scigliano, *South Vietnam,* 51–55.

53. Kahin, *Intervention,* 95.

54. The full name for the Can Lao was *Can Lao Nhan Vi Cach Mang Dang* (Personalist Labor Revolutionary Party).

55. Kahin, *Intervention,* 96–97. On January 6, 1956, Diem introduced Ordinance No. 6. According to its language, anyone considered a danger "to the defense of the state and public order" could be arrested. Diem later promulgated the notorious Law 10/59, which went into effect on May 6, 1959. Under its provisions, anyone who committed or aimed to commit sabotage, or infringed upon the security of the state, or belonged to a subversive organization, would be sentenced to death by special military courts within three days of being charged, and there would be no appeal. Young, *Vietnam Wars,* 56, cites figures of 50,000 prisoners and 12,000 killed.

56. Race, Jeffrey, *War Comes to Long An* (Berkeley: University of California Press, 1972), 55–61. Race compiled a detailed study of the forces in conflict in southern Vietnam within Long An, a strategic Mekong Delta province lying south and west of Saigon. He documents the failure of Diemist land reforms in Long An.

57. Scigliano, *South Vietnam,* 104–5, 120–24. At the time of Diem's ascension to power in the South, about 40 percent of rice lands were owned by 2,500 people, one-quarter of 1 percent of the rural population. Tenant rentals were commonly 50 percent of the crop, and tenants often had to furnish their own equipment, water buffalo, labor, seeds, and anything else needed to produce the crop. There were 1,584 French landowners expropriated, and about 111,000 tenants received the lands, about 10 percent of South Vietnam's tenant farmers.

58. Kahin, *Intervention,* 99.

59. Herring, *America's Longest War,* 63.

60. Duiker, *The Communist Road,* 172–73.

61. Kahin, *Intervention,* 103.

62. Turley, *The Second Indochina War,* 7–9.

63. Ibid., 21.

64. Duiker, *The Communist Road,* 175.

65. Interview with Dr. Pham Thi Xuan Que on videotape in "America's Mandarin," one of the documentaries in the "Vietnam: A Television History," cited in note 48 above. She said "hound dogs" was the term for Nhu's secret police.

66. Race, Jeffrey, "The Origins of the Second Indochina War," *Asian Survey* (May 1960): 381 ff.

67. Duiker, *Communist Road,* 184.

68. Ibid., 184; quote is from Millett, Allan R., and Maslowski, Peter, *For the Common Defense: A Military History of the United States of America* (New York: Free Press, 1984), 545.

69. Ibid., 186–90. Ho Chi Minh and his colleagues knew about the vast destructiveness of the Korean War, both north and south, caused by U.S. firepower, particularly from the aeriel bombing of cities. They wanted to avoid a similar fate for Vietnam.

70. Turley, *The Second Indochina War,* 24–25; Porter (ed.), *Vietnam Documents,* vol. 2, Document 21, 44–46, "Communique of the 15th Plenum of the Lao Dong," May 13, 1959. This communique reflects the crucial decision made by the Communist leaders to permit armed struggle in the south as part of the insurgent strategies to undermine Diem's GVN. The DMZ was created at the Geneva Conference in July 1954. It was a buffer zone five miles wide dividing the northern regroupment zone (North Vietnam) from the southern regroupment zone (South Vietnam).

It extended from the South China seacoast to the village of Bo Hu Su along the Ben Hai River, and due west from there to the Laotian border at the 17th Parallel of north latitude.

71. Duiker, *The Communist Road,* 190–93; Young, *Vietnam Wars,* 66–68.

72. Doyle et al., *Passing the Torch,* 157–59.

73. Duiker, *The Communist Road,* 194.

74. Turley, *The Second Indochina War,* 30–31.

75. Hess, *Vietnam,* 68.

76. Pike, Douglas, *Vietcong: The Organization and Technique of the National Liberation Front of South Vietnam* (Cambridge, MA: MIT Press, 1966), 77–84, 109–18; Duiker, *The Communist Road,* 197.

77. Porter, *Vietnam Documents,* vol. 2, Document 37, 86–89. "Manifesto of the South Viet Nam National Front for Liberation," December 1960, 86–89. The moderate nature of its program was to serve as a bridge linking the Communists and non-Communist nationalists in a common cause, the overthrow of the "disguised colonial regime of the U.S. imperialists" and the American "lackey, the dictatorial Ngo Dinh Diem administration."

78. Duiker, *The Communist Road,* 196–98.

79. Ibid., 198; Kolko, *Anatomy of a Revolution,* 126.

80. Turley, *The Second Indochina War,* 31–32; Kolko, *Anatomy of a Revolution,* 128–29.

81. Pike, *Vietcong,* 136–50.

82. Porter, *Vietnam Documents,* vol. 2, Document 27, 68–70, "Address by Lao Dong Party Secretary Le Duan," April 20, 1960. Duan's speech is the most authoritative public statement of Hanoi's evolving policy toward the south. It stressed that Hanoi wanted above all else to avoid a war that would bring in the Americans and engulf North Vietnam.

83. Race, Jeffrey, *War Comes to Long An,* 113–30. In his detailed study of the revolutionary dynamics in a crucial province, Race shows how Diemist military forces and local officials could not stem the rising tide of revolutionary violence in Long An. Local officials were killed, kidnapped, or driven off. Insurgents took control of many districts, gave land to poor peasants, reduced taxes and land rents, established village self-defense forces, and gathered intelligence.

84. Hess, *Vietnam,* 68.

85. Rust, William J., *Kennedy and Vietnam: American Vietnam Policy, 1960–1963* (New York: Da Capo Press, 1985), 1–20; Spector, *Advice and Support,* 369–71; and Kahin, *Intervention,* 123–26.

86. Spector, *Advice and Support,* 349–61.

87. Porter, *Vietnam Documents,* vol. 2, Document 31, 75–78, "Memo from Ambassador Elbridge Durbrow to President Ngo Dinh Diem," October 14, 1960. In a tactfully worded, lengthy memo, Ambassador Durbrow, who had cleared the memo with Secretary of State Christian Herter beforehand, suggested many reforms for President Diem to make. Diem ignored Durbrow's memo.

88. Herring, *America's Longest War,* 70–71.

89. Isaacs, Arnold R., *Without Honor: Defeat in Vietnam and Cambodia* (New York: Vintage, 1984), 159.

90. Ibid., 155–56.

91. Hess, *Vietnam,* 69.

92. Ibid., 69–70.

93. Isaacs, *Without Honor,* 164–68.

94. Hess, *Vietnam,* 70–71.

95. Doyle et al., *Passing the Torch,* 186–87.

96. Herring, *America's Longest War,* 3d ed., 49–50.

97. Young, *Vietnam Wars,* 58–59.

98. Gravel, Mike, ed., *The Pentagon Papers: The Defense Department History of U.S. Decision Making in Vietnam* (Boston: Beacon Press, 1971), vol. II, 22; Baritz, Loren, *Backfire: Vietnam—The Myths That Made Us Fight, the Illusions That Helped Us Lose, the Legacy That Haunts Us Today* (New York: Ballantine, 1985), 16. According to Baritz: "South Vietnam was an American invention. . . . What was invented was not the place called South Vietnam, obviously, but the idea about the place." The southern military zone never evolved into a nation whose people shared a common culture, purpose, or identity.

99. Hess, *Vietnam,* 60–63.

CHAPTER 4

Raising the Stakes

Vietnam represents the cornerstone of the Free World in Southeast Asia, the keystone to the arch, the finger in the dike. . . . Vietnam is crucial to the free world in fields other than military. Her economy is essential to the economy of Southeast Asia; and her political liberty is an inspiration. . . . We must assist the inspiring growth of Vietnamese democracy and economy.

John F. Kennedy

COLD WAR CRISES

When John F. Kennedy took the presidential oath of office on January 20, 1961, the world appeared to be entering the most perilous stage in its history. The ceaseless global Cold War struggle between the United States and the Soviet Union raged on. At several points—Berlin, Cuba, the Congo, and Laos, the two superpowers verged on confrontation. In Asia and Africa, Third World nations were breaking free from colonialism; they struggled to establish stable governments and develop modern institutions. The reckless and erratic Soviet Premier Nikita Khrushchev saw possibilities for advancing Soviet interests in the turmoil and chaos generated within the emerging nations of the Third World. In a speech delivered a few days before Kennedy's inauguration, Khrushchev vowed his support for anticolonial "wars of national liberation." The Soviet leader, emboldened by Soviet breakthroughs in space and missile technology in the late 1950s, crowed that Communism was superior to capitalism and told anxious Americans that their grandchildren would sleep under a Communist moon. Kennedy, sensing the American Cold War angst during his 1960 presidential campaign, had attacked what he called the "horse and buggy" policies of the Eisenhower administration that he charged had permitted the American economy to stagnate and had allowed the Soviets to gain the initiative in space-age technology. Kennedy vowed to "get the country moving again."

To rally the nation to face the challenges he saw, Kennedy struck an alarmist note in his inaugural address. The new president sounded the theme of a nation embattled, facing crises around the world, with the fate of the Free World hanging on the outcome of the long twilight struggle between the Soviet Union and the United States. He warned that the time was short, that the perils were grave, and that the news would get worse before it got better. But he also struck a pose of gallant defiance: He welcomed the challenge "of defending freedom in its hour of maximum danger." And he warned the Soviet leaders,

> Let every nation know, whether it wishes us well or ill, that we shall pay any price, bear any burden, meet any hardship, support any friend, oppose any foe to assure the survival and success of liberty.[1]

In responding to what he perceived as Khrushchev's challenge, Kennedy made an unlimited commitment to defend freedom around the globe.

Despite evidence of a growing rift between China and the USSR, Kennedy and his senior advisers embraced the containment ideology held by his predecessors, Eisenhower and Truman. The New Frontiersmen viewed Communists forces as an interlocked threat that must be checked by the United States around the globe. Kennedy and his men also shared a penchant for action. They eagerly picked up the gauntlet that Khrushchev had thrown down and sought arenas in which to challenge Soviet initiatives. The new secretary of defense, Robert McNamara, a Republican and former president of Ford Motor Company, called for the largest peace time increase in defense spending in U.S. history. The United States immediately embarked on a crash program to build up both its strategic nuclear arsenal and its conventional military forces.

Sensing the need for a greater variety of responses to Cold War challenges, the Kennedy administration expanded its strategic capabilities. It scrapped the Eisenhower doctrine of "massive retaliation," replacing it with the concept of "flexible response," strategic versatility that permitted a calibrated U.S. response to any Soviet-backed uprising without having to risk a nuclear confrontation with the Soviet Union. Recognizing that the Third World would be the principal Cold War battleground of the 1960s, the new administration sought to develop a counterinsurgency capability to neutralize Soviet support for revolutionary uprisings. President Kennedy also wanted to eliminate the "conditions in which Communism flourished," placing emphasis on developing programs of economic and technical assistance for Third World nations that "would channel revolutionary forces into peaceful, democratic paths."[2]

Kennedy and his advisers viewed Vietnamese Communism as an advance arm of Chinese and Soviet Communism that was absolutely dependent on them for its sustenance. They failed to understand that Vietnamese revolutionary nationalism rested on a largely autonomous national foundation.[3] To the New Frontiersmen, South Vietnam remained a domino threatened by external aggression, whose fall would imperil other Southeast Asian nations and threaten the vital national security interests of the United States and its allies in Europe and Asia.

As a senator, Kennedy had been a strong backer of Ngo Dinh Diem; he had consistently supported the Eisenhower policy of keeping Vietnam partitioned and maintaining a non-Communist state in its southern half. Kennedy quickly made ensuring the survival of South Vietnam a top foreign policy priority, confident that the new counterinsurgency forces that he planned to deploy to Vietnam would enable Diem to defeat the insurgents and demonstrate that Soviet-sponsored wars of national liberation could not succeed in the Third World.

Other factors strengthened Kennedy's commitment to retaining a non-Communist government in southern Vietnam. His thin margin of victory in the 1960 election made him vulnerable to Republican charges that he was "soft" on Communism. Ironically, he had leveled similar charges at Eisenhower during the recent campaign, and he knew full well that Nixon and other Republican leaders would be quick to retaliate if he should appear irresolute in the pursuit of anti-Communist foreign policy objectives or if the Communists should make advances anywhere in the world. As a Democratic president, he also felt vulnerable to the legacy of McCarthyism and memories of the "loss of China." Further, the Bay of Pigs fiasco in Cuba, occurring early in his presidency, probably reinforced his inclination to take a tough anti-Communist stance in Southeast Asia.[4]

But Kennedy's first Southeast Asian challenge came in Laos rather than in Vietnam. Eisenhower had warned his youthful successor that Laos was the most acute Cold War crisis of the moment and had told him that if Laos were lost, the entire Far East would soon follow. The old general discussed both the costs and benefits entailed if it became necessary to intervene militarily to save that country from a Communist takeover.[5] In Laos, General Sananikone's right-wing government verged on collapse as Kennedy took office, and the young president had to act quickly to try to salvage it.

Kennedy considered military intervention in Laos in March 1961, then decided against it after conferring with the Joint Chiefs of Staff (JCS). The Joint Chiefs warned the president about the pitfalls of a land war in Asia. They told Kennedy that if Washington sent troops to Laos, it was likely that China would also send forces. If the United States did intervene militarily, the Joint Chiefs recommended that it be full-bore; hit them with everything we had—60,000 troops, air power, even nuclear weapons—and be prepared to engage the Chinese. Otherwise stay out.[6] Kennedy stayed out.

Probably Kennedy's failure to intervene in Cuba at the time of the Bay of Pigs fiasco killed any possibility of sending troops into Laos. How could Kennedy explain to the American people his willingness to send troops to Laos 9,000 miles away if he was unwilling to send them to Cuba 90 miles away? Kennedy was also aware of the unpromising political situation in Laos. He did not hold General Sananikone in very high regard, nor did he perceive him as being a terribly promising instrument with which to fight America's Cold War battles in Southeast Asia.[7] Renouncing the military option in Laos, Kennedy sought a political resolution of the civil war.

The Soviets and the British agreed to reconvene the Geneva Conference and to try to work out a negotiated settlement among the Pathet Lao, neutralist, and pro-Western groups in Laos. In May 1961, the three Laotian factions began negotiations at Geneva. Eventually, they worked out an agreement that created a tripartite coalition government. The agreement was signed on July 23, 1962.[8] According to its terms, Laos became a neutral nation governed by a coalition under Prime Minister Prince Souvanna, with the pro-Western and Communist factions sharing power. The new coalition government was a fragile creature that favored the *Pathet Lao* and its North Vietnamese backers, who kept thousands of troops in eastern Laos in violation of the Geneva agreement.[9] The Communists controlled the eastern half of the country, including two provinces bordering Vietnam containing major infiltration routes along the developing Ho Chi Minh Trail. Kennedy also violated the 1962 Geneva agreement on Laos when he ordered the CIA to expand military operations in that country. The U.S.-sponsored "secret war" in Laos escalated as the CIA recruited 9,000 Hmong tribesmen to strike against the Ho Chi Minh Trail complex that ran along the Laotian southern corridor for hundreds of miles.[10]

As he opted for a political settlement in Laos, Kennedy increased the U.S. commitment to South Vietnam because Diem's position continued to deteriorate. Kennedy had received a pessimistic report from General Landsdale stating that the southern insurgents were increasing their numbers, extending their control over more and more terrain and villages, and getting closer to their goal of toppling Diem's government. Landsdale called for an increase in U.S. aid to the GVN and a 20,000-man increase for the ARVN. He also recommended that the South Vietnamese armed forces be taught quickly how to confront the revolutionaries with the "tactics and strategy of unconventional warfare."[11]

Despite their rising worries over Diem's survivability, for most of their first year in office Kennedy officials continued Eisenhower's policies in South Vietnam. In May 1961, Kennedy approved actions to try to shore up Diem's deteriorating position. He ordered an increase in the MAAG contingent in South Vietnam by 100 advisers, approved the 20,000-man increase for the ARVN, and sent in 400 Special Forces troops (Green Berets) to train South Vietnamese forces in counterinsurgency tactics. He also dispatched Vice President Lyndon Johnson to South Vietnam to assure Diem of continuing U.S. support.

In addition, the president authorized covert operations against North Vietnam. South Vietnamese paramilitary units were sent into the DRV on espionage, sabotage, and psychological warfare missions. They also attacked enemy supply lines and staging areas. Kennedy also established a task force headed by Deputy National Security Adviser Walt Rostow to consider additional measures that the United States might have to take if the Communist threats to Laos and South Vietnam increased. Rostow's recommendations included bombing North Vietnam, blockading its ports, and sending U.S. combat forces to South Vietnam.[12] The president's actions in the spring of 1961 represented a minimal response that did not move the U.S. commitment in Vietnam much beyond the levels achieved under Eisenhower. They were mainly intended to shore up Diem's government, buy time, keep options open, and enable Kennedy and his advisers to deal with U.S. foreign policy crises elsewhere.

In the fall of 1961, events forced President Kennedy to give greater attention to Vietnam. Hanoi increased the rate of infiltration of regroupees into the South. The NLF forces escalated their military campaigns, threatening to overrun the Mekong Delta. VietCong main force units also launched a major offensive in central South Vietnam. They seized Phuoc Vinh, the capital of the Phuoc Long province, 60 miles northwest of Saigon. The NLF regular forces attacked other provincial towns in the central highlands. President Diem, frightened by the rising level of military activity, called for additional U. S. military aid. The Joint Chiefs of Staff considered sending U.S. combat forces to the embattled country.[13]

Kennedy, hesitant to send U.S. combat forces to Vietnam, instead sent his personal military adviser General Maxwell Taylor, accompanied by Walt Rostow, on a fact-finding mission. Taylor's findings, submitted to the president on November 3, were starkly pessimistic: Diem's government was ineffective and unpopular. The ARVN forces refused to take the offensive against the insurgents. Taylor recommended that the

Figure 4.1   Vietnamese trainees watch as U.S. Ranger Lt. Bruce G. Smally instructs Corporal Y. Bhung on how to use a bayonet. The U.S. Special Forces are training *Montagnard* tribesmen to combat VietCong guerrillas. 8/25/62. *Source:* CORBIS. © Bettman/CORBIS.

United States undertake a "limited partnership" with the GVN. Specifically, he recommended that Washington significantly increase its military support for Diem and upgrade the performance of GVN paramilitary and local defense forces in order to free the ARVN regulars for combat against the NLF forces. He also recommended sending 8,000 U.S. combat troops.[14]

While administration officials were debating Taylor's report, Kennedy received another recommendation, this one written by Undersecretary of State Chester Bowles and Averell Harriman, the chief American negotiator at Geneva. Bowles and Harriman frankly doubted Diem's ability to survive, and they opposed increasing the U.S. commitment to the GVN. They believed that the causes of Diem's decline were primarily political; his failing government could not be saved by U.S. military action. Bowles and Harriman proposed instead that Kennedy seek a negotiated settlement in Vietnam. They called for an expanded agenda at Geneva, currently dealing with Laos, to work out a negotiated solution for Vietnam based on the 1954 Geneva Accords. Other administration voices joined Bowles and Harriman in proposing a negotiated settlement of the Vietnam issue.[15]

Kennedy's advisers had given him clear choices for Vietnam. He could either expand the U.S. commitment in an effort to seek a military solution or he could try for a negotiated settlement. Kennedy quickly ruled out a negotiated settlement for Vietnam. Having already opted for negotiations on Laos, having suffered the Bay of Pigs fiasco, and having accepted the Berlin Wall, Kennedy feared that a decision to seek a political settlement in Vietnam would send the wrong signal to Khrushchev and other Soviet leaders who already believed Kennedy was not tough enough to stand up to Soviet pressure tactics. Adding to his concern, Kennedy had recently met with Khrushchev for a series of talks in Vienna. Kennedy feared that the Soviet leader had misread him, that he had mistaken his civility and restraint for weakness. Kennedy also assumed that he would face domestic political reprisals from his anti-Communist flank if he opted for negotiations on Vietnam as well as on Laos.

On the other hand, the president refused to send U.S. combat troops, which would significantly raise the American commitment in South Vietnam. He believed that the introduction of U.S. combat forces might jeopardize the Laotian negotiations at Geneva. Kennedy was skeptical that combat forces could solve Diem's problems, believing that the South Vietnamese themselves would have to defeat the insurgents. Kennedy also feared that once U.S. soldiers engaged in combat and took casualties, the pressure to send more troops would be intense. Diem himself did not welcome combat troops. He wanted increased U.S. financial support and equipment to strengthen his own forces, not U.S. armies fighting in his country.[16]

Rejecting both negotiations and an immediate dispatching of U.S. combat troops, Kennedy tried to solve the Vietnam dilemma by choosing the cautious middle ground. Influenced by a memo from Secretary of State Dean Rusk and Secretary of Defense Robert McNamara, the president rejected Taylor's proposal to send U.S. ground combat forces. But Kennedy approved Taylor's proposals to increase significantly the number of U.S. military advisory and combat support personnel going to Vietnam. In addition, Washington sent helicopter, transport, and reconnaissance aircraft to add firepower and mobility to Diem's army. Kennedy authorized the use of napalm and the Air Force began the aerial spraying of defoliants to deny the VietCong ground cover and food crops. Kennedy also approved funding to increase the ARVN force levels and to upgrade their training and equipment. Further, Washington endeavored to improve the performance of South Vietnamese district forces and local security forces.

The President hoped these middling actions would arrest the steady political and military erosion occurring in South Vietnam. He also knew that the large increases in the number of U.S. advisory and support personnel would violate the Geneva Accords of 1954. Washington feared the Communists could gain a propaganda windfall from the American violations of the agreements. Accordingly, in December 1961, the State Department issued a White Paper that claimed that renewed aggression by Hanoi, which violated the Geneva agreements, justified U.S. escalatory actions in South Vietnam.[17]

Kennedy's mildly escalatory decisions in November 1961 formed the basis of the U.S. Vietnam policy for the remainder of his presidency. It also established a pattern of responses. Despite his bold rhetoric, Kennedy was a cautious Cold Warrior in action. He preferred to make short-term responses to immediate problems. He usually tried to split the difference between his hawkish and dovish advisers, between the National Security faction and the State Department faction.

Because many Kennedy administration officials believed that Diem's inept and repressive government itself was a major cause of the insurgency and an obstacle to defeating it, all of their aid increases were approved with the proviso that Diem would take actions to reform his government and broaden his base of support. But Diem resisted U.S. pressures to get him to reform his administration and to make his army fight the insurgents more aggressively. He made it clear to U.S. Ambassador Frederick Nolting that South Vietnam's governance was an internal matter beyond the province of U.S. officials. He told Nolting bluntly that the GVN "did not want to be an American protectorate."[18] The ambassador quickly yielded to Diem and did not press him to make reforms.

The persistent refusal of Diem and his successors to make reforms that would have made their governments more responsive to the welfare of the peasants who made up the large majority of the South Vietnamese population was a major cause of the ultimate Communist victory and the American defeat in South Vietnam. In Diem's case, it was much more than obsolete ideology, stubbornness, and arrogance. He and Nhu believed that they knew how to run their government better than their U.S. advisers, and they resented and rebuffed U.S. efforts to intervene in what they regarded as an internal matter. They also perceived that America had committed itself to their cause and would continue to provide them with support even if they did not make the requested reforms. They understood that the Americans preferred stability and continuity above all else. Further, they knew that the Americans would not pressure them severely to make changes while they were under the stress of insurgent assaults because U.S. officials did not want to undermine their fragile regime and thereby facilitate a rebel victory.

But there were other, more fundamental reasons why Diem and all subsequent leaders of South Vietnam, mostly army generals, could never make the necessary reforms that might have strengthened their governments and improved their chances for long-term survival. These factors also shed light on the underlying South Vietnamese political limits that continually frustrated U.S. efforts in Vietnam and ensured the eventual U.S. defeat and the demise of South Vietnam. Diem and all of his successors did not respond to U.S. requests for reform because they could not do so, at least not without grave risk to their survival.

In the first place, they would lose legitimacy, the perceived right to govern, in the eyes of their own people if they appeared to be puppets, doing what their American masters dictated. That was a charge consistently made against them by Hanoi and NLF propagandists. Second, the South Vietnamese governments, whether headed by a civilian or general, were essentially military dictatorships. Their power, their ability to govern, depended mainly on the support of powerful senior military officers whose loyalty had to be purchased. Any effort to move beyond the generals and reach out to other classes with land reform, a wider suffrage, or village autonomy risked provoking a coup d'état.[19]

There was another dilemma that U.S. officials concerned to reform South Vietnamese governments could never overcome. Genuine reform that might have broadened a regime's popular base also would have risked bringing to power a leader who might have sought a cease-fire, opted for negotiations with NLF officials, formed a neutralist coalition government, and asked the Americans to leave. U.S. officials regarded such possibilities as tantamount to an American defeat because they believed that such a government would soon be dominated by NLF leaders who would eventually seek a reunion with Hanoi. In short, a succession of South Vietnamese governments dared not reform, and American officials dared not push them too hard toward reform. These unresolved (and unresolvable) political dilemmas constituted an integral part of the American ordeal in Vietnam.

A LIMITED PARTNERSHIP

Kennedy's November 1961 decisions to violate the military provisions of the 1954 Geneva agreements and to increase significantly U.S. military support levels for the GVN were intended to keep Diem in power, at the same time keeping the American commitment in South Vietnam limited, preserving the administration's freedom of action, and maintaining U.S. control of events in Vietnam. Kennedy was not trying to win in Vietnam; he was doing only enough not to lose. By opting for the limited partnership, he revealed that he was not prepared to make the tough decisions: either try to negotiate a settlement and withdraw or send large numbers of U.S. combat forces to try to win the war in South Vietnam.

Kennedy had inherited a commitment in South Vietnam from Eisenhower. He would not abandon it, fearing the loss of U.S. prestige and power *vis-à-vis* the Soviet

Union and political damage to his administration at home if he did. The costs of pulling out appeared to him greater than the costs of getting in deeper.[20] Without realizing it, Kennedy had "maintained the momentum of American involvement,"[21] a momentum that neither he nor his successor could arrest before the United States plunged into a large and lengthy war.

To implement the newly formed limited partnership with the GVN, the United States rapidly expanded its military presence in southern Vietnam. A reorganized and expanded military mission, the Military Assistance Command, Vietnam (MACV), commanded by General Paul Harkins, replaced the MAAG. Thousands of American advisers poured into South Vietnam during 1962. Hundreds of U.S. helicopters, reconnaissance, and transport aircraft arrived, with American pilots and maintenance personnel on board. Giant M-113 armored personnel carriers arrived to haul the ARVN forces into battle. Special Forces units moved into the central highlands to train *Montagnards* in various kinds of counterinsurgency operations. American advisers accompanied ARVN forces into combat zones, and American helicopter pilots flew ARVN troops into battle. Although U.S. forces were officially limited to advisory and support roles, Americans on the ground and in the air increasingly found themselves in combat situations as the war escalated. By the summer of 1962, U.S. soldiers were fighting and dying alongside of their ARVN counterparts in South Vietnam.[22]

During the first half of 1962, bolstered by the large increases in U.S. advisers, support personnel, and equipment, the South Vietnamese army took the offensive against the VietCong insurgents. Using helicopters flown by American pilots, ARVN commanders moved into VietCong strongholds northwest of Saigon and in the U Minh forest along the Gulf of Thailand. South Vietnamese Air Force (VNAF) pilots incinerated villages with napalm and defoliated crops and livestock. The ARVN 7th Division attacked a guerrilla stronghold in the Plain of Reeds, 80 miles southwest of Saigon, killing scores of VietCong during three days of fighting. In July, ARVN forces launched a major offensive in the Kien Hoa province. A month later, ARVN forces, supported by U.S. helicopters, invaded the Ca Mau peninsula.[23]

The ARVN mounted larger offensives against VietCong strongholds later in the year. In November, a force of more than 2,000 troops, transported by over 50 U.S. helicopters, launched a full-scale attack in War Zone D, northwest of Saigon. It was the advent of the helicopter more than any other contribution the Americans made to the GVN war effort during the 1962 buildup that enhanced the fighting abilities of the ARVN forces. Helicopters, which began arriving in Vietnam in December 1961, transformed the war. They were flown on combat assault missions, provided transport and ferry services, and supplied Special Forces camps deep in the central highlands.

As the conflict expanded in 1962, U.S. advisers discovered that there was not just one war in South Vietnam, but several, each with its own terrain, methods of warfare, and strategic importance. The Mekong Delta, a watery world of flat expanses, rice paddies, and irrigation canals, dominated by the many tributaries of the Mekong River, constituted one war region. Travel in the delta regions was mostly by boats and sampans.

In 1962, the VietCong had about 10,000 main force troops and at least that many guerrilla irregulars in the delta. Operating out of bases located in remote, impenetrable swamps, the insurgents were almost immune from attack and enjoyed uncontested mobility in this strategic region containing 60 percent of the South Vietnamese population and producing about 75 percent of its annual rice crop.[24]

Beginning about 50 miles north of Saigon and running north for almost 200 miles, and varying in elevation from 500 to over 3,000 feet, lay the mountain plateaus of the central highlands. Here, another kind of war raged. Dominating central Vietnam, the highlands were sparsely inhabited by the *Montagnard* tribes. The VietCong often recruited the *Montagnards,* historically hostile to the Vietnamese, who regarded the *Montagnards* as primitives. Since troops could not operate effectively in the highlands without *Montagnard* support, both the Americans and the GVN tried to wean the *Montagnards* away from the insurgents. By spring of 1962, several ARVN divisions were deployed in the central highlands to try to contain the Communists, because the forces that could control this region held the key to the strategic security of the populated coastal enclaves.[25]

North of the central highlands lay the jagged peaks of the Truong Son Mountains, a rugged wilderness of rain forests, steep ridges, and roaring rivers. In this region, South Vietnam narrowed to a width of 30 to 60 miles. Lying just below the DMZ and bordering Laos to the west, the Truong Son Mountains were a major infiltration route for the VietCong. The rugged peaks rising to 8,000 feet were virtually inaccessible to ARVN forces. The guerrillas dominated the region, frequently overrunning ARVN units and ambushing their reconnaissance patrols.[26]

At the same time that its armies, with enhanced U.S. support, went after the VietCong, the GVN implemented a "strategic hamlet" (*ap chien luoc*) program. Strategic hamlets were designed by Eugene Staley and promoted by a British advisory mission headed by Sir Robert Thompson, who had used strategic hamlets to defeat a Communist insurgency in Malaya during the mid-1950s. Through the strategic hamlets, Thompson planned to complement the ARVN military effort by offering the Vietnamese villagers physical security and economic development. Peasants would be removed from areas of VietCong activity to secure villages defended by ARVN forces initially, and then later by specially trained local militia. Civic action teams would restore village self-government, and implement social and economic programs that would benefit the villagers.

American counterinsurgency enthusiasts supported the strategic hamlet program. They understood that to defeat the VietCong insurgency, it would be necessary to cut it off from its popular base in the rural villages. Winning the war in the villages, winning the villagers' hearts and minds, required more than weapons; it required furnishing the peasants with positive economic and social incentives for supporting the South Vietnamese government. Before these programs could be implemented, the GVN would have to guarantee the physical security of the villagers, both to insulate them from insurgent attacks and to deny the guerrillas access to provisions and recruits. Kennedy administration officials believed that the strategic hamlet program promised to separate the VietCong from the villagers and would thereby kill the rebellion.[27] Washington believed that strategic hamlets would rectify the GVN's most serious political weakness, its lack of support among the peasantry.

Diem embraced the idea of isolating the VietCong from the rural population. Under the rubric of Operation Sunrise, the first fortified villages were under construction in March 1962 in the Ben Cat district of the Binh Doung province, a heavily forested VietCong stronghold 40 miles northwest of Saigon. The ARVN forces dispersed the insurgents. By summer, several strategic hamlets had been carved out of the jungle, accommodating over 3,000 people. The new villages were equipped with schools, medical clinics, markets, and a defense force.[28]

Diem hailed the strategic hamlet program as the ultimate solution to the problems of rural pacification and reconstruction. Diem's brother Nhu was particularly enthusiastic and became the driving force behind the program. He saw the strategic hamlets not only as a means of isolating the people from the VietCong and regaining loyalty to the GVN via social and economic development, but also as vehicles for social control, political indoctrination, and ideological transformation. With the villagers under the control of the GVN, Nhu planned to convert all of them to his philosophy of Personalism. During the summer of 1962, Operation Sunrise was expanded to other provinces, and by the end of the year, Diem and Nhu had made it a national program. They declared 1962 to be the "year of the strategic hamlet."

SOCIAL REVOLUTION IN THE SOUTH

The initiative seized by the ARVN forces during 1962 proved temporary. Despite using helicopters and having U.S. advisers integrated into the command and staff structure of the South Vietnamese forces at every level, the ARVN forces were prone to operational failures. VietCong riflemen learned how to bring down helicopters with small arms fire. It proved difficult for the South Vietnamese military to locate and trap the elusive VietCong guerrillas amidst the swamps and paddy lands of the delta. Peasants sympathetic to the insurgents would inform the guerrillas of ARVN or provincial force movements, giving them ample time to escape. The large-scale ARVN sweeps through VietCong-infested regions usually netted few casualties, prisoners, or captured weapons and stores. As soon as the South Vietnamese forces withdrew, the VietCong returned to reestablish their networks. VietCong tactics could neutralize and occasionally defeat ARVN-U.S. technology. The VietCong also made good use of intelligence and mobility to offset ARVN-U.S. firepower.

During the latter half of 1962, the insurgents built up their forces and continued to make gains in the northern Mekong Delta region. The delta was split into northern and southern halves by the Bassac River, one of the many tributaries of the Mekong. Historically, the southern Mekong Delta region had been a Communist stronghold since the days of the Vietminh. During 1962, the VietCong and GVN forces fought for control of the people and resources of the northern half. The VietCong gradually gained the ascendancy.

During this time, the NLF more than compensated for the substantial increase in U.S. military aid going to the South Vietnamese forces. The number of main force units the VietCong could field expanded. The size of their maneuver battalions increased, and their training, discipline, and operational capabilities improved. Their recruits came mainly from the ranks of the southern peasantry, although their forces were significantly enhanced by about 5,800 infiltrators coming into the south via the Ho Chi Minh Trail during 1962.[29] Most of these infiltrators were regroupees, southerners who had gone north in 1954 and 1955. They constituted highly motivated, thoroughly indoctrinated, specially trained cadres who moved into leadership positions within the VietCong ranks. Insurgent firepower increased, coming mostly from captured U.S. weapons acquired when the rebels overran ARVN outposts or ambushed small units. The insurgents also purchased U.S. weapons from some ARVN officers who were quite willing to do business with the VietCong. They also obtained some modern Chinese weapons, such as automatic rifles and mortars, which had been brought down the Ho Chi Minh Trail. VietCong planners devised tactics to counter the heliborne assaults of the ARVN forces. As their tactical sophistication improved, the guerrillas proved more willing to stand and fight the South Vietnamese forces.[30]

The escalating conflict in the vital northern Mekong Delta region came to a head early in 1963 during the Battle of Ap Bac, the most important battle of the developing war in southern Vietnam.[31] In late December, ARVN forces learned of the presence of a heavy concentration of enemy troops near the hamlet of Ap Bac, located in the Dinh Tuong province forty-five miles southwest of Saigon. A golden opportunity appeared for the ARVN 7th Division, led by Colonel Bui Dinh Dam, a Diem favorite, to attack and destroy a major VietCong force. The Americans considered the 7th Division to be the finest fighting unit in the South Vietnamese army. Instead, the battle that occurred on January 2, 1963, turned out to be a stunning rebel victory and an ARVN fiasco. It revealed all of the shortcomings of the South Vietnamese armed forces and served as an ominous sign of the future.[32] It also thrust into prominence the senior U.S. military adviser to the ARVN 7th Division, Lieutenant Colonel John Paul Vann, one of the American heroes of the Vietnam War.[33]

The ARVN battle plan called for South Vietnamese forces to launch a three-pronged attack on rebel troops. The 11th Regiment Battalion from the 7th Division, helilifted to the battle site, was to attack from the north. Two companies of Civil Guard troops, provincial forces under the command of the Province Chief, Major Tho, also a Diem favorite, attacked from the south. In addition, a company of the 7th Division, transported in M-113s and commanded by Captain Ba, another Diem protege, would assault from the west. These attacks were to be supported by artillery fire and tactical bombers, with reserve forces standing by to be helicoptered in, if required. Circling overhead in his L-19 spotter plane, Colonel Vann, advising Colonel Dam, would coordinate the attacks.

Figure 4.2   The Ho Chi Minh Trail. *Source:* Public Domain.

The planned assault resembled an open claw, and inside the claw, dug into the Ap Bac treeline, was the VietCong 514th Battalion, a main force outfit of approximately 320 soldiers, reinforced by local guerrillas. Against the 3,000 ARVN and provincial troops, supported by armor, artillery, helicopters, and bombers, the 514th had only automatic rifles, two 30-caliber machine guns, grenades, and a few light mortars. They also had limited stores of ammunition, only enough for about one day of fighting.[34] As the battle began, it appeared that the heavily outnumbered and outgunned rebels, having no exit, would be quickly overwhelmed and destroyed.

The ARVN 11th Regiment Battalion made their helicopter landings to the north, uncontested. VietCong forces, probing south, encountered the provincial troops. A fierce firefight ensued before the VC retreated to their tree line. Major Tho ordered his Civil Guards, who had been roughed up by the rebels, to halt their advance. Colonels Dam and Vann then brought in the reserve force to land west of the Ap Bac tree line. The VietCong riflemen opened fire on the approaching helicopters, 10 slow, heavy-bodied H-21s carrying the troops, and 5 sleek new Bell HU-1 gunships (nicknamed Hueys) flying escort. The VC hit 14 of the 15 ships, shooting down 5 helicopters with rifle fire. The reserve forces that landed sustained heavy casualties, and the survivors were immediately pinned down in the paddy fields by fire coming from the tree line. The company of M-113s, commanded by Captain Ba, was delayed for hours by Captain Ba's caution. When it finally arrived, it was ineffective against the entrenched VietCong forces.[35] Guerrillas armed only with small arms fire were able to neutralize the 10-ton armored behemoths, because the ARVN soldiers lacked effective leadership, discipline, and tactical competence.

Colonel Vann, observing from the air, exhorted Colonel Dam to order both Major Tho and Captain Ba to move their troops forward to assault the tree line. They both refused to obey Dam's orders. Vann then requested an airborne unit from Saigon to be brought in to try to salvage the battle. But the order for the paratroopers had to go through Major General Huynh Van Cao, formerly the 7th Division commander and now the commander of IV Corps, with control over military operations in the northern Mekong Delta. Cao, whose rank owed more to his political connections than to his professional competence, delayed calling in the airborne forces for several hours, then landed them at a site that permitted the VietCong forces to withdraw from the field during the night. Under secret orders from Diem to keep ARVN casualties low, Cao chose defeat at Ap Bac to protect his career rather than seek the victory that could have been his.[36]

What could have been a major ARVN victory turned instead into a significant victory for the NLF and its forces. It was much more than a military success for the VietCong, who had stood and fought against superior forces. It was a smashing psychological victory that NLF propagandists used to recruit more troops and to win the allegiance of more hamlets to their cause. Ap Bac also signaled that the momentum of the expanding war had shifted to the NLF. By the summer of 1963, many of the villages of the strategic northern Mekong Delta either supported the NLF or took a neutral stance.[37] The GVN mainly controlled only towns and cities scattered over the region.

For the ARVN forces, "Ap Bac epitomized all the deficiencies of the system."[38] The battle served as a paradigm for military failure. For Diem, the political loyalty of General Cao and Colonel Dam represented, above all else, coup insurance. He wanted the 7th Division available to rush to Saigon if necessary to repel possible challenges to his regime by dissident ARVN generals. Diem was determined to keep ARVN battle casualties low. He and his brother Nhu believed that both the November 1960 coup attempt and another attack on Diem's life in February 1962, when two disgruntled Vietnamese Air Force pilots had bombed his palace, had been provoked by casualties sustained by ARVN forces fighting the rebels. Diem preferred political survival to waging an aggressive war against the VietCong in the countryside. General Cao and Colonel Dam preferred losing a battle to risking Diem's displeasure and dismissal from their commands. It was a matter of priorities, and Diem considered unhappy ARVN generals more dangerous foes then the NLF insurgents supported by Hanoi. For Diem and his family oligarchs, the key to remaining in power lay in retaining a favorable balance of loyal ARVN forces and in keeping U.S. economic and military support. Diem and his brothers assumed that the United States, the world's preeminent power, would never let their anti-Communist government fall to Hanoi's instruments of conquest.

Ap Bac revealed the long-present shortcomings of an army whose leaders were more expert at playing politics than at fighting battles. According to Colonel Wilbur Wilson, U.S. senior adviser to III Corps, "The generals got to be generals by virtue of their ability in political intrigue, not as a result of their ability to lead men."[39] Further, the officer class of Diem's army came mostly from urban middle- and upper-class families, often Catholic and French-speaking. They had no nationalistic feelings for South Vietnam, nor had they identified with the struggle to defeat French colonialism. Most had served with the French forces fighting the Vietminh. These officers generally held their enlisted troops, who were mostly peasant conscripts or mercenaries, in contempt.

It dismayed Colonel Vann to discover that ARVN officers were indifferent to the welfare of the troops entrusted to their commands, and they did not want to lead their troops into battle. Further, Ap Bac demonstrated the pitfalls of going to war with troops who were afflicted with low morale and whose performance suffered from a lack of training and discipline. Many ARVN soldiers openly admitted that they were afraid of the guerrillas, considered themselves inferior to them, and did not want to engage them in a firefight. The ARVN troops also lacked positive incentives for fighting, and their leaders failed to provide them with any. Colonel Vann and the other American advisers discovered that they were trying to wage war against the Vietcong guerrillas "with an army that suffered from an institutionalized unwillingness to fight."[40]

By contrast, at Ap Bac, the NLF forces had stood their ground against fearsome weapons and troops that outnumbered them 10 to one, and they had fought with great tenacity for a cause in which they believed, a cause for which they were willing to die. Above all, Ap Bac "underlined the limits of U.S. Power" in Vietnam.[41] U.S. wealth, military technology, and advisory leadership could not compensate for the deficiencies of an army that did not want to fight and whose leaders were under orders not to incur many casualties.

While Saigon's armed forces were losing ground to the insurgents in the northern Mekong Delta, the much-vaunted strategic hamlet program was coming unraveled in the same region. Most delta peasants resented being removed from their ancestral lands. They refused to move and had to be forcibly relocated, many to hamlets whose security could not be guaranteed. Few young men of military age moved because they were either avoiding conscription or had joined the VietCong. Many of these insecure hamlets were infiltrated by the VietCong. Even in the secure hamlets, many of the programs that were supposed to bind the people to Saigon were never implemented. Promised land reforms were not implemented. Many relocated peasants ended up losing ancestral lands that they had been forced to abandon, for which they received little or no compensation from GVN officials. Even though the United States provided ample funds for promised strategic hamlet social services, most were never implemented because of official corruption. "The strategic hamlets were more akin to concentration camps than communities."[42] In areas where the strategic hamlets were more successful, VietCong terrorists often attacked the villages, intimidated the people, and kidnapped or murdered Diemist officials.

The main reason that the strategic hamlets failed was that Diem and Nhu viewed them primarily as a means of extending their political control over the rural population, rather than as furnishing an opportunity to provide the peasants with positive incentives for supporting the South Vietnamese state. They were not trying to win the "hearts and minds" of peasants, they were trying to coerce and indoctrinate them. Rural Vietnamese could find little in the strategic hamlet program that worked for their benefit. Even though South Vietnamese officials generated rigged statistics that vastly exaggerated the number of strategic hamlets constructed and their resident populations, the GVN continued to lose popular support at the rice-roots level throughout the latter half of 1962 and into 1963.[43]

The decline in the ARVN's military effectiveness and the failures of the strategic hamlet program reflected the political deterioration occurring in South Vietnam from mid-1962 to mid-1963, despite the large military escalations of the Kennedy administration.[44] The NLF guerrillas continued to grow in numbers and to enhance their military capabilities. More important, VietCong political cadres continued to gain the support of increasing numbers of villagers in the countryside. The military actions of the guerrillas supported and advanced the political goals of the insurgency. Always, the VietCong fighters and political cadres worked in tandem, coordinating their activities to achieve their military-political objectives.

There were many reasons why increasing numbers of South Vietnamese peasants chose governance by Hanoi-backed NLF officials over that provided by American-backed GVN officials in 1962 and 1963. In part, the peasants reacted to the political shortcomings of many Diemist officials: their repressiveness, corruption, and ineptitude, as well as their lack of genuine interest in the peasants' needs and problems. The GVN simply never gave many villagers any good reason to support it and often provided very good reasons to reject it. In part, the villagers reacted against the ARVN and provincial troops, who failed to provide them with physical security and who sometimes abused the peasants, stole their food, rice crops, tools, and animals. Often, indiscriminate ARVN use of artillery and aerial bombing injured, maimed, and killed civilians, destroying their homes. The abuses and failures of the strategic hamlet program angered and alienated many peasants. In part, villagers were coerced and intimidated into at least passive support for the rebels. The NLF use of terror, which included kidnappings and selective assassinations of Diemist officials, landlords, collaborators, informers, and spies, often carried out with great brutality, could be very effective. The NLF propagandists also played on the xenophobia of the peasants, invoking bitter memories of French colonialism and linking the Diem government and its American patrons to the hated colonial past.[45]

But skilled NLF organizers also developed many positive incentives with which to win over the villagers, whose support was absolutely crucial to their cause. Highly disciplined party cadres often practiced the "three withs": They lived with the villagers, they ate with the villagers, and they worked with them in the rice fields. These cadres were trained to treat the villagers with courtesy, to listen to them, and to respond to their needs. The NLF cadres often gave land confiscated from Diemist landlords to landless peasants. They helped peasants market their crops. They improved public health, sanitation, educational, and maternity services. They restored traditional village autonomy. They organized farmers, women, and young people into village associations under local leadership. They appealed to the traditional Vietnamese values of family and communalism and to the strong nationalist feelings of the peasants. In propaganda terms, the VietCong cadres were liberating the people from Diemist taxation, repression, corruption, and subservience to the American imperialists.

In 1962 and 1963, a revolution directed by the Hanoi Politburo was taking root and gathering momentum in many parts of the southern Vietnamese countryside. Villages, although remaining physically within the country nominally governed by Ngo Dinh Diem, had been removed politically from his authority and removed militarily from the control of his army. These villages were now administered by NLF cadres. The cadres also organized the villagers for self-defense. These "combat villages" provided the basis for the integrated political-military campaign that the NLF would wage for over a decade. The revolution that had been underway in Vietnam since 1945 and had verged on completion in 1954, only to be thwarted by the partition of the country, the subsequent American intervention, and the establishment of the Diem government, had revived as the 1950s ended, and was clearly gaining momentum in the early 1960s.[46]

Even though the political and strategic situation in southern Vietnam was rapidly deteriorating, Washington saw no reason for reappraising its policy. In Saigon, both Ambassador Nolting and MACV Commander Paul Harkins proclaimed that progress was being made. Secretary of Defense Robert S. McNamara, returning from a trip to Vietnam in November, reported that "every quantitative measure that we have shows that we are winning the war."[47] At a December 12, 1962, press conference, President Kennedy spoke optimistically about the war. Premier Diem pronounced the counterinsurgency program a success and insisted that the GVN military forces were containing the insurgents in the countryside. Diemist officials prepared bogus elaborate color-coded maps and fabricated body counts that misled gullible U.S. officials in Saigon and Washington.

The wall of U.S. and GVN official optimism was breached by some younger members of the American press corps assigned to cover the Vietnam War. Because these journalists accompanied the ARVN forces into the field and interviewed advisers like Colonel Vann, who talked frankly with them about the outcome of Ap Bac and other engagements, they discovered that Saigon was losing the war in the Mekong Delta. The ablest of these young journalists included David Halberstam of the *New York Times;* Neil Sheehan, a reporter for United Press; Malcolm Brown; and Charles Mohr.

Their articles denounced the Diem regime, calling it both inept and corrupt, and they held Diem primarily to blame for the failing GVN effort. They called the strategic hamlet program a sham. They challenged official statistics that inflated both the number of strategic hamlets constructed and the number of VietCong killed.[48] Halberstam filed stories describing the military and political gains that the rebels were making in the northern Mekong Delta.[49] Diem, enraged by the Americans' critical reportage, struck back at his journalistic critics by expelling several journalists employed by NBC, CBS, and *Newsweek.* Despite pleas from Ambassador Nolting to resinstate them and his warnings that banning the journalists would cost Diem valuable popular support in the United States, the South Vietnamese leader refused to lift the ban.[50]

To harried U.S. officials in Saigon, and to the Diem family, any stories in the American press that deviated from the official line of optimism and progress toward inevitable victory over the Communists were considered to be giving aid and comfort to the enemy. U.S. officials denied the journalists' accounts and accused them of hurting the American–South Vietnamese war effort. General Harkins, who insisted that Ap Bac had been an ARVN victory, accused Halberstam of being unfair to Diem and of writing lies to make him look bad.[51] President Kennedy, who was trying to hide both the growing U.S. involvement in the civil war in South Vietnam and any bad news emanating from the war zone from the American people, was angered by Halberstam's columns. Kennedy tried to get *New York Times* publisher Arthur O. Sulzberger to recall him. Sulzberger rebuffed the president, and Halberstam stayed in Vietnam.[52] The reporters responded to these attacks and pressures by accusing U.S. officials of deceiving the American people about the growing U.S. involvement in battles that were being lost.[53]

The main reason the young journalists were so critical of the performance of the ARVN forces in the field and of Diem's corrupt and inept government was because these writers believed in the cause and wanted the South Vietnamese and their American advisers to win. They all sought the same goals. The journalists were patriotic supporters of America's Vietnam policies, not adversaries. Browne and Sheehan were U.S. Army veterans. Halberstam was an Army reservist. The Marines later awarded Charles Mohr a Bronze Star for bravery during the battle to reclaim Hue in February 1968. Like Colonel Vann, who befriended them, they were Cold Warriors, ideological anti-Communists who believed in the U.S. cause in Vietnam and who wanted the GVN to defeat the NLF insurgents and their North Vietnamese backers. But they saw through the lies and phony statistics of Saigon officials and the fatuous U.S. official optimism based on Diemist deceptions. What the reporters were trying to do was warn Washington and the American people that the war was failing. Unless Diem and Nhu were replaced or radically altered their approach to governance and war, the war would surely be lost.[54]

Behind the declarations of official optimism, internal reports told a more realistic story of growing tension between Diem and U.S. officials. The relationship between the GVN and Washington deteriorated in 1963. Both Diem and Nhu were alarmed by the rapid buildup of the American advisory apparatus. Diem was infuriated by a policy that gave U.S. military advisers control over the distribution of aid to the provinces; Diem demanded that these advisers be recalled. Diem and his brother also resented the assertiveness of many Americans, which they often interpreted as arrogance and a desire to take over conduct of the war against the rebels. The CIA reports sent to Washington confirmed the political deterioration occurring in the delta region and elsewhere.[55] Colonel F. P. Serong, an Australian counterinsurgency expert, sent a secret report to General Harkins describing the failure of the ARVN forces to provide security for the rural population.[56] U.S. officials continued to press Diem to make democratic reforms, which he correctly feared would undermine his regime. These U.S. pressures provoked Diem's brother Nhu to public criticism about the pushy Americans. During 1963, the American-GVN partnership became increasingly strained. Within the United States, some government officials were losing faith in Diem and calling for a coup to rid the country of the failing leader and his family.[57]

Senator Mike Mansfield, an Asian scholar and a long-time supporter of Diem, at President Kennedy's behest, led a fact-finding trip of several senators to Vietnam in December 1962. Upon his return, Mansfield warned Kennedy that the war in Vietnam was becoming an American war that could not be justified by current U.S. security interests in Southeast Asia. He reported that the U.S. escalations had made the Diem regime more unstable and ARVN forces less able to contain the growing NLF insurgency. Additional efforts necessary for the survival of the GVN would have to come from Saigon, not Washington, and if they were not forthcoming, the United States should either reduce its commitments to South Vietnam or get out. Mansfield told the president that the United States was in danger of being drawn "inexorably" into the doomed role and bloody fate of the French colonial armies in Southeast Asia.[58] Kennedy angrily rejected Mansfield's recommendations. He had no intention of walking through the door that Mansfield opened for him. Kennedy continued the U. S. military buildup in South Vietnam during the first half of 1963. He also continued to support Diem's government, despite the growing rift between U.S. officials and their South Vietnamese clients.[59]

THE DECLINE AND FALL OF NGO DINH DIEM

Suddenly, the Buddhist crisis exploded in Hue, which marked the beginning of the end of the Ngo Dinh family oligarchy. The crisis erupted on May 8, 1963, when government troops fired into a crowd protesting a Diemist law forbidding the flying of religious flags celebrating the 2,527th anniversary of the Buddha's birth. Nine people were killed. Two days later, thousands of Buddhists took to the streets to protest the shootings and to demand religious freedom. Diem responded by rejecting their demands and jailing the Buddhist leaders. He denied that his soldiers had fired on the demonstrators; he blamed the shootings on the VietCong. Diem's rigid and deceptive response provoked additional demonstrations. Major opposition to Diem's floundering regime shifted from the countryside to the cities and came from Buddhist monks, not Communist cadres.

The Buddhist revolt reached a new dimension on June 11, when an elderly Buddhist monk, Thich Quang Duc, immolated himself in front of large crowds at a busy intersection in downtown Saigon. American news photographers and reporters, alerted beforehand by Buddhist leaders, were at the scene, and soon horrific pictures and accounts of the burning monk made the front pages and television news highlights in America and around the world.[60] Americans, many of whom had previously given little thought to Vietnam, appalled by the images of self-immolation, gained insight into the depth and passion of the Buddhist opposition to Diemist rule. World opinion, shocked by the dramatic photograph, criticized Americans for supporting a government that persecuted religious worshippers. Quang Duc's flaming sacrifice made the political crisis in Vietnam in the summer of 1963 a big story in the American news media. Many of the news stories emanating from Saigon sharply criticized Diem's repressive actions. U.S. officials brought intense pressure on Diem to rescind the ban and conciliate the Buddhists. But Diem was unresponsive to their pleas. His brother Ngo Dinh Nhu continued to denounce and redbait the Buddhists. Nhu and his wife also advised Diem to ignore the American demands and suppress the Buddhist revolt.[61]

The Buddhist rebellion, which was more a political than a religious uprising, had long been in the making. Its roots lay in the mass emigration from the North following the Geneva agreements of July 1954, when a million Catholics streamed south to form a popular base of support for Diem's emerging government. Under Diem's family rule, Catholics received favored treatment and enjoyed special privileges and opportunities. Priests enjoyed political influence; most district and province chiefs were Catholics. South Vietnam's 1.6 million Catholics constituted a favored minority in a country in which about 11 of its 14 million people were Buddhists.[62]

The Buddhist uprising in Hue reflected not only the passions of the moment, but also the accumulated resentments deriving from years of discrimination and social repression. The rebellion also reflected a growing militancy on the part of younger, more

Figure 4.3 The Buddhist revolt against the Diem family's rule intensified when Thich Quang Duc, an elderly monk, immolated himself by fire on a busy downtown Saigon street on June 11, 1963. Dramatic photographs of the gruesome event made the front pages and television news highlights around the world. *Source:* AP/Wide World Photos.

political monks, who were determined to challenge Diemist proscriptions and to seek a greater role in public life. Thousands of high school and college students, traditionally apolitical, took to the streets in Saigon and Hue to support the Buddhists. Many ARVN soldiers, themselves Buddhists, sympathized with the protesters.

The Buddhists did not present a coherent list of demands, and there were divisions within their ranks, but generally they called for Diem's removal, an end to American intrusions in Vietnamese affairs, and a neutral South Vietnam governed by a coalition of factions looking toward peaceful reunification with the North. Diem refused all but token concessions.[63] Madame Nhu inflamed the crisis with her shrill denunciations of the Buddhists and ghastly humor: She told a CBS news reporter that the Buddhists had only "barbecued a bonze with imported gasoline."[64] She also offered to furnish the gasoline and matches for more immolations. By midsummer, the war against the VietCong had virtually halted, and South Vietnamese society appeared on the verge of disintegrating. The demonstrations and fiery sacrifices continued. A war inside of a war beckoned.

On the night of August 21, Diem and Nhu perpetrated a series of wanton acts that sealed their fate. Nhu's American-trained praetorian guards, assisted by local police forces, raided pagodas in several cities. Temples were desecrated, 1,420 monks were arrested, and dozens more were killed or injured.[65] Alarmed ARVN generals began to plot the overthrow of the Ngo Dinhs before chaos engulfed everyone and the VietCong won their revolution by default.

Several coup plots were percolating during that tumultuous summer of 1963 in Saigon. Some of them had been underway prior to the pagoda raids. The earliest dated from the end of June and had been started by Tran Kim Tuyen, Diem's diminutive national intelligence chief. Tuyen was helped by Colonel Do Mau, director of Military Security Services. Junior officers joined the plot as well and U.S. agents encouraged the coup plotters. Nhu's assaults on the pagodas were driving the army officers, many of whom were Buddhists, and the Americans, together.[66]

Sensing the danger to the regime posed by the developing alliance between U.S. officials and dissident army officers, Nhu embarked on a bizarre scheme to preserve his family's power. He sought a rapprochement with the NLF and Hanoi. He succeeded in making contact with Hanoi. It is impossible to tell from the available evidence whether Nhu was serious about a rapprochement with the Communists; he may have only been trying to outmaneuver the Americans. But he may have been trying to make serious moves toward an accommodation with the enemy and to oust the Americans whom he detested. U.S. officials in Saigon operated on the assumption that Nhu's gestures toward Hanoi were genuine. His weird actions only increased the growing resolve of some U.S. officials to get rid of him and his outspoken wife, and Diem too, if the president insisted on retaining close ties to his brother and sister-in-law.[67]

The chief planner of the coup that eventually toppled Diem was Major General Tran Van Don, the commander of the ARVN. He worked closely with Lieutenant General Duong Van "Big" Minh, who would head the new government if the coup succeeded. Don made contact with U.S. officials through an old friend, CIA agent Lucien Conein, who became the principal liaison between the generals and U.S. officials as the coup plot developed.

On August 24, a group of anti-Diem officials within the State Department sent a cable to the newly appointed American ambassador to Saigon, Henry Cabot Lodge. Lodge was instructed to give Diem a chance to get rid of Nhu, but, if Diem refused, the message indicated that Diem himself might have to go. Lodge also was instructed to inform the dissident generals that the United States was prepared to abandon Diem if he continued to prove uncooperative and that Washington would support a replacement government. Secretary of State Rusk and President Kennedy approved sending the cable to Lodge.[68]

After meeting with the South Vietnamese president several times, Lodge sized up Diem as being rigid and unreformable. He also perceived that Diem would never separate himself from his brother and sister-in-law. In Lodge's view, a coup that rid South Vietnam of the Ngo Dinh family rule remained the best hope for winning the war against the VietCong. Working through Conein, Lodge assured the generals planning Diem's overthrow that they would have U.S. support if the *coup d'état* succeeded. Lodge also sent President Kennedy a secret cable on August 28 informing him that the United States "was launched on a course from which there is no respectable turning back; the overthrow of the Diem government."[69] But the generals, unable to gain the support of key officers commanding troops in the vicinity of Saigon, and fearful of Nhu's machinations, aborted the coup in late August, placing it on indefinite hold.

About the time that the coup plotters were backing off, Kennedy received an unsolicited offer from French President Charles de Gaulle to mediate the crisis in Vietnam. De Gaulle proposed a comprehensive solution that included America's withdrawing its troops, establishing a neutral government for South Vietnam, and having North and South Vietnam resume relations. It was a solution based on the Geneva Accords of 1954. Hanoi and Saigon both expressed an interest in de Gaulle's proposal; Kennedy abruptly rejected the French offer. De Gaulle's proposal represented an ironic reversal; he was suggesting that it was time for America to end the war in Vietnam that it had snatched from the French back in 1954, after failing to get the French to continue the fight.[70] De Gaulle, the seasoned statesmen, tried to warn Kennedy of the pitfalls of intervening in Vietnam. Kennedy was not interested in being warned, least of all by the imperious Charles de Gaulle. The French record of fighting bitterly to cling to an empire in Southeast Asia and the Maghreb, especially Algeria, was not instructive. In any case, Kennedy was irrevocably committed to continuing the American effort to establish a non-Communist state in the southern half of Vietnam, with or without Ngo Dinh Diem.

Meanwhile, South Vietnam continued to disintegrate. Diem would not conciliate the Buddhists and their supporters. The Kennedy administration remained deeply divided over how to handle the deepening crisis that threatened to lose the war and collapse South Vietnam. Resorting to his usual *modus operandi* when faced with tough decisions, President Kennedy dispatched another fact-finding mission to South Vietnam. The mission was headed by Marine General Victor Krulak, a counterinsurgency expert working for the Joint Chiefs of Staff, and Joseph Mendenhall, a State Department specialist on Far Eastern affairs.

Their reports only added to Kennedy's confusion. General Krulak's exuded optimism. He reported that the coup had failed, that the ARVN forces were winning the war in the countryside, and that the United States should continue its support of Diem. By contrast, Mendenhall's report was starkly pessimistic. He reported that South Vietnam was verging on a breakdown, that a religious war between Catholics and Buddhists threatened, and that the war against the VietCong could not be won by the Diem government. Kennedy, obviously exasperated, asked them, "You two did visit the same country, didn't you?"[71]

Kennedy, frustrated by the inability of U.S. officials to manage the chaotic political life of South Vietnam, nevertheless was not prepared to consider seeking a negotiated settlement or extricating the United States from what increasingly appeared to be a no-win situation. He also did not want to bomb North Vietnam, send American combat forces, or take over the political life of the country. He and his advisers were so preoccupied with day-to-day crisis management in South Vietnam that they had lost the capacity to think in terms of long-range U.S. interests in Southeast Asia or to confront fundamental issues. Kennedy was not prepared to consider any plan of action that might involve the abandonment of a long-standing American commitment in southern Vietnam or the Americanizing of the war. "The administration drifted along, divided against itself, with no clear idea where it was going."[72]

Kennedy, following weeks of indecision, in early October sent still another fact-finding team, which was headed by Robert McNamara and General Maxwell Taylor, to appraise the general political and military situation in South Vietnam. Their report "badly misjudged the actual conditions in South Vietnam."[73] They reported that the war effort had made great progress since 1962. But it simply was not true that the ARVN was winning the war; in fact, the South Vietnamese army was steadily losing territory and villages to the VietCong at the time McNamara and Taylor made their visit. The NLF controlled much more territory and population in the fall of 1963 in the Mekong Delta region than it had 18 months earlier. McNamara and Taylor reported that prospects for a coup against Diem were slim, even though the coup planners were again busily at work on the plot that would topple Diem within a few weeks. The report also exaggerated the effectiveness of applying selective pressures to Diem to get him to stop persecuting the Buddhists and rebuild his base of support among the urban elites. In contrast, Ambassador Lodge had a clear grasp of the dire political situation in South Vietnam. He understood that Diem was unreformable and would never separate himself from Nhu, but McNamara and Taylor ignored Lodge's views in their report to the president.[74]

Despite its misperceptions and faulty judgments, Kennedy embraced the recommendations of the McNamara-Taylor report, adopting a policy of applying selective pressures against Diem. Kennedy cut off the funds to support some Special Forces under Nhu's control. He also recalled the CIA station chief in Saigon, John Richardson, who was known to be friendly with Ngo Dinh Nhu. These measures, intended as such by Kennedy, were taken as signals by General Don and the other coup planners to accelerate their plotting and seek greater support from the Americans. Lodge, through Conein, assured the conspirators that the United States would do nothing to hinder the coup and would extend military and economic support to any new regime that broadened its base of popular support, effectively prosecuted the war, and cooperated with U.S. officials.[75]

The Kennedy administration still remained hopelessly divided over whether to support Diem or the coup planners. Vice President Johnson, McNamara, and General Harkins continued to support Diem. State Department officials believed that Nhu and Diem had to go and supported the coup plotters. "Kennedy himself vacillated, adher-

Figure 4.4 As the political crisis in South Vietnam deepened during the fall of 1963, President John F. Kennedy conferred with his two leading advisers, special military representative General Maxwell Taylor and Secretary of Defense Robert McNamara, both of whom had just returned from a fact-finding trip to Saigon. *Source:* CORBIS.

ing to the policy of not overtly supporting a coup, but not discouraging one either."[76] He relied on Lodge, who was on the scene and who backed the coup plot. For several weeks, the coup conspirators plotted while U.S. officials fretted indecisively. As the *coup d'état* became imminent, Kennedy's chief concerns appear to have been that it might fail or that if it succeeded, that U.S. officials be capable of plausible deniability. Lodge reassured the nervous president that the coup would succeed and that any new government would be an improvement over Diem and Nhu.[77]

As October 1963 came to an end, Saigon seethed with rumors, plots, and counterplots. General Don and his coconspirators had planned their coup scrupulously. They had secured the support of key generals commanding troops in the vicinity of Saigon. They neutralized the forces of generals remaining loyal to the Ngo Dinhs and established a precise timetable of operations. Nhu, knowing a coup attempt was nigh, but not knowing precisely which generals and troop units were involved, schemed furiously to flush out the conspirators, even going so far as to concoct an elaborate fake coup that involved one of the generals who, unbeknownst to Nhu, was part of the real coup.

The *coup d'état* that destroyed the Diem regime began on November 1 at 1:30 P.M. Saigon time. The coup leaders moved their forces into place, seizing control of key military and communication facilities. Once certain that a coup against them was underway, Diem and Nhu, from a command post inside the presidential palace, tried frantically to contact ARVN units that they thought still remained loyal to them. They quickly discovered that all had either joined the coup, had been jailed or killed, or could not get their forces to Saigon. Although trapped, Diem and Nhu refused the generals' repeated demands to surrender. They tried unsuccessfully to lure the coup leaders to the palace for consultations, a stalling device that had worked to thwart the November 1960 coup attempt.

At 4:30 P.M., as the coup went forward, Ngo Dinh Diem phoned Ambassador Lodge, who was staying at the American embassy:

Diem: Some units have made a rebellion and I want to know what is the attitude of the U.S.?

Lodge: I do not feel well enough informed to be able to tell you. I have heard the shooting, but am not acquainted with all the facts. Also, it is 4:30 A.M. in Washington and the U.S. Government cannot possibly have a view.

Diem: But you must have some general ideas. After all, I am Chief of State. I have tried to do my duty. I want to do now what duty and good sense require. I believe in duty above all.

Lodge: You have certainly done your duty. As I told you only this morning, I admire your courage and your great contribution to your country. No one can take away from you the credit for all you have done. Now I am worried about your physical safety. I have a report that those in charge of the current activity offer you and your brother safe conduct out of the country if you resign. Had you heard this?

Diem: No. (*Pause*) You have my phone number.

Lodge: Yes. If I can do anything for your physical safety, please call me.

Diem: I am trying to reestablish order. (*Hangs up.*)[78]

Diem no doubt inferred the American position from Lodge's offer of asylum: U.S. officials were supporting the coup and would do nothing to prevent it from succeeding. The United States was abandoning an ally it had installed in power back in 1954 and 1955; one it had supported for nearly a decade.

At about 7:00 P.M., Diem and Nhu exited the palace through a secret underground passageway and fled to the home of a friend, a wealthy Chinese merchant residing in the Cholon district. Hours later, ARVN troops loyal to the coup leaders overwhelmed the guards and occupied the presidential palace. The next morning, Diem and Nhu, after talking with various supporters, phoned General Don's headquarters. They offered to surrender in exchange for pledges of safe conduct. Don accepted their offer, although he told them their surrender would have to be unconditional.

General Minh dispatched two jeeps and an armored personnel carrier to fetch the deposed leaders. He also dispatched his personal bodyguard Captain Nhung, with secret instructions to assassinate Diem and Nhu. The deposed leaders were taken prisoner in front of a small chapel near the house of their friend and placed in the back of the personnel carrier. Their hands were tied behind their backs. Captain Nhung joined the bound brothers in the back of the vehicle. When the armored car returned to coup headquarters, Diem and Nhu were no longer among the living. They had both been shot in the back of the head. Nhu had also been stabbed several times. As Nhung hopped out of the armored car, he saluted General Minh and whispered, "Mission accomplie."

The victorious rebels quickly went after the rest of the Ngo Dinh family leaders. Archbishop Ngo Dinh Thuc fled to the Vatican. Ngo Dinh Can was arrested in Hue and executed shortly thereafter by a firing squad. Madame Nhu survived the bloodbath only because she was traveling in the United States when the coup occurred. The coup leaders believed that it was necessary to eradicate the Ngo Dinh family because they feared Diem and Nhu still had some popular support and might find a way to return to power if they remained alive. Diem and Nhu were buried in unmarked graves somewhere in Saigon.[79]

In Saigon, news of the successful *coup d'état* brought a joyous response. People poured into the streets to celebrate the overthrow of a tyrant whose power base, at the time of his downfall, had shrunk to a handful of family members, a few government bureaucrats, some police and military retainers, and the Catholic minority. In Saigon, citizens cheered the ARVN soldiers who had taken part in the coup and, assuming that U.S. officials had ordered the coup, praised all Americans they encountered on the streets.

U.S. official spokesmen in Saigon and Washington claimed to have known nothing about the coup and insisted that they had had no part in it. They said it was an internal political matter involving only quarreling factions of Vietnamese politicians. In fact, the Americans were deeply implicated in the coup. They were aware of it from its inception, and they had encouraged it. Lucien Conein met often with the plotters and functioned as a conduit among the generals, Lodge, and Washington. Conein was with General Don the day Diem was overthrown.[80] Without American financial support, promises of noninterference, and most of all, pledges to continue to provide economic and military aid to any replacement government that would emerge from a successful coup, the coup would never have occurred.

President Kennedy had not ordered Diem's or Nhu's deaths. When he heard the news that Diem and Nhu had been murdered, his faced turned white and he fled the Oval Office. He had been one of Diem's earliest supporters and strongest champions. He had sought his replacement as head of state not his murder.[81] But no one had taken any steps to ensure the brothers' survival other than making contingency plans for granting them asylum prior to removing them from the country. No one told Don and Minh that U. S. officials wanted Diem and Nhu kept alive.

The response in Hanoi to the coup was mixed; the overthrow of Diem both resolved some problems and created new ones for the Communist leadership. The coup had rid South Vietnam of an uncompromising anti-Communist zealot who had also staunchly opposed the French. Diem had been a leader with some claim to rival Ho Chi Minh as a symbol of Vietnamese nationalist aspirations. The successful coup also confirmed Hanoi's claims that the Diem regime was a corrupt, unpopular regime that had lost all right to rule. On the other hand, the Communists had to be concerned because the new government, a military junta led by General Minh, had a potential for achieving a broader base of support. Minh was a southerner and a Buddhist who had been one of the leaders of a coup that had overthrown a tyrant.[82] It would be more difficult to sustain an insurgency that would require greater assistance from the North. Ominously, the new government had the strong backing of the Americans, and General Minh pledged to prosecute vigorously the war against the NLF. Hanoi anticipated an enlarged American presence in the South and a consequent escalation of the conflict. The Communist leadership worried, lest northern economic development be endangered by the costs of a larger war in the South and perhaps U.S. air attacks north of the 17th Parallel.[83]

An expanded conflict also posed problems for Hanoi in its relations with the two major Communist powers, the Soviet Union and China. The Soviets had backed off their support of anticolonial "wars of national liberation" and were preaching the doctrine of "peaceful coexistence" with the United States. China, bidding to take over leadership of the Third World, championed the cause of national liberation in the early 1960s. Hanoi's increased involvement in the southern insurgency and possible conflict with the United States appeared to align the Vietnamese Communists with China and against the Soviet Union.[84]

A Failed Partnership

Ironically, Washington's support for the coup weakened rather than strengthened the security of South Vietnam. It ushered in a protracted period of political instability in South Vietnam that hindered counterinsurgency efforts and was a major cause of the large-scale U.S. military intervention in 1965 that Americanized the war. U.S. officials who had supported the coup were so caught up in the process that they had given little thought to what kind of leaders might come to power after Diem's downfall. They were so convinced that Diem and Nhu had to be removed from power that they just assumed that whoever replaced them would be an improvement.

American complicity in the coup strengthened the U.S. commitment to South Vietnam and "tied the United States to all succeeding regimes."[85] President Johnson, who had supported Diem and argued against the coup, believed that Kennedy's involvement in the coup was the worst error made by the United States during its long involvement in Vietnam. The coup made the United States directly responsible for the fate of successive South Vietnamese governments. It also set into motion a train of events that "eventually forced President Johnson in 1965 to choose between accepting defeat or introducing American combat forces."[86]

Three weeks after the coup, Kennedy's assassination overshadowed the murders in Saigon. At the time of his death, Kennedy's Vietnam policy was in disarray and his administration was divided over what to do about the failing war against the VietCong. Kennedy loyalists and several scholars have argued that had Kennedy lived, he was planning to extricate the United States from South Vietnam sometime in 1965 and that there would have been no American war in that country.[87] But in the final months of his presidency, Kennedy repeatedly reaffirmed the American commitment in Vietnam. In a televised interview with Walter Cronkite, broadcast on September 2, 1963, Kennedy invoked the classic Cold War rationale for the U.S. involvement in southern Vietnam:

> Those people who say that we ought to withdraw from Vietnam are wholly wrong, because if we withdraw from Vietnam, the Communists would control Vietnam. Pretty soon Thailand, Cambodia, Laos, Malaya would go and all of Southeast Asia would be under the control of the Communists and under the domination of the Chinese.[88]

Three days later, in another television interview, Kennedy told David Brinkley that the United States would remain in Vietnam to check Chinese expansionism in Southeast Asia. Shortly before he died, the President told Ngo Dien Diem that the United States gave the highest priority to defeating the Communist insurgency in South Vietnam. On the day he died, in a noontime speech that Kennedy would have delivered at the Dallas Trade Mart, he planned to once again affirm the American commitment in Vietnam. He would have told the assemblage of businessmen that Americans "dare not weary of the task" of supporting South Vietnam no matter how "risky or costly" that support might be. In all of his public statements, Kennedy consistently reaffirmed a strong commitment to the U.S. effort in Vietnam to the end. He never once suggested to any of his senior civilian or military advisers that he might be thinking about disengaging from Vietnam. Lyndon Johnson never got the impression that Kennedy had any intentions of pulling out of Vietnam. Johnson went to his grave believing that what he did in Vietnam was what Kennedy would have done, had he lived.[89]

No one can say with certainty what Kennedy might have done in Vietnam had he lived; all efforts to do so represent exercizes in counterfactual historical speculation. Had he lived, he probably would have continued U.S. incremental escalations in South Vietnam to prevent disaster until he was reelected in November 1964. In the summer of 1965, having to face the same crisis that Johnson had to confront and the same stark choices—accept a Communist victory in Vietnam or undertake a major military escalation that amounted to an American takeover of the war—Kennedy and his senior advisers, all of whom stayed on board to help forge Johnson's Vietnam policy, would probably have done what Johnson did. Had he lived, President Kennedy probably could not have avoided an American war in Vietnam. It is unlikely that Kennedy was prepared to pull out and present the NLF and Hanoi with a victory in Vietnam that would have also given the Chinese and the Soviets a major Cold War ideological victory. At home, Richard Nixon, Barry Goldwater, and other prominent Republican leaders would have exploded in denunciations of a Democratic bug-out in Southeast Asia and blamed them for the "loss of Indochina" to the Communists. If one of John Kennedy's major political goals was to set the stage for a Robert Kennedy candidacy for the presidency in 1968; it is hard to imagine that he would risk fatally compromising his brother's bid by handing the Republicans "the loss of Indochina" to the Communists.

What Kennedy might have done can never be known. What can be known is the Vietnam policy of his abbreviated presidency. "Kennedy bequeathed a terrible legacy to his successor."[90] Kennedy was a conventional Cold Warrior. He embraced a strong anti-Communist ideology; he was committed to containment, and he believed in the domino theory.[91] He and his senior advisers believed unquestioningly that retaining a non-Communist South Vietnam was vital to the strategic security of the United States and its allies in Southeast Asia. Kennedy and his advisers acted on the presumption that Washington knew best what should be done in Vietnam. In the name of the ongoing struggle with the VietCong, Americans claimed the right to intervene as they chose. They supported the overthrow of the Diem government primarily because it refused to follow their advice—ease up on the Buddhists, reform the government, and most of all more vigorously prosecute the war against the VietCong.[92] U.S. officials appeared serenely confident that they would somehow muddle through and prevail. The most important consequence of the Kennedy administration's words and deeds was to increase sharply the American stake in Vietnam from 1961 to 1963 and to put the United States on course for a major war in Southeast Asia.

Vietnam represented President Kennedy's "great failure in foreign policy."[93] "Vietnam stands as the most tragic legacy of the global activism of the Kennedy era."[94] During his abbreviated presidency, Kennedy gave Vietnam only sporadic attention. Vietnam was rarely near the top of his list of foreign policy crises to be managed. The ongoing Cold War with the Soviets, especially showdowns in Berlin and Cuba, preoccupied the young leader. Vietnam policy was often left to advisers, principally McNamara, Taylor, Walt Rostow, and McGeorge Bundy. Kennedy does not appear to have known very much about the country or to have shown much interest in Vietnam for most of his presidency. He never asked hard questions or made tough decisions. Only his brother Robert could do that. Robert Kennedy once asked at a National Security Council meeting, What if no South Vietnamese government could resist a Communist takeover? If it could not, he stated, then America should extricate itself from the region.[95] The president never confronted that potentiality; he reacted to Southeast Asian crises and improvised policy on an ad hoc basis.[96]

The president preferred to take cautious middle courses. His middle courses of action managed to stave off disaster and significantly increase the U.S. commitment to Vietnam. During Kennedy's presidency, the levels of economic and military aid to the GVN rose significantly. At the time of the coup, South Vietnam was costing the United

States $1.5 million per day, and there were 16,500 military advisers in the country, including counterinsurgency forces. Some of these advisory forces engaged sporadically in combat. When Kennedy took office, there had been about 650 U.S. military personnel in South Vietnam; on the day of his death there were about 16,700.[97] When Kennedy took office, the NLF controlled about half of the villages within South Vietnam; on the day of his death, they controlled many more, especially in the strategic Mekong Delta region. Kennedy "bequeathed to his successor a problem eminently more dangerous than the one that he had inherited from Eisenhower."[98]

Kennedy continued the Eisenhower policies in Vietnam, but he significantly upped the ante and instigated a small-scale limited American war. The Indochina interventions of the Eisenhower and Kennedy administrations revealed an American tendency to think about Vietnam in terms of Cold War abstractions rather than to understand concrete Vietnamese cultural, social, political, and strategic realities. U.S. officials gave primacy to global Cold War factors and persistently underplayed particular, local, Vietnamese historical forces. Americans tried to understand events in Vietnam using paradigms generated by their Cold War ideological predilections, not by indigenous Vietnamese realities. U.S. Cold Warriors failed to understand that it was not possible to create a nation out of part of a nation by an act of political will if that part of a nation lacked historical and cultural bases for existence. Washington persistently failed to understand that Communism had aligned itself with Vietnamese nationalism, that the national revolution that U.S. officials tried for 30 years to thwart had deep Vietnamese roots. Revolution in Vietnam was not a Chinese and Soviet Cold War strategy.

Americans also failed to understand the extent to which they were perceived as outsiders meddling in the internal affairs of the Vietnamese people and the consequent liabilities and limits imposed on their actions by that perception. Two thousand years of history had taught the Vietnamese to distrust and fear foreign imperial powers. U.S. officials persisted in viewing the Vietnamese national revolution as foreign aggression, when in fact the VietCong insurgency originated as an indigenous reaction to repression by the American-backed Ngo Dinh family regime. The Americans were the outsiders in South Vietnam, not the VietCong. That insurgency and the threat to its survival posed by the Diem government in turn provoked an initially reluctant response from the Communist leaders in Hanoi, who felt compelled to assume command of the rebellion that was occurring in the southern part of their country and to use it as a vehicle to bring about national reunification.

The Americans were prisoners of their Cold War ideologies that superimposed a false set of abstractions on Indochina realities. Consequently, the Americans could not only never defeat the Vietnamese national revolution, they could never understand why they were losing. They could not understand why a succession of U.S.-backed South Vietnamese governments could never establish their legitimacy, win the hearts and minds of the rural population, govern, or fight effectively. U.S. officials understood that their mission was to stem the tide of expansionist Communism in Indochina; to a large majority of Vietnamese and to much of the rest of the world, Americans appeared to be replacing the French in opposing Asian self-determination and preserving Western influence in Southeast Asia.

Just as a European diasporic society had created their own nation in the New World, Americans intended to replicate that achievement in the unpromising political geography of southern Vietnam. However, Americans tried to do the impossible in southern Vietnam; they tried to determine the political destiny of its people and change the course of its history

Notes

1. Excerpts from Kennedy's inaugural address are taken from a copy of the speech printed in Sorensen, Theodore C., *Kennedy* (New York: Harper & Row, 1965), 275–78. Kennedy misread Krushchev's remarks about Soviet support of anticolonial wars of national liberation. The Soviet leader was not flinging down his gauntlet before Kennedy; he was responding to challenges from Mao and trying to assert Soviet leadership in the Third World.
2. Herring, *America's Longest War,* 74–75.
3. Kahin, *Intervention,* 126.
4. Ibid., 127
5. It is impossible to know precisely what Ike told his successor about Laos at this meeting. The most plausible analysis is by Fred I. Greenstein and Richard H. Immerman. They suggest that Eisenhower did not make any specific recommendations for action, rather he talked about the potential costs and benefits of military intervention in Laos. He, in effect, left that decision to the incoming administration. Greenstein, Fred I., and Immerman, Richard H. "What Did Eisenhower Tell Kennedy about Indochina? The Politics of Misperception," *Journal of American History* 79 no. 2 (September 1992): 568–87. See also Porter (ed.), *Vietnam Documents,* vol. 2, Document 38, 90–92, which is a memo of the July 19 meeting between Eisenhower and Kennedy; Clifford, Clark, "A Vietnam Reappraisal," *Foreign Affairs* 47 (July 1969): 604–5; Parmet, Herbert, *JFK: The Presidency of John F. Kennedy* (New York: Penguin, 1983), 81; Schulzinger, *Time for War,* 99.
6. Schlesinger, Arthur Meier, Jr., *A Thousand Days: John F. Kennedy in the White House* (Greenwich, CT: Fawcett, 1965), 309–11.
7. Cooper, Chester, *The Lost Crusade: America in Vietnam* (New York: Dodd, Mead, 1970), 191–92; Young, *Vietnam Wars,* 78.
8. Protocol to the Declaration of the Neutrality of Laos, July 23, 1962, in Porter (ed.), *Vietnam Documents,* vol. 2, Document 77, 156–60. The nations attending the Geneva conference signing the protocol included Burma, Cambodia, Canada, the People's Republic of China, the Democratic Republic of Vietnam (North Vietnam), France, India, the Kingdom of Laos, Poland, the Republic of Vietnam (South Vietnam), Thailand, the Soviet Union, Great Britain, and the United States. The protocol reads that all foreign troops and paramilitary forces were to be removed within 30 days. In actuality, 750 U.S. MAAG forces departed as did a few Soviet pilots. The 10,000 plus PAVN troops remained in Laos in violation of the protocol.
9. O'Ballance, Edgar, *The Wars in Vietnam: 1954–1980* (New York: Hippocrene, 1981), 28–31.
10. Herring, *America's Longest War,* 78.
11. Doyle et al., *Passing the Torch,* 181. Kennedy had a special interest in counterinsurgency. He believed that it would be the most effective instrument available for checking Third World guer-

rilla forces. He moved to beef up U.S. Special Forces training programs that had begun under the Eisenhower administration in the late 1950s. At the president's direction, special warfare training centers began preparing U.S. soldiers to challenge guerrillas in the jungles and mountains of Laos and Vietnam.

12. Sheehan, Neil; Smith, Hedrick; Kenworthy, E. W.; and Butterfield, Fox, *The Pentagon Papers: The Secret History of the Vietnam War* (New York: Bantam, 1971), "National Security Action Memorandum 52," 126–27.

13. Doyle et al., *Passing the Torch,* 191–93; O'Ballance, *Vietnam Wars,* 42–43.

14. Cablegram from General Taylor to Kennedy, November 1, 1961, printed in Porter (ed.), *Vietnam Documents,* vol. 2, Document 70, 140–42. Taylor recommended sending an 8,000-man military force to repair the extensive damage caused by recent floods; forces that could also perform combat missions. Kennedy rejected his suggestion. See also Sheehan et al., *The Pentagon Papers,* Documents 26, 27, 28, and 29, 141–50.

15. Karnow, *Vietnam,* 248.

16. Kahin, *Intervention,* 134.

17. Herring, *America's Longest War,* 84; Berman, Larry, *Planning a Tragedy: The Americanization of the War in Vietnam* (New York, W. W. Norton, 1982), 16–23; Pelz, Stephen, "John F. Kennedy's 1961 Vietnam War Decisions," *Journal of Strategic Studies* 4 (December 1981): 356–85; Department of State, *A Threat to Peace* (Washington, DC: U.S. Government Printing Office, 1961), the State Department White Paper documenting Hanoi's violations of the Geneva Accords exaggerates the amount of Hanoi's support for the NLF and it contradicts CIA intelligence findings. The Rusk-McNamara memo dated November 11, 1961, appears in Sheehan and others, *The Pentagon Papers,* 150–53.

18. Quoted in Herring, *America's Longest War,* 84.

19. Blaufarb, Douglas, *The Counterinsurgency Era* (New York: Free Press, 1977), 85–88; Gravel, *Pentagon Papers,* Vol. II, 123. John Kenneth Galbraith told President Kennedy that Diem would never reform his government because he could not. If he agreed to reforms, it would lessen his power and he would be thrown out of office.

20. Gelb, Leslie H., with Betts, Richard K., *The Irony of Vietnam: The System Worked* (Washington, DC: Brookings Institution, 1979), 75–79; Pelz, Stephen, "John F. Kennedy's 1961 Vietnam War Decisions," 356–85.

21. Doyle et al., *Passing the Torch,* 197.

22. Tuchman, *March of Folly,* 299. The Eisenhower administration observed the 1954 Geneva Accords limits on foreign military personnel in South Vietnam. There were about 650 American advisers in South Vietnam in January 1961. By the end of the year, there were over 3,000 advisers and support personnel, 9,000 by the end of 1962. At the time of Kennedy's death, there were about 16,700.

23. O'Ballance, *The Vietnam Wars,* 43–44; Miroff, Bruce, *Pragmatic Illusions: The Presidential Politics of John F. Kennedy* (New York: David McKay, 1976); Maitland, Terrence; Weiss, Stephen; and the editors, *Raising the Stakes* (Boston: Boston Publishing, 1982), 19–21.

24. Blaufarb, *Counterinsurgency Era,* 113–15.

25. Maitland et al., *Raising the Stakes,* 23.

26. Ibid.

27. Kahin, *Intervention,* 140–41; Herring, *America's Longest War,* 85–86; and Duiker, *The Communist Road,* 201–3; Miroff, *Pragmatic Illusions,* 158–60.

28. Maitland et al., *Raising the Stakes,* 14–15, 18–19.

29. O'Ballance, *The Vietnam Wars,* 43; Hess, *Vietnam,* 74.

30. Sheehan, Neil, "Annals of War: An American Soldier in Vietnam: Part 2, A Set-Piece Battle," *New Yorker* 64, no. 19 (July 1988): 35–36; Halberstam, David, *The Making of a Quagmire: America and Vietnam during the Kennedy Era,* rev. ed. (New York: Knopf, 1988), 56–66; Hess, *Vietnam,* 74.

31. The Vietnamese word for hamlet is *ap.* The main action during the Battle of Ap Bac took place in the tree line near the village of Bac.

32. Halberstam, *Quagmire,* 72–73.

33. John Paul Vann arrived in South Vietnam in March 1962, soon becoming the senior adviser to the ARVN 7th Division. He quickly established himself as one of the ablest officers in the U.S. Army. He returned to the states after his year's tour as adviser and retired from the army. Deeply committed to the American cause in Vietnam, Vann returned in 1965 as a civilian official. Until his death in June 1972, Vann was the most effective American adviser involved in counterinsurgency and pacification activities.

34. For accounts of the Battle of Ap Bac, see Sheehan, Neil, *A Bright Shining Lie: John Paul Vann and America in Vietnam* (New York: Random House, 1988), 203–65; Palmer, Dave Richard, *Summons of the Trumpet* (New York: Ballantine, 1978), 37–51; and Halberstam, *Quagmire,* 67–81.

35. Sheehan, "Annals of War, Part 2," 58–60.

36. Ibid., 60–63; Halberstam, *Quagmire,* 76–81.

37. O'Ballance, *The Vietnam Wars,* 43–47; Duiker, *The Communist Road,* 214–15.

38. Halberstam, *Quagmire,* 79.

39. Colonel Wilson is quoted in Clarke, Jeffrey J., *Advice and Support: The Final Years, 1965–1973* (Washington, DC: U.S. Government Printing Office, 1988), 47.

40. Quote is from Sheehan, *A Bright Shining Lie,* 90; see also Halberstam, *Quagmire,* 52–55; Clarke, *The Final Years,* 162–63.

41. Hess, *Vietnam,* 75; Sheehan, "Annals of War, Part 2," 62.

42. Hess, *Vietnam,* 74.

43. Hilsman, Roger, *To Move a Nation* (New York: Delta, 1967), 87–88. Hilsman, a State Department official and counterinsurgency expert, was initially a strong supporter of the strategic hamlet enterprise. By summer of 1963, Ngo Dinh Nhu claimed that two-thirds of the South Vietnamese population resided in secure strategic hamlets. A more realistic figure would have been 5–10 percent; Blaufarb, *Counterinsurgency Era,* 116–27; Pike, *VietCong,* 61–73, 102. According to Pike, NLF cadres kidnapped an 9,000 officials and murdered 1,700 in 1962, and kidnapped 7,200 and murdered 2,000 in 1963.

44. Porter, *Vietnam Documents,* vol. 2, Document 87, 169–74, "Short-term Prospects in South Vietnam," extract from a memo by Roger Hilsman, December 3, 1962. Hilsman noted the deterioration of internal security in South Vietnam occurring in 1962.

45. Maitland et al., *Raising the Stakes,* 37–41.

46. Ibid., 42–47; Young, *Vietnam Wars,* 84–86.

47. Ball, George, *The Past Has Another Pattern* (New York: W. W. Norton, 1982), 339.

48. Hallin, Daniel C., *The Uncensored War: The Media and Vietnam* (New York: Oxford University Press, 1986), 43–48.

49. See article titled "Vietnamese Reds Gain in Key Area," which appeared under Halberstam's byline on the front page of the August 15, 1963, *New York Times;* Rust, *Kennedy in Vietnam,* 81–84; Sheehan, Neil, "In Vietnam, the Birth of the Credibility Gap," *New York Times,* October 1, 1988, 15.

50. Schulzinger, *A Time for War,* 115–16.

51. U.S. Army Military History Research Collection, "Senior Officers Debriefing Program, Conversations between General Paul D. Harkins and Major Jacob B. Cough, Jr.," recorded at Carlisle Barracks, PA, 53;*Young,* Vietnam Wars, 90–92.

52. Karnow, *Vietnam,* 296–97.

53. Halberstam, *Quagmire,* 148–55, gives his account of the press controversy; Miroff, *Pragmatic Illusions,* 157–58.

54. Sheehan, "In Vietnam, the Birth of the Credibility Gap," 15; Knightley, Phillipp, *The First Casualty* (New York: Harcourt Brace Jovanovich, 1975), 376–83; Sheehan, Neil, *A Bright Shining Lie: John Paul Vann and America in Vietnam* (New York: Random House), 315–16.

55. Kahin, *Intervention,* 143–45; Young, *Vietnam Wars,* 94–95.

56. Maitland, *Raising the Stakes,* 56.

57. Young, *Vietnam Wars,* 94.

58. Extract of "Report to the President on Southeast Asia-Vietnam," by Senator Mike Mansfield, December 18, 1962, in Porter (ed.), *Vietnam Documents,* vol. 2, Document 88, 174–76.

59. Kahin, *Intervention,* 146–47.

60. David Halberstam witnessed Quang Duc's self-immolation. *Quagmire,* 113.

61. This means "reverend," or "the reverend." Madame Nhu's given name was Le Tran Xuan, meaning "beautiful spring."

62. Shaplen, *Lost Revolution,* 191–92.

63. Ibid.

64. Videotape, "America's Mandarin," from the television series, *Vietnam: A Television History.*

65. Kahin, *Intervention,* 152.

66. Shaplen, *Lost Revolution,* 197–201.

67. Kahin, *Intervention,* 153–56; Hammer, Ellen J., *A Death in November: America in Vietnam,* 1963 (New York: E. P. Dutton, 1987), 221–30. Hammer has examined all the pertinent documents and she cannot tell if Nhu was serious about seeking a rapprochement with Hanoi.

68. Sheehan and others, Cablegram from the State Department to Ambassador Henry Cabot Lodge in Saigon, August 24, 1963, Pentagon Papers, Document 35, 194–195. Its key passages: "U.S. government cannot tolerate situation in which power lies in Nhu's hands. Diem must be given chance to rid himself of Nhu and his coterie. (If in spite of all your efforts, Diem remains obdurate and refuses, then we must face the possibility that Diem himself cannot be preserved." Roger Hilsman drafted the cable.

69. Kahin, *Intervention,* 159–160; Hearden, Patrick J., *The Tragedy of Vietnam* (New York: Harper Collins, 1991), 95–96; excerpts from the Lodge cable are quoted in Olson and Roberts, *Where the Domino Fell,* 101.

70. Young, *Vietnam Wars,* 102.

71. Hilsman, *To Move a Nation,* 501–50.

72. Herring, *America's Longest War,* 102; Paul Kattenburg, a State Department expert on Vietnam, recalled being present at a National Security Council meeting held August 31, 1963, attended by Rusk, McNamara, Taylor, Johnson, and Robert Kennedy, as they discussed how to handle the crisis in South Vietnam. Kattenburg was appalled at their lack of knowledge about the culture and history of Vietnam, their lack of knowledge of the political situation and the war in Vietnam, and their inability to understand the identification of nationalism and Communism in Vietnam. Because of their lack of understanding, they were incapable of fashioning a coherent or effective Vietnam policy. Kattenburg's observations are taken from an interview cited in Gibbons, William Conrad, *The U.S. Government and the Vietnam War,* vol. 2 (Princeton, NJ: Princeton University Press, 1986), 161–62.

73. Herring, *America's Longest War,* 103.

74. Porter, *Vietnam Documents,* vol. 2, Document 109, 201–3, extract from "Report of the McNamara-Taylor Mission to South Vietnam," October 2, 1963.

75. Kahin, *Intervention,* 171; Young, *Vietnam Wars,* 100–101; Giglio, James N., *Presidency of John F. Kennedy* (Lawrence: University of Kansas Press, 1991), 251–52. See 239–54 for an excellent brief analysis of Kennedy's Vietnam policy.

76. Herring, *America's Longest War,* 104.

77. Sheehan et al., *Pentagon Papers.* See Documents 48–58, 213–31.

78. Ibid., "Lodge's Last Talk with Diem," Document 59, 232.

79. Shaplen, *Lost Revolution,* 208–11. Shaplen says about $600,000 was funneled through the U.S. embassy to the coup leaders, who used the money to bribe key generals stationed near Saigon into supporting the coup.

80. Interview with Lucien Conein recorded on videotape, "America's Mandarin," from the television series, *Vietnam: A Television History.* In 1972, the Senate Committee on Foreign Relations investigated U.S. complicity in the coup that overthrew Ngo Dinh Diem. The committee found extensive U.S. involvement. Senate Committee on Foreign Relations, *U.S. Involvement in the Overthrow of Ngo Dinh Diem, 1963,* 92nd Congress, 2nd session (Washington, DC: U.S. Government Printing Office, 1972).

81. Schulzinger, *A Time for War,* 122. Hersh, Seymour, *The Dark Side of Camelot,* a highly critical account of the Kennedy Presidency, cites an interview with Lucien Conein in which he states that Kennedy "must have known" that Diem would perish in the coup. But Hersh cited no other evidence other than Conein's deductive account.

82. Duiker, *The Communist Road,* 219–21.

83. Hess, *Vietnam,* 77.

84. Ibid.

85. Berman, Larry, *Planning,* 28.

86. Ibid. General William C. Westmoreland agrees with Johnson that Kennedy's involvement in the coup that destroyed Diem was a serious error that locked America into a war to defend South Vietnam. Rosen, James, "What's Hidden in the LBJ Tapes," *Weekly Standard,* September 19, 2003, says that President Johnson believed, erroneosly, that Kennedy had ordered the murder of Diem and Nhu

87. O'Donnell, Kenneth P., and Powers, David F.; with McCarthy, Joe, *Johnny, We Hardly Knew Ye: Memories of John Fitzgerald Kennedy* (Boston: Little, Brown, 1972), 15–17. Hilsman, *To Move a Nation,* chap. 34: "If Kennedy Had Lived?" 524–537. Hillman says that had he lived Kennedy would probably have opted for a negotiated settlement before he would have Americanized the war. William J. Rust, *Kennedy in Vietnam: American Vietnam Policy, 1960–1963,* believes that had Kennedy lived there would have been no American war in Vietnam. John M. Newman, *JFK and Vietnam: Deception, Intrigue, and the Struggle for Power* (New York: Warner, 1992), insists that Kennedy would never have placed U.S. combat troops in Vietnam and that he was planning to withdraw all American military advisers by the end of 1965.

88. Quoted on videotape, "Lyndon Johnson Goes to War, 1964–1965," from the television series, *Vietnam: A Television History.*

89. The excerpt from the speech Kennedy intended to deliver at the Dallas TradeMart comes from Schulzinger, *A Time for War,* 125.

90. Ibid., 122.

91. Giglio, *Presidency of John F. Kennedy,* 240.

92. Herring, *America's Longest War,* 3d ed., 119; Hammer, *Death in November,* 211.

93. Schlesinger, Arthur M., Jr., *A Thousand Days* (Greenich, CT: Fawcett, 1965), 909–10.

94. Walton, Richard J., *Cold War and Counter-Revolution: The Foreign Policy of John F. Kennedy* (Baltimore: Penguin, 1972), 201.

95. Hilsman, *To Move a Nation,* 501; Schlesinger, Arthur Meier, Jr.,*Robert Kennedy and His Times* (Boston: Houghton Mifflin, 1978), vol. 2, 746–47.

96. Rust, *Kennedy in Vietnam,* x. In an interview given after his brother's death, Robert Kennedy said that the president never considered either withdrawal or large-scale military intervention in Vietnam. When asked what John Kennedy would have done if the government of South Vietnam appeared about to fall to the Communists (the situation Johnson faced in the summer of 1965), Robert Kennedy, confirming the short-term, ad hoc, and cautious nature of the Kennedy Vietnam policy, said that his brother would have faced that problem when he came to it. John Kennedy at the time of his death probably had not made up his mind about what to do in Vietnam.

97. Young, *Vietnam Wars,* 103. Those who believe that had he lived Kennedy would have withdrawn U.S. forces from Vietnam and there would have been no American Vietnam war make much of NSAM 263 issued October 3, 1963. NSAM 263 announced that the U.S. military mission would be mostly completed by the end of 1965 and that 1,000 troops could be withdrawn by the end of 1963. The primary reason that the U.S. military mission was not completed and the troops not withdrawn as scheduled was because the military situation deteriorated. The VietCong, supported by regular North Vietnamese Army forces, taking advantage of the political chaos reigning in South Vietnam, pressed ever closer to victory in 1964 and 1965. About a thousand U.S. military advisers did come home, but they belonged to a construction battalion whose mission had been completed and Kennedy had ordered them replaced by other soldiers.

98. Herring, *America's Longest War,* 107.

CHAPTER 5

America Goes to War

I knew from the start that I was bound to be crucified either way I moved. If I left the woman I really loved—the Great Society—in order to get involved with that bitch of a war on the other side of the world, then I would lose everything at home. . . . But if I left that war and let the Communists take over South Vietnam, then I would be seen as a coward and my nation would be seen as an appeaser and we would both find it impossible to accomplish anything for anybody anywhere on the entire globe.

Lyndon B. Johnson

THE SAME ONLY MORE

Lyndon Johnson and his senior foreign policy advisers operated within an international diplomatic environment that they perceived to be changing as they turned their attention to Vietnam following Kennedy's death in late November 1963. The Sino-Soviet split appeared to be irrevocable; some U.S. officials believed that the two major Communist powers might have a war one day. The Sino-Soviet split also bore directly upon the expanding war in southern Vietnam. Hanoi supported China in its conflicts with the Soviets and "Soviet influence in Vietnam was negligible."[1] The United States no longer faced an international Communist monolith bent on world domination; the Soviet-Chinese conspiracy had fragmented into quarreling moieties.

Relations between the United States and Soviet Union had improved markedly since their confrontation in Cuba in October 1962 over Soviet efforts to install nuclear-capable intermediate range missiles in Cuba aimed at the United States. Negotiating a nuclear test ban treaty and grain deals with the Soviets in mid-1963 encouraged some

U.S. officials to hope for a lasting *détente* with the USSR. But the United States continued its policy of nonrecognition of China, trying to isolate the PRC from international life. U.S. officials saw China as an expansionist state seeking to assert leadership of revolutionary forces in Southeast Asia and elsewhere among other Third World nations.

To U.S. officials, Southeast Asia appeared especially vulnerable to Chinese intrusions in late 1963. South Vietnam was descending into political chaos in the aftermath of Diem's death. Both leftist and rightist forces challenged the fragile neutralist government of Laos. In Cambodia, Prince Sihanouk had cast off both U.S. aid and offers of protection. In Indonesia, Sukarno was seeking Chinese support for his war against a pro-Western government in Malaysia, a country in which China had supported an insurgency during the early 1950s. Washington feared that China might try to exploit the political disorder in countries along China's southern periphery and that the food-short Chinese might be tempted to overrun the rich rice baskets of Southeast Asia.

The winds of change blowing in other regions of the world heralded the dawning of a more polycentric world order in late 1963. In Western Europe, De Gaulle was challenging the U.S. dominance of the NATO alliance and was trying to reassert French influence in Vietnam. Rioting, revolution, and rising anti-Americanism in Latin America fueled U.S. fears of a spreading Castroism within a region long dominated by the "Yanqui" colossus. Birthing pains among African nations emerging from a colonial past posed threats to world stability. A superpower confrontation in the Congo had been averted in 1961 by a United Nations intervention.

U.S. officials feared that the Communist powers might become involved in some of these Third World trouble spots and that such interventions could bring, *inter alia,* confrontations with the United States and the threat of nuclear war. It is within this context of a more fluid, unstable, and polycentric world order, in which the chief threat to American strategic interests appeared to emanate from Chinese expansionism in Southeast Asia, that Johnson and his senior advisers forged their Vietnam policies.

President Johnson inherited from his late predecessor both a strong commitment to the survival of a non-Communist South Vietnamese state and a group of advisers who had orchestrated that commitment. A brilliantly successful domestic politician, Johnson was initially neither very knowledgeable about nor confident of his grasp of foreign affairs. The methods that had worked for him at home—a subtle amalgam of strong-arm politics, favors, flattery, and compromise to form coalitions based on a consensus of all interested parties—could not be applied to the international realm. In contrast to his mastery of domestic political processes, Johnson often found himself beyond his depth when conducting U.S. foreign policy. Compounding his difficulties in Southeast Asia, in addition to the frustrating limits on U.S. power to influence events in that troubled region, was Johnson's profound ignorance of the history and culture of the Vietnamese people. He never grasped the dynamics of the Vietnamese revolutionary war strategy, nor did he ever comprehend the ideologies or psychologies of its leaders. He persisted in trying to understand the peculiarly Vietnamese dynamics of national revolution by applying the Procrustean concepts of the U.S. anti-Communist Cold War ideology.

To a greater degree than Kennedy, Johnson relied on the knowledge and judgment of his senior foreign policy advisers. From late-1964 to mid-1965, during which time Johnson transformed "a limited commitment to assist the South Vietnamese government into an open-ended commitment to preserve an independent, non-Communist South Vietnam,"[2] and took his nation to war, the men who most influenced the shaping of Southeast Asian policy were a coterie of Kennedy holdovers: Secretary of Defense Robert S. McNamara, National Security Adviser McGeorge Bundy, Secretary of State Dean Rusk, and U.S. Ambassador to South Vietnam Maxwell Taylor. Johnson "had inherited the policy and the men who made it."[3] Of these men, McNamara, through his *ex officio* clout, forceful personality, and a keen analytic mind, which absorbed enormous amounts of factual data, exerted the greatest formative influence on Johnson's Vietnam policy.

Vietnam did not dominate Johnson's presidency during his first year; he had entered the White House committed to fighting another kind of war than the one raging in southern Vietnam. Early in his presidency, he had declared "unconditional war on poverty in America."[4] Johnson intended the fight against poverty to be an integral part of what he labeled a "Great Society," a broad range of welfare, social reform, and civil rights legislation that he would soon propose to Congress.[5] In Johnson's expansive view, his Great Society would fulfill the social vision of the New Deal by eradicating residual poverty and racial injustice. The new president would use the powers of the federal government to bring the 40 million Americans still denied equal access to the American dream into the socioeconomic mainstream. Creating his Great Society would also ensure Johnson, a man of vaulting ambitions and possessor of an outsized ego, an honored place in the national memory. It would be his great legacy.

It is one of the many ironic dimensions of the American Vietnam ordeal that Lyndon Johnson, the man whose highest goal had been to expand the American system to include all its citizens, felt compelled to Americanize the war in Southeast Asia, a foreign war that soon curtailed his domestic war on poverty, slowed the march of civil rights, and strangled his Great Society. The war in Southeast Asia that President Johnson and his advisers set in motion eventually claimed the lives of over 58,000 of their fellow citizens, a disproportionately high number of whom had come from the ranks of the disadvantaged classes, whom Johnson had committed himself to helping. From the ranks of the strongest supporters of Johnson's ill-fated Great Society reform program would come some of the most cogent critics of his Vietnam War policies.

Johnson and his advisers quickly embraced the U.S. commitment in Vietnam, considering it an integral part of the Kennedy agenda that the new President, in his first speech to the American people, had pledged to continue.[6] Like Truman, Eisenhower, and Kennedy before him, Johnson considered Southeast Asia a vital strategic interest of the United States. He brusquely dismissed any suggestions that the region might be of only marginal importance or that the United States might consider withdrawing from South Vietnam. Two days after becoming president, he boldly asserted, "I am not going to lose Vietnam. I am not going to be the president who saw Southeast Asia go the way China went."[7]

Although Johnson embraced immediately the U.S. commitment in South Vietnam, he shared Kennedy's reluctance to invest large amounts of U.S. military power in the region. He did not want to fight another land war in Asia, nor did he want to bomb the North. He feared that large-scale U.S. military intervention would undermine the ability of the South Vietnamese forces to fight their enemies aggressively. The new president also feared that the injection of U.S. combat forces into the Vietnam War would provoke adverse reactions throughout the world and trigger uprisings of domestic opposition that could stifle his domestic reform program and cost him the 1964 presidential election. He rejected initial proposals from the Joint Chiefs of Staff to "undertake major air and ground operations against North Vietnam."[8] Johnson understood the dilemma that had plagued his predecessor concerning U.S. Vietnam policy: "Doing more, doing less, or doing the same all entailed enormous risks."[9]

Within 48 hours of Kennedy's death, Johnson held a full-scale briefing on Vietnam, which was attended by all of his senior foreign policy advisers. He was informed that the new military government of South Vietnam was struggling. It was not broadening its base of support, and the war was going badly for ARVN forces in many provinces. At this meeting, Johnson opted for a continuation of Kennedy's policy of sending U.S. military advisers to South Vietnam, along with substantial amounts of economic and military aid. In addition, he approved the conduct of covert operations within eastern Laos and North Vietnam. The conferees drafted a National Security Action Memorandum (NSAM 273) stressing the continuity of policy between his and his predecessor's administrations:

> It remains the Central Objective of the United States in South Vietnam to assist the people and government of that country to win their contest against the externally directed and supported Communist conspiracy.[10]

The NSAM 273, along with subsequent increases in the number of advisers and the amount of aid going to South Vietnam, and a step-up of covert operations against the DRV, constituted Johnson's Vietnam policy for the first year of his presidency. Johnson adopted a policy of doing the same that Kennedy had done, only doing more of it.

COUP SEASON

As Johnson reaffirmed the U.S. commitment to Saigon, General Minh, the leader of the Military Revolutionary Council (MRC), the new ruling junta in South Vietnam, rid his country of the last vestiges of Ngo Dinh family rule. General Minh unshackled the press, emptied Ngo Dinh Nhu's political prisons, and restored Saigon's vibrant café and night life. Saigon once again became a cheerful and noisy cosmopolitan city. And once again, the city's fragmented political life erupted. Religious sectarians, students, labor leaders, intellectuals, socialists, and especially the Buddhists and Catholics, quarreled heatedly over the political future of their unstable and fragile state.

In the South Vietnamese countryside, the VietCong continued to enhance its control of people and territory.[11] In December 1963, meeting in Hanoi in a special session, the Central Committee of the Lao Dong, after much debate among the delegates, enacted a series of resolutions that decisively influenced the course the insurgency in South Vietnam would take over the next 18 months. The Central Committee issued a directive calling for an escalation of the southern insurgency and for increased support for the revolution from the DRV. The Communist leaders knew that they were running out of regroupees to send south and that they could not win the war without a major commitment of their own military forces. They issued new directives stressing that winning the insurgency in the South was not only a task for southerners, it was a task for all the Vietnamese people, North and South. Preparations were made to improve the Ho Chi Minh Trail complex and to infiltrate PAVN units into southern Vietnam.

The Communist leadership decided that the time had come to move toward the final stage of the revolutionary struggle, a general counteroffensive paralleled by popular risings in the cities that would topple the South Vietnamese government. They realized their escalations ran the risk of a war with the United States, but they hoped their efforts would bring about the rapid collapse of the South Vietnamese government and the forced withdrawal of their American patrons without a fight. The aging revolutionary leaders in Hanoi made a huge miscalculation; they gambled and lost. Their efforts to bring about a more rapid demise of South Vietnam and force the Americans out provoked a major war with the United States that delayed the completion of the Vietnamese national revolution for more than a decade, cost an estimated 3 million lives, and brought extensive physical destruction to their nation.[12]

The new Saigon government alarmed U.S. officials when it quickly demonstrated a penchant for acting independently. It soon proved to be more interested in seeking a negotiated settlement of the conflict than in fighting the PLAF forces. Hoping to move the conflict in South Vietnam from the military to the political plane, the MRC sought the support of rural elements, the sects, Buddhists, and even some of the factions within the NLF. The Saigon generals opposed any proposals by Americans to increase the U.S. advisory role in the conduct of ARVN operations or to expand the war against the NLF. They also opposed U.S. plans for taking the war to the North, especially a bombing campaign against North Vietnam.

General Minh and his colleagues believed that the appeal of the VietCong had been lessened by Diem's overthrow and that the rural population would be more responsive to government programs administered by local officials acting independently of the Americans. A conciliatory approach that had the villagers' interests at heart would be more effective than Diemist corruption, repression, and the strategic hamlets. The MRC would strive to form a government of national reconciliation that would seek to coexist peacefully with Hanoi. Most members of the Military Council, including generals

Minh and Don, had formerly served in the French colonial forces, and they were responsive to French President Charles De Gaulle's offer to help the Vietnamese achieve a peaceful reunion of their country, free of external influences, including America influence. Ultimately Minh and most of his colleagues would have looked to a neutralist coalition government with the NLF.

Johnson administration officials, both in Saigon and Washington, angrily rejected the prospect of French intrusion into Vietnamese politics, a cease-fire, negotiations with NLF elements, and the formation of a neutralist coalition government that might ask the Americans to leave. Such possibilities risked the collapse of the American rationale for intervention in southern Vietnam that had prevailed for a decade. Washington held neutralization of South Vietnam in anathema; in their view, it would be tantamount to defeat, because it would leave the Communists in a dominant position throughout Indochina, "a situation that would have adverse effects throughout Southeast Asia."[13]

From Washingtron's perspective, the political and strategic situation in southern Vietnam deteriorated rapidly in the months following Diem's demise. The Buddhists and Catholics, the most powerful political factions in Saigon, waged bitter internecine warfare. In the rural areas, provincial governments verged on collapse. The remaining strategic hamlets were being dismantled, often by their peasant occupants who viewed them more as internment camps than havens.[14] The NLF continued to expand its influence in the South. The MRC proved incapable of governing the fractious politicians of South Vietnam and unwilling to fight the VietCong.

The coup that had destroyed Diem's family oligarchy had also deepened the divisions among U.S. officials concerned with the conduct of U.S. Vietnam policy. Military officials, particularly MACV Commander General Paul Harkins, who had opposed the coup, in turn opposed the new government because of its unwillingness to fight the NLF aggressively. Ambassador Lodge, who had spearheaded the U.S. support of the coup that destroyed Diem, backed Minh and the other MRC leaders and tried to isolate Harkins from policy affairs.

Minh's junta was not destined to remain in power for long, nor to have much of an opportunity to try its conciliatory approach in the countryside. During the brief reign of the MRC, tensions and rivalries persisted among ARVN leaders, including members of the ruling council. One of these leaders, Major General Nguyen Khanh, who had supported the coup but was not a member of the ruling council, began plotting his own coup to overthrow the Minh-Don group. Khanh was motivated by his fears that the current leaders could not manage the war against the PLAF. He was supported by General Harkins and some members of Harkins's military advisory group, particularly Colonel Jasper Wilson. Wilson helped shift the balance of power among ARVN commanders toward Khanh and he kept Harkins informed of the plot's progress. Khanh's coup also enjoyed the tacit support of Taylor and McNamara, who wanted to be rid of leaders they perceived as inept, pro-French neutralists unable to either fight or govern effectively.[15] The bloodless coup that brought Khanh to power occurred on January 30, 1964. President Johnson, having opposed the overthrow of Diem, was pleased with the advent of Khanh, who appeared eager to cooperate with U.S. officials and get on with the war.

Khanh's bid for power opened the coup season in southern Vietnam. There would be five more coups during the next year, and South Vietnam would have seven governments in 1964 alone. As the succession of coups made a travesty of South Vietnamese political processes and poisoned political life, U.S. officials pleaded with their charges to maintain at least a semblance of political stability. Without a stable government in Saigon, U.S. officials feared that the war against the VietCong could be lost.

Hoping that he was the man to rally his people and turn the war around, U.S. officials supported General Khanh. Khanh also appealed to the Americans because he was the first South Vietnamese leader who promised to accept their advice. McNamara and Taylor accompanied Khanh on a barnstorming tour of South Vietnam, a public relations effort designed to sell the little-known leader to his own people. The trio appeared at rallies in several cities, with Khanh standing in the middle, flanked by Taylor and McNamara, both raising Khanh's arms in triumphalist displays of Allied unity. At these rallies, McNamara liked to shout *"Vietnam Muon Nam"* (Vietnam a thousand years), but he failed to achieve the proper pitch and pronunciation. To many Vietnamese in the audience, McNamara's shoutings sounded like "Southern duck wants to lie down."[16] These rallies may have had the opposite effect from that intended by the Americans. They made Khanh, a short, squat man standing between two tall U.S. officials, appear inconsequential, even undignified.

Back from his efforts at promoting General Khanh, McNamara submitted a pessimistic report to Johnson on March 16, 1964. In his report, McNamara noted the deterioration of the political and military situation in the South, occurring since Diem's downfall. He estimated that the VietCong now controlled about 30 to 40 percent of the territory. In 22 of 43 provinces the VietCong controlled at least 50 percent of the land area. McNamara also noted that in many areas administered by Saigon, much of the population had no interest in supporting the ARVN cause. Village defense forces refused to fight, deserted, and often joined the VietCong. The ARVN desertion rates and draft dodging were high, while the VietCong were energetically recruiting new forces in many of the rural provinces. Displacing Minh with Khanh had not arrested the growing antiwar and neutralist sentiment among people residing in Saigon-controlled areas, especially among the Buddhists. To revive the nearly moribund war effort, McNamara recommended increasing the size of ARVN forces, augmenting U.S. economic and military aid, and developing a plan for taking the war to North Vietnam.[17]

The next day, Johnson met with the National Security Council to consider McNamara's recommendations. After a brief debate, Johnson decided to implement most of McNamara's proposals, a decision that amounted to continuing the U.S. advisory role in South Vietnam on an expanded scale. National Security Action Memorandum 288 (NSAM 288), issued on March 17, restated the American goal: to preserve an independent, non-Communist South Vietnam, which was necessary to prevent all Southeast

Asia from turning Communist and to prove to the rest of the world that Communist wars of national liberation could be curtailed. The NSAM 288 called for a national mobilization plan to put South Vietnam on a war footing and for major increases in the number of ARVN forces. The memorandum also approved increases in various U.S. aid programs and in the number of U.S. military advisers serving in South Vietnam.[18]

At about the same time that Johnson implemented McNamara's recommendations, an interagency study group, working under State Department auspices, proposed a series of military operations against North Vietnam. The study group's most important recommendation was aerial bombing. Bombing would put military pressure on the North, threaten to destroy their nascent industrial economy, and demonstrate U.S. power and resolve to the Khanh government, Hanoi, Beijing, Moscow, and the rest of the world. The urge to take the war north had many roots, but apparently the prime concern was to bolster the flagging morale of the South Vietnamese leaders. William Bundy, a member of the interagency group, also drafted a proposed Congressional resolution authorizing the president to wage war against North Vietnam.[19]

In late May the Joint Chiefs proposed a sequence of carefully graduated military operations against North Vietnam. The Joint Chiefs' scenario incorporated many of the recommendations of the State Department's interagency group. These proposals included bombing missions and the mining of North Vietnamese ports. The Joint Chiefs also recommended that these military operations be accompanied by consultations with U.S. allies and that Congress enact a resolution authorizing the president to do "whatever is necessary with respect to Vietnam." The proposed scenario stressed the gradualist, restrained, and limited nature of these military actions. The operations were not designed to destroy North Vietnam; they were only intended to persuade Hanoi to stop supporting the insurrection in South Vietnam by threatening the Northerners with ever greater punishment if they did not. How much punishment the North received would be up to them, because at each step of the way they would be given a chance to call off their support of the southern insurgency.[20] "The bland language of the scenario masked a stern reality: However modern and reasonable it sounded, the logic of calibrated response was the logic of the rack, articulated in the language of games theory and the accountant's spread sheet."[21] The Joint Chiefs' scenario also revealed a growing tendency among U.S. officials to look to North Vietnam for a solution that continued to elude them in South Vietnam. Further, the proposals showed a growing tendency to resolve South Vietnam's serious social, economic, and political problems by military means.[22]

By June 1964, Johnson had available a scenario prepared by the Joint Chiefs, recommending a carefully calibrated series of military operations against North Vietnam designed to force them to abandon their support of the revolution raging in South Vietnam or gradually incur extensive damage to their industrial sectors. In addition to these contingency plans prepared by his senior military advisers, the president also had a draft copy of a proposed Congressional resolution authorizing him to take the war to North Vietnam. Johnson, who believed that Harry Truman had made a serious mistake when he failed to seek congressional approval for the Korean intervention in 1950, planned to seek a congressional authorization if and when he decided to take the war to North Vietnam.

But Johnson was not ready to widen the war in Vietnam at that time. He continued to be reluctant to shift his emphasis from social reform at home to waging a major foreign war. He doubted that military power alone could solve South Vietnam's many unresolved problems. He could not be certain that the proposed military measures would cause North Vietnam to abandon the southern insurgents. Even if Hanoi did stop supporting the NLF, the VietCong might be able to continue their rebellion indefinitely unless the Khanh government mounted an effective counterinsurgency campaign. Johnson could not count on strong congressional, media, or public support for making war on North Vietnam without advance preparation or a clear cause. Rather than adopt the Joint Chiefs' scenario for war against North Vietnam in June 1964, Johnson authorized instead an increase in the covert campaign against North Vietnam that he had approved at the outset of his presidency. These operations, code-named Operations Plan 34-Alpha (OPLAN 34-A), included air and naval surveillance missions and commando raids against radar sites and coastal military installations. In addition, Johnson also ordered U.S. pilots to attack Pathet Lao positions along the Laotian panhandle to disrupt North Vietnamese supply lines that ran through that area.[23]

As he authorized the step-up in covert operations against North Vietnamese targets, Johnson also sent a warning to Hanoi via Blair Seaborn, the Canadian representative on the International Control Commission (ICC). Seaborn was instructed to tell the North Vietnamese leadership to stop supporting the VietCong effort in South Vietnam or the United States would attack North Vietnam with devastating results. The DRV Premier Pham Van Dong, meeting with Blair, defiantly told him to tell the U.S. leaders that the DRV would continue to support the NLF until it prevailed. He also told Seaborn that the American choices in Vietnam amounted to either continuing indefinitely a war they could not win or accepting a neutral South Vietnam and withdrawing.[24]

Despite the great expectations of McNamara, Taylor, and his other American sponsors, General Khanh quickly showed himself as an ineffective leader and war manager. The people did not rally to his leadership in the towns and cities. Saigon's numerous political factions continued their quarrels with each other and with Khanh. In the countryside, the VietCong continued to maintain the initiative, and their military forces grew larger and more aggressive. The insurgents, as they continued their assaults on ARVN forces, also launched terrorist attacks against U.S. advisers. The North Vietnamese continued their support of the revolutionaries in the South.

By the summer of 1964, Johnson was gearing himself up for a reelection battle at a time when there was growing concern within the Congress and among segments of the American public about Vietnam. A television documentary produced by CBS reflected rising public worries about what the Johnson administration intended to do in Vietnam if the VietCong continued to gain ground and the Saigon government continued to decline. Johnson decided to wait until after the election to confront the Vietnam conundrum. Delay would also permit him to seek reelection as a moderate but firm peace candidate offsetting the appeal of his belligerent hawkish challenger, conservative Republican Senator Barry Goldwater. Besides, any major commitment of U.S. military forces in Vietnam could only be sold to the American people as a response to overt acts of war against U.S. forces by the North Vietnamese or the National Liberation Front, and none appeared forthcoming.[25]

IN DUBIOUS BATTLE

During the first few days of August 1964, a series of controversial incidents took place in the Gulf of Tonkin involving U.S. and North Vietnamese naval forces. These incidents brought about the implementation of many of the proposed military actions against North Vietnam, including the first U.S. bombings of North Vietnamese targets. They also brought about the enactment of a resolution that granted President Johnson the equivalent of a blank check to wage war in Vietnam. The bombing raids and rapid passage of the congressional resolution convinced the Communist leaders in Hanoi that the United States was planning to wage a major war in Vietnam, a war against them as well as against the National Liberation Front forces in South Vietnam.

On Sunday morning, August 2, three North Vietnamese torpedo boats attacked the destroyer USS *Maddox,* which was engaged in an electronic surveillance mission, code-named DESOTO patrol, off the coast of North Vietnam. Two nights earlier, South Vietnamese patrol boats had attacked North Vietnamese military and radar installations on the offshore islands of Hon Me and Hon Nieu, in the vicinity where the *Maddox* was patrolling when it was attacked. The South Vietnamese raids were part of the series of OPLAN 34-A covert operations that the CIA and military intelligence groups periodically conducted against North Vietnam to harass the North Vietnamese. The North Vietnamese naval command, probably linking the DESOTO patrol with the earlier night's OPLAN 34-A assaults, ordered its boats to attack the *Maddox,* whose patrol route at times brought it to within eight miles of North Vietnam's mainland coast and within four miles of its offshore islands.[26]

In a brief encounter, *Maddox* opened fire with its three-inch and five-inch guns, badly damaging one of the attacking boats. Naval aircraft operating from the nearby carrier USS *Ticonderoga* attacked the torpedo boats, firing rockets and strafing them with 20 mm cannons. They inflicted damage on all three as the boats headed back toward their bases. The *Maddox* sustained very minor damage (one enemy 14.5 mm machine-gun bullet pierced one of its aft electronic gunfire directors).[27]

In Washington, 10,000 miles away, President Johnson reacted angrily but with restraint to the news of an attack on a U.S. warship. Some of his advisers called for retaliatory air strikes against North Vietnamese targets. One of those officials who favored this course of action was the newly appointed U.S. ambassador to South Vietnam, General Maxwell Taylor. General Khanh also called for air strikes against North Vietnam.[28]

Resisting pressures to bomb North Vietnam, Johnson instead directed the Navy to order the *Maddox* to resume its patrols, this time joined by another destroyer, the

Figure 5.1 The U.S. Destroyer *Maddox* was engaged in electronic surveillance along the coast of North Vietnam when it was attacked by North Vietnamese torpedo boats on August 2, 1964. *Source:* AP/Wide World Photo.

USS *Turner Joy*. The destroyers continued to cruise along North Vietnamese shores, but were careful to get no closer than 16 miles. The Pentagon put U.S. combat forces on alert and a U.S. fighter-bomber squadron in Thailand was strengthened. Johnson also took the precaution of using a recently installed "hot line" to tell the Soviets not to be alarmed by the presence of two U.S. warships in international waters just off the coast of North Vietnam. The President took these military actions to assert traditional U.S. claims to freedom of the seas and to demonstrate to the North Vietnamese officials that the United States was not intimidated by the torpedo boat assaults.

Johnson had been notified that additional OPLAN 34-A raids were scheduled for the same general area the night of August 3. His advisers had also informed him that they believed that the North Vietnamese patrol boats had attacked the *Maddox* because their leaders apparently connected the DESOTO patrol with the OPLAN 34-A attack. Even though U.S. officials denied that there were any connections between the patrols and the commando raids, Johnson knew that ordering the destroyers to resume their patrols risked additional attacks on the U.S. warships. Johnson was not trying to provoke a fight with North Vietnam, but he was not going out of his way to avoid one either.[29]

At 7:15 P.M., on the evening of August 4, Captain John J. Herrick, onboard the *Maddox,* the commander of the DESOTO operation, received a warning from the National Security Agency (NSA) that three North Vietnamese boats operating in the vicinity of Hon Me Island were preparing to attack the two destroyers. At 7:46 P.M., the *Maddox* picked up a radar contact traveling at high speed about 35 miles to the north. The two ships, the *Maddox* and *Turner Joy,* wheeled about and headed southeast in the direction of the *Ticonderoga,* about 200 miles away, with the *Maddox* in the lead and the *Turner Joy* following 1,000 yards astern. About 30 minutes later, both destroyers, spotting three more radar contacts, went to general quarters and called for air support. Shipboard analysts evaluated the blips on their radar screens as North Vietnamese patrol boats attempting to set an ambush for the destroyers. Six aircraft soon arrived overhead from *Ticonderoga,* having been dispatched 50 minutes earlier, and they searched the area but could find no enemy boats. At 9:34 P.M. the confusion began. Both destroyers, now 60 miles from the North Vietnamese coast and 180 miles north of the DMZ, began shooting at radar targets. Herrick also began sending messages stating that his ships were under attack. The sonar operator on board the *Maddox* reported many torpedoes in the water. Crewmen on board both ships reported that they saw torpedo wakes in the water.[30] Almost everyone onboard the two destroyers believed at the time that they were under attack. They were mistaken. There was no second attack.

There were clouds, rain storms, heavy surface fog, and it was a moonless night. Twenty-knot winds churned the sea. Surface visibility was near zero. Herrick's attack reports were based on evaluations of radar and sonar contacts. Naval aircraft flying cover over the two destroyers at low altitude and searching for the alleged attacking boats could never find them, nor did the pilots ever see any torpedo wakes, even though they could easily spot the wakes of the destroyers.[31]

For two hours, the two destroyers zigged and zagged furiously around an area of the Gulf of Tonkin in efforts to avoid what their officers and most crewmen thought were torpedo attacks. They fired hundreds of rounds of three- and five-inch shells at their unseen targets, laid depth charges at shallow depths, and even tried to ram their invisible attackers. The Navy pilots, on orders from the destroyers, fired missiles into the ocean at unseen targets. Herrick, trying to evaluate the confusing situation, dispatched a later message expressing his doubts that either of the destroyers had been attacked the night of August 4. He stated that he believed that enemy patrol boats had attempted an ambush earlier in the evening, but that it never occurred because Herrick had maneuvered his ships away from the ambush area. He urged a complete evaluation of the night's events before any further action was taken. He attributed the radar and sonar contacts to weather effects, and to his crew's inexperience and anxiety.[32]

While the two destroyers raced around in Gulf of Tonkin waters firing at unseen targets, in Washington, Johnson, informed that a second attack in two days had been made on U.S. ships on the high seas, ordered retaliatory air strikes against North Vietnamese targets. He concluded that the North Vietnamese were trying to make the United States look weak and ineffectual, like a "paper tiger." President Johnson also decided that it was a propitious moment to have his long-awaited congressional resolution enacted. McNamara, the chief architect of Johnson's evolving war policy, took charge of preparing the reprisal attacks. While the Joint Chiefs of Staff readied a strike execute order, McNamara sought confirmation that the second attack had occurred. He discounted Captain Herrick's cautionary message. He asked Admiral U.S. Grant Sharp, Commander of the Pacific Fleet (CINCPACFLT), about the latest reports from the destroyers. Admiral Sharp, who had not read Herrick's cautionary message at the time McNamara called him, told McNamara that there was little doubt that a second attack had occurred. The evidence that convinced McNamara that there had been a second attack came from NSA radio intercepts of North Vietnamese naval communications, which had been made during the battle. While the military prepared the air strike plan and McNamara sought his confirmation, other officials finalized the wording of the resolution to be sent to Congress. Johnson meanwhile met with congressional leaders to inform them of the incidents and to solicit their support for the resolution that would sanction the retaliatory attacks.[33]

Three years after the United States had gone to war in Vietnam, the Senate Foreign Relations Committee conducted a full-scale investigation of the Gulf of Tonkin incidents. Several of its members challenged the validity of the August 4 attack. McNamara, testifying before the committee, insisted that the NSA intercepts proved that the attack in question had taken place. Electronic intelligence experts who have seen the intercepts have refuted McNamara's contention. Ray S. Cline, former CIA deputy director of intelligence, who carefully analyzed the contents of the NSA intercepts, concluded that the messages received at the time of the second attack, because of the time differences involved, were after action reports on the first attack occurring on August 2.[34] Louis Tordella, a former deputy director of the NSA, after a careful analysis of the same intercepts, reached the same conclusion.[35]

Years later, James B. Stockdale further undermined McNamara's credibility concerning the Gulf of Tonkin incidents. On August 2, 1964, Commander Stockdale was the flight leader of the aircraft that had driven off the patrol boats attacking the *Maddox*. On August 4, when the second attack was supposed to have occurred, Stockdale also led the flight that provided supporting cover for the two destroyers that dark and stormy night out in the Gulf of Tonkin. Stockdale has written a revealing account of the events of that controversial night in the Gulf of Tonkin:

I had the best seat in the house from which to detect boats—if there were any. I didn't have to look through surface haze and spray like the destroyers did and yet I could see the destroyers' every move vividly. Time and time again I flew over the *Maddox* and the *Joy*, throttled back, lights out, like a near-silent stalking owl, conserving fuel at a 250-knot loiter speed. (When the destroyers were convinced that they had some battle action going, I zigged and zagged and fired where they fired.) The edges of the black hole I was flying in were still periodically lit by flashes of lightning—but no wakes or dark shapes other than those of the destroyers were ever visible to me.[36]

Ironically, on August 5, 1964, Stockdale led one of the raids against North Vietnam retaliating for an attack that he knew had never occurred. He remembered thinking at the time that Washington officials had acted hastily and irrationally. Five days later, Stockdale was visited by two of McNamara's assistants who asked him if there had been any boats attacking the destroyers the night of August 4! He told them that he never saw any. President Johnson voiced his doubts that a second attack had occurred a few days after ordering the retaliatory raids when he told George Ball, "Hell, those dumb, stupid sailors were just shooting at flying fish." However, Johnson ordered the DESOTO patrols to continue, but he also separated them from OPLAN 34-A raids. On the night of September 18, there occurred a replay of the August 4 incident, complete with radar and sonar contacts, reports of torpedoes in the water, ships firing at unseen targets, aircraft flying overhead unable to spot any enemy boats, and advisers calling for more retaliatory raids. Johnson, cautious this time, refused to order more sorties against North Vietnamese targets.[37]

But McNamara, in the crisis atmosphere prevailing in Washington on August 4, 1964, preferred quick action to restrained analysis. At a short National Security Council Meeting, McNamara confirmed the second attack for the president, and plans for the retaliatory raids were finalized. President Johnson wanted the reprisal raids timed so that they would be occurring at the same moment he would be explaining to the American people why he had ordered the bombing of North Vietnamese targets. He told the American people that he had ordered the raids to retaliate for "open aggression on the high seas against the United States of America." He also reassured the public, by noting that "We seek no wider war."[38]

But the air raids, code-named PIERCE ARROW, were delayed; the first planes attacked their targets 90 minutes after the president's speech. Naval aircraft from the *Ticonderoga* and *Constellation* flew 64 sorties against four North Vietnamese naval bases and an oil supply facility. The raiders destroyed or damaged several boats and did significant damage to the oil storage complex. During the strikes, two U.S. aircraft were shot down. One pilot was killed and the other, Lt. (j.g.) Everett Alvarez, was captured. He was the first of 826 American pilots and air crewmen known to have been captured by the North Vietnamese, and he spent eight and one-half years as a prisoner of war.[39]

On August 5, the resolution was sent to Congress. The next day the Senate committees on Foreign Relations and Armed Services met in joint session to consider it. Senator William J. Fulbright, chairman of the Foreign Relations Committee, presided over the hearings. Johnson urged Fulbright to move the resolution through quickly so it would have the maximum impact. The president assured his friend that he planned no wider war after the retaliatory raids. At the committee hearings, McNamara presented the administration's version of the events. McNamara portrayed the ambiguous incidents occurring in the Gulf of Tonkin as clear and simple acts of aggression: They were unprovoked attacks against U.S. ships engaged in routine patrols in international waters. He made no mention of the OPLAN 34-A raids, and he did not tell the senators that the destroyers were on spy missions. Although he was aware that the North Vietnamese may have presumed a linkage between the OPLAN 34-A raids and the DESOTO patrols, McNamara told the senators that he could give no rational explanation for the attacks. He portrayed them as irrational acts of aggression.[40]

All but one of the senators on the two committees accepted McNamara's duplicitous version of the Gulf of Tonkin incidents. The lone challenge came from Oregon's Wayne Morse. An anonymous Pentagon leaker had informed Morse of the OPLAN 34-A raids and DESOTO patrols. Morse tried to link the clandestine raids with the attacks on the ships. McNamara categorically denied that there could be any connection and reiterated that the Maddox was on a routine patrol in international waters both times it was attacked.[41] No other senators were interested in pursuing Morse's line of questioning. The committees voted 31 to one to send the resolution to the full Senate; Morse cast the lone dissenting vote.

The next day, Fulbright, who would turn against the war within a year and become the Senate's most prominent dovish critic of Johnson's policy, guided the resolution rapidly through the full Senate, allowing only perfunctory debate. Long accustomed to routinely approving presidential foreign policy initiatives and sharing the administration's view that the United States had to respond to acts of aggression against its armed forces, nearly all of the senators approved the resolution unquestioningly. And nearly all appeared unconcerned about the possible uses a president might make of it.

Although he supported the resolution, Senator Frank Church of Idaho observed that U.S. policy toward Vietnam was "more a product of our own addiction to an ideological view of world affairs . . . rather than a policy based on a detached and pragmatic view of our real national interests." Maryland Senator Daniel Brewster asked Fulbright if the resolution would approve sending armies to fight in Vietnam. Fulbright told him that it would. Wisconsin Senator Gaylord Nelson proposed an amendment making it clear that Congress, by passing the resolution, was not authorizing a change in the U.S. advisory role in Vietnam, nor approving an expansion of the American commitment in South Vietnam. Fulbright, who agreed in principle with Nelson, talked him out of adding the amendment by telling him that it would only cause confusion and delay. Kentucky's John Sherman Cooper asked Fulbright if the resolution would grant the president the power to take the country to war. Fulbright, who later repudiated the role that he played in rushing the Gulf of Tonkin resolution through the Senate, replied that it would. Fulbright also observed that while he did not believe that President Johnson intended to bomb North Vietnam, the resolution allowed him to do so. Fulbright also acknowledged that in case the president decided to involve United States in a full-scale war in Vietnam, he probably would not seek a declaration of war from Congress. In that case, the resolution would serve as a formal declaration of war.[42]

Senator Morse continued to oppose the resolution. He was joined by 83-year-old Alaska Senator Ernest Gruening, who opposed the broad grant of power to the president conveyed by the resolution. Greuning had earlier denounced the American efforts in southern Vietnam:

> All Vietnam is not worth the life of an American boy. The United States is seeking vainly in this remote jungle to shore up self-serving corrupt dynasties or their self-imposed successors, and a people that has demonstrated that it has no will to save itself.[43]

Knowing that the resolution would soon clear the Senate overwhelmingly, Senator Morse denounced the Johnson administration. He charged that the United States had provoked the attacks by escorting the South Vietnamese boats close to North Vietnam's shores. He also accused U.S. officials of covering up South Vietnam's attacks on North Vietnam's military installations. He further accused Washington officials of violating the United Nations charter by refusing to seek a peaceful resolution of the conflict and by bombing North Vietnamese targets in retaliation for the attacks on U.S. destroyers. With remarkable prescience, Senator Morse forecast a disastrous outcome for the U.S. involvement in Indochina similar to the French catastrophe. He predicted the United States would soon be engaged in full-scale war in Vietnam, having to deploy hundreds of thousands of combat forces and necessarily incurring tens of thousands of casualties. He also predicted that the American people would one day repudiate the current administration for its perfidy and folly in the Gulf of Tonkin, and would vindicate his and Senator Gruening's votes against the resolution. He concluded his extraordinary speech with the observation that the days of Western dominance in Asia were over: "Like the European countries before us, we must find a way to withdraw gracefully from Vietnam."[44]

With only Morse and Gruening dissenting, the Senate approved the resolution 88 to two. The House had previously passed it unanimously, 416 to zero. House members showed no interest in questioning or debating the resolution, or any possible ramifications that might occur after its enactment. The news media accepted official versions of the events and editorialized in support of the retaliatory raids. A public opinion poll released on August 10, the same day Johnson signed the resolution, showed that 85 percent of the public supported the air strikes. Prior to his ordering the raids, a majority of Americans had held negative views of Johnson's handling of Vietnam. His actions transformed the public's views of his presidency and significantly increased his prospects for winning the upcoming election. Johnson's approval ratings in the polls shot up from 42 percent to 72 percent. All of the indicators denoted a nation that was unified in its support of the attacks on the North Vietnamese.[45] When Senators Gruening and Morse sought reelection, they were both defeated.

The resolution that Johnson would later use as a congressional authorization for the Vietnam War had an Orwellian official title: The Joint Resolution to Promote the

Maintenance of International Peace and Security in Southeast Asia. It soon became known as the Gulf of Tonkin resolution. The key language in the 300-word document that granted Johnson the authority he later used to wage a war in Vietnam follows:

> The Congress approves and supports the determination of the President, as Commander-in-Chief, to take all necessary measures to repel any armed attacks against the forces of the United States and to prevent further aggression. The United States is therefore prepared, as the President determines, to take all necessary steps, including the use of armed force, to assist any member or protocol state of the Southeast Asia Collective Defense Treaty requesting assistance in defense of its freedom.[46]

Johnson intended that the reprisal raids and the prompt congressional passage of the resolution should serve several political purposes. The administration sent General Khanh and his South Vietnamese critics a message that America was determined to back his shaky government. At home, by demonstrating that the president could defend U.S. interests in Vietnam without expanding the war, Johnson silenced Republican presidential challenger Arizona Senator Barry Goldwater, who had previously urged Washington to step up the war and send additional ground troops to South Vietnam. Goldwater had no choice but to support the air strikes and vote for the resolution. By neutralizing Goldwater, Johnson effectively removed the war issue from the upcoming election campaign. The first congressional debate on Vietnam had brought "a near-unanimous endorsement of the president's policies and provided him an apparently solid foundation upon which to construct future policy."[47]

Washington also intended that the air raids send Hanoi a message: The United States stood firm in support of its ally, General Khanh. They were also a warning to Ho Chi Minh and his colleagues that if the North Vietnamese continued to support the southern insurgency, they could expect to lose their nascent industrial economy to American bombs.

But Hanoi did not react as Johnson and his advisers expected. They read the retaliatory raids as a sign that the United States intended to try to extricate itself from its failed policy in South Vietnam by expanding the war to the North. The men in Hanoi viewed the raids as a prelude to a major American war. They believed that U.S. officials were preparing to send ground troops to the South and to bomb the North, and perhaps to invade North Vietnam as well. Although unhappy about the prospects of a war with the United States that they had hoped to avoid, the Communists leader affirmed their continuing support of the southern insurgency. Pham Van Dong met with Canadian ICC representative Seaborn for a second time on August 10. Dong told Seaborn to tell Johnson that the DRV would fight the United States if war came. Hanoi also decided to send regular combat forces to South Vietnam. Soon, three regiments, about 4,500 men, were on their way to war. These regiments represented the first PAVN regulars to be sent South.[48]

   Although they successfully rallied popular support for the reprisal raids, Johnson and McNamara had misled both the Congress and the public. Later, when Senator Fulbright and other congressional leaders realized they had been deceived, they turned against a war they had come to believe that Johnson and McNamara had tricked them into approving. Fulbright was especially bitter, believing Johnson had deliberately misled him by indicating, at the time the president asked him to steer the Gulf of Tonkin resolution through the Senate, that his administration had no intentions of subsequently taking America to war.

   The DESOTO missions, aligned with the OPLAN 34-A raids, were provocative to the North Vietnamese, whether their alignment was deliberate or inadvertent. The incident of August 2, when North Vietnamese gunboats attacked the *Maddox,* lasted 15 to 20 minutes and caused only minimal damage. The August 4 incident never occurred. It was only imagined by nervous and inexperienced sailors, most of whom had never been in a combat situation before. At the time that he ordered the retaliatory raids, Johnson and his leading advisers sincerely believed that a second attack had taken place. In the short run, the Gulf of Tonkin events were timely and served Johnson administration purposes.[49]

   The president had also expanded the U.S. commitment in Vietnam to include not only defending South Vietnam, "but also to responding to North Vietnamese provocations."[50] The long-standing barrier against taking the war north of the DMZ had been breached. PIERCE ARROW represented both a culmination and a prologue. It was the capstone of the U.S. policy that limited American involvement in Vietnam to an advisory role that had been in place for a decade; it also foreshadowed the abandonment of that advisory role and the escalations that led to direct intervention in Vietnam.[51] The American response to the Gulf of Tonkin incidents, characterized by official confusion, faulty judgment, and duplicity, was a crucial link in the chain of events that eventually plunged the United States into a full-scale war in Vietnam. With the air raids, followed by Hanoi's decision to send regular troops south, both "the United States and North Vietnam had moved toward the brink of conflict."[52]

   Johnson did not, as many Americans later suspected, seek the congressional resolution as a blank check for bringing the United States into a war to which he had already committed himself after his reelection. Johnson was not seeking a predated declaration of war. In August 1964, Johnson still hoped that the United States could sustain a non-Communist government in southern Vietnam without having to fight an American war in that region. He rejected his advisers' periodic suggestions that he should order more bombings of North Vietnam. He clung to that hope throughout his fall campaign for reelection. Johnson did not want to be a war president. Following his election, he intended to concentrate on implementing that wide range of social legislation that he had earlier labeled the Great Society. He feared that a war would divide Americans and undermine his reform program. In 1964, Johnson had reduced defense expenditures. The number of military personnel serving on active duty had decreased and monthly draft calls were reduced. But Johnson's hope of avoiding a major war in Vietnam rested on two illusions:

that the latest South Vietnamese leader could build a stable government and defeat the VietCong and that Hanoi could be pressured into renouncing the August 1945 revolutionary vision of a united Vietnam free of Western influence.[53]

THE ELECTION OF 1964

Vietnam was not a prominent issue in the 1964 presidential campaign, in part because of Johnson's politically adroit reaction to the Gulf of Tonkin incidents, but also because public interest in Vietnam was still relatively slight. The news media rarely gave the events of Vietnam extensive coverage in the fall of 1964. The conflict to date had been characterized by relatively small-scale, low intensity warfare. The U.S. role was limited; costs and casualties were comparatively light. Most Americans were uninformed and unconcerned about *la guerre sale* occurring in a small, poor country located in a remote corner of the globe.[54] The 1964 election campaign focused on domestic issues and on the question of which candidate would make the better leader.

The president made few campaign appearances until late September, and when he made speeches, he made only a few references to Vietnam. Johnson hoped these scanty remarks about Vietnam would persuade the American public that he did not intend to expand the U.S. role in Southeast Asia. He appeared to commit himself to not sending U.S. combat troops to fight a land war in Asia. At Eufaula, Oklahoma, on September 25, he said, "We don't want our American boys to do the fighting for Asian boys. We don't want to get involved in a nation with 700 million people and get tied down in a land war in Asia."[55]

He cleverly played on public fears of Goldwater's recklessness when he told a crowd in Akron, Ohio, on October 21:

> Sometimes our folks get a little impatient. Sometimes they rattle their rockets some, and they bluff about their bombs. But we are not about to send American boys nine or ten thousand miles away from home to do what Asian boys ought to be doing for themselves.[56]

These remarks, taken out of context, would appear to be explicit promises by Johnson not to Americanize the Vietnam War. In the years that followed, after the United States was enmeshed in a controversial war and Johnson had become a controversial leader, these remarks, made during the heat of the 1964 campaign, would provoke bitter accusations that the president had lied to the American people about his intentions in Vietnam in order to achieve his reelection.

But when these and other speeches are read closely, it is clear that Johnson injected qualifiers and other ambiguous remarks into his texts. In his campaign speeches, Johnson also stated that America would not abandon its commitments in Vietnam. He hinted that he might change his mind later about bombing North Vietnam and that he might even send U.S. combat troops.[57] These rhetorical escape hatches represented the efforts of a canny politician who knew that he had obtained the necessary authority from Congress to commit America to war in Vietnam if he determined that he must.

At the same time, to ensure his reelection by a landslide margin, Johnson gave his audiences false assurances that he would never take the nation to war in Indochina when he really knew that he might have to in the near future. While he did not talk about this possibility during the reelection campaign, he knew that the situation in South Vietnam was fluid and deteriorating. He was also involved with the contingency planning by his advisers for bombing North Vietnam and for sending U.S. combat troops to South Vietnam.

Johnson's rhetorical subterfuges worked. Senator Fulbright and many leftist radicals, who would become some of the most passionate critics of the American Vietnam War, campaigned for Johnson in 1964. He obtained his landslide victory in November, crushing Barry Goldwater. The Democrats rolled up their largest congressional majorities since the glory days of the New Deal. But many Americans would later turn against the war, in part because they no longer trusted the man in the White House who appeared to have plotted war while promising peace.

ROLLING THUNDER

During the months between the Gulf of Tonkin incidents and Johnson's landslide victory on November 3, 1964, political turmoil prevailed in South Vietnam. The NLF forces continued to take control of more and more of the country. On August 16, General Khanh, taking advantage of a period of euphoria generated in Saigon by the U.S. retaliatory attacks on North Vietnam, tried to acquire dictatorial powers. Buddhists and students took to the streets to protest this power grab and forced Khanh to back down. In September, Lam Van Phat, an ARVN general who had previously been a waiter in an elegant Paris restaurant, attempted to overthrow Khanh. Ambassador Taylor intervened in the chaotic South Vietnamese political process to deflect Phat's bid for power.

With Taylor's blessing, a countercoup, led by a group of younger officers called the "Young Turks," which included Nguyen Cao Ky, Nguyen Van Thieu, and Nguyen Chanh Thi, restored Khanh to power. In October, the generals selected a civilian, Harvard-educated Tran Van Huong, former mayor of Saigon, as prime minister. General Khanh stepped down to become commander-in-chief of the South Vietnamese armed forces in return for his promise to stay out of politics. Despite his pledge, Khanh and the Young Turks remained the powers behind the new civilian leadership. When asked at a press conference who the best man was to lead South Vietnam effectively, Huong paused, smiled, and said, "You got me there."[58]

While the political turnstiles were spinning in Saigon during the fall of 1964, the PLAF escalated the war. On October 11, three VietCong battalions attacked ARVN forces in the Tay Ninh province, northeast of the capital city, and they inflicted heavy casualties. On October 31, VietCong guerrillas attacked Bien Hoa airport on the outskirts of the capital city. Mortar shells rained down on the airfield, killing four U.S.

servicemen and wounding 72 others. The VC also destroyed five B-57 bombers and damaged 22 other U.S. aircraft. The VietCong assault on the Bien Hoa Airport amounted to a major shift in guerrilla tactics. For the first time in the developing war, they directly attacked a U.S. military installation. Ambassador Taylor noted the shift in tactics and notified President Johnson. Taylor called the attack "a deliberate act of escalation and a change in the ground rules." He recommended that Johnson should order an appropriate act of reprisal against a DRV target. But Johnson, with the elections still two days away, did not order any retaliatory strikes. Later in the month, the NLF forces mounted their largest offensive of the war to date. In two weeks, two VietCong regiments occupied most of Binh Dinh, a key populous coastal province and long-time insurgent stronghold.[59] Again there was no U.S. response. As November 1964 ended, President Johnson and his advisers had to confront a major crisis in Vietnam: the greater failure of the same policy he had inherited from Kennedy.

As 1964 approached its end, the Communists were close to victory in Vietnam for the third time in 20 years. They had been there in August 1945, when the Japanese occupation came to an end, only to have the French return. They got close again in June 1954, following Dien Bien Phu, only to be denied victory by major power diplomacy and the U.S. intervention in southern Vietnam. They would be denied victory once again by the U.S. decision to Americanize the war during the first half of 1965. Direct American intervention forced Hanoi "to resort to a higher level of revolutionary war, but it did not substantially resolve the underlying political problems in the GVN or arrest the seemingly inexorable slide of the South toward Communism."[60] Another decade would pass before the Communists would again approach victory. In 1975, there would no longer be anyone able and willing to deny them their long-sought goal.

As the political coherence and military capability of the South Vietnamese government rapidly eroded in late 1964, it was evident to Johnson's advisers that the policies they had been shaping since they had come to office with Kennedy in 1961 had failed. But since their reputations were so closely tied to these policies, it was extremely difficult for them to detach themselves from these policies and conceive of other policy tracks, such as distancing the United States from the Saigon regime, reducing the American commitment, seeking a negotiated settlement, or even withdrawing and permitting the collapse of South Vietnam. Even if these advisers could have imagined such alternatives, and even if such policies might have been seen as serving the long-term national interest, such proposals would have shown their previous counsels to have been incorrect, and it might have cost some of them their jobs. In addition, by the end of Johnson's first year in office, many of the skeptics who might have tried to warn the president about the futility and dangers of military escalation were no longer in government service. Since Kennedy's death, they had either resigned or Johnson had dismissed them from office. Thus, Johnson heard fewer dissenting voices and was exposed to a narrower range of options than was his predecessor.[61]

Johnson's advisers perceived escalation as the only way to protect the U.S. commitment in which they all had a personal stake.[62]

Most important decision makers firmly believed that the costs to the United States position in the Cold War competition with the Soviets and China of a Communist victory in South Vietnam far exceeded the costs of greater U.S. involvement in the war.[63]

By the end of November, Johnson's senior advisers had formed a consensus to bomb North Vietnam. According to its various advocates, bombing the DRV could achieve a variety of goals. In their judgment, it would interdict the infiltration of men and material into South Vietnam, and boost morale in Saigon. It would also induce Hanoi to abandon the insurgency in the South by punishing North Vietnam so severely that its leaders would soon understand that they could not hope to support the PLAF, except by incurring unacceptable losses.[64]

There also was a schism among Johnson's advisers about the kind of bombing campaign proposed for North Vietnam. This division pitted the president's civilian advisers against his military advisers. The civilians, led by McNamara and Assistant Secretary of Defense for International Security Affairs John T. McNaughton, called for a limited air war, for gradually applying air power to North Vietnam. Starting with a few carefully selected minor targets, this kind of air war was devised to send Hanoi a signal that it must either stop supporting the NLF or face the gradually increasing destruction of its country. The controlling assumption among the gradualists was that at some point the increasing pain inflicted upon the North Vietnamese by the bombing would induce Hanoi to abandon its support of the revolution in South Vietnam rather than see its military facilities, infrastructure, and industrial sectors destroyed. The gradualists also designed the bombing to give Johnson maximum flexibility; he could increase or decrease the pressure in response to Hanoi's behavior. The gradualist campaign was also perceived as safer; its advocates believed it would not provoke Chinese or Soviet entry into the conflict.[65] It would be a "slow squeeze," designed to save South Vietnam from North Vietnam.

Military advocates of bombing, led by Air Force Chief of Staff General John P. McConnell and Admiral Ulysses S. Grant Sharp, urged Johnson to launch a "fast squeeze" from the beginning. They wanted full-scale air attacks on North Vietnam's military bases, transportation systems, and industries. They argued that only a massive and intense bombing campaign could force Hanoi to the bargaining table on U.S. terms. They believed that only fear of national extinction would force Hanoi to abandon the revolution in South Vietnam.[66]

As Johnson's top civilian and military advisers quarreled among themselves about how best to escalate the war, one insider strongly opposed bombing North Vietnam. George Ball, undersecretary of state, the number-two man in the State Department, had previously studied the effects of strategic bombing on Germany during World War II and knew its limitations. Ball did not believe bombing would either weaken North Vietnam's war-making ability or demoralize its population. He had also served in the French embassy during the Franco-Vietminh War and understood the nature of the political-military struggle in Vietnam. He doubted that bombing North Vietnam was the proper counter to the Hanoi-supported revolution in South Vietnam. He also doubted that bombing North Vietnam could raise morale in South Vietnam.

Ball raised some challenging issues: Suppose, he asked, that Hanoi stopped supporting the NLF. Could the ARVN forces, given the current disarray in Saigon, defeat them, even if the VietCong had to go it alone? He pointed to the risks entailed by bombing: Suppose, in retaliation for the bombing, the North Vietnamese invaded South Vietnam in force? The United States would either have to send its armies or accept a Communist victory. No matter how it was done, gradually or all-out from the start, Ball warned Johnson that bombing could bring the Chinese and the Soviets into the war; it could also heal the rift between the two major Communist powers. Most important, he warned Johnson that once he started down the escalatory road, the United States would not be able to control events. He suggested that negotiations, with all of their risks, including their leading to a neutral government in the South and an American departure, better served the national interest than any scenario likely to come from bombing. For Ball, the wiser course for Washington to take, however painful it might appear to Johnson's hawkish advisers, was to seek a political solution and get out of Vietnam.[67]

Figure 5.2   The establishment Dove, George Ball, shown here holding a press conference, was a senior adviser to both President Kennedy and President Johnson. Ball consistently opposed Americanizing the Vietnam War and, Cassandra-like, warned of the disasters that would befall the United States if it persisted. Tragically, both Kennedy and Johnson disregarded his warnings. *Source:* CORBIS. Neg. #: U1608037.

The ultimately disastrous U.S. military intervention in Vietnam proved that George Ball's counsel had been correct. Why then did his warnings, like Cassandra's, go unheeded by Johnson and all his other senior advisers in the fall of 1964? The best answer is that they considered a Communist victory in South Vietnam to be unacceptable. Rejecting withdrawal or negotiations, they insisted that bombing was necessary to avert a complete collapse in Saigon. "The administration turned to air power as the only acceptable solution to an urgent problem."[68]

Johnson's civilian advisers also prevailed over the military proponents of all-out bombing. On November 27, 1964, an interagency Working Group of the National Security Council, headed by William Bundy, developed a gradualist bombing campaign to be implemented in two stages. Phase one, which would last for 30 days, called for air strikes along the major infiltration routes in eastern Laos and for reprisal strikes against North Vietnam in response to NLF attacks on U.S. installations or personnel. While phase one bombings were being carried out, Ambassador Taylor would try to get South Vietnam's squabbling politicians to resolve their differences. Once Saigon's politics were stabilized, phase two would kick in. It would be a systematic aerial war of rising intensity carried out against North Vietnamese military targets that would last for several months or until Hanoi abandoned the insurgency in southern Vietnam.[69]

Johnson delayed implementing phase one bombing mainly because of the persisting political instability in South Vietnam. He told his advisers that he would not order any bombing of North Vietnam until the South Vietnamese politicians had put their political house in order and were able to take the war to the insurgents. Johnson's reluctance to order the bombing reflected his lack of confidence in the shaky Saigon government. Perhaps Johnson's hesitation was also a sign of Ball's influence? Perhaps they were the yearnings of an instinctively cautious politician looking for a way out of the Vietnamese trap with honor and minimal damage at home and abroad?

Ambassador Taylor conveyed Johnson's concerns to the top echelons of Saigon's fractious military and civilian leadership: There would be no bombing of North Vietnamese targets until South Vietnam had a stable government. Some of the generals either ignored or did not fully understand Taylor's message, because in mid-December Air Marshal Nguyen Cao Ky and General Nguyen Chanh Thi made a bid for power that amounted to another coup attempt. President Johnson, informed that yet other coup was underway in Saigon, exclaimed, "I don't want to hear anything more about this coup shit! I've had enough of it, and we've got to find a way to stabilize those people out there!"[70]

Taylor, furious at Ky's and Thi's blatant display of political irresponsibility in the face of imminent danger, gave the South Vietnamese generals a traditional army-style chewing out.

> I made it clear that all the military plans which I know you would like to carry out are dependent on government stability. Now you have made a real mess. We cannot carry you forever if you do things like this. . . . You people have broken a lot of dishes and now we have to see how we can straighten out this mess.[71]

The South Vietnamese generals were infuriated by Taylor's tactless reproach, although he managed to persuade them to support Huong's government. Meanwhile, the Buddhists, sensing the war-weariness and desires for a negotiated settlement among many segments of the population, launched a new wave of protests, including more immolations by fire. The Buddhists also called for Ambassador Taylor to resign. In Hue, riotous students attacked the U.S. Information Service Library.[72] The protests had taken on a distinctly anti-American as well as an antigovernment cast. U.S. officials once more feared that a government that would be willing to negotiate with the NLF and favor the expulsion of Americans might arise from the chaos that had become the political norm in Saigon. General Khanh fed these fears by making overtures to some of the Buddhist factions and parroting some of their anti-American sentiments. The CIA reported that Khanh also made contact with NLF elements, further alarming his American patrons, who had become increasingly skeptical of both his reliability and competence.

While confusion reigned in the streets of Saigon, VietCong forces continued their terrorist attacks on U.S. installations and inflicted a series of defeats on ARVN forces. On Christmas Eve 1964, the VietCong bombed the Brinks Hotel in downtown Saigon in which U.S. officers were billeted. The blasts killed 2 officers, and wounded 38 Americans and 13 Vietnamese. On New Year's Day, at Binh Gia, about 40 miles southeast of Saigon, two of ARVN's elite units, a Ranger battalion and a Marine battalion, were chewed up by forces of the VietCong 9th Division, the first PLAF main force unit to reach divisional size.[73] At Binh Gia, there were 445 South Vietnamese and 16 American casualties against only 32 confirmed VietCong casualties.[74] Again there was no U.S. response to these attacks. On January 6, 1965, Ambassador Taylor sent an extremely pessimistic assessment of the situation in South Vietnam to President Johnson. Taylor feared a political collapse was imminent and that a neutralist government reflecting a Khanh-Buddhist alliance could come to power in Saigon. Such a government would negotiate with the NLF unless a bombing campaign against North Vietnam was implemented immediately.[75]

For more than a year, Hanoi had been pursuing a strategy in southern Vietnam designed to win the war in the countryside, foment popular uprisings in the cities, and bring down the struggling South Vietnamese government. They intended to supplant the RVN with a coalition dominated by the NLF that would adopt a neutralist stance internationally, tell the Americans to get out of Vietnam, and seek a peaceful reunion with the North. In early 1965, it appeared to the Communist leadership that they were close to achieving their goals. Political chaos reigned in Saigon and the ARVN forces were increasingly demoralized and ineffective. Since Johnson authorized the retaliatory air strikes in early August following the Gulf of Tonkin incidents, he had been restrained, unwilling to order further air raids for any of the VietCong attacks, even attacks on U.S. installations and advisers. Johnson's restraint encouraged Hanoi's leaders to believe that they might be able to achieve their objectives without a major war with the Americans, that Johnson would adhere to the pledges he made during the recent presidential campaign in which he appeared to promise the American people that he sought no wider war in Vietnam.

But Johnson's advisers, including Taylor, in a classic inversion of logic, now argued that the reason for delaying the bombing, Saigon's chronic political instability, had become the main reason for implementing it immediately! George Ball has commented on his colleagues' logical inversions:

> I was not surprised when my colleagues interpreted the crumbling of the South Vietnamese government, the Vietcong's increasing success, and a series of defeats of South Vietnamese units not as proving that we should cut our losses and get out, but rather that we must promptly begin bombing to stiffen the resolve of the corrupt South Vietnamese government. It was classical bureaucratic casuistry. A faulty rationalization was improvised to obscure the painful reality that America could arrest the galloping deterioration of its position only by the surgery of extrication: We must, they argued, commit our power and prestige ever more intensely to stop the South Vietnamese government from falling completely apart, negotiating covertly with the Liberation Front or Hanoi, and ultimately asking us to leave. It was Catch-22 and the quintessence of black humor.[76]

Despite the mounting pressure being applied by both his civilian and military advisers, Johnson continued to delay implementing the bombing campaign against North Vietnam. Guided by his political intuitions, he was not convinced that it should be undertaken as long as the South Vietnamese political situation remained so unstable and the war effort appeared so unpromising. However, Pleiku changed Johnson's mind. Early on the morning of February 7, 1965, VietCong fighters fired artillery rounds at the barracks of an U.S. Marine base at Pleiku in the central highlands. The VC also attacked a nearby helicopter base at Camp Holloway. Nine Americans died and 137 were wounded in the assaults.[77] The VietCong also destroyed or damaged 22 helicopters and fixed-wing aircraft. Within a matter of hours, Johnson had ordered the Joint Chiefs to implement FLAMING DART, a series of reprisal air strikes against preselected North Vietnamese targets. For two days, U.S. Navy and South Vietnamese aircraft flew retaliatory strikes against DRV sites located just north of the DMZ.

Undeterred by these air strikes, the VietCong struck again on February 10. They attacked a hotel that housed members of the 140th Maintenance Detachment, an Army aircraft repair unit, at Qui Nhon, a coastal city 85 miles east of Pleiku. After the assaults, rescuers pulled 23 bodies and 21 wounded soldiers from the rubble.[78] Again, Johnson retaliated, this time with heavier air strikes against military targets in North Vietnam. This time Washington did not characterize the air strikes as tit-for-tat reprisals, but called them generalized responses to a continuing pattern of aggressive acts. "The administration had moved from reprisals to a continuing, graduated program of air attacks against North Vietnam."[79]

McGeorge Bundy, who was visiting Vietnam at the time of the Pleiku attack, wrote Johnson a long memo calling for the implementation of sustained bombing.

Bundy asserted that if a systematic bombing campaign were not undertaken, the South Vietnamese cause would be lost within six months to a year and the Communists would control all of Vietnam. He admitted that the bombing campaign might fail, but Washington had to try it in order to preserve its credibility as a great power in world affairs. On February 13, 1965, Johnson authorized ROLLING THUNDER, a systematic, gradually expanding bombing campaign using both American and VNAF aircraft to strike at North Vietnamese targets. ROLLING THUNDER represented a major U.S. escalation of the expanding war.[80]

But Pleiku served more as a pretext than as a cause.[81] Johnson's change of heart occurred mainly because his advisers had finally convinced him that if the bombing campaign were not undertaken, the GVN would simply collapse. Johnson conceded that taking the war north could provide the Saigon government with a reprieve and give it a chance to stabilize itself. Beginning with sporadic strikes against minor targets just north of the DMZ, Johnson gradually expanded the air war against North Vietnam until it became a systematic, large-scale effort that struck major targets all over the country. ROLLING THUNDER, the U.S. and VNAF air war against North Vietnam, had begun.

A large majority of Americans supported this latest U.S. escalation of the war. A Gallup poll taken at the outset of ROLLING THUNDER showed 67 percent of the public supported the bombing of North Vietnam. Nearly all Congressional Democrats supported the President's actions, except for the two senators, Wayne Morse of Oregon and Ernest Gruening of Alaska, who had voted against the Gulf of Tonkin resolution back in August 1964. Republicans likewise strongly supported ROLLING THUNDER, including Barry Goldwater, the Republican presidential candidate whom Johnson had so badly mauled in the recent election. All prominent newspapers, including the *New York Times,* editorially supported the bombing of the North. However, the nation's most influential newspaper columnist, Walter Lippmann, doubted that bombing North Vietnam would be effective. He called for the neutralization of South Vietnam. Privately, Lippmann told McGeorge Bundy, Johnson's national security adviser, one of the foremost advocates of bombing, that the situation in South Vietnam was hopeless.[82] As always, Johnson's in-house Cassandra, George Ball, dissented and prophesied disaster. Ball opposed the bombing and any other escalations of the expanding war that the President might be entertaining.

As Washington made its decisions to initiate an air war against North Vietnam, the political sands in Saigon shifted once again. On February 14, General Khanh appointed Phan Huy Quat, a physician, as prime minister. Quat quickly selected a new cabinet that included four other doctors. U.S. officials quickly dubbed Quat's government the "medicine cabinet." A few days after the medicine cabinet took office, another coup attempt erupted, led by Colonel Pham Ngoc Thao and General Lam Van Phat, who had been the instigator of the failed coup attempt in September 1964. They intended to oust General Khanh from his position as commander of the ARVN. But Air Marshal Ky used his control of the air force to disperse the coup forces.

But Marshal Ky and General Thieu, the leaders of the Young Turks, hitherto aligned with Khanh, then convened a meeting of the Armed Forces Council. The council voted to remove Khanh from his position as commander-in-chief of ARVN and to affirm its support for Quat and his medicine cabinet. Khanh tried to rally ARVN generals to his support, but he failed. Colonel Wilson, who had helped Khanh come to power 13 months earlier and whom Khanh trusted, persuaded him to resign and leave the country. The Young Turks, who wanted to depose Khanh because of his growing alliance with the Buddhists and his efforts to establish contacts with NLF elements, brought Khanh's erratic one-year reign to an end.

Ambassador Taylor, who had backed the Young Turks, had also wanted to be rid of Khanh because he was skeptical that a Khanh-controlled government could be relied on to support the air war against North Vietnam. Ambassador Taylor feared that Khanh might seek a neutralist alternative to continuing the war.[83] General Westmoreland, the MACV commander who also backed the coup, believed that Ky and Thieu had staged a mock coup in order to depose Khanh: a farce to humiliate Khanh and show the other generals that he no longer had control of the South Vietnamese army.[84] Khanh's departure cleared the way for the Young Turks, who, with American blessings, would soon become the military rulers of South Vietnam. After a long period of instability, turmoil, and chaos, Washington believed that a government was finally emerging in Saigon that would follow American advice and enthusiastically support the widening American war. Ironically, the Young Turks appealed to the harried U.S. officials in Saigon precisely because they could not achieve what the Americans were ostensibly endeavoring to accomplish: the creation of an independent nation-state in southern Vietnam that could defeat the revolutionaries and block the further expansion of Communism.

DAHLIAS AND GLADIOLI

When ROLLING THUNDER began, administration officials confidently expected that it would quickly bring Hanoi to its senses. It would take only a few weeks, at most a few months, of bombing before the North Vietnamese Communists abandoned the southern insurgents. Ho Chi Minh and his associates, awed by the power and destructive potential of America's arsenal of high-tech air weapons systems, would quickly capitulate rather than risk losing their industrial and transportation infrastructures. But the high hopes of the Americans in the efficacy of their aerial campaign were soon dashed. The air war quickly proved ineffective. ROLLING THUNDER achieved none of its expected goals. Its failure rebutted the predictions of Johnson's senior advisers that a gradualist bombing campaign against North Vietnam would save the GVN from impending military defeat and political collapse. It failed to bring Hanoi to the bargaining table on American terms. Supplies from North Vietnam for the PLAF continued to pour into many parts of South Vietnam. A State Department Intelligence Note on the effects of bombing found that the air strikes had not diminished the morale of the North Vietnamese people. In fact, State Department analysts found that the U.S. bombing had increased North Vietnamese resolve and enabled the North Vietnamese leaders to tighten their control over the populace.[85] Bombing North Vietnam also failed to bolster morale in South Vietnam, failed to halt the entropic tendencies of Saigon politics, and failed to grant a reprieve to the GVN from the steadily increasing NLF military and political offensives. "The military and political fabric of the southern regime continued to un-ravel even more rapidly than before."[86]

President Johnson had hoped that bombing North Vietnam would obviate the sending of U.S. combat forces into South Vietnam, but the restrained manner in which he implemented the air war against North Vietnam ensured that it could not. Gradually taking the war to North Vietnam increased rather than decreased the pressures on Washington to send troops into South Vietnam. Soon after the bombing campaign had begun, Johnson's advisers pressed him to move to the second escalatory stage: sending in U.S. combat forces. The troops were needed to protect U.S. air bases in South Vietnam from NLF attacks. More ominously, bombing had also provoked the introduction of additional PAVN forces into South Vietnam.[87] ROLLING THUNDER brought about what its opponents feared, massive ground retaliation by the North Vietnamese, without bringing about what its proponents sought, the DRV to the conference table on terms then acceptable by the United States.[88]

There is a direct linkage between the gradually expanding bombing campaign against North Vietnam and Washington's decision to send the first U.S. combat troops to South Vietnam. General Westmoreland, fearing PLAF attacks against the large American air base at Danang, requested two battalions of Marines to provide ground security for that facility.[89] The MACV commander had no faith in ARVN forces that had been assigned to protect the air field.

Ambassador Taylor initially opposed Westmoreland's request for troops on several grounds. Citing the French experience, Taylor questioned whether American troops could fight a guerrilla war successfully in Southeast Asian jungles. He also believed that the introduction of U.S. combatants would tempt the ARVN commanders to unload more of the burden of the fighting onto the Americans. He could foresee American combatants taking full responsibility for the war "amid a population grown as hostile to [the] American presence as it had been to the French."[90] Most of all, Taylor worried that the introduction of even a small contingent of U.S. combat forces with a specific and limited mission would remove an important limit on U.S. involvement in South Vietnam, a limit that U.S. officials had observed since the beginning of the Indochina wars. It would be a foot in the door to an ever-widening commitment, and once that first step was taken, it would be very difficult to hold the line.[91]

Washington ignored Taylor's prophetic objections. Johnson promptly approved General Westmoreland's request for security forces that had previously been endorsed by Admiral Sharp, the man in charge of the air war and Westmoreland's immediate superior in the chain of command. Johnson's crucial decision to send American ground

Figure 5.3   U.S. Marines storm ashore on March 8, 1965, at Da Nang Beach in South Vietnam. They were the first of more than 2.7 million young men and women who would serve in South Vietnam over the next seven years. The Marines landed in Vietnam to strengthen the defenses of Da Nang Air Base against Communist forces. *Source:* AP/Wide World Photos.

combat forces to South Vietnam was made without much deliberation, planning, or thought about its possible consequences.

The landing of American troops that transformed the Vietnam War and the U.S. role in it occurred on the morning of March 8, 1965 at a beach south of Danang. At 9:03 A.M., Marine Corporal Garry Powers leaped from his amphibian landing craft, waded through ankle-deep water, and jogged up the wet sand. He was the first of the more than 2.7 million young men and women who would serve in South Vietnam over the next seven-and-one-half years. As wave after wave of Marines streamed ashore in full battle gear that warm spring morning, they encountered throngs of pretty Vietnamese girls who placed leis of yellow dahlias and red gladioli around their necks. The mayor of Danang made a welcoming speech celebrating the festive occasion. Overhead, helicopter gunships searched for VietCong snipers in the nearby jungle-covered hills.[92]

As Taylor had predicted, a few weeks after the Danang landings, military commanders were urging Johnson to take the next step. Westmoreland, fearing security threats to other U.S. military installations and disturbed by intelligence reports that the NLF planned "to seize a large sector of the Central Highlands, there to establish a government to challenge Saigon's, and drive eastward to the coast to cut South Vietnam in two," asked Washington for two Army divisions, one to deploy in the highlands, the other to send to the Saigon area.[93] Admiral Sharp, Army Chief of Staff Harold Johnson, and other members of the JCS, impatient with what they viewed to be Johnson's too cautious approach to the war, all endorsed General Westmoreland's request for additional combat forces.

President Johnson had come face to face with the dilemma that his predecessors who had previously involved the United States in Vietnam—Truman, Eisenhower, and Kennedy—had all managed to evade: either accept the collapse of the South Vietnamese government and the defeat of the American cause or send large numbers of U.S. combat forces into that country. Johnson and his advisers had trapped themselves. They had ruled out the options of withdrawal, negotiations, or an all-out air war against North Vietnam. Knowing that the gradualist air war was not producing the desired results, nor was it likely to any time soon, Johnson and his advisers knew that if they did not send combat forces quickly, the GVN would probably go under before year's end. Having convinced themselves that defeat for the South Vietnamese regime would result in unacceptable diplomatic disasters for the United States in Southeast Asia and around the globe, and having convinced themselves that the loss of South Vietnam would also activate a vicious right-wing political assault on their liberal Democratic administration at home, Johnson and his advisers could only accept the ineluctable logic of their policy formulations and agree to send more combat forces.

On March 29, a gray Renault sedan stalled on Saigon's Vo Di Nguy, a street running along one side of the American embassy compound. Within minutes, 300 pounds of plastic explosives packed in the trunk of the car erupted into a giant fireball. The powerful blast extensively damaged the embassy. It killed 20 and injured over 100 people, who were either working in the embassy, were passersby, or were dining in restaurants across the street from the American headquarters. As dazed and bleeding embassy staff members stumbled out of the wrecked building, only to encounter the litter of bodies in the street, Saigon police shot and killed the VietCong terrorist who had deliberately stalled the explosives-laden car near the embassy.[94]

Two days later, President Johnson met with members of the NSC to review U.S. Vietnam policies. On April 2, he made a series of decisions that moved America closer to war: 20,000 additional combat troops would be sent to Vietnam and the air war against the North would be expanded. A major effort to create a multilateral force to intervene in South Vietnam would also be mounted. South Korea, Australia, and New Zealand would be asked to send troops to Vietnam. Most important, additional Marine combat units would be deployed in the vicinity of Danang, and their mission would be expanded to include offensive operations against VietCong forces within a 50-mile radius of the Marine bases.[95] The Marine mission had made a crucial transition from static defense to offensive mobile operations.

On April 6, 1965, McGeorge Bundy issued NSAM 328, implementing Johnson's decisions. On that date, there were about 27,000 U.S. troops in South Vietnam, most of them noncombatants. Within a few weeks, thousands of combat troops would be pouring "in country." Confronted with a choice, as he put it in his own words, "of running in or running out of Vietnam," Johnson chose to run in. While he expanded the U.S. military presence and changed its mission from advice and static defense to limited offensive operations against the NLF forces, Johnson chose not to inform the American people of those important moves. At a press conference, he stated, "I know of no far-reaching strategy that is being suggested or promulgated."[96]

As the air war against North Vietnam expanded and the first ground combat troops were being sent into South Vietnam, public opinion polls showed that a large majority of Americans supported the continuing U.S. efforts in Vietnam.[97] Johnson's escalations drew broad popular support; influential media editorials all supported the president's actions. But it was also during the spring of 1965 that vocal critics of Johnson's war policies surfaced: not only those who criticized him for doing too much, but also those who attacked him for not doing enough. The words "hawk" and "dove" entered the emerging public discourse on the war. The words were not precise descriptive terms, but they identified the two emerging strands of public opinion critical of the administration's war policies. Hawks favored a stronger military effort, an all-out air war and the sending of more U.S. combat forces. Doves called for an end to the bombing of North Vietnam and opposed the sending of U.S. combat forces to South Vietnam. Many doves also wanted a negotiated settlement of the conflict, followed by U.S. withdrawal.

The first vocal opposition to the war appeared on university campuses. Professors at the University of Michigan, Harvard, and the University of California at Berkeley staged "teach-ins" featuring speakers who attacked Washington's war policies. Academics opposed to the war staged a national teach-in modeled on those held on university campuses. Telephones linked 122 colleges to a national debate on the war staged at the Sheraton hotel in Washington, DC. The highlight of the national teach-in featured a debate between Professor Robert Scalapino, a political scientist from the University of California, Berkeley, who defended U.S. policy in Vietnam, and George Kahin, director of Southeast Asian studies at Cornell, who mounted a dovish critique of that policy.[98] On April 17, the Students for a Democratic Society (SDS) organized the first antiwar protest march. About 15,000 people, mostly college students, gathered in the nation's capital to demonstrate their opposition to the developing U.S. war in Vietnam.

Aware of the growing hawkish and dovish criticisms of his Vietnam policies, President Johnson, on the evening of April 7, delivered a major speech at The Johns Hopkins University in which he reaffirmed the American commitment to South Vietnam. Johnson attempted to silence his critics on both ends of the political spectrum. He tried to appear tough enough to satisfy the hawks, but soft enough to give the doves hope. He told the American people, "we are there because we have promises to keep . . . we are also there to strengthen world order," and "we are there because there are great stakes in the balance." He forcibly stated that the United States would remain in Vietnam as long as was necessary to protect South Vietnam and that he would use whatever force was necessary to repel aggression. But he also stated that the United States remained ready for "unconditional discussions" if they would lead to a peaceful settlement.

Johnson's talk of his readiness for unconditional negotiations consisted mostly of rhetoric, a public relations gesture. Neither he nor his advisers had given any thought to the form or substance of such talks had they occurred. The President added that when the war was over and South Vietnam could live in peace without fear of aggression from North Vietnam, the United States would sponsor a billion-dollar developmental program for the Mekong River valley, a kind of "TVA for Southeast Asia" that would include North Vietnam.[99]

In his speech, Johnson was trying not only to persuade Americans to support his Vietnam policies, but to find the right mix of sticks and carrots that would persuade Ho Chi Minh to settle on U.S. terms. Before he gave his speech Johnson had told presidential aide Bill Moyers: "Old Ho, he can't turn that down." Moyers later said, "If Ho Chi Minh had been George Meany, Lyndon Johnson would have had a deal."[100]

The public responded favorably to the president's speech at the Johns Hopkins University. Reactions in Congress were mostly supportive. Media editorializing was generally enthusiastic. The thousands of letters and telegrams sent to the White House ran five-to-one in favor of the president. But his words failed to satisfy or silence most hawks or doves. Soon after the speech, the term "credibility gap" appeared in the media to describe the skepticism voiced by some journalists and politicians over whether the Johnson administration was being entirely candid about its present Vietnam policies.[101]

On April 8, unexpectedly responding to Johnson's offer of unconditional discussions put forth in the Johns Hopkins speech, North Vietnam's premier, Pham Van Dong, offered Hanoi's bases for negotiations. It consisted of four points:

1. The United States would have to accept the 1954 Geneva Accords: stop all acts of war against North Vietnam and withdraw all of its forces from South Vietnam.
2. Until Vietnam was reunified, the Geneva Agreements must be strictly observed; that meant no alliances with any foreign power for either zone, no foreign bases and no foreign military personnel in either zone.
3. The internal affairs of South Vietnam must be settled in accordance with the program of the NLF.
4. The peaceful reunification of Vietnam would be achieved by the people of both zones without any foreign interference.[102]

Washington regarded Hanoi's terms as unacceptable. Johnson and his advisers were especially concerned about point 3, which they understood as calling for a NLF takeover of the South Vietnamese government. Notwithstanding their rejection of specific DRV proposals, it is doubtful that the Johnson administration was seriously interested in a negotiated settlement of the conflict in April 1965. Washington feared that the South Vietnamese government was too weak militarily and politically to risk a negotiated settlement, although for political reasons they knew they had to appear to want a settlement. Johnson understood that if two-thirds of the American population supported his Vietnam policies in the spring of 1965, two-thirds also favored a negotiated settlement of the war. But at that time, Johnson intended to apply more military power in hopes of strengthening the position of the GVN so that future negotiations might bring about a settlement on terms acceptable to Washington. In the meantime, Washington sought to buy time. A short bombing pause from May 13 to May 18 did not elicit any reduction in PLAF activity, nor did it entice Hanoi into modifying its negotiating stance. But it defused some of Johnson's domestic critics, who accused Washington of not wanting negotiations, which may have been its main purpose.

But Hanoi was probably not really serious about negotiations either in April 1965; it probably did not anticipate Washington's accepting its four-point program as a basis for negotiations. The North Vietnamese leaders were proposing terms more to improve relations with the Soviet Union, who had endorsed the four-point peace program and whose economic and military assistance would be crucial in a protracted war with the United States, than to settle the conflict in Vietnam.

Both sides, regardless of what they said for public relations purposes, made nonnegotiable demands that each knew were unacceptable to the other: The United States would not compromise on its insistence that an independent non-Communist South Vietnamese state be allowed to exist in the southern part of Vietnam. Hanoi would not compromise its goal of a NLF-dominated coalition government taking over in South Vietnam, which they believed would lead inevitably to the peaceful reunification of Vietnam under Communist control. By summer, both sides had abandoned their diplomatic sparring and were going after each other on the battlefield.[103]

On April 20, McNamara, Taylor, the Joint Chiefs, and other high-ranking U.S. officials met in Honolulu to chart the next phase of the U.S. military buildup in South Vietnam. Since Washington had agreed to send some combat forces to South Vietnam, Taylor had opposed increasing their numbers and had been trying to confine those troops "in country" to security patrols in the immediate vicinity of coastal air bases. General Westmoreland's staff challenged Taylor's enclave concept. They asserted that his enclave strategy represented "an inglorious static use of U.S. forces in overpopulated areas with little chance of direct or immediate impact on the outcome of events."[104]

In Honolulu, Westmoreland, backed by the Joint Chiefs, requested 17 additional Army maneuver battalions, specifically, the 173rd Airborne Brigade, and all necessary support forces; he also wanted authorization to deploy them in unrestricted offensive operations. With McNamara leading the way, the conferees worked out a compromise. Taylor abandoned his opposition to further combat deployments. Westmoreland got his infantry battalions plus an additional 40,000 troops, including 7,000 "Third Country" forces from South Korea and Australia. But the MACV commander accepted Taylor's proposal that the troops would be assigned to four enclaves that would be established at Chu Lai, Qui Nhon, Quang Ngai, and Bien Hoa.[105]

The next day, President Johnson approved the troop increases and their assignment to the four enclaves. Altogether, an additional 82,000 soldiers were ordered to join the 33,500 already serving in South Vietnam. The Honolulu decisions, although they did not meet all of the military's operational demands, significantly increased the number of U.S. combat troops in South Vietnam and "marked a major step toward a large-scale involvement in the ground war."[106] The senior U.S. officials meeting there acknowledged that bombing North Vietnam could never force the North Vietnamese and NLF to abandon their war against Saigon. These advisers believed that U.S. forces had to take over and fight the war on the ground if the South Vietnamese were to have a chance to stabilize.[107]

As the Johnson administration made the decisions that moved America closer to full-scale war in the spring of 1965, Washington responded to a crisis in the Dominican Republic. In late April, Johnson, told that pro-Castro elements had infiltrated a revolutionary movement making a bid for power in the Dominican Republic, sent 23,000 U.S. Marines and Army infantrymen to suppress the revolt. U.S. forces blocked the rebellion and succeeded in stabilizing the politics of the country. The explanation Johnson gave to the American people for the military intervention was to protect American lives that were endangered by the uprising. The Organization of American States (OAS) later sent a peace-keeping force and U.S. forces were withdrawn. Elections were held in the Dominican Republic in 1966, and a government came to power that protected U.S. strategic and economic interests in that country.

Polls taken at the time of the intervention showed that public opinion strongly supported the U.S. military incursion, although liberals and foreign critics denounced the intervention, which violated the charter of the OAS and abrogated the long-standing U.S. pledge to refrain from direct military intervention into any Latin American country. The Dominican campaign was limited in duration, and only 26 American lives were lost (about 3,000 Dominicans died during the fighting). Success in the Dominican operation probably encouraged Johnson to try more of the same in Vietnam, and he assumed that similar success there would silence any domestic or foreign critics.[108]

On May 4, Johnson asked Congress for $700 million to support U.S. military operations in Vietnam. Johnson made it clear to the lawmakers that he would regard a vote for the money as an endorsement of his Vietnam policies. Even though Johnson's evasive and ambiguous rhetoric made it difficult for many legislators to understand just what Johnson's Vietnam policies were at this time or what his future intentions might be, they could not vote against funding for American soldiers already in the field. Both houses approved the appropriation quickly, without signficant debate. Johnson would later insist that this vote on the appropriation bill and the Gulf of Tonkin resolution refuted dovish critics who claimed that he never gave Congress a chance to pass judgment on his Vietnam policies.[109]

In South Vietnam, despite the bombing, increased U.S. aid, and the introduction of U.S. combat forces, ARVN forces verged on disintegration. Desertion and draft avoidance rates were high. The politicized ARVN officer corps had virtually given fighting the war over to the Americans and were concentrating on doing what they did best—engaging in constant political intrigue and using their military positions to enrich themselves and their families. The PLAF forces, strengthened by the addition of PAVN regulars now fighting in South Vietnam, went on the offensive. In the Phuoc

Long province, northwest of Saigon, VietCong regiments attacked a Special Forces camp at Dong Xoai and also attacked Song Be, the provincial capital. At Ba Gia, in the coastal province of Quang Ngai, another VC regiment destroyed two ARVN battalions. In the central highlands, NLF forces overran several district towns and besieged a Special Forces camp at Duc Co, a remote site in the Pleiku province. With ARVN losses running high and its military organization nearing collapse, General Westmoreland concluded that only the rapid, large-scale introduction of U.S. combat forces could avert defeat.[110]

If the South Vietnamese military were ailing, its political leaders were nearly terminal. The fifth Saigon government within a year came to power when the Young Turks overthrew the medicine cabinet of Phan Huy Quat in early June. Taylor and Westmoreland were glad to see Quat go. His supporters included a faction of Buddhist monks who wanted to end the war. Quat also opposed the introduction of large-scale U.S. combat forces into his country. The new government was headed by a military directorate of 10 senior ARVN officers led by a triumvirate: Air Marshal Ky, General Thieu, and General Thi. All were pro-American and all favored Americanizing the war. Ky became prime minister, and Thieu became head of the military forces.[111]

Logically, the Ky government represented the *reductio ad absurdum* of the South Vietnamese political process. The regime could hardly be called a government at all; it consisted of a committee of generals who did not represent any South Vietnamese groups in the political sense. Having no political base and with much of its armed forces incapable of fighting, the new government could survive only with massive American economic, diplomatic, and military support. In the name of self-determination and to ensure the continuation of the war against the NLF and the PAVN forces in South Vietnam, Washington supported a political facade in Saigon. In order to survive in power, the Saigon government was forced to surrender control of its war to the Americans.

AMERICANIZING THE WAR

In early June, Westmoreland and the JCS requested an additional 150,000 troops. They also called for abandoning the modified enclave strategy and supplanting it with an offensive strategy. They warned that anything less than a rapid, large-scale commitment of U.S. forces with the freedom to fight aggressively risked imminent defeat in South Vietnam. Among Johnson's senior civilian advisers, only George Ball opposed a major commitment of U.S. ground combat forces to Vietnam. In mid-July, Robert McNamara, after another of his many trips to Saigon, confirmed the military leaders' warnings that a failure to act decisively would probably mean defeat for the GVN within a few months. He also told Johnson that vigorous U.S. involvement in the war could avoid defeat in the short run and probably produce a favorable settlement in the long run. McNamara recommended sending an additional forty-four battalions, which would bring the total U.S. force level in Vietnam to 179,000 by year's end.[112] McNamara's recommendations triggered a week of intensive discussions among the president and his senior advisers that stretched from July 21 to July 28, during which "Johnson made his fateful decisions, setting the United States on a course from which it would not deviate for nearly three years and opening the way for seven years of bloody warfare in Vietnam."[113]

Although he made the momentous decisions that Americanized the Vietnam War, Johnson rejected the military's call for an all-out air war, mainly because he feared it would provoke Chinese military intervention, as had happened in Korea. He committed 175,000 combat troops to South Vietnam. Johnson also granted Westmoreland the authority to send U.S. troops into combat in any situation where the MACV commander deemed their use necessary to strengthen the GVN forces.

The decision to send large numbers of U.S. combat forces amounted to an open-ended commitment to defend South Vietnam. The amount of force required and the length of time needed to defeat the enemy would depend on Hanoi's response to the U.S. buildup and the Communists' willingness to raise their own stake in the war's outcome. Johnson had committed America to a war of indeterminate size and duration.[114]

These presidential decisions, most influenced by McNamara's memos and the secretary of defense's oral arguments, made in the sequence of discussions held over seven days in late July, are among the most important decisions ever made during the long history of U.S. involvement in Southeast Asia. During the last week of July 1965, the president decided that American boys would henceforth have to do what, during his presidential campaign in 1964, he had told his fellow citizens that only Asian boys would do: fight a land war in Southeast Asia. These July decisions, the nearest thing to a formal decision for war in Vietnam ever made by U.S. officials, represented the culmination of a year and a half of debate and indecision over America's Vietnam policy.

The Chairman of the Joint Chiefs, Earle Wheeler, urged President Johnson to put the nation on a war footing by calling the Reserves and National Guard to active duty. The president refused to mobilize the Reserves and National Guard because he feared that such an act might precipitate a divisive congressional debate that would undermine the coalitions he was forming to enact Great Society legislation. McNamara, the *primus inter pares* among Johnson's senior advisers, urged him to declare a state of national emergency, seek a tax raise, and place the July decisions squarely before the American people. Johnson refused to take any of these actions for several reasons. He did not want to alarm the major Communist powers. He did not want to put his domestic reform agenda at risk by dividing and distracting Congress or the American people. He did not want to provoke discussions about implementing wartime economic controls, and he did not want to stir the passions of the American people. The president chose to take the nation to war by stealth.[115] He decided to fight the Vietnam War on the side, to avoid raising taxes, and to use the Gulf of Tonkin resolution as the functional equivalent of a war declaration.[116]

As Johnson and his top echelons made their decisions for war, they ignored the supposed object of everyone's concern, America's South Vietnamese ally. The generals in Saigon were never involved in or even consulted about the decisions to inaugurate ROLLING THUNDER or later to send large contingents of U.S. ground combat forces to South Vietnam. The generals would be briefed on the steps being taken and their acquiescence expected. Indeed, Generals Ky and Thieu had no choice but to support these decisions, since their survival in power depended on the Americans maintaining a strong military presence in South Vietnam and their continuing high levels of military and economic assistance. "The Americans came in like bulldozers and the South Vietnamese followed their lead without a word of dissent."[117]

On the morning of July 28, Johnson met with congressional leaders. At noon, he held a televised press conference. He continued to mislead Congress, the media, and the American people about his Vietnam decisions. The president insisted that he had not authorized any change of policy, implying that the American role in Vietnam continued to be that of advising and supporting the South Vietnamese forces, when in fact he had committed the United States to a major war. While acknowledging that he was sending 50,000 more troops, doubling draft calls, and bringing the total U.S. forces in South Vietnam to about 125,000, Johnson downplayed his intention to send more soldiers later. He also made no mention of his agreement to allow General Westmoreland to deploy U.S. forces into any combat zone that the U.S. field commander deemed necessary.

President Johnson quietly took the nation to war during the fourth week of July 1965 by indirection and dissimulation. At the time, because of Johnson's deceptions, many Americans did not realize that their nation was going to war. Most of those who understood that America was entering a war probably did not give it much thought. They assumed now that the United States was in the war, it would be a relatively short, small-scale affair with the powerful, well-equipped, and well-trained U.S. combat forces easily gaining the inevitable victory over the outgunned Communist forces. A poll taken at the time America went to war asked citizens to predict how they believed the war would end. Eighty percent predicted it would end quickly with a victory for the United States and its South Vietnamese allies. No one, not a single respondent, predicted it would end with an American defeat and withdrawal. No one predicted that it would end with a Communist victory. To Americans in the summer of 1965, an American defeat or a Communist victory in Vietnam were inconceivable outcomes.

"Displaying the consummate skill that had become his trademark, Johnson in the last week of July [1965] shaped a consensus for his Vietnam policy in his administration, in Congress, and in the country."[118] The president saw himself as rejecting both the extremes of withdrawal and rapid escalation. Instead, he believed that he was taking the middle course of measured escalation, solidly supported by a large majority of Americans. Johnson was also deceiving himself. Beneath the consensual surface, relatively few Americans understood or strongly supported his Vietnam War policies. Many people probably supported the war at the time, simply because President Johnson appeared to be a capable leader; they trusted his leadership and also they anticipated quick victories at minimal cost. When war costs and casualties vastly exceeded anticipated levels and the conflict endured far longer than anyone had expected, Johnson's carefully crafted consensus collapsed into quarreling factions of hawks and doves surrounding confused and frustrated American citizens.

Johnson and his advisers forged a Vietnam War policy that rested upon a number of myths and misperceptions, some of which they had inherited from previous administrations. Some of Johnson's advisers understood that international relations were more complex and dynamic in 1965 than they had been in the 1950s. They understood the implications of the Sino-Soviet split, and they sensed that emerging polycentrism heralded a breakup of the bipolar world dominated by the United States and the USSR. But the president and his advisers remained thralls of the containment ideology and its domino correlative, just as the Truman, Eisenhower, and Kennedy administrations before them. Most of Johnson's aides perceived Ho Chi Minh as an agent of Chinese expansionism. They believed the line against Communism had to be drawn and held in southern Vietnam, lest all Southeast Asia become vassal to the Asian colossus and American and Allied interests in that crucial region be undermined. They believed America would be humiliated if it withdrew from Vietnam. They feared China and the USSR, emboldened by an American debacle, would support Third World insurgencies wherever they appeared. Wars of national liberation could not be suppressed or contained. America would lose credibility in the world; its allies would be demoralized, and they would no longer trust the United States to honor its commitments.

Additional considerations underpinned Washington's determination to hold the line in Southeast Asia to prevent the fall of the dominoes to Communism. Johnson administration officials did not want the economic resources of Southeast Asia to fall into Communist hands. They intended to preserve the rice lands and raw materials of that region for integration into the world economic system, particularly for access by the Japanese and America's NATO allies. U.S. officials also retained a sense of mission about their country's role in world affairs. They saw themselves as champions of a noble cause destined to triumph in Southeast Asia.[119] Perhaps an implicit cultural ethnocentrism also influenced U.S. officials as they forged an interventionist Vietnam policy: Americans, given their superior know-how, noble intentions, vast wealth, and advanced technology, would take over the fighting. They would show their inefficient and passive Vietnamese wards how to fight and win a major war, and how to establish a stable, modern state.

Johnson and his advisers also embraced the McCarthyite myth that had haunted liberal Democrats since the Chinese revolution of 1949. To them, it was axiomatic that the loss of any additional territory in Southeast Asia to Communism spelled political disaster. The loss of southern Vietnam to the Communists would galvanize a political backlash led by Republicans and southern Democrats that could destroy Johnson's beloved Great Society and cost him the upcoming election. Johnson was determined not to replicate the fate that had befallen Truman in the early 1950s when he let the United States get bogged down in the Korean War.

Johnson's ignorance of Vietnamese history, culture, and politics, an ignorance shared by his senior advisers, coupled with his habit of thinking in terms of simplistic

Cold War cliches, led him to misunderstand the nature of the revolutionary insurgency in southern Vietnam. Johnson never understood that Ho Chi Minh and his revolutionary Communist movement embodied Vietnamese nationalism much more so than did the succession of corrupt and inept military dictatorships that the United States backed. He did not understand that the Hanoi-backed insurgency in southern Vietnam enjoyed widespread popular appeal, in part because it expressed Vietnamese nationalistic aspirations to be free of foreign influences. All the president could see was Communist aggression orchestrated from Hanoi in service of the foreign policies of Beijing and the Kremlin that he felt compelled to stop.

Although Johnson and his senior advisors made pivotal decisions during the last week of July that meant America's taking over the Vietnam War, they did not develop a coherent war strategy. Thus, the future roles in the war of the South Vietnamese forces and the future roles of the U.S. forces remained ill-defined:

> Boiled down to its essence, American "strategy" was simply to put more U.S. troops into South Vietnam and see what happened.[120]

Johnson and his aides also made a series of faulty judgments as they took the nation to war. They seriously underrated their enemy. They underestimated Hanoi's popular support, ferocious determination, political discipline, fighting ability, and diplomatic skill. They could never bring themselves to admit that a comparatively small, poor Asian nation, even with substantial assistance from China, the Soviet Union, and the Eastern Bloc, might withstand a large-scale application of U.S. military power for years. Accustomed to a long history of American successes in fighting major foreign wars and waging the Cold War against the Soviet Union, Johnson and his senior advisers could not even consider the possibility that they might not prevail once they committed the United States to full-scale war in Vietnam.

Likewise, they overestimated the strategic capabilities of the U.S. military forces, both in air and ground operations. Without accurately accessing the capabilities of their enemies or the particular limitations and obstacles U.S. military forces would encounter in Vietnam, Johnson and his advisers simply assumed that the application of sizeable amounts of U.S. military force would be sufficient to bring victory. In addition, having drastically underestimated the future size, cost, and duration of the war that they instigated in late July 1965, Washington necessarily overestimated the willingness of the American people to go on year after year passively paying in lives and dollars for a military stalemate.[121]

Johnson and his senior military and civilian advisers evidently regarded Vietnam as another Cold War "problem," analogous to stemming Soviet expansionism in central Europe following World War II. But containment in Europe had built upon solid nationalistic foundations, stable governments, and revamped prosperous industrial economies. There were also a myriad of economic and cultural ties between the United

States and those European countries, and they shared the same perceptions of a common problem. Further, there were obvious linkages of shared national interests in containing the spread of Communism in Europe, which was equated with halting Soviet imperialism.

Containment, which worked in Europe, could not work in Vietnam because none of the conditions that made it work in Europe were present in Vietnam. U.S. policy in Vietnam ignored, even contradicted Vietnamese history. The major theme of Vietnamese national history is resistance to foreign intrusion, manipulation, and control. It is the crucial component of their national identity. To most Vietnamese, Americans appeared to be foreign invaders following a path previously trod by the Chinese, French, Japanese, and others, all of whom had eventually been driven out of the country. Had the U.S. officials who made the fateful decisions in July 1965 to wage a major U.S. war in Vietnam been more familiar with Vietnamese history and culture, they might have understood that Vietnamese antagonism toward the Chinese made it unlikely that they would seek to advance Chinese interests in Southeast Asia. U.S. officials might have also understood the internal political history of Vietnam that enabled the Vietminh to seize control of the nationalistic movement. It had led the resistance to the Japanese and then defeated the French efforts to reimpose colonialism in a bloody war that lasted for eight years. Modern Vietnamese history endowed the North Vietnamese and the Viet-Cong with nationalistic legitimacy, and it also underscored the inherent limits of the American project of nation-building in southern Vietnam.[122]

Johnson understood his Vietnam War strategy to be a holding action which was essentially defensive in nature. He was not trying to defeat North Vietnam or destroy the NLF. But he would punish the North Vietnamese from the air, and the U.S. combat forces on the ground in South Vietnam would prevent the Communists from winning the revolution. He believed that, in time, Hanoi would reach its threshold of pain, would grow weary of punishment and persistent failure, abandon the NLF, and agree to let South Vietnam live in peace. Without fully considering the consequences, Washington had chosen to wage a limited defensive war against a determined foe waging an unlimited strategic offensive for the highest of stakes: national reunification and independence from foreign influences.

In the short run, Johnson's centrist leadership was brilliantly successful in forging a consensus among his advisers, Congress, the media, and the American people in support of Americanizing the Vietnam War at the end of July 1965. Simultaneously, he also succeeded in pushing landmark Great Society measures through Congress—among them Medicare/Medicaid, the Voting Rights Act, and federal aid to education. Johnson gambled that a measured escalation of the bombing of North Vietnam and a limited commitment of ground combat forces to South Vietnam would enable him to achieve his military and political goals in Southeast Asia soon enough to allow him to fulfill his commitment to social justice at home. He believed America could afford to fight a limited war in Vietnam at the same time it completed the New Deal at home. He refused to choose between the Great Society and the war in Vietnam; he refused to choose between being a leader of war and a leader of social reform. Johnson's western frontier faith in American omnicompetence led him to believe that the United States could afford both "guns and butter." In his own words, "I wanted both, I believed in both, and I believed that America had the resources to provide for both."[123]

But in the long run, the price paid for seeking this middle-of-the-road consensus was military stalemate in Vietnam and political stasis at home, "a middle road of contradictions and no priorities for action."[124] Johnson, who went to war in Vietnam to save the Great Society, later had to sacrifice the Great Society to pay for the Vietnam War.

In the summer of 1965, Washington began sending its armies off to fight a major land war in Southeast Asia. It was a war that Johnson had not sought, had hoped to avoid, but, rather than accept defeat of the American cause in Vietnam, had felt compelled to undertake.

NOTES

1. Herring, *America's Longest War,* 113.
2. Ibid., 108.
3. Halberstam, David, *The Best and the Brightest* (Greenwich, CT: Fawcett, 1969), 424–27. Halberstam affixed the ironic label, "the best and the brightest," to the men who crafted America's disastrous Vietnam policy. The "best and brightest" included Rusk, McGeorge Bundy, McNamara, Taylor, and Westmoreland, as well as Kennedy and Johnson. The quote that Johnson inherited both a Vietnam policy and the men who made it is from Young, *Vietnam Wars,* 105.
4. Gelb and Betts, *Irony of Vietnam,* 97. The Johnson quote is from the videotape, "Lyndon Johnson Goes to War, 1964–1965," from the television series, *Vietnam: A Television History.*
5. Leuchtenburg, William, *A Troubled Feast: American Society Since 1945* (Boston: Little Brown, 1983), 138.
6. Moss, George, *America in the Twentieth Century* (Englewood Cliffs, NJ: Prentice Hall, 1989), 340.
7. Halberstam, *Best and Brightest,* 364.
8. Ibid., 116.
9. Schulzinger, *A Time for War,* 124.
10. Sheehan et al., *Pentagon Papers,* Document 60, 232–33, "Excerpts from National Security Action Memorandum 273," November 26, 1963, Bornet, Vaughn Davis, *The Presidency of Lyndon B. Johnson* (Lawrence: University of Kansas Press, 1983), 66–68.
11. Maitland et al., *Raising the Stakes,* 94–96.
12. Turley, *The Second Indochina War,* 57–60; Duiker, *The Communist Road,* 221–23; and Doyle, Edward; Lipsman, Samuel; Maitland, Terrence; and the editors of Boston Publishing, *The North* (Boston: Boston Publishing, 1986), 40–43, a volume in the series The Vietnam Experience; Hess, *Vietnam,* 77; Herring, *America's Longest War,* 3d ed., 122.
13. Quote taken from Hess, *Vietnam,* 78; Kahin, *Intervention,* 183–91.
14. Hess, *Vietnam,* 74.
15. Kahin, *Intervention,* 194–207.
16. Quoted in Maitland and others, *Raising the Stakes,* 100–101.
17. Sheehan et al., *Pentagon Papers,* Document 63, 277–83, "McNamara Report on Steps to Change the Trend of the War," March 16, 1964. In the report McNamara identifies the greatest

weakness in the present situation to be "the uncertain viability of the Khanh government." Schulzinger, *A Time for War,* 140.

18. Sheehan et al., *Pentagon Papers,* Document 64, 283–85, "Excerpts from National Security Action Memorandum 288 'U.S. Objectives in South Vietnam,'" March 17, 1964. By the end of 1964, there were 23,300 U.S. advisers in South Vietnam, an increase of about 7,000 for the year.

19. Young, *Vietnam Wars,* 109–10.

20. Ibid., 113; Clodfelter, Mark, *The Limits of Air Power: The American Bombing of North Vietnam* (New York: Free Press, 1989), 42–43. President Johnson prohibited military actions that might threaten North Vietnam's survival or might appear to the Chinese and Soviets to threaten North Vietnam's survival. Johnson and other administrative spokesmen repeatedly announced publicly that the United States had no intention of destroying the Hanoi regime; they also gave repeated assurances through private and diplomatic channels.

21. Quoted from Young, *Vietnam Wars,* 113.

22. Porter, *Vietnam Documents,* vol. 2, Document 151, 283–85, "Draft Resolution on Southeast Asia," June 11, 1964. The resolution was written by William Bundy, assistant secretary of state for far eastern affairs.

23. Hess, *Vietnam,* 79.

24. Porter, *Vietnam Documents,* vol. 2, Document 155, 291–92, "Notes by Canadian ICC Representative Blair Seaborn on Meeting with Pham Van Dong," June 18, 1964. Blair noted that Dong told him that the choices in Vietnam were either *a guerre a outrance,* which the United States could not win, or neutrality. Herring, George (ed.), *The Secret Diplomacy of the Vietnam War: The Negotiating Volumes of the Pentagon Papers* (Austin: University of Texas Press, 1983), 8–9; and Goodman, Allen E., *The Lost Peace* (Palo Alto, CA: Hoover Institution Press, 1978), 19–20.

25. The CBS television documentary, "Vietnam: The Deadly Decision," was broadcast April 1, 1964.

26. The main primary source for the Tonkin Gulf incidents occurring between August 1 and August 5, 1964, is the U.S. Congress, Senate, Committee on Foreign Relations, "Hearings on the Gulf of Tonkin, the 1964 Incidents," 90th Congress, 2d Session, February 1968 (Washington, DC: U.S. Government Printing Office, 1968). The official account can be found in Marolda, Edward J., and Fitzgerald, Oscar P., *The U.S. Navy and the Vietnam Conflict,* vol. 2: *From Military Assistance to Combat, 1959–1965* (Washington, DC: U.S. Government Printing Office, 1986), 393–462; Moise, Edwin E., *Tonkin Gulf and the Escalation of the Vietnam War* (Chapel Hill: University of North Carolina Press, 1996). See 76–82 for Moise's meticulous reconstruction of events occurring Sunday afternoon, August 2, 1964, in the Gulf of Tonkin.

27. *U.S. News and World Report,* "The 'Phantom Battle' that Led to War," *U.S. News and World Report* (July 23, 1984), 59–60. North Vietnamese claimed their coastal territory extended 12 miles into the Gulf of Tonkin; the United States recognized a three-mile limit.

28. Kahin, *Intervention,* 214–15.

29. Porter, *Vietnam Documents,* vol. 2, Document 163, 301–2. "Telegram from Rusk to Taylor," August 3, 1964. Rusk told Taylor, "We believe that present OPLAN 34-A activities are beginning to rattle Hanoi, and the *Maddox* incident is directly related to their effort to resist these activities."

30. Ibid., Document 170, 313–15, "Chronology of Events Relating to the Gulf of Tonkin Incidents By Joint Reconnaissance Center, U.S. Navy," August 10, 1964 (extract) "The Phantom Battle," 61–62; Davidson, Phillip B., *Vietnam at War: The History, 1946–1975* (Novato, CA: Presidio, 1988), 317–20.

31. *U.S. News and World Report,* "The Phantom Battle," 62–63.

32. Ibid., 63; Maitland et al., *Raising the Stakes,* 159; see Moise, *Tonkin Gulf,* 106–42, for a painstaking reconstruction of the confusing and bizarre events that occurred during the evening of August 4 in the Tonkin Gulf. Moise's meticulous research demonstrates beyond reasonable doubt that there was no second attack on the U.S. ships.

33. Kahin, *Intervention,* 222.

34. Interview recorded on videotape, "Lyndon Johnson Goes to War, 1964–1965," from the television series, *Vietnam: A Television History.*

35. *U.S. News and World Report,* "The Phantom Battle," 64.

36. Stockdale, James B., and Stockdale, Sybil, *In Love and War* (New York: Harper & Row, 1984), 3–36. Stockdale is quoted in Kahin, *Intervention,* 223.

37. *U.S. News and World Report,* "The Phantom Battle," 66. Hanoi has always denied that there was a second attack; it insists that it was fabricated by the U.S. National Security Agency.

38. Kahin, *Intervention,* 223–25; Johnson quoted in Olson and Roberts, *Where the Domino Fell,* 117.

39. *U.S. News and World Report,* "The Phantom Battle," 65.

40. Maitland et al., *Raising the Stakes,* 160–61.

41. *U.S. News and World Report,* "The Phantom Battle," 65–66.

42. Gelb and Betts, *Irony of Vietnam,* 103–4; Hoopes, Townsend, *The Limits of Intervention: How Vietnam Policy Was Made—and Reversed—During the Johnson Administration* (New York: W. W. Norton, 1987), 26; Schulzinger, *Time for War,* 219.

43. Quoted in Olson and Roberts, *Where the Domino Fell,* 118.

44. Senator Wayne Morse's lengthy speech is recorded in the *Congressional Record,* 88th Congress, 2d Session, August 7, 1964, 18413–27. A synopsis of his speech appears in Schulzinger, *A Time for War,* 152–53.

45. Eighty-five percent of the public approved of Johnson's decision to order retaliatory air raids against North Vietnamese targets. Polls cited in Schulzinger, *A Time for War,* 39, and Herring, *America's Longest Wa*r, 123. O'Keefe, Kevin J., in an unpublished paper on print media coverage of the Gulf of Tonkin incidents, found that most newspaper and newsmagazine accounts of those events were uncritically accepting of official versions and were nearly unanimous in their editorial support of President Johnson's actions.

46. Porter, *Vietnam Documents,* vol. 2, Document 167, 307, "The Gulf of Tonkin Resolution," August 7, 1964.

47. Herring, *America's Longest War,* 123.

48. Young, *Vietnam Wars,* 123.

49. Gelb and Betts, *Irony of Vietnam,* 101.

50. Davidson, *Vietnam at War,* 322.

51. Herring, *America's Longest War,* 125.

52. Hess, *Vietnam,* 80.

53. Ibid., 81.

54. Herring, *America's Longest War,* 126.

55. Quoted in Goldman, Eric, *The Tragedy of Lyndon Johnson* (New York: Dell, 1968), 279.

56. Quoted in ibid., 281.

57. Goldman calls Johnson's rhetorical insertions "escape hatches."

58. Maitland et al., *Raising the Stakes,* 162–63; Huong's quote is recorded on videotape, "Lyndon Johnson Goes to War, 1964–1965," from the television series, *Vietnam: A Television History.*

59. Davidson, *Vietnam at War,* 323; Taylor quote found in Olson and Roberts, *Where the Domino Fell,* 12.

60. Duiker, *The Communist Road,* 233.

61. Kahin, *Intervention,* 245–46; Thomson, James B., "How Could Vietnam Happen? An Autopsy," *Atlantic* 221 (April 1968), 50–52. Officials who resigned or were dismissed included Paul Kattenburg and Roger Hilsman. Thomson, an East Asia specialist, left the government for Harvard in 1966.

62. Thomson, "How Could Vietnam Happen?" 52; Gallucci, Robert, *Neither Peace nor Honor: The Politics of American Military Policy in Viet-Nam* (Baltimore, MD: Johns Hopkins University Press, 1975), 35–58.

63. Schulzinger, *A Time for War,* 162.

64. Herring, *America's Longest War,* 124; Duiker, *The Communist Road,* 236.

65. Davidson, *Vietnam at War,* 336–39.

66. Ibid., 339–40; Millett and Masloski, *For the Common Defense,* 54.

67. Ball, George W., "A Light That Failed—Top Secret: The Prophecy the President Rejected," *Atlantic,* 230 (July 1972), 33–49. The substance of the article is a memo Ball wrote October 5, 1964, which Johnson read. Ball hoped to get Johnson and his advisers to examine the erroneous assumptions underlying U.S. Vietnam policies and to realize that there were other options available besides escalation. Ball failed and left office in 1966. Schulzinger, *A Time for War,* 163, suggests George Ball suffered Cassandra's fate.

68. Herring, *America's Longest War,* 126.

69. Sheehan et al., *Pentagon Papers,* Document 88, 373–78. "Final Draft Position Paper Produced by Working Group." Key members of the group besides William Bundy included John McNaughton, George Carver, Marshall Green, and Vice Admiral Lloyd Mustin.

70. Remarks attributed to Johnson by Jack Valenti in an interview recorded on videotape, "Lyndon Johnson Goes to War, 1964–1965," from the television series, *Vietnam: A Television History.*

71. Sheehan et al., *Pentagon Papers,* Document 89, 379–81, "Account of Taylor's Meeting with Saigon Generals on Unrest," December 24, 1964.

72. Herring, *America's Longest War,* 129.

73. Davidson, *Vietnam at War,* 333–34.

74. Kahin, *Intervention,* 262.

75. Ibid., 263–65.

76. Ball, George W., *The Past Has Another Pattern* (New York: W. W. Norton, 1982), 389–90. Ball is quoted in Kahin, *Intervention,* 275; Berman, *Planning a Tragedy,* 45–52.

77. Davidson, *Vietnam at War,* 335–36.

78. Maitland et al., *Raising the Stakes,* 170–71.

79. Herring, *America's Longest War,* 129; Young, *Vietnam Wars,* 137–38. The maze of memos generated by Johnson's senior civilian and military advisers between November 1964 and February 1965, as they forged U.S. Vietnam policy that culminated in the decision to initiate an air war against North Vietnam, reveals a bureaucratic worldview that had few points of reference to Vietnamese political and strategic realities. The terms of the paper debate waged among these high echelons, George Ball excepted, were defined by the prime goal they had set for themselves in Vietnam, and this goal in turn derived from the Cold War ideological consensus they all embraced. The goal, of course, remained the creation of a non-Communist state south of the 17th Parallel to stop the spread of Communism in Southeast Asia. The U.S. foreign policy-making elite were not capable of critically examining two other assumptions that nearly all of them shared: A Communist takeover of South Vietnam was unacceptable and defeat for the American cause in Vietnam could not be allowed to occur.

80. Sheehan et al., *Pentagon Papers,* Document 92, 423–27, "McGeorge Bundy Memo to Johnson on Sustained Reprisal Policy," February 7, 1965. The tone of Bundy's memo is grim. Even as he advocates bombing, he concedes that it might fail to improve the situation in South Viet-

nam; Clodfelter, *Limits,* 58–63. On February 27, 1965, the State Department issued a White Paper rationalizing the bombing campaign as a response to North Vietnamese aggression against South Vietnam.

81. McGeorge Bundy referred to incidents such as Pleiku as "streetcars." If you don't catch it, another will come along soon.

82. Schulzinger, *A Time for War,* 172.

83. Kahin, *Intervention,* 294–305.

84. Westmoreland, William C., *A Soldier Reports* (New York: Dell, 1976), 123–24.

85. The State Department note is cited in Berman, *Planning a Tragedy,* 51.

86. Quote is from Kahin, *Intervention,* 306; Sheehan et al., *Pentagon Papers,* Document 97, 440–41, "McCone Memo to Top Officials on Effectiveness of Air War."

87. Davidson, *Vietnam at War,* 324–25.

88. Kattenburg, Paul, *The Vietnam Trauma in American Foreign Policy, 1945–1975* (New Brunswick, NJ: Transaction, 1980), 131–32. Kattenburg is quoted in Berman, *Planning a Tragedy,* 51–52.

89. Westmoreland, *A Soldier Reports,* 157.

90. Ibid., 157–58.

91. Porter, *Vietnam Documents,* vol. 2, Document 195, 364–65, "Telegram from Taylor to Rusk," March 18, 1965.

92. Maitland and others, *Raising the Stakes,* 174–75. Corporal Powers was assigned to the Third Marine Amphibious Force. Its 3,500 personnel under the command of General Lewis Walt came ashore along Danang's beaches March 8, 1965.

93. Westmoreland, *A Soldier Reports,* 161.

94. Maitland et al., *Raising the Stakes,* 183–84.

95. Sheehan et al., *Pentagon Papers,* Document 98, 442–443, "Order Increasing Ground Forces and Shifting Mission," April 6, 1965. According to Item 11: "The actions themselves should be taken as rapidly as practicable, but in ways that should minimize any appearances of sudden changes in policy. . . . The President's desire is that these movements and changes should be understood as being gradual and wholly consistent with existing policy."

96. Quoted in Maitland and others, *Raising the Stakes,* 184.

97. Poll cited in Turner, *Dual War,* 116.

98. Goldman, *Tragedy of Lyndon Johnson,* 476–77; Young, *Vietnam Wars,* 156–57.

99. Johnson's statements from his Johns Hopkins speech are cited in Turner, *Dual War,* 128–29.

100. Moyers's quote is from an interview recorded on videotape, "Lyndon Johnson Goes to War, 1964–1965," from the television series, *Vietnam: A Television History.*

101. Turner, *Dual War,* 131–32.

102. Hanoi's Four Points are reprinted in Gettleman, Marvin E.; Franklin, Jane; Young, Marilyn; and Franklin, Bruce (eds.), *Vietnam and America: A Documented History* (New York: Grove, 1985), 274–75.

103. Kattenburg, *Vietnam Trauma,* 130–33; Duiker, *The Communist Road,* 241–42.

104. Quoted in Westmoreland, *A Soldier Reports,* 166.

105. Porter, *Vietnam Documents,* vol. 2, Document 198, 370–71, "Memorandum for the President by McNamara," April 21, 1965; Doyle, Edward; Lipsman, Samuel, and the editors of Boston Publishing, *America Takes Over* (Boston: Boston Publishing, 1982), 10–11, a volume in the series, The Vietnam Experience.

106. Herring, *America's Longest War,* 132.

107. Schulzinger, *A Time for War,* 174.

108. Moss, *America in the Twentieth Century,* 348–49; Young, *Vietnam Wars,* 153.

109. Herring, *America's Longest War,* 135.

110. Morrocco, John, and the editors of Boston Publishing, *Thunder from Above: Air War, 1941–1968* (Boston: Boston Publishing, 1984), 81–83, a volume in the series The Vietnam Experience. Clarke, *The Final Years,* 48. By June 1965, ARVN was suffering about 2,000 battle casualties per month and losing an additional 10,000 men a month from desertions. Total manpower losses outstripped gains from recruiting and conscription.

111. Clarke, *The Final Years,* 22–23. According to Clarke, during 1964–1965, a rising group of younger officers, most in their late thirties and early forties, displaced the older generals who had overthrown Diem. These Young Turks emerged as the new arbiters of power in Saigon. Thieu, Ky, and Chi were the leaders of these new men of power.

112. Westmoreland, *A Soldier Reports,* 179–82; Sheehan et al., *Pentagon Papers,* Document 105, 456–58, "McNamara's Memo on July 20, 1965, on Increasing Allied Ground Force." The memo was drafted on July 1 and revised July 20.

113. Herring, *America's Longest War,* 138–39.

114. There are detailed accounts in Kahin, *Intervention,* 366–401; and in Berman, *Planning a Tragedy,* 105–53, that anatomize the decision-making process of July 21 to July 28, 1965, which plunged America into a land war in Asia. Clark Clifford, a friend of Johnson's, and Senator Mike Mansfield joined with George Ball to try to warn the president of the perils of getting involved in a major war in Southeast Asia. He rejected their advice. See also Schandler, Herbert Y., *The Unmaking of a President: Lyndon Johnson and Vietnam* (Princeton, NJ: Princeton University Press, 1977), 30–31.

115. Herring, *America's Longest War,* 139–40.

116. Summers, Harry G., Jr., *On Strategy: A Critical Analysis of the Vietnam War* (New York: Dell, 1982), 49–50; Young, *Vietnam Wars,* 160.

117. Herring, *America's Longest War,* 3d ed., 153–54.

118. Ibid., 142.

119. Hess, *Vietnam,* 87–88.

120. Quoted in Clarke, *The Final Years,* 106.

121. Summers, *On Strategy,* 142–43.

122. Hess, *Vietnam,* rev. ed., 86.

123. Johnson quoted in Young, *Vietnam Wars,* 158.

124. Gelb, Leslie, "Vietnam: The System Worked," *Foreign Policy* 3 (summer 1971): 164.

CHAPTER 6

A Chain of Thunders

Front line combat in Vietnam was remarkably similar to the battles fought by those soldiers on the point who charged the Bloody Angle at Spotsylvania, who stormed the Nazi fortifications along the Siegfried Line, who broke through the Japanese defenses before Manila, and who assaulted the Chinese and North Korean entrenchments on Pork Chop Hill. The casualty figures tell the story.

Harry G. Summers Jr.

THE CONCEPT OF LIMITED WAR

Americans went to war during the summer of 1965, confident that the Vietnamese insurgents could not withstand for long the application of U.S. military power. They assumed that the United States needed to do little more than flex its high-tech military muscles and it would triumph in Southeast Asia. President Johnson expected a relatively quick and cheap U.S. victory that would save South Vietnam, allow him to implement his Great Society, and preserve his broad-based consensus supporting containment of Communism abroad and social reform at home.

Two and one-half years later, the nation found itself mired in a frustrating and costly war. As 1967 drew to a close, Washington had committed 486,000 troops to Vietnam and was spending over $2 billion per month on the conflict. Despite these large investments of their nation's manpower and wealth, far in excess of what anyone had anticipated when the war began, many Americans perceived that the United States was not winning the war in Vietnam. To them, the conflict appeared to be stalemated; they faced the dismaying prospect of a protracted war with ever mounting costs and casualties. Many citizens concluded that it had been a mistake for the United States to have become involved in the Vietnam War.

During most of 1967, support for the conflict and for Johnson's leadership was declining among the Congress, the media, and the public. A debate between the hawks and the doves over Johnson's war policy was building in Congress and echoing in the streets. Within the White House, presidential advisers were dividing into hawkish and dovish factions. Facing rising war costs, Congress was abandoning Johnson's Great Society reform program. Widening social fissures heralded the breakdown of consensus. In Newark, Detroit, and elsewhere, angry black rioters torched entire blocks of cities. Violence in Vietnam bred violence at home.

The prime cause of America's entanglement in a stalemated war of increasing magnitude was the failure of U.S. officials to develop effective strategies for achieving national political objectives within a limited war milieu.[1] Traditionally, U.S. military leaders have not devoted themselves to the development of grand strategy, specifically with the development of the military means required to achieve particular national goals. "The Americans had won every war since the Civil War by an overwhelming combination of superior manpower and weight of materiel, a superiority which minimized the importance of strategy."[2]

As the Cold War rivalry between the United States and the Soviet Union intensified in the aftermath of World War II, both sides built up potent nuclear and thermonuclear arsenals. Strategists in both nations spawned new strategic theories as they struggled to control these extraordinarily powerful weapons. Within America, given the absence of military theorists, strategic analysts for the nuclear age were recruited from civilian ranks. At institutes and "think tanks," civilian theorists fashioned strategic concepts for the nuclear era. For the most part, military professionals ignored the theories propounded by civilian strategists, considering them arcane intellectual exercizes irrelevant to solving the practical problems of war fighting in the atomic age.

One of the fashionable theories developed for the nuclear age by civilian strategists was the concept of limited war. It rested on two foundational principles: first, that a nuclear war with the Soviet Union had to be avoided at all costs, for it could never be won given the immense destructive power of the nuclear weaponry possessed by both sides; and, second, that the United States must contain Communism, which was spreading in the Third World via local, small-scale revolutionary wars, backed by the Soviets and the Chinese. Limited warfare assumed the gradual application of economic and military assistance, diplomatic pressure, covert operations, and military force at the site of insurrections. Limited-war doctrine called for the employment of these instrumentalities with restraint and skill. A deft touch was required to use just enough and the right mix of persuasion, money, aid, and force necessary to defeat a rebellion and contain the spread of Communism, without provoking a response from the USSR or China that could escalate to a nuclear confrontation.

The theory of limited war received its first real-world application during the Korean conflict. That war started when North Korea, seeking to bring the entire country under its control, invaded South Korea on June 25, 1950. President Truman, assuming that the North Korean invasion was supported, perhaps directed, by the Soviet Union to further Soviet expansionist ambitions in Asia, quickly made the decision to intervene militarily. U.S. objectives were not only to defend South Korea against Communist aggression, but to contain the spread of Communism without provoking a confrontation with the Soviets that could lead to World War III.

Caught by surprise and reacting to the Chinese intervention in the Korean War five months after the war began, U.N. Commander General Douglas MacArthur wanted to undertake military initiatives against China. He ran up against the civilian proponents of limited war who insisted on confining the U.N. forces to the Korean battlefield.[3] MacArthur and his supporters chafed at the limitations placed on U.N. forces, while their Chinese adversaries freely used their homeland for logistical support, aircraft bases, and sanctuaries.

A dispute over the objectives for which the Korean War was being fought lay at the core of the conflict between MacArthur and Truman. MacArthur wanted to inflict a major defeat on China and liberate all of Korea from Communism. Truman sought the limited political objective of restoring the status quo, of ensuring the survival of a non-Communist South Korea below the 38th Parallel. His overriding concern was the avoidance of a confrontation with the Soviets, then aligned with China. Truman relieved MacArthur of his command when MacArthur publicly criticized the Truman administration's limited war strategies and political objectives. This dispute between civilian and military leaders, which erupted during the Korean War over strategies and objectives, foreshadowed similar conflicts that occurred during the Vietnam War.

Following the end of the Korean War, a decade would pass before America would again resort to limited war in order to contain the spread of Communism in Asia. But, in Vietnam, American limited war strategists came up against a sophisticated revolutionary war strategy employed by the North Vietnamese and the NLF. In the Korean War, U.S. forces had only engaged in conventional war against the North Korean and Chinese armies. During 1962 and 1963, President Kennedy cautiously pursued a small-scale, low-intensity limited war policy in Vietnam, based on furnishing the South Vietnamese government with diplomatic, economic, and military assistance, accompanied by the use of covert operations, counterinsurgency tactics, and the deployment of thousands of U.S. military advisers. Following Kennedy's assassination, Lyndon Johnson immediately embraced the limited U.S. commitment in Vietnam and gradually expanded it.

During the first half of 1965, to stave off the imminent collapse of the South Vietnamese government, Johnson rapidly escalated the conflict, first by bombing North Vietnam, and when that strategy quickly proved ineffective, by sending large numbers of U.S. ground combat forces to fight the VietCong and PAVN forces in southern Vietnam. Johnson chose to expand drastically the limited war, which he had inherited, rather than to accept the Kennedy administration's failure to develop an effective strategy to enable the South Vietnamese government to survive.

At the time that Johnson made these escalatory decisions, he could not know that he had committed U.S. forces to a long, costly, and ultimately losing war. One of the many causes of that eventual disaster would be defects inherent in the U.S. concept of limited war, as well as in its application to Indochina. Washington's efforts to fight a limited war in Vietnam were also complicated by disputes among Johnson's civilian and military advisers over how best to implement military strategy. The architects of America's limited war in that region never improvised a grand strategy to counter the sophisticated strategy used by their determined foes.

In August 1965, an operations study prepared for the Joint Chiefs defined four major U.S. objectives in Southeast Asia. They included enabling the GVN to extend its control over all of that country lying south of the 17th Parallel, defeating the PLAF and NVA forces fighting in South Vietnam, forcing Hanoi to withdraw its forces from the South and renounce its support of the southern insurrection, and deterring Chinese expansion into Vietnam, Indochina, or anywhere in Southeast Asia.[4]

But U.S. policy makers never developed the strategies to accomplish most of these objectives. One reason for their failure was their unwillingness to order a total mobilization of U.S. human and economic resources. Vietnam would be a limited war for limited ends, using limited assets.[5] Another cause of failure lay in the incompatibility of U.S. military strategies in Vietnam. Johnson limited the American military effort in Vietnam so as not to provoke Chinese or Soviet military intervention. On the other hand, he counted on a comparatively quick and easy victory over the NLF and Hanoi. Having limited the use of U.S. military power to avoid war with China and a possible nuclear confrontation with the USSR, and having seriously underestimated the enemy's capacity to resist U.S. power, Washington "did not confront the crucial question of what would be required to achieve its goals until it was bogged down in a bloody stalemate."[6]

When the United States was eventually forced to curtail the air war and withdraw its ground combat forces from Vietnam because public opinion would no longer support a war that involved sustaining massive American casualties and costs for an indeterminate period of time, the GVN remained totally dependent on U.S. economic and military aid, military advisers, and air and logistics support for its survival. After the U.S. aid programs were reduced and military support was withdrawn, PAVN forces overwhelmed the demoralized GVN army, and South Vietnam was quickly extinguished on the last day of April 1975.

Having surrendered the formulation of limited war strategy to civilian analysts, Johnson's military advisers had no choice but to go along with it. But his military advisers resented the restrictions civilian officials imposed on the air war against North Vietnam, restrictions they believed prevented them from inflicting enough damage to force Hanoi to stop supporting the southern insurgency. The military continually pressured Johnson to intensify the air war against North Vietnam. But the president feared that the military's call for full-scale bombing attacks risked Chinese military intervention, a risk Johnson, with vivid memories of Korea, refused to run.

Although they exercised tight control over the selection of targets for the air war against North Vietnam, civilian leaders in Washington, other than confining the ground war to the territory of South Vietnam, left the framing of strategies for its conduct to the Joint Chiefs and to General Westmoreland.[7] Initially, Johnson's military advisers accepted these geographic limits imposed on the ground war because Westmoreland did not have enough combat forces or a sufficiently developed logistics support system for conducting operations within South Vietnam and simultaneously undertaking cross-border operations into Laos, Cambodia, and southern North Vietnam. In time, military leaders would also challenge some of the civilian restrictions imposed on the ground war, which they viewed as needlessly delaying the achievement of U.S. objectives in Southeast Asia.

WAR OF ATTRITION

General William Westmoreland was the "key American military actor in the Vietnamese drama."[8] As Commander of the Military Assistance Command—Vietnam (COMUS-MACV), Westmoreland held tactical command over the American war that began in the summer of 1965. He and his staff devised the strategy of attrition that was in place from July 1965 until President Nixon supplanted it with Vietnamization in August 1969. During his tour of duty in Vietnam, General Westmoreland won the most important campaign of the American Vietnam war, the Tet-68 Offensive, a series of battles in which RVNAF (Republic of [South] Vietnam Armed Forces) and U.S. forces destroyed the PLAF and severely damaged the VietCong's political infrastructure in many districts.

Westmoreland has been called the "inevitable general."[9] From the outset of his military career, he appeared destined for distinction. Westmoreland compiled a superb World War II record, serving as an artillery officer with the 9th Infantry Division, which saw extensive action in North Africa, Normandy, and Germany. He also fought in Korea, where he reached the rank of brigadier general at the relatively youthful age of 38. After Korea, he continued to advance his career with choice assignments, including a tour as superintendent of the U.S. Military Academy. Westmoreland assumed command of U.S forces in Vietnam in June 1965. The Vietnam War proved to be a difficult and frustrating experience for the inevitable general. He became a controversial figure, often the target of criticism, most often from doves, but also from hawkish critics who believed his strategy of attrition could never produce victory in Vietnam.[10]

Westmoreland quickly decided to use an attrition strategy. Attrition played to the American strengths—firepower and mobility, and it minimized U.S. casualties. Westmoreland believed that the American people would never support a war fought with large numbers of young conscripts, if they sustained heavy casualties and did not attain victory within a comparative short time frame. Attrition warfare also promised an opportunity for winning the war more quickly than protracted counterinsurgency operations. Denied by the exigencies of the American limited-war policy of an opportunity to wage

Figure 6.1 The inevitable general, William C. Westmoreland, the U.S. field commander in Vietnam from 1965 to 1968. Here, COMUSMACV arrives at Camp Evans helicopter pad where he spoke with a group of newsmen. *Source:* CORBIS. Neg.#: U1593714.

a war of annihilation by invading North Vietnam, Westmoreland believed that attrition campaigns in South Vietnam were the next best available strategy. Westmoreland also felt that he had no choice but to use an attrition strategy, because North Vietnam was committing its main force units to the war in South Vietnam.[11]

Westmoreland's attrition strategy was quickly endorsed by Army Chief of Staff Harold Johnson, by the Joint Chiefs, and by civilian leaders, including Secretary of Defense McNamara and President Johnson. But "the Army applied the doctrine and force structure it had developed for conventional contingencies in Europe and Korea against insurgent forces practicing a form of revolutionary warfare."[12] A major reason for the failure of the Americans to gain more than a military stalemate in the Vietnam War after years of large-scale warfare was their reliance on a conventional strategy against adversaries who employed unconventional war strategies that enabled them to fight a protracted war and avoid defeat at the hands of a much more powerful army. The strategy of gradual escalation forced the U.S. forces to fight a lengthy and indecisive war of attrition, the kind of war for which Giap's unconventional strategy of protracted warfare was precisely suited.

As Westmoreland and his staff planned it, his strategy of attrition was to unfold over three phases, anticipating a decisive U.S. victory by the end of 1967. During phase one, U.S. troops would be used to protect the developing American logistics system—military bases, air fields, roads, and lines of communication. Westmoreland also believed that U.S. combat forces would have to be committed to battle during this first phase, because enemy main force units operating in the vicinity of Saigon and in the central highlands continually attacked GVN forces. Westmoreland viewed the military situation in the summer of 1965 as precarious. The VietCong controlled half the territory and population of South Vietnam. The VC offensives launched in May were destroying ARVN units at the rate of one battalion per week, and the insurgents were overrunning many district headquarters. The PAVN offensives in the central highlands sought to take control of that vital region and threaten the coastal cities. Typically, political chaos reigned in Saigon. A South Vietnamese political collapse and a VietCong victory before the end of the year both appeared possible. Westmoreland's objectives during phase one were to protect the populated areas, thwart enemy operations, and halt the downward slide of the war in the South.[13]

Assuming that the military situation could be stabilized by the end of 1965 and that the South Vietnamese would have stopped losing by then, Westmoreland's planners called for phase two to begin. U.S. forces would take the initiative and, wherever possible, eliminate the enemy's base camps and sanctuaries. These large-unit sweeps into enemy basing areas were to be the tactical operations that came to be known as "search and destroy" missions. Westmoreland assumed that by attacking key enemy basing areas, he could force the VietCong main units to fight, giving the U.S. forces an opportunity to use their superior firepower to "find, fix, and finish the enemy." U.S. forces would also provide security for an expanded pacification effort. The length of phase two would depend on U.S. force commitments and the enemy's response to the U.S. efforts. General Westmoreland estimated that phase two would last about a year. It was assumed that the back of the insurgency would have been broken by the end of phase two. Phase three would begin in 1967; it would essentially be a mopping-up exercise. Remaining insurgent forces would be annihilated or pushed back to remote areas, where they would pose no threat to village security or GVN forces. During phase three, the pacification program would be extended throughout South Vietnam.[14]

U.S. planners assumed that the tasks of pacification and building up the GVN military forces would be pursued during all three phases. They expected that by the time the U.S. war of attrition was completed, most of the people of South Vietnam would be living in villages, free of VietCong pressure. They also assumed that the GVN military forces would be strong enough to handle any lingering security threats to South Vietnam. With the VC forces neutralized and PAVN units forced back into North Vietnam, Hanoi would have to negotiate a settlement on U.S. terms. American combat forces would be withdrawn.[15] As the American war in Vietnam unfolded, Westmoreland's strategic plan would prove impossible to implement fully for many reasons.

As Westmoreland began deploying U.S. combat units during the summer of 1965, his operations were hampered by inadequate logistical support systems. President Johnson's failure to mobilize the Reserves and National Guard and to rely completely on increased draft calls and enlistments to meet the expanding manpower needs of the rapidly escalating war created serious problems for Westmoreland. The regular U.S. Army had few engineering, logistics, and service units on active duty. Military planners had assumed that in the event of war, Reserve and National Guard units would be mobilized to provide these crucial support services. When Johnson, ignoring the advice of the Joint Chiefs and Robert McNamara, refused to call the Reserves or National Guard to active duty for political reasons, many units found their ammunition in short supply.[16] Other combat units arrived under strength and without all of their weapons, equipment, or supplies.

At the time the American war in Vietnam began, South Vietnam possessed only one deep-water port, the commercial docks located fifty miles inland at Saigon. Since warehouse and storage areas were not equipped to handle the massive influx of war materiel, military supplies piled up on Saigon docks. VietCong sappers destroyed huge quantities of the arriving U.S. supplies. South Vietnamese workers stole equally large quantities of material for their use, for sale on the black markets, or to sell to the Viet-Cong. For the rest of 1965, Westmoreland had to delay the tactical deployment of maneuver units because of inadequate logistics support.[17]

Working under adverse conditions, the Seabees, the Army Corps of Engineers, and civilian contractors constructed additional deep-water ports, warehouses, jet-capable air fields, roads, and bridges. The world's most productive economy was soon sending a cornucopia of equipment and supplies over 9,000 miles to its warriors fighting in Vietnam. The 1st Logistical Command developed a superb supply system that not only kept American soldiers supplied with ammunition, weapons, tanks, and planes, but also with toilet paper, shaving lather, fresh socks, beer, pizzas, soft drinks, and ice cream.[18] Within a year, Westmoreland had accomplished "what has properly been called a logistics miracle. The Americans who fought in Vietnam were the best fed, best clothed, best equipped army that the nation, or any nation, had ever sent to war."[19]

But serious problems inherred in the logistics success story. U.S. troops were so well supplied with luxuries that many of them quickly lost enthusiasm for the hardships of extended field operations. The supply system was also expensive and wasteful. Sometimes soldiers expended enormous amounts of ammunition to kill one enemy soldier. The promiscuous use of firepower was also responsible for many accidental deaths. A large number of troops were killed by "friendly fire" from U.S. aircraft, artillery, mortars, and machine guns. Many other U.S. troops were also killed in the numerous accidents involving the storing, handling, transporting, and guarding of ammunition. Finally, the effort necessary to make the U.S. Army the best-supplied in history tied up large numbers of military personnel in noncombat activity.[20]

SEARCH AND DESTROY

Although Westmoreland had few combat units and U.S. logistics were still in the chaotic stage, he felt he had to attack VietCong units operating in some areas in order to take the pressure off beleaguered ARVN forces that were verging on disintegration. On June 27, troops of the 173rd Airborne Brigade, the first U.S. Army unit to see combat in Vietnam, climbed aboard helicopters at the Bien Hoa Air Base on the outskirts of Saigon. They were accompanied by a battalion of Australian soldiers and several battalions of

ARVN infantry. Westmoreland was sending the 173rd and their allies on the war's first search-and-destroy mission. They were flown into War Zone D, a jungle-infested area thirty-five miles northwest of Saigon that had long been a VietCong stronghold. The VietCong chose not to engage the green U.S. sky troopers or their allies on that operation. After two days of inconclusive skirmishing, the troops returned to Bien Hoa. "This American foray 27 June locked the United States into a ground war in Asia."[21]

The 173rd Airborne Brigade made several more incursions into War Zone D during the ensuing months, each of them ending much like the first: withdrawal after a few days of skirmishing with an elusive enemy not much interested in a real fight. In early November, the troops of the 173rd once more helicoptered into War Zone D. One of the soldiers gave the operation the sarcastic name of HUMP. ("Hump," "humping," and "humping the boonies" were the soldiers' terms for long and exhausting marches over rugged jungle-covered terrain in hot, humid weather under the heavy weight of rucksacks crammed with extra rations, water, and ammunition.) But Operation HUMP turned out to be a fierce and brutal campaign. In a remote region of War Zone D, several Airborne platoons ran into a large force of VietCong hiding in the thick jungle. This time the VC wanted a fight. The combat was intense, some of it savage hand-to-hand fighting. The noise level from rocket, machine gun, and automatic rifle fire was so high that officers and noncoms had to convey orders to their men by hand signals. Both forces sustained heavy casualties in a daylong battle that ended when the VietCong broke contact and disappeared into the jungle.[22]

The first big battle of the developing American war occurred in I ("Eye") Corps, the northernmost combat sector controlled by the 3rd Marine Amphibious Force, under the command of General Lewis Walt.[23] On August 15, 1965, Marine intelligence learned from a VietCong deserter the exact location of the 1st Vietcong Regiment. It was holed up in hamlets on the Batangan Peninsula, 15 miles south of a new Marine base at Chu Lai in the Quang Ngai province. General Walt concluded that the regiment posed a threat to Chu Lai, and he ordered the Marines to attack it.[24]

Quickly, the Marines organized a large-scale amphibious assault, code-named Operation STARLITE[25] on the VietCong positions. An assault battalion of the 3rd Marines landed on the sandy peninsula to pin the enemy against the sea. Another battalion came ashore in the enemy's rear. The two Marine battalions slowly worked their way forward over several days, squeezing the VietCong between them. As the Marines advanced, aircraft strafed and naval gunfire bombarded the VC positions. The Viet-Cong regiment was destroyed; about 700 enemy troops were killed. The Marines lost 50 dead and 150 wounded.[26]

Ia Drang: The Battle That Transformed a War

Operations STARLITE and HUMP served as preliminaries for the most important battle of phase one of the war of attrition. One of the defining battles of the U.S. Vietnam War occurred in a remote region of the central highlands between October 18 and

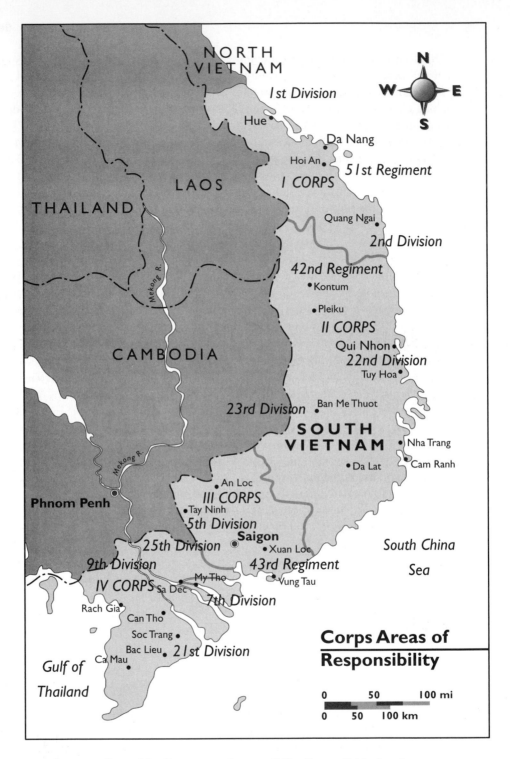

Figure 6.2 Corps areas of responsibility. *Source:* Public domain.

November 24, 1965. Westmoreland's chief worry during the summer of 1965 was that a PAVN offensive would conquer the central highlands, drive to the coast, and sever Saigon from the northern provinces, in effect cutting the country in half. He planned to counter the NVA drive with the 1st Air Cavalry Division (air mobile) based at An Khe. Westmoreland wanted the Air Cavalry to beat back the PAVN thrust and keep open Route 19, the main highway running from Pleiku to Qui Nhon.

The 1st Cavalry brought a new concept to warfare; it combined infantry, artillery, and aviation functions into one unit possessing 435 helicopters. Because rugged terrain and remote locations posed no obstacles for the Air Cavalry, they appeared to be the best force to blunt the PAVN offensive. The stage was set for the first battle of the war pitting North Vietnamese regulars against an elite American combat force.[27]

By early October, General Giap had committed three NVA regiments to the campaign, the 320th and 33rd, with the 66th held in reserve in Laos. These units were joined by some crack VietCong main forces. On October 19, the 320th and 33rd struck a U.S. Special Forces camp at Plei Me on the Cambodian border, 25 miles southwest of Pleiku, and ambushed an ARVN relief column sent to help the embattled defenders. The NVA regiments then lay siege to the Special Forces camp. Their objective was to destroy Plei Me, perhaps other camps in the area, and capture Pleiku. The North Vietnamese would then be positioned to strike east toward the coast. Westmoreland countered with the Air Cavalry, which supported the ARVN relief force with air and artillery attacks. U.S. firepower inflicted heavy casualties on the enemy and broke the siege of Plei Me.[28]

With their opening gambit checked, the PAVN forces retreated to the west. Westmoreland ordered the 1st Air Cavalry to search out and destroy the NVA forces. He was taking a gamble. The air mobile concept had never been tested in combat. The 1st Cavalry was under strength. Many of its soldiers were weakened from bouts with malaria, and many of their helicopters were not operational. The Air Cavalry would have to operate in unfamiliar and rugged terrain dominated by jungle-shrouded mountains. Even the open spaces between the jagged peaks were covered with shrubs and elephant grass as high as a man's head. The search area, the Ia Drang Valley, covered about 1,500 square miles of desolate country inhabited only by a Montagnard tribe, the Jarai.[29]

The first phase of the Battle of the Ia Drang lasted from late October to November 14. It consisted of searches punctuated by brief and violent clashes whenever the Americans located NVA units. The largest of these battles occurred on November 6, when two Air Cavalry companies ran into an NVA ambush. Both sides were bloodied in a brief but brutal firefight.[30] Another week of sporadic clashes preceded the most significant battles of the Ia Drang campaign.

By November 10, the PAVN forces had eluded their pursuers and had made their way to the sheltering crevices of the Chu Pong massif, a mountain range at the southern end of the Ia Drang Valley near the Cambodian border. There they planned to regroup for another assault on the camp at Plei Me. As the NVA forces took refuge in the Chu Pong Mountains, Major General Harry W. O. Kinnard, the Air Cavalry commander, ordered air searches of the area around the massif. After aerial reconnaissance,

Kinnard ordered the 1st Battalion, 7th Cavalry, to attack the largest landing site in the valley at the foot of the mountains, named "Landing Zone X-ray."[31] The 1st Battalion helicoptered in on November 14. Inadvertently, the 1st Cavalry had launched its attack right in the midst of a NVA staging area. The PAVN commander, General Chu Huy Man, instantly ordered the 66th and 33rd NVA regiments to counterattack. The climactic phase of the Battle of the Ia Drang was joined.

Within a few hours, the 1st Battalion was engulfed "in fighting as fierce as any ever experienced by American troops."[32] Lieutenant Colonel Harold G. Moore Jr., commanding the embattled battalion, brought in air strikes and artillery support. Moore also urgently requested reinforcements. The NVA rained rocket and mortar fire on Landing Zone X-ray in an effort to deny the 1st Battalion its reinforcements. Despite heavy fire, another battalion landed at Landing Zone X-ray to join the fight. For three days, fighting raged in the vicinity of Landing Zone X-ray, an area about the size of an American football field. The two U.S. battalions beat back repeated attacks by one of the NVA regiments that was trying to overrun their perimeter. The combat was intense, "resulting in savage, close quarter fighting, sometimes in hand-to-hand combat. One U.S. soldier was found dead, his hand clutching the throat of a dead enemy infantryman."[33]

Air Cavalry pilots flew in and out of the landing zone under heavy fire, bringing in ammunition and supplies, and hauling out wounded and dead soldiers. Air Force

Figure 6.3 The body of a slain comrade is carried to an evacuation helicopter by soldiers of the U.S. 1st Cavalry Division in the Ia Drang Valley early in the week of November 15, 1965. Photographer: Peter Arnett. *Source:* AP/Wide World Photo. Neg.#: APA4579987.

pilots bombed and strafed enemy positions. Artillery, hauled to nearby firebases by powerful CH 47 Chinook cargo helicopters, rained thousands of rounds on the North Vietnamese. B-52 strategic bombers flying out of Guam, each carrying a 36,000-pound payload, used for the first time in support of ground operations, pounded the NVA positions.[34]

The battle of the Ia Drang ended on November 17 when the North Vietnamese withdrew from the major battle sites and retreated into Cambodia. Forbidden by the rules of engagement then in place from pursuing a retreating enemy into neutral territory, General Kinnard had no choice but to let them go. Over the next few days, occasional firefights ensued between the air cavalrymen and straggling NVA units, the last occurring on November 24. Soon afterward, the Americans also withdrew from the river valley and were flown back to their base at An Khe. U.S. officials estimated that the North Vietnamese lost 3,561 soldiers killed and more than 1,000 wounded of the 6,000 that they had committed to battle. The three enemy regiments were decimated. The PAVN threat to the central highlands had been eliminated; 305 U.S. soldiers had been killed during the five weeks of fighting.[35]

U.S. forces won a significant victory at Ia Drang. General Westmoreland and his chief of operations, General William Depuy, both strongly committed to an attrition strategy, found confirmation for their views in the favorable ratio of U.S. to enemy losses which they fixed at 12:1. Both generals were convinced that search-and-destroy missions would eventually defeat both the VietCong and PAVN forces fighting in South Vietnam. Seasoned in the meat-grinder battles of World War II, Westmoreland and Depuy were convinced that they could bleed the enemy to death over the long haul of attrition warfare. They believed that they could soon achieve the "cross-over point," when they would be killing North Vietnamese soldiers at a faster rate than they could be replaced. The Battle of the Ia Drang locked the attrition strategy in place for nearly four years.[36]

The campaign also vindicated the air mobile concept; henceforth, helicopter assaults would be the mainstay of U.S. tactics in Vietnam.[37] Over the years of America's longest war, over a million soldiers would ride into battle aboard Huey helicopters, and the familiar "whup, whup, whup" of their whirling rotors would become the most enduring soundtrack of the Vietnam War.

But military analysts concerned themselves with some of the implications of the Battle of the Ia Drang. They wondered about the accuracy of the estimates of enemy casualties that, according to some skeptical soldiers on the scene, were merely WEGs (wild-eyed guesses) that probably drastically inflated the numbers.[38] They also wondered why the 1st Cavalry so quickly abandoned the Ia Drang Valley after the weeks of hard fighting, leaving the region vulnerable to future PAVN infiltrations. They were not reassured by the army's explanation that the valley had no strategic significance and that the chief purpose of the operation had been to kill as many enemy soldiers as possible.

The Ia Drang campaign also signaled that the Vietnam War was entering a new phase; it had evolved into two parallel wars. The long-standing conflict between the

GVN forces and the VietCong for control of the countryside continued. "Superimposed on the older war was the more recent and more conventional struggle between the NVA and the Allied forces."[39] Future battles would require more U.S. forces and would portend higher U.S. casualties. "A major part of the war in Southeast Asia had thus become Americanized, as vividly demonstrated by the Ia Drang campaign."[40]

The Battle of the Ia Drang also revealed that the Air Cavalry had a serious tactical limitation. Once out of their helicopters and on the ground, U.S. combat units were immobilized. The lightly armored NVA troopers used their foot mobility to outmaneuver the Americans. Only if the NVA attacked could the Americans engage them in battle, and only then could the Americans, using their far greater firepower, inflict more casualties than they took. But if the enemy chose to elude U.S. assault units, as the VietCong troops had done repeatedly in War Zone D earlier in the year, and as the retreating NVA troops did for two weeks in the Ia Drang River Valley, the Air Cavalry troops could not force a fight because they were not willing to leave their landing zones to go plunging off into the jungle in pursuit of their more mobile enemy. Throughout the Ia Drang campaign, the NVA had retained the tactical initiative. If the PAVN forces wished to evade the U.S. forces or engage in brief, small-scale firefights, they had the maneuverability to do so. How would U.S. search-and-destroy missions attrite a mobile enemy that could retain the tactical initiative and control the terms of engagement?[41]

Senior NVA commanders in Hanoi also took note. Their infantry had gone up against the most modern weapons systems the high-tech superpower could throw at them and they had survived. They could use their foot mobility to evade the U.S. firestorm and could retreat to the Cambodian sanctuaries to avoid annihilation. For them, Ia Drang amounted to a significant victory. The outcome of the Battle of the Ia Drang also convinced General Giap and his associates that North Vietnam would win the war eventually. Protracted warfare, the people's war strategy, would inevitably defeat air mobile tactics. The NVA would avoid taking unsustainable casualties. They would be patient; they would retain the tactical initiative. They believed they could eventually wear down the Americans and break their political will. The war would become unpopular with the American people, and the U.S. soldiers would have to leave South Vietnam—just like the Chinese and the French had been forced to leave previously. Once the Americans were gone, the NVA and VietCong forces would then quickly dispatch the puppet forces of the GVN and victory would be theirs.[42]

The civilian leader directing the American Vietnam War also derived lessons from the Battle of the Ia Drang. Secretary of Defense Robert S. McNamara was briefed by Generals Westmoreland and Kinnard immediately after the campaign. What he grasped was the most important message coming out of that crucial battle: Vietnam was going to be a long and difficult war. "The Vietnam War had just exploded into an open-ended and massive commitment of American men, money, and materiel."[43]

Following his briefings, McNamara drafted two secret memos for President Johnson in which he stated that in the aftermath of the Ia Drang battle, the United States had two options in Vietnam: It could arrange for a negotiated settlement and withdraw, or it could drastically increase the number of U.S. combat forces currently in Vietnam to try and win the war. If America opted for escalation, there could be 600,000 U.S. troops fighting in South Vietnam by 1967 and U.S. casualties could exceed 1,000 per month. Even so, in McNamara's estimation, the chances of defeating the North Vietnamese and VietCong forces would be no better than one in two or one in three.[44] The secretary of defense, having observed the failure of the gradualist bombing campaign against North Vietnam and having grasped the full implications of Ia Drang, was fast losing any expectations of a relatively quick and easy victory. As 1965 ended, McNamara, the chief architect of the American Vietnam War, was losing faith in that war.

A WIDER WAR

At year's end, General Westmoreland had achieved the objectives of phase one of his strategic war plan. The military situation had stabilized. He had 184,000 U.S. troops in South Vietnam and more were on their way. The VietCong found they could not sustain the momentum they had built up earlier in the year. The PAVN offensive in the central highlands had been blunted. The ARVN forces had stopped losing the war. Since the advent of U.S. combat forces during the summer of 1965, most war news had been favorable to the American side. Within the United States, the war continued to enjoy widespread popular support. *Time* named General Westmoreland its "Man of the Year" for 1965.

If it was true that the Allies had stopped losing by year's end, it was also true that they were far from winning the war. Even as security in South Vietnam had been strengthened in many areas, enemy infiltration had increased. About 20,000 NVA troops were fighting in South Vietnam, constituting one-third of the enemy's combat-effective troops. U.S. intelligence officials put the total enemy strength at year's end at 221,000, far more troops than ever before. The VietCong/PAVN forces had matched every U.S. escalation. Intervention had saved the GVN from imminent collapse, but had also transformed a revolutionary conflict into a prolonged and lethal international war.[45]

There were few major battles in South Vietnam during 1966, although there were many small-scale firefights all over the country. Although fighting occurred everywhere, it was concentrated in the areas where the Vietminh and their successors in the NLF were strongest: in the northern provinces and in the areas northwest and southwest of Saigon. In the northern sector, U.S. Marines engaged frequently in combat operations against VietCong forces and also defended the region just below the DMZ from NVA attacks. Westmoreland could not implement phase two of his attrition strategy according to the planned schedule for 1966 primarily because manpower shortages delayed his buildup of combat forces. His policy of limiting soldiers to a one-year tour in the combat zone also delayed the U.S. buildup and was a continuous source of manpower instability throughout the war. Further, most of the arriving troopers and their officers had never seen a moment's combat. Their training in the states before arriving "in country" had not prepared them for the rigors of warfare. Westmoreland spent most of the year acclimating, training, and building up the U.S. combat force levels. He was preparing his troops for the large-scale operations that would characterize the fighting during 1967.

U.S. troops also had to adapt to the unique conditions of the Vietnam battlefield. Unlike World War II or Korea, the Vietnam conflict was a frontless war. There were no territorial objectives to be taken. There was no vital center of enemy resistance to be destroyed; all of South Vietnam was a fluid battlefield. Military operations had to be highly mobile, multilinear, and nondirectional.[46] Battles occurred throughout the entire country. They could occur wherever and whenever the VC or PAVN forces picked a fight. They could occur in remote, sparsely populated highlands or borderlands, or amid the populous Mekong Delta and coastal regions. The American objective in these sporadic encounters was to attrite as many of the enemy as possible while using their superior air mobility and firepower to minimize their own casualties. Westmoreland never had enough combat effectives to occupy an area after a battle, so, inevitably, the U.S. forces would be withdrawn after a campaign had ended. Enemy forces often returned to these areas soon after the American pullout because there were no available ARVN forces to secure and pacify these areas, or because the ARVN forces available were ineffective in securing and pacifying these areas from which the enemy had been cleared. In such a formless war, the only measures of "winning" were statistics: the number of enemy soldiers killed, captured, or persuaded to surrender; of enemy weapons captured; and of enemy equipment, supplies, and food stores destroyed. It was a war of numbers, numbers that never added up to a U.S. victory before popular support for the war collapsed and time ran out.

In the fall of 1966, the United States mounted its largest search-and-destroy mission, Operation ATTLEBORO, which prefigured the big-unit war of 1967. In late October, General Westmoreland sent a large Allied force consisting of the 1st Infantry Division, units from two other U.S. infantry divisions, the 173rd Airborne Brigade, and a large contingent of ARVN troops into War Zone C. War Zone C was an area northwest of Saigon in the Tay Ninh province that bordered Cambodia. It had been a VietCong stronghold for years. The VietCong 9th Division, accompanied by a NVA regiment, had attacked a Special Forces outpost in that region and then overran a relief column sent to assist it.[47]

In a series of battles spread over a month, the 22,000-man allied force, supported with B-52 strikes and artillery, killed over 1,100 enemy soldiers and captured tons of food, weapons, and supplies before driving their adversaries across the border into Cambodia. U.S. commanders declared ATTLEBORO to be a victory, citing the 15:1 kill ratio they achieved. PAVN commanders noted that while their forces were depleted, they were not annihilated. They also noted that their forces retained the tactical initiative, controlled the fighting, and broke off engagements when they sensed they were taking unacceptable casualties. Most important, North Vietnamese commanders understood that Allied search-and-destroy operations, while destructive, did not permanently deny them the use of basing areas. As soon as the Allies withdrew, and the bombing and artillery bombardments ceased, the Communists returned. If ATTLEBORO were an Allied victory, it was only temporary and limited.[48]

As 1967 dawned, Westmoreland was more convinced than ever that large-scale search-and-destroy missions such as Operation ATTLEBORO provided the means for the destruction of North Vietnamese regular forces and VietCong main force units. He believed subsequent ATTLEBORO-type operations would lead to eventual Allied victory. He "forged jumbo operational plans as the dominant pattern of strategy for the upcoming year."[49] Even though hundreds of small-scale operations would continue all over South Vietnam during the year and account for over 90 percent of the combat operations involving U.S. forces.

Westmoreland had at his disposal 390,000 U.S. soldiers, including seven divisions, two airborne and two light infantry brigades, an armored regiment, and a Special Forces group. They were supplemented by "third country" forces from South Korea, Australia, and New Zealand. In addition, ARVN, which had expanded rapidly in 1966, could field eleven divisions. Total RVNAF (Republic of [South] Vietnam Armed Forces), in addition to the ARVN units, included territorial forces, security forces, local troops, and irregulars. Westmoreland's Combined Campaign Plan for 1967 assigned RVNAF the tasks of securing and pacifying areas under their control, while the U.S. forces carried the brunt of the fighting against the Communists. His objectives included securing South Vietnam's borders and beating back NVA attacks across the DMZ, neutralizing the VC forces in War Zones C and D, eradicating VietCong sanctuaries in the vicinity of Saigon, defending the strategic central highlands against PAVN incursions, driving the VC and PAVN forces back from the populated regions, and providing security for the populated regions of South Vietnam.[50]

The first of the 1967 big-unit campaigns occurred in a region about 30 miles northwest of Saigon, in a strategic area sandwiched between War Zones C and D called the Iron Triangle, which served as a staging area for VC attacks against GVN installations in the vicinity of Saigon. The Iron Triangle, bounded on two sides by rivers and on a third by a jungle, incorporated about 40 square miles of nearly impenetrable territory covered by trees, vines, and shrubs. Underneath the dense growth lay miles of tunnels, caverns, and chambers, some of which dated from the Vietminh campaigns against the Japanese during World War II. Thousands of insurgents could inhabit this subterranean labyrinth, an inviolable sanctuary, seemingly immune from counterattacks or efforts at destruction. On the fringe of the region, nestled in a loop of the Saigon River, lay the village of Ben Suc, many of whose estimated 3,500 residents had been VietCong or VietCong supporters for years.[51]

Wanting to eliminate once and for all the threat to the Saigon regime posed by the VietCong redoubt buried within the recesses of the Iron Triangle, General Westmoreland in early January 1967 launched a massive operation, code-named CEDAR FALLS, lasting three weeks and involving 30,000 U.S. and ARVN forces.[52] The first phase of the operation was to dispose of the threat posed by the villagers of Ben Suc. If, according to VietCong doctrine, the people are the "sea" in which the guerrilla "fish" must swim, MACV strategists concluded that permanently eliminating the threat posed by the VietCong forces marshaled in the Iron Triangle necessarily involved "draining the sea" by removing the villagers and razing the village, leaving the VC "fish" to flop about and perish.

On January 8, 1967, an armada of U.S. transport helicopters suddenly descended upon Ben Suc. Instantly, a force of hundreds of American and ARVN soldiers surrounded the village. They met with little resistance from the sullen villagers. Although the arrival of the helicopters caught them by surprise, most of the VietCong fighters in the village at the time escaped. All of the villagers were rounded up and transferred to a refugee camp at Phu Loi, near Phu Cuong, fifteen miles downriver. Specially trained destruction teams then moved in. Giant caterpillar tractors, called Rome plows, fitted with wide bulldozer blades, cleared huge swatches of jungle, exposing the tunnel complexes. Demolition teams destroyed the houses above the ground and the tunnel complexes below. Within a few days, "the village of Ben Suc no longer existed."[53]

While Ben Suc was being demolished, U.S. combat forces ranged across the Iron Triangle searching for VietCong units. Because the VC commander chose not to engage the American forces, most of the VC fighters scattered and fled. Despite the corps-sized operation, the superior American mobility, and the vastly greater U.S. firepower, the VietCong retained the tactical initiative.

During the three weeks of the CEDAR FALLS operation, about 700 VietCong were killed and another 700 were either captured or turned themselves in under the *chieu hoi* (open arms) program, run by the GVN, which granted amnesty to VietCong defectors. U.S. forces also destroyed enemy structures, equipment, and food supplies. Volunteers from the 1st Infantry Division's special chemical unit, nicknamed the "tunnel rats," combed the nearly 12 miles of tunnels that were exposed at various locations in the Iron Triangle. Among their discoveries were a power station, a fully equipped field hospital, a weapons factory, and a regional PLAF headquarters.[54]

The entire region was then bombed, shelled, strafed, and burned to destroy any remaining structures or tunnels that could be of use to the VietCong. In an effort to deter VietCong reentry into the Iron Triangle, the area was declared a "free fire zone," which meant that artillery and air strikes could be made in the region without prior approval of GVN officials and without warning to its inhabitants. As the Allies departed the Iron Triangle, they were convinced that they had dealt the VietCong a devastating setback. They had rendered one of the enemy's long-time bastions and staging areas unusable and had severed the VietCong connections with the people inhabiting its vicinity. They soon discovered that "they were wrong."[55]

The VietCong quickly returned to the Iron Triangle. They rebuilt and resupplied their base and once again threatened the region around Saigon. The razing of Ben Suc and the forced relocation of all of its residents amounted to an admission that the ARVN forces were failing to pacify the peasants. Some villagers were killed and others were brutally treated by ARVN soldiers while relocating them. Most of the villagers lost their homes, their ancestral lands, and all of their possessions except for what they could carry with them. They found conditions in the refugee camp at Phu Loi miserable. Initially, each family was allotted only ten square feet of living space in hastily constructed shelters. About all CEDAR FALLS brought the Saigon government "was a devastated forest and a horde of hostile refugees."[56]

About a month after CEDAR FALLS, Westmoreland mounted a larger operation called JUNCTION CITY in War Zone C. The U.S. soldiers made special efforts during JUNCTION CITY to trap VietCong combat units and force a fight with them, thus avoiding a repetition of CEDAR FALLS, when most of the VC slipped through their grasp. But the VietCong mostly avoided combat during JUNCTION CITY, and the bulk of their forces fled across the Cambodian border. Even so, over a three-month period, American officials reported about 3,000 enemy soldiers killed.[57] But War Zone C was not neutralized, the VietCong 9th Division was not put out of the war, and no serious efforts were made to pacify the villagers living in the region. War Zone C continued to be used as a VC basing area after the Allied withdrawal.

One dimension of the ground war that limited the effectiveness of JUNCTION CITY was the rules of engagement civilian leaders imposed on U.S. troops fighting in Vietnam. Even though both the VC and the NVA forces repeatedly violated Cambodian neutrality, U.S. forces were never allowed to pursue their enemies into Cambodia or attack any Cambodian-populated areas. The VietCong 9th Division commander, aware that U.S. mobility and firepower had eliminated the inviolability of VC basing areas inside of South Vietnam, took his troops into adjacent Cambodian sanctuaries where they joined PAVN combat units.

But Westmoreland's forces had to stop at the Cambodian border. The rules of engagement in effect confined them to defensive efforts aimed at attriting a resourceful, mobile enemy who could escape beyond the fixed boundaries of the ground war in southern Vietnam to regroup and then renew attacks on GVN targets in South Vietnam. U.S. military commanders vainly sought to modify these rules of engagement to permit U.S. troops to pursue opposing forces to their destruction or until they surrendered, even if that meant some fighting on Cambodian soil and inflicting damage and casualties on that neutral nation.[58]

While Operations CEDAR FALLS and JUNCTION CITY were being conducted in III Corps Tactical Zone in the vicinity of Saigon, to the north, in II Corps Tactical Zone, battles for control of the central highlands raged. Units of the 4th Infantry Division under the command of Major General William R. Peers, operating out of their base camp at Pleiku, battled forces from the 1st and 10th NVA divisions. In Kontum province, small units from both sides engaged in fierce firefights of short duration amid "some of the most difficult tropical terrain in the world."[59] There, among huge trees, as tall as 250 to 300 feet, where little sunlight filtered through a triple-canopied jungle even at midday, PAVN regulars chose where and when to attack U.S. forces. The Americans counterattacked, trying to kill as many of the enemy as they could, often sustaining heavy losses themselves. Both sides lost many soldiers in vicious jungle-mountain warfare.

Figure 6.4 U.S. troops of the 7th and 9th divisions wade through marshland during a joint operation in South Vietnam's Mekong Delta, April 1967. *Source:* AP/Wide World Photos.

In other action in the central highlands, General Peers deployed units of his 4th Division along the South Vietnamese border in western Pleiku. His objective was to deny invading PAVN forces access to South Vietnam's strategic heartlands. From April to October, U.S. and NVA troops fought a series of battles in the rolling tropical plains of western Pleiku near the Cambodian border. The hard-fighting U.S. forces succeeded in beating back numerous NVA thrusts. By October, General Peers discerned that the major Communist push would be an invasion of Kontum province, directly north of Pleiku.[60] There, one month later, occurred the Battle of Dak To, a decisive battle that determined the outcome of the campaigns waged for control of the central highlands during 1967.

Dak To was the site of a U.S. Army Special Forces camp set amid towering mountains in central Kontum province. The camp lay in a valley ringed by 6,000-foot peaks and ridges. Fighting had begun during the summer, when NVA forces had entrenched themselves in bunker complexes along the hilltops and ridgelines above the camp. For months, grueling battles took place in the vicinity of Dak To between forces from the 24th NVA Division and Allied forces that included the 3rd Brigade of the 1st Cavalry

Division and some elite ARVN ranger units. In early November, a battalion of the 173rd Airborne and a brigade from the 4th Infantry Division were flown in to join the battle.

During the first two weeks of November, U.S. patrols made contact with the NVA units, enabling the American troops to call in artillery barrages, tactical aircraft, and high-flying B-52s to pound the enemy positions. On November 17, the fighting around Dak To intensified when a patrol from the 173rd Airborne Brigade came upon the 174th NVA Regiment entrenched in bunker complexes running along the eastern slope and the summit of a peak known on American maps as Hill 875. Hill 875 lay 12 miles west of the Special Forces camp, about two miles from the point where the borders of South Vietnam, Cambodia, and Laos merge.[61] "The fight for Hill 875 would ultimately climax the Battle for Dak To, as well as the 1967 campaign for the highlands."[62]

The 2nd Battalion, 503rd Infantry, of the 173rd Airborne was ordered to move in and clear the enemy from Hill 875. It took five days of hard fighting to secure the mountain. During the battle, the paratroopers of 2nd Battalion lost so many men that another airborne battalion and units of the 4th Infantry Division had to be brought in. On November 23, the Americans reached the summit of Hill 875, only to discover that the defenders had abandoned their positions during the night. The 174th had accomplished its mission, which had been to cover the withdrawal of the NVA forces retreating into Cambodia and Laos.[63]

The taking of Hill 875 ended the Battle of Dak To. U.S. officials estimated that during the campaign, the North Vietnamese lost about 1,400 KIA (killed in action) compared with 289 American and 49 ARVN dead.[64] The Battle of Dak To was also the last of the border campaigns in the central highlands for the year. The Allied forces had repulsed the NVA invaders. The strategic central highlands remained under South Vietnamese control.

As the border battles raged in Pleiku and Kontum provinces for control of the central highlands, to the north in I ("Eye") Corps Tactical Zone the Marines held the line against efforts by the NVA units to infiltrate across the DMZ into northern South Vietnam. Along Route 9, a dirt road that ran east-west across the country's northernmost province of Quang Tri, from the sandy coastal plains to the mountainous border with Laos, the Marines had constructed a series of fire support and patrol bases at Dong Ha, Cam Lo, Khe Sanh, and Lang Vei. The facility at Khe Sanh already served as a Special Forces camp. Teams of *Montagnards,* involved in the secret war in Laos that aimed at interdicting enemy supplies coming down the Ho Chi Minh Trail, operated out of Khe Sanh. Route 9 roughly paralleled the DMZ, and most of the Marine firebases lay 10 to 15 miles south of the DMZ. Forward of these firebases, perched on a hill 3 miles south of the DMZ near Con Thien (Hill of Angels), the Marines had constructed their most important firebase.[65]

Sporadically, artillery batteries from the NVA 325th C Division shelled the northern firebases. In April 1967, a regiment from the 325th occupied several hills in the vicinity of Khe Sanh in preparation for an attack on the camp. The Marines, in a series of vicious hill fights, drove the PAVN forces from the heights and ended that threat to

Khe Sanh.[66] In September, NVA forces besieged Con Thien. Artillery and rocket barrages on Con Thien and a nearby base at Gio Linh were followed by infantry assaults that tried to overrun the Marine perimeters.

U.S. forces eventually broke the sieges of Con Thien and Gio Linh with a combination of massed firepower and aggressive ground tactics. A combination of artillery and naval gunfire, tactical aircraft strikes, and B-52 bombings hit the enemy positions along the DMZ. Marine troopers, using claymore mines, machine guns, and automatic rifles, beat back the PAVN charges, inflicting severe casualties. The hellish Battle of Con Thien ended on October 20. American estimates of NVA losses for that battle were 2,000 KIA. Over 200 Marines died in the conflict.[67] At year's end, the Marines still retained all of their forward bases. Fighting hard, they had withstood sieges, repelled infantry assaults, and blocked all NVA efforts to infiltrate units across the DMZ.

Within a few months, the Americans would discover that the bloody campaigns initiated by the NVA forces at Dak To and Con Thien in the fall of 1967 were part of General Giap's strategic plan to lure American forces into remote border regions in central and northern South Vietnam in preparation for the surprise VietCong/PAVN assaults on the country's cities and towns during the Tet campaign of early 1968.

Westmoreland's attrition strategy during 1967 had accomplished major objectives. U.S. troopers had pushed many of the VC main force units and guerrillas away from populated areas, forcing them to flee to remote regions of the country, or seek refuge in Cambodian sanctuaries to avoid destruction. VietCong-controlled areas in South Vietnam had been significantly reduced. The VietCong discovered they no longer had any safe havens inside South Vietnam; nowhere were they safe from the reach of American firepower.

The NVA forces were driven out of the central and northern border provinces of South Vietnam, often with heavy casualties. As 1967 ended, American officials estimated that 180,000 enemy soldiers had been killed since 1965. Assuming a sizable official inflation of body counts, it is clear that U.S. forces had inflicted severe losses on the enemy while keeping their own losses comparatively light. The number of PLAF volunteers declined, forcing the NLF to rely on conscription, which many villagers resented. U.S. combat forces and Westmoreland's aggressive tactics prevented a GVN collapse and VietCong victory, both of which probably would have occurred before 1965 ended, if not for the massive American intervention.

But the U.S. attrition strategy also had limits, and it was grounded on some dubious assumptions. Westmoreland assumed that U.S. forces would be able to use their superior firepower and mobility to destroy enemy forces at a greater rate than they could be replaced, at the same time keeping U.S. casualties low. But despite Westmoreland's big-unit campaigns of 1967, the war remained essentially one of small-unit warfare. For these small-unit battles, the VC and NVA units usually retained the tactical initiative. They determined where and when they wanted to fight and for how long. If their casualties reached unacceptable levels, they broke off battles and melted into the jungle. The U.S. forces could use their massive firepower to inflict heavy casualties, but they could not annihilate their enemies. For the duration of the American war in Vietnam, "the pace of fighting was dictated by the North Vietnamese and by the Vietcong, not by the United States."[68]

The VC and NVA also exploited the restrictions placed on U.S. forces. They knew that U.S. troops could not pursue them and that U.S. aircraft could not strike them whenever they sought the safety of their cross-border sanctuaries in Cambodia and Laos. They also took advantage of the weather, when heavy rains, thunderstorms, and thick fog hampered U.S. air operations. When they were trapped or cutoff, and knew that retreat was impossible, both the VietCong and PAVN troops found they could nullify the U.S. firepower advantage by swiftly closing with the American troops and fighting at close quarters.[69]

MACV planners did not anticipate the remarkable ability of the Communists to absorb huge manpower losses and continue the war. Despite suffering proportionately far greater casualties than the armies of most nations that have lost wars in the twentieth century, the VietCong and NVA forces carried on the fight year after year. The MACV planners also could not foresee that their pursuit of victory via the strategy of attrition amounted to an open-ended U.S. military commitment that might eventually require more forces than President Johnson would find politically acceptable to send to Southeast Asian battlefields. Finally, they failed to anticipate that rising U.S. casualties, although proportionally and absolutely far lower than the losses of either the NLF or PAVN forces, would become the major cause of the Vietnam War's growing unpopularity in the United States.[70]

As 1967 ended, the U.S. forces had not defeated their enemies, nor were the NVA or VietCong anywhere close to being defeated. Despite substantial losses, the Vietcong and NVA forces not only survived, but increased in numbers. They matched all of the U.S. escalations of the conflict. The U.S.-AVRN forces never reached the cross-over point, or even came close.

Many VietCong guerrillas retained their capability of operating within the populated regions. The NLF's political infrastructure remained intact. Many of the NLF political cadres retained their ties to the villagers. In South Vietnam, as 1967 ended, thousands of insurgent "fish" continued to swim in the South Vietnamese "sea." U.S. soldiers had won all of the major battles since the Battle of the Ia Drang, but they were not close to winning the war. In the summer of 1965, General Westmoreland had estimated that the war could be won by the end of 1967. By the end of 1967, he had nearly 500,000 soldiers fighting a stalemated war.

Attrition warfare also had several adverse consequences that hindered the U.S. effort at nation-building in South Vietnam. Bombing and artillery fire disrupted the South Vietnamese rural economy, diminished rice production, inadvertently killed civilians, and generated millions of refugees. The refugees were herded into squalid camps or else they fled to the suburbs and cities, where they survived as an uprooted fringe population representing potential VietCong fifth columns.[71] At any given time during the American war in Vietnam, between 4 and 5 million people, representing 25 to 35 percent of the South Vietnamese population, became refugees. Many suffered from serious diseases: malaria, tuberculosis, and dysentery. Others had serious wounds that left them permanently disfigured or disabled.

The disintegration of their traditional ways of life coupled with the often desperate circumstances of the refugees made many Vietnamese yearn for an end to the war. There was also the terrible ironic consequence: mass immiseration of the refugees also contributed to the growing sense that the Americans were disrupting and ruining the lives of many of the people they had come to help. The U.S. war weakened the social fabric of a fragmented nation and further alienated people from a fragile government that had never enjoyed the support of much of the rural population. The American takeover of the war represented an implicit expression of U.S. officials' lack of confidence in the South Vietnamese military forces, and it further undermined the resolve of the ARVN troops.[72]

THUNDER FROM THE AIR

ROLLING THUNDER, the strategic air war waged by the U.S. Air Force, the air attack arm of the U.S. Navy, and the RVNAF against North Vietnam, which began on March 2, 1965, paralleled the ground war raging in South Vietnam. Initially, the air war against the North was a strictly limited affair. President Johnson himself selected the targets on a weekly basis, allowing air commanders to choose the specific times for the raids during that time span. During the first weeks of ROLLING THUNDER, attacks were confined to military targets, mostly south of the 20th parallel. In time, the air war against North Vietnam evolved in phases. "During each phase, a different emphasis was placed upon targets, and the scope and intensity of the attacks varied as well."[73] During the first phase implemented in the spring and summer of 1965, allied planes also attacked infiltration routes in North Vietnam just above the DMZ to try to destroy the ability of the North Vietnamese to infiltrate men and supplies into South Vietnam in support of the VietCong insurgency.

It quickly became evident to the planners of ROLLING THUNDER that the gradualist bombing campaign of limited scope had failed to reduce appreciably North Vietnam's ability to infiltrate men and supplies into South Vietnam. Hanoi also gave no indication that it was ready to negotiate an end to the war on anything like American terms. Conceding the air war's ineffectiveness, General Earle Wheeler, chairman of the Joint Chiefs, advised President Johnson to intensify the aerial campaign, order more sorties, and strike at key North Vietnamese military and industrial targets. After a brief debate in July 1965 among senior administration officials in which George Ball, the hawks' nemesis, was the only adviser to oppose escalating the air war, Johnson ordered

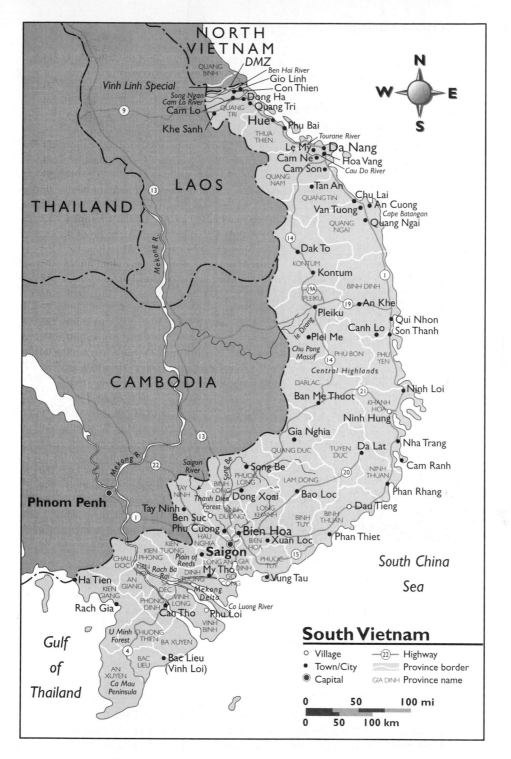

Figure 6.5   Map of South Vietnam. *Source:* Public domain.

major increases in the number of air strikes. He also expanded the target list. For the rest of 1965, Johnson and McNamara gradually expanded the air war against North Vietnam, although they refused to order an all-out air assault to try to destroy the war-making ability of North Vietnam, as called for by the Joint Chiefs and Admiral U.S. Grant Sharp, the commander of ROLLING THUNDER.[74]

As 1965 ended, it was evident to both U.S. civilian and military leaders that the air war had failed to accomplish its strategic goals, even though it had evolved into a large-scale operation involving thousands of sorties monthly. The target list had expanded to include military bases, transportation systems, and supply depots, as well as intensified bombing of the major infiltration routes out of North Vietnam. Intelligence data confirmed that Hanoi was infiltrating more men and supplies into the south than ever before, and North Vietnam also continued its strong backing of the southern insurgency. Further, U.S. intelligence sources showed that the bombing, far from hurting the morale of the North Vietnamese people, had united them with their government.[75]

Johnson's military advisers blamed the continuing failure of the air war on the self-imposed restrictions of civilian leaders. But Secretary of Defense Robert McNamara remained confident that at some point the gradually escalating bombing campaign would reach a point where Hanoi would stop supporting the southern insurgency rather than continue to absorb punishment. President Johnson still believed in the air war as a means to secure his political goals in Vietnam, but he realized that bombing could not bring him the relatively quick and easy victory that he had anticipated.[76]

After Johnson ordered a bombing pause from December 24, 1965, to February 1, 1966, in a futile effort to get negotiations going, both the air war and the debate over it resumed. Once again the Joint Chiefs pressured McNamara to escalate the bombing, but they changed their plan from interdiction to bombing North Vietnam's POL (petroleum products, i.e., gasoline, oil, and lubricants) storage facilities located near the cities of Hanoi and Haiphong. The Joint Chiefs understood oil to be the vital element in North Vietnam's ability to infiltrate men and materiel into South Vietnam. By early 1966, U.S. intelligence estimates had placed five NVA regiments in South Vietnam. Supplying these forces required the DRV to expand its truck fleet. By destroying North Vietnam's oil supply, the Joint Chiefs reasoned that they could stop the trucks from supplying the NVA and NLF forces fighting in South Vietnam. Since North Vietnam possessed no oil wells and no refineries, all their oil was imported, most of it via Soviet tankers that docked and offloaded their cargoes at the port of Haiphong. Prior to distributing it, most of the oil was stored in giant tank farms on the outskirts of the city. The Joint Chiefs insisted that destroying these storage tanks and those near Hanoi would cripple North Vietnam's ability to sustain the revolution in South Vietnam. Admiral Sharp concurred.[77]

Pentagon analysts studied the POL bombing proposals for months. Since the sites were located near cities, there was a high risk of civilian casualties. The oil storage areas were also defended by antiaircraft batteries, surface-to-air missiles (SAMs), and North Vietnamese air force fighters. The danger of heavy U.S. aircraft losses was great.

Johnson also worried that such a major escalation of the war might provoke Hanoi to expand the war in South Vietnam, or worse, it might bring the Chinese and the Soviets into the conflict.

After months of discussion, Johnson's military and civilian advisers finally convinced him that raids on North Vietnam's POL facilities were necessary. Johnson approved them, although he retained misgivings. On the day the first attacks were carried out, a distraught president, fearful that they might somehow go wrong, told his daughter, Luci, "Your daddy may go down in history as having started World War III."[78]

On June 29, 1966, Navy fighter-bombers from USS *Ranger* on YANKEE STATION in the Gulf of Tonkin and Air Force fighter-bombers flying out of bases in Thailand struck three POL sites "in the heart of North Vietnam."[79] U.S. officials considered these initial attacks highly successful. They were the first air strikes near Hanoi and Haiphong, and they caught the enemy by surprise. Facilities near the two cities accounting for about 60 percent of North Vietnam's POL storage capacity were destroyed, with the loss of only one American plane. Polls showed the American public strongly backed the POL raids, and Johnson's popularity rating jumped 12 points, from 42 percent to 54 percent. America's European allies were less enthusiastic about the POL raids, and Prime Minister Harold Wilson of Great Britain publicly dissociated himself from the attacks.[80] The Soviet Union and China both condemned the air strikes and promised increased aid to North Vietnam, but made no gestures toward intervention.

Delighted with the bombing results and the public's response to them, and relieved that the Chinese and Soviets reacted moderately, Johnson ordered additional POL strikes. During July and August 1966, Navy and Air Force planes attacked oil storage facilities in the North Vietnamese heartland. By September 4, the POL campaign had ended, and 75 percent of Hanoi's oil storage capacity had been destroyed. Soviet-Bloc tankers that hauled in Hanoi's POL supplies could no longer offload their cargoes in Haiphong because American bombers had destroyed the port's pumping equipment.[81] But North Vietnamese air defenders made American pilots and air crewmen pay a high price for the July and August POL campaigns. Antiaircraft batteries and SAMs downed over 70 U.S. aircraft during those two months. Hoa Lo Prison in Hanoi, given the ironic nickname of the "Hanoi Hilton" by the U.S. flyers, became the residence for years for dozens of American pilots and crewmen shot down over North Vietnam while flying POL missions.

Analysts monitoring the POL operations concluded that the attacks constituted a strategic failure. Having anticipated the raids long before President Johnson finally ordered them, the North Vietnamese had decentralized their POL supply systems. Stored in 50-gallon drums in small camouflaged sites near major transportation arteries, dispersed POL supplies proved hard to find and extremely costly to destroy. Although the air strikes knocked out a high percentage of Hanoi's oil storage capacity, they destroyed only a small amount of their POL stores. The POL imports via rail from the Soviet Union through China quickly replaced the losses. Analysts also discovered that only a small percentage of North Vietnam's POL requirements were needed to keep the supply trucks rolling south, and the NVA had more than enough oil and gasoline for themselves.[82]

At the conclusion of the U.S. POL campaign, a joint CIA-DIA (Central Intelligence Agency–Defense Intelligence Agency) report found that Hanoi retained "the capability to continue support of activities in South Vietnam at even increased combat levels."[83] McNamara also commissioned a study of the second phase of ROLLING THUNDER by the Institute for Defense Analysis (IDA), an independent agency from outside of the government, composed of forty-seven distinguished American scientists. The IDA report, known as the Jason Summer Study, was bluntly critical of strategic bombing. Whatever damage ROLLING THUNDER had done to North Vietnam's facilities and equipment had been more than offset by the increased flow of economic and military aid from the Soviet Union and China. IDA scientists not only found the POL campaign to have failed, they doubted that any amount of strategic bombing could either appreciably reduce North Vietnam's infiltration of men and supplies to the southern war theater or induce Hanoi's leaders to call off their support of the revolutionary war in South Vietnam:

> It must be concluded therefore, that there is currently no adequate basis for predicting the levels of U.S. military activity that would be required to achieve the stated objectives—indeed, there is no firm basis for determining if there is any feasible level of effort that would achieve these objectives.[84]

The failure of the POL raids ended Robert McNamara's advocacy of increased bombing. He now viewed the Vietnam War as a stalemate and became convinced that President Johnson should seek a negotiated end to the conflict. He believed that no amount of military pressure the United States could conceivably apply could break the political will of the North Vietnamese and force them to abandon their support of the revolutionaries in southern Vietnam. For the remainder of his tenure as secretary of defense, McNamara refused or scaled back the military's subsequent requests for additional troops.[85] He began to identify with the small but growing number of Washington officials who were becoming disenchanted with the U.S. war policy in Vietnam. In time, these doves came to outnumber the hawks among Johnson's advisers.

To substitute for the bombing campaign that they perceived as a failure, the scientists who had drafted the Jason Summer Study proposed building an electronic barrier of wire, mines, and sensors across the DMZ and the segment of the Ho Chi Minh Trail complex that wound through the Laotian panhandle as the most effective way of reducing infiltration into South Vietnam.[86] McNamara became a powerful advocate of the electronic barrier, which was later partially built, as an alternative to the bombing of North Vietnam.

McNamara's turn toward dovishness set off another debate in Washington over the effectiveness of the bombing campaign against North Vietnam. The Joint Chiefs, wedded to the belief that if enough bombing were done against enough targets soon enough it would be effective, continued to call for escalating the air war against North Vietnam. Since the POL raids had failed to diminish North Vietnam's ability to supply its forces and the VietCong fighting in the South, the military leaders shifted their advocacy. They now called for a vastly expanded bombing campaign to destroy North Vietnam's electrical industry, port facilities, and locks and dams. "They aimed to wreck the enemy economy to produce a prostrate foe."[87]

McNamara assumed the leadership of the advocates of scaling back the bombing campaign. Johnson was caught in the middle of his advisers' intramural dispute. By the spring of 1967, after the failure of another bombing pause calculated to start the negotiations process, Johnson, siding with his military advisers, escalated the air war. ROLLING THUNDER entered its third phase, which included air strikes against hitherto exempted major industrial targets: electrical production plants and North Vietnam's only steel factory. U.S. aircraft also mined North Vietnamese harbors and estuaries and bombed previously off-limits targets near the Chinese border. "ROLLING THUNDER grew fangs."[88] Polls showed the American public strongly supported the expanded air war that aimed to destroy North Vietnam's industrial economy.[89]

For the rest of 1967, U.S. aircraft attacked industries supportive of the war effort, including electrical-generating plants, petroleum storage facilities, military installations, transportation support facilities, and air defense systems. ROLLING THUNDER spared few North Vietnamese targets of any economic or strategic consequence. The air war raged at peak intensity as measured by the scope of permissible targets, numbers of sorties flown, and bomb tonnage dropped. Johnson had granted the Joint Chiefs and Admiral Sharp permission to hit most of the targets that they had been demanding to attack since ROLLING THUNDER began in March 1965. President Johnson, many of his civilian advisers, the Joint Chiefs, Admiral Sharp, and the air commanders all believed that the damage inflicted by the air war, coupled with the success of Westmoreland's big-unit war in South Vietnam, would eventually "cause Hanoi to yield to American terms."[90] The third phase of ROLLING THUNDER lasted until April 1, 1968, when, in the throes of a political crisis created by the Tet-68 campaigns, President Johnson deescalated the air war.

The Tet-68 Offensive mounted by the VietCong and PAVN forces proved dramatically that the bombing campaign "to interdict the flow of men and supplies to the South had been a signal failure."[91] Most of the resources necessary for the enemy to mount and sustain a large-scale campaign had flowed down the Ho Chi Minh Trail, despite the intensive bombing of North Vietnam. The magnitude of the Tet-68 Offensive stunned the advocates of ROLLING THUNDER and shattered their conviction that the air war had curtailed North Vietnam's ability to infiltrate men and materiel to the South and weakened their will to fight.[92]

ROLLING THUNDER, the gradually expanding air war waged against North Vietnam for three years, from March 2, 1965 through March 31, 1968, failed. It failed to interdict North Vietnamese supply routes to the South, and it failed to weaken either

North Vietnam's fighting capabilities or its determination to support the war in South Vietnam. The Joint Chiefs, Admiral Sharp, and the air commanders always insisted that political restrictions imposed by civilians had caused the air war to fail. But during the third phase of the air war, most of the targets in North Vietnam that the Joint Chiefs claimed to be of economic or military significance were either destroyed or damaged before Tet-68 occurred. ROLLING THUNDER, even when waged at its maximum intensity for nearly a year, neither stopped the flow of goods and fighters to South Vietnam nor broke Hanoi's will. The North Vietnamese, while absorbing immense damage and losses from the sustained U.S. air war waged against it, not only continued its war effort in southern Vietnam, but also they expanded it. They infiltrated some 35,000 troops south during 1965, the first year of the aerial war. In 1967, when the expanded air war raged at its most destructive levels, North Vietnam sent 90,000 soldiers into South Vietnam.[93]

Johnson's military advisers also insisted that had the bombing campaign been intense from the outset, North Vietnam would not have had time to develop its air defenses, disperse its industries and POL stores, or prepare its people to withstand the air war. Hanoi would have been forced to abandon its support of the southern revolution, or risk national extinction. Although it necessarily remains forever in the realm of counterfactual speculation, it is possible that an all-out effort from the start might have rendered ROLLING THUNDER more effective. But it is also true that when ROLLING THUNDER began, Hanoi's leaders expected that U.S. aircraft would soon attack industrial targets and bomb population centers. They quickly mobilized all of their resources to defend against an unrestricted air war. They also prepared for an American invasion of North Vietnam and for a protracted war. They prepared for far worse than they ever got or that the Joint Chiefs and Admiral Sharp ever proposed delivering, and never did they indicate that they were prepared to end their support of the southern rebels or that they could not infiltrate the supplies and people into South Vietnam that the war in that region required. Further, an all-out air assault that threatened to destroy North Vietnam could have provoked Chinese or even Soviet intervention, a possibility that no responsible policymaker in Washington dared ignore. Finally, an all-out air assault would have created more international and domestic opposition to the war:

> There is no basis to saying with any certainty that air power unfettered by political considerations would have "won" the air war in Vietnam. Various outcomes of a more rapid escalation [were] possible, not all of them favorable to victory.[94]

Military analysts have suggested additional reasons for the failure of ROLLING THUNDER besides the political controls clamped on U.S. air operations over North Vietnam by civilian officials. The unconventional type of warfare waged by the enemy contributed to the failure of the air war. A conventional air war waged against North Vietnam could not defeat an enemy waging guerrilla warfare in South Vietnam. There were three major reasons why the effort to interdict Hanoi's supply efforts failed: (1) the minimal needs of the NVA and NLF forces fighting in South Vietnam, (2) North Vietnam's excess resupply capabilities, and (3) the supplies pouring into North Vietnam from China via rail and from the Soviet Union and Eastern Bloc countries via ship.[95] Destroying North Vietnam's rudimentary industrial economy had no discernible effect on either its capacity or its will to wage a guerrilla war against the RVN.

ROLLING THUNDER grew from 25,000 sorties flown in 1965 to 79,000 in 1966 and to 108,000 in 1967. During that time, U.S. aircraft dropped 643,000 tons of bombs and inflicted an estimated $600 million worth of damage on North Vietnam.[96] It crippled the country's nascent industrial sector and disrupted its agriculture. Several cities in southern North Vietnam were leveled, and others sustained severe damage. The government diverted thousands of people from agricultural work to air defense activities. To keep its transportation system functioning, an estimated 100,000 people were recruited to repair roads, railroads, and bridges. Women workers made up more than half of the people in work brigades and repair crews, which were continually at work for the duration of the air war against North Vietnam.

It was also vitally important for Hanoi to keep the railroad links to China open. An estimated thousand tons of supplies came daily from China. Thousands of Chinese workers worked alongside their Vietnamese allies to keep the railroad open and the supplies flowing to Vietnam. Food supplies diminished, and only extensive aid from the USSR and China enabled millions of North Vietnamese to maintain even a subsistence-level diet. The quality of available education and health care in North Vietnam declined. Although Washington never adopted a policy of directly targeting civilians, the bombing campaign nevertheless claimed approximately 50,000 civilian casualties out of a population of 17 to 18 million.[97]

ROLLING THUNDER eventually proved to be exceedingly costly. Before Johnson ordered the bombing of North Vietnam halted on October 31, 1968, America lost 950 planes costing about $6 billion. A Pentagon study found that in addition to manpower and aircraft losses, every dollar's worth of damage inflicted on North Vietnam cost the American taxpayers $9.60 in 1966.[98] There were other costs: Captured U.S. pilots and air crewmen provided Hanoi's leaders with a bargaining chip that they later used in negotiating with American officials. ROLLING THUNDER also gave the Communists a propaganda advantage that they exploited to influence world and American public opinion. Robert McNamara, disillusioned by the failure of the air war, wrote in a memo to President Johnson:

> The picture of the world's greatest superpower killing or seriously injuring 1,000 non-combatants a week, while trying to pound a tiny, backward nation into submission, (is not a pretty one).[99]

Although opinion polls showed that a large majority of Americans consistently supported the air war against North Vietnam for its duration, the growing number of domestic opponents of the war seized on ROLLING THUNDER. Doves denounced it as expensive, futile, and wrong. They denounced the extensive damage done to homes, small businesses, and schools, and the loss of civilian lives. Administration spokesmen defended the bombing; they claimed it was precision bombing that destroyed only military targets. They dismissed Hanoi's claims that thousands of civilians were being killed by the bombing as so much Communist propaganda.

Angry North Vietnamese officials invited U.S. journalists to come and see for themselves. In December 1966, Harrison Salisbury, a prominent *New York Times* journalist, traveled to North Vietnam. His dispatches from Hanoi highlighted the extensive civilian casualties and widespread destruction to civilian structures. Salisbury's reports, which refuted Washington's claims that only military targets were struck, were widely read and fueled the growing antiwar movement.

By the summer of 1967, President Johnson had to confront a sizable antiwar movement that derived much of its furious energy from its reactions to the air war. Both the civilian and military advocates of ROLLING THUNDER had assumed that the destruction or the threat of destruction of North Vietnam's industrial sector would cripple Hanoi's ability to supply the insurgents fighting in South Vietnam and persuade it to negotiate an agreement permitting South Vietnam to survive as a stable, non-Communist state. That assumption turned out to be one of the gravest errors in judgment made by the officials who led the United States to war.

AERIAL ATTRITION WARFARE

While ROLLING THUNDER unfolded against North Vietnam, the United States waged a large-scale air war in South Vietnam against the VietCong. Air operations in South Vietnam were an integral part of the U.S. attrition strategy. Although the American media gave the ground war in South Vietnam far more coverage, the war leaders in Washington considered the accompanying air war to be just as important. The southern air war reflected the same logic that underlay the aerial campaign against North Vietnam: that America would use air power extensively to force Hanoi to stop its aggression in South Vietnam. The air war in South Vietnam also suffered from the same misjudgments: underestimating the enemy's determination and ability to counter U.S. air power.[100] The air war in South Vietnam was also much larger, lasted far longer, and was much more diversified than the bombing campaign against North Vietnam.

Strikes against guerrilla bases and supply routes constituted two-thirds of the U.S. air operations undertaken in southern Vietnam. These preplanned attacks, based on aerial reconnaissance and intelligence reports, attempted to deny the VietCong "safe havens where they could train and rest troops, store ammunition and food, and plan offensive operations."[101] Giant B-52 Stratofortresses from the Strategic Air Command (SAC) often participated in these air strikes against guerrilla strongholds and supply lines. Code-named ARC LIGHT, the flights of B-52s, initially flying from Andersen Air Force Base on the U.S. island territory of Guam, 2,800 miles away, approached their targets at altitudes varying from 30,000 to 36,000 feet. The giant bombers were both invisible and inaudible to observers on the ground; they combined the element of surprise with devastating power. A flight of six B-52s, each plane capable of carrying from 18 to 27 tons of bombs and using a carpet bombing technique in which all of the bombs were released according to a predetermined pattern, could saturate a target area in a matter of seconds. "Carpet bombing could change the face of the earth."[102] The ARC LIGHT strikes often caused enormous destruction and heavy casualties. The B-52s constituted the most frightening weapon in the hi-tech U.S. arsenal deployed by the U.S. in Vietnam War. After surviving a B-52 assault, a terrified VietCong guerrilla called carpet bombing "the chain of thunders."[103]

If U.S. air strikes were scheduled for populated areas or sites near populated areas, clearance had to be granted by South Vietnamese officials, either by the province chief or by the military commander responsible for the area. Friendly populations were supposed to have advance warning that the area in which they resided had been designated a target area. Although U.S. officials denied it, air attacks in or near populated areas claimed civilian casualties, as proven by examinations of hospital admissions records. Advance warning was not always provided and not always understood when furnished.[104] Subject to approval by South Vietnamese officials, areas known to be controlled by the VietCong and not inhabited by friendly villagers were designated "free fire zones." These areas could be bombed without clearance from local officials or without warning to any inhabitants who might be in the area.[105]

After the preplanned strikes against guerrilla sanctuaries and supply lines, the most frequent kind of missions flown in South Vietnam were close air support operations carried out by air force, Marine, and army pilots, who usually flew from air fields

Figure 6.6 Giant B-52 strategic bombers were the most feared weapons systems in the American arsenal. Here a B-52 Stratofortress releases a load of 750-pound "iron bombs" during an intense phase of the Battle of the Ia Drang, November 1965. Photographer: USAF. *Source:* AP/Wide World Photos. Neg.#: APA4414251.

in South Vietnam. These strikes provided crucial added fire power for ground combat forces locked in battle with VietCong units.[106] These missions also helped keep down U.S. casualties. These close-in attacks were called in by ground commanders or forward air controllers (FACs) flying over the combat area. The FACs would mark the location of enemy forces with smoke flares to guide the pilots as they roared in to fire rockets, 20-mm cannons, air-to-ground missiles, or to drop iron bombs, phosphorous bombs, or napalm canisters on their targets.

Along with its preplanned strikes and close support missions, the Air Force also conducted an extensive campaign of aerial defoliation, code-named Operation RANCH HAND, in South Vietnam to deprive the guerrillas of their forest cover and to destroy VietCong food crops. Defoliation was a civilian counterinsurgency program initiated by President Kennedy on a small scale in 1962, over the objections of his senior military advisers who feared the United States might be accused of resorting to chemical or biological warfare.[107] As the war escalated, Operation RANCH HAND expanded rapidly. U.S. Air Force C-123s, specially fitted with 1,000-gallon tanks and bars of spray nozzles attached to the undersides of their wings, flew hundreds of sorties during the years 1965 to 1967. Over the door of the RANCH HAND briefing room at Tan Son Nhut Air Base hung a plaque with the sardonic inscription, "Only You Can Prevent Forests."[108]

Crews aboard the RANCH HAND C-123s used a variety of herbicides on their missions. The different types of herbicides were identified by color-coded bands encircling the drums containing the chemicals. The defoliants including agents Orange, White, Purple, Pink, and Green. Agent Orange proved to be the most versatile, effective, and widely used herbicide. It contained an extremely toxic chemical agent, 2,4,5-T (Dioxin). One C-123 could haul 11,000 pounds of Agent Orange that it dispensed over a 300-acre target area in about four minutes. Within a few weeks, all of the plants, shrubs, and trees in the sprayed area had withered, turned brown, and died. Lush, green forests turned quickly into barren, brown moonscapes following a RANCH HAND spraying. During 1967, the peak year of Operation RANCH HAND, Air Force crews sprayed about 1.5 million acres, 40 percent of which were croplands. Before the defoliation campaign ended, more than 100 million pounds of chemicals were sprayed over millions of acres of South Vietnamese forests and crops. Operation RANCH HAND destroyed about one-half of South Vietnam's timberlands and left behind unknown human costs.[109]

Operation RANCH HAND in time became controversial. On June 26, 1969, a report appeared in a South Vietnamese newspaper alleging that a toxic ingredient found in Agent Orange caused birth defects in children born to women who had been exposed to the herbicide. Later that year, a study by the National Institute of Health presented evidence that the wives of U.S. airmen who had been exposed to Agent Orange gave birth to a disproportionate number of deformed babies. The affected families were eventually paid about $175 million by the chemical companies that produced the herbicide for the Air Force. A study done under the auspices of the American Association for the Advancement of Science to investigate the effects of spraying in Vietnam found that

Figure 6.7   Two Air Force C-123s on a defoliation mission over jungle terrain in South Vietnam during Operation RANCH HAND conducted by the 12th Air Commando Squadron. The C-123 planes are spraying the jungle canopy with defoliation liquid. *Source:* CORBIS. Neg.#: BE045742.

some of the forested areas that had been sprayed with Agent Orange had not regenerated. On April 15, 1970, the Defense Department suspended the use of Agent Orange. The last RANCH HAND mission, using other herbicides, flew from Tan Son Nhut Air Base on January 7, 1971.[110]

Years after the Vietnam War had ended, scientific researchers were still trying to determine the specific effects that exposure to Dioxin could have on people. Veterans, exposed to Agent Orange during the war, have reported recurring health problems, including skin rashes, breathing dysfunctions, various kinds of cancers, and birth defects in their children, which they believe came from their exposure to Dioxin. A class action suit against the Veterans Administration brought by veterans who were exposed to Agent Orange while serving in Vietnam was settled out of court in 1985.[111]

Another facet of the U.S. air wars in Indochina entailed air operations within neutral Laos. The air war in Laos was an inevitable outgrowth of the long U.S. involvement in that country that dated back to Eisenhower's presidency. Following the 1962 Geneva Accords that created a neutral Laos, the United States provided substantial military and economic assistance to the royalist government headed by Prince Souvanna Phouma. Meanwhile, the Pathet Lao continued its war against that government. The ongoing war in Laos got entertwined with the larger war in Vietnam because the Ho Chi Minh Trail ran through the mountainous regions of eastern Laos. The North Vietnamese stationed troops in this remote region to assist in the movement of troops and supplies along the Ho Chi Minh Trail; they also armed and trained the Pathet Lao forces. Washington, while publicly supporting the government of Souvanna Phouma, also used the CIA to train Hmong (Meo) tribesmen to fight the Pathet Lao.

In addition to fighting a secret war in Laos using indigenous proxies, the United States began an extensive bombing campaign in that country in 1964. At the beginning of 1965, the southern panhandle of Laos, which shared a 450-mile-long border with Vietnam, had been turned into a major supply corridor supporting VietCong military operations in South Vietnam. A few months before ROLLING THUNDER began against North Vietnam, President Johnson ordered U.S. aircraft to interdict traffic coming south along the components of the Ho Chi Minh Trail running through the Laotian corridor. The bombing campaign in Laos gradually expanded until it reached a volume of 3,000 sorties per month during the fall of 1967. From 1964 through 1967, U.S. aircraft dropped an estimated 450,000 tons of bombs in Laos.[112]

The air war waged in Laos from 1965 through 1967, like its counterpart waged against North Vietnam, also failed strategically. Bad flying weather and rugged jungle-covered mountainous terrain continually hampered U.S. air operations. Because the Ho Chi Minh Trail through Laos consisted of a vast web of small roads and trails, most of which were invisible from the air, U.S. pilots could only interdict a portion of the weapons, military supplies, and soldiers coming into South Vietnam. "Sweating porters moved heavily burdened bicycles down the narrow trails, under the cover of a visually impenetrable canopy of foliage."[113] Enemy countermeasures and self-imposed restrictions on the bombings further reduced the effectiveness of the air war in Laos. At the height of the U.S. aerial campaign against the segments of the Ho Chi Minh Trail running along the Laotian corridor, despite suffering sizeable losses of trucks, bicycles, and personnel, the North Vietnamese were infiltrating more supplies and personnel into South Vietnam than ever before.

The Other War

While rapidly escalating the Vietnam War and transforming America's failed advisory role into a full-scale military effort to suppress the VietCong insurgents and to discourage their North Vietnamese backers, U.S. officials strongly supported the Ky regime's efforts to build a new nation in southern Vietnam. Ky's performance as prime minister pleasantly surprised Washington. He managed to survive in office, and the chronic instability that had plagued South Vietnamese politics since the anti-Diemist coup of November 1963 subsided. The June 1965 coup that brought Ky to power would prove to be South Vietnam's last. In February 1966, to escape from the growing opposition to the Vietnam War among senators led by William Fulbright, who was holding hearings before the Senate Foreign Relations Committee on all aspects of the administration's war policy, Johnson traveled to Honolulu with his senior advisers to meet with General Ky and other high South Vietnamese officials.

On February 6, in Honolulu, Johnson publicly embraced Ky and urged him to emphasize what Johnson called "the other war" in South Vietnam: building a South Vietnamese nation, developing the South Vietnamese economy, improving the lives of the Vietnamese people, and winning the allegiance of the villagers.[114] Ky, who had been briefed by U.S. officials before coming to Hawaii, made a speech replete with ambitious plans for revitalizing South Vietnam's economy and ensuring a prosperous and free nation. Johnson, delighted by Ky's speech, wrapped his arm around the South Vietnamese leader and told him, "Boy, you speak just like an American!"[115] At the conclusion of the conference, through a joint communique, Johnson and Ky pledged to work for the welfare of the ordinary people and to bring about the end of poverty, disease, and ignorance in South Vietnam. It gave pacification a powerful momentum that lasted for the duration of the American war in Vietnam.[116]

Ky, emboldened by Johnson's public show of support at Honolulu, returned to Vietnam determined to strengthen his grip on the South Vietnamese government. Backed by U.S. officials, Ky persuaded the Military Directorate to dismiss a powerful rival,

Figure 6.8 The leaders meet and confer in Honolulu, February 6, 1966. In foreground Secretary of Defense Robert McNamara talks with President Nguyen Van Thieu. In the background President Johnson confers with Premier Nguyen Cao Ky.
Source: AP/Wide World Photos. Neg.#: APA1364635.

one of the triumvirs, General Nguyen Chanh Thi, the I Corps commander. The I Corps area included Danang and Hue, South Vietnam's second and third largest cities. Ky's firing of Thi provoked a major political crisis in South Vietnam, resulting in a brief civil war that occurred inside the war already raging in South Vietnam.

The Buddhists, quiescent for nearly a year under the leadership of Thich Tri Quang, who had formed a loose confederation of dissidents called the Struggle Movement, suddenly erupted. Their revolt quickly spread to Danang, Saigon, and other South Vietnamese cities. The Buddhists also revived their demands for free elections and a restoration of civilian rule. Other disaffected groups joined their movement, including students, trade unionists, religious sectarians, and even dissident army and police elements. Eight Buddhist monks and a nun committed self-immolation by fire in support of the movement. Although they were careful not to make their ultimate political goals explicit, the Buddhists hoped that the elections would bring a coalition government to power in South Vietnam that would end the war, negotiate a settlement with the NLF, and expel the Americans.[117]

Henry Cabot Lodge, having replaced Maxwell Taylor, was back in Saigon for another stint as the U.S. ambassador to South Vietnam. Lodge feared that free elections could bring a neutralist government to power that would proceed to negotiate an end to the war and throw the Americans out. Lodge endorsed Ky's efforts to suppress the Buddhists and their supporters, as did General Westmoreland and President Johnson. They wanted the civil war-within-a-war suppressed as quickly as possible before South Vietnam completely unraveled.

When the Buddhists had risen against the Diem regime three years earlier, U.S. officials had supported them, mainly because the Kennedy administration had perceived Diem and his brother Nhu as being uncooperative. The Ngo Dinh brothers had rejected American advice and had been unwilling either to reform their government or prosecute vigorously the war against the PLAF. But in the spring of 1966, with the U.S. stake in the Vietnam War far greater than it had been during the Diem era, Ky and Thieu had cooperated with U.S. officials and strongly supported the expanded U.S. war effort against the NLF and the North Vietnamese. Whatever their shortcomings, U.S. officials backed the generals, because they feared that if the Buddhists, or political leaders supported by the Buddhists, came to power, they would seek negotiations with the NLF and possibly the North Vietnamese.

Assisted by General Westmoreland, Ky moved against the Buddhists. On the morning of April 5, 1966, U.S. C-130 transports flew 2,000 ARVN troops into the Danang air field. Ky, personally leading two battalions of ARVN Marines, announced that he had come to "liberate Danang." Ky's show of force, designed to overawe his opponents, only provoked them. General Thi and the local ARVN commander, General Nguyen Van Nhuan, joined the rebels. General Nhuan used his troops to confine Ky's forces to the Danang Air Base. He also warned Ky that if he tried to move his troops out of the air base there would be fighting. Ky was forced to back down. He announced that he would withdraw his troops from Danang and seek a rapprochement with the

Buddhists. After meeting with Buddhist leaders, General Thieu, Ky's chief of state, announced that elections for a constituent assembly would be held within a few months and that civilian government would soon be restored. Reacting to these concessions from the military government, Tri Quang and the other Buddhist leaders called off their protests.[118]

By canceling their protests, the Buddhists played into the hands of the wily Ky and Thieu, who never intended to keep their promises. Confident of U.S. support, they were stalling for time until they could mount a larger effort against the rebels. On May 15, 1966, Ky launched another assault on Danang. With U.S. aircraft again providing logistic support, Ky sent in larger forces armed with tanks, artillery, and other heavy weapons. Ky's forces took control of the mayor's office, Danang's one radio station, I Corps headquarters, the police station, and key military installations. There followed two days of bitter and intense fighting in the streets of Danang, during which hundreds of soldiers and protesters were killed. Ten more Buddhist monks and nuns killed themselves in fiery acts of self-immolation. Ky's heavily armed forces crushed the revolt.[119] His forces also suppressed the dissident movement in Saigon, but Hue, the center of the Buddhist resistance movement, remained in rebel hands.

The Struggle Movement's actions took on a decidedly anti-American coloration in Hue. Angered by the U.S. backing of Ky, the dissidents sacked the U.S. consulate and burned the United States Information Service (USIS) library there. They also unfurled banners demanding the ouster from Vietnam of all foreign influences, including American. Soon thereafter, Ky's forces assaulted the dissident positions in the former imperial capital. By June 19, Hue was once again under government control. Tri Quang was arrested along with hundreds of bonzes, students, and other protesters. The Buddhist political movement was crushed. Ky and Thieu, rescinding their promises to hold elections within a few months, announced that the military junta would remain in power until elections took place sometime in 1967. The Ky-Thieu regime, with strong support from U.S. officials, had proven too powerful for the Struggle Movement to bring down.

American soldiers were both baffled and angered by the internecine struggle occurring at a time when the U.S. military effort in Vietnam was rapidly expanding, American troops were doing most of the fighting, and U.S. casualties were growing. One U.S. soldier angrily asked, "What are we doing here? We're fighting to save these people, and they're fighting each other!"[120] But the Buddhist revolt had little impact on the continuing war between the RVNAF and PLAF. The VietCong were caught by surprise by the Struggle Movement and did not support it or take advantage of it.

The suppression of the Buddhist uprising signaled the end of the Buddhists as a major factor in South Vietnamese politics. The ARVN generals had defeated their last major political rivals; the possibility of a civilian alternative to military rule in South Vietnam no longer existed. After three years of political conflict that had begun with the coup that brought down the Diem regime, during which none of a succession of governments could provide even the rudiments of political leadership, a measure of stability was returning to South Vietnam's civic life. Following the suppression of the

Figure 6.9   A nun administers first aid to Buddhist protester. *Source:* CORBIS.
Neg.#: U1569662.

Buddhists, the Vietnamese people living under the control of the RVN perceived that
the rule of the generals could not be challenged as long as the Americans maintained
such a powerful presence in their country and backed the military rulers.

The middle ground that the Buddhists had been building up between the Saigon
military and the NLF was cut away and prospects were destroyed for anything resembling a viable "third force."[121] Politics in South Vietnam had been polarized. The people's practical choices were reduced to either rule by the ARVN generals or by the
NLF-Hanoi forces, a prospect that had no appeal for millions of South Vietnamese citizens who were neither Communists nor supporters of military dictators.

U.S. officials, in addition to committing more troops to the expanding war against
the PLAF and NVA forces, had to inject American power into the areas of South Vietnam under the RVN's administrative control. Given the absence of indigenous support
for the RVN, it was necessary for American forces to provide guarantees that the South
Vietnamese governmental apparatus would remain in the hands of Vietnamese willing
to support American policies and goals. U.S. officials often staffed RVN agencies and
programs at the provincial and district levels. The RVN took on more of the attributes

of an American dependency in 1966. Consequently, NLF propagandists could more easily portray the Americans as the hated colonial successors of the departed French.

Following the suppression of the Buddhists, both U.S. and South Vietnamese officials tried to implement effective pacification programs among the rural population of South Vietnam. To U.S. officials, pacification had become a catch-all term that referred to all of the nonmilitary aspects of the war. As U.S. ground combat forces took over the bulk of the fighting in South Vietnam, the South Vietnamese armed forces, both ARVN and territorial troops, were assigned major responsibility for pacification support. In practice, pacification support usually meant using local South Vietnamese forces to provide area security for the villagers, while the American forces engaged VietCong main force units. Sometimes U.S. combat forces, especially Marines assigned to I Corps, provided area security for the villagers. Pacification could also refer to the myriad of civilian programs that provided the rural population of South Vietnam with schools, health services, and economic assistance—whatever might improve the quality of their lives, wean them from the allure of the NLF, and bind them closer to the government of South Vietnam.

Responding to American pressure, with funding and expert advice provided by U.S. officials, the Ky government implemented a Revolutionary Development program (RD). Consciously imitative of the NLF cadres, 59-person Revolutionary Development teams were sent into South Vietnamese villages. Team personnel were trained to provide physical security for the villagers, assist in government reorganization and political development, establish schools and literacy programs, and aid in social and economic development.[122] They lived among the people and "carried out hundreds of tasks to build popular support for the government and to undermine the VietCong."[123]

As had been the fate of earlier pacification efforts, Revolutionary Development generally failed. Cadres were hastily trained, and there were never enough teams available to service all of South Vietnam's hamlets and villages. District officials sometimes undercut the Revolutionary Developmental teams' efforts; sometimes ARVN troops extorted money from the villagers and stole their pigs and chickens. The most serious problem was the absence of physical security. Since U.S. troops were preoccupied with the war against the VietCong main force units, providing village security devolved upon the ARVN forces. But they were incapable of supplying adequate security in many areas. In some locales, ARVN troops were the security problem. In insecure areas, the VC terrorists kidnapped and murdered thousands of RD cadres in 1966 and 1967.[124]

The failure of Revolutionary Development also raised three fundamental questions about the RVN's approach to pacification:

1.   Pacification could not succeed as long as corrupt officials and rogue ARVN units continued to prey upon the villagers. And there was no evidence that Ky's regime seriously intended to reform itself and eliminate these abuses.
2.   Given the peasant preoccupation with land owning, land reform would have to form the heart of any long-range pacification program that hoped to win the allegiance of

the peasantry. Ky's lack of commitment to land reform and his responsiveness to the interests of large local landowners ensured the continuing failure of Revolutionary Development.

3. To overcome the fragmentation of South Vietnamese society and the alienation of the rural masses from the ruling urban elites, villagers would need to have been given a sense of participation, an active involvement in the government, for pacification to work. The peasants would have had to see people from their villages rising to positions of authority within the government system to identify with the GVN, to connect its operations to their interests and welfare. Ky's government never tried to breach the profound divisions existing within the South Vietnamese social structure by recruiting district or provincial officials from the villages.

In April 1967 President Johnson, to promote pacification, folded it into Westmoreland's command (MACV). All civilian and military agencies involved with pacification now came under the administrative control of a hybrid agency called Civil Operations and Revolutionary Development Support (CORDS). The MACV deputy placed in charge of CORDS was Robert W. Komer, an energetic civilian bureaucrat nicknamed "Blowtorch" because of his aggressive management style. Komer reorganized and revitalized the American approach to pacification. He improved the liaison with South Vietnamese civilian and military officials responsible for pacification programs. He also established the Hamlet Evaluation System (HES), a computerized reporting system to monitor and quantify the progress of pacification in the countryside. Komer also worked closely with CIA officials and the RVN district and provincial leaders to put greater emphasis on identifying and neutralizing the VietCong political infrastructure that enabled the insurgency to maintain its ties to the villagers.[125]

While it pursued the will-o-the-wisp of pacification following the suppression of the Buddhists, the South Vietnamese military regime also implemented democratic political reforms, but in carefully limited fashion to ensure that the generals retained control of the government. Pressure for drafting a constitution and holding elections came mainly from the Johnson administration. Washington wanted to legitimatize the South Vietnamese government in American eyes and thereby gain increased domestic support for the expanding war.

In early 1967, South Vietnamese voters elected a constituent assembly. The newly elected assembly, assisted by U.S. constitutional scholars, drafted a new constitution modeled on the American Constitution. It created a bicameral legislature, but it granted the executive branch most of the powers of government and permitted the president to assume dictatorial powers in the event of an emergency that could be declared at his discretion. Further, the president needed only to obtain a plurality of the votes to be elected. This provision prevented opposing candidates from joining together in a runoff to defeat the government's candidate.[126]

Elections under the new constitution were held in September 1967. The most serious political conflict that occurred during the campaign pitted the supporters of General Ky against the supporters of General Thieu to see which man would head the government ticket. The showdown occurred when they attended an intense two-day caucus consisting of forty-eight ARVN generals. For two days the generals did what they did best—they engaged in emotional, often tumultuous politicking. When the last speech had been made and the last threat delivered, Thieu emerged the victor. Thieu ran for president with Ky as his vice-presidential running mate.

They were challenged by ten civilian candidates. Since Communists and neutralists were barred from seeking office, Buddhists were boycotting the election, and the opposition consisted of obscure men with local followings, Thieu and Ky were running under conditions that made their defeat extremely unlikely. Even so, the Thieu-Ky ticket received only 35 percent of the vote. They were embarrassed by the electoral performance of a political unknown, Truong Dinh Dzu, a wealthy lawyer running on a platform calling for negotiations with the National Liberation Front, who came in second with 17 percent of the vote.[127]

Their slender electoral victory did not give the Thieu-Ky regime greater legitimacy, a broader political base, or increased political power. Two-thirds of South Vietnam's carefully circumscribed electorate preferred alternatives to Thieu and Ky. It is possible that if all of the South Vietnamese people had been permitted to vote in a genuinely free election, they might have registered a preference for a government that would have sought to negotiate an end to the war and to expel the Americans. Thieu and Ky survived in power not because their government was popular or intrinsically powerful but because it had the backing of the Americans.

U.S. officials convinced themselves that the September 1967 election demonstrated that democracy had come to South Vietnam and that the Thieu-Ky regime had achieved a popular base of support. Most South Vietnamese voters held a different view. They understood that they had participated in a carefully staged political show mainly to please their American patrons. "Many Vietnamese regarded the entire process as an American-directed performance with a Vietnamese cast."[128] U.S. officials had tried to keep a low profile; they had endeavored to let the South Vietnamese develop their own version of democratic elections. But in the end, the Americans interferred enough to poison the whole political process. The new government neither validated democracy nor respected the rights of its opponents. But the Thieu-Ky victory, however dubious it might be within a Vietnamese political context, meant that the military junta would remain in power, Americans would remain in South Vietnam, and the war would go on. Behind the democratic facade and U.S. officials' spin, the South Vietnamese leaders provided brutally authoritarian government.

From mid-1965 to the end of 1967, while the Americans escalated both the air war against North Vietnam and the ground war in South Vietnam, the South Vietnamese government failed to eliminate its underlying political weaknesses. Pacification floundered, and the Thieu-Ky regime remained a narrowly based military directorate dependent on continuing American support to remain in power. The large-scale U.S. military effort could not compensate for the continuing failure of the South Vietnamese to erect a strong, stable, and popular government or to build a viable nation. The American war proved either irrelevant to nation-building or exacerbated its problems. The continuing political failures of the Saigon regime were a major cause of the eventual U.S. failure in Vietnam.

The impact of the U.S. war, with its half million troops, thousands of civilians, and billions of dollars, strained and disrupted the South Vietnamese economy.[129] Saigon became a boomtown whose prosperity was based on a single industry, war. The former "Paris of the Orient" became a crowded, noisy metropolis, its streets clogged with traffic and its hotels, restaurants, bars, nightclubs, casinos, and brothels teeming with American soldiers, civilian advisers, journalists, and tourists. Many Saigonese found work providing services to the Americans and to their fellow Vietnamese who profited from the war economy. Corruption became a way of life for many South Vietnamese officials. They siphoned off large amounts of U.S. aid in a variety of ways. In many cases, U.S. agencies paid millions of dollars for imaginary goods and services that were never provided. The black market became a big business trafficking in huge amounts of stolen American consumer goods, weapons, and illegal currency exchanges.[130] For years, one could buy anything in Saigon; anything, that is, but hearts and minds, victory, or peace.

As the U.S. presence in South Vietnam expanded, tensions between the Americans and Vietnamese increased. Because of their profound cultural differences, the Americans and Vietnamese had to struggle to understand each other across a vast chasm of mutual ignorance and misperceptions. The exigencies of fighting a war and building a nation exacerbated the already tense relations between the two allies. Because the VietCong had infiltrated every echelon of both the government's civilian agencies and its armed forces, security leaks posed chronic problems. U.S. commanders were forced to keep all Vietnamese off of their major bases and to withhold details of major military operations from their ARVN counterparts in order to maintain security.

"The paradox arose of the Americans fighting on behalf of an army (and a government) that they treated with disdain, even contempt." U.S. soldiers often spoke openly and contemptuously of their South Vietnamese allies. They wondered why the enemy's soldiers often seemed braver and fought harder than the ARVN forces. A stark contradiction evolved between the official political objectives for which Americans were fighting in Southeast Asia—the freedom and independence of the South Vietnamese people and the reality of a war in which Americans often bypassed both the RVN and its military forces as they designed and carried out U.S. campaigns aimed at defeating the VietCong and the NVA.[131]

The apparent indifference of many Vietnamese to the welfare of U.S. soldiers who were dying in battle trying to protect them infuriated American troops. The uncanny ability of the villagers to avoid mines and booby traps that killed and maimed U.S. soldiers led many troops to assume that these people cooperated with the enemy or that they were the enemy. U.S. soldiers, upon entering a village after taking fire from it or its vicinity, unable to tell which of its inhabitants were "friendlies" and which were VietCong or VietCong sympathizers, tended to assume that all of the villagers were either real or potential enemies.[132]

Diplomatic Charades

As the American war in Vietnam expanded, pressures for a negotiated settlement of the conflict also escalated. From mid-1965 until the end of 1967, White House officials estimated that as many as 2,000 individual efforts were made to begin peace talks between Washington and Hanoi. President Johnson claimed in his memoirs that he personally followed 72 negotiation initiatives.[133] Neither side dared to ignore the many diplomatic efforts initiated by third parties concerned with bringing together American and North Vietnamese negotiators to halt the war, but they consistently refused to make the concessions necessary to initiate serious peace talks. The more both sides invested in the conflict, the less willing they were to consider negotiating. The escalating military stalemate bred a diplomatic impasse as both sides manuevered to score "PR" points with the international community and world public opinion.

Hanoi repeatedly denounced U.S. involvement in Vietnam as a violation of the 1954 Geneva Accords. North Vietnamese leaders insisted that the United States would have to cease all acts of war against Vietnam, dismantle its bases, and remove all of its military forces before any talks could begin. They further insisted that the political destiny of South Vietnam would be determined in accordance with the program of the National Liberation Front. The Saigon regime would be replaced by a coalition government dominated by the NLF. Hanoi's leaders clearly indicated that they considered the question of Vietnam's unity to be fundamental and nonnegotiable: "The unity of our country is no more a matter for negotiations than our independence."[134]

According to the view from Hanoi, there was no role for the United States to play in determining the political destiny of South Vietnam. America would have to withdraw all of its troops from that country, after which the RVN would doubtless collapse or be overthrown. Hanoi would then proceed to unify Vietnam under its control. Ho Chi Minh believed that great power diplomatic interests and the U.S. intervention in South Vietnam after Geneva had deprived the Vietminh of the political dividends that should have accrued from their military victory over the French, which was control of an independent and unified Vietnam.

The Communists were determined never to entrust their political future to others again. This time, they would determine the political outcome of the Vietnam War, that is, the current phase of a war that had been going intermittently since 1946. Hence, they made American withdrawal from Vietnam a precondition for negotiations and declared the unity of Vietnam to be a nonnegotiable item. Given the battlefield realities existing during the 1965 to 1967 period, Hanoi's diplomatic stance did not represent the negotiating position of a nation seriously concerned with a diplomatic resolution of the Vietnam War. It reflected the diplomatic posturing of leaders who were determined to win the war and confident that in time they would.

Washington promulgated its negotiating position at the beginning of 1966. Johnson, planning to escalate the air war against North Vietnam, halted the bombing during the Christmas holiday. He combined the bombing halt with a diplomatic offensive, sending administration officials around the world and across America to explain that the United States was ready to negotiate with Hanoi without insisting that they meet any preconditions. But the United States offered to halt the bombing of North Vietnam only after Hanoi had stopped infiltrating men and supplies into South Vietnam. Washington would withdraw all of its troops from South Vietnam only after an "acceptable political settlement" had been reached.

While agreeing that the political destiny of South Vietnam would have to be worked out by the South Vietnamese themselves, Washington refused to allow the NLF to join any South Vietnamese government. They would allow their views to be represented, but only after Hanoi stopped all "acts of aggression." "Beneath these ambiguous words rested a firm determination to maintain an independent, non-Communist South Vietnam."[135] Johnson's insistence that he favored unconditional negotiations masked a U.S. diplomatic stance that was no more acceptable to Hanoi than its positions were to Johnson. McNamara also acknowledged that part of Johnson's motivation for halting the bombing was to prepare American and world public opinion for more escalations.[136] Johnson did not expect Hanoi to accept his overtures.

Hanoi promptly denounced the U.S. bombing pause as a sham and rejected Johnson's terms for negotiations. The North Vietnamese regarded Vietnam as one country. They dismissed as a species of political fiction Washington's claim that a sovereign nation with a legitimate government existed in the southern half of Vietnam. They sharply differentiated between what they regarded as illegitimate American interventions into the affairs of their country and their own legitimate involvement in Vietnam's internal affairs. Hanoi refused to consider performing any reciprocal acts to get the Americans to halt the bombing and insisted that only their negotiating positions offered a basis for a correct political settlement of the war.[137] Johnson, anticipating the rebuff, resumed the air war against North Vietnam on January 31, 1966.

In 1966 and 1967, even though both sides remained far apart and neither country appeared willing to make the kinds of concessions that might have brought them closer to negotiations, various third parties tried to bring Hanoi and Washington to the bargaining table. One of these initiatives involved the Polish diplomat Januscz Lewandowski. He persuaded U.S. officials to offer North Vietnam a proposal that he claimed would circumvent Hanoi's refusal to consider reciprocal actions in return for a bombing halt. In exchange for the United States halting the bombing, Hanoi would only have to give private assurances that they would stop their infiltration into South Vietnam within a reasonable time. When U.S. officials could verify that the infiltration had in fact stopped, Washington would freeze its combat forces at current levels, and negotiations between the two sides could begin.[138]

Lewandowski's initiative, code-named MARIGOLD, never had a chance. A few days before the Polish envoy was scheduled to meet for talks with Communist leaders in Hanoi, Johnson ordered U.S. aircraft to bomb rail yards near the center of the capital. Some of the planes inadvertently bombed nearby residential neighborhoods and caused civilian casualties. Hanoi, assuming that Johnson was combining a new negotiating proposal with an expanded bombing effort, refused to meet with Lewandowski. It is unlikely that Hanoi was prepared to accept the Polish diplomat's formula had the air attacks not occurred. But the bombing killed whatever prospects MARIGOLD may have had, because the North Vietnamese refused to be pressured into negotiations, or to give the appearance of being pressured into negotiations. Lewandowski had to abandon his efforts, and "the Polish initiative ended in fiasco."[139] In 1967, a peace initiative developed by British Prime Minister Harold Wilson that attempted to employ the good offices of Soviet President Alexei Kosygin met a similar fate.

During the period when both sides were expanding their war effort, all third-party initiatives, however well-intentioned or balanced, were destined for failure. Starting negotiations between Washington and Hanoi depended mainly on the willingness of the belligerents to compromise. Neither was prepared to do so because each side remained confident that it was going to win the war and that it would then be in a position to force the other side to make concessions that would be tantamount to accepting political defeat. Leaders in Washington and Hanoi both strove to appear responsive to all serious peace proposals. They also tried to exploit those proposals for propaganda purposes to make it appear that their adversary was the one pressing the war, was not interested in genuine negotiations, and was the aggressor.

During the summer of 1967, as both international and domestic pressures for a negotiated settlement intensified, each side became slightly more flexible. Johnson sent a Harvard professor of international relations, Henry Kissinger, to Paris to meet with French intermediaries who had long-standing personal connections with North Vietnam's two principal leaders, Ho Chi Minh and Pham Van Dong. The two Frenchmen, Herbert Marcovich and Raymond Aubrac, had previously met with both leaders in Hanoi. Both Ho and Dong denounced the United States, but appeared to hold out hope for a diplomatic resolution of the conflict and suggested that reunification might occur over an extended period of time. In secret meetings, code-named Pennsylvania, with the Frenchmen, Kissinger was sufficiently encouraged to relay an administration offer to the Communist leaders: Washington would stop the bombing with the understanding that a pause would lead promptly to the start of productive talks between U.S. and North Vietnamese officials. While the secret talks occurred in Paris, Johnson, in a major speech delivered in San Antonio, Texas, on September 29, indicated that he would stop the bombing if it would lead to the start of productive peace talks.

For the next two months, both sides danced around the issue of when a U.S. bombing halt should occur, what reciprocal acts would be required of the North Vietnamese, and what negotiations might achieve. Johnson, not trusting the North Vietnamese, and responding to the concerns of his more hawkish senior advisers, continued the bombing. The North Vietnamese leaders, not trusting the Americans, reverted to their long-held position that the United States would have to halt all bombing of North Vietnam unconditionally and then perhaps talks could begin.[140] The Pennsylvania talks collapsed. Johnson remained committed to maintaining a pro-Western government in power in

South Vietnam. Hanoi remained committed to unifying all of Vietnam under its control. Negotiations could not begin to bridge that gulf in 1966 or 1967.

Both countries continued to try to win the war to control the political destiny of South Vietnam. There is no reason to assume that any of the peace initiatives could have succeeded no matter how adroitly they were handled, given the unwillingness of the belligerents to make concessions. Because both sides indulged in diplomatic charades. "The search for negotiations with Hanoi between 1965 and 1968 is one of the most fruitless chapters in U.S. diplomacy."[141] Johnson's judgment was essentially sound when he concluded that Hanoi was not willing to negotiate an end to the war on terms that he could accept, and therefore the many diplomatic initiatives undertaken in 1966 and 1967 were destined for failure.[142]

WAR AT HOME

At the time the Johnson administration made its fateful decisions during the spring and summer of 1965 to mount an air war against North Vietnam and to send ground combat forces to fight in South Vietnam, decisions that committed the United States to fighting a major war in Southeast Asia, a large majority of American families enjoyed a life of unprecedented material abundance and comfort. The affluent, mostly white middle class created by the post–World War II economic expansion maintained an abiding faith in American institutions. A wide consensus that cut across most political, economic, and social lines believed that the United States had successfully waged the Cold War against the Soviet Union and its clients. The Communist threat to the Free World had been contained. Nearly all Americans were accustomed to supporting their political leaders and trusted them to make the right foreign policy decisions and to keep the citizenry informed of their actions.[143]

Within a few years controversy over the Vietnam War, linked to the Civil Rights movement and other insurgencies, had fundamentally altered the American social and political landscape. Most every institution was affected—universities, Congress, the presidency itself, the major political parties, the armed forces, the media, trade unions, and the churches. The Cold War consensus had been shattered irretrievably. Americans were profoundly divided, confused, and distressed. By the summer of 1967, public opinion polls revealed that large numbers of Americans no longer trusted their political leaders or believed that they were waging the Cold War effectively.[144] Most Americans had become disenchanted with the Vietnam War and called for its speedy conclusion; however, they disagreed vehemently among themselves about how to end the controversial war.

The Johnson administration, by taking the nation to war in Vietnam, had also simultaneously called forth domestic opposition to its war policies. A diverse peace movement, recruited from left-wing radical and liberal groups that had coalesced in the mid-1950s to try to defuse the Cold War and to ban atmospheric testing of nuclear weapons, formed the core of the emerging opposition to the Vietnam War. Between 1963 and 1965, peace advocacy in this country was reoriented from "ban the bomb" rallies to protesting the growing U.S. war in Vietnam.

To call the various organizations and activities constituting the opposition to the expanding war in Vietnam during 1965 to 1967 a "movement" can be misleading, for the term implies a coherency of organizational structures and a congruency of tactics, strategies, goals, and ideologies that never existed among the diverse antiwar groups. Typically, they were action-oriented gatherings of people committed to ending the war in Vietnam and often were involved in other reform causes such as civil rights and women's liberation. Some organizations, such as the SDS, generated a sophisticated political analysis and ideological rationale for their antiwar activities, but most antiwar activists did not. Few antiwar protesters had well-defined institutional affiliations or embraced a coherent ideology or politics. However, all protesters felt a strong personal commitment to the cause, and it was that passionate commitment that gave the antiwar movement what political cohesion it possessed. Antiwar organizations did not usually recruit members nor did citizens affiliate with them in any formal sense. "There was no way to join; you simply announced or felt yourself to be a part of the movement—usually through some act like joining a protest march."[145] It was this sense of a purposeful togetherness, of belonging to a community organized for political action that attracted many young people, many who were enrolled in the nation's colleges and universities, to become involved in antiwar activities.

A schism quickly appeared between liberal and radical antiwar activists and persisted for the duration of the movement. Protesters divided over both strategies and goals. Liberals sought to strengthen U.S. international leadership for peace in the world; radicals indicted the United States as the major source of war and injustice in the world. Liberals called for the rule of international law and the strengthening of the United Nations; radicals wanted to liberate and empower poor people, both at home and abroad. Liberals sought to change American foreign policy; radicals wanted a fundamental transformation of the structures of power and wealth within the United States and the world. Liberals were committed to political action, to working within the established political system via electoral action and citizen lobbying; radicals were committed to direct action and acts of civil disobedience against an unjust society. Liberals sought a negotiated settlement of the Indochina conflict—a settlement that would end the fighting, phase out the American involvement, and restore political stability to that part of the world. Radicals demanded an immediate U.S. disengagement from Indochina: "America—Out of Vietnam—NOW!" became their rallying call.[146]

At a deeper level, the divisions within antiwar ranks between liberals and radicals turned on a debate over American values and institutions, and over the meaning of American culture itself. Could American institutions be reformed? Radicals thought not. They believed that American politics had to be radically transformed; some radicals thought it was time for a second American revolution that would be part of a global revolution. In combination with angry African Americans, radicalized students, and others, militants sought to create new political structures and build a new political movement outside of the mainstream political institutions. Just as the VietCong, whom they supported, were resisting illegitimate authority in the jungles of Southeast Asia, domestic radicals would liberate the American people from homegrown tyrannies. The radical antiwar movement was an integral part of, the cultural revolution that swept America during the late 1960s. Domestic political and cultural upheavals and radical antiwar activism reciprocally energized one another.

Liberals, by contrast, believed the problem was not with American culture, but with the U.S. Vietnam War policy. Liberals did not want to remake America; they wanted to end a war they believed was futile and unnecessary. They did not take sides in the war, but sought to end it. Liberal antiwar activists did not try to restructure American politics. They tried to work within a political system they regarded as sufficiently flexible and open, which could be used to bring about a change in the government's Vietnam War policy.[147] Liberal antiwar activists, who were always far more numerous than their radical counterparts, considered the radical analysis of American culture and politics seriously flawed. They also considered radical calls for a new American revolution as unnecessary and quixotic. For their part, militants considered liberal pacifists naive believers in a bankrupt political system that caused wars and exploited poor people within "Amerika" and the Third World.

As the American war in Vietnam expanded, hawkish critics of Johnson's war policies occupied a prominent place in the developing debate over the war. Hawks, a mix of conservative Republicans, southern Democrats, and Cold War liberals, devout believers in the containment ideology, viewed the conflict in Vietnam as a crucial component of the global struggle with Communism for control of the planet's political future. Hawks felt strongly that America must hold the line against Communist aggression, lest an important ally in Southeast Asia succumb to the Red tide. Hawks believed that if South Vietnam fell to the Communists, the Soviets and Chinese would press their advantage elsewhere in that strategically important region. Additional allies and neutral nations would fall to Communism, and the security of America itself would be undermined in time. Hawks, convinced that the United States possessed the military power to demolish the VietCong and North Vietnamese forces if the wraps were removed, were frustrated by the restraints that civilians had clamped on U.S. military forces. They demanded that President Johnson "do whatever was necessary to attain victory."[148]

During the first three years of the American war in Vietnam, 1965–1967, Johnson was much more responsive to hawkish critics of his war policies than he was to dovish protesters. He viewed hawks as more influential politically and more likely to reflect mainstream public opinion than liberal and radical antiwar protesters.

Opposition to the war took various forms from 1965 to 1967. The earliest protests were the aforementioned teach-ins and the first antiwar demonstration staged in the nation's capital by SDS in the spring of 1965. It was the bombing of North Vietnam that aroused antiwar activists more than any other aspect of the government's war policy. During that year there were comparatively few antiwar activists and few protest demonstrations. Public opinion polls taken during the first year of the American war in Vietnam consistently showed strong popular support for the conflict. Most Americans still expected a U.S. victory; no one imagined a Communist victory.

Polls also reflected intense popular resentment of the antiwar protesters.[149] One factor that provoked intense negative responses to antiwar demonstrations was the participation of youthful adherents of the 1960s counterculture in some of the protest movements. These "hippies," with their outlandish costumes and bizarre forms of protest, added a satirical quality to the antiwar movement, sometimes turning it into street theater of the absurd. Hippies sometimes disrupted antiwar demonstrations, provoked police reprisals, and further alienated the peace movement from the American society they proposed to change. Administration officials and the prominent media focused on these comparatively few countercultural protesters, inflaming the already intensely negative popular response to the fledgling antiwar movement.

In February 1966, Senator Fulbright held televised hearings on all aspects of the administration's war policy before his Foreign Relations Committee. Fulbright and his dovish colleagues grilled administration defenders, such as Secretary of State Dean Rusk. They also provided George Kennan, General James Gavin, and other prominent critics of the war a national forum for vetting their dissenting views. Kennan, one of the principal architects of America's Cold War foreign policy, who in 1946 had coined the term "containment," scathingly dismissed Vietnam as one of the most marginal regions in the world and of utterly no consequence for U.S. foreign policy makers. He observed that the United States could best serve its national interests and strenghten its standing among its major allies by liquidating its military involvement in Southeast Asia as rapidly as possible. Millions of Americans watched the hearings. A book-length publication of all transcripts of the hearings became an instant best-seller. Fulbright's hearings gave antiwar sentiment a legitimacy that it had previously lacked and strengthened the ranks of the critics of the U.S. Vietnam war policy.[150]

Within the nation there was less antiwar activity in 1966 than in 1965. Public opinion polls continued to show strong popular support for the war. The antiwar movement remained small, internally divided, local, diverse, and diffuse. Peace liberals organized for political action during the fall 1966 elections. In Berkeley, California, antiwar activist Robert Scheer challenged a liberal Democratic congressional incumbent who supported the war. Scheer lost badly, and most liberal antiwar political efforts failed. The antiwar movement continued to operate at the political margins and had no measurable impact on public opinion, Congress, or on administration war policy.[151]

The big winners in the fall 1966 elections were the Republicans, coming back from the debacle of 1964. Republicans gained forty seats in the House and picked up seven senators. In California, a newcomer to electoral politics, former screen actor and television host Ronald Reagan, was elected governor by a landslide margin. Reagan, a Goldwaterite Republican, attracted enthusiastic popular support by running on a conservative platform that called for victory in Vietnam and condemned black militants, student radicals, antiwar protesters, and hippies. Vietnam was rarely an explicit issue in most 1966 election campaigns. What killed the Democrats was the white backlash

Figure 6.10 Secretary of State Dean Rusk (center, back to camera) is being questioned by members of the Senate Foreign Relations Committee, chaired by J. William Fulbright (center), on the conduct of the war in Vietnam. Photographer: Wally McNamee. *Source:* CORBIS. Neg.#: WL005367. © Wally McNamee/CORBIS.

against the urban riots by African Americans during the summers of 1965 and 1966. White working-class ethnic voters, many of them trade union members, began deserting the Democrats in large numbers. They opposed civil rights legislation and antipoverty programs, and they loathed the urban rioters and antiwar protesters.

For most Americans during 1966, the Vietnam War was not yet a major cause for concern. It was still a faraway war that was financially profitable, and it gratified the American penchant for anti-Communist crusades. The U.S. economy was booming, living standards for most Americans had never been higher, and few Americans had to make any sacrifices for the war. American youngsters were much more involved with rock 'n' roll music than a war in some faraway Southeast Asian country most had never heard of. A large majority of Americans united in support of the war to maintain an anti-Communist government in Saigon, although they disagreed over whether the goal could be better achieved by military escalation or negotiations.[152] But as 1966 was ending, the first signs of war weariness appeared, and there was growing dissatisfaction with the government's war policy.

By the spring of 1967, any illusions Americans had about achieving a quick and easy victory in Vietnam had largely receded. America found itself mired in an escalat-

ing military stalemate in Indochina. Nor could the United States get an acceptable political solution to the conflict, given the battlefield realities, the grave political weaknesses of the RVN, and the negotiating stance taken by Hanoi. U.S. casualties announced
on March 10, 1967—232 killed in action and another 1,381 wounded, over 1,600 casualties in all—were the highest yet for any week of the war. A few days later, Congress
passed a $20 billion supplemental appropriations bill to pay for the rapidly escalating
costs of the war.[153] At the time, polls showed that a majority of the American public was
still supportive of the war, and the prominent national media continued to back the government's policy.

As 1967 unfolded, opposition to the war increased rapidly and public support for
the conflict eroded. Mainstream press coverage of the war was becoming more independent of government influence, and more critical of U.S. policy. Antiwar rallies,
marches, and demonstrations increased in size, occurred more frequently, and developed
more militant tactics during 1967, the first year of significant nationwide protest against
the Vietnam War. On April 15, the Spring Mobilization Committee, a coalition of liberal and radical protest leaders, staged large antiwar demonstrations in San Francisco
and New York City. About 50,000 people participated in the San Francisco demonstration and as many as 200,000 people converged on New York's Central Park for an
afternoon of speeches and music.[154] Protesters gathered daily in front of the White
House to chant, "Hey, hey, LBJ, how many kids have you killed today? and "Ho, Ho,
Ho Chi Minh, [the] NLF is going to win."[155]

The most prominent civil rights leader, Dr. Martin Luther King Jr., joined the antiwar ranks during the spring of 1967, adding greatly to the peace movement's sense of
growth and momentum. In a sermon delivered at New York's Riverside Church on
April 4, 1967, the Nobel laureate established himself as a leading spokesman for the
peace cause. He blamed America for the war and called for a speedy end to the fighting. He urged all men of humane conviction to protest the war in whatever way was appropriate. He declared that Vietnam was "a symptom of a far deeper malady" that
caused the United States, in the name of anti-Communism, to oppose the rightful demands of oppressed people everywhere who were seeking freedom and dignity. King
claimed that anti-Communism had caused America to stray from its commitments to
brotherhood and peace, and he called upon his country to return to its rightful home.[156]

Another prominent African American also defied the government's war policy.
Heavyweight boxing champion Muhammad Ali, a devout member of the Nation of
Islam sect, refused induction into the Army on religious grounds. Government attor-
neys argued successfully that "Black Muslims" were not eligible for conscientious objector status because they did not oppose all wars, only particular wars. Ali's draft
board pronounced his religious views "insincere" and refused his request for a defer-
ment. Ali replied

> It would be no trouble for me to accept on the basis that I'll go into the armed services box-
> ing exhibitions in Vietnam, or traveling the country at the expense of the government, if

it wasn't against my conscience to do it. I wouldn't give up the millions that I gave up and my image with the American public, If I wasn't sincere.[157]

Ali was convicted of draft evasion in June 1967, stripped of his heavyweight title, and sentenced to five years in prison. He stayed out of prison on bond until the Supreme Court overturned his conviction on a technicality. Ali lost five of his prime years as a professional athlete for his refusal to be drafted. He became one of the controversial iconic personalities of the Vietnam War era, admired by opponents of the war and reviled by its supporters.

Alarmed by the rising antiwar protest activities taking place in the spring of 1967, government officials struck hard at their critics. They charged that the antiwar movement was funded and led by Communists and that antiwar protest demonstrations encouraged America's enemies to fight on. Johnson ordered the Federal Bureau of Investigation (FBI) and the CIA, in violation of its charter, to investigate prominent antiwar organizations and individuals. The Secret Service, the IRS, and the Justice Department were also involved in probing protest organizations and prominent individuals. Although CIA agents later told Johnson they could find no evidence that either foreign or domestic Communists controlled the antiwar movement, the president falsely claimed that they had.[158] FBI agents infiltrated many antiwar organizations. The FBI also used *agents provocateurs* to provoke violent confrontations with police and to take other violent actions that discredited antiwar organizations in the public's eyes.[159] The government's public relations strategy was to try to diminish the significance of the antiwar demonstrations by emphasizing how few people were involved in protest activities and by depicting them as a radical fringe of hippies and Communists. Most of the national news media followed the government's lead in redbaiting and belittling the antiwar movement.

By the summer of 1967, public opinion polls were getting harder to read. Polls also revealed both mass citizen apathy and ambivalence concerning the war. Nearly half of the citizens polled did not know enough about the Vietnam War to express an informed opinion. Although still supportive of the war effort, a majority of Americans no longer expressed confidence in Johnson's leadership nor expected the war to end any time soon. For the first time, a majority of respondents said U.S. involvement in the Vietnam War was a mistake. More and more Americans revealed a yearning for an end to the war and liked the idea of turning the conflict over to the South Vietnamese.[160] Most Americans in the summer of 1967 were neither hawks nor doves: "If any bird symbolized the growing public disenchantment with Vietnam, it was the albatross." A housewife succinctly expressed the contradictory attitudes generated by the war: "I want to get out but I don't want to give up."[161]

Media editorials and congressional leaders increasingly voiced criticisms of U.S. Vietnam policy. Polls registered a widening "credibility gap," as a pervasive mistrust of government spread through the body politic. Some Americans saw the Vietnam War as only the most dramatic symbol of a spreading malaise infecting American society, a society increasingly marked by race riots, street demonstrations, and violent crime. The Vietnam War was coming home during that long hot summer of 1967. As the American consensus fractured and civility disappeared from public life, people feared that the Great Society was becoming a sick society.[162]

One of the earliest forms of antiwar protest was expressed in opposition to the draft. Attacking conscription offered protesters a dramatic way to show how the war directly touched American families. Radical pacifists staged the first public draft card burning ceremony in New York's Foley Square on October 28, 1965.[163] As the Vietnam War expanded in 1966 and 1967, the size of monthly draft calls grew larger, and the number of conscripts being sent to fight in Vietnam increased. The number of young people resisting conscription also increased. Voluntary associations offering draft counseling proliferated. A new do-it-yourself literary genre appeared: manuals and handbooks instructing readers how to apply for conscientious objector status and other kinds of deferments and exemptions from military service. A radical historian, Staughton Lynd, emerged as a leader of the militant antidraft movement, urging young men to oppose conscription and support draft resistance. The SDS also supported draft resistance as an effective means of attacking the Vietnam War.[164]

The draft had become a generational obsession by 1967. Opposition to conscription was widespread; there were many means available and young men resisted, evaded, or avoided the draft for a variety of reasons. A large majority of young men who came of draft age during the Vietnam War era avoided military service.[165] Most of these evaders found legal means of avoiding the draft. They obtained deferments or exemptions by exercising their legitimate rights under the prevailing conscription system. Others manipulated the system to achieve their deferments or exemptions. Motivated primarily by a desire to avoid the Vietnam-era draft, they went to college, got married and fathered children, or obtained jobs in "critical" (exempted) occupations. Medically fit young men, aided by draft counselors and sympathetic doctors, found ways to obtain deferments, often on psychological grounds.

The success of millions of mostly middle- and upper-middle-class young men in evading the conscription system either legitimately or illegitimately highlighted a fundamental reality: the conscription system in place during the Vietnam War era was riddled with inequities. The basic source of all draft inequities derived from a fact of political demography—the potential pool of draft-eligible young men between 1964 and 1973, an estimated 27 million people—vastly exceeded the number who enlisted or were conscripted, approximately 9 million people. Aware that all the branches of military service required far fewer men than the available pool could provide, the director of the Selective Service, General Lewis Hershey, designed a system of "channeling" men into certain occupations and professions. Using the draft as a lever, Hershey pressured young men to remain in colleges and universities, enter certain critical occupations, which were often linked to the military-industrial complex, or to enter professions that served national health and safety interests.[166]

Hershey's system worked well enough during the period of peace following the end of the Korean War in 1953 until the American takeover of the war in Vietnam during the summer of 1965. During that time, all military manpower needs were mostly met by volunteers, and draft calls were comparatively low, averaging from 8,000 to 12,000 per month. Only the army used the draft, although the other military services benefited from enlistees, who facing the draft, figured they could do better by volunteering for service in the Navy, Marines, Air Force, or Coast Guard. But there were always hidden class inequities structured into the vitals of the conscription system that were exposed when the Vietnam War became controversial, draft calls rapidly expanded, and casualties mounted.

The dilemma of who served when only a comparative few were needed was resolved by complex processes that permitted most middle- and upper-middle-class young men to avoid military service if they were determined to do so. These processes necessarily shifted the burden of fighting the Vietnam War to youths from lower-middle-class, working class, minority, and poor backgrounds. The vast majority of U.S. conscripts who fought in the Vietnam War were drawn from the lower rungs of the American social ladder. They were the young men who were either too poor, too uneducated, too unskilled vocationally, or whose families were too lacking in political clout to avoid the war. The draftees who had to fight the U.S. Vietnam War were a cross section, not of the entire society, but of its lower-income and disadvantaged classes. Going to the Vietnam War was the price paid by many young men who lacked the connections and resources to avoid conscription.[167]

Other draft-eligible young men chose drastic methods of avoiding the draft and the war. Thousands of young men refused to register for the draft upon turning age 18. Hundreds of thousands refused induction when called. About 40,000 fled the country, mostly to Canada, to avoid military service. Some, in desperation, maimed and mutilated their bodies to disqualify themselves from military service. A handful of young men, adopting the protest method of South Vietnam's Buddhist monks and nuns, publicly immolated themselves.[168]

Many draft-age young men joined the Reserves or the National Guard to avoid active duty and a possible tour in Vietnam. But during the peak years of the war, when monthly draft calls ranged between 30,000 and 50,000 selectees, nearly all Reserve and National Guard units had filled up and most had long waiting lists. Applicants usually needed political connections to get into one of those draft sanctuaries.

It was always possible that the Reservists and National Guardsmen could be called to active duty and be shipped off to Vietnam at any time. But President Johnson, rejecting the advice of his senior military advisers and Secretary of Defense McNamara, refused to activate most of these forces. His refusal accorded with his desire to fight a limited war that would have a limited domestic impact. Had he activated the Reserves and the National Guard, he would have provoked a firestorm of protest from many influential citizens and lost the support of many members of Congress. Most Reserve and National Guard units remained havens for affluent draft evaders for the duration of the war. A high percentage of draft-eligible college graduates and professional athletes could be found in the ranks of the Reserves and the National Guard during the Vietnam War.[169]

Several draft-eligible young men who became prominent American political leaders in the decades following the Vietnam War, used various strategies to avoid a possible combat assignment. A future vice president, J. Danforth Quayle, was one of the many affluent young men who obtained a coveted National Guard assignment and side-stepped a possible tour of duty in Vietnam. A future president, George W. Bush, benefiting from his family's political connections, joined the Texas Air National Guard. Another future president, Bill Clinton, manipulated the conscription system to avoid military duty altogether.

In California, several antiwar organizations planned a Stop the Draft Week for mid-October 1967. On Monday, October 16, as newly drafted young men arrived in buses for their physical examinations and induction into the Army, a peaceful sit-in was held at the entrance to the Oakland, California Induction Center at 5:00 A.M. After the group refused orders to leave, the police moved in and arrested over 100 demonstrators. The next day, by 6:00 A.M., 3,500 militants, many affiliated with the SDS, surrounded the entrance to the induction center. After refusing police orders to disperse, they were attacked by the police. The entrance to the induction center was cleared within a few hours. Scores of demonstrators were injured and over 20 people were hospitalized. On Friday, perhaps 10,000 militants showed up and for hours blocked the entrance to the induction center. They were confronted by a force of over 2,000 police. Some demonstrators blocked streets, fought with police, and disrupted traffic over a 20-block area of the city. Many demonstrators and police were injured during the day-long melee.[170]

A week after the demonstrations at the Oakland Induction Center, the nation witnessed the largest yet antiwar demonstration, held in the nation's capital. On October 21, the National Mobilization Committee and other antiwar organizations staged a rally in front of the Lincoln Memorial in Washington, DC, attended by an estimated 100,000 people. It was a warm and sunny fall afternoon and the atmosphere was festive, like a picnic. Many people gave speeches; bands played and people sang. The protesters were mostly young, white, and middle class. Some 50,000 demonstrators marched slowly across the Arlington Memorial Bridge to a large parking lot north of the Pentagon where they held another rally. A group of perhaps 4,000 militant protesters attempted unsuccessfully to "invade" the Pentagon, the nerve center of the U.S. war effort. Most of the demonstrators, disinclined to engage in civil disobedience and disruptive tactics, or to provoke confrontations with soldiers and police, left the area after a few hours. That night, government troops attacked the remaining militants in the parking lot and reclaimed the area. Hundreds of protesters were arrested and scores were hospitalized.[171]

Administration officials and most political leaders fiercely assailed the demonstrators as did most news media commentators. Polls taken at the time showed that Americans overwhelmingly agreed that antiwar demonstrations hurt the U.S. war effort, aided the Communists, and harmed the antiwar cause. Even though the antiwar movement remained weak and marginalized, there was little prowar enthusiasm. Most Americans did not like antiwar activists, but they increasingly did not like the Vietnam War either, and polls showed that they were pulling away from it.[172]

The growing public controversy over the war paralleled deepening divisions within Johnson's administration over his war policy. The Joint Chiefs and General Westmoreland had joined forces in the spring of 1967 in an effort to enlarge the war. Confident that his war of attrition would eventually produce victory, Westmoreland requested 200,000 additional troops to expand the ground war against the VC/NVA forces. The Joint Chiefs strongly endorsed his troop request, and they asked again for a mobilization of reserve forces. They also sought authorization for cross-border operations into Cambodia and Laos to clean out the VC/NVA sanctuaries in these neutral nations bordering southern Vietnam. They further proposed an invasion across the DMZ. In addition, they asked for an expanded air campaign against North Vietnam and for permission to mine North Vietnam's major ports. Only such measures, they argued, could defeat the rebels and force Hanoi to abandon its support of the southern insurgency.[173]

These escalatory requests by the military collided with moves by some of Johnson's civilian advisers, led by McNamara, to curtail the bombing of North Vietnam, hold the line on ground troops, and seek a negotiated settlement of the conflict that would allow the United States to extricate itself gracefully from Vietnam. McNamara and other civilian officials in the Defense and State Departments had been disillusioned by the failure of both the air war against North Vietnam and the ground war in South Vietnam to defeat the VietCong, discourage Hanoi, or strengthen the Saigon regime.

Johnson found himself caught amidst the divisions among his senior advisers. His political instinct was to seek a middle course between the hawks and doves. He refused most of the requests of the Joint Chiefs, except for expanding the air war against North Vietnam, but he agreed to send Westmoreland 55,000 additional troops. He rejected McNamara's suggestion to scale back the U.S. war effort, having lost confidence in his secretary of defense's judgment.[174] Johnson's war policy decisions were based more on domestic political considerations than they were on strategic criteria. His decisions amounted to a continuation of his policy of graduated escalation. He perpetuated the military stalemate without confronting the flaws within the U.S. strategy of limited war.

Following the October protest demonstrations, Johnson mounted a vigorous public relations campaign designed to bolster popular support for his war policy. He believed that the U.S. forces were winning the war. The reports Johnson received from MACV headquarters constantly reported news of progress: of the large numbers of the enemy killed, of the supplies captured, and of the villages pacified. Johnson discounted the critics of the war among the Congress, the media, the antiwar groups, and the general public. He regarded them as uninformed, lacking in nerve, and, in the case of antiwar activists, disloyal. Johnson tended to personalize criticisms of his war policy, and he deeply resented them. He believed that if his critics only understood what he was trying to do, they would support him enthusiastically.[175]

Presidential aides formed a citizens committee headed by former presidents Truman and Eisenhower to rally public opinion behind the war. Johnson met with an informal advisory group composed of elder statesmen. These former top officials, dubbed the "wise men," endorsed Johnson's war policy, although they voiced concern about spreading public disenchantment with the war.

Johnson also brought Ambassador Ellsworth Bunker and General Westmoreland home to make upbeat speeches about Vietnam. Both officials exuded confidence and optimism. Ambassador Bunker provided the Senate Foreign Relations Committee with an upbeat assessment of the war. General Westmoreland told a National Press Club audience, "We have reached an important point when the end begins to come into view." In answer to a question following his speech, Westmoreland said he believed America could begin phasing down the level of U.S. forces and turn more of the fighting over to the ARVN.[176] Soon after Westmoreland's speech, Johnson held a press conference, passionately defending his war policy, insisting that America must honor its commitments, and stating that U.S. forces were making progress.[177] He exhorted the American people to stay the course and to hang tough—that victory was in sight. Westmoreland, back in Vietnam, announced that the enemy had suffered such severe losses that it could no longer mount an offensive anywhere in Vietnam.[178]

As government officials appealed for support of the Vietnam War and told Americans that victory was coming, dovish critics, most of them academic experts, attacked the government's war policy. In lectures, speeches, essays, articles, and books, they unrelentingly indicted a war policy they thought was wrong, counterproductive, and not serving the national interest in Southeast Asia. They constantly proposed alternatives: halt the bombing of North Vietnam, recognize the National Liberation Front, and seek a negotiated solution to the problem of who should rule in South Vietnam.

Although publicly vowing to continue to press for victory in Vietnam and exhorting his fellow Americans to stay the course, Johnson privately was not so optimistic. He read top-secret CIA reports that noted that the NLF and NVA forces had adapted their tactics to the expanded U.S. war effort and showed no signs of being defeated or demoralized. He began to consider a change in his Vietnam strategy during the fall of 1967. Influenced by McNamara, other civilian advisers, and some of the more cautious "wise men," Johnson began to reappraise his war policies with an eye toward reducing U.S. casualties and transferring greater responsibility for the ground war to the South Vietnamese armed forces. He still remained committed to winning the war and to saving South Vietnam from a Communist takeover, but his thoughts pointed toward a different strategy, which an official in President Nixon's administration would years later call "Vietnamization."[179]

President Johnson, whatever he may have been thinking in the privacy of his study, in all of his public appearances and pronouncements concerning his Vietnam War policy, remained strongly committed to winning the American war in Vietnam. As 1967 ended, the administration appeared to be winning the propaganda campaign for the hearts and minds of the American people. The principal audience for the dovish critique of the war consisted mainly of a relatively small educated elite who embraced liberal or radical politics. Efforts by liberal Democrats to challenge Johnson's war policy from within the government were ineffective. Even though it was cracking at the edges, Johnson's centrist consensus still held. Polls showed that hawks significantly outnumbered doves. Johnson remained determined to prevail in Vietnam and was confident that he would. He also remained confident that he could hold the center and hold Congress.[180]

But the American people would continue to support the war only as long as President Johnson could convince them that victory was nigh. Neither Johnson nor the American people could know that for six months the Communists had been planning a major offensive designed to "liberate" South Vietnam and force the Americans out of that country. As 1967 ended, they readied their forces to launch it. The Tet-68 Offensive would be the most important military campaign of the American war in Vietnam. It would shatter all hope of imminent American victory, transform the American political scene, and provoke a major crisis in Washington. It would also convince millions of Americans that their government was fighting a war that it could not win.

NOTES

1. Thompson, James Clay, *Rolling Thunder: Understanding Policy and Program Failure* (Chapel Hill: University of North Carolina Press, 1980), 10–11; Summers, *On Strategy,* 18.
2. Davidson, *Vietnam at War,* 337.
3. Ibid., 338.
4. Clarke, *The Final Years,* 106.
5. Thompson, *Rolling Thunder,* 11.
6. Herring, *America's Longest War,* 145.
7. Krepinevich, Andrew F., Jr., *The Army and Vietnam* (Baltimore, MD: Johns Hopkins University Press, 1986), 165; Palmer, Bruce, Jr., *The 25-Year War: America's Military Role in Vietnam* (New York: Simon and Schuster, 1985), 174–77.
8. Davidson, *Vietnam at War,* 369.
9. Furguson, Ernest B., *Westmoreland: The Inevitable General* (Boston: Little, Brown, 1968).
10. Ibid., Davidson, *Vietnam at War,* 369–86; essay in Summers, Harry G., Jr., *Vietnam War Almanac* (New York: Facts on File, 1985), 357–59.
11. Westmoreland, *A Soldier Reports,* 186–93.
12. Krepinevich, *Army and Vietnam,* 164.
13. Westmoreland, *A Soldier Reports,* 187–88; Clarke, *The Final Years,* 102.
14. Ibid.
15. Ibid.
16. Stanton, Shelby L., *The Rise and Fall of an American Army: U.S. Ground Forces in Vietnam, 1965–1973* (New York: Dell, 1985), 21.
17. Ibid., 23.
18. Palmer, Dave Richard, *Summons of the Trumpet* (New York: Ballantine, 1978), 111–13.
19. Herring, *America's Longest War,* 151.

20. Stanton, *Rise and Fall,* 23; Palmer, *Summons of the Trumpet,* 169–70. The ratio of noncombat to combat troops within the U.S. force structure in Vietnam was six to one. In early 1969, U.S. troop levels in Vietnam peaked at 543,000. At the time, only about 75,000 of these troops directly engaged in combat.

21. Quoted in Davidson, *Vietnam at War,* 349–50; Doyle et al., *America Takes Over,* 40; Stanton, *Rise and Fall,* 44.

22. Stanton, *Rise and Fall,* 45–46.

23. General Walt in turn was under COMUSMACV's (Westmoreland's) command authority. South Vietnam was divided into four combat sectors: I ("Eye") Corps, II Corps (the central highlands), III Corps (Saigon and vicinity), and IV Corps (the Mekong Delta). MACV directly controlled U.S. combat operations in Corps II, III, and IV. The South Vietnamese army also had a corps commander in each zone and the U.S. Army and ARVN generals and their staffs coordinated operations in each corps zone.

24. Stanton, *Rise and Fall,* 34–35.

25. Operation STARLITE was originally named SATELLITE.

26. Boettcher, Thomas D., *Vietnam: The Valor and the Sorrow* (Boston: Little, Brown, 1985), 317–19; Stanton, *Rise and Fall,* 34–39.

27. Summers, Harry G., Jr., "The Bitter Triumph of Ia Drang," *American Heritage Magazine* (January/February 1984): 56–58.

28. Palmer, *Summons of the Trumpet,* 119–20.

29. Herring, George C., "The 1st Cavalry and the Ia Drang Valley, 18 October–24 November 1965," in Heller, Charles E., and Stofft, William A., *America's First Battles* (Lawrence: University Press of Kansas, 1986), 313–14. Ia was the Jarai word for "river"; Moore, Lt. Gen. (Ret.); Harold G., Jr.; and Galloway, Joseph, *We Were Soldiers Once and Young: Ia Drang—The Battle That Changed the War in Vietnam* (New York: Random House, 1992), 29–34.

30. Heller & Stofft, *America's First Battles,* 315.

31. Summers, "The Bitter Triumph of the Ia Drang," 53.

32. Westmoreland, *A Soldier Reports,* 204.

33. Herring, "*The 1st Cavalry and the Ia Drang Valley,*" 318; Westmoreland, *A Soldier Reports,* 204–05; and Davidson, *Vietnam at War,* 360–62.

34. Morrocco, *Thunder from Above,* 88–93; Palmer, *Summons of the Trumpet,* 128–30; Moore and Galloway, *We Were Soldiers Once,* 124–39.

35. Herring, "The 1st Cavalry and the Ia Drang Valley," 319; Westmoreland, *A Soldier Reports,* 204; Moore and Galloway, *We Were Soldiers Once,* 402–3.

36. Summers, Harry G., Jr., "The Bitter Triumph of Ia Drang," 58, suggests that, ironically, the victorious campaign at Ia Drang contributed to the eventual American defeat in Vietnam. It gave American soldiers a sense of invincibility; after Ia Drang, they believed that all they had to do was to keep fighting battles and they would inevitably win the war.

37. Krepinevich, *The Army and Vietnam,* 168–69; Stanton, *Rise and Fall,* 57–58; Morrocco, *Thunder from Above,* 171.

38. Herring, "The 1st Cavalry and the Ia Drang Valley," 323.

39. Palmer, *Summons of the Trumpet,* 140.

40. Clarke, *The Final Years,* 124.

41. Thompson, W. Scott, and Frizzel, Donaldson D., eds., *The Lessons of Vietnam* (New York: Crane, Russak, 1977), 73–74; Palmer, *Summons of the Trumpet,* 323.

42. Moore and Galloway, *We Were Soldiers Once,* 399.

43. Ibid., 400.

44. Ibid., 400–401.
45. Duiker, *The Communist Road,* 239; Turley, *The Second Indochina War,* 66.
46. Stanton, *Rise and Fall,* 76–77.
47. Westmoreland, *A Soldier Reports,* 234; Krepinevich, *The Army and Vietnam,* 190–91.
48. Rogers, Bernard W., *Cedar Falls–Junction City: A Turning Point* (Washington, DC: U.S. Government Printing Office, 1974), 73–74; Stanton, *Rise and Fall,* 101–2; Hess, *Vietnam,* rev. ed., 95.
49. Stanton, *Rise and Fall,* 125.
50. Ibid., 126. MACV officials estimated total enemy combat strength at 285,000 at the end of 1966.
51. Schell, Jonathan, *The Real War* (New York: Pantheon, 1987), 59–74; Morrocco, *Thunder from Above,* 172; Palmer, *Summons of the Trumpet,* 168–71.
52. Westmoreland, *A Soldier Reports,* 268–69.
53. Schell, *Real War,* 86–121; Doyle et al., *America Takes Over,* 105.
54. Ibid., 107–8.
55. Palmer, *Summons of the Trumpet,* 176.
56. Schell, *Real War,* 133–88; quote is from Doyle and others, *America Takes Over,* 108.
57. Rogers, *Cedar Falls–Junction City,* 154–57; Westmoreland, *A Soldier Reports,* 269.
58. Stanton, *Rise and Fall,* 127–29.
59. O'Ballance, *Wars in Vietnam,* 108; Stanton, *Rise and Fall,* 150.
60. Stanton, *Rise and Fall,* 161.
61. Westmoreland, *A Soldier Reports,* 313. Hills on U.S. Army maps are designated according to their height in meters. Hill 875 was 875 meters high.
62. Stanton, *Rise and Fall,* 164.
63. Ibid., 165–68; Doyle et al., *America Takes Over,* 182.
64. Westmoreland, *A Soldier Reports,* 312–13; Davidson, *Vietnam at War,* 469.
65. Stanton, *Rise and Fall,* 170–71.
66. Westmoreland, *A Soldier Reports,* 263–64.
67. Ibid., 265–66; Doyle et al., *America Takes Over,* 160–61; O'Ballance, *Wars in Vietnam,* 107.
68. Thompson, Robert, *No Exit from Vietnam* (New York: David McKay, 1969), 135; Gibson, *Perfect War,* 109, cites a National Security Council study stating that throughout 1966 and 1967, 75 percent of all battles were the enemy's choice of time, place, and duration.
69. Krepinevich, *The Army and Vietnam,* 167. Krepinevich believes that the fatal flaw of Westmoreland's attrition strategy was that it could not force the enemy to engage in big unit fights.
70. Mueller, John E., "The Search for a 'Breaking Point' in Vietnam: The Statistics of a Deadly Quarrel," *International Studies Quarterly* 4 (December 1980): 497–519. General Giap has estimated PAVN manpower losses for the war at 600,000 soldiers killed. If his guess was accurate, North Vietnam lost about 3 percent of its prewar population. For America to have sustained an equivalent loss, its battle deaths would have had to reach about 7 million, a figure that would have been inconceivable to any rational American. One of the major reasons for the failure of the U.S. attrition warfare strategy in Vietnam was because North Vietnam was willing to absorb huge personnel losses and still continue the war indefinitely.
71. Herring, *America's Longest War,* 155–56. By 1968 the American war in the countryside had created an estimated 5 million refugees. The urban population of South Vietnam swelled from 15 percent in 1964 to 40 percent by 1968.
72. Schandler, *The Unmaking of a President,* 31–32; Herring, *America's Longest War,* 155; Schulzinger, *Time for War,* 193–94.
73. Thompson, *Rolling Thunder,* 35; Clodfelter, *Limits,* 63–64.

74. Morrocco and others, *Thunder from Above,* 64–65.

75. Palmer, *Summons of the Trumpet,* 156–57.

76. Thompson, *Rolling Thunder,* 45–48; Clodfelter, *Limits,* 71–72.

77. Clodfelter, *Limits,* 92–93.

78. Quoted in Morrocco and others, *Thunder from Above,* 127.

79. Ibid., 128; Mersky, Peter B., and Polmar, Norman, *The Naval Air War in Vietnam* (New York: Kensington, 1981), 118–121.

80. Clodfelter, *Limits,* 98.

81. Morrocco et al., *Thunder from Above,* 130–31.

82. Clodfelter, *Limits,* 99.

83. Porter, *Vietnam Documents,* vol. 2, Documents 261 and 262, 466–70, "Intelligence Memoranda by the Directorate of Intelligence, CIA," May 12 and May 23, 1967. Gallucci, *Neither Peace nor Honor,* 64–70; Thompson, *Rolling Thunder,* 51–53.

84. Sheehan and others, *Pentagon Papers,* Document 117, 506–7, "Vietnam Bombing Evaluation by Institute for Defense Analysis."

85. Clodfelter, *Limits,* 99–100.

86. Turley, *The Second Indochina War,* 97; Stanton, *Rise and Fall,* 174–75; Schulzinger, *A Time for War*, 211.

87. Quote is from Clodfelter, *Limits,* 101.

88. Palmer, *Summons of the Trumpet,* 162; Porter (ed.), *Vietnam Documents,* vol. 2, Document 263, 470–72, "Memorandum for McNamara by the Joint Chiefs of Staff," JCSM-30767, June 2, 1967.

89. Clodfelter, *Limits,* 105. A Harris poll taken February 13, 1967, showed that 67 percent of the American public supported ROLLING THUNDER.

90. Quote is from Ibid., 112.

91. Thompson, *Rolling Thunder,* 64; Clodfelter, *Limits,* 84.

92. Clodfelter, *Limits,* 112.

93. Sharp, Ulysses S. G., *Strategy for Defeat: Vietnam in Retrospect* (San Rafael, CA: Presidio Press, 1978). Admiral Sharp argued that an intensive bombing campaign could have won the war. But in 1965 the rate of infiltration into South Vietnam had been 1,500 men per month; in 1966, 4,500 men per month; in 1967, as the air war intensified, the rate of infiltration increased to 6,000 men per month. In January 1968, on the eve of the Tet Offensive, 20,000 men infiltrated into South Vietnam.

94. Littauer, Raphael, and Uphoff, Norman, eds., *The Air War in Indochina,* rev. ed. (Boston: Beacon, 1972), 36. The passage is also quoted in Thompson, *Rolling Thunder,* 64; Lewy, *America in Vietnam,* 389–96. By 1967 China was undergoing its Cultural Revolution; it was less able to intervene in North Vietnam, but Johnson would never rule out that possibility.

95. Clodfelter, *Limits,* 117–18. ROLLING THUNDER destroyed 65 percent of North Vietnam's oil storage capacity, 59 percent of its power plants, 55 percent of its bridges, 9,821 vehicles, and 1,966 railroad cars. In the fall of 1967, when the air war raged at its most intense level, there were about 55,000 NVA troops in South Vietnam and about 250,000 VietCong forces.These forces engaged in battle infrequently and the PLAF got much of its required supplies from southern villagers. The NVA and VietCong required 34 tons per day of supplies from North Vietnam. Seven 21D 2-ton trucks could haul that daily requirement, which represented less than 1 percent of the daily tonnage imported from China and the Soviet Union by rail and by sea. An all-out air war waged indefinitely could never have seriously hindered Hanoi's resupply capability, given the small needs of the troops fighting in the South and Hanoi's huge excess resupply capacity made possible by Chinese and Soviet assistance.

96. Ibid., 134–36.

97. Turley, *The Second Indochina War,* 95–96.

98. Enthoven, Allen C., and Smith, K. Wayne, *How Much Is Enough? Shaping the Defense Program, 1961–1968* (New York: Harper & Row, 1971); Coldfelter, *Limits,* 131. One of the major operational controls that limited the effectiveness of ROLLING THUNDER missions was the formidable air defense system gradually developed by the North Vietnamese. It included 200 SAM missile sites, 7,000 antiaircraft guns, and 80 MiG fighters. American aviators had to operate against the most sophisticated and deadliest air defense system ever erected in the history of aerial warfare.

99. Sheehan and others, "Secretary McNamara's Position of May 19 on Bombing and Troops," *Pentagon Papers,* Document 129, 580.

100. Thayer, *War without Fronts,* 79–86; Morrocco et al., *Thunder from Above,* 74.

101. Morrocco et al, *Thunder from Above,* 84.

102. Ibid., 88–89.

103. Ibid.

104. Thayer, *War without Fronts,* 129–32.

105. Ibid.

106. Ibid., 83–84.

107. Morrocco, *Thunder from the Air,* 85.

108. Buckingham, William A., Jr., *Operation Ranch Hand: The Air Force and Herbicides in Southeast Asia, 1961–1971* (Washington, DC: U.S. Government Printing Office, 1982).

109. Herring, *America's Longest War,* 151.

110. Boettcher, *Vietnam,* 258–59; Morrocco et al., *Thunder from Above,* 180.

111. Jacobs, James B., and McNamara, Dennis, "Vietnam Veterans and Agent Orange," *Armed Forces and Society* 13 (fall 1986): 57–79.

112. Morrocco, *Thunder from Above,* 180; Hess, *Vietnam,* rev. ed., 121.

113. Scheck, William, Lt. Col., "During the Struggle between $6 Million Aircraft and $15 Bicycles Along the Ho Chi Minh Trail, the Bicycles Won" *Vietnam* 13, no. 5 (February 2001): 14.

114. Sheehan et al., "Johnson's Remarks to Officials of U.S. and Saigon at Honolulu," *Pentagon Papers,* Document 111, 495–96.

115. Quoted in Karnow, *Vietnam,* 444.

116. Blaufarb, *Counterinsurgency Era,* 232–33.

117. Kahin, *Intervention,* 413–114; Clarke, *The Final Years,* 128–29.

118. Kahin, *Intervention,* 423–425.

119. Doyle et al., *America Takes Over,* 78–79; Clarke, *The Final Days,* 136.

120. From interviews with soldiers on videotape "America Takes Charge, 1965–1967," from the television series, *Vietnam: A Television History.*

121. Kahin, *Intervention,* 432.

122. Blaufarb, *The Counterinsurgency Era,* 225–29.

123. Herring, *America's Longest War,* 158.

124. Ibid., 158–59. There were 3,015 RD personnel kidnapped or murdered during a seven-month period in 1966.

125. Blaufarb, *The Counterinsurgency Era,* 229–31; Herring, *America's Longest War,* 159; Davidson, *Vietnam at War,* 431–32; Clarke, *The Final Years,* 209–12; Andrade, Dale, *Ashes to Ashes: The Phoenix Program and the Vietnam War* (Lexington, MA: Lexington Books, 1990), 58–63.

126. Herring, *America's Longest War,* 159–60.

127. Karnow, *Vietnam,* 451–52.

128. Shaplen, Robert, *The Road from War: Vietnam, 1965–1971* (New York: Harper & Row, 1971), 151; also quoted in Herring, *America's Longest War,* 160.

129. Herring, *America's Longest War,* 161.

130. Ibid., 162; Hess, *Vietnam,* rev. ed., 99. In 1954, Saigon had a population of 550,000; in 1961, 1 million. In December 1967, U.S. officials estimated that 2,200,000 people lived within the city and another 1 million in the suburbs of Gia Dinh province.

131. Schandler, *The Unmaking of a President,* 31–32. Interviews with soldiers recorded on videotape, "America Takes Charge, 1965–1967," from the television series *Vietnam: A Television History.*

132. *Ibid.*

133. Goodman, *The Lost Peace,* 23–26.

134. Quoted in Gareth Porter, ed., *A Peace Denied: The United States, Vietnam, and the Paris Agreement* (Bloomington: Indiana University Press, 1975), 29; also quoted in Herring, *America's Longest War,* 165.

135. Herring, *America's Longest War,* 166.

136. Goodman, *The Lost Peace,* 28.

137. Ibid., 35–36.

138. Karnow, *Vietnam,* 493–94; Goodman, *The Lost Peace,* 39–42.

139. Herring, *America's Longest War,* 167.

140. Turner, *Lyndon Johnson's Dual War,* 191–98; Doyle et al., *America Takes Over,* 136–37; Schulzinger, *Time for War,* 250–52.

141. Goodman, *The Lost Peace,* 24.

142. *Ibid.*

143. Schulzinger, *A Time for War,* 215.

144. Ibid., 215–16.

145. Quoted in DeBenedetti, Charles; with Chatfield, Charles (assist. author), *An American Ordeal: The Antiwar Movement of the Vietnam Era* (Syracuse, NY: Syracuse University Press, 1990), 75.

146. Ibid., 25–26, 97.

147. Ibid., 117.

148. Herring, *America's Longest War,* 170.

149. DeBenedetti, *American Ordeal,* 119–127, 135–136; Small, Melvin, Johnson, Nixon, and the Doves (New Brunswick, NJ: Rutgers University Press, 1988), 31–33. Most Americans thought opposition to the war to be illegitimate. They viewed the protesters as aiding the enemy and undermining American troops fighting in Vietnam. They especiallly resented male university students who joined the ranks of antiwar activists, considering them to be a privileged elite of cowards and traitors.

150. Doyle et al., *America Takes Over,* 141–52.

151. DeBenedetti, *American Ordeal,* 151–52, 157; Small, *Johnson, Nixon, and the Doves,* 75.

152. DeBenedetti, *American Ordeal,* 162.

153. Schandler, *The Unmaking of a President,* 49.

154. DeBenedetti, *American Ordeal,* 175–76.

155. Quoted in Herring, *America's Longest War,* 173.

156. King's April 4, 1967, sermon was published as "A Declaration of Independence from War" in *Ramparts,* 5, no. 11 (May 1967): 33–37.

157. Moss, George, "The Vietnam Generation, 1964–1973," unpublished essay, 1984, 13; Baskir, Lawrence M., and Strauss, William A., *Chance and Circumstance: The Draft, the War, and the Vietnam Generation* (New York: Random House, 1978), 63, 79, 97.

158. DeBenedetti, Charles, "A CIA Analysis of the Antiwar Movement: October 1967," *Peace and Change,* 9 (spring 1983): 31–41. According to the CIA report to Johnson on the peace activists, "Many have close Communist associations but they do not appear to be under Communist direction." Despite the report, Johnson met with a bipartisan congressional group including House minority leader Gerald Ford on October 24 and told them that he had a "secret" report that

documented Communist control of the October 21 march on Washington. Johnson believed that the antiwar movements were controlled by Communist organizers in the service of Moscow, Beijing, and Hanoi.

159. Gitlin, Todd, *The Whole World Is Watching: Mass Media in the Making and Unmaking of the New Left* (Berkeley: University of California Press, 1980), 186–89.

160. DeBenedetti, *American Ordeal,* 179.

161. Both quotes are from Herring, *America's Longest Wa*r, 174.

162. Oberdorfer, Don, *Tet! The Turning Point in the Vietnam War* (New York: Da Capo Press, 1971), 79–81; Herring, *America's Longest War,* 174–75; Mueller, *War, Presidents, and Public Opinion,* 112–13. Three times during 1967 the Gallup poll asked people: Do you think the Johnson administration is or is not telling the public all it should know about the Vietnam war? Each time only 21 to 24 percent answered yes; 65 to 70 percent answered no.

163. DeBenedetti, *American Ordeal,* 128–29.

164. Ibid., 165–67.

165. Moss, "The Vietnam Generation," 3–7. Between August 10, 1964, when President Johnson signed the Gulf of Tonkin Resolution formally making the Vietnam conflict an American war, and March 28, 1973, when the last American soldier exited Vietnam, 18 million draft-eligible young men avoided military service. Of these 18 million, 11 million obtained deferments or exemptions, 4 million drew high lottery numbers during the two years that the lottery draft operated, and another 3 million young men avoided military service because Selective Service lost or mishandled their files.

166. Schulzinger, *A Time for War,* 238–39.

167. Ibid., 5–6; Baskir and Strauss, *Chance and Circumstance,* 8–10.

168. Baskir and Strauss, *Chance and Circumstance,* 62–90.

169. Moss, "The Vietnam Generation," 9.

170. Powers, Thomas, *Vietnam: The War at Home* (Boston: G. K. Hall, 1973), 236–38; DeBenedetti, *American Ordeal,* 196.

171. Powers, *Vietnam: The War at Home,* 238–40; DeBenedetti, *American Ordeal,* 197–98; and Norman Mailer, *The Armies of the Night: History as a Novel, the Novel as History* (Cleveland, OH: World Publications, 1968).

172. DeBenedetti, *American Ordeal,* 198–99. Americans, by a 3:1 margin, thought that antiwar demonstrations were acts of disloyalty against American boys fighting in Vietnam and that the demonstrations encouraged the Communists to fight harder. Some 70 percent thought the demonstrations hurt the antiwar cause.

173. Sheehan et al., "Westmoreland Cable to Joint Chiefs on Troop Needs," March 28, 1967, *Pentagon Papers,* Document 123, 560–65; "Joint Chiefs Report to McNamara on Troops Needs," April 20, 1967, Document 124, 565–67; and "Notes on Johnson's Discussion with Wheeler and Westmoreland," April 27, 1967, Document 125, 567–69.

174. Karnow, *Vietnam,* 507–8.

175. Oberdorfer, *Tet!* 98–99.

176. Quoted in Karnow, *Vietnam,* 514; Schlandler, *The Unmaking of a President,* 62; Small, *Johnson, Nixon, and the Doves,* 120–24. Neither Westmoreland nor Johnson ever used the phrase "We can see the light at the end of the tunnel." It was coined by Henry Cabot Lodge.

177. Quoted in Turner, *Lyndon Johnson's Dual War,* 205.

178. Dougan, Clark; Weiss, Stephen; and the editors of Boston Publishing, *Nineteen Sixty-Eight* (Boston: Boston Publishing, 1983).

179. Herring, *America's Longest War,* 3d ed., 200–201.

180. Small, *Johnson, Nixon, and the Doves,* 178. Polls showed a 6 percent increase in public support for Johnson's war policy at year's end.

CHAPTER 7

Year of the Monkey

For twenty years first the French and then Americans have been predicting victory in Vietnam. But for twenty years we have been wrong. The history of conflict among nations does not record another such lengthy and consistent chronicle of error. It is time to discard so proven a fallacy and face the reality that a military victory is not in sight, and that it probably will never come.

Robert Kennedy

SURPRISE ATTACK!

Taking advantage of the cease-fire called to celebrate Tet, the beginning of the lunar new year and Vietnam's most important holiday, some 84,000 VietCong and NVA soldiers launched simultaneous attacks during the early morning hours of January 30, 1968,[1] extending from the demilitarized zone in the north to the Ca Mau peninsula in the south. They attacked Saigon, 5 of the 6 largest cities, 36 of 44 provincial capitals, and 64 of 242 district capitals. Within South Vietnam's beleaguered towns and cities, ARVN forces, its ranks depleted by the absence of many soldiers who went home for the holidays, fought to defend governmental and military installations, the major targets of the enemy assaults. The offensive caught the Allied command by surprise. Convinced that any enemy assaults would occur on the northernmost provinces and the Marine base at Khe Sanh, the Allied leaders "could not conceive of an attack of the magnitude of what occurred during the Tet holiday."[2]

Although caught by surprise, RVN and U.S. troops quickly recovered and counterattacked effectively. Using their superior firepower and mobility, they were able to expunge the VietCong and PAVN forces from the towns and cities. Nearly everywhere they repulsed the attackers quickly, usually inflicting severe losses. Almost nowhere did the attackers have time to secure their positions, and they did not receive any significant support from the residents. General Westmoreland quickly judged the Communist offensive to be a complete military failure.[3] Tet-68, the largest and most important campaign of the American Vietnam war, amounted to a major military defeat for the VietCong and NVA forces.

But news of the Tet *coup de main* broke like a thunderclap across America. The fact that the enemy could mount a major military effort all over South Vietnam and catch the Allies by surprise shattered all illusions of impending American victory in the war. Tet suggested that all the years of bombing, attrition warfare, pacification, body counts, and computer printouts that claimed, by all quantitative measures, that the United States was winning the war, had not meant a thing. In the wake of Tet, millions Americans realized that the United States had involved itself in a stalemated war in Southeast Asia.

Although suffering major military reverses, Hanoi scored a decisive political victory over the United States and its RVN allies.[4] Tet constituted a major turning point in the Vietnam War. After Tet-68, President Johnson felt compelled to scale back the bombing of North Vietnam and put a ceiling on the number of U.S. ground combat forces committed to South Vietnam. The Communist offensive forced Washington to confront the reality that it was fighting a war that it was not winning, nor was likely to win at any reasonable cost. Because President Johnson was eventually forced to abandon the strategy of graduated escalation to resolve a political crisis, the first few months of 1968 are the most important in the entire history of the long U.S. involvement in Vietnam.

Tet-68 represented Hanoi's belated response to the Americanization of the war that had occurred in the summer of 1965. Washington's decisions to escalate the conflict in South Vietnam posed a severe challenge to the Vietnamese revolution. Given U.S. firepower, the Communist leaders understood that any effort on their part to match Westmoreland's strategy of attrition would cost them heavy casualties and would also run the risk of extending the war to North Vietnam. But if they did not respond vigorously to the American threat, the Communist leaders feared that the southern insurgency could be slowed, postponing the achievement of Hanoi's goals of revolution and reunification of the country.[5]

The decision to respond to the U.S. military buildup was made in December 1965 at the Twelfth Plenum of the Central Committee of the Lao Dong meeting in Hanoi. Knowing they probably could not defeat the Americans militarily, Hanoi's leadership opted for a strategy of protracted struggle, of "people's warfare." Eschewing the possibility of military victory in the near future, they discerned two enemy political weaknesses they believed they could exploit: the inherent instability of the Saigon regime and the potential softness of public support for the Vietnam War within the United States.[6]

To exploit these perceived weaknesses, the directive issued at the close of the Twelfth Plenum called for the Lao Dong to mobilize the armed forces and the Vietnamese people to foil the war of aggression of the U.S. imperialists, in order to defend

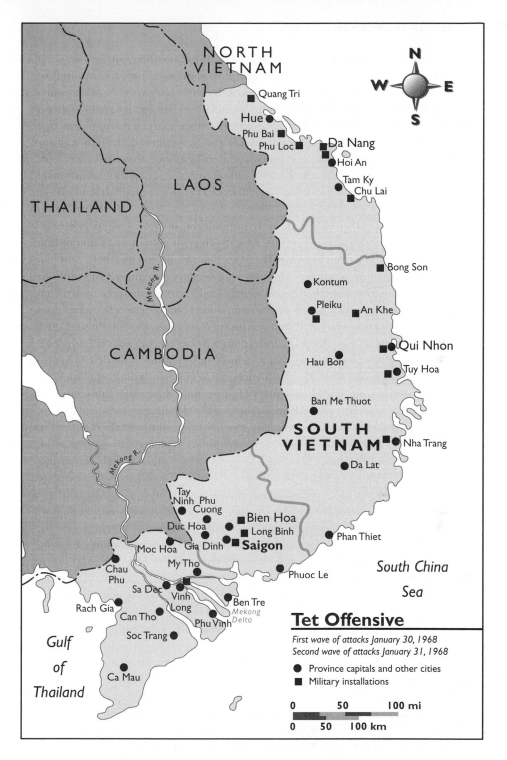

Figure 7.1 The Tet-68 Offensive. *Source:* Public domain.

the North, liberate the South, complete the national people's democratic revolution in the whole country, advancing toward the peaceful reunification of the country.[7]

Senior NVA military commanders publicly endorsed the Politburo's strategy of protracted warfare, which amounted to countering Westmoreland's strategy of attrition with an attrition strategy of their own. They aimed at keeping the tactical initiative, keeping pressure on both the American and GVN forces, and inflicting a high level of costs and casualties on both. The implementation of Communist-style attrition warfare in the South was the prime responsibility of one of its chief advocates, General Nguyen Thi Thanh, the aggressive commander of the PLAF forces.[8]

Throughout 1966 and into 1967, General Thanh vigorously pursued Hanoi's protracted warfare strategy. The Communists incurred severe losses, while attaining few desirable strategic or political results. U.S. and RVN forces won all major battles. U.S. troop levels continued to increase, and Westmoreland aggressively pursued his big-unit style of attrition warfare. The U.S. antiwar movement had no discernible impact on Johnson's determination to bomb North Vietnam or on his decision to fight a gradually escalating ground war. Thanh's strategy also failed to induce Washington to seek a negotiated solution. The GVN, with all of its deficiencies, appeared to be more stable in the spring of 1967 than when Hanoi had implemented the protracted war strategy. Many VietCong units and some NVA units fighting in South Vietnam had been decimated. Others had been driven out of South Vietnam into Cambodia or Laos, or were forced to take refuge in sparsely populated peripheral areas in the central highlands. The NLF infrastructure controlled fewer villages and less territory in South Vietnam than it had at the time the Twelfth Plenum had decided to fight attrition with attrition.[9]

Disappointed with the results of the protracted war strategy and convinced that victory could come only from a combined general offensive and popular rising of the South Vietnamese, Hanoi's leaders, in the spring of 1967, decided that a major offensive should be launched the following year. General Thanh took charge of the planning until his death, which could have resulted from U.S. bombing that occurred on July 6, 1967. Planning for the new strategy continued under his successor, General Pham Hung. Final approval of the General Offensive–General Uprising was given at the Lao Dong's Fourteenth Plenum, in November 1967.[10]

Hanoi's leadership convinced itself that the political situation in South Vietnam had evolved to a point where a revolutionary uprising could occur in response to a successful Communist offensive. They viewed the Buddhist revolt that had taken place in Danang and Hue during the spring of 1966 as an indicator that the Saigon government was ripe for overthrowing. The Communist leaders expected the military victories achieved during the intended offensive to trigger an uprising that would be led in the towns and cities by VietCong cadres.[11] If the general uprising succeeded, the RVN would be overthrown. It would be replaced by a coalition government dominated by the NLF. There would be a cease-fire, and the Americans would be forced to withdraw from South Vietnam. The country could then proceed toward reunification and complete the national revolution the Vietminh had begun in 1945.

The Lao Dong leaders believed their offensive strategy had a reasonable chance of success. Even if it fell short of total victory, they expected it to shake the foundations of the RVN by undermining the faith of the South Vietnamese in the ability of their government to protect them, "thus increasing the likelihood of a negotiated settlement favorable to the revolutionary cause."[12] By taking the war out of the jungles and paddies and into the cities, they would show that all parts of South Vietnam were vulnerable; there were no safe havens and no one was immune from attack. They hoped to send a message to the Americans that they had involved themselves in a war that they could not win, at least at any reasonable price. The Communist leaders saw their strategy of the General Offensive–General Uprising (*Tong Cong Kich–Tong Khoi Nghia,* or *TCK–TKN)* as a calculated gamble. It would replace the strategy of protracted warfare that had shown little promise of achieving desired goals after more than two years of bloody stalemate.

The Communists launched phase one of *TCK–TKN* in October 1967 with a series of assaults along the periphery of South Vietnam. They struck at Song Be and Loc Ninh near the Cambodian border, at Dak To in the central highlands, and at Con Thien, just south of the DMZ. Their goals were to inflict casualties and draw U.S. forces away from populated areas to these sparsely populated border regions, which would leave the urban populations of South Vietnam unprotected from the Tet assaults planned for phase two. These peripheral attacks were powerful, fighting was fierce, and casualties were heavy on both sides. In every area, the Communists were beaten and forced to retreat to their cross-border sanctuaries. Communist losses, though substantial, achieved their purpose; they induced Westmoreland to move a substantial number of U.S. and ARVN forces away from populated areas.[13]

By late fall 1967, the U.S. military command in Saigon, noting that the rate of infiltration down the Ho Chi Minh Trail had increased sharply, suspected that the Communists were preparing for a major offensive early in 1968. Captured enemy documents and interrogations of VC and NVA defectors confirmed these suspicions. Westmoreland concluded that the main enemy offensive would occur in I Corps, just south of the DMZ. He believed the Communists would try to capture the two northernmost provinces of South Vietnam, Quang Tri and Thua Thien, which were separated from the rest of South Vietnam by mountains reaching to the sea. Westmoreland strengthened the U.S. forces at Khe Sanh and other forward bases near the DMZ. He did not consider Saigon or the other cities of South Vietnam to be facing any serious dangers. As a show of confidence in the improving South Vietnamese forces, the MACV had entrusted the defense of Saigon and other urban areas to ARVN.[14]

On January 10, Lieutenant General Frederick Weyand, commander of III Corps, warned Westmoreland that intelligence data indicated that the enemy was shifting his forces from the border regions to Saigon and to other cities in South Vietnam. Weyand's views were confirmed by General Philip Davidson, the head of the MACV's intelligence division. In response to these warnings, Westmoreland moved some U.S. forces to the vicinity of Saigon and placed others in the corridors running from the Cambodian border toward the capital. He also persuaded General Thieu to keep half of his ARVN forces on duty during the Tet holidays. These precautionary moves possibly saved Saigon from an enemy takeover during Tet. But Westmoreland remained convinced that the major enemy push would come in the north and that it would occur before the Tet holidays.[15]

Phase two of *TCK–TKN,* which Americans knew as the Tet-68 Offensive, began shortly after midnight on January 30, when PLAF/NVA forces launched a nationwide assault on South Vietnam's cities and towns. At 2:45 A.M., a squad of nineteen VietCong commandos on a suicide mission blasted a hole in the wall surrounding the U.S. embassy compound in downtown Saigon, and then entered the courtyard. From their position inside the compound they could threaten the embassy's main buildings. But U.S. reinforcements arrived quickly and a fierce battle was joined. Six and one-half hours later all of the VC commandos were killed or captured. By 9:00 A.M. the embassy was secure.

At 9:30 A.M., standing amid the rubble and litter of bodies, General Westmoreland held an impromptu press conference. He insisted that the Allied forces had everything under control; Communists all over South Vietnam were being beaten back and slaughtered. Some journalists wondered how Westmoreland could be so confident of victory when VietCong commanders had managed to get inside the U.S. embassy, the citadel of American power in Vietnam and supposedly the most secure place in the whole country. Although it was of no tactical consequence and it resulted in a quick defeat for the VietCong, the firefight inside embassy walls had a dramatic impact in the United States. Americans were shocked to learn that an enemy supposedly on its last legs could bring the war to the symbolic heart of American power within South Vietnam's capital. General Westmoreland, standing amid the shards of battle inside the embassy compound, became one of the enduring images of the Tet-68 offensive in American minds.[16]

Within hours of the embassy assault, other VietCong forces attacked targets in or near Saigon, including the presidential palace, the headquarters of both the MACV and

Figure 7.2 With dead American soldiers lying in the foreground, U.S. security forces take cover behind a wall at the entrance to the U.S. Embassy compound in downtown Saigon. Photographer: Hong Seong-Chan. *Source:* AP/Wide World Photos. Neg. # APA4439024.

the South Vietnamese joint general staff at Tan Son Nhut Air Base, the RVN's radio station, and the air base at Bien Hoa. In every instance, the attackers were driven off and suffered heavy losses. Some ARVN units, under severe pressure, fought effectively. They were reinforced by U.S. troops, who used their superior firepower to inflict severe casualties on the outgunned VietCong. Nothing remotely resembling a popular rising occurred in Saigon.[17]

The VietCong's attacks left Saigon's inhabitants shocked and dazed. Their sense of security, their feeling that they were safe from a remote conflict that only engulfed the countryside had been shattered as they experienced the contagion of war firsthand. The fighting within the city did extensive damage to sections of Saigon. Thousands of families were left homeless in the wake of the fighting that had saved them from a possible Communist takeover.

Everywhere in South Vietnam, local VietCong units attacked urban centers in force. In Nha Trang, a coastal city of 120,000 about 180 miles north of Saigon, enemy soldiers attacked a naval training center. The VietCong forces struck targets in Kontum and Pleiku, two central highlands cities. At Danang, ARVN and U.S. forces, alerted by a VietCong defector that an attack was imminent, met the enemy on the outskirts of the city. In none of these assaults did the attackers accomplish their missions. They were driven back everywhere, with heavy losses.[18]

In the Mekong Delta, that vast watery expanse that constituted South Vietnam's rice bowl, the VietCong attacked 13 of 16 provincial capitals and many of the district capitals. The ARVN forces generally performed ineffectively in the delta region, and U.S. forces had to be rushed to many towns and cities to drive out the attackers. An estimated 5,000 VietCong were killed and hundreds were captured during the fighting in the delta. Most of the local guerrillas and political cadres were wiped out.[19]

The ferocity of the fighting during Tet-68 climaxed at Hue. In a battle lasting a month, two NVA regiments and two VietCong elite battalions battled eight U.S. and 13 ARVN battalions in one of the most savage battles of the war. "The furor of the Tet-68 Offensive would become symbolized by the catastrophic destruction incurred in this grim city struggle."[20]

Hue, located near the coast midway between Danang and the DMZ, had an official population of 100,000, swollen by the influx of thousands of war refugees, at the time of the Tet-68 Offensive. The Perfume River runs through the city, with two-thirds of the population living north of the river, mostly within the walls of the Citadel (Old City), and one-third residing south of the river in the Westernized New City. Until Tet, Hue had remained free of war. Both sides had treated it with respect, and Hue was considered an open city.[21] There was a sizable U.S. presence in Hue, and many other foreigners lived and worked there. It was the most beautiful of Vietnam's cities, with its unique blend of traditional and cosmopolitan cultures.

On the morning of January 31, about 7,500 NVA/VietCong fighters, achieving complete tactical surprise, overwhelmed the ARVN defenders and took control of the Citadel, once the home of the Nguyen emperors, and much of the New City within a few hours. Two U.S. Marine companies from Phu Bai, a few miles south of Hue, joined with ARVN forces to counterattack the next day. The counterattack stalled in the face of determined NVA/VC resistance. Over the next few days, both the Americans and South Vietnamese augmented their forces in Hue. Starting on February 5, naval gunfire from ships of the Seventh Fleet, positioned offshore, pounded targets inside the Citadel from a range of 15 miles. Both VNAF and U.S. aircraft napalmed and strafed targets within the Old City. On the ground, Marine rifle companies advanced from house to house in savage fighting.[22]

By February 9, the Marines had reclaimed the sectors of the city lying south of the river, and the ARVN units had reclaimed much of the Citadel. But in the southeastern sector of the Citadel, including the Imperial Palace, the NVA/VC forces held a series of strong points. The Communists inflicted heavy casualties on the attacking South Vietnamese. The hard-pressed ARVN troops were joined by elements of the 1st Battalion, 5th Regiment, U.S. Marines, on February 12. For days the carnage of close combat took a deadly toll on both the ARVN forces and the U.S. Marines. On Febru-

Figure 7.3 U.S. Marines hold a stone tower position overlooking a street in Hue, Vietnam's ancient imperial capital, in February 1968, during the Tet-68 Offensive. *Source:* AP/Wide World Photos. Neg. # APA4057083.

ary 24, elements of the 3rd ARVN Regiment raised the RVN flag over the Citadel and the battered remains of the Palace of Perfect Peace. It took the Allies another week of scattered fighting to crush isolated pockets of resistance and round up NVA/VC stragglers. The Battle of Hue ended on March 2, 1968.

Over 8,000 soldiers on both sides died in the monthlong battle. Seventy-five percent of the city's population was rendered homeless. The stench of death hovered over the littered landscape. The exhausted survivors gazed in horror at the remains of Hue, the once-proud and lovely imperial city, which had been blasted into corpse-strewn rubble. "The beautiful city was a shattered, stinking hulk, its streets choked with rubble and rotting bodies."[23] Hue had been saved, but destroyed.

Concurrent with the Battle of Hue, the Communists had occupied Gia Hoi, a sector of the city lying north of the Perfume River and east of the walled Citadel. Within Gia Hoi, the Communists established a provisional government and set about implementing their revolution. Cadres organized groups of students, workers, and teachers into administrative units. The Communists used terror to destroy the established government of the city. They purged Gia Hoi of all "reactionary elements" by liquidating anyone who had an affiliation with the Saigon regime. They summarily executed about 3,000 people, often in brutal fashion, or they buried them alive.[24]

The victims of NLF "hit squads" included officials of the national government, city officials, civil servants, community leaders, military personnel, police, priests, and teachers. Foreign victims included many Americans, Germans, Filipinos, Koreans, and nationals of other countries. In November 1969, President Nixon cited the Communist mass murders committed during their Tet-68 occupation of Hue as a justification for his policy of gradually withdrawing U.S. troops from South Vietnam. He asserted that if the United States withdrew its forces precipitously, as many Americans were demanding, the massacre at Hue would become a prelude for a nightmare, a bloodbath of massive proportions.[25]

SIEGE AT KHE SANH

Before the Battle of Hue ran its course, the Communists had launched phase three of *TCK–TKN* in a remote corner of the Quang Tri province, 60 miles northwest of the battered former imperial city. Two elite PAVN divisions, the 304th and 325-C, lay siege to the U.S. Marine base at Khe Sanh. The base, perched on a plateau near the corner formed by the DMZ and the Laotian border, blocked enemy infiltration along Route 9. Four battalions of the 26th Marines, under the command of Colonel David E. Lownds, reinforced by one battalion of ARVN Rangers, 6,000 men total, defended the main base and surrounding hill strong points at Khe Sanh. They faced an estimated 30,000 to 40,000 PAVN troops.

General Giap had planned phase three to be the capstone of *TCK–TKN*. If the phase two attacks on the cities succeeded in bringing about popular uprisings and the collapse of the Saigon regime, Giap's divisions would try to drive the U.S. Marines out of Khe Sanh. If the NVA forces succeeded, they could end the Second Indochina War with a stunning military victory.[26]

The Battle of Khe Sanh received extensive media coverage within the United States. Americans feared for the lives of the Marines, who were crowded into their isolated outpost, subjected to intensive artillery and mortar bombardments, and seemingly in danger of being overrun. Journalists noted uneasily that Khe Sanh resembled Dien Bien Phu, the French fortress the Vietminh had isolated and overrun in May 1954. The fall of Dien Bien Phu had been a catastrophic defeat for the French. It had destroyed their will to continue the Franco-Vietminh War. Would history repeat itself at Khe Sanh? Would the United States suffer its first major defeat of the Second Indochina War? If such a military disaster occurred, would it be the end of the American Vietnam war? President Johnson fretted that Khe Sanh might be lost to the Communists. Asserting that he did not want "any damn Dinbinfoo" on his watch, Johnson anxiously raised the possibility of using tactical nuclear weapons to save Khe Sanh if the enemy verged on overrunning it.[27]

The fears of the journalists and President Johnson were exaggerated. Khe Sanh bore only a superficial resemblance to Dien Bien Phu. There was never any serious danger of the NVA forces overrunning the base or driving out the Marines. General Giap had been able to defeat the French at Dien Bien Phu in 1954 for two major reasons: he had had superior firepower, and he had been able to cut the aerial lifeline to the fortress. But, at Khe Sanh, the combination of American air power and artillery fire gave the Americans a vast superiority over the NVA forces, and Giap's forces could not interdict Westmoreland's air supply system to the base. In fact, one of the reasons Westmoreland had installed the Marines at Khe Sanh was because he hoped to lure Giap into a set-piece battle. Confident that the Marines, supported by artillery and aircraft, could hold the base against whatever forces the NVA committed to battle, Westmoreland viewed Khe Sanh as the ideal place to call the awesome U.S. firepower into play. If Giap's forces took the bait and tried to overrun Khe Sanh, Westmoreland believed they would be cut to pieces by artillery fire and bombing.[28]

The siege of Khe Sanh began on the morning of January 20, 1968, when NVA forces hit the base and its hilly outposts with barrages of artillery, rocket, and mortar fire. The Battle of Khe Sanh developed as a full-scale conventional campaign fought between two national armies in an important arena of the war. The I Corps Tactical Zone, consisting of the five northernmost provinces of South Vietnam (Quang Nam, Quang Tin, and Quang Ngai, in addition to Quang Tri and Thua Thien) was the largest and most complex combat area in South Vietnam. Within that region, the enemy mounted a potent mix of insurgent and conventional tactics that often put severe pressures on the allied forces. During 1967, the fighting in I Corps accounted for half of the enemy KIAs, and the Marines suffered half of the U.S. KIAs for that year.[29]

Westmoreland reacted to Giap's siege of Khe Sanh by executing Operation NIAGARA, which had been prepared for use against the NVA in the event they attacked the base. Operation NIAGARA represented a mighty concentration of firepower com-

Figure 7.4 Khe Sanh: A panoramic view of the sandbagged perimeter bunkers. U.S. Marine defenders held on to the remote outpost lying below the DMZ during a 77-day siege by North Vietnamese regulars. *Source:* CORBIS.

posed of B-52s, tactical aircraft, and artillery directed at the enemy positions.[30] As the Battle of Khe Sanh unfolded, artillery duels between PAVN and Marine gunners, round-the-clock air raids on the NVA positions, and vicious firefights whenever enemy units attacked one of the surrounding strong points were daily occurrences. On February 7, a Special Forces camp at Lang Vei, south of Khe Sanh, was destroyed by NVA forces using Soviet PT-76 light tanks. It was during the Khe Sanh campaign that the enemy first used armor in South Vietnam. The loss of Lang Vei enabled the NVA to put more pressure on the Marines defending Khe Sanh. Three weeks later, the key battle of the Khe Sanh campaign took place. From February 29 to March 1, following the heaviest enemy artillery barrage of the campaign, a regiment of the NVA 304th attacked Khe Sanh from the east. But U.S. artillery and bombers decimated the regiment before any of its units reached the base perimeter.[31]

The destruction of the 304th regiment marked the turning point in the battle. Although there were harassing attacks made by the enemy over the next several days, the NVA mounted no more major assaults on Khe Sanh. The PAVN forces began withdrawing by March 11. Giap apparently decided to pull his forces back from Khe Sanh because of the failure of the phase two campaigns and because he had concluded that the U.S. forces could not be beaten at Khe Sanh. There would be no replication of Dien

Bien Phu if that had been Giap's objective. Scattered fighting occurred in the vicinity of the base until the end of the month. A relief force reached Khe Sanh on April 8, allowing Colonel Lownds and his troops to leave the base. The siege of Khe Sanh had lasted seventy-seven days; it had claimed the lives of more than 200 Marines. Estimated NVA losses exceeded 10,000 killed or wounded.[32]

When the Tet-68 Offensive ran its course, President Johnson proclaimed it "a complete failure." And Tet was in many ways a significant victory for the United States and South Vietnam. In addition to their losses at Khe Sanh, the mostly futile country-wide assaults during the Tet-68 Offensive cost the attackers horrendous casualties. From January 29 through March 31, 1968, combined VietCong and PAVN losses may have exceeded 58,000 KIA, nearly 70 percent of the forces committed to the campaigns! The VietCong, who had staged most of the attacks, "were largely destroyed as an effective military menace to the South Vietnamese government."[33] The PLAF main force units had to be reconstituted, using NVA regulars who infiltrated south down the Ho Chi Minh Trail during the next six months. Compared with the egregious losses sustained by the Communists during Tet-68, U.S. and ARVN casualties were light, altogether about 3,400 killed and wounded.

In many provinces, much of the VietCong political infrastructure, which had been painstakingly erected over the years, was destroyed during the Tet-68 battles. The VietCong cadres had come out into the open to organize the uprisings that were expected to follow the assaults on the towns and cities. The expected uprisings never materialized, and the VietCong cadres were eliminated. Nowhere in South Vietnam cities and towns were the VietCong attackers welcomed by the South Vietnamese people, nor did any defections from GVN political or military ranks occur. In fact, many of the ARVN forces fought well, despite being caught by surprise.[34] After Tet, there was no chance the Saigon regime would be overthrown by a revolution from within South Vietnam. After the spring of 1968, the Vietnam War became, for the most part, a conventional war between the main forces units of the allies and the NVA/PLAF. U.S. military leaders considered Tet-68 the greatest victory of the war for the American and ARVN forces. In the wake of his greatest success, having taken advantage of an opportunity to badly hurt the enemy, General Westmoreland was eager to mount a major counteroffensive and win the war.[35]

STALEMATE

But the Tet-68 campaigns proved to be the great paradox of the American Vietnam War. Tet-68 turned out to be a short-term tactical U.S. victory that prepared the way for the long-run strategic defeat of the American cause in Southeast Asia. Ironically, Tet-68, the greatest U.S. mlitary victory of the long war, was the beginning of the end of the U.S. intervention in Southeast Asia.

The scope, scale, and intensity of the VietCong Tet-68 Offensive shocked most Americans, who had been led to believe that the VietCong were about finished. Nightly, television news beamed the sights and sounds of fierce battles in the streets of Saigon and Hue into American living rooms. America's most respected television news anchor, Walter Cronkite, reacted to the Tet attacks by asking rhetorically: "What the hell is going on? I thought we were winning the war?" Viewers watched VietCong commandos fighting inside the American embassy compound; they watched General Westmoreland's impromptu press conference held in the embassy courtyard amidst the rubble and the dead VietCong sappers; and they witnessed the summary execution of a VietCong terrorist by General Nguyen Ngoc Loan, chief of South Vietnam's National Police, on a cobblestone street in Saigon. Daily press reports filed from cities all over South Vietnam highlighted the surprise attacks and the extensive destruction that they caused. Initial wire stories, later corrected, exaggerated the Communist successes and contributed to the confusion and widely shared sense that Tet had been an Allied disaster.[36]

A quotation from an Associated Press (AP) report had tremendous impact. On February 7, Air Force Major Chester I. Brown conducted a press tour through the shattered Mekong Delta town of Ben Tre. The town had been occupied by the VietCong.

Figure 7.5 Brigadier General Nguyen Ngoc Loan, chief of the South Vietnamese National Police, summarily executes a VietCong terrorist on a street in Saigon during the Tet-68 Offensive. NBC television also broadcast the execution on its nightly newscast on February 2, 1968. Photographer: Eddie Adams. *Source:* AP/Wide World Photos.

U.S. troops were called in to reclaim the town. To eject the VietCong, the Americans used heavy artillery and helicopter gunships that leveled most of the town's buildings and killed many of its inhabitants. Surveying the remains of Ben Tre, Brown matter-of-factly told AP reporter Peter Arnett, "It became necessary to destroy the town to save it."[37]

Major Brown's Orwellian phrase encapsulated a basic contradiction of the U.S. war effort in South Vietnam. Ostensibly, Americans were fighting in Vietnam to protect the freedom of the South Vietnamese people and enable them to build a nation. But American weaponry was destroying part of the South Vietnamese social fabric in the process of trying to liberate it. The military means overwhelmed the political ends. For many of the residents of Ben Tre, the real-world alternative to rule by the VietCong was death and destruction at the hands of their saviors. If America had to destroy its friends in order to save them, of what use was the war to us, or, *a fortiori,* to our friends? Major Brown's remark "seemed to epitomize the purposeless destruction of the war."[38] The phrase gained wide currency in the United States and became one of the staples of antiwar discourse for years.

While the media stressed the surprising power of the enemy offensive, official cables to Johnson and other leaders in Washington presented a more realistic account of Tet-68. From his reading of the secret cable traffic, Johnson knew the VietCong had suffered heavy casualties, the ARVN troops were fighting effectively, and the urban populace was not rallying to the NLF banner. Johnson, knowing Tet was a significant allied tactical victory, tried to counter the sensational media coverage and reassure the American people.[39] He held a press conference on February 2 to pronounce the Communist offensive a complete failure. Administrative officials appeared on public affairs programs and made speeches around the country to convey the message that Tet was a great allied victory and a disastrous Communist defeat.

The Johnson administration's public relations efforts to salvage popular support for the U.S. Vietnam War policy in the aftermath of the Tet assaults failed. Much of the press and the public continued to regard Tet as a disaster. What administration spokesmen did not understand was that it was not that journalists or the American people thought Communists were winning the Tet battles. That was not the problem. The public was shocked by the fact that the Tet Offensive could occur. Tet-68 exploded all of the official reassurances that the United States was winning the war, the VietCong were on their last legs, and the war would end soon. To many Americans, Tet confirmed what they already suspected, that the United States had locked itself into an endless war that was consuming ever-rising numbers of lives and dollars. Public opinion polls showed that popular discontent with the war increased sharply in the aftermath of the Tet-68 Offensive.[40]

Despite their outward show of confidence, Johnson and his senior advisers had been shaken by the Tet-68 Offensive. They also were alarmed by the prospect of further offensives in South Vietnam and by Communist initiatives in other parts of the world. On January 23, just before Tet, the North Koreans had seized an intelligence-gathering ship, the USS *Pueblo,* operating near their coast, after having tolerated such espionage operations for years. At about the same time, South Korean police discovered an assassination plot against South Korean President Chung Hee Park, which had been masterminded in North Korea. CIA operatives warned that the Soviets might provoke another crisis over Berlin, a perennial Cold War flash point. Washington also received reports of increased unrest in the Middle East.[41] Johnson worried that the Tet-68 attacks, including the siege at Khe Sanh, were parts of a worldwide Communist effort to score Cold War victories over the United States and its allies.

Johnson's military advisers responded to Tet by proposing to widen the war. The Joint Chiefs wanted to expand the bombing campaign against North Vietnam. But Johnson, concerned above all with holding Khe Sanh, refused to take any additional military actions against North Vietnam. He asked General Westmoreland if he needed any additional troops to prevent a defeat at Khe Sanh. Westmoreland replied that he did not. But he was concerned about his logistic ability to support the forces that he had committed to I Corps, and he requested some additional airlift and helicopter support.[42]

In early February 1968, Army General Earle Wheeler, the chairman of the Joint Chiefs, had much on his mind besides Vietnam. In Johnson's willingness to send Westmoreland whatever additional forces he might need to avoid a politically damaging defeat at Khe Sanh, Wheeler saw an opportunity to rebuild the American strategic reserve and replenish U.S. military forces stationed elsewhere in the world. The deployments to Vietnam had not been based on the military demands of the situation, but on the forces available without calling up the Reserves and the National Guard. The NATO forces assigned to Germany and the forces committed to South Korea had all been been skeletonized and stripped of their best officers and noncoms in order to send more troops to the Vietnam War.[43]

Faced with Communist threats in North Korea and Berlin, and perhaps elsewhere, the Joint Chiefs had concluded that U.S. strategic assets had been stretched too thin by Vietnam. General Wheeler, believing Tet would force Johnson's hand, thought he could persuade Johnson to take the politically risky step of mobilizing the Reserves and of putting the country on a full-war footing. Wheeler maneuvered Westmoreland, who had initially declined Johnson's offer of more combat troops, into requesting additional forces. Then the Joint Chiefs put pressure on Johnson to provide the forces not only for Vietnam, but to restock the stateside strategic reserve so the military would be better positioned to meet Communist threats to U.S. interests elsewhere. They were especially concerned that American NATO commitments not be sacrificed on the altar of Vietnam.[44] They were disappointed when Johnson deferred their request to mobilize the Reserves and agreed to send General Westmoreland a force of only 10,500 troops, which could be provided without calling up the Reserves.

Wheeler pursued his goal of a mobilization of the Reserves, which he believed was necessary to enable the United States to meet the military demands of the Vietnam War and to fulfill its other strategic commitments in a dangerous world. He obtained Johnson's approval to travel to Vietnam to assess General Westmoreland's immediate and future manpower needs. After conferring, Westmoreland and Wheeler came up with a planned troop request designed to meet both the MACV's Vietnam needs and defend other U.S. interests in the world. The troop request consisted of three force packages: The first increment of 108,000 men would be sent to Vietnam by May 1, 1968. Additional increments of 42,000 and 56,000 men would be sent by September 1 and December 1, respectively, 206,000 men total. But only the first increment would be sent to Vietnam for sure. The other two increments would constitute the strategic reserve in the United States, which was not to be deployed in Vietnam unless the North Vietnamese mounted a successful offensive.[45]

Wheeler presented the troop request to Johnson on February 28, 1968. He accompanied his report with a pessimistic appraisal of the military situation in Vietnam that contradicted General Westmoreland's previous optimistic appraisals. Wheeler told Johnson that the initial Tet attacks nearly succeeded in a dozen places, that the ARVN forces had been thrown on the defensive, and that pacification had suffered serious setbacks. "In short it was a very near thing."[46] Wheeler also told Johnson and his civilian advisers that Westmoreland would need to augment his forces significantly if he was to respond effectively to the challenges posed by Tet-68: to counter the enemy offensive, to eject the NVA forces fighting in I Corps, to restore security to the towns and cities, to restore security in the populated regions of the countryside, and to regain the initiative with a counteroffensive of his own. To accomplish all of these objectives, Wheeler insisted that Westmoreland would require large numbers of additional troops.[47] By accentuating the negative aspects of the military situation in Vietnam, Wheeler tried to pressure Johnson into supporting a call-up of the reserves, part of which would be used to replenish depleted U.S. force levels elsewhere.

The magnitude of the troop request stunned Johnson and his civilian advisers, and Wheeler's pessimistic assessment of Tet alarmed them. Departing Secretary of Defense Robert McNamara, the *bête noire* of the hawks to the end, "in his valedictory meeting as a member of the cabinet," strongly opposed sending more U.S. troops to Vietnam. McNamara said that feeding another 200,000 soldiers into combat would merely be doing more of the same. The North Vietnamese, as they had previously, would simply match the American escalation with one of their own. McNamara pointed out that bombing had consistently failed to impair the Communists' ability to infiltrate whatever men and supplies they required. He believed the key to improving the situation in South Vietnam was not to send more U.S. troops but to increase the resources and responsibilities of the South Vietnamese army.[48]

At the February 28 meeting, General Wheeler confronted the president with two bitterly unattractive choices. If Johnson met the Army's request for an additional 206,000 troops, it would mean transcending the parameters of limited war that the president had set. The Reserves would have to be mobilized to provide the manpower, and the economy would have to be put on a war footing to meet the vastly increased expenditures. That would mean tax increases and probably economic controls. Worse, Johnson would have to take these politically unpalatable actions in an election year, and at a time of rising domestic opposition to the war. But if he refused the military's request for increased troop levels in Vietnam, he would be sending a clear signal to friends and foes alike that the upper limits of the U.S. military commitment in South Vietnam had been reached. He would be acknowledging that American strategic goals had either been abandoned or pushed far into the future.[49] Further, with U.S. military forces stationed around the world having already been stretched dangerously thin to provide the 536,000 troops currently in Vietnam, failure to meet the Army's request for 206,000 additional soldiers might render the U.S. government incapable of responding effectively to threats to its strategic interests elsewhere.

Johnson, shocked by General Wheeler's report, refused to make such a critical decision on the spot. He asked his new secretary of defense, Clark M. Clifford, who was attending the meeting, to head a study group to examine all facets of the troop request. Johnson told Clifford to study the matter thoroughly and carefully, then to give him "the lesser of evils."[50]

Johnson's directive to Clifford inaugurated the most important debate over what action to take in Vietnam ever undertaken within any administration during the long U.S. involvement in Southeast Asia. For the first time, there would be a reappraisal of all aspects of the U.S. Vietnam War policy. During the reassessment process, hawks and doves waged a bureaucratic war for the heart and mind of Lyndon Johnson. Everyone at the meeting that day sensed that a decisive moment in the war had arrived. They also knew Clark Clifford was the man who more than any other was going to determine on which side of the historic divide President Johnson would choose to walk. Would Johnson decide to escalate or to back off? The outcome of a major war hung in the balance.

Although he was a newcomer to Johnson's inner circle, Clifford was also a seasoned Democratic Party insider. He had managed Harry Truman's 1948 campaign when the feisty president had scored his famous upset over the consensus favorite Thomas Dewey. Clifford also had been a valued adviser of President Kennedy. Prior to appointing him to replace McNamara, Johnson had often sought Clifford's advice on a whole range of issues.[51] Clifford was an establishment centrist who had embraced the Cold War ideology characteristic of his generation of political leaders. He had supported Johnson's Vietnam War policy since its inception. Johnson brought Clifford on board as McNamara's replacement primarily because he had assumed that his new defense secretary would loyally continue to back his war policy.

Unbeknown to Johnson, Clifford had already begun to have doubts about the validity of the domino theory, which was the chief ideological rationale for the U.S. war effort in Vietnam. In September 1967, Johnson had sent Clifford to accompany Maxwell Taylor on a trip to Asia to persuade several of the U.S. allies in that region to increase their troop commitments in Vietnam. Clifford was surprised to learn that the leaders of Thailand, the Philippines, South Korea, New Zealand, and Australia neither wished to send more troops to Vietnam nor felt particularly threatened by the fact that North Vietnam had over 100,000 troops in South Vietnam. Clifford asked himself, If these Asian and Pacific island nations proximate to the Vietnam War felt no fear of Communist expansion, could it be that U.S. officials had exaggerated the potential threat to the stability of these countries posed by the Communist revolution in Vietnam?

Clifford also had kept in touch with influential friends in corporate board rooms and law offices across the land. Until Tet, these powerful men had generally supported the administration's war policy. After the Communist offensive, many had turned dovish. Worried about the stalemated war, growing political disunity, and signs of economic decline, they opposed any further escalations of the war. Some thought it was time for America to cut its losses and get out of Vietnam. Their opinions had an impact on Clifford,[52] who was already questioning the U.S. war policy as he replaced McNamara.

To help him complete the task Johnson had given him, Clifford quickly formed a task force, which included several of the president's senior civilian and military advisers: Dean Rusk, Secretary of the Treasury Henry H. Fowler, Undersecretary of Defense Paul Nitze, Director of the CIA Richard Helms, National Security Adviser Walt Whitman Rostow, General Wheeler, and General Taylor. The Clifford Task Force turned immediately to examining the Army's request for 206,000 additional troops, as well as the means by which it could be met. The major problem was that all previous troop requests had been fulfilled without mobilizing Reserve forces. But it was precisely this political barrier that would have to be broken to meet the military's latest demands. Such a large troop increase also would have an adverse impact on the economy and require large cuts in Great Society programs. Foreign aid would be gutted.[53] Several task force members further pointed out that, in their judgment, sending large numbers of additional troops would probably be futile. North Vietnam would match the U.S. escalation with one of their own, as they had previously.

As the task force members studied the troop request, officials from the Defense Department, the CIA, and the State Department systematically destroyed the rationale for the Joint Chiefs' troop request and began to challenge the Vietnam War policy itself. A Department of Defense official, Alain Enthoven of Systems Analysis, called the troop request another "payment on an open-ended commitment." In his view, sending additional U.S. combat troops to South Vietnam would not bring an earlier end to the war, attrite the enemy, or erode Hanoi's will to fight.[54]

Clifford began to ask fundamental questions about the American Vietnam policy, many of which Johnson had never raised, questions that were exceedingly difficult to answer precisely. By raising these basic issues, Clifford broadened the task force's focus. Although the task force had been formed to study the military's request for more troops, it began to reappraise the entire U.S. Vietnam war effort. To Clifford, the most important question was not how to send 206,000 more troops to Vietnam, but rather should America continue on its present course in Vietnam? Clifford raised other fundamental questions about the U.S. war policy and discovered that senior officials either could not provide answers or furnished him with inadequate answers:[55]

1. Will 200,000 more troops win the war? No one could be sure.
2. If not, how many more will be needed to win and when? No one knew.

3. Can the enemy respond with a buildup of their own? They could and they probably would.
4. What would be involved in committing 200,000 more men to Vietnam? A Reserve call-up of up to 280,000 men, increased draft calls, and an extension of tours of service for most men on active duty.
5. How much would it cost to meet the latest troop request? An estimated $2 billion per month.
6. What would be the impact on the economy? Credit restrictions, tax increases, and probably wage and price controls. It would also worsen the balance of payments and lower the value of the dollar.
7. Can the bombing stop the war? No, not by itself.
8. Would stepping up the bombing decrease U.S. casualties? Very little, if at all.
9. How long must we keep sending U.S. troops and carrying the main burden of combat? Nobody knew. The South Vietnamese forces are far from ready to replace the U.S. forces.

During his review, Clifford asked General Wheeler for a presentation of the military plan for attaining victory in Vietnam. General Wheeler told him that there was no military plan for victory. Astonished, Clifford asked him why. Wheeler told him that there was no plan because U.S. forces operated under three major political restrictions: They could not invade North Vietnam because such action would possibly bring the Chinese into the war. They could not mine Haiphong, North Vietnam's principal port, because Soviet ships might be sunk. They could not pursue the enemy into Laos and Cambodia because such initiatives would widen the war. Clifford then asked, given these restrictions, how could America hope to win the Vietnam War? Wheeler replied, without enthusiasm, that eventually the enemy would reach a point when it would decide it could not continue the war because it could no longer tolerate the damage that the strategy of attrition was inflicting. Clifford then asked General Wheeler how long he thought it would take for the current attrition strategy that was in place to induce Hanoi to abandon the insurgency in South Vietnam. Wheeler would not attempt an estimate.[56]

Following days of analysis of the Vietnam War policy, Clifford concluded with a series of observations that starkly revealed the bankruptcy of the U.S. strategy of limited war in Southeast Asia:

> I could not find out when the war was going to end; I could not find out the manner in which it was going to end. I could not find out whether the new requests for men and equipment were going to be enough, or whether it would take more and, if more, how much; I could not find out how soon the South Vietnamese forces would be ready to take over. All I had was the statement, given with too little self-assurance to be comforting, that if we persisted for an indeterminate length of time, the enemy would choose not to go on. And so I asked, "Does anyone see any diminution in the will of the enemy after four years of our having been there, after enormous casualties, and after massive destruction from our bombing?" The answer was that there appeared to be no diminution in the will of the enemy.[57]

Following his extensive discussions with many civilian and military leaders, Clifford concluded that the most probable outcome of sending 206,000 more troops to Vietnam would be to raise the level of combat and casualties. "I was convinced that the military course we were pursuing was not only endless, but hopeless."[58] Sending more troops would further Americanize the war and leave the United States further than ever from its goal of achieving an independent South Vietnam. Clifford therefore concluded that the United States should send no more troops to South Vietnam. Instead, the American goal "should be to level off our involvement and work toward gradual disengagement."[59] Having made his decision, Clifford set out to try to convince President Johnson that the time had come to alter course in Vietnam. Clifford knew Johnson would have to abandon his policy of gradual escalation because it was not working. Nor did it show any promise of ever working. It also was limiting America's ability to meet strategic commitments elsewhere in the world, weakening the economy, and dividing the American people.

JOHNSON AGONISTES

Johnson received the Clifford Task Force's report on March 4. It contained General Wheeler's recommendation that the troop request should be met. But to achieve the goal of 206,000 additional troops in Vietnam during 1968, the report made clear to Johnson that he would have to call 262,000 Reservists to active duty, increase draft calls, and extend the tours of most men currently serving on active duty.

More significantly, the task force's report also called for a reassessment of the U.S. Vietnam policy, especially in relation to U.S. global strategic interests. It hinted that America would have to establish a limit for its involvement in Vietnam and abide by it. The report also asserted that no amount of additional U.S. troops in Vietnam could achieve American objectives there unless the South Vietnamese government achieved a broader popular base and fought more effectively.[60] Clifford hoped the report would cause Johnson to focus on the fundamental questions of U.S. Vietnam policy raised by the Wheeler-Westmoreland troop request issue. He also hoped to sow seeds of doubt in Johnson's mind about the wisdom of continuing to escalate the war.

The president carefully read and pondered over the report for several days. He discussed what he should do in Vietnam with several advisers, including members of the task force. Rostow urged him to go all out and make a maximum effort to win the war. Johnson's initial reaction to the Communist Tet Offensive had been to do just that. He was angry, and he wanted to strike back. Johnson also believed that an aggressive post-Tet counteroffensive, coupled with an intense bombing campaign, could break Hanoi's will. He felt ready to mobilize the Reserves, not only for Vietnam but also to strengthen the overall American strategic posture in the world. He wanted to unleash Westmoreland and have him pound the VietCong remnants and battered North Vietnamese forces into submission.

Figure 7.6 The man who turned the Vietnam War around. In March 1968, Clark Clifford, the new secretary of defense, helped persuade Lyndon Johnson to abandon the failed strategy of graduated escalation and replace it with an early version of Vietnamization. *Source:* AP/ Wide World Photos. Neg. # APA3068015.

What partially deterred him from striking back hard was the Clifford Task Force's report. Johnson was persuaded to make any further commitment of U.S. forces to Vietnam contingent upon the South Vietnamese government improving its capabilities for governing and fighting. Johnson agreed that the South Vietnamese leaders should be informed that continued American support for their cause would depend on their willingness to assume a greater burden of the fighting. Johnson's willingness to send the message to Thieu and Ky that they would have to do more of the fighting indicated that there was significant movement in Washington's policy toward the concept of Vietnamization that would later be embraced by the Nixon administration.

Johnson also knew that Westmoreland was already taking the offensive against the enemy with the U.S. forces he had on hand.[61] MACV did not appear to have an immediate need for additional forces to take the fight to the Communists and hold Khe Sanh. Johnson also responded positively to a proposal from Rusk to consider curtailing the bombing of North Vietnam. Rusk persuaded Johnson that a partial bombing halt might offset some of the domestic opposition to the war, and it could even elicit a favorable response from the North Vietnamese that would move both sides closer to negotiations.[62] By March 7, Johnson was moving toward two new positions: setting a troop ceiling for Vietnam and ordering a partial bombing halt. In the "Battle for

Lyndon Johnson," Rostow, Wheeler, and the other hawks appeared to be losing ground to Clifford and the growing number of doves among them.

Whatever possibility remained of Johnson sending large numbers of additional troops to Vietnam diminished when *New York Times* reporters Hedrick Smith and Neil Sheehan broke the story on March 10 that Johnson was considering a troop increase of 206,000 troops.[63] The impact of the *Times*'s scoop, which penetrated the veil of secrecy Johnson had draped over the top-secret deliberations, was dramatic. White House spokesmen denied, unconvincingly, that the president was considering such a large troop request from General Westmoreland. Johnson's credibility gap widened. A storm of public criticism erupted. If Tet were such a great allied victory, people demanded to know, why did General Westmoreland need 200,000 more troops? Other influential print and electronic media voices editorialized against the proposed troop increase and called for changes in the Vietnam War policy. The day after the *Times* broke the sensational story, Senator Fulbright, on live television, grilled Rusk for hours about the administration's plans for sending more troops to Vietnam. Fulbright ended his interrogation by warning Rusk that any further escalations of the war had better be cleared with Congress.

Dramatic evidence of flagging Congressional support for the Vietnam War surfaced shortly after the *Times* story broke. Clark Clifford and General Wheeler conferred with hawkish leaders on the House and Senate Armed Services Committees. These people, mostly conservatives, all Cold Warriors who had been staunch supporters of the war effort to date, told Clifford and Wheeler that they could not support a Reserve call-up or a large increase in the number of U.S. troops fighting in Vietnam. Senator Richard Russell, a close friend of Johnson, and one of the most powerful senators on Capitol Hill, made a profound impression on Clifford when he told him and General Wheeler that he believed the United States had made a serious mistake by involving itself in Vietnam in the first place. Clifford wondered, If Senator Russell and his fellow hawks did not support a troop increase, then who would?[64]

"The Tet Offensive . . . legitimated the Vietnam War as a political issue." It "liberated politicians, journalists, and commentators from their previous commitments to the war."[65] The search for alternative war policies became a legitimate, even obsessive, political preoccupation. Because 1968 was a presidential election year, the war became an integral part of the electoral process. The search for alternatives, for a way out of a war that had become unpopular and seemingly unwinnable, unpopular mainly because it appeared unwinnable, had become the leading issue of the embryonic presidential race. Presidential candidates from both parties began to criticize Johnson, his war policy, and the proposed troop increase.

The first of these candidates to challenge the president was an obscure Democratic senator from Minnesota, Eugene McCarthy. McCarthy had no money, no organization, and apparently no serious ambition to be president. He was an introspective, philosophical, even mystical personality, more comfortable writing poetry or discussing profound questions of human existence with close friends than roaming the Senate corridors or campaigning for votes. But McCarthy felt compelled to offer his presidential candidacy to opponents of the Vietnam War as a conduit through which their opposition to that war could flow into the developing presidential election. When the Minnesota senator entered the New Hampshire presidential primary, scheduled for March 12, the pundits wrote off his quixotic challenge. They expected the upstart maverick to be crushed by the master politician in the White House who, despite his credibility gap and the albatross of war, retained all of the powers of presidential incumbency and possessed the consummate political skills to use them.[66]

McCarthy, running on a single issue, opposition to the Vietnam War, surprised everyone with a strong showing in New Hampshire. Aided by hundreds of young volunteers who went door-to-door in the snow on his behalf, McCarthy came within 500 votes of defeating President Johnson in a state where the electorate had hawkish inclinations. McCarthy's surprise showing came as a political revelation. Analysts read the New Hampshire results as evidencing far greater public dissatisfaction with the war and with Johnson's leadership than anyone had realized. McCarthy's strong showing exposed Johnson's political vulnerability at the outset of the presidential campaign. If a political lightweight like McCarthy could almost beat President Johnson in a hawkish state, what might a more formidable antiwar candidacy do nationwide? The Democratic primary election results "buoyed the hopes of the president's critics in both parties."[67]

At the time, everyone interpreted McCarthy's strong showing in New Hampshire as a vote for peace, a vote for disengaging from Vietnam. But postelection studies have solved the mystery of how an unknown dovish candidate could have done so well in a hawkish state against the president. Among McCarthy voters in the 1968 New Hampshire primary, a three-to-two majority actually favored escalating the American war effort. In the November elections, more New Hampshire voters who had previously cast their votes for McCarthy in the Democratic primary voted for the hawkish third-party candidate George Wallace than for either Democrat Hubert Humphrey or Republican Richard M. Nixon.

The hawks of New Hampshire voted for the dovish McCarthy, either because he was the only protest candidate running and they did not care about his ideology or, more likely, because he was *not Lyndon Johnson.* These angry New Englanders voted for McCarthy because it was the best way they could send a message repudiating Johnson's war policy and leadership.[68]

McCarthy's strong showing in New Hampshire lured a much more powerful dovish presidential candidate into the political arena four days later, New York Senator Robert F. Kennedy. He had plenty of money, an experienced and savvy campaign organization, name recognition, and a vast personal following among the American electorate. With Kennedy's entry into the 1968 Democratic presidential race, Johnson knew he now faced a long and divisive battle for his party's nomination. Even if he managed to beat back Kennedy's challenge and win renomination, Johnson would be taking a badly divided Democratic Party into the general election against Richard Nixon,

Figure 7.7   Senator Eugene McCarthy campaigns on Main Street in Manchester, New Hampshire, March 9, 1968. McCarthy, the candidate of choice among young people and other antiestablishment voters, opposed the Vietnam War. Photographer: Walter Green. *Source:* AP/Wide World Photos. Neg. # APA3619723.

the probable Republican nominee. Nixon could be expected to make the increasingly unpopular war and the growing disorders in American society the leading issues. Public opinion polls, taken at the moment Kennedy and McCarthy began their challenges to his leadership, showed Johnson at the lowest point of popularity since he had assumed the presidency.

After New Hampshire came the Wisconsin primary, set for March 19. All three candidates' names would be on the Wisconsin ballots. Johnson's political advisers informed him that recent polls taken in that midwestern state showed both McCarthy and Kennedy positioning themselves to beat him. The Wisconsin voters, more dovish than New Hampshire's electorate, viewed McCarthy and Kennedy as peace candidates and saw Johnson as a war candidate. His political advisers told the president that if he wanted to retrieve his candidacy, he would have to make a dramatic gesture toward peace in Vietnam.

On top of the disturbing political news in New Hampshire and Wisconsin, Johnson also heard some disconcerting economic news. The inflation rate was rising because of increased war spending and Congress's continuing refusal to enact the president's proposed surtax to reduce the deficit. The consumer price index in 1967 rose more than it had in any year since the Korean War. Increased federal spending for the Vietnam War also exacerbated the nation's spiraling balance-of-payments deficit. A gold crisis loomed during late 1967, when the British were forced to devalue the pound sterling. Many currency speculators sold their dollars, causing a run on the gold markets. During the first half of March 1968, the central banks of various countries had to supply almost $500 million in gold to help stabilize the dollar's value, to which all other currencies were pegged. American banks alone had sold over $300 million worth of gold by March 14. The administration had to grapple with the gold crisis at the same time it struggled with its failed Vietnam War policy.

A financial crisis was averted only by an emergency joint effort by the treasurers and central bankers of several countries, who created a system of monetary exchanges that temporarily curtailed gold selling on the free market.[69]

The jittery international money market sent a signal to Treasury Secretary Henry Fowler. Fowler told Johnson that if the United States were to send 206,000 additional troops to Vietnam, as requested, it would cost $2.5 billion in 1968 and $10 billion in 1969. These war expenditures would add another $500 million to the balance-of-payments deficit, require a major tax increase, and force deep cuts in funding for many Great Society and foreign aid programs. He warned the president that if the requested troops were sent to Vietnam and Congress did not take the painful political medicine of major tax increases and deep spending cuts in an election year, the United States would be risking the collapse of the dollar and a serious international financial crisis. International trade would be disrupted. The U.S. economy and those of its major trading partners could suffer serious damage. It could bring on a recession or depression.[70]

By mid-March, a combination of strategic, political, and economic considerations convinced Johnson that he could not approve the deployment of 206,000 additional troops to Vietnam. Meanwhile, Allied forces were holding their own. The NVA assault on Khe Sanh was ending, Hue had been reclaimed, and intelligence data indicated that there was little likelihood of further PLAF/NVA assaults against South Vietnamese cities. Domestic opposition to any large increase in U.S. forces in Vietnam was both widespread and deeply entrenched, even among many hawks.

President Johnson also continued to consult with his advisers, including Rostow and Rusk, who supported his war policy. On March 17 and March 18, Johnson made two speeches in which he defended his war policy and attacked his critics. He stated his determination to press on, to win the war, and he urged all Americans to support the U.S. soldiers fighting in Vietnam. The two speeches failed to elicit any noticeable popular support. Johnson's political advisers told him that the two speeches had damaged his reelection prospects in Wisconsin and that he must make some conciliatory gestures toward peace if he hoped to salvage his presidency. Johnson and his speech writers also worked on a major speech to be delivered to the American people on March 31, in which he would announce his decision on the troop request and inform the nation of his policy for the post-Tet phase of the Vietnam War.

Meanwhile, the "wise men," who included some of the principal architects of America's Cold War foreign policy, had decided that Johnson's Vietnam War policy was threatening to harm seriously the national interest. These distinguished and powerful men had given Johnson a vote of confidence at their November 2, 1967, meeting. But the Tet-68 Offensive and the sharp fall-off in popular support for the war, coupled with the gold crisis, had convinced them to press for disengagement from Vietnam before the war did irreparable harm to the nation's global security interests.

The most influential of the "wise men"—Dean Acheson, Averell Harriman, and Paul Nitze—wanted a "review of Johnson's war policy within the larger context of America's global national security concerns."[71] These elder statesmen, all Europeanists, believed that Washington had committed too many assets to an area of only peripheral importance and was in danger of neglecting vital U.S. interests in Europe. The limited war in Vietnam had gotten out of control, and it was time to restore the limits. It was time to phase down our commitments and, better yet, get out. It was time to refocus on our top priorities—ensuring the strategic security and continuing prosperity of Europe. It was time to restock U.S. NATO forces, save the dollar, and stabilize the European gold markets. The old Cold Warriors joined forces with Clark Clifford and together they worked behind the scenes to try to change administration war policy.

Johnson also was inclined to move in two new directions: send only token U.S. troop increases to Vietnam, which could be raised without necessitating a major Reserve call-up; and take actions to build up the military forces of South Vietnam. On March 22, the president officially rejected General Westmoreland's request for 206,000 troops. For the first time, Johnson had to put a cap on the number of American forces he would commit to Vietnam; he closed the open-ended commitment he had made in July 1965. On March 24, Johnson approved sending Westmoreland a mere 13,500 additional troops. They would turn out to be "the last increment of American military manpower committed to the Vietnam War."[72] In South Vietnam, the generals were responding to U.S. pressures. Draft calls were raised, and Thieu announced that ARVN forces would be augmented by adding 135,000 men.

The president also announced that he was recalling General Westmoreland from the field. He was bringing him back to Washington to become the Army's new Chief of Staff. To replace him, Johnson appointed General Creighton W. Abrams, Westmoreland's deputy, as the new MACV commander. Although Johnson's removal of Westmoreland from his command was widely construed as a dismissal, it was not. In fact, Westmoreland was promoted. He would henceforth be the most senior general in the U.S. Army. Although Westmoreland had come under criticism for his prophecies of victory and for failing to anticipate the Communist Tet-68 Offensive, he still retained Johnson's trust and respect. Having placed limits on the number of troops he was willing to commit to the war, Johnson's removal of Westmoreland, the general who wanted a large increase in combat forces and who wanted to undertake an offensive campaign designed to win the war, was inevitable. Johnson's removal of Westmoreland from the war zone put an exclamation point on his decision to end the policy of gradual escalation.

Clark Clifford, convinced the United States could never win the Vietnam War because of the powerful political and economic forces that were imposing limits upon U.S. military activity, was determined to set the United States on a decscalatory course in Vietnam. Clifford also was alarmed by the growing domestic unrest and loss of support for the war among the nation's legal and financial elite with whom he customarily socialized. Clifford worked with Acheson and Harry McPherson, Johnson's head speech writer. Together they "waged an unrelenting battle for the president's mind."[73]

On March 25, the "wise men" gathered at the State Department. They had come to try to salvage America's global foreign policy, which they had constructed in the years following World War II. It was an elaborate network of military bases around the world, regional alliances, and global commitments. It had been stretched to the breaking point by the war the United States was waging in Vietnam. The Tet-68 Offensive and gold crisis had exposed American vulnerabilities and defined limits to American power to order world affairs. The "wise men" spent the day in meetings with Rusk and Rostow from the State Department, with CIA Director Richard Helms, and with Generals Wheeler and Depuy. These officials briefed the "wise men" on the current diplomatic, military, and nation-building dimensions of the Vietnam War.

The next day, the "wise men" assembled for lunch in the White House to present their views to Johnson. The president had previously met with their most influential member, Dean Acheson. Acheson, who also had held extensive discussions on the war with Clifford and some of Johnson's other senior advisers, told the president that neither the time nor the assets were available to accomplish American military objectives in Vietnam. The force of 500,000-plus Americans currently in South Vietnam could neither expel the NVA nor subdue the VietCong. Acheson also told the president that public opinion would never support an expanded war effort, nor would it support the present level of military activity indefinitely. Acheson further stated his judgments that the ineffective ground war had to be changed, that the bombing of North Vietnam had to be halted, and that the war must be ended as soon as possible without sacrificing the American commitment to South Vietnam.[74]

The president went around the table, holding frank conversations with many individual "wise men" at the March 26 luncheon. While a few still supported Johnson's war policy, most sounded variations on Acheson's themes: They were convinced action had to be taken to reduce U.S. commitments in Vietnam and find a way out. They agreed that a troop increase would be folly and that the South Vietnamese military must shoulder a greater burden of the fighting. They told the president that they believed that the war was stalemated and that the United States could not afford to commit any more assets to Vietnam without doing serious harm to its national economy and global interests. They also told him that neither Congress nor most of the American people would support any further escalations of the conflict.[75] Following their individual conversations with the president, McGeorge Bundy then summed up the collective wisdom of the "wise men" for Johnson:

> The majority feeling is that we can no longer do the job we set out to do in the time that we have left. . . . We must begin to take steps to disengage. When we last met, we saw reasons for hope. We hoped then there would be slow steady progress. Last night and today the picture is not so hopeful.[76]

Johnson was shaken by what he heard at lunch that day. The "wise men," all of whom had previously supported his policy as recently as last November, had mostly spoken against it. Ironically, many of the "wise men," including Bundy, had advised Johnson for years to pursue the war policy that they were now counseling him to abandon. Tet-68 and the gold crisis had transformed the once-hawkish U.S. foreign policy Establishment into a flock of cooing doves. They now saw Johnson's war policy as hopeless and advised him to cut his losses and get out. The Republic of South Vietnam would have to learn to defend itself. The American foreign policy establishment was attending its last hurrah. It was not only abandoning the Vietnam War, but also it was abandoning its role in the formulation of U.S. foreign policy. Walt Rostow pronounced the American establishment dead. Lyndon Johnson put it more crudely: "The Establishment bastards have bailed out."[77]

For Johnson, who had become personally involved in this profound political crisis, the remarks of the "wise men" came as excruciating revelations. When they had first gathered, he expected them to support his war policy and urge him to carry on as they always had previously. But most had turned against the war. They advised him to phase out U.S. involvement and turn the war over to the South Vietnamese forces. During the final week of March, Johnson had to shoulder personally the responsibility for the greatest American foreign policy failure in the nation's history.

Johnson's dramatic meeting with the "wise men" on March 26 finally persuaded him to accept the realities that he had resisted for weeks: The Tet Offensive had significantly increased opposition to the war in America among elite groupings, including emboldened clergy, prominent laymen, influential media editorial writers, and members of Congress. Further escalation of the war was politically impossible. The gold crisis of March 1968 convinced Johnson that further escalation of the war could bring financial disaster. It could unhinge the dollar and undermine trade between the United States and its major European partners. Johnson would either have to scale down the war or court political and economic disaster.[78]

Following the March 26 meeting, Johnson worked on his speech, which was scheduled to be delivered to the nation on March 31. Clifford was involved in the speech-writing process, working with Harry McPherson. During the final days before it was to be given, Clifford played a key role in determining both the content and tone of the most important speech about the Vietnam War Johnson ever delivered.[79]

Johnson spoke on Sunday evening, March 31, from the Oval Office. He spoke more slowly and more softly than usual. The weary president announced four major decisions that changed the course of the Vietnam War and had a decisive impact on American political life.

1. Johnson repeated the offer of negotiations that he had made the previous September at San Antonio. He would halt all bombing of North Vietnam, whenever that action would lead to productive negotiations. As a conciliatory gesture and as a first step to deescalate the Vietnam War, Johnson announced an unconditional partial bombing halt. All bombing north of the 20th parallel would be stopped immediately.
2. Johnson told the American people of his decision to send only 13,500 additional support troops to Westmoreland over the next five months. He was rejecting Westmoreland's request for a major troop increase. There would be no further escalation of the ground war in South Vietnam.
3. Johnson stated that the U.S. effort in Vietnam would henceforth focus on expanding and improving the military capabilities of South Vietnam's armed forces and that they would gradually assume a greater responsibility for defending themselves.
4. As Johnson approached the end of his speech, he acknowledged that there was disunity in the country. He warned Americans of the perils of disunity and then concluded his speech with a stunning pronouncement, which he said he hoped would restore unity:

With America's sons in the fields far away, with America's future under challenge right here at home, with our hopes and the world's hopes for peace in the balance every day, I do not believe that I should devote an hour or a day of my time to any personal partisan causes or to any duties other than the awesome duties of this office. . . . Accordingly, I shall not seek, and I will not accept, the nomination of my party for another term as your president.[80]

Even though Johnson had been seriously considering retiring from office long before the Tet-68 and gold crises had occurred, he had not discussed that possibility with any of his associates, friends, or journalists. He had suffered a near-fatal heart attack in 1955, and he knew heart disease ran in his family on his father's side. The president, if he were to seek reelection and win, feared he would not live out his second term. He had no desire to join the bruising battle for renomination with Eugene McCarthy and Robert Kennedy, which would divide the Democratic Party. He also had no desire to join the even more brutal battle with Richard Nixon, the likely Republican Party nominee, which would exacerbate the deep divisions within the nation created by the controversial war. But the embattled president had kept these thoughts and misgivings to himself. Almost no one, foreign observers, political commentators, hawks, doves, Clifford, nor most of Johnson's other advisers had anticipated his resignation. Whether they were cheered or dismayed by the prospect, everyone had simply assumed the inevitability of his candidacy for reelection. Johnson had caught the pundits, the politicos, the nation, indeed the world, by surprise.

Three days later, Hanoi declared its readiness to have its delegates make contact with American representatives so that they could both decide how and when to end all bombing and other acts of war against the DRV. Although surprised by Hanoi's prompt response, Washington responded positively to the DRV's gesture. Talks between Washington and Hanoi opened in Paris on May 13. These negotiations began a diplomatic process that would, many years later, bring the U.S. war in Vietnam to a close.[81] On April 4, the Pentagon formally denied Westmoreland's request for 206,000 more troops and placed a ceiling of 549,500 on U.S. troop deployments to South Vietnam.[82] The open-ended military commitment had been officially closed.

Although the Tet-68 Offensive left the Communists with devastating defeats and horrendous casualties, cost them a good deal of their political infrastructure in South Vietnam, and created a million additional refugees; it brought them a tremendous political victory within the United States that eventually forced President Johnson to abandon his strategy of graduated escalation. He replaced it with an early version of what would later be called "Vietnamization" by his successor Richard M. Nixon.

TURNING POINT

Tet-68 was the major turning point of the American Vietnam War. In its wake there occurred a fundamental shift in U.S. war policy that brought the first steps toward the deescalation of American involvement in Indochina. Johnson's dramatic change of direction had been brought about by domestic political developments, by economic and financial considerations, and by the efforts of Clark Clifford and the "wise men," who persuaded him to change course. Tet-68 had forced the U.S. foreign policy-making elite to confront the stark reality that their limited war strategy of graduated escalation could not achieve U.S. objectives in Southeast Asia. They understood that the Vietnam War could not be won at any reasonable price that the American public was willing to pay. They also saw that if the administration were to continue to escalate the conflict, serious and permanent damage could result, both to the American economy and to the U.S. global foreign policy based on containing Communism. In the weeks following Tet-68, the "wise men" persuaded the president to abandon his failed war policy. "March 31, 1968, marked an inglorious end to the policy of gradual escalation."[83]

The combination of Johnson's March 31 speech and the opening of negotiations with the Communists in Paris six weeks later gave many Americans the sense that the war in Vietnam was coming to an end. No doubt they expected that there would be more battles and that negotiations would be strained at times. Peace would not occur immediately. Nor would the troops be coming home that spring. But a subtle shift in thinking occurred. Americans began to talk about the war in the past tense; they began to think of the Vietnam conflict as history. Public approval of Johnson's conduct of the war rose sharply in the wake of his speech. He appeared to have joined the ranks of his dovish advisers and now sought peace in Vietnam rather than military victory. That he had also announced his intention to retire at the end of his current time and not seek re-election reinforced the spreading public perception that the end of the American war in Vietnam was coming.

But the president never intended nor could he foresee that his March 31 decisions would alter the course of the war or determine its outcome. He did not see himself as abandoning U.S. goals nor initiating any fundamental policy changes. He remained powerfully committed to what he understood to be stopping North Vietnamese aggression and to achieving an independent non-Communist state in southern Vietnam. He viewed the partial bombing halt, the leveling off of the American military role in South Vietnam, and the building up of the South Vietnamese armed forces as being steps toward the achievement of U.S. goals in South Vietnam, while at the same time placating public opinion at home. He was seeking a politically sustainable war policy.

At the time, Johnson did not believe the North Vietnamese would respond positively to the partial bombing halt any time soon, so he would have the option of resuming the air war against North Vietnam in the future when perhaps the political climate at home would be more supportive of such actions. Johnson viewed his actions announced in the March 31 speech as political accommodations that were needed to buy time for his policies to work. Johnson was repositioning himself politically to persevere in a righteous cause that he believed protected the vital security interests of the United States in Southeast Asia. For the remainder of his presidency, despite what he may have said or implied in his March 31 speech, Johnson prosecuted the war as vigorously as he could in a continuing effort to win a military victory. In tandem with the "wise men," Clark Clifford had persuaded Johnson to alter his war policy on March 31, but they failed to shake his commitment to a U.S. military victory in South Vietnam or to undermine his belief that his strategy of limited war would one day achieve it.

Johnson did not understand that his March 31 decisions set in motion a process that eventually "unraveled our Vietnam commitments."[84] Tet was a watershed. After Tet, a U.S. military solution was no longer possible in South Vietnam, primarily because the American people no longer had the patience or willingness to continue furnishing the vast resources still required to attain it. Although Johnson did not realize it, after Tet, only a political solution to the Vietnam War was possible.[85] Johnson's partial bombing halt also initiated a diplomatic process that would one day bring an end to the American war in Vietnam, a denouement that would open the door to an eventual Communist victory. In the short run, Tet proved to be a major U.S. tactical victory and a severe Communist defeat. But in the long run, Tet-68 turned out to be a crucial Communist political victory and a fatal U.S. strategic defeat.

At the time Johnson made his fateful decisions to end the policy of graduated escalation of the Vietnam War, the United States retained over 1 million troops stationed abroad in more than 40 countries. Since 1945 America had enmeshed itself in a global network of treaties and military alliances. By March 1968 the military forces required to defend U.S. strategic interests around the globe had been stretched dangerously thin in order to send 536,000 troops to South Vietnam. The Joint Chiefs were especially worried about the military's ability to meet its NATO commitments, which remained the key American strategic interest in the world. The powerful U.S. economy that sustained both American global commitments and the war in Vietnam showed signs of decline. The gold crisis threatened to undermine the value of the dollar and disrupt world commerce. The practical limits on the total military assets that the world's richest and mightiest nation-state could afford to commit to its limited war for limited goals in Southeast Asia had been reached by March 1968, the pivotal month of the entire war.

America's per capita gross domestic product (GDP) was at least 100 times larger than Vietnam's, which was one of the poorest countries in the world. Although the U.S. thermonuclear arsenal had the capability of obliterating Vietnam and its people within a matter of hours, America could not apply enough of its awesome military power to achieve the strategic goals it had set for itself. In addition to competing global strategic commitments, economic and financial strains, and rising domestic opposition, the refusal of America's SEATO allies to commit more troops to the Vietnam cockpit during the fall of 1967 further limited the U.S. Vietnam war effort.

The inefficient and class-biased conscription system strained to furnish the 40,000 to 50,000 young men that were required monthly for military service in 1968 because of the exemptions and deferments factored into the Selective Service, and because of the wholesale draft avoidance and resistance occurring at the time. The number of soldiers provided by the draft was insufficient to meet the replacement needs of the U.S. Armed Forces stationed around the world in 1968, much less to continue a large-scale military buildup in South Vietnam had one been ordered in the aftermath of Tet.[86] The insufficiencies of the draft, combined with Johnson's refusal to mobilize the Reserves, deprived the American military services of the manpower needed to meet its global strategic commitments and simultaneously fight a major war in Vietnam.

Nor could the United States use nuclear weapons to augment its conventional firepower, because its leaders feared both the domestic and worldwide reaction to their use on a nation of poor Asian peasants who posed no direct threat to U.S. security interests. American public opinion polls showed consistent popular opposition to resorting to nuclear weapons in Vietnam. In addition, U.S. military planners did not see any need to use nuclear weapons because of the adequacy of their conventional weaponry, because of the absence of suitable targets, and because they were reluctant to inflict mass casualties on civilian populations. Another inhibition on the possible use of nuclear weaponry was the desire not to alarm or anger the Soviets and Chinese, who might feel compelled to intervene militarily in Vietnam, or worse, to respond in kind. No doubt any kind of Soviet or Chinese nuclear retaliation represented an extremely remote threat, but it was one that could not be absolutely discounted.

In March 1968, a confluence of powerful historical forces forced Washington to abandon its policy of graduated escalation in pursuit of military victory in Vietnam. Given the limits imposed on the size of the war effort America could mount in Vietnam in the spring of 1968 and after, and given the protracted warfare strategy employed by a resourceful and resolute enemy supported by China, the Soviet Union, and the Eastern Bloc, a military victory in Vietnam was beyond available American strength.

THE TELEVISED WAR

Television coverage of some of the fierce Tet battles highlighted the fact that Vietnam was America's first televised war, the first war to be shown night after night in American living rooms. For years, color video had brought Americans the sights and sounds of men at war. The Vietnam War was also the first major war the United States had ever lost. Many Americans believe that television was a major cause of the U.S. defeat in Southeast Asia. That is, they believe that America lost history's first televised war precisely because it was televised. They embrace a myth for which there is no supporting empirical data and which cannot withstand critical scrutiny.

There are two versions of the myth that television news coverage caused America to lose the war. The first version, a liberal or dove view espoused mainly by journalists and some leftist intellectuals who opposed the Vietnam War, holds that television news coverage of the conflict exposed the American viewing public to the brutal realities of an unjust war. It brought Americans news of war crimes committed by U.S. soldiers; it exposed the tyrannical, corrupt, and incompetent governments in Saigon that the U.S. backed for 20 years; and it exposed efforts by American leaders to mislead the American public about the war. In this dovish view of television coverage of the war, journalists braved the wrath of their own government to help bring a halt to an unjust and a futile war. The other version of the myth, the conservative or hawkish view embraced by many Americans, including General Westmoreland and journalist Robert Elegant, insists that America lost a war in Vietnam that it could have won.[87] These hawks have blamed the defeat on the mass media, particularly the television news networks, for turning American public opinion against the war and eventually forcing an American withdrawal from Vietnam, which allowed the Communists to overwhelm the South Vietnamese defenders and take over the entire country in the spring of 1975.

Westmoreland has stated that the news media, especially television, snatched defeat from the jaws of victory in the aftermath of Tet-68, just when the Allies had a battered enemy on the ropes and was ready for the kill. He has asserted that a golden opportunity to mobilize U.S. military resources for a maximum effort to win the Vietnam War in a year or two was lost because television news coverage of the Tet campaigns turned the public against the war in early 1968 and prevented Johnson from escalating the conflict.[88] Westmoreland's stab-in-the-back thesis holds that powerful and hostile media, particularly television news coverage, were primarily responsible for the American strategic defeat in Vietnam.[89]

The thesis that the media, particularly television, were responsible for losing the Vietnam War, or were a major cause of the American defeat in Vietnam, whether advanced by doves or hawks, is groundless and untenable for a host of reasons. Most historians of the Vietnam War and most analysts of mass media coverage of the war dismiss it as being without merit.[90]

Television news coverage of the Vietnam War up to the time of Tet was overwhelmingly favorable; television journalists consistently represented American soldiers as fighting aggressively and winning every major battle en route to inevitable victory in the war.[91] During the first few years of television coverage of the war, the networks rarely showed American soldiers getting killed or wounded. Remarkably little American blood got spilled on television prime-time news. Typical video sequences of combat action showed U.S. troops moving across rice paddies or showed an air strike from a distance. Sometimes one heard the muted sounds of rifle fire or the rhythmic whup-whup-whup of helicopter rotors. Often the televised reports direct from the field were after-action accounts; stories filed after firefights had occurred. Americans got to see a sanitized, edited version of war.[92]

The only public opinion poll that ever asked people how watching television news coverage of the Vietnam War influenced their attitudes toward the war found that 83 percent of the respondents said they felt more hawkish after watching the news.[93] At the time this poll was taken—July 1967—other polls showed that 50 percent of Americans believed that U.S. entry into the war had been a mistake.[94] These polls demonstrated that opposition to the Vietnam War and to Johnson's war policy was growing despite, not because of, television news coverage, which was highly favorable at the time.

Television news coverage of the war became more critical during the Tet-68 battles, and, for the first time, television provided viewers with a steady diet of live-action coverage of the carnage. Viewers witnessed the destructiveness and brutality of war, of American soldiers fighting and dying in the streets of Saigon and Hue. But evidence from public opinion polls taken soon after the Tet attacks have undermined Westmoreland's thesis. At a time when the media exaggerated the tactical gains made by the enemy, portrayed Tet as a great shock and disaster for America, and showed American soldiers being killed in combat, public opinion polls registered temporary rises in popular support.[95]

Proponents of the stab-in-the-back thesis often cite Peter Braestrup's writings to substantiate their charges. Braestrup, a former Marine officer, Vietnam journalist, and media scholar, produced a massive study of the media coverage of Tet. He found that during the first few days of the Tet Offensive, the public was misled into thinking that the VietCong were winning, when in fact they were losing, and losing badly, almost everywhere. He has criticized journalists for their inaccurate and misleading stories. To Westmoreland, Braestrup's critique proved that distorted media coverage misled Americans and turned a tactical victory into a major defeat that eventually cost America a war it could have and should have won.[96]

But a careful reading of Braestrup's study has shown that he furnishes the proponents of the stab-in-the-back thesis neither aid nor comfort. Braestrup himself did not embrace the thesis and has challenged those who did.[97] He took pains to make clear that he did not charge either print or television journalists with biased coverage during Tet. He has never said that Tet-68 coverage by either the print or television journalists, however deficient in the early stages, turned public opinion against the Vietnam War. In fact, he believed such claims were impossible to substantiate: "No empirical data exist to link news coverage with changes in public opinion."[98]

Braestrup contended that skewed media coverage of the Tet campaigns exacerbated a growing political crisis in Washington that would have occurred even if those journalistic accounts had been clinically accurate. He believed it was Johnson's indecisive leadership in the weeks following Tet that caused the decline of popular support for the war that occurred in March 1968. For Braestrup, changes occurring in public opinion of the Vietnam War in the weeks following Tet were caused by failures of political leadership, not by television news or other media coverage of the battles.[99] Ironically, the administration's propaganda efforts in the fall of 1967, which were aimed at convincing Americans that the United States was winning the war, that the VietCong verged on defeat, and that the conflict would end soon, magnified the public shock and disillusionment that occurred during the Tet campaigns and widened the credibility gap.

When trends in public opinion on the Vietnam War have been matched with trends in television news coverage of the conflict, it has been shown that a majority of the American people turned against the Vietnam War before television news coverage of the conflict became predominantly negative. Despite their shift to a more negative emphasis in their television coverage of the war during and after Tet, on the whole, the network television news coverage continued to be more positive than negative until the fall of 1969. A majority of Americans had developed dovish views on the Vietnam War long before then.[100] Television coverage of the war lagged behind public opinion.

The increasingly critical television coverage of the war that occurred at the time of Tet and after represented a response by media journalists to public opinion, not an effort to shape it. What turned television coverage against the war after Tet-68 was growing antiwar sentiment among U.S. soldiers serving in Vietnam, increasing numbers of public officials speaking out against the war, and growing disillusionment with the war among the American people. The stab-in-the-back theorists, in their haste to make the media into a scapegoat, have inverted the relationship between television news coverage of the Vietnam War and public opinion concerning the war and presidential leadership. Westmoreland, Elegant, and many others failed to understand that it was public opinion that influenced television news coverage of the war much more than it was television coverage that influenced public opinion on the war.

As public support for the war dropped, television news coverage became more critical. But the news networks were merely catching up to what their viewers were already thinking about the war and the U.S. leadership; they were not telling them what to think. When Walter Cronkite, the most popular and influential television anchor during the Vietnam War era, declared at the end of his newscast on the evening of February 27, 1968, that the war was a stalemate, the erstwhile supporter of the war was aligning his views with those of his Middle American constituents. Numerous public opinion polls show that Cronkite told Americans nothing that a large majority of them did not already believe.

The stab-in-the-back theorists also face another difficulty. Westmoreland's insistence that victory was within the U.S. grasp following Tet, if Johnson had only sent the requested troops and taken the other escalatory steps called for at the time, was dubious. At the time, Clark Clifford, most Pentagon analysts, and the "wise men" had concluded that Hanoi had both the political will and military assets to match any and all U.S. post-Tet escalations. Hanoi could also count on the Chinese, who might have intervened militarily if the North Vietnamese ever faced military defeat or national extinction. Had Johnson escalated the war after Tet, had he sent the 206,000 troops requested by the Pentagon, and had he ratcheted up the air war, he most likely would not have achieved strategic victory within a year or two. Most likely, Washington would only have attained a continuing military stalemate at a far higher level of costs and casualties. Such a continuing costly stalemate in Vietnam would have brought intensified opposition, political polarization, and violent conflict within the United States that could have seriously undermined American political stability. It would also have raised taxes, jacked up the inflation rate, weakened the dollar, worsened the gold crisis, disrupted U.S. foreign trade, and seriously damaged U.S. global foreign policy interests, especially NATO.

The fundamental problem with the stab-in-the-back thesis is that it represents a failure of historical understanding. Powerful political, economic, and strategic forces determined the outcome of the Vietnam War and caused the eventual American strategic defeat. The role of the media, including television news coverage, in determining that outcome was inconsequentiial, so inconsequential it cannot be measured. Television news coverage of the war did not turn the American people against it. It was the course taken by the Vietnam War—the United States had locked itself into a stalemated conflict of rising casualties and costs—coupled with a loss of confidence in the integrity and competence of government officials, all of which was highlighted by the surprise Tet-68 Offensive that turned most Americans against the Vietnam War.

Public opinion turned the media, particularly television news, against the war. Had the cathode ray tube never been invented, had censorship been imposed on Vietnam War news, and had all of the journalists covering the war in Southeast Asia been cheerleaders for the Allied side, public opinion would have turned against the Vietnam War just as it did against the Korean War. The Korean War was popular when UN forces appeared to be rolling toward an easy victory over the North Koreans in the fall of 1950. Following the surprise Chinese intervention in late November 1950 and the subsequent stalemated warfare that went on for years, public opinion polls consistently showed that a majority of Americans did not support the Korean War. Yet television news was in its infancy during the Korean War. Most U.S. households did not have television sets, war news from Korea was heavily censored, and U.S. war correspondents were all supportive of the UN effort.[101]

Those who praise or blame the television networks for the American defeat in Vietnam promulgate a myth that may serve hidden ideological agenda, but they do not explain why the United States lost a war.

TALKING AND FIGHTING

The talks between American and North Vietnamese representatives that began in Paris on May 13, 1968, deadlocked instantly. President Johnson, doubting the talks could be productive, and wary of Communist propaganda, demanded concessions from Hanoi in exchange for a complete bombing halt. The American delegation, led by Averell Harriman, refused to accept any cease-fire terms that would require the withdrawal of U.S. forces from South Vietnam while allowing the Ho Chi Minh Trail to remain open and allowing PAVN forces to remain in South Vietnam. The American negotiators also refused to consider any political settlement of the conflict that did not guarantee the continued survival of a non-Communist government in South Vietnam. The North Vietnamese delegation, headed by Xuan Thuy, quickly rejected the American demand for a reciprocal deescalation to completely stop the bombing. Hanoi also rejected any cease-fire proposals that would limit its ability to support the war in South Vietnam and refused to consider any political solution that allowed the Thieu-Ky regime to survive.

Given the fact that the military initiative in South Vietnam had passed to the Allies in the months following the Tet Offensive, the North Vietnamese probably were not interested in conducting substantive negotiations at that time. They preferred to wait until the political and military balance shifted toward their side. Hanoi's approach to the Paris talks was to use them as part of a larger strategy of talking while fighting. It intended to use the negotiations underway in Paris to achieve a complete bombing halt, to highlight differences between the Americans and South Vietnamese in an effort to drive the Allies apart, and to exploit the antiwar sentiment within the United States that was growing rapidly in the wake of Tet.[102] Hanoi coordinated its diplomacy with its war effort. For the Communists, negotiations were not a means for ending the war, they were part of an integrated military-political-diplomatic strategy designed to achieve their major objectives: the withdrawal of the Americans, the overthrow of the Thieu-Ky regime, and the creation of a coalition government in South Vietnam. For Hanoi, the negotiations were another way to win the Vietnam War. They had agreed to the Paris talks to try to achieve objectives via negotiations that they could not achieve by fighting, particularly obtaining a complete bombing halt.

Since both sides refused to make the necessary compromises required to move the negotiations forward, the Paris talks proved sterile for months. Meanwhile, the United States pressed its war in South Vietnam. The year 1968 was the bloodiest of the American Vietnam War. More U.S. combatants fought in more battles that year than in any other. During 1968, more than 14,000 American soldiers were killed and 150,000 were wounded, the highest totals for any year of the war.

The number of battle deaths would have been far higher if it had not been for the remarkable medical support U.S. combat soldiers received for the entirety of the long war. "American servicemen and women fighting in Vietnam received the best medical care in the history of warfare."[103] The key to success in saving the lives of often badly wounded soldiers, many of whom would have died in previous wars, lay in the excellent support system the Army established and the extraordinary care provided by doctors, nurses, and other medical personnel. The helicopter medical evacuation system, known as aeromedevac or medevac, "evolved into a complex system of transporting critically wounded servicemen from a live battle site to a medical facility within as little as twenty minutes."[104] There they would be treated for shock and infection, stabilized, and resuscitated. Their wounds would be stitched up, burns would be treated, and amputations would be performed if required. After a stay of from three to five days, patients would be transferred to rear hospitals, usually in Japan.

Figure 7.8   Members of the 101st. Airborne Division carry a wounded man to a UH-1D Medevac helicoptor during the assault on Hill 937 in the A Shau Valley. Photographer: Lieutenant Thomas Devine. *Source:* U.S. Army Photo. Neg. # SC651398.

Between 7,500 and 11,000 American women served in the Vietnam War, all of them volunteers. Eighty percent of these women served as Army, Air Force, and Navy nurses. About half of the 1,300 women who were assigned to nonmedical work were enlisted personnel. They served as clerks, air traffic controllers, photographers, and cartographers. Their tour of duty was usually for one year, and like all military personnel during the Vietnam War, they were rotated in and out of Vietnam on an individual rather than a unit-by-unit basis.

All nurses were officers, and they had to be at least 21 years old to be assigned to a combat zone. Although they were never legally assigned to combat roles, women serving as nurses in forward hospitals often came under enemy fire. Eight American women were killed in Vietnam, and dozens were wounded.

The women who served as nurses experienced a different kind of war. Working 12-hour shifts, six days a week, in trauma units at forward hospitals, they immersed themselves in the carnage of war. Many women found their initial experiences emotionally devastating. Many of the savagely wounded soldiers were 19-year-old boys just a few months removed from care-free civilian life in the States. Nurses often wept at the tragedy of youngsters burned, disfigured, and crippled before they had had a chance to enjoy the fullness of life. But the camaraderie of the trauma units and the understanding that they were helping young people in desperate need strengthened the nurses.

Unlike many of the combat soldiers, who grew progressively disillusioned as the war went on, the nurses all felt a strong sense of accomplishment. Their morale remained high. Military commanders valued their professional skills. MACV promulgated standing orders that in the event of an enemy attack on a forward hospital, the nurses were to be evacuated before the patients. Many nurses volunteered for multiple tours of duty in Vietnam. Years afterward, nurses occasionally reminisced about their war experiences. They surely did not miss the horrors of war, the agony of badly wounded soldiers; but they did miss the adrenaline rushes and the companionship. Above all, they missed the feelings of satisfaction that came from performing life-saving work under extremely stressful, often dangerous circumstances.[105]

Shortly after Tet, Westmoreland mounted the largest search-and-destroy operation of the war: Forty-two American and thirty-seven ARVN armored and infantry battalions scoured the countryside around Saigon trying to locate and eliminate the VC/NVA units that had survived Tet. Eventually, the 110,000 Allied troops involved in the gigantic operation formed a ring of steel around Saigon.[106]

During the latter half of 1968, the American Vietnam war was characterized by hundreds of battalion-sized operations and thousands of actions involving companies and platoons. In countless small unit operations, U.S. forces attempted to locate and destroy enemy forces all over South Vietnam. While these land battles raged, specially trained Army and Navy units waged riverine warfare against VietCong guerrillas amid the watery wastes of the Mekong Delta.[107]

Although the air war against North Vietnam had been curtailed, aerial warfare in South Vietnam reached a new intensity during 1968. The number of air strikes flown

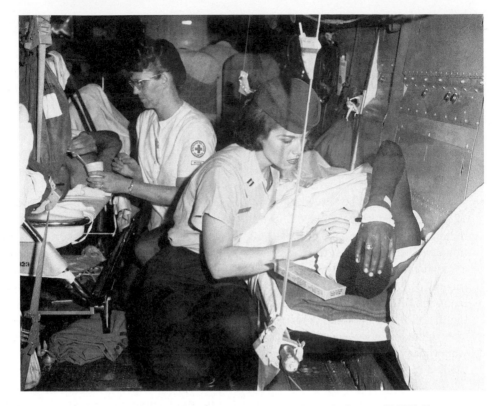

Figure 7.9 Nurses attend the wounded onboard an aircraft. *Source:* CORBIS. Neg. # BE082133. Copyright: Bettmann/CORBIS.

against guerrilla sanctuaries and supply lines increased as Air Force and Navy bombers that had been committed previously to raiding North Vietnam's military and industrial sites joined the air war in South Vietnam. After Tet, carpet bombing raids on enemy positions by cells of B-52s trebled. U.S. planes also stepped up their bombing of the Ho Chi Minh Trail. As the air war against North Vietnam diminished, the air wars in South Vietnam and Laos intensified.[108]

U.S. military action also included assaults into the border regions adjacent to many of the South Vietnamese cities that the VietCong and PAVN forces had attacked during Tet. One of the most spectacular operations occurred in the I Corps Tactical Zone following the vicious fighting to reclaim Hue. U.S. forces struck a NVA staging area in the A Shau Valley, which lay in the southwestern corner of the Thua Thien province adjacent to the Laotian border. Remote and rugged, the A Shau Valley had been a Communist stronghold for years. It was from that region that NVA forces had attacked the northern provinces as well as the city of Hue. The MACV officials feared that the enemy might use the A Shau to launch additional attacks, so they mounted an operation, code-named DELAWARE, to destroy the PAVN bases in the valley. Two battalions of the U.S. 7th Cavalry, the 1st and the 5th, helilifting in to attack the NVA, ran into the fiercest air defenses encountered in South Vietnam. Ten assault helicopters were shot down, and another 13 were severely damaged by deadly fire coming from antiaircraft batteries lodged in the hills and mountains that ringed the valley.[109] In addition to the air defenders of the A Shau, helicopter and fixed-wing aircraft pilots had to contend with some of the most hazardous flying weather of the entire war. Dense fogs, thick clouds, and driving rainstorms generated by the summer monsoons often reduced visibility in the target areas to near zero.

Sweeps by the 7th Cavalry troops failed to find many NVA forces. The NVA had chosen not to fight and had slipped into cross-border sanctuaries in nearby Laos. But the Americans captured sizable amounts of food and stores the departing enemy had left behind. After the 7th Cavalry was pulled out, elements from Major General Melvin Zais's elite 101st Airborne, the famed "Screaming Eagles," air-assaulted into the A Shau Valley in an effort to catch the NVA returning to their bases. The 101st also failed to find many PAVN soldiers who wanted to stand and fight.[110] By the end of August 1968, the Americans had withdrawn from the A Shau Valley, and the North Vietnamese had returned.

In addition to action in the A Shau Valley, U.S. troops also fought along the northern border in the vicinity of the DMZ. The Marines' main objective in this region, following their successful defense at Khe Sanh, remained sealing the border against enemy infiltration. Marine units patrolled Route 9, attacking and counterattacking any North Vietnamese forces trying to infiltrate the northern provinces. One of the fiercest of many battles occurring in this area took place near Con Thien, on October 25. In a seven-hour fight, an armored company completely destroyed a North Vietnamese bunker complex.[111] The NVA suffered many losses during the latter half of 1968 in the vicinity of the DMZ, but they nevertheless managed to achieve a stalemate.

MASSACRE AT MY LAI

Extensive fighting also occurred in the southern part of I Corps, in the Quang Ngai province. One of the most gruesome tragedies of the Vietnam War occurred in this region when U.S. soldiers, using pistols, automatic rifles, and grenades, massacred an estimated 400 to 500 civilians at two hamlets, My Lai and My Khe, on March 16, 1968. Both hamlets composed part of Son My village, near the coast in the Son Tinh district of the Quang Ngai province. The soldiers who massacred the women, children, and old men of My Lai belonged to the 1st and 2nd Platoons of Charlie Company, 1st Battalion, the 11th Infantry Brigade, which was attached to the Americal Division under the command of Major General Samuel Koster.[112]

The Americal Division suffered from grave command and control problems, stemming from poor training and a lack of leadership, from division down to platoon level, which permitted civilian mistreatment to occur. Some elements of its 11th Infantry

Brigade were little better than organized bands of thugs, with the officers eager participants in the body count game.[113]

After the perpetration of the atrocities, members of the brigade and divisional staffs succeeded in covering it up for a time. The American people did not learn of the hideous incident for over 20 months, until late November 1969, and then from independent media sources who exposed the Army's attempted cover-up.[114] An official U.S. Army board then conducted a thorough 16-month-long investigation of the incident and its cover-up. Fourteen officers were found to be complicit in covering up war crimes. Additionally, 13 soldiers, 4 officers, and 9 enlisted men were charged with committing war crimes and crimes against humanity. Subsequently, all of the soldiers accused of war crimes either had the charges against them dropped, or they were acquitted, except Lieutenant William Calley. Calley's 1st Platoon was estimated to have killed over 200 of the villagers that lethal day in My Lai. A court martial convicted Calley of mass murder.[115]

The mass murders at My Lai and My Khe were a grotesque consequence of many factors: a formless war of attrition in which military success was measured statistically by counting corpses; small-unit actions fought in populated regions against an enemy that relied on village support to sustain its insurgency; the frustrations of fighting a war

Figure 7.10 Bodies of women and children lie in a ditch near the village of My-Lai-4. Photographer: Ronald Haeberle. *Source:* Getty Images/Time Life Pictures.

that appeared both unpopular and unwinnable; race prejudice, which encouraged many U.S. soldiers to regard Vietnamese peasants as "gooks," as less than fully human; the fear, rage, and hatred arising from fighting an enemy that set deadly mines and booby traps that maimed and killed GIs; an enemy who after attacking melted into the jungle or merged into the rural population; paranoia arising from the inability of U.S. soldiers to tell friendly villagers from enemies and therefore to assume that they all were real or potential foes; and the poor leadership, inadequate training, lack of discipline, and the thuggery that characterized the 11th Infantry Brigade.

After learning of the massacre, some Americans worried about how many other My Lais might have gone undetected. They feared that perhaps the only unique feature of the My Lai massacre was its discovery. Some also wondered if the U.S. military might have had a policy of targeting civilians suspected of aiding the enemy. In various forums, hundreds of Vietnam veterans claimed they had participated in, witnessed, or heard of mass atrocities committed against civilians in South Vietnam. Some people found cold comfort in the fact that the VietCong forces were guilty of systematic atrocities and the cold-blooded murders of thousands of civilians. There also was a troubling inconsistency in finding one young junior officer guilty of mass murder in a war where long-range artillery fire and aerial bombing had killed thousands of civilians since the Americanization of the war. In the eyes of many Americans, William Calley was more a scapegoat than a war criminal.

"The extent of American atrocities in Vietnam cannot be established with any precision."[116] According to available evidence and testimony, U.S. soldiers frequently committed atrocities against Vietnamese civilians, and they became more frequent in the years after Tet as discipline and morale plummeted. However, the MACV never had an official policy of targeting civilians nor even of informally sanctioning attacks under certain circumstances. Killing, attacking, or using unnecessary force against civilians in situations where they posed no danger to U.S. military personnel was illegal, and always in violation of extant rules of engagement. Even the thugs of the Americal Division knew that what had occurred at My Lai and My Khe was both illegal and wrong, which is why they covered it up with falsified reports and sham inquiries. Most U.S. combat soldiers serving in Vietnam did not commit atrocities against civilians, nor is there hard evidence that there were any other My Lai–type massacres where American troopers deliberately murdered hundreds of old men, women, and children.[117]

Six weeks after the massacres at My Lai and My Khe, the VietCong launched another wave of attacks against Saigon and other South Vietnamese cities. The fighting in and near Saigon was vicious and lasted for weeks. It was not until early June that the ARVN and U.S. forces crushed all remaining enemy resistance. Like its vastly larger predecessor, the VietCong mini-Tet Offensive also failed. There was a third, even weaker, round of VietCong urban assaults in August that Allied intelligence anticipated and an American preemptive strike easily crushed.[118]

These subsequent smaller enemy offensives showed that the VietCong were feeling the effects of their terrible losses sustained in February. They fought in smaller units, avoided direct attacks on U.S. installations, and were forced to use younger and less-experienced fighters. More and more NVA troopers had to be fed into the depleted VietCong main force units. In the aftermath of their defeats at Tet, the North Vietnamese Politburo had to refashion its military strategy. It abandoned offensive operations and reverted to defensive tactics. During the latter half of 1968, enemy actions were largely confined to sporadic standoff rocket and mortar attacks on Allied positions.[119]

THE FAILURE OF REFORM

In the fall of 1968, General Abrams abandoned the strategy of attrition warfare that had been in place since 1966 in South Vietnam. He shifted the American focus from small-scale combat operations to pacification and Vietnamization. With negotiations underway in Paris, U.S. and South Vietnamese officials launched an accelerated pacification program to bring as many of South Vietnam's villages as possible under the control of the Saigon government. U.S. combat forces formed security shields to prevent VietCong forces from entering populated areas. Allied officials focused their efforts in the areas where the VietCong had suffered their worst losses and could not thwart the accelerated Allied pacification efforts. The CORDS and South Vietnamese officials also stepped up the *Chieu Hoi* program that offered amnesty to VietCong defectors and, with assistance from CIA officers, they implemented the PHOENIX program, an intelligence-gathering operation aimed at exposing and neutralizing the VietCong infrastructure.[120] Pacification made little progress for the rest of 1968. Saigon controlled only a few more villages at year's end than it had before the Tet Offensive erupted, and there was no way to tell for sure whether all of the people living in "friendly" villages genuinely supported the GVN and the U.S. military effort.

Simultaneously with its enhanced pacification efforts, the United States pressed forward with Vietnamization. Efforts were made to expand and modernize the South Vietnamese armed forces. Authorized force levels were increased from 685,000 to 850,000, and South Vietnamese soldiers were provided with more modern weapons. There was noticeable improvement in the performance of the ARVN forces by the end of the year, but fundamental deficiencies persisted. Draft evasion and desertion remained both chronic and massive. There was also no discernible enthusiasm for Vietnamization on the part of South Vietnamese leaders. Having become quite comfortable with U.S. soldiers doing most of the fighting and dying for them, Thieu and Ky appeared to be in no hurry to alter the situation.[121] South Vietnam's leaders had not been consulted before Johnson decided that Vietnamization would be the new focus of the post-Tet American effort.[122] Neither GVN political desires nor RVNAF military capabilities had anything to do with the U.S. decision to begin the process of Vietnamization. American domestic political exigencies forced Johnson to turn to Vietnamization.[123]

The surprisingly effective performance of some of the ARVN units during the Tet battles had given U.S. leaders in Washington and Saigon some grounds for hoping that Vietnamization might work, that the South Vietnamese government would, in time, develop the capacity to defend itself. But there was never any realistic basis for believing that the RVN could ever carry out Vietnamization successfully. The main reason American soldiers were fighting in Vietnam was because Washington did not believe the South Vietnamese could defend themselves against the insurgency directed from Hanoi. Nothing had really changed since Tet. Most of the ARVN troops who had fought hard during the Tet battles did so because they were fighting for survival, not because they had suddenly become patriots or brave, aggressive warriors. They displayed the "back-to-the-wall courage of the cornered."[124]

The fundamental reality that foreclosed any possibility of a successful Vietnamization program lay in the fact that General Thieu and Marshall Ky's power depended on maintaining the loyalty of a coterie of ARVN generals who held their commands because of their political reliability, not because they were competent warriors. The price that the leaders of the RVN would have had to pay for eliminating incompetence and corruption within their civilian and military bureaucracies would have been a fall from power. Insistence on reform would have amounted to committing political suicide. Because the South Vietnamese government and army remained rotten at their cores, and because American leaders neither had the leverage nor will to impose radical reforms on South Vietnam's leadership elites, no amount of U.S. economic and military support could ever make Vietnamization work well enough to defeat their resourceful and implacable enemies.[125]

Despite the stepped-up Allied military activity, the accelerated pacification program, and the beginnings of Vietnamization, the military and political balance in South Vietnam had changed little as 1968 ended. The VietCong forces had suffered severe losses, were much weaker, and controlled fewer villages and a smaller portion of the South Vietnamese population than they had before the Tet Offensive. But much of the VietCong infrastructure remained intact. U.S. military operations after Tet inflicted heavy losses on the enemy, destroyed staging areas, and disrupted supply lines; but the NVA/VC main force units remained intact, still formidable foes at year's end.

As historian Ronald Specter has noted of the Tet-68 campaigns and the fighting that continued throughout the year, "The battles of 1968 were decisive . . . because they were so indecisive."[126] Popular support for the war within the United States continued to decline: Congressional opposition grew stronger. Morale and discipline within the U.S. Army continued to erode. The Communists rebuilt their military and their political infrastructure.

The Saigon government's performance improved somewhat during 1968. It was stronger and more stable after Tet than it had ever been. Many of the South Vietnamese people, angry at the Communists for violating the Tet truce and for attacking their cities, turned to the Thieu government. Many city residents, hitherto smug in their sense of safety from the ravages of war and apathetic toward the government, now felt vulnerable and understood that their security depended on the ARVN forces. Thieu's government actively involved citizens in repairing the extensive damage incurred by South

Vietnam's cities during Tet. His government also launched new programs to combat corruption and curb rampant inflation.

By mid-summer 1968, Thieu, with U.S. support, had gained the upper hand over his archrival, General Ky. Thieu's anticorruption program was one-sided; it aimed chiefly at the corruption of Ky's supporters and ignored the corrupt practices of Thieu loyalists. Thieu gradually replaced cabinet members and province chiefs loyal to Ky with military men loyal to him. The political savants, who frequented the sidewalk cafes of Tu Do Street, began calling Thieu "the little dictator."[127]

But chronic political weaknesses persisted in South Vietnam. Tet generated nearly a million new refugees to add to those already inhabiting the slums, back-alley labyrinths, and suburban hovels of Saigon and other cities. The massive needs of the war refugees went largely unattended. Land reform in South Vietnam stalled because Thieu favored large landowners. Corruption at all levels of the Saigon government and military persisted. The Buddhists, the sects, and other non-Communist political groupings refused to support the RVN. The Saigon regime, despite a few cosmetic gestures toward civilian rule, remained, in essence, a military dictatorship. Another of the Tu Do Street savants commented on the status of the RVN after Tet: "The dung heap is the same. Only the flies are different."[128] There were other problems stemming from Vietnamization, and the U.S. negotiations with Hanoi exacerbated tensions between U.S. and Saigon officials. The South Vietnamese feared and resented what appeared to them as U.S. efforts to impose a settlement on them and then get out, leaving the RVN at the mercy of the Vietcong and the NVA.[129]

THE ELECTION OF 1968

The tensions in South Vietnam paralleled the political turmoil in the United States during that turbulent year. The 1968 presidential election evolved amidst a backdrop of the worst violence, social conflict, and political polarization seen in America since the Civil War. The Vietnam War had combined with domestic insurgencies to create profound schisms between white and black, affluent and poor, young and old, "hippies" and "straights," hawks and doves, and practitioners of what was called the "new politics" and members of the political Establishment. Political and cultural warfare raged in the streets of many of America's cities. Robert Kennedy, seeking the Democratic nomination as an antiwar candidate, and Richard Nixon, seeking the Republican nomination, both feared the institutional framework of the world's oldest democracy might not be able to contain the powerful centrifugal forces threatening to spin out of control.[130]

Racial tensions increased sharply during the first few months of 1968. More race-related disturbances occurred then than in any previous year, and authorities braced themselves for another summer of urban rioting. The Southern Christian Leadership Council (SCLC), headed by Dr. Martin Luther King Jr., began a Poor People's campaign to protest poverty, discrimination, and the Vietnam War, which was draining funds from civil rights and antipoverty programs. On the evening of April 4, King, the apostle of nonviolent social change and gentle critic of the Vietnam War, was assassinated as he stood on a balcony outside of a Memphis motel room. That night the inner cities of America exploded in fury as news of King's murder reached them. Some 75,000 federal troops and National Guardsmen joined local police and sheriffs to suppress the uprisings in 130 cities. Forty-six people, mostly African Americans, were killed, shot by police and the National Guard, and thousands of people were injured. In Chicago, Mayor Richard Daley ordered police to "shoot to kill" arsonists and looters. In the nation's capital, the site of some of the worst rioting, looting, and burning, barbed-wire barriers and machine-gun emplacements surrounded government buildings to protect them from any attacks.[131] Machine-gun mounts on the steps of the nation's capitol eloquently expressed the torment of a profoundly divided people.

Until Tet-68, the large majority of the nation's nearly 7 million college students had been apolitical, and unquestioningly prowar. In its aftermath, many were in a rebellious mood. Dozens of demonstrations convulsed college campuses during the spring of 1968, most of them related to the Vietnam War. Students protested the presence of ROTC programs. Recruiters from the military services, the CIA, and corporations with Pentagon contracts were harassed and picketed.

The most violent uprising occurred in April at Columbia, one of the most distinguished universities in the country. On this prestigious Ivy League campus, black militants joined with antiwar radicals to protest both the university's complicity with the Vietnam War and its plans to construct a new gymnasium in an area that would require the relocation of African Americans living in apartments on the building site. During the demonstration, students occupied campus buildings and refused orders to vacate them. University officials called in the New York City police, who forcibly removed the students. In the process, hundreds of students were arrested, and about 150 were injured. Following the police action, student protesters called a strike that forced the university to curtail its spring 1968 semester. Student uprisings also occurred in other countries during 1968. A worker-student revolt in France nearly brought down the government.[132]

From April to early June, Eugene McCarthy and Robert Kennedy waged a spirited primary campaign for the Democratic presidential nomination in the aftermath of Johnson's withdrawal speech. A third candidate for the Democratic nomination, Vice President Hubert Humphrey, knowing he had no chance against McCarthy and Kennedy in many of the primaries because he supported Johnson's Vietnam War policy, quietly lined up delegates from the states that did not hold primaries. Johnson, who hated Kennedy and did not believe McCarthy had the qualifications to be president, promoted Humphrey's candidacy.

Kennedy, passionate and charismatic, beat McCarthy in most of the primaries because of his remarkable ability to appeal to voters across class and cultural boundaries: to African American voters, Hispanics, and the disadvantaged generally, as well as to ethnic working-class voters and activist liberal intellectuals. Kennedy was the only prominent white politician in the country who had any credibility at all with African American citizens during those profoundly troubled times. McCarthy, cerebral and cool, who appealed mainly to well-educated, middle-class liberals who constituted the traditional reform elements in American politics, beat Kennedy only once, in the Oregon primary on May 25.

Next up was the important California primary. After a hard fight, Kennedy won a narrow victory. But shortly after delivering a victory speech to his supporters in the ballroom of the Biltmore Hotel in Los Angeles in the early morning hours of June 5, he was assassinated by Sirhan Sirhan, a Arab nationalist who hated Kennedy because of his strong support of Israel.[133] Another senseless killing once again intensified widely shared fears that anarchy and civil conflict would overwhelm the American political process. Kennedy's murder appeared to show that the last lines of reason and restraint within American politics had been breached. With his murder, the antiwar forces within the Democratic party lost any chance to capture their party's presidential nomination.

Political violence in America during the tormented year of 1968 climaxed in Chicago at the time of the Democratic Convention. Radical elements within the antiwar movement, the National Mobilization to End the War in Vietnam (MOBE) and the Youth International Party ("Yippies") planned a series of demonstrations in Chicago to protest the Vietnam War. The demonstrations were timed to coincide with the Democratic Convention to be held during the last week of August. Chicago's Mayor Daley, the host of the Democratic Convention, vowed that antiwar demonstrators would not disrupt his city or its convention. The stage was set for the most violent confrontation between antiwar protesters and police of the entire Vietnam War era. Daley himself was a strong opponent of the Vietnam War and had been a backer of the late Robert Kennedy, but he was committed to suppressing the antiwar activists.

In the days preceding the convention, thousands of youthful antiwar activists filtered into Chicago, gathering mainly in Lincoln Park, far from the convention site at the International Amphitheater near the stockyards. To meet the anticipated threat to law and order, Mayor Daley mobilized his entire 12,000-man police force. In addition, the governor of Illinois assigned 5,649 members of the National Guard to round-the-clock duty in Chicago, and President Johnson ordered 5,000 federal troops be flown to Chicago if they were needed. The assembled police, National Guard, and federal troops outnumbered the protesters, whose numbers never exceeded 10,000 to 12,000.[134]

Tension built during the days of the Democratic Convention, which convened at the Amphitheater on Saturday, August 24. There were skirmishes in the parks between protesters and police. For several days, the police and National Guard succeeded in keeping the demonstrations miles from the convention site and nearby hotels, where the delegates were staying and where various candidates for the presidential nomination had set up their headquarters.

The convention was controlled by Humphrey's supporters. They easily defeated efforts by a coalition of antiwar delegates to adopt a peace plank for the party platform. After a few hours of emotional debate, the convention adopted a plank that endorsed President Johnson's policy. Humphrey was nominated on Wednesday evening, August 28. The major antiwar candidate, Senator Eugene McCarthy, finished a distant second.

Chicago exploded the night Humphrey was nominated. About 5,000 protesters gathered in Grant Park across the street from the Hilton Hotel, where most of the delegates were staying. Encircled by National Guardsmen, mobs of demonstrators broke through barriers at various points and fanned out into the nearby Loop. They in turn were attacked by mobs of police, using clubs, mace, and tear gas. The violent scene was illuminated by spotlights and recorded by television cameras and news photographers. Protesters taunted the police by shouting, "The whole world is watching, the whole word is watching." Some of the police chanted "kill, kill, kill" as they charged the crowds. There is evidence that the Chicago police planted *agents provocateurs* among the protesters to incite them to more violent actions thus incurring more punishment from the police. Police also indiscriminately attacked luckless tourists and passersby caught in the melee, as well as television cameramen and newspaper photographers who were recording the orgy of violence. The entire Walpurgis Night of horrors was telecast to a nation that watched in amazed disbelief. Senator Abraham Ribicoff, viewing the nightmare scenes on a television monitor inside of the convention hall, condemned Mayor Daley's use of "Gestapo tactics." The forces of law and order won the "Battle of Chicago," but there were lots of casualties on both sides. Over 1,000 people were injured, including 192 policemen, and 662 people were arrested.[135]

Many who witnessed the violence on television were fearful that American fascism might be wearing the dark-blue uniform of the Chicago police. A far larger number of viewers endorsed the police attacks on demonstrators, whose radical politics and countercultural lifestyles they perceived as intolerable threats to the good order and public morality of American civilization. The violence surrounding the Democratic Convention dramatized the ominous fact that there could be no peace in America until peace came to Vietnam. Journalist I. F. Stone observed, "The war is destroying our country as we are destroying Vietnam."[136]

The violent events in Chicago shattered the radical antiwar movement and strengthened political conservatives who had been making a comeback from the Goldwater debacle of 1964. The "Battle of Chicago" also played into the hands of Republican presidential candidate Richard Nixon, who had been nominated at the orderly Republican convention in Miami three weeks before the Democrats' tumultuous gathering. In his acceptance speech, a poised and confident Nixon had sounded the themes that would highlight his fall campaign: the need for national unity, the demand for "law and order," and the urgent need for peace in Vietnam, although not peace at any price.[137] These themes would have strong appeal to millions of voters yearning for the return of social peace and for an end to a hated war.

A strong third party candidate with a large popular following, Governor George Wallace of Alabama, the American Independence Party leader, also entered the race for the presidency in 1968. Although he voiced hawkish sentiments, Wallace called for a negotiated settlement of the Vietnam War. He also championed traditional values and the work ethic. But his main issue was playing to white antipathy toward civil rights measures and antipoverty programs. Wallace had a remarkable talent for voicing the fears

Figure 7.11 War in the Streets of Chicago. Police battle demonstrators near the Hilton hotel on Chicago's Michigan Avenue, August 28, 1968, outside the Democratic convention on the night Hubert Humphery was nominated. *Source:* CORBIS. Neg. # U1605074.

and resentments of working-class whites, especially young men. When the general campaign began in September, polls gave Nixon a 15 percent lead over Humphrey, and also showed that Wallace commanded considerable popular support.

The 1968 fall presidential campaign turned only partly on the issue of the Vietnam War. The conflict in Vietnam "was enmeshed in a web of racial tensions and barely articulated discontents."[138] None of the three major candidates had a clearly defined stance on the war; all took carefully qualified and nuanced positions that ultimately differed little from one another. All favored a negotiated settlement of the conflict that would end the fighting and preserve a pro-Western government in South Vietnam. Neither the millions of hawks who favored more bombing and a more aggressive ground war nor the flocks of doves who favored an immediate U.S. pullout of Vietnam had a candidate to vote for. Nixon, well ahead in all of the polls, refused to discuss Vietnam for fear of complicating the Paris talks. Nixon and especially his vice presidential running mate, Maryland Governor Spiro T. Agnew, spent much time calling for "law and order" and denouncing antiwar activists, black militants, and hippies.

Humphrey, whose candidacy had emerged from the political ruins of Chicago, appeared to have no chance when the electoral contest began. He headed the ticket of a party profoundly divided over the Vietnam War. He had little money and no national campaign organization. He was repudiated by the antiwar liberals who had been defeated at the Democratic Convention. These dovish politicos scorned his loyal support of Johnson's war policy. Humphrey wanted to take a more independent stance; he favored a complete bombing halt, but Johnson refused to allow him to propose it. Humphrey's campaign slogan, "The Politics of Joy," sounded absurdly inappropriate to the joyless mood prevailing in the country. For weeks his campaign floundered along.

But as the 1968 election entered its final month, Humphrey's campaign suddenly sprang to life. Even though he did not seek Johnson's permission, Humphrey separated himself from the administration's war policy and endorsed a total bombing halt. Eugene McCarthy belatedly endorsed Humphrey, and many antiwar Democrats returned to the party fold; they preferred a flawed liberal to their nemesis, Nixon. As Humphrey's campaign gained momentum, Nixon's hitherto smooth-running campaign appeared to stall. Nixon, worried by Humphrey's late surge, hinted that he had a plan for ending the Vietnam War, but claimed that he could not disclose its details lest he compromise its future effectiveness. Wallace's popular support in the north declined as trade union leaders campaigned vigorously for Humphrey. Polls taken throughout October showed Humphrey steadily closing the gap, with Nixon and Wallace fading.

Johnson, who despised Nixon, and knowing that a dramatic peace gesture could put the Democratic candidate over the top, spoke to the American people on Thursday evening, October 31. The president announced a complete halt of all bombing of North Vietnam effective at midnight on October 31, five days before the election, and he implied that a peace settlement was coming soon. Peace talks were scheduled to begin on November 6, the day after the election. Johnson was persuaded to halt all bombing of North Vietnam by Averill Harriman, one of the "wise men," who had told Johnson that a bombing halt would clear the way for the start of substantive negotiations with Hanoi.

The Communists had indicated informally that they were prepared to begin serious peace discussions within a few days of a complete bombing halt, and that they would also accept the Saigon government's presence at the Paris talks. The United States, in return, had agreed to accept a representation from the NLF. General Abrams assured Johnson that a bombing halt would pose no threat to Allied forces in South Vietnam, especially since Johnson had promised Abrams that he would shift the aircraft engaged in bombing North Vietnam to the aerial war against the Ho Chi Minh Trail in Laos.[139]

Johnson's election-eve speech propelled Humphrey's candidacy forward. Public opinion polls taken over the final weekend before Tuesday's scheduled vote showed Nixon's lead had evaporated. The pundits pronounced the election "too close to call." A Harris poll released on Saturday, November 1, three days before the election, showed Humphrey ahead of Nixon by 40 percent to 43 percent.[140] Humphrey appeared poised to pull off the biggest political upset since Harry Truman had defeated Thomas Dewey twenty years earlier.

But behind the scenes, complex political maneuvering may have thwarted Humphrey's belated drive for the presidency. Anna Chennault, the Chinese-born widow of the leader of the famed Flying Tigers, and a strong supporter of Nixon, contacted the South Vietnamese ambassador to the United States, Bui Diem. She told Diem to advise General Thieu not to participate in any negotiations until after the elections because a Nixon presidency would negotiate better terms for South Vietnam than a Humphrey presidency.

On November 1, General Thieu, aware that the unilateral U.S. bombing halt had not required any reciprocal deescalations by Hanoi, announced that South Vietnam would not attend the Paris talks. Thieu's rubber-stamp National Assembly condemned President Johnson's "betrayal of an ally." Americans sadly realized that Johnson's peace initiative was not going to halt the war. Another Harris poll, taken on Monday, showed Nixon had regained the lead. Informed of the efforts of the Nixon camp to prevent the beginning of peace talks, Johnson chose not to publicize the connections between Thieu and Nixon, which might have embarrassed the Republicans and given Humphrey the victory.[141]

Although it is impossible to calculate precisely the impact of the collapse of the peace initiative on the presidential vote, and no doubt a myriad of domestic issues influenced the outcome, Thieu's last-minute demurral may have given Nixon his thin margin of victory. Out of 73 million votes cast, his winning margin was a scant 510,000. Nixon received 43.4 percent of the vote, Humphrey 42.7 percent.

But it is unlikely that most American voters viewed the election as a referendum on Johnson's war policy. That policy itself was perceived, erroneously, by most voters as having become dovish in the aftermath of Tet. Voters could not discern much difference among Nixon, Humphrey, and Wallace's policy positions on the war. Nixon may have been narrowly preferred because he was viewed as being better qualified for the presidency and because the nation was becoming more conservative in the wake of the war and social disorder. The antiwar movement was a casualty of the politics of war in 1968. Its radical wing shattered and disintegrated into extremist, violent, and quarreling factions. Its liberal wing was mostly coopted by the Democrats into supporting the ambiguous war policy of Hubert Humphrey.[142]

Following two weeks of intense U.S. pressure and promises of continuing support, Thieu reluctantly agreed to send a delegation to the Paris talks. There followed a debate that went on for weeks over the shape of the negotiating table and the positioning of the four delegations at the table. By the time negotiations involving the four concerned parties began, Johnson's administration had entered its final days.

Although it may have cost Humphrey his chance to win the 1968 presidential election, "It seems highly doubtful that South Vietnamese intransigence sabotaged an opportunity for a peace settlement."[143] Hanoi's new flexibility coming toward the end of 1968 did not extend beyond getting the bombing halted, which it managed without having to make any concessions in return. On the substantive issues, Hanoi would have probably accepted nothing less than a U.S. withdrawal and the end of the Thieu regime, both of which were unacceptable to Johnson. In the fall of 1968, neither Washington nor Hanoi was prepared to make the kinds of concessions that might have brought peace to Vietnam. The Tet Offensive and its violent aftermath had only hardened the diplomatic impasse over the key issues that had prevailed for years.

As the Year of the Monkey ended, most Americans yearned for an end to the bloody and stalemated war. Those who expected the incoming administration of Richard Nixon to bring an early end to the conflict would be bitterly disappointed, and they would discover that their Vietnam ordeal was destined to endure another four years.

NOTES

1. Tet is a celebration of the beginning of the lunar new year. It is the most important Vietnamese holiday. During the Vietnam War it was customary for both sides to observe a 36-hour cease fire during Tet, and 1968, the Year of the Monkey, was to be no exception.

2. Stanton, *Rise and Fall, 220.* Palmer, Bruce, Jr., *The 25-Five War: America's Role in Vietnam* (New York: Simon and Schuster, 1985), 78–79. One of the reasons MACV was surprised by the size of the enemy forces involved in the Tet-68 attacks was because their intelligence reports had underestimated both enemy strength and the rate of infiltration into South Vietnam. Adams, Samuel, "Vietnam Coverup: Playing with Numbers," *Harper's* (May 1975), 41, accuses Westmoreland of deliberately undercounting the VietCong in order to deceive civilian leaders in Washington into thinking America was winning the Vietnam War. A CBS video documentary, "The Uncounted Enemy: A Vietnam Deception," broadcast January 23, 1972, leveled the same charge. In response, General Westmoreland filed a libel suit against CBS that was eventually settled out of court. Larry Berman has shown in *Lyndon Johnson's War: The Road to Stalemate in Vietnam* (New York: W. W. Norton, 1989), 111–13, that there was no conspiracy by Westmoreland to deceive Johnson, McNamara, or any other high officials. Quote is from Hess, *Vietnam,* 106.

3. Oberdorfer, *Tet!* 34.

4. Brodie, Bernard, "The Tet Offensive," in Frankland, Noble, and Dowling, Christopher, eds., *Decisive Battles of the Twentieth Century* (London: 1976), 319–21.

5. Duiker, *The Communist Road,* 240.

6. Porter, *Vietnam Documents,* vol. 2, Document 222, 416, "Letter from Le Duan to Nguyen Chi Thanh, Commander-in-Chief of the PLAF," March 1966; Duiker, *Communist Road,* 242.

7. Quoted in Duiker, *The Communist Road,* 242–43.

8. Doyle, Edward; Lipsman Samuel; Maitland, Terrence; and the editors of Boston Publishing, *The North* (Boston: Boston Publishing, 1986), a volume in the series The Vietnam Experience, 52–56; Duiker, *The Communist Road,* 248.

9. Davidson, *Vietnam at War,* 434–41.

10. Duiker, *The Communist Road,* 263–64; Oberdofer, *Tet!* 42–43.

11. Porter, *Vietnam Documents,* vol. 2, Document 268, 477–80, "Directive from Province Party Standing Committee to District and Local Party Organs on Forthcoming Offensive and Uprisings," November 1, 1967. This document shows that the Communists were not depending on spontaneous risings of the people in the towns and cities at the time of the Tet-68 General

Offensive. The directive reveals detailed plans for coordinating military attacks on RVN offices with organized political activity by cadre leaders.

12. Duiker, *The Communist Road,* 264–65.
13. Krepinevich, *The Army and Vietnam,* 237–38; Duiker, *The Communist Road,* 265–66.
14. Westmoreland, *A Soldier Reports,* 411–16.
15. Ibid., 410–21.
16. Oberdorfer, *Tet!* 2–40; Olson and Roberts, *Where the Domino Fell,* 184.
17. Stanton, *Rise and Fall,* 208–16.
18. Ibid., 228–33; Oberdorfer, *Tet!* 122–31.
19. Stanton, *Rise and Fall,* 231–33.
20. Quote is from ibid., 221.
21. Summers, *Vietnam Encyclopedia,* 199–200.
22. Stanton, *Rise and Fall,* 228.
23. Quote is from Palmer, *Summons of the Trumpet,* 228–29. Some 9,776 of Hue's 17,134 houses were destroyed and another 3,169 seriously damaged. Thousands of civilians were killed during the month-long battle for Hue. Young, *Vietnam Wars,* 217–19.
24. Krepinevich, *The Army and Vietnam,* 250; Oberdorfer, *Tet!* 232.
25. President Nixon made his remarks during a speech delivered to the American people on the evening of November 3, 1969.
26. Palmer, *Summons of the Trumpet,* 215–16; Davidson, *Vietnam at War,* 551–54.
27. Johnson is quoted in Pisor, Robert, *The End of the Line; The Siege of Khe Sanh* (New York: Ballantine, 1982), 100, and 121–22; Westmoreland, *Soldier Reports,* 444–45; Davidson, *Vietnam at War,* 564–66. All discuss the possible use of tactical nuclear weapons at Khe Sanh. In an interview published in *Vietnam,* vol. 13, no. 5 (February 2001), 27–32, General Walter T. Kirwan, who, shortly after the Communist Tet-68 offensive, assembled a MACV staff team to considerable possible uses of tactical nuclear weapons, reminisces about that experience.
28. Davidson, *Vietnam at War,* 552–53.
29. Stanton, *Rise and Fall,* 235–38; Davidson, *Vietnam at War,* 552–53.
30. Davidson, *Vietnam at War,* 558–59.
31. Stanton, *Rise and Fall,* 238–42.
32. Davidson, *Vietnam at War,* 559–61; Pisor, *End of the Line,* 233–38.
33. Stanton, *Decline and Fall,* 233.
34. Pike, Douglas, *War, Peace, and the Vietcong* (Cambridge, MA: MIT Press, 1969), 125–27; Schandler, *The Unmaking of a President,* 77–78.
35. According to Oberdorfer, *Tet!,* who cites official U.S. and South Vietnamese figures, 58,373 PLAF and PAVN soldiers died between January 29 and March 31, 1968. During that time, 4,954 RVNAF soldiers, and 3,895 Americans from all branches of the armed forces, were killed.
36. Oberdorfer, *Tet!* 158–71; Schandler, *The Unmaking of a President,* 80–81.
37. Quoted in Oberdorfer, *Tet!* 184. Arnett was the only journalist to hear Major Brown's remark, and it was Arnett's wire service account that put the famous quote into circulation. Kendrick, Alexander, *The Wound Within: America in the Vietnam Years, 1945–1974* (Boston: Little Brown, 1974), 251.
38. Quote is from Herring, *America's Longest War,* 192.
39. Schandler, *The Unmaking of a President,* 83.
40. Hess, *Vietnam,* 109.
41. Johnson, *The Vantage Point,* 382–86.
42. Schandler, *The Unmaking of a President,* 92–97.
43. Davidson, *Vietnam at War,* 492–96.

44. Ibid., 497–98; Kolko, Gabriel, *Anatomy of a War: Vietnam, the United States, and the Modern Historical Experience* (New York: Pantheon, 1985), 313–15.

45. Schandler, *The Unmaking of a President,* 105–11; Davidson, *Vietnam at War*, 497–505.

46. Porter, *Vietnam Documents,* vol. 2, Document 279, 501–04, "Report of the Chairman, Joint Chiefs of Staff, General Earle G. Wheeler, on the Situation in Vietnam," February 27, 1968; Sheehan et al., *Pentagon Papers,* 615–21.

47. Porter, *Vietnam Documents,* vol. 2, Document 279, 501–4.

48. Schandler, *The Unmaking of a President,* 118–19. The quoted material is on 119.

49. Ibid., 120.

50. Johnson, *The Vantage Point,* 392.

51. Ibid., 235–36.

52. Clifford, Clark M., "A Viet Nam Reappraisal: The Personal History of One Man's View and How It Evolved," *Foreign Affairs,* 47 (July 1969), 606–7.

53. Schandler, *The Unmaking of a President,* 138–40.

54. Alain Enthoven's quote is found in Herring, *America's Longest War,* 3d ed., 213.

55. Questions and answers are taken from Clifford, "A Vietnam Reappraisal" 610–11.

56. Ibid., 611.

57. Ibid., 611–12.

58. Ibid., 613.

59. Ibid., 613.

60. Porter, *Vietnam Documents,* vol. 2, Document 230, 505. "Memorandum for the President from the Clifford Group" (extract); Schandler, *The Unmaking of the President,* contains a detailed description of the draft memo for the president, 167–76. The draft was written by William Bundy and Paul Warnke.

61. Johnson, *The Vantage Point,* 396–98.

62. Ibid., 398–401.

63. Sheehan, Neil, and Smith, Hedrick, "Westmoreland Requests 206,000 More Men, Stirring Debate in Administration," *New York Times,* March 10, 1968, 1.

64. Schandler, *The Unmaking of a President,* 211.

65. Both quotes come from ibid., 220.

66. McCarthy, Eugene J., *The Year of the People* (New York: Doubleday, 1969), 67–72; White, Theodore H., *The Making of a President, 1968* (New York: Atheneum, 1969), 83–85.

67. Schandler, *The Unmaking of a President,* 223.

68. Converse, Philip E.; Miller, Warren E.; Rusk, Jerold G.; and Wolfe, Arthur C., "Continuity and Change in American Politics: Parties and Issues in the 1968 Election," *American Political Science Review* 63 (December 1969), 1,083–92; Moss, *News or Nemesis,* 95–96. Sandbrook, Dominic, *Eugene McCarthy: The Rise and Fall of Postwar American Liberalism* (New York: Knopf, 2003), passim, argues that McCarthy's crusade failed to shorten the war, but it did hasten the self-destruction of the old liberal Democratic Party governing majority by driving millions of working class white voters into the Republican Party and George Wallace's American Independence Party. Sandbrook also points out that it was never the intention of McCarthy to wrest the presidential nomination away from Johnson; he was only trying to frighten Johnson into changing his policy and ending the war.

69. Collins, Robert M., "The Economic Crisis of 1968 and the Waning of the American Century," in *American Historical Review* 101, no. 2 (April 1996), 396–422. See also Johnson, *The Vantage Point,* 314–18.

70. Collins, "Economic Crisis of 1968," 407–18; Joseph, Paul, *Cracks in the Empire: State Politics in the Vietnam War* (Boston: South End Press, 1981), 265–66.

71. Herring, *America's Longest War*, 3d ed., 223.

72. Schandler, *The Unmaking of a President*, 236.

73. Clifford, "A Vietnam Reappraisal," 613–14; Schandler, *The Unmaking of a President*, 243–46, 251.

74. Johnson, *The Vantage Point*, 409–13; Oberdorfer, *Tet!* 294–95.

75. The "wise men" present at the decisive March 25 White House meeting included Dean Acheson, George Ball, McGeorge Bundy, Douglas Dillon, Cyrus Vance, Arthur Dean, John J. McCloy, General Omar Bradley, General Matthew Ridgway, General Maxwell Taylor, Robert Murphy, Henry Cabot Lodge, Abe Fortas, and Arthur Goldberg. Kolko, *Anatomy of a War*, 313–20.

76. McGeorge Bundy quote was found in Olson and Roberts, *Where the Domino Fell*, 192–93.

77. Johnson is quoted in Morris, Roger, *An Uncertain Greatness: Henry Kissinger and American Foreign Policy* (New York: Harper & Row, 1977), 44.

78. Johnson, *The Vantage Point*, 417–18; Sheehan, *A Bright Shining Lie*, 721–22; and Kolko, *Anatomy of a War*, 318–20. Melvin Small, *Johnson, Nixon, and the Doves*, 129–61, argues that the activities of the antiwar movement strongly influenced Johnson's decision to abandon his strategy of graduated escalation.

79. Johnson, *The Vantage Point*, 420–21.

80. Johnson's March 31 speech is printed in *Public Papers of the President of the United States, Lyndon B. Johnson, 1968–1969*, vol. 1 (Washington, DC: U.S. Government Printing Office, 1971), 469–76. Key passages, with analysis, are in Schandler, *The Unmaking of a President*, 282–87. Johnson resigned mainly because if he had not stepped down then, neither the American people nor Hanoi would have believed that his proposals were anything more than election year ploys.

81. Goodman, *The Lost Peace*, 65–67.

82. Schandler, *The Unmaking of a President*, 288–89; Kolko, *Anatomy of a War*, 333–37. The Communist leaders had not anticipated the great uproar that the Tet-68 campaigns caused within the United States nor their political impact. When they realized that even though they had suffered major losses, the American political defeat was even greater, they were euphoric. They also realized that they had been lucky—that the timing of the attacks coincided with the dollar crisis that together caused the American political elite to lose its stomach for the Vietnam War and to persuade Lyndon Johnson to abandon his policy of graduated escalation. The Communist leaders have always maintained that the Tet-68 Offensive was the turning point of the war with the Americans, the decisive triumph of their war effort.

83. Quote is from Herring, *America's Longest War*, 207.

84. Schandler, *The Unmaking of the President*, 319.

85. Kissinger, Henry, "The Vietnam Negotiations," *Foreign Affairs*, 47 (January 1969): 214–16.

86. Moss, "The Vietnam Generation," 6–8, 10–12.

87. Westmoreland, *A Soldier Reports*, 427–28, 438–39, 471–72, 554–57; Elegant, Robert, "How to Lose a War: Reflections of a Foreign Correspondent," *Encounter* (August 1981), 73–74.

88. Westmoreland, *A Soldier Reports*, 427–28, 438–39.

89. Kimball, Jeffrey P., "The Stab-in-the-Back Legend and the Vietnam War," *Armed Forces and Society* 14 (spring 1988): 438–39.

90. There is a large and generally excellent literature on the media coverage of the Vietnam War. Daniel C. Hallin, *The Uncensored War: The Media and Vietnam* (New York: Oxford University Press, 1986); and George Donelson Moss, "News or Nemesis: Did Television Lose the Vietnam War" in *A Vietnam Reader: Sources and Essays* (Englewood Cliffs, NJ: Prentice Hall, 1991) both show that television news coverage of the Vietnam War did not turn the American people against the war. William Hammond, a historian at the Army's Center of Military History, has written two books about the military and the media: *Public Affairs: The Military and the Media, 1962–1968* (Washington, DC: U.S. Government Printing Office, 1989) and *Public*

Affairs: The Military and the Media, 1968–1973 (Washington, DC: U.S. Government Printing Office, 1996). Hammond believes that media coverage of the war, whether favorable or unfavorable, had only a minor influence on public perceptions of the war.

91. Hallin, *Uncensored War,* 110.
92. Patterson, Oscar, III, "An Analysis of Television Coverage of the Vietnam War," *Journal of Broadcasting* 28 (fall 1984): 401–2.
93. The poll appeared in *Newsweek,* July 10, 1967, 20–24.
94. Mueller, *Wars, Presidents, and Public Opinion,* 88–89.
95. See Table 4.6 showing policy preferences in Vietnam appearing in Mueller, *Wars, Presidents, and Public Opinion,* 107. Public opinion polls taken in early February, immediately after the Tet attacks, showed that the number of people calling themselves hawks rose from 56 percent to 61 percent and the number calling themselves doves dropped from 28 percent to 23 percent.
96. See Braestrup, Peter, *Big Story: How the American Press and Television Reported and Interpreted the Crisis of Tet 1968 in Vietnam and Washington,* 2 vols. (Boulder, CO: Westview Press, 1977).
97. Braestrup, Peter, "The Press and the Vietnam War," *Encounter* (April 1983), 92.
98. Braestrup, Peter, "The Tet Offensive—Another Press Controversy: 2," in Harrison Salisbury, ed., *Vietnam Reconsidered: Lessons from a War* (New York: Harper & Row, 1984), 167–68.
99. Ibid., 171.
100. Mueller, *War, Presidents, and Public Opinion,* 91, cites a poll taken in September 1968 showing 48 percent of Americans favoring a dovish position, and 43 percent favoring a hawkish position. This is the first time any poll showed that doves outnumbered hawks. It was probably Johnson's indecisive leadership that caused the sharp drop in public support for the war.
101. Ibid., 23–114; Moss, *News or Nemesis,* 35–43.
102. Goodman, *The Lost Peace,* 65–68; Karnow, *Vietnam,* 566.
103. Quote is from Sasaki, Dr. Clarence T., "Holding Death at Bay," *Vietnam* 5, no. 2 (August 1992), 35.
104. Ibid., 35–40. Of the 97,659 soldiers who received serious wounds in Vietnam, the mortality rate was 2.5 percent, compared with 4.5 percent for World War II and 4.0 percent for Korea. Quote is from Hood, Jonathan Davis, and Buesseler, John Aure, Colonel. M.D., U.S. Army (ret.).
105. Marshall, Kathryn, *In the Combat Zone* (New York: Penguin, 1987), 3–13; Norman, Elizabeth M. *Women at War: The Story of Fifty Military Nurses Who Served in Vietnam* (Philadelphia: University of Pennsylvania Press, 1990), 21–35.
106. Stanton, *Rise and Fall,* 259–60.
107. Ibid., 255, 259, 262–63.
108. Morrocco, *Thunder from Above,* 184–86.
109. Doughan, Clark; Weiss, Stephen; and the editors of Boston Publishing, *Nineteen Sixty-Eight* (Boston: Boston Publishing, 1983), 142–44, a volume in the series The Vietnam Experience; Stanton, *Rise and Fall,* 248–49; Palmer, *Summons of the Trumpet,* 263–64.
110. Stanton, *Rise and Fall,* 249–50.
111. Ibid., 251–54.
112. Lewy, *America in Vietnam,* 324–25; Dougan, *Nineteen Sixty-Eight,* 79.
113. Stanton, *Rise and Fall,* 258.
114. An independent journalist, Seymour M. Hersh, exposed the Army's cover-up of the My Lai massacre. See his book, *Cover-Up: The Army's Secret Investigation of the Massacre at My Lai 4* (New York: Random House, 1972).
115. "Conversations between Lt. General William R. Peers and Lt. Colonel Jim Breen and Lt. Colonel Charlie Moore," in Oral History Collection of U.S. Army Military History Institute, Carlisle Barracks, PA, 33–44, 56–58; Peers, William R., *The My Lai Inquiry* (New York: W. W. Norton,

1979), passim; Palmer, *25-Year War,* 85–86, 170–71; Stanton, *Rise and Fall,* 258. Calley was initially sentenced to life imprisonment at hard labor. Following lengthy reviews of his case in both military and civilian courts, his sentence was first reduced to twenty years, then to ten years. After serving 26 months, most of which was spent in an apartment rather than a stockade, he was paroled in 1974 and walked away a free man.

116. Lewy, *America in Vietnam,* 311.

117. Ibid., 324–31. Lewy has carefully studied the issue of American war crimes and atrocities committed during the Vietnam War. See his chapter 9, "Atrocities: Fiction and Fact," 307–42, and chapter 10, "The Punishment of Atrocities and War Crimes," 343–73; also see Westmoreland's views, *Soldier Reports,* 494–501. In October, 2004, the Toledo (Ohio) *Blade,* a family owned newspaper, devoted 15 pages over four days to an exhaustive expose of an elite Army unit known as the Tiger Force. The Tiger Force, a 45-man platoon attached to the 101st Airborne, operating in and around the Quang Ngai province in South Vietnam's fiercely contested Central Highlands, murdered hundreds of noncombatant men, women, and children from May to November 1967. In 1971, Army investigators conducted a lengthy inquiry that eventually concluded that eighteen Tiger Force personnel had participated in war crimes. No one was ever charged and the investigation was quietly shut down in 1975.

118. Porter, *Vietnam Documents,* vol. 2, Document 285, 512–16, "COSVN Directive," June 10, 1968; Palmer, *Summons of the Trumpet,* 264–65; Stanton, *Rise and Fall,* 259–63.

119. Duiker, *Communist Road,* 276–78; Davidson, *Vietnam at War,* 540–44. During the first six months of 1968, Hanoi lost an estimated 100,000 PLAF and NVA troops, about half of their entire strength at the beginning of the year.

120. Blaufarb, *Counterinsurgency Era,* 266–74; Andrade, *Ashes to Ashes,* 81–97. The PHOENIX program, 1968–1972, that operated in South Vietnam to neutralize the VietCong political infrastructure in the villages became controversial. Its critics, testifying before congressional investigating committees, accused the CIA and its South Vietnamese counterparts of operating a barbarous assassination program outside the framework of law, morality, and bureaucratic accountability. Andrade has refuted these charges. He concedes that there were plenty of abuses; people were often imprisoned, tortured, and murdered without cause. But he shows that the intent of the program was to identify and neutralize the VCI. In 1969 and 1970, the PHOENIX program achieved considerable success in eliminating or disrupting the revolutionary infrastructure in some districts of South Vietnam. But it was too small, too inefficient, and never got the support it needed from RVN officials to cripple significantly the insurgency.

121. Clifford, "Vietnam Reappraisal," 614; Herring, *America's Longest War,* 212–13.

122. Davidson, *Vietnam at War,* 531.

123. Herring, *America's Longest War,* 208.

124. Davidson, *Vietnam at War,* 531.

125. Ibid., 532; Bluefarb, *Counterinsurgency Era,* 302–5.

126. Herring, *America's Longest War,* 213.

127. Quoted in Dougan et al., *Nineteen Sixty-Eight,* 126; Davidson, *Vietnam at War,* 544–47; Lipsman, Samuel; Doyle, Edward; and the editors of Boston Publishing, *Fighting for Time* (Boston: Boston Publishing, 1983), 88–90, a volume in the series The American Experience.

128. The unidentified Saigonese is quoted in Dougan et al., *Nineteen Sixty-Eight,* 123.

129. Herring, *America's Longest War,* 214–15.

130. Schlesinger, Arthur M., Jr., *Robert Kennedy and His Times,* vol. 2 (Boston: Houghton Mifflin, 1978), 930–31.

131. DeBenedetti, *American Ordeal,* 217–18; Moss, *America in the Twentieth Century,* 370.

132. O'Neill, William L., *Coming Apart: An Informal History of America in the 1960s* (New York: Quadrangle, 1971), 289–91; DeBenedetti, *American Ordeal,* 217–18.

133. Schlesinger, *Robert Kennedy,* 955–56.

134. Moss, *News or Nemesis,* 96–99.

135. Hodgson, Godfrey, *America in our Time: From World War II to Nixon: What Happened and Why* (New York: Vintage, 1976), 370–72; DeBenedetti, *An American Ordeal,* 223–28. Immediately after they broadcast images of the violence taking place in the streets of Chicago, the three television networks were deluged by letters, telegrams, and phone calls by irate viewers. By an eight-to-one margin, the viewers condemned the demonstrators and what they perceived as biased television reportage favoring the protesters. During the ensuing two weeks, Mayor Daley received 75,000 letters from all over the country; 90 percent of them praised his police. Public opinion polls showed that 56 percent of the people approved of Daley's handling of the disorders and 71 percent thought that his security measures were justified.

136. Dougan et al., *Nineteen Sixty-Eight,* 175; Stone is quoted in DeBenedetti, *An American Ordeal,* 228.

137. Dougan et al., *Nineteen Sixty-Eight,* 176. During 1968, antwar sentiment was growing within the U.S. Armed Forces. Desertion rates increased. Forty-three soldiers stationed at Fort Hood, Texas, refused to go to Chicago during the Democratic convention. Antiwar coffeehouses and underground newsletters appeared on U.S. military installations.

138. Quote is from DeBenedetti, *An American Ordeal,* 235.

139. Johnson, *Vantage Point,* 513–29; Goodman, *Lost Peace,* 69–73. The eventual scaling back and cessation of the air war against North Vietnam had ominous consequences for the inhabitants of Laos. Bombing sorties against targets in the Laotian panhandle and the Plain of Jars, an area in northeastern Laos controlled by the Pathet Lao, escalated in 1968.

140. Dougan et al., *Nineteen Sixty-Eight,* 180.

141. Schulzinger, *Time for War,* 271–72; Hess, *Vietnam,* rev. ed., 112. President Johnson met with General Thieu in Honolulu in July 1968 to reassure him that the United States would never support the establishment of a coalition government in South Vietnam. Johnson also promised that South Vietnam would be represented in any negotiations. Kimball, Jeffrey, *Nixon's Vietnam War* (Lawrence: University Press of Kansas, 1998), 56–62, has the best brief analysis of Nixon's behind-the-scenes intrigues to sabotage the peace talks and ensure his victory. Kimball's book is much the best study of Nixon's involvement with Vietnam, dating from his vice presidency and continuing through the summer of 1974, when he was forced to resign the presidency and return to private life.

142. DeBenedetti, *An American Ordeal,* 235–36. Many Humphrey supporters believe that Nixon's meddling cost him the election.

143. Quote is from Herring, *America's Longest War,* 219.

CHAPTER **8**

A War to End a War

We designed a war we were going to lose, and we managed to lose it the way we designed it.

Newt Gingrich

NIXON AND KISSINGER

Tet-68 transformed American politics and also transformed the American Vietnam war. President Johnson, his leadership discredited and heading a party badly split over an increasingly controversial war was forced to remove himself from politics, in effect resigning at the end of March 1968. Amidst the most turbulent backdrop since the Civil War, a divided electorate chose a resurrected Richard Nixon to lead the nation out of the morass of Vietnam and to restore peace both at home and abroad.

Nixon had been a hawk on the Indochina wars. As vice president, he had called for U.S. military intervention in May 1954 to save the French at Dien Bien Phu. In 1955, he had stated that expansionist China posed the greatest threat to U.S. strategic interests in Southeast Asia and that it might become necessary to use nuclear weapons to halt Chinese aggression. Nixon strongly backed the Johnson administration when it committed America to war in Vietnam during the summer of 1965. In 1966, and again in 1967, Nixon opposed calls for negotiations with Hanoi. He believed that such calls only encouraged the Communists to continue fighting. Nixon insisted that negotiations should occur only after all NVA forces had been driven from South Vietnam.[1]

During the 1968 presidential campaign, Nixon had frequently criticized Johnson's gradualist use of military force in Vietnam because it had produced neither military victory nor a negotiated settlement of the war. Conceding that a military victory was no longer possible, Nixon suggested that the road to a negotiated settlement of the Vietnam War ran through Moscow, not through Hanoi. Because Nixon believed North Vietnam could not continue its war in South Vietnam without Soviet backing, Washington should work for "a broad political accommodation with the Soviet Union—for *detente*"[2] to reduce or to end Soviet aid to North Vietnam. He stated that if the Soviets wanted Hanoi to end its war in South Vietnam, the North Vietnamese would have no choice but to negotiate its conclusion.

Asserting that ending the Vietnam War was necessarily the top national priority, Nixon stressed the importance of ending the war honorably and in such a fashion that the U.S. withdrawal from Vietnam would never be or even appear to be an American defeat. For him, the maintenance of an independent non-Communist South Vietnamese government was crucial. Ensuring a free South Vietnam was a major American commitment and a vital national interest. Preserving South Vietnam was also necessary for the United States to maintain its credibility as a great power with both friends and foes. How America ended its war in Vietnam would determine if there would soon be another war or if the world would enjoy a generation of peace.

As his campaign for the presidency developed, Nixon had suggested that if he were elected, he would move on a variety of nonmilitary fronts, that he had a plan, which he refused to disclose in detail, for ending the war.[3] But once in office, it became evident that President Nixon did not have a plan, secret or otherwise, for ending the Vietnam War. He brought to the White House only a few general principles pertaining to a settlement that he had formulated over the years.

The new president gradually improvised a Vietnam strategy during his first year in office. Some of Nixon's ideas concerning the Vietnam War were similar to the views of Henry A. Kissinger, who became Nixon's national security adviser. Kissinger, while a professor at Harvard, had written extensively on foreign policy and national security issues. He had also accepted special diplomatic assignments from Lyndon Johnson, most notably the aforemention operation Pennsylvania, a failed effort to negotiate a cease-fire with Hanoi during the summer of 1967. Kissinger's realist theories of international relations were favored by the foreign policy establishment, whose members tended to dislike and distrust Richard Nixon. Kissinger shared Nixon's view that the first order of foreign policy business must be the phasing out of the American Vietnam war and that it had to be done in an honorable fashion. But Kissinger had never been an enthusiastic supporter of the U.S. military intervention in Vietnam. He believed Johnson and his advisers had made a serious error in geopolitical judgment when they decided to send U.S. combat forces to Vietnam in 1965; they had sought a military solution to a political problem. But in 1969, Kissinger argued that how or why America had gotten into the war no longer mattered because "ending the war honorably is essential for the peace of the world."[4]

Nixon's approach to Vietnam "was an integral part of an effort to redefine America's global strategy."[5] Both Nixon and Kissinger envisioned a world in which the major powers, including the Communist powers, maintained a stable world order, in which they would all have a vested interest. Nixon and Kissinger believed they could provide the leadership that would enable the United States to maintain its primacy within this new world order. The two American leaders sought to improve relations with the Soviet Union and to move toward normal relations with China, ending 20 years of hostility between the Peoples Republic and the United States. Both Nixon and Kissinger, who quickly became Nixon's chief foreign policy adviser and envoy, shared the conviction that they must extract the United States from what had become a major liability.[6]

They also believed that to accomplish their major foreign policy goals they would have to concentrate the power to conduct American foreign policy into their hands. Achieving such power required bypassing the National Security Council and the bureaucracies in the Defense Department, the State Department, and the CIA. They believed that an energetic and decisive foreign policy could come only from the new partnership forming in the White House, in consultation with a few senior advisers. Early in his presidency, Nixon told Kissinger, "You and I will end the war."[7]

Nixon and Kissinger understood that Johnson's modus operandi, decision making by consensus, had been a slow and cumbrous process. Further, consensus required a variety of lowest common denominator decisions, which often reflected the bureaucratic interests of senior officials. Consensus decisions were expressions of the power balance within Johnson's administration among members of the Joint Chiefs, the State Department, the Defense Department, the CIA, and the National Security Council, whether or not such decisions made strategic or diplomatic sense. Nixon and Kissinger both were certain that they possessed the requisite expertise to rise above the miasma of bureaucratic consensus politics. They believed that only they could make the bold, decisive moves needed for ending the American war in Vietnam, reorienting U.S. relations with China and the Soviet Union, and achieving a stable and peaceful world order that accorded with U.S. strategic interests.

Nixon and Kissinger found that their power and options were more limited than they had supposed, and that many of their assumptions and ideas proved invalid. They discovered that they had limited freedom of maneuver, even less than their predecessors, because of a multiplicity of factors: the stalemated war, Hanoi's protracted war strategy and absolute refusal to modify its objectives, Soviet unwillingness to prod Hanoi to end the war, General Thieu's fears that any settlement that America might make with Hanoi threatened his country's prospects for survival, and powerful domestic constraints.

Nixon's narrow victory in the November 1968 election carried with it no mandate whatsoever. Because of the presence of a strong third-party candidate George Wallace, Nixon won the presidency by only a plurality (with 43 percent of the popular vote). Fifty-seven percent of the voters preferred a candidate other than Richard Nixon for president of the United States. Congress remained firmly in the control of large Democratic majorities. Many liberal Democratic congressmen and senators were now freed from the inhibitions of having to support Johnson's war. They could be expected to prod Nixon's administration to seek a negotiated end to the war and to challenge any initiatives he might undertake to expand or widen the war.[8]

Public opinion polls taken in early 1969 showed that large majorities of Americans wanted a quick end to the U.S. war and favored an early withdrawal of all U.S. forces. But most Americans did not want to see the United States defeated in Vietnam, and they believed that it was important to stop the spread of Communism in Southeast Asia. They also wanted the South Vietnamese to take responsibility for their own defense and survival. The same people who wanted a quick end to a war also wanted to win the war but not see it escalated. While wanting to stop the spread of Communism in Southeast Asia, they also exhibited little concern for the welfare of the South Vietnamese people or much regard for the survival of their government.[9] Such a tangle of conflicting views may have defied logic, but they set limits to what Nixon and Kissinger could do as the two labored to forge a new U.S. strategy for Vietnam.

The new president and his chief adviser confronted dilemmas as they struggled to improvise a U.S. Vietnam policy and the strategies required to make it work. Any terms acceptable to Hanoi for ending the war were unacceptable to them, to their allies in South Vietnam, to the U.S. congressional majority, and to a majority of the American people. Domestic criticism of the costs of the war put pressure on the President to withdraw U.S. troops, but unilateral American force withdrawals also encouraged Hanoi to refuse to make any concessions to achieve a settlement Nixon could accept.

Johnson had passed on to his successors a war that could neither be won nor ended, except on terms that amounted to a major American defeat. Nixon and Kissinger would not accept such an outcome in 1969. In fact, the Nixon administration and the American people would endure four more years of war in Indochina before they could accept the unacceptable, accept what had been inevitable since Tet-68, perhaps inevitable since the U.S. intervention in southern Vietnam in the summer of 1954: eventual strategic defeat. Washington finally accepted it in January 1973, only by disguising that defeat within the rhetoric of "peace with honor." "Peace with honor glossed over the ineffable strategic reality of the American Vietnam war: American withdrawal from the war and the survival of the South Vietnamese government . . . had always been contradictory objectives."[10]

VIETNAMIZATION

As he had promised the American people, Nixon turned his attention immediately to Vietnam. He told his chief of staff, Harry R. "Bob" Haldeman, that he was not going to be like Lyndon Johnson and vowed "to end the war in Vietnam fast." As the new president set out to end the war, he ruled out the two extreme solutions: immediate withdrawal or massive escalation. Nixon understood from the beginning of his presidency that his only feasible option was an American withdrawal.[11]

For Nixon, the only significant question concerned the way America withdrew. Would it be precipitous, an ignominious American defeat, or would it be measured and honorable, assuring the survival of South Vietnam? Nixon had joined the conservative Republican assault on the Truman administration for "losing" China during the early 1950s, and like his predecessor Lyndon Johnson, the new president "feared the domestic upheaval that might accompany the fall of South Vietnam to communism."[12] The long delay in ending the war arose from Nixon's preoccupation with how the war was to be terminated and with what consequences, domestic and international.

The long delay in ending the war also ensued because for years the North Vietnamese leadership adhered to their goals of bringing down the South Vietnamese government, replacing it with one dominated by the NLF, forcing the Americans out, and reuniting the country under their control. The aging revolutionaries in Hanoi never forgot the outcome of the Geneva conference in 1954 in which great power diplomacy deprived them of a victory they had won on the battlefields of Vietnam. They were determined to control their own political destiny, and they had no interest in negotiating an end to the war on any terms that Nixon and Kissinger could accept. For four years, from January 1969 to January 1973, Nixon and Kissinger waged a slow, bitter American retreat from Indochina, and they called it "peace with honor."

Shortly after assuming office, Nixon sent a letter to the North Vietnamese leaders expressing his desire for peace. He proposed as a first step the mutual withdrawal of "external forces" (United States and NVA) from South Vietnam and the restoration of the DMZ as a boundary between the two countries of North Vietnam and South Vietnam. He also proposed, at Kissinger's suggestion, that the Paris negotiations follow a two-tiered approach, with Washington and Hanoi concentrating on mutual troop withdrawals, while Saigon's representatives and the NLF negotiated a political settlement of the civil war. At the same time Nixon sent his letter to Hanoi, he sent Kissinger to tell the Soviet ambassador to the United States, Anatoly Dobrynin, that a peace settlement in Vietnam must precede any accommodation between the United States and the Soviet Union. That is, the American Vietnam war must end before *detente* could occur. To signal to both Hanoi and Moscow that his administration would not be bound by the old limits, Nixon accompanied these diplomatic initiatives with the bombing of VC/NVA sanctuaries in the eastern provinces of Cambodia bordering southern Vietnam.[13]

The bombing also represented a response to another Communist offensive carried out in many districts and provinces of South Vietnam on February 22, 1969, and it also fulfilled a long-standing request of the Joint Chiefs to strike at VC/NVA bases in Cambodia that lay beyond the reach of Allied troops. Johnson had always rejected the Joint Chiefs' request out of his fear of widening the war. The bombing operation, code-named MENU, began on March 18 with B-52s bombing the VC/NVA Cambodian sanctuaries in several locales.

The MENU operation began with a BREAKFAST phase. As the war went on and the bombing of Cambodia continued, BREAKFAST was followed by LUNCH, LUNCH by SNACK, SNACK by DINNER, DINNER by DESSERT, and DESSERT by SUPPER. Nixon ordered intermittent bombing raids on Cambodia through August 1969. Sometimes the bombing raids were followed by lightning cross-border raids by teams of Special Forces operatives. The air raids and ground attacks had the combined effect of driving the North Vietnamese deeper into the Cambodian interior. After August, the bombing continued on a regular basis until May 1970, when air strikes in Cambodia began openly in support of Allied ground operations against North Vietnamese bases.[14]

Fearing an adverse reaction from Congress and the American people because the bombings occurred in a neutral country and represented a widening of the war, both geographically and politically, the Nixon administration went to great lengths to try to keep them hidden. Air Force officials in charge of the bombings constructed elaborate systems of phony records of sorties supposedly flown against authorized targets in South Vietnam to account for the expenditures of fuel and ordnance used on the secret raids into Cambodia. An elaborate system of dual bookkeeping was set up, which made it appear that the bombs hitting the Cambodian sanctuaries of the enemy were instead falling on targets inside of South Vietnam.[15]

When William Beecher wrote an account of the secret bombing of Cambodia that appeared in the *New York Times* on May 9, 1969, Nixon suggested to Kissinger that the informant could have been someone on the National Security Council staff. Kissinger concurred. The next day, the president, with Kissinger's approval, ordered FBI director J. Edgar Hoover to wiretap the phones of 11 National Security Council staff members and four members of the news media whom he suspected of leaking information about the bombing to the paper.[16]

In May 1970, at the time of the American incursion into Cambodia, Nixon ordered the bombing of target sites in North Vietnam and also tried to keep this action secret. After another press leak, the *New York Times* ran a story about the renewed bombing of North Vietnam. Once again, Nixon ordered wiretaps put on the phones of officials and journalists that he suspected. In July 1971, the *New York Times* began publishing the "Pentagon Papers," a secret Defense Department internal history of the long U.S. involvement in Vietnam, given to them by former Defense Department officials Daniel Ellsberg and Anthony Russo. To stop further press leaks and to discredit Ellsberg, White House officials formed a special security unit, the "Plumbers."

President Nixon, increasingly frustrated by his inability to end the Vietnam War and convinced that his policies, even his ability to govern, were under attack from his "enemies" in the federal bureaucracies, in Congress, in the media, and in the universities, ordered the "Plumbers" to take whatever actions were necessary to stop press leaks. Wiretapping had led to the formation of the "Plumbers." It was a natural progression from the actions of the "Plumbers" to the "dirty tricks" of the 1972 presidential election, one of which was the Watergate burglary and its attempted cover-up. The genesis of the Watergate scandals that eventually destroyed the Nixon presidency lay in Nixon's siege mentality arising from his inability to forge a rapid end to the Vietnam War, which led him to countenance illegal measures intended to squelch his political opponents. When Nixon ordered the wiretapping of the phones of NSC staffers and journalists in May 1969, he unwittingly began a process that would destroy his presidency and mar his historical reputation five years later.

None of Nixon's and Kissinger's initial efforts to end the Vietnam War produced any noticeable results. Neither the VC/NVA February offensive nor the secret U.S. bombing of Cambodia changed the military balance in Vietnam. The stalemate on the battlefield was matched by a continuing diplomatic standoff in Paris. The Soviets did not cooperate as expected; they made no effort to persuade Hanoi to end the war. Both the North Vietnamese and South Vietnamese governments rejected the U.S. proposal for a mutual withdrawal of U.S. and PAVN forces from South Vietnam. The Saigon government refused to recognize or negotiate with representatives of the NLF. The war went on. "At the heart of the U.S.-North Vietnamese conflict remained the status of South Vietnam."[17]

Perceiving that his initial efforts to end the war had failed, Nixon used a televised speech on May 14, 1969 in which he called for a cease-fire throughout Indochina to be followed by the withdrawal of all U.S. and North Vietnamese troops from South Vietnam within a year. He proposed a comprehensive eight-point Vietnam peace plan that he hoped would break the diplomatic logjam. Most of the eight points referred to the proposed troop withdrawal and other military matters. The president also tried to resuscitate the two-tier formula, separating the military and political dimensions of the struggle, by stating that "the political settlement is an internal matter that ought to be decided by the South Vietnamese themselves."[18]

Nixon followed his speech with a trip to Midway Island in early June, where he met with General Thieu. After conferring with Thieu, Nixon announced on June 8 that he was immediately recalling 25,000 American troops from Vietnam. U.S. disengagement from Southeast Asia had begun. The large-scale withdrawal of American forces from Vietnam was part of a new "Nixon Doctrine" of limited U.S. involvement in Third World revolutionary wars. Henceforth, the United States would provide economic and military assistance, but the host country would have to furnish its own troops. The United States would help, but the host country would have to defend itself. Implementation of the Nixon Doctrine meant there would be no more Vietnams. In a larger context, the Nixon Doctrine represented an effort to downsize American global foreign policy commitments, to align U.S. commitments with its ability to meet them. Lest Hanoi or the Soviets read the wrong message into the troop pullout, Nixon followed his Midway Island pronouncements with several speeches attacking antiwar critics and affirming that his administration would keep America's commitments abroad.[19]

During the first six months of his presidency, Nixon set the pattern that would prevail for the next four years. He declared military victory to be unattainable, but also vowed that the United States would never leave Vietnam without a negotiated settlement that permitted the South Vietnamese government to survive. Beginning in June 1969, the withdrawal of U.S. troops, which Nixon linked to progress in negotiations and Vietnamization, did not please either hawk or doves, yet provided each side with some encouragement. The pace of withdrawal was too slow for doves and too fast for hawks, but gave some hope to doves that the U.S. war would eventually end and gave reas-

Figure 8.1   President Nixon and General Thieu holding a press conference on Midway Island June 8, 1969. Following their meeting, Nixon announced that he was immediately recalling 25,000 U.S. troops from Vietnam. *Source:* CORBIS. Neg # U1645066-19. © Bettmann/CORBIS.

surance to hawks that there would not be a precipitate U.S. withdrawal followed by a collapse of the South Vietnamese government.

But these diplomatic and military moves also failed to extract the slightest concessions from Hanoi. The Communists could neither be pressured nor lured into altering their basic negotiating stance. They reiterated the peace terms they had maintained since talks had begun in May 1968: the total and unconditional withdrawal of all U.S. forces from Vietnam and the replacement of the Thieu government with a provisional government.[20]

On the battlefield, the VC/NVA continued its protracted war strategy. The war went on, although the scale and intensity of fighting declined during the year, casualties dropped, and Hanoi pulled some of its forces back across the DMZ. The North Vietnamese were prepared to wait out the Nixon administration, confident that declining domestic support for the war would eventually force Washington to withdraw the U.S. forces, just as the loss of support at home had forced the French to withdraw their forces from Indochina during the previous war.[21] Hanoi's leaders understood that if the U.S. forces did not win, in time, they would lose; the North Vietnamese had only not to lose, and in time they would win. Hanoi confidently embraced General Tran Hung

Dao's dictum, which he pronounced in 1284 as his forces outlasted the invading armies of China, the reigning superpower of that era, "Time is always in our favor."[22]

By the summer of 1969, it was evident that the strategies Nixon and Kissinger had brought to Washington to end the American Vietnam war had failed to deliver the promised result. Nixon had never set a specific date for ending the war, but he and Kissinger expected that their mix of threats, secret back-channel diplomatic maneuvers, and efforts to involve the Soviets would bring an end to the American Vietnam war within a year from the date they took office. But by the summer of 1969, congressional criticism of the continuing war was on the rise, and the peace movement, quiescent since the violence in Chicago, geared up for fall demonstrations.

Fearful that domestic discontent would undermine his efforts to get Hanoi to negotiate an acceptable agreement, Nixon turned to what he called his "go for broke" strategy, an all-out effort to end the war, either by a diplomatic agreement or by the use of military force. Through French intermediaries, the president sent a personal message to Ho Chi Minh urging a settlement, but with the added warning, amounting to an ultimatum, that if no progress were made by November 1, he would have no choice but to resort to "measures of great consequence and force."[23] Nixon sent Kissinger to see Dobrynin again to warn him that there remained little time for a peaceful solution to the impasse at Paris.

Nixon also directed Kissinger to form a select National Security Council study group to develop plans for a "savage, punishing" blow aimed at North Vietnam.[24] Nixon and Kissinger sought that one decisive stroke that would destroy the will of the North Vietnamese to continue the war in South Vietnam. Kissinger told the select group at their first meeting in early September, "I can't believe that a fourth-rate power like North Vietnam doesn't have a breaking point."[25] By the end of the month, the group had developed a thick loose-leaf notebook of attack plans, code-named DUCK HOOK. DUCK HOOK included mining Haiphong Harbor, implementing a naval blockade of the North Vietnamese coast, and saturation bombing of both military targets and major cities. In addition, the planners considered more drastic operations such as invading North Vietnam, bombing the Red River dikes to flood the major rice-growing region of North Vietnam, and closing down the rail supply lines to China. The DUCK HOOK planners also analyzed possible uses of tactical nuclear devices in North Vietnam.[26] Not averse to using press leaks himself if they could advance his policies, Nixon let journalists know he was considering a range of military options. Nixon probably intended the leaks as warning signals to Moscow and Hanoi that the time left for diplomacy had grown short and that his patience had worn thin. Nixon also vowed to a congressional delegation that he would not be the first president to lose a war.[27]

Nixon's "go for broke" strategy also failed. Hanoi could not be intimidated, although the Communists did agree to hold secret talks with the Americans outside of the framework of the Paris negotiations. On August 4, 1969, Kissinger met privately with Xuan Thuy for the first of what would prove to be a long series of secret talks between Kissinger and DRV envoys, lasting until the Paris Agreement was negotiated in January 1973. At that first meeting, Thuy rejected all of Kissinger's proposals, dismissed Nixon's epistolary ultimatum to Ho Chi Minh, and repeated Hanoi's refrain that there could be no agreement until the United States had removed all of its troops from Vietnam and had sacrificed the Thieu government.[28] On August 15, Ho Chi Minh formally replied to Nixon's letter. The North Vietnamese leader ignored the ultimatum, rejected Nixon's overtures, and restated Hanoi's basic position, insisting that it was the only correct formula for peace. Hanoi radio infuriated the President by wishing the American peace movement splendid success with its upcoming demonstrations.[29]

By fall 1969, Nixon, angered by Hanoi's intransigence and by dovish antiwar critics whom he believed encouraged North Vietnam's resistance to his diplomatic overtures, faced stark choices: He could undertake a major military escalation of the war, or he could beat a humiliating diplomatic retreat. His gut reaction was to strike back at his enemies. He wanted to hurl U.S. air power at the North Vietnamese and blockade their ports. But he was advised by Secretary of State William Rogers and Secretary of Defense Melvin Laird not to escalate the war because such action would doubtless arouse the doves in Congress, the press, the academies, and the streets. Additionally, Kissinger's select group of strategic planners concluded that air strikes and a blockade would probably not wring any concessions from Hanoi nor diminish its ability to support the war in South Vietnam. A strong U.S. military operation directed against North Vietnamese targets would also suggest that Nixon was trying for a military victory in a war that he had promised to phase out. Nixon had to abandon his plan to strike a decisive blow against the Communists. Discovering that military escalation would probably not be effective, unwilling to make concessions that compromised his notion of peace with honor, and facing rising domestic opposition and impending peace demonstrations, Nixon found himself without a Vietnam policy.[30] All of his secret plans for ending the war quickly had come to naught. The war went on and the North Vietnamese showed no signs of faltering or wanting to negotiate on terms that Nixon and Kissinger could accept.

Caught in a bind largely of his own making, Nixon could only fall back on Vietnamization, the policy he had inherited from Johnson. Having discovered that his and Kissinger's strategics could not end the war, Nixon convinced himself that Vietnamization could. The United States would withdraw its military forces from South Vietnam while continuing to provide substantial military and economic assistance to the GVN to build it up to a point where it could deflect the VC/NVA attacks and survive on its own. Nixon believed that if he could rally the American people behind him, accelerate the buildup in South Vietnam, and persuade Hanoi that America would never abandon Thieu, then he might be able to convince North Vietnam's leaders that it would be to their advantage to negotiate an acceptable settlement with the United States in the short run, rather than have to deal with a strong South Vietnamese government in the long run.

Vietnamization was attractive to Nixon and Kissinger as their fall-back route to an honorable peace. The real-world results of Vietnamization would be three more years of war for Americans, with thousands of additional U.S. battle deaths, additional multi-billion dollar expenditures, and continuing domestic turmoil. For Vietnamese, the results included extensive physical destruction, economic disruptions, a million more refugees, hundreds of thousands of civilian and military casualties, and continuing social misery, and in the end, the collapse of the South Vietnamese state and a victory for the North Vietnamese and VietCong. En route to those outcomes, Nixon's presidency would be destroyed, the second U.S. administration to fall victim to the ordeal of Vietnam.

Mobilizing against War

While Nixon sought a Vietnam War policy, liberal antiwar activists organized the Moratorium and the New Mobilization, the largest antiwar demonstrations ever staged in America. The leadership of the Vietnam Moratorium Committee (VMC) was liberal; many of its organizers had worked for Eugene McCarthy or for Robert Kennedy during the 1968 Democratic presidential campaign. The VMC leaders like Sam Brown wanted to reach beyond the college campuses and into the cities, towns, and workplaces of America, hoping to mobilize the broadest possible coalition of antiwar citizens to get them to engage in legal and traditional protests all across the country. People were encouraged to take the day off from business as usual to discuss the war with fellow workers and what might be done to end it. Brown and his fellow organizers believed that the sheer size and variety of protests would put maximum pressure on the Nixon administration to bring the Vietnam War to a speedier conclusion. Many leading intellectuals, and prominent dissidents supported the Moratorium. Twenty-four Democratic senators and Averill Harriman added their support to the cause. The Moratorium also had the support of most of the peace movement, except for its most militant factions.[31]

On M-Day, on Saturday, October 15, 1969, demonstrations occurred all over the country. Between 500,000 and 1 million people participated; 100,000 citizens gathered in Boston Common to hear speeches and listen to music. In a large parade in Manhattan, Wall Street financiers walked alongside housewives, civil rights leaders, hippies, and disillusioned Vietnam veterans. Philadelphia hosted a myriad of antiwar events. The moratorium was widely observed in the Midwest, largely ignored in the South. In Denver 3,000 marchers braved falling snow and chilling winds to march on the state capital. In California, 20,000 citizens gathered on the sunny UCLA campus for a day of antiwar programs. The major Moratorium events around the country received live and generally fair media coverage. In Vietnam, groups of U.S. soldiers stationed at various sites wore black armbands to show their support for Moratorium Day. For the first time, the antiwar movement had joined the war.[32]

To publicize his indifference to the Moratorium demonstrations, Nixon let it be known that he planned to spend Saturday afternoon watching a football game on television. He also canceled draft calls for November and December because his Vietnamization policy significantly reduced military manpower needs. He also dismissed General Hershey, the controversial doyen of the Cold War era draft, replacing him with a civilian bureaucrat, Curtis Tarr. Tarr acted quickly to defuse protests against the Selective Service. He ended most student deferments, supplanting them with a lottery draft system. Under the new system, young men, upon turning 19, drew numbers from 1 to 365, based on their birth dates. If an individual drew a low number, say 1 to 50, he would probably be exposed to the draft. Drawing a number between 50 and 100 meant that he might. People who drew numbers 101 or higher generally avoided military service during the three years that the lottery draft was in place. The new, random system removed some of the class inequities from the draft, and it also significantly reduced the ranks of young men likely to engage in antiwar activities. It also largely eliminated the draft as a source of controversy and protest for the remainder of the Vietnam War.[33]

In between the Moratorium and the New Mobilization, scheduled for November 13 to 15, the Nixon administration launched its counteroffensive against its antiwar critics. The president unleashed his feisty vice president, Spiro T. Agnew, who went on the oratorical warpath. Agnew lambasted what he termed the "liberal establishment press," accusing the media of biased and negative coverage of Nixon administration activities and its Vietnam War policy. He labeled these newscasters "an effete corps of impudent snobs who characterize themselves as intellectuals."[34]

Nixon followed Agnew with a major televised address to the nation the evening of November 3. It was the longest and most important speech of his presidency to date. He timed the speech so it fell midway between the moratorium and the new mobilization. His chief goals were to declare war on the antiwar movement and to rally the American people in support of his Vietnam War policy. The president called his antiwar critics an irrational minority trying to thwart the will of the large majority of the American people. He defended the American Vietnam war. He cited the commitments to Vietnam made by three previous administrations, and he vowed to stay in Vietnam until America achieved an honorable and lasting peace.

Nixon also used the speech to spell out his Vietnamization policy. He insisted that it would produce an honorable peace by enabling the South Vietnamese to save themselves while he withdrew U.S. forces and reduced American casualties. Citing the Communist mass murders at Hue during the Tet-68 campaign and the thousands of deaths in North Vietnam that had accompanied land reform during the mid-1950s as precedents, the president invoked the chilling specter of a bloodbath facing the South Vietnamese, especially the 1.5 million Catholics among them if the United States precipitously pulled out its forces and left the South Vietnamese people at the mercy of the Communists. He appealed powerfully to the American people's patriotism, to their sense of honor, and to the ideal of American greatness. He concluded his speech with a stirring call for support for Vietnamization by the mass of the American people, whom he called "the great silent majority," ending with "North Vietnam cannot humiliate the United States. Only Americans can do that."[35]

With his speech, the president regained the initiative and put his critics in the Congress, the press, and the peace movement on the defensive. Nixon sold the American people a policy that he claimed would produce an honorable peace and save

American lives. By calling attention to and labeling the "silent majority," Nixon broadened his base of support and gave millions of Americans a new political identity. Pro-Nixon rallies appeared in a number of cities. Polls taken soon after his speech showed that 77 percent of the American people supported Vietnamization. Another poll showed that by a six to one margin the American people agreed that antiwar demonstrations harmed prospects for peace in Vietnam.[36] Many antiwar senators and Congressmen climbed aboard the Vietnamization bandwagon. Nixon, delighted with his success, boasted that he "had floored those liberal sons of bitches with the TV speech," and "we've got those liberal bastards on the run now; we've got them on the run and we're going to keep them on the run."[37]

Nixon and Agnew's successful counteroffensive complicated preparations for the New Mobilization. Organization was further hindered by factional infighting among radical and liberal antiwar activists. Eventually a slate of varied activities was scheduled to take place across the nation from November 13 to 15. One of the first demonstrations was the March against Death. Marchers began near the Arlington National Cemetery, led by drummers playing a funeral roll. Solemnly marching across the Memorial Bridge, in single file, each participant carried a lighted candle and a placard inscribed with the name of one of the 45,000 American soldiers who had died in the Vietnam War. They marched to the White House; as they passed, each parader paused to shout the name of the dead warrior inscribed on his placard. The procession then continued down Pennsylvania Avenue to the Capitol where each marcher placed his placard in a waiting coffin and blew out the candle. For 36 hours the procession wound its mournful way until all 45,000 of the dead had been memorialized.[38]

In addition to the March against Death, many other antiwar activities occurred from November 13 to 15 as the New Mobilization unfolded. The Reverend William Sloane Coffin led an ecumenical prayer service for peace at the National Cathedral in Washington. In San Francisco, an estimated 150,000 people paraded for peace. On Saturday, November 15, the largest protest demonstration in American history took place in the nation's capital. A huge crowd of perhaps 350,000 people gathered at the Mall by the Lincoln Memorial. This human wave then flowed down Pennsylvania Avenue past the White House, which was barricaded by a huge circle of busses, and onto the grounds of the Washington Monument. This huge assemblage of mostly white, mostly young demonstrators appeared to pay fitful attention to a parade of speakers. The protesters were much more interested in the cast from the hit Broadway musical *Hair*, who showed up to sing a medley of their songs. The emotional highpoint of the demonstration occurred when the vast assemblage of humanity joined Peter, Paul, and Mary to chant John Lennon's haunting refrain, "All we are saying / is give peace a chance." For more than 10 minutes, the huge crowd was caught up in the hypnotic power of the chant.[39]

Despite the large numbers of participants and the spectacular events themselves, the New Mobilization appeared to have minimal impact on public opinion and none on the war policy of the Nixon administration. Nixon's "Silent Majority" speech and Agnew's rhetorical assaults on the news media had their desired effect because there

Figure 8.2 The New Mobilization peace parade passes along Pennsylvania Avenue from the Capitol building on November 15, 1969. The peace rally (an estimated 350,000 people) gathered at the Washington Monument to protest the Vietnam War. *Source:* AP/Wide World Photos.

was no live television coverage of the events, and the events of the New Mobilization received limited coverage on the nightly network newscasts. Public opinion polls revealed that three-fourths of Americans disapproved of the protest demonstrations. Polls also showed that 60 percent of Americans agreed with President Nixon that antiwar demonstrations aided the enemy and made Washington's efforts to achieve peace in Vietnam more difficult.[40]

Most Americans, however frustrated and angry they might be with the war, resented antiwar demonstrators even more. Part of the popular disgust with antiwar activists was driven by the people's yearnings for an end to controversy. After nearly a decade of upheaval, most Americans longed for a return to domestic tranquility. Many of the protesters themselves were fatigued. They were weary from too many protests of a seemingly endless war and exhausted from challenging a government that harassed, rebuked, or ignored them. Many quietly resumed their private lives, abandoning what appeared to them futile efforts to influence public opinion, change government policy, and stop an unjust war.

THE FAILURE OF VIETNAMIZATION

It proved much easier for President Nixon to manipulate American public opinion by slamming the antiwar movement and by claiming that Vietnamization would produce peace with honor than for U.S. and South Vietnamese officials to turn Vietnamization into an effective policy. There was some improvement in RVNAF forces in 1969 and 1970. Force levels were increased, from about 820,000 soldiers in 1968 to over 1 million by 1970. They were also equipped with modern weapons, including M-16 rifles and more powerful artillery. Some ARVN units, when properly led, and even some district and local forces, fought effectively. The South Vietnamese air force and navy were both enhanced. Pay and conditions of service were improved for all branches of the South Vietnamese armed forces.

But the improved version of the RVNAF still suffered from a large array of serious problems. Systematic corruption and mass desertion persisted. Paper force levels looked impressive, but they were inflated by 15 to 20 percent because ARVN commanders padded unit rosters with the names of nonexistent soldiers to collect additional money. The ARVN generals also collected large sums of money from affluent Vietnamese, who paid bribes to avoid military service. In addition, Vietnamization required a modern South Vietnamese army. A modern army required large numbers of competent officers, experienced noncommissioned officers, and skilled people to perform a wide variety of tasks and missions. Furnishing the RVNAF with all of the officers and manpower demanded by the Vietnamization process required an elaborate network of training installations, skilled instructors, and equipment. Neither the skilled personnel nor good training facilities were available in sufficient numbers to give Vietnamization a chance to succeed. "ARVN remained an inept instrument riddled with political intrigue and corruption."[41]

Another fundamental problem plagued Vietnamization. The backbone of the ARVN was supposed to be its infantry divisions, but these divisions lacked mobility. Each division served in its home area, and most of its personnel were recruited from its home area. Often family and dependents accompanied the soldiers into the field, resulting in hovels and tent cities that appeared alongside division cantonments. The ARVN infantry divisions were essentially static territorial units, unavailable for offensive operations or counterattacks. With soldiers' families clustered around the camps, an enemy attack guaranteed disaster, mass desertions, and incredible confusion as soldiers fled their units to help their wives and relatives to safety.[42]

Although President Nixon did not realize it, Vietnamization rested on a fantasy: that these motley home guards masquerading as maneuver units could be molded into a modern strike force that would be able to hold its own against the disciplined battle-tested units of the NVA. Possibly, with enough time, at least some of the RVNAF deficiencies—its lack of capable officers and noncoms, its lack of skilled manpower, its lack of training facilities, and its lack of maneuverability—could have been corrected. However, irresistible political pressures on Nixon to end U.S. involvement in the war guaranteed that Vietnamization could never have nearly enough time to succeed. "Vietnamization can be seen in its true light—an American self-serving illusion."[43]

THE FAILURE OF PACIFICATION

During 1969 and into 1970, one aspect of nation-building appeared to be flourishing: the accelerated pacification program under the direction of William Colby, who had replaced Robert Komer as head of CORDS. General Abrams strongly backed pacification and deployed U.S. units to help provide village security. General Thieu also enthusiastically supported many pacification programs. Additional villages and hamlets were reclaimed from the VietCong. By the end of 1969, an estimated 80 percent of the rural population lived in secure or relatively secure areas. In many areas of South Vietnam, the threat posed by the insurgency receded. The number of VietCong defectors, both soldiers and cadres, rose significantly.

Project PHOENIX neutralized the VC infrastructure in some areas. Members of the clandestine VC apparatus were identified, imprisoned, often tortured during interrogations, and in many cases, killed. Both the number and quality of the VC/NVA forces appeared to decline. Many villages developed their own local governments and self-defense forces. Traditional village councils were reinstated in many locales. Roads were opened, bridges were repaired, schools were established, and hospitals were built. Thieu instituted a major land reform program called "Land to the Tiller," which reduced the size of maximum holdings and redistributed thousands of hectares of excess lands to landless peasants. New strains of livestock were introduced; peasants received tractors, steel plows, and other modern farm equipment. The rural economy improved; rice production increased in 1969 in South Vietnam for the first time in years.[44]

But a closer look at pacification during its heyday reveals its serious shortcomings and limitations. Much of the so-called progress in various pacification programs derived from inflated or phony statistics compiled by corrupt South Vietnamese bureaucrats. Hence the numbers of villages considered under the control of the South Vietnamese government, the number of VC defectors, the amount of VC infrastructure neutralized, and the number of landless peasants given land were all exaggerated. Pacification efforts from 1969 to1970 suffered from two related problems: First, most programs represented belated efforts to achieve a quick fix. There was never enough time to implement programs designed to provide long-term solutions to fundamental problems. Second, there were never enough honest and competent officials to make these programs work. Pacification programs were always vitiated by the corruption and incompetence that riddled the South Vietnamese bureaucracies.[45]

On the battlefield, the scale and intensity of fighting declined during 1969. General Abrams shifted U.S. strategy from large-scale search-and-destroy operations to small-unit patrolling and pacification. Because Hanoi deliberately avoided large-scale combat, General Abrams assigned more of his forces to the tasks of pacification and to the support, training, and advisory missions involved in preparing the RVNAF forces to take over responsibility for defending themselves. The MACV commander also dismantled his divisions, breaking them down into small platoon and company-sized task forces in order to assign them patrol, reconnaissance, and territorial security missions. He ordered small-scale offensives mounted against enemy basing areas near the DMZ and along the Laotian and Cambodian borders. These offensives attacked NVA supply depots and supply lines; their objective was to attrite the enemy's logistics system and thereby keep them on the defensive.

General Abrams succeeded in uniting the disparate dimensions of the U.S. war effort in Vietnam. He fused the war of attrition, previously a big-unit war aimed at destroying enemy bases and personnel, with Vietnamization and nation-building. For the first time since the American war in Vietnam had begun, U.S. forces implemented an integrated strategy. They were fighting one war now instead of two.[46]

Most of the fighting in the Vietnam War after 1969 consisted of small-unit combat occurring in the more remote and sparsely populated regions of South Vietnam, involving South Vietnamese and North Vietnamese forces. Because they retained the tactical initiative, the NVA forces usually controlled the scale and tempo of the fighting. They initiated most of the combat and usually inflicted heavier casualties on the South Vietnamese forces than they incurred. American battle deaths decreased sharply in 1969; but RVNAF casualties remained high.[47]

HAMBURGER HILL

One of the most notorious battles of the American Vietnam war occurred in late spring 1969. It has passed into history as the Battle of Hamburger Hill, a name apparently provided by one of the soldiers who had to fight it. In March, the MACV intelligence officers had noted that the NVA forces were again building up their logistics systems in the forbidding A Shau Valley, ostensibly preparing for offensive operations in I Corps. General Zais's "Screaming Eagles," the 101st Airborne (Air Mobile), were ordered back into the area to destroy them.

During April and early May, soldiers from units of the 101st that had been helilifted into the A Shau Valley found several new supply caches and other evidence of a PAVN logistical buildup taking place in the area.[48] On May 10, a combined force of U.S. Marines and the 101st Airborne's 3rd Brigade, 187th Infantry air assaulted into a rugged area of thickly jungled mountains along the west side of the A Shau Valley near the Laotian border. The next day, soldiers in B Company of the 187th Infantry discovered that the NVA forces had fortified a series of ridges cloaked in thick jungle. These ridges appeared on American maps as Hill 937. Hill 937 was known to the Vietnamese as Dong Ap Bia (Mount Ap Bia). As B Company troops advanced up the slopes of Dong Ap Bia, they were hit by concentrated machine-gun fire coming from enemy bunkers dug into the crests of the montane ridges. B Company was forced to withdraw; artillery and air strikes were called in to pound the NVA positions. Thus began a fierce 10-day battle for Dong Ap Bia, which Americans would soon know as Hamburger Hill.[49]

On May 13, two companies of the 187th's 1st Battalion tried to take the hill, only to be driven back by withering rocket and machine-gun fire from the bunker occupants, two battalions of the 29th NVA Regiment. The men of the 187th were reinforced, and they attacked again, only to be driven back once more. There was a pause in the fighting while the enemy bunkers were subjected to intensive artillery fire and air strikes for 36 hours. On May 18, two battalions made another assault of the hill, one going up the southern slope, the other up the northern slope. The weather halted this attack. Heavy rains had turned the hillside, denuded of foliage by the artillery fire and bombing, into mud. The soldiers, as they tried to advance up the mountain, kept slipping and sliding back down the slopes. Finally, on May 20, following another sustained artillery and air bombardment of the enemy positions, a four-battalion force reached the crest of Dong Ap Bia, only to discover that the NVA troops had abandoned the bunkers. They had slipped away during the night. A few days after the hill had been taken, orders came down to abandon it.

The Battle of Hamburger Hill received extensive press coverage and quickly ignited public controversy. The men of the 101st had fought hard and taken heavy casualties for a objective that was quickly abandoned. Many troopers bitterly criticized the command decision that had required the seemingly pointless sacrifice of many men. Journalists vetted the soldier's complaints. Senator Edward Kennedy of Massachusetts called the battle "senseless and irresponsible."[50] General Zais defended the action; he stated that the 101st Airborne's mission had been to seek out the enemy and destroy them wherever they were found. Zais pointed out that the enemy had lost an estimated 650 KIA during the 10-day fight, whereas U.S. battle deaths at Dong Ap Bia totalled 56, a kill ratio of better than 10 to one.[51]

Figure 8.3   Troops of the 101st Airbourne Division jump out of a helicopter to assist in fighting at Dong Ap Bia, which became known as "Hamburger Hill," 5/18/69. *Source:* Center of Military History, U.S. Army.

Hamburger Hill turned out to be the last campaign of the now-abandoned attrition strategy, and it was also the last battle of the Vietnam War in which victory was determined by a body count. In reaction to the controversy aroused by the battle, President Nixon ordered General Abrams to hold down American casualties in future battles. At the heart of the controversy over Hamburger Hill were not so much questions of tactics or casualties, but of what kind of war Americans were now waging in Vietnam and for what goals. The conflict was no longer a war of search and destroy, of attrition. It had mutated into a war based on a new strategy of small-unit warfare aimed at destroying enemy logistics systems, fused with pacification and nation-building efforts. The Battle of Hamburger Hill had occurred during the transitional period.

An Army in Decline

"Not only were American troops leaving South Vietnam, but the offensive spirit was leaving the American army."[52] The bitterness expressed by some of the soldiers of the 101st Airborne over the fighting at Dong Ap Bia was a sign that America was beginning to reap a bitter harvest from its lengthy and inconclusive war in Southeast Asia—the progressive demoralization of the U.S. Army ground forces serving in Vietnam. Until 1968, the U.S. armed forces in Vietnam had fought well. The army that America sent to fight the Vietnam War was the best the nation ever had and was undoubtedly the best army in the world. The troops were the healthiest, the most intelligent, the best educated, and the best trained in U.S. military history. They were equipped with powerful and effective high-tech weapons, and they were supported by a remarkable logistics system that made them the best-fed and best-supplied soldiers in the history of warfare. Wounded soldiers received better medical treatment quicker than any soldiers who had ever fought a war. They were led by competent professionals at all levels, from sergeants to generals. Troops fought aggressively, with great tenacity, in pursuit of their objectives. Their morale was high, their discipline taut. They believed in the cause for which they fought, and they remained confident of victory. They won every major battle they fought, and they nearly always inflicted far heavier casualties on their enemies than they sustained.

The decline of the American army that began in 1968 and got progressively worse in 1969, 1970, and 1971 was caused by a multiplicity of factors and circumstances.[53] Nixon's Vietnamization policy was a major cause of the breakdown in morale and discipline. The President emphasized his commitment to seeking a negotiated peace, of not trying to win a military victory. U.S. troop withdrawals reinforced the notion that America was pursuing a no-win policy in a war that would probably end soon for the United States. Soldiers began asking themselves, Why fight? Why get wounded or killed in a war that Washington is not trying to win? A sardonic rhetorical question gained wide currency after 1969: Who wants to be the last soldier to die in Vietnam? As they watched U.S. troops being pulled out of Vietnam, many soldiers cared only about surviving their year in "'Nam" and returning to the "real world" (the United States) alive. "Shorttimer's fever," especially among soldiers with a few weeks to go on their year's tour, had become widespread by 1969. Its symptoms included an acute fear of being killed or seriously wounded, a reluctance to engage in combat, a generally poor performance of all duties, a rebellious attitude toward military authority, and withdrawal from social activities with buddies.

By 1969, the class-biased Selective Service had delivered an army of conscripts to Vietnam, who were pulled out of predominantly lower-middle-class, working-class, and disadvantaged backgrounds. The fact that most middle-class and upper-middle-class youths were avoiding the war was itself a source of resentment and declining morale among the troops in the field. The soldiers manning rifle companies in Vietnam understood the price they were paying for being poor and poorly educated, without employable skills, and for possessing no political clout. They had to fight a war that most of their more affluent countrymen were avoiding. It also appeared to them that they had been drafted to fight a war that a majority of their fellow Americans no longer believed in, and that their government no longer was trying to win.[54]

By 1969, the quality of both the officer and noncommissioned officer corps had declined. In 1965, the officer corps had been made up mainly of career professionals and Reserve Officer Training Corps (ROTC) graduates. The unpopularity of the Vietnam War caused a severe reduction in ROTC enrollments, and, by 1969, dozens of

ROTC programs had been expelled from college campuses. To make up the shortages, the U.S. Army was forced to turn to Officer Candidate School (OCS) products, who generally possessed lower educational attainments and leadership abilities.

The noncommissioned officer corps had severe shortages of experienced sergeants by 1969. Promising young privates were hurried through twenty weeks of stateside advanced training and given sergeants' stripes. These young, inexperienced buck and staff sergeants, called "Instant NCOs" or "shake'n'bakes," were then rushed to Vietnam and thrown into combat. Platoons of "grunts" (the most frequently used nickname that Army and Marine combat infantrymen gave themselves) sometimes found themselves going into combat led by 22-year-old second lieutenants who were just out of OCS and inexperienced 20-year-old "shake'n'bake" sergeants who had just arrived from Stateside.[55]

Army personnel practices during the Vietnam War era exacerbated problems created by assigning young and inexperienced officers and noncoms to combat units. The Army wanted to build up a large pool of officers with combat experience; captains and majors were given six-month tours as company and battalion commanders. Many of these inexperienced officers proved to be ineffective leaders in combat; sometimes their mistakes cost soldiers fighting under their commands their lives. Just about the time these officers had acquired battlefield experience and were becoming effective leaders, they were reassigned to rear-echelon desk jobs to complete their year's duty in Vietnam. Because of the constant turnover in the company and battalion commander positions, there was an instability in these critical leadership positions. Worse, some of these officers were concerned only with advancing their careers, with "getting their tickets punched." These officers did not care about the welfare of the men they were assigned to lead. When ordering the men under their commands to fight, they hovered over the battlefield in command helicopters, safely above the fray. Soldiers sometimes refused to put their lives on the line for officers whose principal combat goal appeared to be compiling a good dossier.[56]

The growing unpopularity of the war and the activities of antiwar protesters also undermined the morale of soldiers serving in Vietnam. Grunts loathed college antiwar protesters, viewing them as a privileged class of cowards and traitors. But the knowledge that millions of Americans no longer believed in the war or supported it with any enthusiasm caused resentment and confusion among many troops, who came to doubt the purpose of the war and whether the sacrifices they were making were worthwhile or even appreciated. They felt abandoned by a nation that was abandoning the war that they still had to fight. By 1969, some soldiers serving in Vietnam had turned against the war and wore the symbols of the stateside antiwar protesters, love beads and peace medallions, on their uniforms. Some soldiers grew their hair long and sprouted full beards, in violation of military dress and appearance codes that increasingly went unenforced in the field. Soldiers sometimes saluted one another with the two-fingered peace sign.[57]

The Army's switch from aggressive big-unit search-and-destroy missions to small-scale holding actions in support of Vietnamization and pacification in 1969 also undermined soldiers' morale and discipline. They grew reluctant to expose themselves to danger on operations they knew were only intended to buy time until the South Vietnamese took over and the Americans went home. "Search-and-evade" operations were added to the tactical repertoires of some squads and platoons. Soldiers sent on patrols were careful to search only areas where they knew the enemy would not be found. Sometimes they did not patrol at all, and they filed a faked report of a search that never took place. Combat refusals increased in 1969 and became more frequent in 1970 and 1971.[58] The cumbersome and overloaded military justice system could not handle the increasing incidence of combat refusals in Vietnam. Punishment for refusing a lawful order to fight was often left to field commanders, who in many cases meted out light punishments or ignored the incidents.

From 1969 on, the U.S. Army appeared to be at war with itself. As morale and discipline ebbed, as search-and-evade tactics and combat refusals increased in frequency, both officers and noncoms who took an aggressive approach to combat or who strictly enforced rules and regulations risked reprisals, even assassinations, at the hands of rebellious troops. Such assassinations had occurred in previous wars, but never so frequently as in the latter years of the American war in Vietnam. A new term came into use: "fragging." The word derived from the use of the fragmentation grenade, a weapon that was readily available, easy to use, and left no fingerprints or other incriminating evidence when used to kill an unpopular officer or a noncom. The Army reported 96 fragging incidents in 1969 and 209 incidents in 1970. In those two years, 75 officers and noncoms lost their lives to assassins who in most cases were never apprehended. Court martials were held in fewer than 10 percent of fragging cases because of the lack of evidence and witnesses. Most soldiers who committed fraggings in Vietnam literally got away with murder.[59]

In addition to fragging, racial violence occasionally racked military installations in Vietnam. By 1969, Army life in Vietnam had become a racial pressure cooker. Many African American soldiers, angry over the discrimination and prejudice they had encountered in civilian society and in the Army, often denounced white attitudes and sometimes denounced whites as well. Whites frequently replied in kind. Some black soldiers, influenced by black nationalist doctrines, developed an African American style of appearance and behavior that white officers, often Southerners with traditional racial attitudes, found threatening. Racial animosity was generally suppressed in combat situations, but in rear basing areas racial enmities sometimes exploded. Race riots, even racially motivated firefights, occurred.[60] Black-white racial conflict was a social pathology that the Army inherited from the civilian society it served.

Desertion was another indicator of decline. Thousands of Vietnam-era soldiers deserted in 1969, 1970, and 1971. Desertions were comparatively rare in combat areas, and very few American soldiers defected to the enemy. Neither the VietCong nor the NVA forces encouraged American soldiers to desert, nor did either usually offer deserters sanctuary.[61] The Communists wanted the Americans to get out of their country, not to join them.

But for every soldier who deserted, many more troops tried to escape through psychological withdrawal by using drugs. By 1969, drug abuse had become a serious problem for the Army in Vietnam. A Defense Department survey conducted in 1969 found that about 25 percent of U.S. soldiers serving in Vietnam were using marijuana.[62] Far worse, U.S. troops began using hard drugs in late 1969 and early 1970, particularly heroin. The heroin came from the mountainous region stretching across northern Laos, northern Thailand, and northeastern Burma, from an area known as the Golden Triangle.[63] High-grade heroin, 80 to 90 percent pure, flowed into South Vietnam via illicit conduits controlled by high officials in the South Vietnamese government. These officials garnered huge profits from selling the severely addictive drug to American GIs. After trying unsuccessfully to get the South Vietnamese police to curtail the flow of drugs, U.S. officials tacitly accepted the South Vietnamese officials' involvement in drug operations. South Vietnamese pushers aggressively sold the nearly pure heroin to soldiers for $2 to $3 a vial, a fraction of the price that diluted heroin sold for on the streets of American cities. By 1970, an estimated 7 percent of U.S. soldiers in Vietnam used heroin regularly; by 1971, between 10 and 15 percent. The Army discovered that it had a heroin plague on its hands, with an estimated 25,000 to 37,000 addicted users.[64]

The gleaming American sword, honed to a keen edge, which had been thrust into South Vietnam in 1965, had become dull and corroded by 1971. The confusions inherent in Nixon's Vietnamization policy, the class-biased conscription system, the decline in the quality of officers and noncommissioned officers, dubious Army personnel policies, the antiwar movement and declining domestic public support for the war, racial tensions, and the contagion of drug use had combined to undermine morale, erode discipline, abrade unit cohesion, and sap the Army's fighting spirit. Other branches of the U.S. Armed Forces serving in Southeast Asia—the Navy, the Air Force, the Marines, and the Coast Guard—also experienced declining discipline and morale, racial conflict, and drug abuse but on much smaller scales. One of the reasons Nixon accelerated the recall of American forces from Vietnam in 1970 and 1971, over the protests of General Abrams and General Thieu, was because of his awareness that the U.S. fighting machine in South Vietnam was disintegrating. It became necessary to remove the Army in order to save it.

WIDENING THE WAR: CAMBODIA

During the spring of 1970, Nixon had to confront the contradictions inherent in his Vietnam War strategy. At home he faced declining popular support for his policies, rising congressional opposition, and more peace demonstrations. Negotiations in Paris remained sterile. Vietnamization proceeded slowly. To appease domestic dissent, Nixon announced a phased withdrawal of 150,000 troops from Vietnam over the next 12 months. Both General Abrams and General Thieu strongly protested the size of Nixon's proposed troop withdrawal. They insisted it would leave the RVN vulnerable to

VC/NVA attacks and that it would retard both Vietnamization and nation-building. The Vietnamese were not consulted, either for planning or implementing Vietnamization. Although President Nixon publicly announced that General Thieu had recommended the proposed U.S. troop withdrawals, Thieu had strongly opposed them. The South Vietnamese leaders, having no choice, reluctantly went along with Vietnamization; they saw it for what it was, a political expedient for the United States. Some Vietnamese dismissed Vietnamization as a U.S. Dollar and Vietnamese Blood Sharing Plan. Most saw it as a fig leaf to cover U.S. abandonment.[65]

Both Nixon and Kissinger also knew that accelerated American troop withdrawals could only stiffen Hanoi's resolve to make no concessions at Paris and to wait until all of the Americans had been forced to leave South Vietnam. On the battlefield, the NVA continued their patient defensive strategy of protracted small-scale warfare. Only when most Americans had departed would General Giap shift to the offensive and move in to destroy the South Vietnamese forces and eliminate the Saigon government.

But an event occurred that caught both Washington and Hanoi by surprise, and it changed the shape of the Vietnam War. The neutralist leader of Cambodia, Prince Norodom Sihanouk, was overthrown by his pro–Western Prime Minister General Lon Nol on March 18, 1970. For years, the Cambodian leader had been able to spare his country and its people from the conflict by accommodating both sides. But with his overthrow, Cambodia's delicate charade of neutrality would soon be replaced by murderous involvement in war.

Sihanouk had come to power in 1954 after leading the nationalist movement that drove out the French. He followed a neutralist line in the Cold War. Neutrality enabled him to extract economic and military aid from both the United States and the Communist powers. For years, Sihanouk kept his small nation at peace and preserved its independence by playing the Chinese Communists and the North Vietnamese off against the Americans and the South Vietnamese.

During the early 1960s, as the United States got more deeply involved in southern Vietnam, Cambodian neutrality took an anti-American tack and tilted toward the Communists. Sihanouk rejected American offers of military aid in 1963 and severed diplomatic relations with the United States in 1965. He allowed the NVA to establish bases in the Cambodian provinces bordering South Vietnam, and he also granted Hanoi the use of the port of Sihanoukville from which they supplied their forces fighting in the southern half of South Vietnam. Trucks and bicycles carried war materiels from the Cambodian port city to staging areas along the Cambodian—South Vietnamese border. In exchange for these privileges, the North Vietnamese looked the other way when Sihanouk used his army to brutally suppress an indigenous Communist insurgency called the Khmer Rouge in 1966. As North Vietnam infiltrated more men and supplies into South Vietnam along the Ho Chi Minh Trail complex, they extended the routes across eastern Cambodia. This region became a vital part of their extended war in the South. Even though neutral Cambodia had become an accomplice in the North Vietnamese war against South Vietnam, Sihanouk allowed American and ARVN forces on occasion to pursue fleeing VC/NVA forces into Cambodia. Sihanouk also tolerated the secret American bombing of the NVA bases and sanctuaries in Cambodia that Nixon initiated in March 1969.[66]

Although caught by surprise, Nixon and Kissinger welcomed the overthrow of Sihanouk, whose behavior had become increasingly erratic; also, Sihanouk's control of events had slipped, and his neutrality policy had become increasingly anti-American in tone. Washington quickly recognized the Lon Nol government and extended U.S. military and economic assistance to Cambodia. The United States also approved South Vietnamese cross-border raids into Cambodia. Lon Nol barred Hanoi from further access to the port of Sihanoukville. He also ordered the Communists to vacate their bases on Cambodian soil and to get out of his country.

Determined to stay in regions that were crucial to the conduct of its war in South Vietnam, Hanoi solidified its control over its Cambodian sanctuaries. NVA forces drove west into Cambodia toward the capital of Phnom Penh to overthrow the Lon Nol government. A CIA report to President Nixon warned that the Communist forces could overthrow the new Cambodian regime. Without strong U.S. action, a domino might fall in Southeast Asia. With Cambodia in Communist hands, the port at Sihanoukville would be reopened and the entire country would become an enemy basing area outflanking the Allied forces in South Vietnam. "The United States had to intervene in Cambodia decisively or see the war change dramatically for the worse."[67]

The deposed Sihanouk quickly cast his lot with the Chinese Communists. From Beijing, he called for the overthrow of Lon Nol's "illegal" regime, for a Pathet Lao victory in Laos, and for a VC/NVA victory in South Vietnam. In Paris, Kissinger met privately with Le Duc Tho, a member of the North Vietnamese Politburo who had replaced Xuan Thuy as Hanoi's chief negotiator in the secret talks. In conversations with Kissinger, Le Duc Tho made it clear that Hanoi had linked the overthrow of Lon Nol's government with the ongoing revolutionary war in South Vietnam. Within Cambodia, to enhance their campaign to overthrow the Lon Nol government, China and Hanoi backed the Khmer Rouge, which had revived in the late 1960s following Sihanouk's efforts to suppress it.[68]

Reacting to the widening war, Nixon believed that the time had come for the United States to make a decisive move in Indochina. For years, MACV, backed by the Joint Chiefs, had called for ground invasions of Cambodia to destroy the VC/NVA border sanctuaries. Johnson had consistently denied the Joint Chiefs' requests because he did not want to widen the war. But Nixon decided that it was now time to go after the sanctuaries. The major targets were 14 North Vietnamese staging areas, which had been off-limits to U.S. and ARVN forces. Two areas were to be attacked: the Parrot's Beak, a section of Cambodian land that jutted into South Vietnam to a point only 30 miles west of Saigon, and the Fishhook, a point of land lying 55 miles northwest of Saigon. The president approved General Abrams's proposal that U.S. forces attack the Fishhook area, while the ARVN forces, supported by U.S. air strikes, would attack the sanctuaries in the Parrot's Beak.[69]

Nixon's decision to send U.S. forces into Cambodia was one of the most controversial actions of his presidency. He sent in the troops to serve a variety of strategic, political, and diplomatic purposes. They would shore up Lon Nol's regime and help keep Cambodia out of Communist hands. They would buy more time for Vietnamization to work in South Vietnam. Nixon decided that the strategic advantages to be gained from the Cambodian incursion outweighed its political liabilities, particularly the domestic controversy he anticipated would be aroused by the action. He also hoped the invasion would put pressure on Hanoi to consider negotiations as an alternative to facing a wider war. Further, Nixon intended to send the Communist leaders a message that he would not be bound by the self-imposed limits of his predecessor; he may have also wished to keep Hanoi guessing about what he might do next.

Nixon also placed the Cambodian crisis in a larger context. He saw it as one of those decisive moments in the Cold War when the will and character of the American people and its leaders were being tested by events and by their enemies. Nixon vowed to meet the challenge; he would show his mettle in the ongoing struggle between the Communist world and the Free World. Nixon was determined to maintain American credibility with both U.S. friends and foes.[70] It was time for the big play that might bring victory in the big game.

Nixon announced his decision to invade Cambodia, and he explained the reasons for the incursion in a televised speech given to the American people on the evening of April 30, 1970. He stated that the invasion did not represent a change in American policy or direction, that it was not an effort to widen the war; rather, it was to protect and facilitate Vietnamization. Nixon claimed the invasion was necessary to save a friendly government from Communist aggression, and that it was necessary to protect U.S. forces still remaining in South Vietnam after the scheduled withdrawal of another 150,000 troops. He also told Americans that one of the major reasons for the invasion was to capture COSVN, the PLAF command center for South Vietnam, located in the Fishhook area of Cambodia. Nixon's tone throughout his speech was belligerent and provocative. In a fighting mood, he defied his critics in the press, the academies, and the Congress: "I would rather be a one-term president than be a two-term president at the cost of seeing America accept the first defeat in its proud 190-years' history." He concluded his speech with some vintage Nixonian Cold War hyperbole: "If, when the chips are down, the world's most powerful nation acts like a pitiful, helpless giant, the forces of totalitarianism and anarchy will threaten free nations and free institutions throughout the world."[71]

As the MACV staffers planned the Cambodian campaigns to destroy the enemy bases in the areas of the Fishhook and Parrot's Beak, and any enemy troops that might try to defend them, they knew that many American combat units had already redeployed to the United States or were scheduled to be redeployed soon. The Cambodian incursion would be the last opportunity for the Allies to mount a large-scale combat operation involving American assets. It would also put the ARVN units to the ultimate test of combat against enemy forces on a foreign battlefield. The Cambodian invasion would therefore furnish an excellent opportunity to measure the progress that Vietnamization had achieved to date.[72]

On April 29, 1970, the ARVN forces, with U.S. air and artillery support, penetrated the Parrot's Beak area. They captured some enemy supplies, but most of the enemy forces in the region eluded the invaders. On May 1, following artillery barrages and heavy bombing by B-52s, a task force of 15,000 U.S. and ARVN armored and infantry battalions entered the Fishhook region accompanied by helicopter gunships and fighter-bomber strike aircraft. The operation was code-named Toan Thang 43. It was the largest operation involving U.S. forces in a over a year. The fighting was not intensive because the VC/NVA forces chose to abandon their bases and supply depots in the region rather than stand and fight against overwhelming forces. Further, the U.S. forces operated in Cambodia under tight ground rules. They had orders to travel no farther than nineteen miles beyond the Vietnamese border, and U.S. commanders had been told to keep U.S. casualties down. The Americans also had orders to be out of Cambodia by June 30.[73]

All U.S. forces had withdrawn from Cambodia by June 29. Operation Toan Thang 43 had been successful. Large quantities of enemy ammunition, weapons, and rice had either been captured or destroyed. All enemy installations and basing facilities had been destroyed. The COSVN operations had been disrupted. But most of the main enemy units had avoided battle. They had retreated to the interior and survived intact.

The pressure on Lon Nol's forces had been eased, and the Cambodian army had gained time to build up its strength. An endangered domino was saved for a time, but the temporary U.S. incursion could not remove the long-run threat to Lon Nol's survival posed by the Khmer Rouge. The VC/NVA losses of men, facilities, weapons, and supplies, plus the closing of the port at Sihanoukville, probably set back their offensive timetable 12 to 15 months. The Cambodian incursion bought time for Vietnamization, for the staged withdrawal of U.S. forces from South Vietnam, and for pacification and nation-building programs. It also put increased pressures on the Ho Chi Minh Trail because it was the sole remaining source of supply for the VC/NVA forces fighting in southern South Vietnam. The Cambodian invasions also eased the danger to the remaining American forces in Vietnam.

But the Allies failed to inflict a decisive defeat on the VC/NVA forces; they disrupted but did not end their use of Cambodian territory.[74] The U.S.-ARVN military intervention also drove the North Vietnamese forces deeper into Cambodia where they joined the growing Khmer Rouge insurgency, thus setting in motion a tragic chain of events that would lead to the fall of the Lon Nol government and to the worst atrocities of the Second Indochina War.

But the gains the Americans and South Vietnamese made from Toan Thang 43 were largely offset by the liabilities of a wider war in Southeast Asia. Even though Nixon had committed himself to winding down the American war in Vietnam, he had expanded the theater of military operations to include another country. Further, the United States had acquired another fragile client in Indochina. Nixon had committed

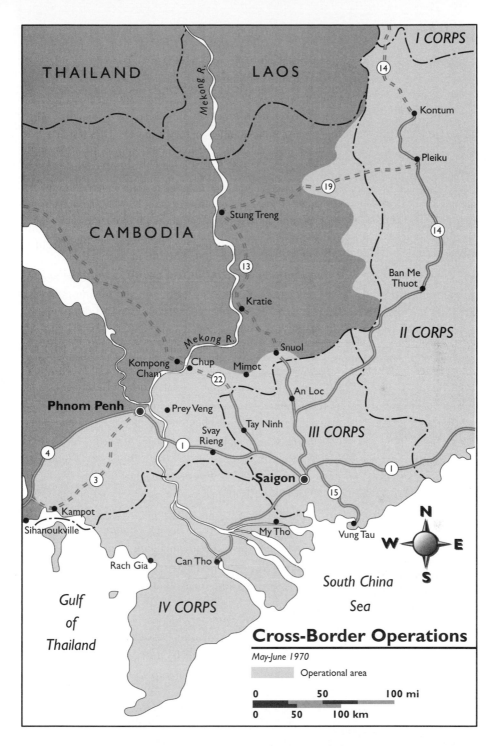

Figure 8.4 Map of the Cross-Border Operations, May-June 1970. *Source:* Public domain.

significant U.S. economic and military resources to help Cambodia defend itself against the VC/NVA and Khmer Rouge attacks, at the same time that he was pulling U.S. forces out of South Vietnam. The American Vietnam war had been expanded; it had become the Second Indochina War. It now encompassed Vietnam, Laos, and Cambodia.

Although American aviators and armored units involved in the Cambodian incursion had fought aggressively when they had the opportunity, some U.S. infantry companies indulged in search-and-evade tactics to avoid combat during Toan Thang 43. One company briefly refused a direct order from its commanding officer to march down a road thought to be infested with enemy soldiers. Most ARVN units involved in the Cambodian incursions performed ineffectively. They failed to fight aggressively. Their armored units developed severe problems because they lacked competent maintenance personnel and sufficient spare parts. They had persistent command and control problems. For example, they failed to coordinate artillery fire with their mobile operations and had to rely on U.S. artillery. Insofar as the Cambodia operation had been a test of Vietnamization, ARVN flunked the test. That failure had ominous implications for the future survival of South Vietnam. After all of the Americans had departed, the GVN would have to face its foes alone.[75]

Figure 8.5 The helicopter war. The Vietnam War was the first in which helicopters were used extensively to airlift troops into combat. Here, riflemen of the U.S. First Air Cavalry Division prepare to board a squadron of "Hueys" (Bell UH-1Ds) at Lai Khe, South Vietnam, for an assault on An Loc, June 13, 1972. *Source:* CORBIS. Neg # BE045823.

CAMBODIAN SPRING

In addition to its many consequences for the Indochina War, the Cambodian incursion had many domestic impacts. It accentuated the growing dissatisfaction with the pace of U.S. troop withdrawals, aroused mistrust of the Nixon administration, brought into the open the latent issue of executive authority to make war, and triggered waves of demonstrations that reverberated for months. Antiwar activists took to the streets, and scores of college campuses from Maryland to California erupted in demonstrations, all protesting the sudden widening of a war that the President had promised to phase out quickly. Most were peaceful, some were not. ROTC buildings were bombed or torched on many campuses, including Yale and the University of Wisconsin. On May 1, President Nixon made some incendiary remarks that infuriated virtually everyone opposing or protesting the war. He referred to those antiwar activists who were "blowing up the campuses" as "these bums."[76] On May 2, radical students at Yale issued a call for a nationwide student strike to demand an immediate U.S. withdrawal from Vietnam.

At Kent State University antiwar protests wrought terrible consequences. On May 1, a crowd of about 500 students gathered at the center of campus to protest the invasion of Cambodia and to denounce President Nixon. That night, thousands of students converged on downtown Kent. Fist fights broke out among patrons at a downtown bar. Soon a riotous mob rampaged through the downtown area, trashing storefronts and smashing windows. Police in riot gear fired tear gas at the rioters and drove them back to the campus. The mayor of Kent declared a state of emergency and requested help from the Ohio National Guard. During the night, the ROTC building on campus was burned. Next day, Troop G of the National Guard moved in to occupy the campus. At a press conference held on May 3, Governor James Rhodes vowed to eradicate the "Communist elements" on the Kent State campus. On May 4, at about noon, following hours of confrontations between students and troops, the Guardsmen suddenly aimed their rifles at a crowd of students, and fired off 61 rounds of live ammunition. When the indiscriminate shooting stopped, four students lay dead and nine had been wounded. Victims included protesters and bystanders; one of the students killed was a young woman on her way to class who walked into the line of fire.[77]

The Kent State killings ignited anger and intensified the anguish over the war and its domestic effects. During the next several weeks over 4 million of the nation's students participated in protest demonstrations against the Cambodian invasion, the killings at Kent State, and President Nixon's war policies. During the "Cambodian spring," nearly half of the nation's colleges and universities recorded protests. About a fifth of the nation's campuses were forced to shut down, some for a few days, and some for the remainder of the spring semester. Governor Ronald Reagan ordered the multicampus University of California system to close for a week. Most protests were peaceful, but some colleges reported signicant violence. On May 6, police shot and wounded several SUNY-Buffalo students and fired tear gas cannisters into campus dormitories. On May

Figure 8.6 Tragedy struck at Kent State University on May 4, 1970. Troops of the Ohio National Guard fired into a crowd of student protesters, killing four. This photo shows a young woman reacting to the death of one of the students. *Source:* CORBIS. Neg.#: BE021214.

14, state police and National Guardsman shot and killed two students in their dorm at Jackson State University in Mississippi. The Cambodian invasion, coupled with the killings on the Kent State campus, had provoked the most massive protests in the history of American higher education.[78]

One of the more bizarre incidents of the Vietnam War era occurred during the weeks of demonstrations and protests that followed the Cambodian invasion and the killings at Kent State. On May 8, more than 100,000 young protesters descended on the nation's capital. That night, President Nixon, unable to sleep and distraught over the outrage his actions in Cambodia had caused, had a driver take him to the Lincoln Memorial where some of the students who had come to Washington were camped out. It was about 4:40 A.M. when the president arrived. Earnestly trying to communicate with those young people, he rambled on about sports, global travel, racial tensions, and his own student days during the 1930s at Whittier College. The students, perhaps too sleepy or too stunned to engage the president of the United States in a dialogue about the Vietnam War, mostly listened. Within about an hour, White House aides, alerted to his whereabouts, arrived and led him away.[79]

Antiwar rallies occurred in other cities. Antidraft actions commonly occurred at various Selective Service sites. Bombs were set off at various federal government installations and military recruitment centers. A bank in Isla Vista, a suburban community near the Santa Barbara branch of the University of California, was burned to the ground. An Army research center on the campus of the University of Wisconsin was bombed.[80] These random terrorist acts represented a kind of chaotic guerrilla warfare being waged against the American war machine by campus-based radicals.

The outbreak of antiwar opposition during May 1970 provoked a backlash among supporters of the administration's war policy. On May 8, construction workers in New York City beat up antiwar demonstrators in New York's financial district. Two weeks later, the head of the New York Labor Council led an estimated 100,000 union members on a march through Manhattan supporting the invasion of Cambodia and denouncing antiwar demonstrators. The "hard hats" waved American flags and sang "God Bless America" as they strode along the streets of New York. Trade unionists in other cities organized rallies and parades in support of the war. A grateful president held a well-publicized meeting at the White House where he warmly received union leaders who supported his war policies.

This eruption of prowar support revealed the class divisions among Americans, which had been exacerbated by the Indochina War. Antiwar activists were recruited mainly from the ranks of the educated middle- and upper-middle classes.[81] Prowar activists mostly came from the ranks of the hardhats, from young men who embraced traditional patriotic ideals and moral values. It pitted those who worked with their hands against those who worked with their minds, the proletariats against the professionals, or aspiring professionals. It was evident by 1970 that many of the sons and daughters of the Establishment had turned against the war while most members of the working classes continued to support it.

The Cambodian invasion also provoked dissent within the Nixon administration and an outburst of Congressional criticism. For the first time, it appeared that Congress might seriously challenge the President's power to wage war in Indochina. Content since the rise of the Cold War to let presidents control foreign and strategic policy, the Senate, being the more dovish branch of Congress, voted to repeal the Gulf of Tonkin resolution.

Many senators believed the resolution had served as a retroactive declaration of war. The Senate's gesture was purely symbolic, however. President Nixon claimed he possessed the authority to wage war based on the war powers clause of the Constitution, and no one challenged him. The Senate also enacted the Church-Cooper amendment, which cut off all funding for military operations in Cambodia, effective on June 30, 1970.[82] The House of Representatives failed to enact the Church-Cooper amendment; hence, it never became law. Republican Senator Mark Hatfield and his Democratic colleague George McGovern introduced an amendment to a military appropriations bill that would have cut off all funding for U.S. military operations in Indochina at the end of the year. It also failed to pass.

None of these congressional actions in 1970 seriously impeded the president's power to wage war, but as harbingers of rising congressional opposition, these actions

Figure 8.7   Construction workers wave flags and anti-Lindsay signs in a demonstration near City Hall in New York City on May 5, 1970. Participants had been angered by New York City Mayor John Lindsay's antiwar sympathies. *Source:* AP/Wide World Photos.

increased the pressure on Nixon and Kissinger to find a way to phase out the American war in Indochina or risk having Congress end it for them. Clearly, the public and congressional responses to the Cambodian invasion had reduced President Nixon's options. Domestic politics prevented finding any new missions for U.S. combat forces and increased the pressure on the Administration to end the war.[83]

Nixon was neither inclined toward nor capable of reconciling his critics. Instead, he attacked them, hard. He accused his congressional critics of prolonging the war and told them that if they restricted his war-making powers, they would be responsible for an American defeat in Indochina. Nixon empowered the FBI, the CIA, and military intelligence agencies to use illegal surveillance techniques against radical antiwar groups.[84] By the summer of 1970, the Nixon White House was exhibiting many of the attributes of a beleaguered fortress. The president and the president's men increasingly held the partisan and perhaps paranoiac view that it was them against all of the administration's enemies in the media, the Congress, the universities, and the antiwar movement, who were trying to undermine Nixon's power to govern.

As the embattled president confronted the firestorm of protest provoked by the Cambodian incursion, any hope that he may have held out for breaking the diplomatic deadlock at Paris was dashed. If the Cambodian operation had been intended to pressure the North Vietnamese into making concessions, then it had the precisely opposite effect of hardening Hanoi's position. The North Vietnamese and NLF delegates walked out of the Paris talks in protest over the American invasion of Cambodia and refused to return until all U.S. troops were pulled out of Cambodia. Le Duc Tho broke off the secret talks with Henry Kissinger. Nixon's announced withdrawal of 150,000 more American forces in April, coupled with the uproar provoked in the United States by the Cambodian incursion, only strengthened Hanoi's determination to continue stalling the negotiations until domestic political pressures forced Nixon to withdraw all U.S. forces from Indochina. Kissinger offered another peace proposal at Paris, a cease-fire in place, to try to move the talks forward, but Hanoi promptly rejected it.[85]

As the fall 1970 midterm elections approached, Nixon campaigned energetically against his Democratic Congressional critics and denounced the antiwar protesters wherever he campaigned. The hard-pressed administration viewed the elections as an opportunity to rally support for Vietnamization and defeat many of Nixon's prominent dovish Congressional critics. Nixon hoped to replace the doves with new people who would support his policies. Vice President Agnew also took to the hustings to campaign energetically against the Nixon administration's numerous opponents. During the two weeks that he actively campaigned, Nixon repeatedly attacked the radical antiwar demonstrators. At a rally in San Jose, California, the president, spotting a large group of young antiwar protesters in the parking lot outside of the auditorium where he had just spoken, climbed onto the hood of his limousine. He extended his arms over his head, flashing the "V-for-Victory" sign.[86]

But Nixon and Agnew's efforts to strengthen administrative support in Congress mostly failed. A few prominent senatorial doves lost, but so did a few hawks. There were not many changes in the House of Representatives either, but even the small changes were not good news for the Nixon White House. Of the 12 congressmen who lost their seats, 10 had been administration supporters. Several newcomers to the House were avowed doves, most notably Bella Absug (Democrat, New York) and Ronald Dellums (Democrat, California), both outspoken peace activists. The 1970 elections turned, like most elections, on many issues besides the war. Insofar as the election could be viewed as a referendum on administration war policies, the president suffered a net loss of support. Both houses of the new Congress remained overwhelmingly Democratic, and the new Congress would prove to be slightly more dovish than its predecessor.

After two years in office, after two years of fighting and diplomatic maneuvering, the man elected president on a promise to bring an end to the Vietnam War discovered to his dismay that the American position in Southeast Asia had deteriorated. Nixon's freedom of maneuver, never very great, had diminished. He could see no way to end the war any time soon on terms that accorded with his conception of peace with honor. The Paris negotiations remained deadlocked. Hanoi had not budged from its positions staked out when negotiations had begun in May 1968. The United States could not drive the North Vietnamese troops out of South Vietnam, and Kissinger could not persuade Hanoi to withdraw them. The war had also been widened. The United States was now supporting a struggling government in Cambodia that was trying to survive the growing Khmer Rouge insurgency backed by North Vietnam and China. In South Vietnam, the RVNAF buildup was faltering. The U.S. troop withdrawal was accelerating. Popular support for Nixon's war policy was ebbing, Congressional opposition was growing stronger, and antiwar protest had been revitalized by the Cambodian incursion and the Kent State killings. As 1970 ended, it was evident that Nixon's improvised policy of Vietnamization was not working nor did it show any promise that it ever could work.

WIDENING THE WAR: LAOS

Although it had been a manifest failure, Nixon, perhaps as much for lack of a feasible alternative as for any other reason, adhered to his policy of Vietnamization. Early in 1971, hoping to calm his domestic critics, he announced another speedup in the timetable of U.S. troop withdrawals. Nixon's announcement drew protests both from General Thieu, who knew that Vietnamization was not working and feared its consequences, and General Abrams, who was concerned for the security of the U.S. forces remaining in South Vietnam. In response to stepped-up NVA infiltration, Nixon also expanded the air war against the Ho Chi Minh Trail complex in Laos and resumed bombing selected targets in North Vietnam, including staging areas north of the DMZ and military targets in the Hanoi-Haiphong area. He also prepared to expand the ground war once again.

The MACV and RVNAF intelligence analysts had detected a heavy stockpiling of enemy military supplies at two sites. One site was about 30 miles west of Khe Sanh, near the Laotian town of Tchepone, and the other was along the South Vietnam—Laotian border, near the northern end of the A Shau Valley. From these two bases, the NVA units could attack the two northern provinces of South Vietnam, Quang Tri and Thua Thien, and threaten the city of Hue. It was a venerable strategy that the North Vietnamese had tried many times in the past, only to be blocked each time by U.S. troops. Some of the deadliest fighting of the entire war had occured during these regional battles. But now, in early 1971, the Americans were leaving Military Region I. (Corps Tactical Zones were renamed Military Regions in July 1970. MR1 was formerly known as I Corps.) How would the South Vietnamese high command respond to this developing threat? Rather than wait for the NVA to attack the northern provinces of their country, General Thieu and his chief of staff, General Cao Van Vien, proposed a preemptive campaign to destroy the two supply sites in order to relieve the enemy pressure building in the northern provinces. The MACV Commander General Abrams approved the proposed ARVN operation, as did President Nixon.

Laos, like Cambodia, was a neutral country, its neutrality formally guaranteed by the 1962 Paris Agreement. But neither side had observed that neutrality from the day it was established, and Laos's weak neutralist government, headed by Prince Souvanna Phouma, could not defend the nation's territorial integrity. The struggle for power within Laos was mainly a dimension of the Vietnam War that had spilled into that hapless country. The CIA had been waging a secret war in Laos since 1963, involving Meo tribesmen. CIA officials trained and supported the Meo in their battles against the Pathet Lao. U.S. aircraft had been bombing targets along the Ho Chi Minh Trail in the Laotian corridor since 1964. The Nixon administration escalated the U.S. air war against Laos in 1969. During the first two years of Nixon's presidency, U.S. bomb tonnage dropped in Laos exceeded the totals for both the Kennedy and Johnson years.

North Vietnamese forces had been occupying part of Laos since the Franco-Vietminh War. They also supported and trained the Pathet Lao. By 1971, the NVA controlled all of the Laotian territory adjoining their own country and occupied the entire Laotian corridor, from which they had expelled the native Laotians, using it as one huge logistics system to support their war in South Vietnam.

General Thieu's and General Vien's main objective for the operation, code-named LAM SON 719, was the destruction of enemy logistics installations and supplies at Tchepone and at a basing area near the northern end of the A Shau Valley. The operational plan also called for holding these facilities for 90 days and for interdicting the flow of supplies down the Ho Chi Minh Trail, then withdrawing from Laos before the rainy season began. The South Vietnamese military leaders calculated that a successful spoiling operation in Laos, when coupled with the destruction wrought in the Cambodian sanctuaries the previous year, would keep South Vietnam free of any enemy offensives for a year and would buy additional time for Vietnamization.[87]

Two factors made LAM SON 719 unique. It was the first major operation since the American war began in 1965 in which ARVN forces would have to fight without American advisers or U.S. combat units accompanying them in battle. U.S. troops stationed just inside South Vietnam provided artillery support. U.S. helicopters and strike aircraft would cover the air above Laos, but on the ground, the South Vietnamese would be on their own. The LAM SON 719 operation would be another test of Vietnamization. South Vietnamese and U.S. officials would find out if the ARVN forces were ready to be weaned from their American dependency. Could they mount a successful invasion into Laos on their own?

The second factor involved the NVA. With the closing of the port at Sihanoukville, the Ho Chi Minh Trail had become the jugular of Hanoi's war in South Vietnam; it was vitally important to the NVA war effort to maintain the flow of men and materiel down the trail network. Anticipating an attack at Tchepone, the hub of the Ho Chi Minh Trail complex running through the Laotian corridor, General Giap had brought in an additional 20,000 well-equipped troops, including 19 antiaircraft battalions, 12 infantry battalions, a tank regiment, and an artillery regiment. Unlike the Cambodian incursion, where the VC/NVA forces fled into the interior to avoid battle with the invaders, the PAVN forces in the vicinity of Tchepone were prepared to fight the South Vietnamese invaders.[88]

On February 8, 1971, units of the ARVN 1st Airborne Division and 1st Armored Brigade under the command of General Hoang Xuan Lam pushed into Laos along Route 9, west of Khe Sanh. The operation encountered trouble from the outset. North Vietnamese agents placed at high levels within the RVNAF command structure had furnished complete details of the operation to the enemy forces in advance. The element of tactical surprise was completely lacking for LAM SON 719. Then the weather turned bad, and the U.S. aircraft could not fly their air support missions for several days.

ARVN politics also intruded to undermine LAM SON 719's chances for success. General Thieu ordered General Lam to proceed cautiously and to not take heavy casualties. Thieu gave this order because the ARVN 1st Airborne was his palace guard; they were his coup insurance. Their destruction would leave him vulnerable to overthrow by his ARVN rivals. General Lam, a poor soldier but an astute politician, obediently

Figure 8.8   South Vietnamese soldiers, in a camouflaged tank, lead an armored column toward the Laotian border. These troops were in the first group that moved down Route 9 and into Laos, beginning an invasion that was aimed at cutting the Ho Chi Minh trail. Photographer: Bettmann Archive. *Source:* CORBIS. © Bettmann/CORBIS.

stopped his columns a short distance into Laos. After the ARVN offensive stopped, the powerful NVA forces attacked.

Over the next two weeks, the NVA augmented its forces and inflicted mounting casualties on the ARVN forces. Worried about the fate of his palace guard, General Thieu ordered General Lam to remove the 1st Airborne from battle altogether and to replace it with an inexperienced RVN Marine division. Thieu's removal of the 1st Airborne further weakened LAM SON 719. The South Vietnamese president, who had originally proposed the Laotian incursion, in effect, had subverted it for reasons of state. In General Thieu's hierarchy of priorities, political self-preservation ranked well ahead of any spoiling operation into Laos against the PAVN forces.[89] Because of Thieu's meddling, LAM SON 719 achieved only a fraction of its goals. The ARVN forces destroyed some enemy supply depots and disrupted NVA logistics along the Ho Chi Minh Trail for a few weeks.

Then came the difficult part of the operation—the tactical withdrawal of the South Vietnamese forces. The RVN forces came under intense pressure from NVA infantry, tank assaults, and artillery barrages. 36,000 battle-hardened NVA troops pursued 8,000 inexperienced ARVN soldiers. General Giap saw an opportunity to inflict a major defeat on the South Vietnamese forces and completely discredit Vietnamization. He ordered all-out assaults on the retreating South Vietnamese.

The ARVN's retreat quickly turned into a rout. In some units, discipline and order collapsed as panic-stricken troops abandoned their equipment and weapons, and fled on foot in the direction of the border. Only the intense use of U.S. air power and heroic efforts by U.S. helicopter pilots, which together inflicted heavy casualties on the attacking NVA forces, suppressed NVA artillery fire, knocked out enemy tanks, hauled in ammunition, and hauled out ARVN troops, kept the headlong retreat from becoming a debacle. Because of the extraordinary U.S. effort, remnants of the thoroughly demoralized ARVN forces returned to South Vietnam. During operation LAM SON 719, 108 American helicopters were lost and another 618 were damaged. Eighty-nine American pilots and air crewmen were either killed or reported missing in action, and another 178 were wounded.[90]

The LAM SON 719 operation proved to be a dispiriting failure for the ARVN soldiers. The U.S. media portrayed the Laotian incursion as a disaster. Television cameras showed American viewers dramatic images of panicky ARVN soldiers straggling back to South Vietnam territory. Reacting to yet another widening of the Indochina War, several senators introduced resolutions aimed at limiting presidential power to conduct military operations in Indochina and cutting off all funds for operations in Cambodia and Laos. None of them passed. "The operation revealed the inherent and incurable flaws of the RVNAF, which doomed any realistic hopes of successful Vietnamization."[91] These flaws included (1) the hopeless incompetence of the ARVN's politicized leadership, starting at the top with General Thieu; (2) the continuing inability of the static home-guard infantry divisions to meet the demands of modern mobile warfare; (3) the lack of professionalism, accentuated by the lack of U.S. advisers who usually coordinated helicopter flights, artillery fire, tank-infantry operations, and air strikes for the ARVN forces; (4) serious problems with communications and maintenance; (5) basic deficiencies in training and discipline; (6) the perennial lack of a fighting spirit when facing NVA troops in intensive combat; and (7) the ARVN's continuing dependence on the American forces. All of these failures again exposed Vietnamization for the illusion that it was.[92] LAM SON 719 was another test of the progress ARVN had made toward Vietnamization. It had flunked again.

In a televised speech delivered on the evening of April 7, 1971, President Nixon told the American people that LAM SON 719 proved that Vietnamization had succeeded. Nixon's portrayal of the Laotian incursion as an ARVN victory made little sense to millions of television viewers who had recently watched video clips showing terrified soldiers clinging to U.S. helicopter skids, desperately trying to return to South Vietnam. The operation had, in fact, proven exactly the opposite. Vietnamization had not succeeded, and there was no possibility that it would ever succeed. The South Vietnamese understood that they had been defeated and understood the dire implications of that defeat for the future of Vietnamization, even if the president of the United States did not. In Saigon, anti-American demonstrations erupted. One poster showed Nixon standing over a pile of dead South Vietnamese soldiers, with a message that Vietnamization meant the sacrifice of South Vietnamese soldiers by the United States. Within the United States, the Laotian incursion revived elements of the antiwar movement. The most notable participants were groups of disillusioned Vietnam War veterans.[93]

WAR WEARINESS

Shortly after the surviving South Vietnamese forces had come reeling back from their ill-fated Laotian incursion, Nixon instructed Henry Kissinger to offer Hanoi some new proposals in Paris that the president hoped would get the stalled peace talks moving. Nixon was motivated to make his new offers by three considerations:

1. He understood that military operations like the Cambodian and Laotian incursions were not likely to force Hanoi to negotiate.
2. Recent talks with the Soviets had been productive; the outlines of a major arms control agreement with the Soviets had emerged from these discussions.
3. Work on the opening to China was promising. A foundation for *detente* with the major Communist powers was being structured. Nixon felt, therefore, that he could afford to be more flexible with Hanoi. He also believed that his prospects for reelection in 1972 depended mainly on his ability to end the Vietnam War. But he also knew that he had to avoid the appearance of rushing to make an election year settlement of the war, so his diplomatic initiative in the spring of 1971 was well timed.

Meeting secretly with Xuan Thuy and Le Duc Tho in Paris, Henry Kissinger offered a new seven-point peace plan. The plan contained two important concessions: Kissinger offered to set a date, December 31, 1971, for the complete withdrawal of all

U.S. combat forces from South Vietnam; he also indicated that America was willing to withdraw its troops without requiring a simultaneous withdrawal of North Vietnamese forces. Since the United States had been unilaterally withdrawing its troops for two years, irrespective of Hanoi's troop deployments, Kissinger's latter proposal was not so much a concession as it was simply an aligning of the U.S. negotiating position with the U.S. military reality. More important, the new proposal separated the military issues from the political issues.[94] Thus, it would be possible for Washington and Hanoi to negotiate a cease-fire and to defer settlement of the major political question over which the long war was being waged—who should rule in South Vietnam—to the postwar period.

Kissinger's new proposals ignited the first serious negotiations between Washington and Hanoi since the talks had begun nearly three years earlier. Intense secret meetings between Kissinger and Le Duc Tho took place over the next three months. Responding to Kissinger's concessions, Tho offered a nine-point plan of his own. It was the first peace plan that the North Vietnamese had ever offered the Americans, and it too contained concessions. Hanoi agreed to release all American POWs by the end of 1971, simultaneously with the departure of all U.S. troops from Vietnam. Also, for the first time, Hanoi did not ask for the removal of Thieu as a precondition for negotiations, only that the United States must stop supporting the South Vietnamese leader.

In subsequent meetings, the status of the Saigon government proved to be the sticking point between Kissinger and Le Duc Tho. Hanoi insisted that Washington disavow Thieu. Nixon refused to abandon Thieu. This latest round of secret talks broke off in September when it became obvious that the impasse could not be resolved.[95] While the new proposals made by both sides had been promising indicators, neither side was yet prepared to make the sort of concessions that would be necessary to secure an end to America's involvement in the Second Indochina War.

As the latest round of secret talks between the Americans and North Vietnamese ended in failure, South Vietnam was preparing to hold its presidential election as called for under the 1967 constitution. General Thieu, acutely aware that he had won the previous election with a plurality of only 35 percent, wanted to win resoundingly this time around. He also was determined to use his powers of incumbency to ensure a landslide victory. Thieu clearly grasped the first principle of South Vietnamese politics: Irrespective of constitutional principles and democratic forms, the man who controls the government always wins elections.

When the 1971 electoral campaign began, General Thieu faced serious challenges from two strong rivals, General Nguyen Cao Ky and General Doung Van "Big" Minh. Either might have been able to defeat Thieu in a free and fair election. General Minh had a mixed following among Buddhists, southern Catholics, non-Communist intellectuals, and civilian politicians. Minh also had obtained the support of the NLF, mainly because he had called for the creation of a coalition government that would include representatives of the Provisional Revolutionary Government (PRG), which had been created by the NLF in June 1969.[96] Ky, hitherto noted for his fanatical anti-Communism, staged a remarkable *volte-face.* He called for recognition of the PRG and supported negotiating an end to the war with the Communist leaders in Hanoi.

But it did not matter what Ky and Minh stood for or who supported them; Thieu used his control of the machinery of government to eliminate them from the presidential race. The United States took a public stance of neutrality during the election. However, behind the scenes, CIA and embassy officials worked to ensure Thieu's landslide reelection. Nixon was not about to risk losing Thieu, whose reelection he saw as essential to protecting U.S. interests in Indochina. The election took place on October 3, 1971. In an election that Americans secretly helped him rig, General Thieu was the only candidate. The ballots provided space only for voting yes for Thieu. Polling was supervised by Thieu's soldiers, and the votes were counted by Thieu's officials. The result: President Thieu was reelected to another four-year term as South Vietnam's president, with 94.3 percent of the vote. From their cafés along Tu Do Street, the savants observed that the man they called "The Little Dictator" had gotten his mandate. But, they asked, a mandate for what?

By 1971, most Americans, regardless of their politics, had become thoroughly sick of the Indochina War and wished only that it would go away. Yet the war and its domestic consequences continued to plague the increasingly war-weary nation. In January and February 1971, Lieutenant William Calley went on trial before a military court for his part in the My Lai massacre that had taken place on March 16, 1968. While Calley was on trial, the Vietnam Veterans Against the War (VVAW), meeting in Detroit, sponsored "Winter Soldier," a forum where over 100 veterans testified that they had committed, witnessed, or heard of My-Lai–type war crimes. On March 31, 1971, a military court convicted Lieutenant William Calley of mass murder for his role in the My Lai massacre and sentenced him to life imprisonment at hard labor. For once, both hawks and doves agreed on something, that Lieutenant Calley had been given a raw deal: hawks, because they believed that no soldier should be convicted in war time for doing his duty; doves, because they believed that Calley had been a sacrificial offering to cover up the fact that many other war criminals went free. President Nixon responded to this wave of sympathy for Calley and commuted the life sentence to three years.

Following Calley's conviction, the VVAW staged one of the most poignant demonstrations against the war in the nation's capital. For five days in late April 1971, disillusioned veterans staged a dramatic protest against the government that continued to wage it. A group of VVAW members, including John Kerry, a decorated war hero, camped out on the Mall and tossed their medals and campaign ribbons onto the steps of the Capitol.[97] Some came in wheelchairs, others were missing an arm or a leg. Some wept, others raged at the war machine that appeared to have a momentum of its own— all made compelling witnesses to the anguish of a controversial war that U.S. officials appeared to be unable to either win or end.[98]

Following the VVAW demonstrations, hundreds of thousands of antiwar demonstrators representing a variety of perspectives, interests, and tactics descended on Washington. Peace spokesmen met with congressional leaders, urging them to take more decisive actions to end the war and to address urgent domestic social needs. In early May, thousands of militant demonstrators rampaged through the streets of the nation's capital in a quixotic effort to shut down the government of the United States because it refused to shut down the Vietnam War. Police, National Guardsmen, and federal troops prevented any major disruptions, and thousands of protesters were arrested.[99]

Not long after the spring demonstrations in Washington had subsided, another dramatic war-related issue commanded public attention. On June 13, the *New York Times* began publishing secret government documents that had been given to *Times* reporter Neil Sheehan by former Department of Defense officials Daniel Ellsberg and Anthony Russo. The documents were part of a Pentagon study that had been undertaken by Ellsberg and his colleagues at the request of Secretary of Defense Robert McNamara. Compiled under the direction of Leslie Gelb, these documents amounted to an in-house secret history of the long American involvement in Indochina that had resulted in the Vietnam War. The massive 47 volume study's official title was *History of U.S. Decision-making Process on Vietnam, 1945–1967.* Quickly dubbed the "Pentagon Papers," their publication caused a furor as people discovered what many dovish critics had suspected all along. Readers discovered that President Kennedy, President Johnson, and other high officials had consistently misled the American people about their actions and intentions concerning the war.

Readers also learned that it was the United States that had often violated or ignored treaties, escalated the war, and spurned peace initiatives. Further, readers discovered that President Kennedy had supported the military coup that had overthrown and murdered Ngo Dinh Diem and his brother on November 1, 1963. Publication of the Pentagon Papers widened the credibility gap. Lieutenant Calley's trial, the continuing antiwar demonstrations, and the revelations of the Pentagon Papers all helped drive popular support for the Vietnam War to an all-time low. In June, a poll recorded 61 percent of respondents stating that U.S. involvement in the war was a mistake. A July poll revealed that two-thirds of Americans believed that America should continue to withdraw its troops, even if the Saigon government collapsed.[100] Once the Pentagon Papers entered the public domain, they shortened the time remaining for President Nixon to end the Vietnam War.

Nixon had tried hard to prevent the publication of the Pentagon Papers. Attorney General John Mitchell had secured a court injunction on the grounds that their publication represented "a clear and present danger" to national security. But Federal Judge Gerhardt Gesell quashed the injunction and the Supreme Court quickly sustained him. A majority on the Supreme Court could not see how publishing the papers compromised national security. They found that publication of the Pentagon Papers represented a clear and present danger only to the reputations of former public officials who had conceived and implemented U.S. foreign policy in Southeast Asia and then misrepresented it to the American people. Nixon, thwarted in his efforts to stop the publication of the Pentagon Papers through the courts, unleashed the Plumbers to plug government leaks. White House counselor John Erlichman ordered a team of Plumbers, led by G. Gordon

Liddy, to break into the office of Daniel Ellsberg's psychiatrist in Beverly Hills to find information that would discredit the man who had leaked the Pentagon Papers to the *New York Times*.[101]

THE NGUYEN HUE OFFENSIVE

As 1972 began, both the battlefields of Vietnam and the American home front were comparatively calm. Only about 140,000 U.S. troops remained in Vietnam, of whom no more than 20,000 constituted combat forces, and more troops would be leaving soon. American battle deaths for 1971 had totaled 1,380, the lowest for any year since the American Vietnam War had begun in 1965. The lottery draft was in place, draft calls were low, and draftees were no longer being sent to Vietnam for combat duty. The air wars continued in North Vietnam, Laos, and Cambodia, but they received little coverage in the news and entailed few U.S. casualties. Aviation warfare did not concern the American public in the urgent way that U.S. ground combat in South Vietnam had in years past. Even in this calmer context, President Nixon's public approval rating remained comparatively low. Fewer than half of those polled approved of his job performance.[102]

Toward the end of January, Nixon made several dramatic announcements. On the 25th, he revealed to the American public that Henry Kissinger had been meeting secretly with North Vietnamese emissaries for six months. He also told the people that the only remaining obstacle to peace in Vietnam was Hanoi's stubborn insistence that General Thieu's government would have to be eliminated before any settlement could be reached. Simultaneously, Nixon announced a new proposal: Within six months of an agreement, the United States would remove all of its forces at the same time the POWs were exchanged. Simultaneously, a cease-fire would go into effect, and new elections would be held in South Vietnam under international supervision. He also indicated that the PRG could participate in these elections. But even as he announced the new proposals, he vowed once again that America would never abandon Saigon.[103] North Vietnam promptly denounced the President's decision to go public with secret negotiations and repeated its demands that the United States must stop supporting Thieu and set a final date for the removal of all of its forces from Vietnam. The peace talks collapsed soon after and were put on indefinite hold.

Even though Nixon's peace proposals did not move negotiations closer to a settlement, and, in fact, had gotten them suspended indefinitely, his remarks did score domestic political points with the American public at the beginning of a presidential election year, which was their prime purpose. Many prominent dovish politicians supported his peace initiative, as did much of the influential media. Public opinion polls showed increasing popular support for the president's negotiating stance.

Three weeks after making his latest proposals for ending the American Vietnam War, Nixon journeyed to China for his historic state visit. Upon his return to the United States in late February, he was delighted to find that his power and prestige as a peacemaker had been greatly enhanced. He looked forward to his trip to Moscow, scheduled for late spring. President Nixon felt confident that he and Kissinger could use his trip to China and his upcoming visit to the Soviet Union in order to link subsequent progress toward *detente* to Moscow's and Beijing's willingness to pressure Hanoi into negotiating an end to the war on terms that Washington could accept.

But the Indochina War was about to resume, larger than ever. General Giap was in the final stages of planning what was going to be the largest offensive operation of the war, a spring invasion of South Vietnam that Hanoi hoped might destroy the South Vietnamese armed forces, bring down the Thieu regime, and force the Americans out of Vietnam. As events unfolded that spring, neither Nixon's diplomatic initiatives nor Hanoi's offensive could accomplish their Indochina goals in 1972, "but they did bring the war into a final, devastating phase which would ultimately lead to a compromise peace."[104]

Hanoi's decision to try once again to break the military stalemate had been reached at the Nineteenth Plenum meeting in January 1971. For several reasons, North Vietnamese leaders calculated that spring 1972 would be an opportune time to launch a major offensive against South Vietnam's military forces. They assumed that political necessity would force President Nixon to continue to adhere to the timetable of scheduled U.S. troop withdrawals and that he would not be able to throw the remaining American combat forces into battle against the invading NVA divisions. Hanoi also believed that a successful offensive would lead to a collapse of the Saigon regime. It would also force Nixon, under pressure to end the war before the November elections, to withdraw all U.S. forces remaining in South Vietnam. Giap perceived that, in the aftermath of its demoralizing defeat in Laos, South Vietnam was especially vulnerable to a powerful military assault.

The six members of the Politburo were old men who had spent their lives in pursuit of their dream, the reunification of their country under their leadership. The prospect of dying with the dream unfulfilled, as had been the fate of their supreme leader Ho Chi Minh on September 3, 1969, filled them with dread. They were "old men in a hurry."[105]

Hanoi's decision to seek an early end to the war also represented the response of the North Vietnamese to the changing international situation. They were wary of the growing *detente* between the United States and the Soviet Union which would be sealed by Nixon's journey to Moscow. They worried lest the Soviets curtail their military assistance or pressure them into accepting American terms for a settlement. The North Vietnamese held memories of 1954 at Geneva, when the Soviets, concerned about improving relations with Western Europe and the United States, joined with the Chinese to force Ho Chi Minh to accept the temporary partition of Vietnam that had led to a costly war with the United States. To Hanoi, spring 1972 looked too much like 1954 *redux*.[106]

Hanoi also was alarmed by Nixon's opening to China, signaled by his historic journey to Beijing. China was suspicious of Soviet ties with North Vietnam and viewed the United States as a counterweight to Chinese tensions with the Soviet Union. China wanted the United States to retain a presence in Southeast Asia to offset Soviet power in that region. In the aftermath of the Nixon visit, Hanoi sensed that the Chinese wanted an end to the Indochina War that would allow South Vietnam to survive, enable the United States to maintain a presence in Indochina, and perpetuate the partition of Vietnam indefinitely.[107]

From Hanoi's vantage point, it appeared that Nixon's and Kissinger's pursuit of a new world order based on *detente* with the major Communist powers was about to yield Washington a major dividend: pressure emanating from both Moscow and Beijing on the North Vietnamese to negotiate an end to the Indochina War acceptable to the Americans, that is, a negotiated settlement that would allow the continued existence of the South Vietnam state. The aged revolutionaries in Hanoi, who had been single-mindedly pursuing the goals of revolutionary nationalism since 1945, viewed their imminent spring offensive as being perhaps their last opportunity to win the war, bring down the Thieu government, and achieve a settlement on their own terms—a settlement that would force the Americans out of Indochina and pave the way for reunification of Vietnam under the rule of the Vietnamese Communist Party leaders.[108]

But during the long interval before the offensive would be ready for launching, the Communists decided to continue their small-scale protracted war strategy, the small-unit struggle for control of villages in South Vietnam. Politburo leaders conceded that the RVN pacification programs, especially land reform, had reduced the areas controlled by the PRG, and that PLAF main force levels were depleted. But the Politburo leadership also knew that in the long run it was the fighting ability of the RVN forces that mattered more than their pacification programs. Once the Americans had departed, Thieu would be forced to rely on his own forces, and the Lao Dong leaders were confident that their 1972 offensive would overwhelm the ARVN.[109]

The Twentieth Plenum, meeting in February 1972, approved Giap's final plans for the spring offensive, scheduled to begin in late March. Although the Communists still considered political action important, they no longer planned for a combination general offensive/general uprising a la Tet-68. Giap hoped the VC cadres could organize rural areas where he had a greater expectation of achieving military victory, but he did not expect there to be any urban risings unless the PAVN main units were in the cities in force to support them.[110]

General Giap launched the spring attacks, called the Nguyen Hue Offensive, in three successive stages, committing altogether a dozen infantry divisions supported by tank and artillery units. About 122,000 NVA soldiers, joined by thousands of VietCong guerrillas, were committed to action. Beginning on March 30, the first wave poured across the DMZ to strike at the ARVN positions in the two northernmost provinces of Quang Tri and Thua Thien. Three of the PAVN divisions, totaling about 30,000 men, equipped with modern Soviet-made weaponry that included rockets, missiles, tanks, and heavy artillery, joined in the massive assaults into the northern provinces.[111]

Once again the Allies were caught by surprise. Although their intelligence officers had been expecting a big NVA offensive, they did not know exactly when and where the attacks would come. They also had not anticipated the size or power of the

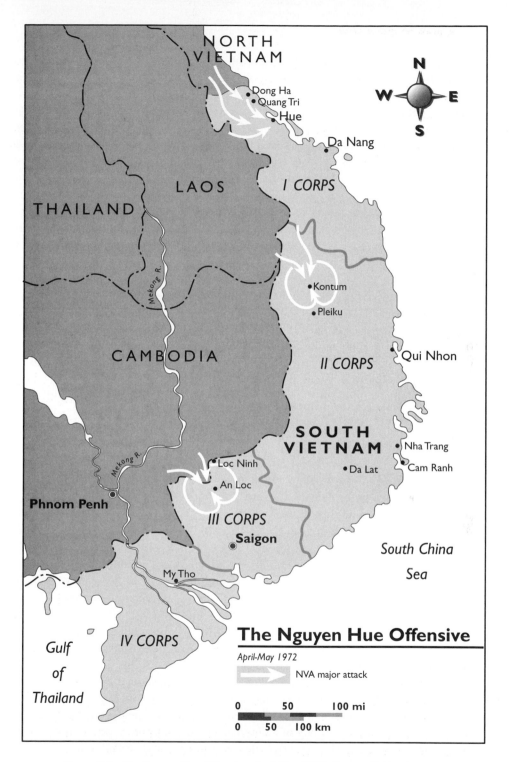

Figure 8.9 The Nguyen Hue Offensive, April–May 1972. *Source:* Public domain.

attack. The ARVN defenses in the two northern provinces had been placed in the hands of the 1st and 3rd Divisions, and they bore the brunt of the NVA assaults. Within a few weeks, the situation in these provinces had become critical. The PAVN forces had overrun the ARVN defensive positions and had wiped out several of their firebases. Compounding the ARVN problems, the incompetent MRI commander, the notorious General Lam of LAM SON 719 shame, ordered the 3rd Division, probably the weakest division in the RVNAF order of battle, to counterattack in the face of superior NVA forces and under terribly unfavorable operational circumstances. They were massacred.

On May 1, the demoralized ARVN troops, accompanied by thousands of frightened family members and panic-stricken civilians, fled in headlong fashion toward the south. The NVA gunners, firing into the fleeing masses, inflicted thousands of casualties on soldiers and civilians alike. On May 1, the provincial capital, Quang Tri City, fell. The entire province lay in NVA hands.[112] The city of Hue, 40 miles south of Quang Tri City, was threatened. U.S. officials in Saigon and Washington feared that the RVN itself might collapse from the pressures generated by the all-out North Vietnamese spring offensive.

Alarmed by the success of the PAVN forces and fearing the fall of Hue and even Danang, General Thieu replaced Lam with General Ngo Quang Truong, probably the finest general in the RVN armed forces. Apolitical, thoroughly professional, and battle-seasoned, Truong was a superb leader who could have commanded troops in any army. He organized a defense for Hue and saved the city, and perhaps saved South Vietnam as well.

Following their successful defense of Hue, the South Vietnamese made retaking Quang Tri City their major military objective of the northern campaign. General Truong built up his forces and in late June launched a counterattack. The Allied assault on Quang Tri brought massive firepower to bear, including U.S. naval gunfire, air strikes, and B-52 bombing runs. Finally, General Thieu ordered the South Vietnamese Marines to go into the city and drive out the NVA forces. After five days of hand-to-hand fighting in the streets and buildings of Quang Tri, the North Vietnamese were expelled. Although extensively damaged, Quang Tri was officially reclaimed by the South Vietnamese on September 16. Arnold Isaacs, an American journalist who witnessed the Battle of Quang Tri filed this description of the aftermath: "When it was finally recaptured Quang Tri was no longer a city but a lake of shattered masonry. . . . It was another case—on a larger scale than ever before—of destroying Vietnam to save it."[113]

The second wave of the Nguyen Hue Offensive began in early April. Two NVA divisions penetrated the central highlands at Dak To and Tan Canh. Within a few weeks, they had beaten the ARVN defenders and had begun a series of attacks on Kontum City. At the same time the NVA forces attacked Kontum, another NVA division, assisted by local VC forces, occupied most of the coastal province of Binh Dinh, a long-time Communist stronghold.[114] Once again, the perennial NVA goal, the bisection of South Vietnam, threatened. If the city of Kontum fell, the NVA forces would link up with the VC/NVA forces in Binh Dinh, and Thieu's country would be knifed in two.

The defense of Kontum City was organized and directed by the legendary John Paul Vann.[115] Vann had returned to Vietnam as a minor civilian official following his retirement from the Army in 1964. By dint of his energy, experience, intelligence, forceful personality, and total dedication to the cause, Vann had worked his way up the bureaucratic ranks to become the leading U.S. adviser in MR2 by 1972. Although a civilian, Vann held the equivalent military rank of a major general. When the RVN MR2 commander, General Ngo Dzu, an accused drug trafficker, suffered a nervous collapse under the stress of the NVA attacks, Vann personally took charge of defending Kontum City.

The Battle of Kontum raged for nearly three weeks. The NVA forces launched a series of frontal assaults on the ARVN defenders. Led by a Vann protege, Colonel Ly Tong Ba, the ARVN defenders repeatedly beat back the NVA attacks. While Colonel Ba's forces were holding the NVA attackers off, Vann called in an air armada of U.S. helicopter gunships, tactical air strikes, and B-52 bombings that decimated the attacking forces. The critical moment in the Battle of Kontum came during the night of May 28, 1972. NVA forces broke through the ARVN defenses and poured into the city. Only round-the-clock bombing by cells of B-52s finally broke the NVA assault, enabling Ba's battered 23rd Division to clear the city.[116]

A few days after achieving his greatest victory, John Paul Vann died in a fiery helicopter crash a few miles south of Kontum City. Vann had given ten years, and finally his life, trying to save South Vietnam from Communist conquest. His body was recovered and flown back to the United States. John Paul Vann was given a state funeral and buried with full honors in a moving ceremony at Arlington National Cemetery. President Nixon praised him and posthumously awarded him the Medal of Freedom, the highest award a civilian could receive, for his heroic service in Vietnam.

The third wave of the Nguyen Hue Offensive struck the Tay Ninh and Binh Long provinces northwest of Saigon in MR3. Three VietCong divisions, the 5th, the 7th, and the 9th, manned mostly by NVA troops and commanded by North Vietnamese officers, poured into South Vietnam from their basing areas in Cambodia. The 5th VC Division took Loc Ninh, a town lying about 80 miles north of Saigon on Route 13, a highway leading straight to the South Vietnamese capital. The ARVN forces fell back to An Loc, a town nine miles south of Loc Ninh on Route 13. Failing to take An Loc by frontal assault, the NVA forces besieged the town. The Battle of An Loc raged for weeks.[117] General Thieu, determined to stop the NVA thrust at An Loc, threw in most of his strategic reserves and his elite airborne forces to bolster the defenses of the besieged town.

The crucial battle for An Loc occurred on the morning of May 11. Units of all three enemy divisions launched attacks on the ARVN defenders. The NVA were hit immediately, first by waves of U.S. and VNAF fighter-bombers and then by B-52 strikes. Thirty B-52 strikes struck the NVA forces within 24 hours. Entire PAVN units, caught in the open by the big bombers, vanished in clouds of dust and debris. Although there was fighting in the vicinity of An Loc for a few more days, the battle was over. The

ARVN forces had held. The key to victory at An Loc had been the effective use of Allied air power, especially the mighty B-52s.[118]

Nixon had reacted quickly and decisively to the North Vietnamese invasion. He and Kissinger both knew that the United States had to move quickly to support the South Vietnamese, or the Saigon regime might very well collapse in the face of the powerful NVA onslaught. Both men understood that it was essential to defeat the North Vietnamese thrusts militarily. If the NVA offensive succeeded, Nixon could not expect the upcoming summit with the Soviets to be productive, nor could he hope to achieve a negotiated end to the Vietnam War on acceptable terms. He believed that a North Vietnamese victory would be a major strategic and diplomatic disaster for the United States that could derail all of his plans for achieving a new world order based on *detente* with the major Communist powers. A Communist victory would also fatally undermine American credibility as a great power in the eyes of both friends and foes.

Nixon perceived that the North Vietnamese had provided Washington with an opportunity to end the war. He saw a chance to implement many of the DUCK HOOK operations that Kissinger's committee had drawn up during the summer of 1969. If Washington moved quickly and decisively, U.S. air power could defeat the offensive and also launch a massive counterattack on the North Vietnamese heartland. Nixon and Kissinger just might be able to force Hanoi to accept a settlement favorable to the survival of South Vietnam.[119]

On April 4, 1972, in an effort to blunt the Nguyen Hue Offensive, Nixon decided to mount an all-out air war against it. He revived the air war against North Vietnam that had been on hold since October 31, 1968. As the North Vietnamese had predicted, Nixon did not consider either sending U.S. combat forces back to South Vietnam or using the few remaining maneuver battalions still serving in the country. The U.S. forces continued to leave South Vietnam while the battles forced by the Nguyen Hue Offensive raged. On April 6, Nixon told the new commander of the 7th Air Force, General John W. Vogt, "I want you to get down there and use whatever air you need to turn this thing around."[120] From around the world, U.S. aircraft carriers and Air Force squadrons raced toward the Indochina War. Additional B-52s flew into Andersen Air Force Base, bringing the combined total of the huge strategic bombers in Thailand and Guam to 210. More than half the B-52s in the SAC were positioned to strike at the NVA invaders. Nixon also ordered the carriers *Constellation* and *Kitty Hawk* to join the four attack carriers already on station in the Gulf of Tonkin, giving the Navy its greatest concentration of airpower in the war.[121]

The revived air campaign against North Vietnam designed by the Navy and Air Force commanders, code-named LINEBACKER, had many diplomatic and strategic goals: (1) to send the North Vietnamese a warning that if Hanoi persisted with its offensive in an effort to win the war, the North Vietnamese could expect to get hit with the most punishing aerial offensive of the war; (2) to cut off North Vietnam from external sources of supply by destroying all of its railroads and harbors; (3) to destroy stockpiles of food, ammunition, weapons, and equipment already in North

Vietnam; (4) to interdict as much as possible the supplies and equipment moving toward the battlefields in South Vietnam, Laos, and Cambodia; (5) to destroy all enemy transportation systems, POL facilities, and power plants; and (6) to wring concessions from the North Vietnamese so that a peace settlement would accord with U.S. and South Vietnamese desires.[122]

On April 10, U.S. aircraft struck supply storage centers near the city of Vinh, about 150 miles north of the DMZ. On April 13, B-52s flying from the large SAC base at U-Tapao in Thailand bombed oil storage sites near Hanoi and Haiphong. It was the first time in the long war that the big bombers had been used in attacks on North Vietnam's two largest cities. On April 16, U.S. bombers accidentally hit four Soviet merchant ships lying at anchor in Haiphong Harbor, killing some Soviet seamen. The Soviets protested the bombing of their ships and the deaths of their sailors, but they did not make a major issue of these events, suggesting to Washington that the Soviets were not going to let the U.S. actions in Vietnam interfere with their upcoming summit meeting with the Americans.

Throughout the months of April and May, U.S. military aircraft flew hundreds of sorties against military targets in North Vietnam. Air Force and Navy tactical bombers flew most of the missions, but B-52s also participated. The LINEBACKER operation exceeded any previous U.S. aerial warfare against North Vietnam. Naval and Air Force pilots flew round-the-clock bombing missions against supply lines, storage facilities, industrial targets, power plants, and other targets considered to have military value. For the first time in the air war, U.S. pilots dropped "smart bombs," laser-guided weapons of devastating precision. Using laser or electro-optical guidance systems, "smart bombs" could destroy targets in heavily populated areas without causing large civilian casualties.[123] In addition to reviving the air war against North Vietnam, Nixon also ordered air attacks against the invading North Vietnamese forces along their northern, central, and southern fronts in South Vietnam. Within 10 days of the launching of the invasions, Allied aircraft were inflicting heavy losses on units of Hanoi's mobilized army on all three fronts. By June the Nguyen Hue Offensive was losing its momentum.

U.S. efforts to separate the North Vietnamese from their Chinese and Soviet sources of supply represented the most risky military move Nixon made during the Vietnam War. Nixon believed he had to take the risk to save South Vietnam from military collapse to preserve *detente* and the chance of an acceptable settlement of the war.[124]

At Nixon's request, Kissinger revived DUCK HOOK. One of DUCK HOOK's original proposals called for the mining of North Vietnam's harbors to interdict all ship traffic into Haiphong and other North Vietnamese ports. But before Nixon ordered the ports mined, he used diplomatic channels to forewarn the Chinese and Soviet leaders of his intentions. The president took these steps to preserve *detente,* to avoid possible reprisals by the major Communist powers, and to reopen secret negotiations with the North Vietnamese emissary Le Duc Tho.[125]

As Nixon applied military pressure to Hanoi, he also applied diplomatic pressure to the Soviets, whom he and Kissinger held responsible for the NVA offensive in South

Figure 8.10   This photo is one of the most enduring and gruesome images of the Vietnam War. Nine-year-old Phan Thi Kim Phuc running down Route 1 naked and screaming in agony from the napalm that had seared her small body. A VNAF pilot attacked Phuc and other children as they fled the village of Trang Bang June 9, 1972. *Source:* Staff photo by Huynh Cong "Nick" Ut. *Source:* AP/Wide World Photos.

Vietnam. The Americans were convinced that Hanoi could never have mounted the operation without the military hardware furnished by the Soviet Union. Kissinger met secretly with Soviet leader Leonid Brezhnev in Moscow on April 20. Before he would consent to talk to Brezhnev about any of the issues of the impending summit, Kissinger insisted that the Soviet leader agree to put pressure on Hanoi to negotiate an end to the war. The U.S. envoy explicitly linked progress toward *detente* to Soviet willingness to persuade Hanoi to accept a compromise settlement of the war. Brezhnev agreed; he wanted nothing to subvert the upcoming summit. However, he protested to Kissinger that he did not have the kind of influence with the Hanoi leadership that the Americans appeared to think he did. He also refused to ask Hanoi to call off its offensive, but he did send a high-ranking envoy to Hanoi to urge the Communist leaders to make peace with the Americans.

Brezhnev also helped Kissinger restart the talks with the North Vietnamese. Kissinger met secretly with Le Duc Tho in Paris on May 2, three weeks before the convening of the Moscow summit. At the time of the meeting, the North Vietnamese offensive was going well. Quang Tri had fallen to the NVA forces, and Kontum and An Loc were under intense attack. Le Duc Tho was confident that the Saigon government verged on collapse, and he believed U.S. air power could not save it. Le Duc Tho was not interested in negotiations that day. Confident of military victory, he rejected all of Kissinger's proposals. He was rigid, arrogant, even rude. The meeting was short and it accomplished nothing.[126]

Disappointed and angered by Tho's response, President Nixon decided to escalate the U.S. air war against the North Vietnamese. He and Kissinger both agreed that only a massive dose of U.S. firepower could deter the North Vietnamese drive for a military victory over the South. Nixon gambled that the Chinese and Soviets both placed greater importance on improving their relations with the United States than they did on retaliating on behalf of their allies in Hanoi. The president growled to his aides, "The bastards have never been bombed like they're going to be bombed this time."[127]

On May 8, in a dramatic televised speech, Nixon announced to a startled nation that he had ordered his most drastic escalations of the war: the mining of Haiphong Harbor, a naval blockade of North Vietnam, and a massive air war against that country. He also used the speech to tell the North Vietnamese that U.S. aircraft would continue to mine ports and interdict lines of communication across the North Vietnamese heartland until Hanoi agreed to release all U.S. POWs and accept an internationally supervised cease-fire. As Nixon spoke to the American people, Navy jets were dropping mines in the narrow 12-mile-long channel connecting the port of Haiphong with the Gulf of Tonkin. Twenty-seven freighters, mostly Soviet, were bottled up at Haiphong. For the next three days, Navy aircraft mined the approaches to North Vietnam's other ports and also to several inland waterways. The blockade quickly cut off the sources of about 85 percent of North Vietnam's war materiel and disrupted all North Vietnamese naval activity.[128]

To the immense frustration of the North Vietnamese, Moscow and Beijing both reacted with restraint to the mining and the renewed bombing of North Vietnam. Nixon and Kissinger had gambled and they had won. They had succeeded in isolating Hanoi from its major allies. Neither the USSR nor China did more than issue *pro forma* criticisms of the U.S. actions, and both privately put pressure on Hanoi to end the war. The two major Communist powers wanted the Vietnam War to end, lest it jeopardize the fruits of *detente* and the major realignment of power then taking place in the world. Hanoi's leaders bitterly observed that the Moscow summit occurred on schedule, even as Operation LINEBACKER was devastating North Vietnam and destroying their army fighting in South Vietnam.[129] Meetings in Moscow between the American and Soviet leaders proved cordial and productive. Nixon and Brezhnev signed several important agreements, including SALT I, new trade agreements, and a new Berlin treaty. President Nixon and Henry Kissinger had carried off the first meeting between a U.S. president and the Soviet leaders in five years, and it was perceived as a major diplomatic success.

Just as the North Vietnamese leaders worried lest their major Communist allies no longer supported their cause, Saigon's leaders feared the U.S. commitment to their cause might also be sacrificed in the name of *detente*. The scale and ferocity of the fighting, the destructiveness of the renewed air war in South Vietnam, and the large numbers of casualties incurred accentuated the already intense levels of war-weariness among South Vietnam's beleaguered population. Millions of South Vietnamese had never supported the Saigon government, its war, or the American effort on its behalf.

The effects of the fighting in the spring and summer of 1972 were to further diminish the ranks of South Vietnamese patriots. More and more people yearned for peace, for an end to the death and destruction afflicting their tortured country, even if it meant a Communist victory. One of the Tu Do Street savants told an American journalist, "We want peace, peace at any cost, peace with Communist rule if necessary."[130] After 20 years of precarious existence, after 20 years of American economic, political, diplomatic, military, and moral support, South Vietnam had failed to evolve a clear national identity. After 20 years, its leaders had utterly failed to project a vision, define a cause, or proclaim a goal that could inspire its citizens to fight a patriotic war.[131] The battle for Quang Tri City, which resulted in huge casualties on both sides, and the city's utter destruction, symbolized the hopeless, endless, and bloody stalemated war.

Within the United States, reaction to Nixon's dramatic war escalations proved comparatively mild. There was a flurry of protest demonstrations, but they did not attract large or militant followings. Doves introduced another round of end-the-war resolutions in the Senate, but none passed. That Nixon had responded so forcefully, yet exempted the use of U.S. ground forces and kept American casualties low, allowed more people to support his actions. The ranks of the antiwar movement had been depleted. Many peace activists were exhausted from years of protesting an endless war. Most U.S. ground combat forces had been withdrawn from South Vietnam and those remaining in that country no longer participated in combat operations. Monthly draft calls were way down and a lottery draft was in place. One of the main energizing sources of antiwar activity had been the draft linked to a fear of being sent to fight and die in Vietnam. Sensing this concern, President Nixon announced in June that no more draftees would be sent to Vietnam unless they volunteered. He also stated that by September 1 there would only be 39,000 U.S. soldiers in Vietnam. Vietnamization not only gradually phased out the American ground combat role in Vietnam, it also gradually phased out much of the activist opposition to the Vietnam War.

Americans did not appear to be much moved by the spectacle of Vietnamese killing Vietnamese during the Nguyen Hue Offensive. Many Americans regarded Nixon's actions as a justifiable reaction to naked aggression, a military invasion of South Vietnam by North Vietnam. Nixon's bold response also attracted considerable popular support. The success of the Moscow summit demonstrated that military escalations did not automatically endanger *detente*. Polls showed strong public support for Nixon's retaliatory actions against the North Vietnamese and for his diplomatic accomplishments in Beijing and Moscow. His public approval rating climbed dramatically.

The Nguyen Hue Offensive had petered out in September when South Vietnamese Marines expelled the last NVA remnants from Quang Tri City. Nixon's decisive response had prevented a South Vietnamese military defeat and perhaps the fall of the Saigon government. Hanoi had undertaken the largest military offensive anywhere in the world since the Chinese had invaded Korea in December 1950. But Hanoi's efforts to use massed forces to overwhelm the ARVN units had met with disaster. General Giap had seriously underestimated the fighting ability of at least some of the ARVN forces. U.S. air power had exacted a ghastly toll. North Vietnam lost over 100,000 troops killed in battle, most of their tanks, and much of their artillery in three months. North Vietnam had been subjected to the most intense bombing campaign of the entire war and sustained heavy damage.[132] PAVN's inadequacies made them vulnerable to such catastrophic destruction. Unaccustomed to mobile, mechanized warfare, they often failed to coordinate their infantry and armor attacks. Their primitive logistics capability could not provide the huge amounts of ammunition, gasoline, and spare parts required to support their offensive effectively. General Giap also appeared not to comprehend the terrible vulnerability of his mechanized forces in an operational situation where the Allied air forces enjoyed absolute control of the air. His army, by far the best the NVA had fielded to date, was destroyed, and his country was battered by the U.S. bombers.

The South Vietnamese also suffered heavy casualties, an estimated 25,000 soldiers killed in three months of fighting. Some ARVN commanders, particularly General Truong and Colonel Ba, demonstrated professional competence in combat situations. Some ARVN units fought courageously and effectively under enemy fire. The VNAF pilots often gave a good account of themselves in many battles. But the PAVN offensive also revealed the continuing shortcomings of the RVN armed forces. Their helicopter and other air transport units proved inadequate. Artillery was poorly coordinated and often inaccurate. Communications and intelligence services remained poor. The ARVN logistics system could never function effectively without U.S. assistance. U.S. advisers directed most of the ARVN combat operations; they were the reinforcing steel rods that held the South Vietnamese army structures together. Many ARVN soldiers continued to perform poorly in combat situations. The ARVN officer corps remained infested with corrupt and incompetent officers. Worse yet, South Vietnam was running out of men. The pool of draft-age men was running dry. Reserve units were depleted, and many regular units could not replace their losses. Shortages of competent officers and noncoms were more acute than ever in the aftermath of the Nguyen Hue Offensive.[133]

The inescapable truth to emerge from the offensive was that ARVN soldiers could neither stop the enemy without significant U.S. air support nor could their counteroffensive have succeeded without it.[134] Once again, Vietnamization had flunked a crucial test. Once again, the ARVN demonstrated that it was unprepared to assume the full burden of defending South Vietnam from the attacks of the VietCong and North Vietnamese forces.

On August 22, 1972, the 1st Battalion of the U.S. 7th Cavalry boarded a plane for Texas. The last U.S. ground combat forces had departed the Vietnam War. It had been seven years five months and fourteen days since the Marines had stormed ashore on the beaches south of Danang on the morning of March 8, 1965, to initiate the ground combat phase of the American Vietnam war. During that long interval, nearly 46,000 American soldiers had died in an effort to secure the survival of the South Vietnamese government. Now the ground combat phase of the war was over for U.S. troops. But as the last contingent of U.S. combat soldiers departed Vietnam, the war between factions of Vietnamese nationalists raged on, its outcome yet to be determined.

Neither Peace nor Honor

Washington and Hanoi, having failed to break the diplomatic stalemate by military means during the summer of 1972, moved during the fall to break the military stalemate by diplomatic means. Although confident of impending victory over George McGovern, the inept Democratic challenger, Nixon wanted to fulfill the promise he had made four years ago to achieve a peaceful settlement of the Indochina War before the November election took place. For their part, the North Vietnamese for the first time in the long war genuinely sought a peace agreement. They had been isolated from their major allies by Nixon and Kissinger's adroit diplomacy. Their army in South Vietnam had been destroyed by U.S. air power and their country was reeling under the heaviest aerial bombardment of the war. Further, some units of the South Vietnamese armed forces had fought with unusual tenacity.

Given these sobering realities, the North Vietnamese were forced to abandon their efforts to achieve a military victory in South Vietnam. They were ready to accept a negotiated settlement, if it did not contravene their long-range goals of replacing the Thieu regime with a coalition government dominated by the PRG, expelling the Americans, and achieving national reunification. The Communist leadership in Hanoi sensed that they might get better terms from Nixon before the election than after his anticipated landslide victory. They wanted to stop the destructive air war raining punishment on their economic and military facilities in order to rebuild for later military operations. They also sought to restrict American military operations in South Vietnam and salvage some of their forces fighting in that region.[135]

Secret meetings between Kissinger and Tho resumed in Paris in mid-July. It was evident from the first meeting that both sides genuinely sought a negotiated settlement of the war. Tho's attitude was much altered from the May 2 meeting; he was polite, respectful, and prepared to yield concessions. That Tho would bargain while U.S. aircraft pounded his country represented a diplomatic breakthrough. Previously, Hanoi had demanded an end to the bombing of their country as a precondition for negotiations. Tho also relinquished Hanoi's other long-standing preconditions: the demand that General Thieu would have to be removed and the withdrawal of all American forces.

In August, while Tho and Kissinger negotiated, President Nixon escalated the air war against North Vietnam. The number of daily sorties quadrupled. More and more "smart bombs" were used to allow U.S. pilots as many precision raids as possible. In September, the Air Force introduced a new all-weather tactical bomber, the F-111, which could fly near the speed of sound at tree-top level in darkness or bad weather. They could strike anytime, anywhere, and without warning.[136] The LINEBACKER operation continued until October 23, when Nixon halted all U.S. bombing of North Vietnam north of the 20th Parallel.

By October 11, Kissinger and Tho had worked out a settlement based on the U.S. concept of a two-tracked agreement that separated the military and political aspects of the conflict. Hanoi agreed to allow General Thieu to remain in power temporarily in exchange for a grant of a political status in South Vietnam to the Provisional Revolutionary Government. Within 60 days of a cease-fire, Hanoi agreed to return all of the American POWs and the United States agreed to withdraw all of its remaining troops from South Vietnam.

Both sides had made concessions. The most painful concession for the Communists had to be renouncing their demand for Thieu's removal. In effect, Hanoi accorded the Saigon government a measure of legitimacy; recognition of Thieu ran counter to the DRV's long-held goal of national reunification under the rule of the Vietnamese Communist Party. Washington's most significant concession permitted all NVA troops currently in South Vietnam to remain. That critical concession meant the Americans had accepted a basic reality of the war. Having failed to drive the North Vietnamese forces out of South Vietnam by military means, they could not hope to get them out via diplomacy. Kissinger also accepted Tho's proposal that a tripartite commission made up of delegates from the RVN, the PRG, and neutralist elements would be created to supervise elections and administer the agreement. All decisions of the tripartite commission would have to be unanimous, which meant that both the Thieu regime and the PRG representatives would retain a veto over the commission's actions.[137] Kissinger tried but failed to get Laos and Cambodia included in the proposed settlement. Significantly, the draft agreement between Kissinger and Tho deferred the key issue, who would rule in South Vietnam, to an unspecified time in the future. Presumably, that matter would be resolved by the tripartite commission after the Indochina War had ended and the Americans had gone home.

With most outstanding issues settled between Hanoi and Washington, Kissinger flew to Saigon to obtain General Thieu's approval of the mid-October agreement, only to discover that the South Vietnamese leader refused to accept it. Thieu and his associates were outraged at what they considered America's arrogant disregard of both their sensibilities and their sovereignty. Kissinger had negotiated a settlement of the war that to South Vietnamese eyes looked like an abandonment of their cause, without consulting them. General Thieu raised several strong objections to the proposed settlement and endeavored to prevent its ratification.

He and his advisers drew up a lengthy list of objections and presented them to Kissinger. Thieu's two most serious concerns were the continued presence of large numbers of North Vietnamese forces in southern Vietnam after the Americans had withdrawn all of their combat forces and the proposed tripartite commission that appeared to him as a coalition government in the making. Thieu was not reassured when Kissinger told him that any North Vietnamese violation of the agreement would provoke an instant and deadly response from the United States. General Thieu preferred that the war in his country continue rather than accept a settlement he believed rendered his nation more insecure than ever. He was also convinced that President Nixon would stand by him and not let Henry Kissinger negotiate his downfall. It was clear that by the fall of 1972 that Saigon had become the chief obstacle to the American exit from the Vietnam War.[138]

Kissinger, concerned primarily with extricating the United States from the war and skeptical of Saigon's prospects for long-term survival, probably hoped "to secure nothing more than a 'decent interval' between an American withdrawal and the resolution of the conflict in Vietnam."[139] Kissinger was angered by Thieu's strenuous opposition to the agreement and viewed the Saigon government as the main impediment to America's exit from Vietnam. When Kissinger returned to Washington, he advised Nixon to sign the agreement without Thieu's approval. Kissinger also attempted to generate momentum for a preelection settlement of the Indochina conflict by announcing dramatically at a special press conference in Washington on October 26 that "We believe that peace is at hand."[140]

But peace was not at hand because President Nixon shared some of Thieu's objections to the mid-October agreement. Nixon had also decided that the United States would have greater leverage with both Saigon and Hanoi following his expected landslide victory over McGovern than before the election. In addition, Nixon discovered that former MACV Commander William Westmoreland and other American military leaders opposed the settlement. Nixon worried continually that any settlement he and Kissinger achieved that appeared to imperil South Vietnam's chances of surviving would provoke a backlash among powerful conservative forces within the United States.

Consequently, Nixon backed Thieu's refusal to sign the agreement. Nixon decided to wait until after his reelection to try to forge an agreement with the North Vietnamese that would improve South Vietnam's prospects for long-term survival. Knowing that he was going to win a huge electoral victory in early November, Nixon would be in a position to force Hanoi to settle on American terms or "face the consequences of what we could do to them."[141] The president's support of General Thieu's intransigence guaranteed that the agreement Kissinger and Le Duc Tho had forged would fail to hold. At the same time that Nixon rejected the settlement, Washington also approved a resupply operation, called operation ENHANCE, for Saigon: Massive amounts of U.S. weapons and equipment were airlifted to South Vietnam—aircraft, tanks, trucks, armored personnel carriers (APCs), and other materiel—to strengthen the RVNAF forces. Nixon also pledged to General Thieu that U.S. negotiators would seek to revise the draft agreement in accordance with his demands.

Nixon confronted an election-eve dilemma. A combination of diplomacy and U.S. firepower had persuaded Hanoi to negotiate an agreement acceptable to Washington.

But the agreement was not acceptable to America's ally in Saigon. General Thieu demanded changes in the accord, which, in turn, were unacceptable to the North Vietnamese. Hence, Nixon viewed both Hanoi and Saigon as obstacles to "peace with honor," that is, disengagement from the war while South Vietnam was still standing.

Following his landslide victory over McGovern on November 7, Nixon moved to resolve the Vietnam dilemma. Kissinger and Le Duc Tho resumed their discussions in Paris. On November 14, President Nixon sent General Thieu a secret letter informing him that Washington would try to renegotiate the pending agreement in accordance with Saigon's wishes. He also promised the South Vietnamese leader that if Hanoi refused to abide by the terms of the agreement and renewed its aggression against the Saigon government, the United States would take "swift and severe retaliatory action."[142] Nixon also dispatched Kissinger's deputy, Alexander Haig, to both reassure and threaten Thieu. Haig promised Thieu increased military aid and more bombing of North Vietnam, but he also made it unmistably clear to the South Vietnamese leader that Washington wanted an agreement with North Vietnam and that all U.S. forces would be out of Vietnam within six months.[143]

In Paris, Kissinger, responding to Nixon's and General Thieu's concerns, introduced many matters for reconsideration that the North Vietnamese assumed had been resolved. Kissinger also proposed major changes that would adversely affect the status of the VietCong and the North Vietnamese forces in South Vietnam. He raised these matters more for the record than because he held out any hope that the North Vietnamese might accept them. Kissinger could not have been surprised when Le Duc Tho and his colleagues, concluding that they had been tricked into approving an agreement the Americans had never intended to keep, angrily rejected all of Kissinger's revised proposals. The North Vietnamese did not believe the Saigon government would have rejected the agreement on their own; they thought, mistakenly, that the Americans had told Thieu to object to the agreement to provide a pretext for Nixon's refusal to accept it.

When Kissinger warned Tho that Nixon, having just won reelection by an overwhelming margin, was prepared to take whatever action he felt necessary to protect U.S. interests in South Vietnam, the North Vietnamese envoy boldly responded to the American's threats by hardening his position. The North Vietnamese even returned to their old stance of insisting that Thieu would have to be ousted as a precondition for any settlement. For weeks, Kissinger and Le Duc Tho negotiated, sometimes tensely, sometimes angrily. On occasion, during these talks, Tho would make concessions and appear to be trying to reach an agreement, only to retract his offer subsequently. During these negotiations Kissinger's moods fluctuated wildly. They swung between optimism that an agreement might be struck and deep pessimism that no agreement was possible. At times he lashed out angrily at the North Vietnamese leaders. Gradually, both sides edged toward an agreement, one similar in most of its provisions to the one they had concluded in early October, which both Thieu and Nixon had rejected.

But Kissinger decided Tho was stalling. He sensed the North Vietnamese sought to avoid an agreement; they were trying to drive a wedge between Washington and

Saigon, forestall further bombing, and wait until the new United States Congress convened in January 1973. The new Congress, controlled by Democrats and in a dovish mood, might cut off all funding for the war and force the Americans to get out of Vietnam. South Vietnam, abandoned by the United States, would then be vulnerable to a future NVA assault. After weeks of futile negotiation, convinced that Hanoi did not want an agreement to come out of the sessions, Nixon directed Kissinger to break off the talks on December 13.[144]

President Nixon had decided it was time to try one more big play—to try to resolve the latest Paris impasse by force. He too was concerned that the incoming Congress would cut off all funding for the American war, effectively ending it and handing the Communists a victory that they had not been able to win on the battlefields of Vietnam. Once again, he demonstrated his willingness to unleash American air power in a campaign known as LINEBACKER II. But LINEBACKER II differed from its predecessor. Whereas LINEBACKER I was designed to destroy North Vietnam's warmaking capacity, LINEBACKER II aimed to destroy Hanoi's will to fight. Nixon had concluded that he would have to shock the North Vietnamese into believing that Washington would not tolerate an indefinite delay in negotiating a peace settlement. The new bombing campaign would also be a spectacular show of resolve to reassure Saigon that the United States remained committed to the goal of an independent South Vietnam.[145] Nixon ordered a powerful air assault against Hanoi and Haiphong. For the first time in the war, he ordered the deployment of B-52s, the most powerful weapons in the U.S. air arsenal, against the two largest cities of North Vietnam. He told the chairman of the Joint Chiefs, Admiral Thomas Moorer, "I don't want any more of this crap about the fact that we couldn't hit this target or that one. This is your chance to use military power to win this war, and if you don't, I'll consider it your responsibility."[146]

To achieve maximum impact, Nixon sent no warning or ultimatum to Hanoi, nor did he go on television to tell the American public why it was necessary to renew the air war against North Vietnam. Starting on December 18, the sky over Hanoi and Haiphong was filled by the largest U.S. air armada of the war. Relying mostly on the B-52s, U.S. aircraft dropped 15,247 tons of bombs, mostly along the 60-mile Haiphong-Hanoi corridor, during 11 days of air attacks. Wave after wave of the B-52s struck warehouses, oil storage facilities, railyards, airfields, power plants, industrial complexes, and SAM-2 sites.

Both Hanoi and Haiphong were well defended; they possessed sophisticated air defense systems that could be expected to bring down a sizable number of the big planes, which composed an integral part of the American strategic deterrent vis-à-vis the Soviet Union. Nixon understood that the SAM-2s would claim many B-52s, but he felt he had to use them to achieve the levels of destruction and psychological impact required to persuade the North Vietnamese to return to the bargaining table. During the course of the 11-day air war, the Soviet-supplied missile systems, some of which were manned by Soviet crews, brought down fifteen B-52s and damaged several others. Ninety-two U.S. pilots and air crewmen were killed or captured.[147]

The LINEBACKER II operation, which the American press quickly dubbed the "Christmas Bombing," provoked furious criticism within the United States and abroad. No effort had been made to prepare the American people for the air war, and most believed that the war was virtually over with only a few details remaining to be resolved before a peace agreement was signed. Hence they reacted with surprise and outrage to the largest bombing campaign of the long war. Even as the United States waged its aerial war, government officials in Hanoi showed visiting U.S. journalists schools, hospitals, and residential areas detroyed or damaged by bombs. Press editorialists and congressional opponents accused Nixon of waging a war against the civilian population of North Vietnam. Senator Edward Kennedy said the air raids "should outrage the conscience of all Americans."[148] European press and government leaders also denounced the U.S. bombing campaign. Swedish Prime Minister Olaf Palme compared the bombing to Nazi atrocities.[149] Congressional critics, on recess for the Christmas holidays, made it clear that when they returned to Washington in January they would cut off all funds to deprive the president of the ability to wage war anywhere in Indochina. Polls showed the bombing brought Nixon's approval rating down to 39 percent, the lowest rating of his presidency.

The LINEBACKER II operation was not a campaign of terror bombing that targeted cities and civilian populations. Only military targets and targets that were not located in densely populated areas were deliberately attacked. The civilian toll for Hanoi was 1,318 killed and 1,216 wounded, and for Haiphong 305 civilians were reported killed. Considering the scale and intensity of the attacks on both cities, these casualty figures were light. American journalists who visited Hanoi and Haiphong after the air war had ceased discovered that civilian property destruction was minor compared with the devastation of targeted areas.[150]

On December 22, Nixon cabled Hanoi that if the North Vietnamese agreed to resume the peace talks, then the United States would stop the bombing. There was no immediate response from the North Vietnamese. On December 26, following a 36-hour respite to observe the Christmas holiday, 120 B-52s, flying out of both Andersen and U-Tapao air bases, attacked Hanoi and Haiphong. It was the most intense day of aerial bombardment in the history of aviation warfare. The next day, Hanoi signaled to Nixon that they were prepared to resume the Paris talks on January 8, 1973. Nixon continued the bombing for two more days. On December 29, he ordered that all bombings north of the 20th Parallel cease at 7:00 P.M. local time.[151] The next day, the president told the American people that the aerial war was over and that peace negotiations would resume in Paris on January 8.

The LINEBACKER II operation had some limited successes. It temporarily reduced Hanoi's war-making capacities and again disrupted its supply lines from China and the Soviet Union. It also sent Hanoi a warning that America would unleash its aircraft in the event that the North Vietnamese violated provisions of the final treaty about to be negotiated. In addition, the firm show of U.S. resolve served to reassure the South Vietnamese and perhaps made General Thieu more willing to accept the final settlement.

But Hanoi returned to the bargaining table mainly because they saw that it was in their interest to do so. The North Vietnamese delegates would likely have returned eventually had LINEBACKER II never occurred. There is no evidence that suggests Operation LINEBACKER II coerced Hanoi to resume the Paris talks.[152]

Negotiations between Kissinger and Tho resumed on January 8, 1973. An agreement was hammered out in six days. Washington again allowed the Communists to maintain an active political and military presence in South Vietnam. Hanoi again accepted the existence of the Thieu regime and allowed continuing U.S. aid to the RVN.[153]

The Christmas Bombing campaign had not produced a settlement that differed in any significant measure from the agreement that had been previously worked out by Kissinger and Tho in mid-October. Despite the pledge to Thieu, Kissinger did not try to obtain the major alterations in the agreement that the South Vietnamese leader had demanded. Nothing of substance had changed between October 1972 and January 1973. There were a few cosmetic changes, but the terms of the final agreement closely followed the October settlement that Nixon had permitted General Thieu to reject.

The most important change in language occurring in the final agreement concerned the DMZ. The North Vietnamese agreed to make explicit reference to it for the first time, but the U.S. negotiators accepted its description as a "provisional and not a political or territorial boundary," which conceded the substance of Hanoi's long-standing view of the DMZ.[154]

More important, the Christmas Bombing campaign did not significantly alter the political or military balance between North and South Vietnam, nor did it improve the chances for the RVN's long-term survival. Whatever Nixon hoped to achieve by the intense 11-day bombing campaign, perhaps a permanent diminution of Hanoi's war-making ability, or perhaps better terms for South Vietnam in the final settlement—all failed to transpire. For all of its sound and fury, the Christmas Bombing campaign proved to be a diplomatic irrelevance.

The president, who sensed that he had no more big plays left in his Indochina playbook, was determined to end the war. Nixon took the best settlement he could get and then imposed it on General Thieu before the new Congress itself ended the American war by cutting off all funding for military action in Indochina. The Christmas Bombing campaign had forced Washington to accept the settlement that Nixon had rejected in October. As John Negroponte, one of Kissinger's aides who had a penchant for irony put it, "We bombed the North Vietnamese into accepting our concessions."[155]

To make the final agreement easier for General Thieu to swallow, Nixon had vastly increased the level of military aid going to the RVN. He also gave the South Vietnamese leader a handwritten promise that the United States would continue to support the Thieu government. Nixon promised in writing that the United States would respond in full force if North Vietnam ever launched another offensive in violation of the peace treaty.

But Nixon again sent Haig to bully General Thieu. He delivered to the South Vietnamese leader a blunt letter Nixon had written demanding that he sign the agreement.

The letter also indicated that Nixon was committed to signing the accords on January 27, "if necessary alone." To put more pressure on the hapless Thieu, the letter also informed him that in the event he did not sign the agreement, Washington would cut off all further assistance to South Vietnam. Thieu, after failing to get the changes he had sought implemented, had no choice but to sign an agreement that he feared and loathed.[156]

Representatives of all four delegations at the Paris talks, the United States, North Vietnam, South Vietnam, and the PRG signed the Agreement on Ending the War and Restoring Peace in Vietnam, usually called the Paris Accords, on January 27, 1973. The Accords had two major divisions: a set of military provisions and a set of political provisions.

The main military provisions of the Paris Accords provided that (1) a ccase-fire throughout South Vietnam would go into effect immediately; (2) at the same time, America would cease all acts of war against North Vietnam and agree to remove, deactivate, or destroy immediately all of the mines that had been laid in North Vietnamese ports, harbors, and waterways; (3) the United States would agree to remove all of its remaining forces, including advisory personnel (about 24,000 people), from South Vietnam and to dismantle all of its bases in that country within sixty days; (4) Hanoi would

Figure 8.11   Ambassador William H. Sullivan (lower right) and Xuan Thuy (upper left) watch as Henry Kissinger (lower center) and Le Duc Tho (second from upper right) initial the Paris Peace Accords on January 23, 1973. *Source:* CORBIS. Neg.#: Be021744.

agree to return all American prisoners-of-war within sixty days; (5) the 150,000 NVA troops currently inside South Vietnam would be allowed to remain; (6) neither the United States nor the North Vietnamese would send more troops to South Vietnam; and (7) two commissions, the Joint Military Commission, made up of representatives from the ARVN and VC/NVA forces, and the International Commission on Control, made up of delegates from Hungary, Poland, Indonesia, and Canada, would enforce the cease-fire provisions of the agreement.[157]

The major political provisions of the Paris Accords provided that (1) the Thieu government and the PRG would both be accorded legitimacy within South Vietnam; (2) both entities would establish a National Council of National Reconciliation and Concord, representing equally the RVN, the PRG, and the "third force" elements in South Vietnam. The council would implement the political aspects of the Accords, including holding elections to determine the future government of South Vietnam. (3) South Vietnam would be declared a free and an independent nation; and (4) all signatories would guarantee that the reunification of Vietnam would be gradual, peaceful, and without coercion.[158]

President Nixon, in a speech from the Oval Office, given a few hours after the Accords were signed in Paris, told the American people that all remaining U.S. troops would be out of Vietnam and all American POWs would be coming home within 60 days. He also stated that "South Vietnam has gained the right to determine its own future. Let us be proud that America did not settle for a peace that betrayed an ally."[159]

If he truly believed his statements, President Nixon was deluding himself. The agreement that had taken so long to consummate served primarily as a vehicle that permitted the United States an exit from the war—we retrieved our POWs and the Thieu government remained in power. But the American extrication, coupled with Nixon's upbeat rhetoric, disguised a disastrous strategic defeat: withdrawal from a war that Washington could no longer hope to win, a war that no longer commanded the support of Congress, the media, or most Americans, and a war that continued on terms increasingly perilous to the survivability of the Saigon government. General Nguyen Cao Ky, who watched President Nixon's televised speech, had a more realistic appraisal of the Paris Accords (he also proved to be an accurate political forecaster):

> I could not stomach it, so nauseating was its hypocrisy and self-delusion. . . . This is an enormous step toward the total domination of Vietnam and there is no reason why the Communists should stop now. . . . I give them a couple of years before they invade the South.[160]

The signing of the Paris treaty occasioned no celebrations or outpourings of joy among the people of South Vietnam or within the Thieu government. The treaty permitted some 150,000 North Vietnamese troops to remain in South Vietnam. The agreement also granted the PRG, the political arm of the PLAF insurgency, a political status in South Vietnam, which meant that the people and areas of South Vietnam under the control of the VietCong had been granted legitimacy and South Vietnam's internal security was further endangered by the presence of ten divisions of enemy troops on its soil.

The January Accords left unresolved the fundamental issue for which the United States and North Vietnam had fought a long and bloody war: the political status, indeed the very existence of South Vietnam. Since the Geneva Accords of July 1954, since the temporary division of Vietnam at the 17th Parallel, Washington and Hanoi had been at odds over who should rule in Southern Vietnam. Having deferred the major question for which the Vietnam War had been fought, one that would determine whether an independent South Vietnam would survive, the Paris agreement presumed that the question would be resolved by political means, sometime in an unspecified future.

But the political mechanisms created to resolve the political issues were inherently unworkable.[161] At the time the Paris agreements were signed, all informed observers understood that the question of who would ultimately have political power in South Vietnam could only be resolved by force. The Paris Accords did not bring a cease-fire; they did not end a war; and they did not save South Vietnam from a Communist takeover. They only ensured that the Vietnam War would go on without the Americans.

Unable to force the Americans out of South Vietnam by military means, Hanoi opted to remove the American forces by diplomacy, which required accepting the continued existence of the RVN for a few years and according the Thieu government legitimacy. But the North Vietnamese had not renounced their long-held revolutionary goals, and they had no intention of abiding by any terms of the Paris Accords that interfered with the attainment of their goals. Hanoi's decision to accept the Paris settlement was based on its assumption that once the Americans had left, the VC/NVA forces could defeat Thieu's regime within a few years. The North Vietnamese also understood that the mechanisms for policing the cease-fire, like the mechanisms for resolving the political issues, were unworkable. Hanoi's leaders believed the South Vietnamese armed forces would never be able to withstand another major NVA offensive on their own; years of Vietnamization had not eliminated the RVNAF's basic flaws or given the South Vietnamese government a broad popular base of support. By Hanoi's reckoning, the RVN would survive only as long as it took North Vietnam to rebuild its forces and mount another offensive, about two or three years. The Paris Accords could only delay for a few years, but they could not prevent, North Vietnam from eventually achieving its military and political objectives.[162]

Only a credible threat of U.S. military retaliation could have enforced the Paris Accords and kept South Vietnam alive indefinitely. But the domestic political reaction to the Christmas Bombing campaign suggested that it had been Richard Nixon's last hurrah. Neither Congress nor the American people would support reentry of American naval and air power into combat anywhere in Indochina, much less advisers or ground combat forces. The Communist leaders concluded that Nixon dared not "risk the political damage that would result from an effort to reimpose U.S. power in South Vietnam."[163] If North Vietnam could not be restrained from military action, if South Vietnam could not defend itself on its own, and if America could not intervene militarily to try to save the RVN, the demise of South Vietnam was inevitable. Nixon's vaunted "peace with honor" in reality meant disguised American strategic defeat delayed by an interval of a few years' duration.

The 1973 Paris Accords, which resembled the 1954 Geneva Accords in many ways, essentially amounted to a deal between Hanoi and Washington. The United States got its POWs back and its remaining troops out of Vietnam. Hanoi got the bombing of its country and the battering of its army halted, and also got the remaining American soldiers out of Vietnam. The Thieu government got nothing, neither peace nor the prospect of a political settlement that could ensure the long-term survival of South Vietnam.

The American and Vietnamese people paid a painfully high price for the illusory peace that Nixon and Kissinger achieved after four more years of war. Many critics of their Vietnam policy maintain that they could have gotten the same terms four years earlier had they been more adroit and flexible diplomatists. Four more years of war had cost more than 15,000 additional U.S. battle deaths, about 150,000 additional South Vietnamese battle deaths, and over 400,000 additional North Vietnamese battle deaths. Hundreds of thousands of civilians in South Vietnam also died during those extra years of war and 2 million more refugees were forced to flee the countryside for the cities and suburbs of South Vietnam. Within the United States, continuing inflation weakened the economy and eroded the living standards of millions of American families. The war also perpetuated and intensified domestic conflicts, dividing Americans, polarizing politics, and poisoning the political atmosphere. The United States emerged from its lengthy involvement in Southeast Asia with its world status and prestige considerably diminished.[164] By the time the United States withdrew all of its soldiers from Vietnam, the morale, discipline, and fighting spirit of its Army had seriously eroded.

The Soviet Union had used the years that the United States had entangled itself in a major war in Southeast Asia to achieve strategic parity with its major Cold War rival. By 1973, many Americans, achingly weary of war and, for that matter, of all international commitments, increasingly embraced a neoisolationist outlook. Nixon himself paid dearly for his prolongation of the Vietnam War. The Watergate scandals, which forced his resignation from the presidency in disgrace, grew out of his inability to end the Vietnam War quickly, as promised. Richard Nixon eventually joined Lyndon Johnson as one of the two most prominent victims of the lengthy American crusade to contain the expansion of Communism in Southeast Asia.[165]

A bizarre follow-up to the Paris agreements occurred in October 1973, when a Nobel Peace Prize committee jointly awarded Henry Kissinger and Le Duc Tho the 1973 Nobel Peace Prize for their efforts to bring an end to the Vietnam War. Kissinger was uneasy about the award, and Le Duc Tho rejected it, pointing out that the war had not really ended. Kissinger later refused to attend the awards ceremony at the University of Oslo and then donated the $65,000 cash prize he received to a scholarship fund established to help the children of U.S. soldiers killed or missing in Vietnam. The Nobel committee had awarded its most prestigious prize to two diplomats who had negotiated a fictitious peace! Even as the committee was announcing its awards, the war raged on and Vietnamese continued to kill Vietnamese in South Vietnam. Former Undersecretary of State George Ball observed, "The Norwegians must have a sense of humor." An American expert on Asian affairs bluntly observed: "There is no peace and we stayed too long." A *New York Times* editorial writer labeled the award, "The Nobel War Prize."[166]

NOTES

1. Ambrose, Stephen E., "Nixon and Vietnam: Vietnam and Electoral Politics," in George Donelson Moss, ed., *A Vietnam Reader* (Englewood Cliffs, NJ: Prentice Hall, 1991), 204–5.
2. Goodman, *The Lost Peace,* 79–80.
3. According to Ambrose, Nixon never said "I have a secret plan to end the war" during the 1968 campaign. The phrase was a journalistic invention. See Nixon, Richard, "Asia after Vietnam," *Foreign Affairs* 46 (October 1967): 111–25; and the excerpts from an undelivered radio speech scheduled for March 31, 1968, in Goodman, *The Lost Peace,* 80–81.
4. Kissinger, Henry, "The Vietnam Negotiations," *Foreign Affairs* 47 (January 1969): 234; Kissinger, Henry, *The White House Years* (Boston: Little, Brown, 1979), 228–32; Kimball, *Nixon's Vietnam War,* 100–102. Kimball shows how both Nixon and Kissinger came to power confident that they could bring an end to the Vietnam War within six months.
5. Quote is from Hess, *Vietnam,* 114.
6. Goodman, *The Lost Peace,* 81; Hess, Vietnam, 114–15; DeBenedetti, 277; Kimball, *Nixon's Vietnam War,* 114–23.
7. The Nixon quote is found in Morris, Roger, *Uncertain Greatness: Henry Kissinger and American Foreign Policy* (New York: Harper & Row, 1977), 156; Lipsman, Samuel, Doyle, Edward, and the editors of Boston Publishing, *Fighting for Time* (Boston: Boston Publishing, 1983) 8, 27–28, a volume in the series *The Vietnam Experience.* See Porter, *Vietnam Documents,* vol. 2, Document 289, 522–29. "National Security Study Memorandum No. 1," January 21, 1969 (extracts).
8. Moss, *America in the Twentieth Century,* 371–73.
9. Polls cited in Mueller, *Wars, Presidents, and Public Opinion,* 92–93.
10. Quote is from Schandler, *Unmaking of a President,* 321.
11. Brandon, Henry, *The Retreat of American Power* (New York: Delta, 1972), 58–59; Goodman, *The Lost Peace,* 85; Schulzinger, *A Time for War,* 275.
12. Herring, George C., "The Nixon Strategy in Vietnam," in Peter Braestrup, ed., *Vietnam as History: Ten Years after the Paris Peace Accords* (Washington, DC: University Press of America, 1984), 51–52; Herring, *America's Longest War,* 3d ed., 245.
13. Lipsman et al., *Fighting for Time,* 30–31; Herring, *America's Longest War,* 225.
14. Kissinger, *The White House Years,* 242–49; Davidson, *Vietnam at War,* 589–94.
15. Crawford, Henry B., "Operation Menu's Secret Bombing of Cambodia," in *Vietnam* (December 1996): 22–28.
16. Kissinger, *The White House Years,* 252–53; Morris, *Uncertain Greatness,* 158–62. According to Morris, Kissinger approved of the wiretaps and gave the names of some officials and journalists whom he wanted wiretapped to FBI agents. Ambrose, Stephen E., *Nixon: The Triumph of a Politician* (New York: Simon and Schuster, 1989), 258–59.
17. Lipsman et al., *Fighting for Time,* 31–32; quote is from Hess, *Vietnam,* 115.
18. Lipsman et al, *Fighting for Time,* 32. Porter (ed.), *Vietnam Documents,* vol. 2, Document 291, 531, "Address on Television by President Richard M. Nixon," May 14, 1969 (extract).

19. Kissinger, *The White House Years,* 271–74; Herring, *America's Longest War,* 226.

20. Goodman, *The Lost Peace,* 87–88.

21. Duiker, *The Communist Road,* 278–83.

22. See epigraph, chap. 1, 5.

23. Copies of Nixon's July 15, 1969, letter to Ho Chi Minh, and the North Vietnamese leader's response, dated August 15, can be found in Szulc, Tad, *The Illusion of Peace: Foreign Policy in the Nixon Years* (New York: Viking, 1978),137, 139. Nixon developed what he called his "madman theory" in his efforts to end the Vietnam War on terms he could accept. He would have aides get the word to Hanoi that the new president was an extreme anti-Communist and mentally unstable, a dangerous man capable of any action in his efforts to end the war—even capable of using nuclear weapons and destroying the Red River dikes that would have flooded Vietnam's most densely populated region. Nixon believed such a ploy could frighten the North Vietnamese leaders into seeking an accommodation with the United States.

24. Quoted in Lipsman and others, *Fighting for Time,* 36.

25. Quoted in Morris, *Uncertain Greatness,* 164.

26. Hersh, Seymour M., *The Price of Power: Kissinger in the Nixon White House* (New York: Summit, 1983), 124–30; Morris, *Uncertain Greatness,* 163–64; Szulc, *Illusion of Peace,* 150–56; Kimball, *Nixon's Vietnam War,* 158–65, is the best brief analysis of the DUCK HOOK contingency planning.

27. Herring, *America's Longest War,* 228.

28. Kissinger, *The White House Years,* 278–83. Henry Cabot Lodge, the head of the U.S. team at the Paris talks, had met privately many times with Xuan Thuy prior to Kissinger's August 4 meeting. These talks had been unproductive.

29. Szulc, Tad, *Illusion of Peace,* 148–49. Nixon, like Johnson, tended to equate criticism of his war policy with subversion. He secretly ordered the FBI, the CIA, and other intelligence agencies to look for connections between the antiwar movement and the enemy.

30. Herring, *America's Longest War,* 228.

31. DeBenedetti, *An American Ordeal,* 248–53.

32. DeBenedetti, Charles, *The Peace Reform in American History* (Bloomington: Indiana University Press, 1984), 180–85; Lipsman et al., *Fighting for Time,* 36–37; DeBenedetti, *An American Ordeal,* 255–57.

33. Schulzinger, *A Time for War,* 281.

34. Quoted in Lipsman et al., *Fighting for Time,* 37.

35. Transcript of Nixon's speech delivered November 3, 1969. The speech also appears in Nixon, Richard M., *Public Papers: Richard M. Nixon, 1969* (Washington, DC: U.S. Government Printing Office, 1971), 901–9. Although the policy itself had been in place for a year and a half, the term "Vietnamization" was coined by Nixon's secretary of defense, Melvin Laird.

36. Polls are cited in DeBenedetti, *An American Ordeal,* 259.

37. Quoted in Szulc, *Illusion of Peace,* 158.

38. DeBenedetti, *An American Ordeal,* 261–62.

39. Ibid., 262–63. One of the people who played a minor role in organizing the huge November 15 Washington protest was a 22-year-old Rhodes Scholar and future president, William Jefferson "Bill" Clinton.

40. Polls cited in ibid., 264.

41. Davidson, *Vietnam at War,* 603–6; quote is from Hess, *Vietnam,* 118.

42. Davidson, *Vietnam at War,* 606–7.

43. Quote is from *ibid.,* 607.

44. Blaufarb, *Counterinsurgency Era,* 264–78; Sheehan, *Bright Shining Lie,* 731–36; Herring, *America's Longest War,* 231–33; Davidson, *Vietnam at War,* 609–12; Andrade, *Ashes to Ashes,* 123–46; and Hess, *Vietnam,* 118.

45. Hess, *Vietnam,* 118–19.

46. Stanton, *Rise and Fall,* 269–70; Davidson, *Vietnam at War,* 612–13.

47. Hess, *Vietnam,* 117–19.

48. Stanton, *Rise and Fall,* 284.

49. Stanton, *Rise and Fall,* 283–88; Lipsman et al., *Fighting for Time,* 17–23; Davidson, *Vietnam at War,* 614–15.

50. Quoted in Lipsman et al., *Fighting for Time,* 22.

51. Transcript of interview with Melvin Zais, General, U.S. Army (Ret.), 1977, Vol III, 575–88, U.S. Army Military History Institute archives, Carlisle Barracks, PA. General Zais had a son fighting in the battle of Dong Ap Bia. General Zais believed that the name, "Hamburger Hill," was suggested by a young Wire Service reporter interviewing a hysterical soldier who had participated in the battle.

52. Davidson, *Vietnam at War,* 615.

53. Ibid., 615–19; Stanton, *Rise and Fall,* 278–80; Lipsman et al., *Fighting for Time,* 92–115; Lewy, *America in Vietnam,* 153–61; Cincinnatus, *Self-Destruction: The Disintegration and Decay of the United States Army during the Vietnam Era* (New York: W. W. Norton, 1981). "Cincinnatus" is the pseudonym used by Cecil B. Currey.

54. Baskir and Strauss, *Chance and Circumstance,* 3–61; Moss, "Vietnam Generation," 4–9.

55. Stanton, *Decline and Fall,* 279–80.

56. Savage, Paul L., and Gabriel, Richard A., "Cohesion and Disintegration in the American Army," *Armed Forces and Society* 2 (spring 1976): 362–71; Baritz, *Backfire,* 294–309; Davidson, *Vietnam at War,* 617–19.

57. Lipsman et al., *Fighting for Time,* 92–96.

58. Ibid., 97–100. A CBS News television documentary portrayed a combat refusal that occurred in April 1970 in War Zone C near the Cambodian border during Operation TOAN THANG 43.

59. Lewy, *America in Vietnam,* 153–58; Cincinnatus, *Self-Destruction,* passim.

60. Lewy, *America in Vietnam,* 154–55; Fiman, Bryan G., et al., "Black-White and American-Vietnamese Relations among Soldiers in Vietnam," *Journal of Social Issues* 31 (fall 1975): 43–46; Lipsman, *Fighting for Time,* 102. African Americans constituted approximately 15 percent of the forces sent to Vietnam from 1961–1972, and Vietnam was the first major foreign war in which the U.S. Armed Forces were fully integrated.

61. Moss, "Vietnam Generation," 14.

62. Cited in Lipsman, *Fighting for Time,* 103.

63. McCoy, Alfred W., with Read, Cathleen B., and Adams, Leonard P., II. *The Politics of Heroin in Southeast Asia* (New York: Harper & Row, 1972), 9.

64. Ibid., 181–85, 217–22. McCoy accuses several high-ranking military officials in the Thieu-Ky government of drug trafficking and he names names. McCoy also charges that U.S. embassy officials refused to investigate these charges and denied that any South Vietnamese officials were involved in drug smuggling.

65. Porter, *Vietnam Documents,* vol. 2, Document 295, 539–41, "Nixon Speech," April 20, 1970 (extract); Herring, *America's Longest War,* 3d ed, 253. Sheehan, Neil, *A Bright Shining Lie,* 741–742, makes the point that Nixon's troop withdrawals saved the army from disintegration.

66. Kissinger, *The White House Years,* 458–61; Lipsman, *Fighting for Time,* 127–30, 138–42; Hess, *Vietnam,* rev. ed., 116–18.

67. Davidson, *Vietnam at War,* 625; Herring, "The Nixon Strategy in Vietnam," 55–56; Lipsman, *Fighting for Time,* 146–47;

68. Kissinger, *The White House Years,* 468–70. William Shawcross, *Sideshow: Kissinger, Nixon, and the Destruction of Cambodia* (New York: Simon and Schuster, 1979), chap. 8 "The Coup," 112–27, has suggested U.S. complicity in the coup that overthrow Sihanouk. He has been vigorously refuted by Henry Kissinger, *The White House Years,* 517–21, see notes, 1484–85. No evidence has ever surfaced connecting the United States to the anti-Sihanouk coup.

69. Davidson, *Vietnam at War,* 625–27; Palmer, *Summons of the Trumpet,* 294–96; Hess, *Vietnam,* rev. ed., 118–19.

70. Szulc, *Illusion of Peace,* 252–60; Lipsman, *Fighting for Time,* 152–53; Herring, *America's Longest War,* 235–36.

71. Transcript of Nixon's speech, April 30, 1970; a copy of the speech is printed in *Nixon, Richard M., Public Papers,* 1970 (Washington, DC: U.S. Government Printing Office, 1971), 405–410.

72. Stanton, *Decline and Fall,* 319–21.

73. Ibid., 322–25; Palmer, *Summons of the Trumpet,* 297–301.

74. Palmer, *Summons of the Trumpet,* 299–301; Stanton, *Decline and Fall,* 324–25; Davidson, *Vietnam at War,* 627–29; Hess, *Vietnam,* 122–23. During Toan Than 43, the VC/NVA lost about 11,000 KIAs, the Allies 976, including 338 Americans. The Allies captured 16,700,000 rounds of small arms ammunition, 23,000 individual weapons, 200,000 rounds of antiaircraft ammunition, and 14 million pounds of rice.

75. Palmer, *The 25-Year War,* 103–4; Stanton, *Decline and Fall,* 324–25; "Vietnam: A War That Is Finished," CBS television documentary first shown to the American public in August 1975.

76. DeBenedetti, *An American Ordeal,* 279.

77. Heineman, Kenneth J., *Campus Wars: The Peace Movement at American State Universities in the Vietnam Era* (New York: New York University Press, 1993), 456–500.

78. Ibid., 249–50.

79. Kimball, *Nixon's Vietnam War,* 218–19; DeBenedetti, *An American Ordeal,* 279–80. President Nixon has an account of the incident in Nixon, Richard M., *RN: The Memoirs of Richard Nixon* (New York: Grosset and Dunlap, 1978), 459–66.

80. Lipsman, *Fighting for Time,* 181–82; DeBenedetti, *An American Ordeal,* 280–82.

81. DeBenedetti, *An American Ordeal,* 281–82.

82. Morris, *Uncertain Greatness,* 199–201.

83. Young, *Vietnam Wars,* 251–52; Hess, *Vietnam,* rev. ed., 120.

84. Brandon, *Retreat of American Power,* 146–49; Herring, *America's Longest War,* 238.

85. Morris, *Uncertain Greatness,* 174–75; Kissinger, *The White House Years,* 968–72; Goodman, *The Lost Peace,* 105–7.

86. DeBenedetti, *An American Ordeal,* 293; Ambrose, *Nixon: The Triumph of a Politician,* 394. When Nixon assumed his triumphalist stance on the roof of the limosine, some of the protesters, enraged at his actions, began hurling rocks and eggs in the direction of the president. He quickly scrambled down and Secret Service agents hustled him into the limosine, which rapidly sped away.

87. Palmer, *Summons of the Trumpet,* 302–3; Stanton, *Decline and Fall,* 333–34; and Davidson, *Vietnam at War,* 637–41. Thieu named the proposed incursion into Laos after Lam Son, the birthplace of Le Loi, a great Vietnamese national hero who, in one of the most famous military campaigns in Vietnamese history, had defeated an invading Chinese army in 1427.

88. Davidson, *Vietnam at War,* 637–42.

89. Palmer, *Summons of the Trumpet,* 304–5.

90. Davidson, *Vietnam at War,* 645–49; Stanton, *Decline and Fall,* 336–37. South Vietnamese losses were heavy: 1,146 battle deaths, 4,236 wounded.

91.   Quote is from Davidson, *Vietnam at War,* 651–52.

92.   Ibid., 652–54; Stanton, *Rise and Fall,* 336–37.

93.   Hess, *Vietnam,* 126.

94.   Kissinger, *The White House Years,* 1016–23.

95.   Porter, *Vietnam Documents,* vol. 2, Document 300, 555–56, "DRV Nine-Point Plan," June 26, 1971; Goodman, *The Lost Peace,* 111–15; Kissinger, *The White House Years,* 1023–31.

96.   Fulghum, David; Maitland, Terrence; and the editors of Boston Publishing, *South Vietnam on Trial: Mid-1970 to 1972* (Boston: Boston Publishing, 1984), 102–4, a volume in the series The Vietnam Experience; Schulzinger, *A Time for War,* 290.

97.   Fulgrun, David; Terrance, *Vietnam in Trial,* 104–8; Herring, *America's Longest War,* 245. Kerry also made a presentation before The Senate Foreign Relations Committee. He called attention to war crimes and atrocities committed by U.S. soldiers against Vietnamese civilians. He confronted the Senators with an unanswerable question: "How do you ask a man to be the last man to die for a mistake?"

98.   DeBenedetti, *An American Ordeal,* 307–8.

99.   Ibid., 309–10; Young, *Vietnam Wars,* 257–59.

100. Polls cited in DeBenedetti, *An American Ordeal,* 310. Ellsberg, a disillusioned defense intellectual turned antiwar activist, hoped that publication of the Pentagon Papers would bring a speedier end to U.S. involvement in the Vietnam war.

101. Haldeman, Harry R., with editorial assistance from Ambrose Stephen, *The Haldeman Diaries* (New York: Putnam, 1994), 300.

102. Schulzinger, *A Time for War,* 292.

103. DeBenedetti, *An American Ordeal,* 324.

104. Quote is from Herring, *America's Longest War,* 246.

105. Hess, *Vietnam,* 127; Clodfelter, *Limits,* 168; quote is from Thompson, Sir Robert, *Peace Is Not at Hand* (New York: David McKay, 1974), 96.

106. Hess, *Vietnam,* 127.

107. Ibid., 127–28.

108. Ibid.

109. Duiker, *The Communist Road,* 288–92.

110. Ibid., 292–93.

111. The three PAVN divisions included the 304th, the 308th, and the 324-B. Consciously emulating their heroic national past, the North Vietnamese leaders named their 1972 spring offensive after Nguyen Hue, who, in 1789, led a surprise offensive against a Chinese army, driving them out of Vietnam.

112. Davidson, *Vietnam at War,* 680–84; Stanton, *Rise and Fall,* 343; and Palmer, *Summons of the Trumpet,* 315–19.

113. Quote is from Isaacs, *Without Honor,* 26.

114. Stanton, *Rise and Fall,* 343–44; Duiker, *The Communist Road,* 293.

115. Reference footnote 31, chap. 4, this book; Sheehan, *A Bright Shining Lie,* 754–85. Sheehan's critically acclaimed best seller is a superb biography of an extraordinary man who spent more time in South Vietnam than any other American civilian or military official.

116. Davidson, *Vietnam at Wa*r, 688–93; Fulghum, *South Vietnam on Trial,* 184–89.

117. Stanton, *Rise and Fall,* 343–44; Davidson, *Vietnam at War,* 693–97.

118. Davidson, *Vietnam at War,* 706–13; Fulghum, *South Vietnam on Trial,* 150–54, 160–67.

119. Nixon, Richard, *RN: The Memoirs of Richard Nixon* (New York: Grosset & Dunlap, 1978), 587; Clodfelter, *Limits,* 153.

120. Quoted in Fulghum, *South Vietnam on Trial,* 142.

121. Clodfelter, *Limits,* 153–54.

122. Ibid., 158.

123. Hess, *Vietnam,* 128–29; Clodfelter, *Limits,* 159.

124. Nixon, *Memoirs,* 590–91; Kissinger, *The White House Years,* 1119–21; Fulghum, *South Vietnam on Trial,* 142–43.

125. Nixon, *Memoirs,* 588–89; Kissinger, *The White House Years,* 1113–14.

126. Fulghum, *South Vietnam on Trial,* 144–45; Goodman, *The Lost Peace,* 118–19; Kissinger, *The White House Years,* 1135–37, 1144–48, 1169–70.

127. Quoted in Herring, *America's Longest War,* 247.

128. Porter, *Vietnam Documents,* vol. 2, Document 305, 566–67, "Address to the Nation by Nixon," May 8, 1972 (extracts); Nixon, *Memoirs,* 605; Clodfelter, *Limits,* 157.

129. Hess, *Vietnam,* 129.

130. Isaacs, *Without Honor,* 27.

131. Hess, *Vietnam,* 130.

132. Summers, *On Strategy,* 134–35.

133. Davidson, *Vietnam at War,* 706–12; Stanton, *Rise and Fall,* 344–45; Fulghum, *South Vietnam on Trial,* 183–84.

134. Quote is from Davidson, *Vietnam at War,* 712.

135. Duiker, *The Communist Road,* 295–96; Goodman, *The Lost Peace,* 120–21; Clodfelter, *Limits,* 170–71.

136. Clodfelter, *Limits,* 161–62, 165–67.

137. Goodman, *The Lost Peace,* 126–29; Lipsman, Samuel; Weiss, Stephen; and the editors of the Boston Publishing, *The False Peace; 1972–1974,* (Boston: Boston Publishing, 1985), 9–13, in the series The Vietnam Experience; Kissinger, *The White House Years,* 1331–59.

138. Kissinger, *The White House Years,* 1366–92; Nixon, *Memoirs,* 702–3; Hess, *Vietnam,* 131.

139. The quote is found in Herring, *America's Longest War,* 252. Kissinger has always emphatically denied he harbored any notion of a peace agreement that would let South Vietnam survive for a decent interval, a few years, before falling to the Communists. Hanhimaki, Jussi, *The Flawed Architect: Henry Kissinger and American Foreign Policy,* (New York: Oxford University Press, 2003) shows Kissinger privately told the Chinese and Russians that all he wanted was a "decent interval" before North Vietnam swallowed the South.

140. Kissinger, *The White House Years,* 1395.

141. Porter, *Vietnam Documents,* vol. 2, Document 315, 581–83, "Letter from Richard Nixon to RVN President Nguyen Van Thieu," November 14, 1972; Nixon, *Memoirs,* 701–7. Quote is taken from Nixon's memoirs, 701.

142. Nixon is quoted in Young, *Vietnam Wars,* 277.

143. Schulzinger, *A Time for War,* 300.

144. Kissinger, *The White House Years,* 1415–46; Nixon, *Memoirs,* 732–33; Goodman, *The Lost Peace,* 151–60; Clodfelter, *Limits,* 179–81; and Porter, *Vietnam Documents,* vol. 2, Document 318, 587–90, "Press Conference Statement by Kissinger," December 16, 1972 (extract).

145. Clodfelter, *Limits,* 182.

146. Quoted in Herring, *America's Longest War,* 253–54.

147. Clodfelter, *Limits,* 186–89. The main reason so many of the B-52s were shot down was inept SAC mission planning. Since the three-plane cells flew at the same altitude and same speed, they had to make wide turns to avoid collisions. The wide turns blanked out their jamming antennae over the SAM sites.

148. Quoted in ibid., 191.

149. Isaacs, Arnold, *Without Honor: Defeat in Vietnam and Cambodia* (Baltimore, MD: Johns Hopkins University Press, 1983), 54–57; Kissinger, *The White House Years,* 1453.

150. Lewy, *America in Vietnam,* 403–4.

151. Clodfelter, *Limits,* 188–89.

152. A recent multiservice study of Operation LINEBACKER II concluded that it was an operational failure, and it did not force the North Vietnamese to return to the Paris talks. See Nostrand, Michael, Lt. Col., U.S. Air Force, et al., "Lessons Learned from LINEBACKER II," in *Vietnam* (October 2000): 38–44, 72.

153. Duiker, *The Communist Road,* 296–97; Goodman, *The Lost Peace,* 160–64; Kissinger, *The White House Years,* 1461–68. The U.S. air war against North Vietnam ended December 29, 1972. The U.S. air war in South Vietnam ended January 27, 1973. The U.S. air war in Laos ended February 22, 1973. The U.S. air war against Cambodia continued until August 15, 1973.

154. Herring, *America's Longest War,* 281.

155. Quoted in Young, *Vietnam Wars,* 279.

156. Hess, *Vietnam,* 134–35; Porter, *Vietnam Documents,* vol. 2, Document 320, 592, "Letter from Nixon to Thieu," January 5, 1973; Nixon, *Memoirs,* 737–51. Nixon wrote two letters to Thieu pledging U.S. support. One dated November 14, 1972, says, "You have my absolute assurance that if Hanoi fails to abide by the terms of this agreement it is my intent to take swift and severe retaliatory action." The second letter dated January 5, 1973, says, "We will respond with full force should the settlement be violated by North Vietnam."

157. Copies of the Agreement on Ending the War and Restoring Peace in Vietnam, January 27, 1973, are reprinted in Goodman, *The Lost Peace,* 188–99. See also Porter, *Vietnam Documents,* vol. 2, Document 324, 599–600. "Letter from Nixon to Pham Van Dong," February 1, 1973. Article 21 of the peace agreement committed the United States to help finance the postwar reconstruction of Vietnam. In the secret February 1, 1973, letter that President Nixon sent to North Vietnam's Prime Minister Pham Van Dong, he promised $3.25 billion in reconstruction aid and another $1.5 billion in commodities.

158. Porter, *Vietnam Document,* vol. 2, Document 324, 599–600; Isaacs, *Without Honor,* 64–68, discusses the major political and military provisions of the treaty, mainly to show that few of those provisions were ever carried out.

159. Isaacs, *Without Honor,* 61; quote from Nixon's speech is found in Olson and Roberts, *Where the Domino Fell,* 251.

160. General Ky's quote is taken from Olson and Roberts, *Where the Domino Fell,* 251.

161. Isaacs, *Without Honor,* 62–63; Herring, *America's Longest War,* 256.

162. Duiker, *The Communist Road,* 299; Davidson, *Vietnam at War,* 730–31.

163. Quote is from Duiker, *The Communist Road,* 299. The epistolary promises that President Nixon made to General Thieu to intervene militarily if the North Vietnamese violated the Paris Accords were secret, unknown to the Congress and the American people. The commitments were never implemented because Nixon was forced to resign the presidency because of the Watergate scandals and Congress refused to honor them.

164. Herring, *America's Longest War,* 256. Kissinger, in a recent book responds to those critics who say that he and Nixon could have ended the Vietnam war years earlier. He says that was not possible because an abrupt American pullout from Vietnam would have encouraged Soviet and Cuban adventurism in Africa, a Soviet invasion of Afghanistan, and Islamic terrorism in the Middle East. Kissinger, Henry, *Ending the Vietnam War: A History of America's involvement in and Extrication from the Vietnam War* (New York: Simon and Schuster, 2002).

165. Kimball, Nixon's Vietnam War, 368–71. Kimball cuts through the self-serving myths and rationalizations perpetuated by Nixon and Kissinger to show that all they achieved with four years of diplomacy and war was a flawed agreement that doomed South Vietnam to early extinction following the U.S. military withdrawal.

166. Quoted in Lipsman et al., *The False Peace,* 119; see also Schulzinger, *A Time for War,* 314.

CHAPTER  9

End of the Tunnel

The . . . .lesson [of Vietnam] is that America must never commit its power and authority in defense of a country of only marginal strategic interests when that country lacks a broadly based government or the will to create one.

George Ball

INDECENT INTERVAL

The war in South Vietnam went on, despite the signing of the Paris Accords, only it now continued without direct American participation. For the revolutionaries, the Paris agreements represented still another in a series of delays going back to their war with France in their three-decades-long effort to unify Vietnam under their control. For the government of General Nguyen Van Thieu, the Paris Accords meant that they would have to fight the revolutionaries alone. Neither side observed the cease-fire and both ignored or deliberately violated many of the other agreements. Neither side made a serious effort to seek a political settlement. The Lao Dong leaders in Hanoi continued to seek the overthrow of the Thieu regime by both political and military means, and to reunify Vietnam under their control. South Vietnam, dependent on U.S. economic and military assistance since birth, struggled to survive after the Americans had departed. President Nixon, engulfed by the Watergate scandal from March 1973 until his forced resignation of the presidency in August 1974, could not keep the promises of support and protection that he had made to General Thieu.

Congress restricted the president's power to intervene militarily in the Indochina War. Congress also drastically curtailed the amount of American economic and military assistance going to South Vietnam, which undermined both the ability and the will of the RVNAF forces to defend themselves. By the end of 1974, the United States had virtually abandoned its long-time client in southern Vietnam. The South Vietnamese economy deteriorated, its people were demoralized, and the military balance of power quickly shifted in favor of the VC/NVA forces. During the spring of 1975, when Hanoi, confident that the United States would not intervene militarily to save the Thieu government, mounted another major offensive, the GVN defenses collapsed with stunning rapidity, and the Thieu government found itself paralyzed and helpless. Neither Kissinger nor Nixon's successor Gerald Ford could convince Congress that it should vote for additional aid funds for the dying nation. Saigon fell to the Communists on April 30, 1975, and the republic of South Vietnam ceased to exist.

The gradual U.S. withdrawal from Vietnam had its parallel in Laos. A cease-fire in Laos followed the January 1973 Paris agreements. The Communist Pathet Lao and the Laotian government agreed to a cease-fire on February 21, 1973. The arrangement did not bring instant peace to that country, but the fighting in Laos had not generated the hatred or destructiveness it had in Vietnam and Cambodia. As John Kenneth Galbraith dryly observed, the people of Laos "have not learned to kill each other like the civilized nations."[1] Laotian Communist leader Prince Souphanouvong and government head Prince Souvanna Phouma were half-brothers who treated each other with respect. Following the cease-fire agreement, the fighting in Laos continued sporadically. American B-52s ended their bombing in Laos on February 22. Ground fighting gradually tapered off, and by April 1973, the long civil war in Laos had ended. On September 12, negotiators signed a protocol that cleared the way for establishing a new coalition government, a government in which the Pathet Lao was the dominant party. Under the new arrangement, the Pathet Lao retained complete control over the areas of the country where its military forces were in control and shared power to administer the rest of the country.

When Cambodia and South Vietnam fell to the Communists in the spring of 1975, the Pathet Lao formally took control in Laos. The Pathet Lao triumph meant that the North Vietnamese had considerable leverage in Laos, because the Laotian Communists had always been closely aligned with the Vietnamese Communist Party. Although the Communist takeover in Laos was kinder and gentler than the Communist triumphs in neighboring Cambodia and Vietnam, it had its violent and repressive aspects. The Pathet Lao sent thousands of supporters of the deposed Phouma government to "reeducation centers." The chief victims of the Communist triumph in Laos were the Hmong, the Meo tribesmen whom the CIA had trained and equipped to fight in the "secret war" in Laos. The Hmong, abandoned by their former American patrons, were forced to flee their native land. About 100,000 Meo ended up in the United States. Most of those who stayed behind were hunted down and killed by the Communists.[2]

In neighboring Cambodia, the Khmer Rouge and Lon Nol's forces waged a furious struggle. The United States had played a major role in the Cambodian civil war that derived from American military and political concerns in Vietnam. Lon Nol had offered the rebels a cease-fire soon after the Paris Accords had been signed, but the

Khmer Rouge leaders, determined to overthrow the Cambodian government, had rejected it. In February 1973, the insurgents appeared to have victory within their grasp. They had isolated Phnom Penh, and their forces had reached the suburbs of the city, a scant five kilometers away. However, an American airlift supplied the city, and, during six months of intensive bombing, U.S. B-52s annihilated the Khmer Rouge forces attacking Phnom Penh. U.S. air power had given Lon Nol's inept army and rickety regime a reprieve. The six-month-long U.S. aerial assault had temporarily destroyed the offensive capability of the Khmer Rouge, but it also severely impacted the Cambodian people. The bombing disrupted the economy, generated 2 million refugees, and contributed to the general disintegration of Cambodian society.

Congress eventually cut off all funds for the U.S. air war in Cambodia, and the B-52s stopped flying on August 15, 1973. The rebels regrouped and resumed their attacks four months later. By early 1974, the Khmer Rouge once again threatened Phnom Penh. This time, Lon Nol's forces were forced to defend their capital city without U.S. air power. The U.S. ambassador in Phnom Penh, John Gunther Dean, concluded that the government's cause was hopeless and that its military forces would be defeated.[3]

HOMECOMING

As the Indochina wars raged on, the American POWs came home. The return of the POWs generated a national celebration. Here was an aspect of the war that a divided nation could unify around. The return of the 591 American prisoners-of-war in February and March 1973 represented the only positive U.S. accomplishment to come out of any postwar negotiations held in accordance with the terms of the Paris agreements. The arrangements called for the POWs to be released in four increments, 15 days apart. The remaining 24,000 U.S. troops on active duty in South Vietnam would depart simultaneously, in four equal-sized increments, spaced 15 days apart. If any snags occurred that delayed the return of the POWs, the remaining U.S. troops would delay their departure from Vietnam.[4]

Called Operation HOMECOMING, the first contingent of 115 prisoners-of-war left Hanoi's Gia Lam Airport on February 12 and were flown to Clark Air Force Base in the Philippines. As they deplaned, some walked briskly, others hobbled painfully down the ramp. Navy Captain Jeremiah Denton, the senior officer among the first group of returnees, who had been held captive for seven years, reached the microphone first. He spoke for all of them when he proudly announced, "We are honored to have had the opportunity to serve our country."

At Clark, the men were given medical examinations and brought up to date on family news and on their current military status. Many aviators were able to enjoy their first American-style meal in years—steaks and banana splits. They were then flown to the United States where they had to endure a media blitz as they were reunited with their families. The other returning prisoners followed in 15 day intervals, until the last men had been repatriated on March 29. Hundreds of small towns and cities across the United States staged heroes' welcomes for individual returnees. There were homecomings, parades, and visits to the White House. President Nixon hosted a gala banquet in honor of the returning POWs.

The POWs had survived the longest captivity of any prisoners in American military history. As prisoners, they also had often been forced to endure deprivation, harassment, and tortures inflicted by their captors. Most of the prisoners endured their agonies heroically, maintaining their military professionalism under extreme duress in accordance with the strict standards of the U.S. Code of Military Conduct. Colonel Fred V. Cherry, the senior African American POW, set an outstanding example. He was tortured for 92 consecutive days after his captors failed to break him by appealing to his "blackness." Colonel Cherry's courageous patriotism earned him a broken rib and a punctured lung.[5]

Another reason for celebrating the returning POWs as heroes reflected the reality that, for most Americans, the homecoming of the POWs was the only positive experience to come out of the long American ordeal in Vietnam. It was the only outcome of the Vietnam War that most Americans could feel any enthusiasm about or take pride in.

On March 30, the last contingent of 5,200 U.S. soldiers remaining in South Vietnam assembled at Tan Son Nhut Air Base on the outskirts of Saigon, in readiness for their flights back to the United States. By April 1, 1973, the only U.S. military personnel remaining in South Vietnam were 159 Marines, who were serving as embassy guards, and another 50 people, who were serving in the Defense Attache Office as permitted by the provisions of the Paris agreement.

The celebrity status accorded the POWs contrasted starkly with the treatment often given to returning ground combat veterans, particularly veterans who returned after Tet-68. They rarely received parades or official welcomes home. Few Americans appeared to appreciate their sacrifice or thanked them for a job well done. They were often ignored by a society that had carelessly sent them off to fight a war that most Americans were ambivalent about or had lost faith in completely. Returning Vietnam combat veterans found themselves to be embarrassing reminders of a war that no one wanted to think or talk about. Worse, some people, opposed to the war, took out their animus toward that conflict by harassing the returning uniformed veterans.

The large majority of returning Vietnam combat veterans were neither war criminals nor head cases. They did not suffer from drug or alcohol addiction, nor did they have acute psychological or physical disabilities. But most veterans had to struggle to come to terms with their war experiences, to readjust to civilian routines, and to reintegrate into American society. They sometimes encountered difficulties completing their educations, finding steady work, and maintaining stable marriages and families. Many also found that they could not discuss their war experiences, or their thoughts and feelings about the war, with their families or close friends. Some veterans retained bitter feelings that their efforts and sacrifices had been meaningless, that they had fought in the service of a cause that had been repudiated or forgotten by most Americans.

Figure 9.1   U.S. Air Force Captain William R. Schwertfeger, Caldwell, Kansas, is welcomed upon his release from a North Vietnamese prison, at Hanoi's Gia Lam Airport by Air Force Colonel Richard Malone, as CMSGT Harry Boles checks off the names of returnees as they pass by. *Source:* AP/Wide World Photos.

Many more felt that they had been sent to fight a war for a good cause, but one for which their government either could not or would not develop a winning strategy.[6]

Surveys have found that thousands of combat veterans continued to be plagued by posttraumatic stress disorder (PTSD) long after the Vietnam War. Veterans afflicted with PTSD suffered a variety of psychological dysfunctions induced by their traumatic wartime experiences. Symptoms included (1) drug and alcohol abuse; (2) recurring nightmares, often reliving horrible war experiences; (3) chronic depression; (4) psychic numbing, the inability to feel any strong emotion; (5) guilt feelings about war actions, or about having survived when their buddies had been killed; (6) the inability to experience intimacy; and (7) unpredictable outbursts of rage and aggressive behavior.[7]

THE POSTWAR WAR

Even as the American POWs came home, the war in Vietnam roared on. The fighting was intense during the two days before the cease-fire was scheduled to take hold on January 28. North Vietnamese and VietCong forces attacked hundreds of villages trying to grab as much territory as they could before the fighting stopped. Washington reacted with the largest aerial campaign since LINEBACKER I. Air Force and Navy aircraft flew hundreds of sorties endeavoring to blunt the Communist assaults.[8] General Thieu also responded with offensive operations designed to reclaim these lands and enhance the total amount of territory and population under the control of the RVN. In February 1973, as the postwar war began, the military situation in South Vietnam favored Thieu's forces. U.S. aid had built up the RVNAF forces until they had become one of the largest and best-equipped armies in the world.

In the spring of 1973, the Thieu government appeared to be in a strong position. As a consequence of successful pacification efforts from 1970 to 1972, coupled with the smashing of the Communist Nguyen Hue Offensive during the summer of 1972, the RVN controlled about 75 percent of the territory and perhaps 80 percent of the 19 million inhabitants of South Vietnam. Communist holdings were confined mostly to the thinly populated western periphery of the country and scattered enclaves in the Mekong Delta, in the central highlands, and along the coast. The RVNAF totaled more than 1 million troops, and they were well equipped, because of the recent lavish American resupply efforts. Both the surviving VietCong forces and the 150,000 North Vietnamese forces in southern Vietnam, still battered and short of supplies from the 1972 campaigns, were no match initially for Thieu's forces. During the first year following the Paris agreements, the South Vietnamese forces not only reclaimed most of the lands and villages grabbed by the Vietcong in the fall of 1972, but also acquired control of some areas that had been in VC hands for years. Thieu was determined to use his military advantage while he had it to try to establish his control over all the land and people of South Vietnam.[9]

Underlying political weaknesses undercut much of the military advantage that Thieu's forces enjoyed over its enemies during 1973. In some regions, authorities loyal to Saigon ruled by day; the VietCong took over at night. The populations of many villages counted as loyal to the RVN were inhabited by villagers who did not trust the Saigon government; they were secret neutralists or supporters of the PRG. Many of the Saigon government's civilian and military bureaucrats assigned to administer districts and villages came from upper-class or urban middle-class backgrounds. Sullen villagers did not identify with these alien bureaucrats or accept their authority as legitimate. The Saigon government's control over much of the rural population of South Vietnam was only nominal.[10]

In April 1973, General Thieu, concerned about the level of support he could expect to receive from the United States now that the war was over for Americans, journeyed to San Clemente, California, to confer with President Nixon and Henry Kissinger. Thieu's visit received little media coverage and most Americans probably did not know that he was in the United States. The POWs were home, and the media were giving the burgeoning Watergate scandals saturation coverage. Vietnam no longer mattered to most Americans. Thieu found Nixon preoccupied with Watergate; the president had a difficult time focusing on the continuing Indochina wars. Nixon promised that the

United States would provide upwards of a $1 billion to modernize the ARVN, and he reassured Thieu that Washington would always stand with South Vietnam.

But Congress, where support for South Vietnam was fading fast, was not about to provide the amounts of funding Nixon promised General Thieu. After San Clemente, Thieu flew to Washington where his visit went virtually unnoticed. Such inattention was in marked contrast to previous visits by South Vietnamese heads of state, which had generated massive publicity and sometimes demonstrations by antiwar activists. Thieu returned to Vietnam worried that the Americans would eventually abandon South Vietnam.[11]

Thieu remained fearful that if the Communists rebuilt their forces and launched attacks in South Vietnam that his forces could not contain, Nixon might not honor his pledge to rescue the RVN. These worries about U.S. support motivated the South Vietnamese leader to press for every advantage over his enemies while he could. Even though all U.S. combat forces had been withdrawn from South Vietnam and Thieu worried about American staying power over the long run, Washington continued to provide strong military support for the Thieu government in 1973. Thousands of former U.S. military advisers continued to work with the ARVN forces, but they had civilian status in order to circumvent treaty provisions. Powerful U.S. naval and air forces remained nearby in the Gulf of Tonkin, in Thailand, and on the island of Guam. Nixon attempted to maintain a credible threat of U.S. reentry into the war to deter Hanoi from treaty violations and aggressive military actions. Thieu took a hard line toward the Communists. He pursued a policy of the "four no's": (1) no abandonment of territory in South Vietnam; (2) no coalition government with the PRG or neutralists; (3) no negotiations with the Communists; and (4) no Communist or neutralist political activities in South Vietnam.[12]

Hanoi, needing a respite from war to rebuild its shattered military forces, confined its activities in South Vietnam largely to politics during most of 1973. The Communists maintained a low level of resistance to Thieu's forces. They also modernized their logistics capability in South Vietnam. They constructed a macadamized highway and an eight-inch oil pipeline running along the border with Laos and Cambodia from the DMZ to Loc Ninh, about 65 miles northwest of Saigon. Hanoi also infiltrated more troops into South Vietnam in violation of the Paris Accords. During the final months of 1973, about 170,000 PAVN and 60,000 VietCong fighters could be found in South Vietnam. They responded to the aggressive tactics of the ARVN with counterattacks of their own. The fighting peaked in October in the Mekong Delta, the Iron Triangle, and in the central highlands. Both sides sustained heavy casualties and the Communists succeeded in reclaiming some traditional strongholds.[13]

During the summer of 1973, the North Vietnamese leaders sought additional help from their major allies, the Soviets and the Chinese. Le Duan, the first secretary of the Lao Dong, traveled to Moscow and Beijing in search of additional military aid. To his dismay, Duan discovered that both the Soviets and the Chinese valued improving relations with the United States more than a Communist victory in Vietnam. They had reverted to the stance they had taken at the Geneva conference in 1954 when they pressured the Vietminh to accept a temporary partition of their country rather than assume control of a united Vietnam. Just as South Vietnam appeared to matter less to U.S. officials than before the Paris Accords, so too a Communist victory in Vietnam now seemed a lower priority to the Soviet and Chinese leaders.[14] Unable to extract additional military aid from either ally, Hanoi was forced to continue its low intensity campaign of resistance to Thieu's military campaigns. However, the Communists were able to stage a series of counterattacks as the year ended and they regained some of the lands they had lost earlier in the year.

Within the United States, the Watergate scandals had seriously eroded Nixon's ability to influence events in Indochina. During 1973, for the first time in the long war, Congress took decisive actions to end all lingering U.S. military activity in Indochina. In June, Congress passed legislation requiring an immediate end to the bombing of Cambodia and all other U.S. military operations in Indochina. Nixon vetoed the measure and the House sustained his veto. Congress subsequently forced a reluctant president to accept a compromise proposal that halted the bombing on August 15.[15] In November 1973, Congress enacted the War Powers Act over another presidential veto. Passage of the act was the culmination of years of effort by congressional opponents of U.S. military involvement in Indochina to restrict the power of the president to commit U.S. forces to war without the advise and consent of Congress. The War Powers Act required the president to inform Congress within 48 hours of any decision to deploy U.S. forces overseas. The new law further mandated that the president must remove these forces within 60 days, unless Congress specifically endorsed their deployment. The War Powers Act, in tandem with the Cambodian bombing cutoff, made it virtually impossible for President Nixon to commit U.S. forces to any further military operations anywhere in Indochina.[16]

By the end of 1973, Nixon was powerless to influence events in Indochina. All of the power that had accrued from his adroit diplomacy, the landslide victory over George McGovern, and achieving the Paris Accords had vanished; they had gone up in the smoke of the Watergate scandals and in the face of congressional assertiveness. With his popular approval ratings reduced to historic lows, Nixon fought grimly for his political survival against a growing army of political foes determined to destroy him if evidence implicating him in the Watergate coverup could be found. He could only watch passively as the Indochina postwar war escalated and the political settlement he had tried to forge for South Vietnam became a dead letter.[17]

During 1974, the military balance in South Vietnam shifted steadily against the ARVN forces even though on paper force levels continued to favor the South Vietnamese heavily over their enemies.[18] The Communists exploited strategic weaknesses of the RVNAF forces. Because of Thieu's efforts to gain control over his whole country, many of his divisions were tied down in static defensive positions. They were vulnerable to attacks wherever the VietCong or PAVN forces chose to strike. By the fall of 1974, Hanoi had put an estimated 285,000 troops in South Vietnam, far in excess of what they were allowed under the Paris Accords. They had also stockpiled huge quantities of war materiel brought down the Ho Chi Minh Trail, which had been transformed into an efficient supply corridor for men, weapons, fuel, and ammunition since the departure of U.S. air power from the war.

THE DECAY OF SOUTH VIETNAM

Meanwhile, South Vietnam's economy began to collapse from a combination of declining American support and internal weaknesses. Corruption, a chronic problem of the GVN since its inception, scaled new heights during Thieu's final years. Corruption involved most senior officials in the GVN military and civilian bureaucracies; it also involved many lower-echelon personnel. Corruption was more widespread in the military, among the officer corps, than elsewhere. Wealthy soldiers purchased safe duty assignments. Promotions were regularly sold to the highest bidders. Pilots demanded bribes before flying combat missions. Supply officers demanded bribes before furnishing food for the troops. Division commanders regularly siphoned off huge sums of money from military payrolls. Presiding at the apex of this vast empire of corruption, General Thieu and his senior military commanders accrued great wealth. Thieu had allowed the corruption system to flourish in order to survive in power. "Corruption had become the glue that held the Thieu regime together."[19]

Official efforts to eradicate or slow the rate of corruption "ranged from the ineffectual to the pathetic."[20] General Thieu felt compelled to tolerate his regime's staggering corruption, since he and his cronies were the prime beneficiaries. Even had he been willing to try seriously to reform his government, he would have failed. Had Thieu tried to remove the corruption from all of his government's civilian and military agencies, the radical surgery required would have killed the patient. It also would have cut out his political power and all major sources of his wealth.

Except for dismissing a few corrupt officials for cosmetic purposes, Thieu chose to cover up his regime's systemic corruption. U.S. officials, led by the last U.S. ambassador to South Vietnam, Graham Martin, went along with the coverup. They either denied that corruption was a serious problem in South Vietnam or insisted that it was being eliminated. If U.S. officials were either blind or complacent about corruption, most South Vietnamese, victimized in countless ways by fraud, bribery, extortion, and graft, were not. Their anger over government corruption was intensified by economic decline, and they complained bitterly about their worsening predicament.

By mid-1974, Thieu presided over a collapsing economy. The rate of inflation had skyrocketed. The cost of living in Saigon had risen 27 percent during the first six months of the year. The price rise for essential commodities was even sharper: rice rose 100 percent, sugar 107 percent, and cooking oil 139 percent. Hyperinflation meant that most soldiers and civil servants were not earning enough to meet the basic needs of their families. "The ultimate expression of the decay of South Vietnam was the widespread black market with the Communist forces."[21] Both the VietCong and North Vietnamese troops were able to get much of their food, medicine, and even weapons from regions under Saigon's control. The sellers' motives were usually mercenary; to make a buck, they sold their enemies what they needed.

At the same time retail prices were shooting up, unemployment was rising rapidly. In 1974, an estimated 1 million people, about one-fifth of the workforce, were without jobs. The piaster was devalued repeatedly against the American dollar; a huge trade deficit evolved that quickly wiped out the RVN's slim foreign reserves. In 1973, a poor rice harvest and an Arab oil boycott had exacerbated South Vietnam's mounting economic miseries. Rice and other food commodities had to be imported; many consumer goods were in short supply. Industries dependent on imported materials slashed their production schedules or, more often, shut down.[22] The South Vietnamese people suffered from an economic double whammy composed of hyperinflation and deep depression; it was stagflation with a vengeance.

The sick South Vietnamese economy was further undermined by the effects of the American pullout. The pullout eliminated about 300,000 jobs, as well as a large annual inflow of dollars. In 1970, U.S. soldiers had spent over $500 million, and in 1971 they had spent over $400 million in South Vietnam. In 1974 they spent less than $100 million.[23] By 1974, economic and social conditions were the worst they had ever been during South Vietnam's twenty-year existence. As corruption and economic decay destroyed the remaining morale and cohesion of South Vietnamese society, the RVNAF, its military shield, also began to give way.

One of the major causes of the RVNAF's decline in 1974 was the deep reduction in the amount of U.S. military assistance going to South Vietnam. Because the huge South Vietnamese army had been trained to fight American-style battles, relying on mobility and massive firepower, it was extremely expensive to maintain and operate; it required an annual budget of $3 to 3.5 billion to sustain it. But the United States provided only $2.3 billion during the fiscal year 1973 and $1.1 billion for 1974.[24]

These drastic aid cuts severely hampered the performance of the South Vietnamese armed forces. Air operations had to be curtailed because of gasoline shortages and the lack of spare parts. Ammunition was in short supply. Unable to fight in the manner in which they had been trained because of equipment and ammunition shortages, the morale of the RVNAF forces, never too high under the best of circumstances, plummeted.

The congressional aid cuts no doubt sapped the strength and morale of the RVNAF forces, but they were not the most important causes of the GVN's growing military weakness. Vietnamization had never worked; that was the inescapable reality. Most of the RVNAF's many shortcomings that had always vitiated its fighting abilities had never been corrected. Desertions probably exceeded inductions in 1974, and the officer corps grew more corrupt and more politicized than ever.

But the fundamental weakness of the South Vietnamese military forces could be found in the realm of politics. The Thieu government in 1974 still suffered from the same chronic problems that had been in place since Diem had come to power back in 1954–1955. It remained what it had been from its beginning, a narrowly based oligarchy dependent for its survival on the political loyalty of senior military commanders. These loyalties had to be purchased—by favors, bribery, and corruption. The Thieu regime never embodied Vietnamese nationalism or became the focus of patriotic feelings. It never won the hearts and minds of most South Vietnamese civilians, nor the loyalty and devotion of most of the men serving in its military forces. Thieu's American connection and his skill at political maneuver had kept him in power for years, but neither he nor his government represented a cause or a purpose, a positive reason for which most soldiers wanted to risk their lives. South Vietnam had always been a nation made up of more cynics than believers, most of whom viewed military service as either an unavoidable disaster or an opportunity for graft. Systemic corruption, the decline of the army, and the reductions in U.S. aid combined to undermine the fragile South Vietnamese political structure. "After two decades of U.S. support, the government of South Vietnam still did not represent any genuine sense of nationhood."[25]

During August 1974, Congress slashed U.S. military aid to South Vietnam still further, and Nixon, his role in the attempted cover-up of the Watergate burglary established, was forced to resign in disgrace to avoid impeachment. Thieu was rapidly running out of American friends, and Americans were even more rapidly running out of reasons for continuing to support his cause.

Thieu soon faced the most serious challenge to his rule since taking office. On September 8, a group of Catholics led by Father Tran Huu Thanh publicly protested the extensive corruption that riddled Thieu's government. Thanh's charges set off a torrent of protest against Thieu and his corrupt regime. Huge demonstrations, similar to the ones that had brought down Diem and Nhu in 1963, broke out in Saigon and other cities. Militant Buddhists again took to the streets to lead popular protests against the government. Thieu made a few efforts to respond to his critics, then cracked down hard on the protesters. He shut down dissident newspapers and his police violently suppressed the protests.[26] Many citizens were bludgeoned into silence; popular support for the RVN was at an all-time low. More and more Saigonese talked openly of seeking an accommodation with the Communists.

The Communist leadership in Hanoi observed the general deterioration of South Vietnamese society and the continuing cuts in American support for Thieu's failing regime. The hawks in the Politburo believed that the time had come for another all-out war in South Vietnam. The doves took a more cautious stance. They wanted to wait and see if the new American president, Gerald Ford, could persuade Congress to restore military aid funds to Thieu's regime. They also wanted to wait and see if Ford would be willing to make good on Nixon's promise to recommit U.S. air power in South Vietnam to save the RVN in the event of another invasion from North Vietnam. Hanoi's hawks and doves both ruled out as politically impossible the possibility that the U.S. might once again commit ground troops to save South Vietnam.

By fall, the Hanoi hawks had won the debate. What clinched the argument favoring another North Vietnamese attack on South Vietnam was the outbreak of popular unrest in Saigon and Hanoi's perception that U.S. domestic public opinion and

Congressional opposition would likely prevent Ford from ordering any further U.S. military interventions into South Vietnam. At a key meeting held in October 1974, the Politburo approved a proposal by General Van Tien Dung, Giap's successor as chief of staff, for a new military offensive scheduled to be launched in South Vietnam in 1975. General Dung had concluded that the war in South Vietnam had reached its final stage. South Vietnam's economy, society, and government were deteriorating. The PAVN forces now enjoyed a clear advantage on the battlefield. Dung's strategic plan called for a two-year campaign that would culminate in the overthrow of the Thieu regime and the creation of a coalition government in 1976.[27]

In the fall of 1974, when Hanoi's leaders looked at the United States, they saw a nation led by an inexperienced president who had not been elected to the office and who appeared to assign Indochina a relatively low priority. They also saw a dovish Congress that was increasingly preoccupied with the deteriorating American economy.[28] Serious internal problems generated by energy shortages and "stagflation" had a far greater urgency for most Americans than a lingering war in Indochina that no longer directly involved U.S. forces.

President Ford viewed such traditional foreign policy issues as relations with the major Communist powers, efforts to break the dismal cycle of periodic warfare between Arabs and Israelis, and in-house quarrels with NATO allies as much more vital to U.S. national interests than a conflict in Southeast Asia that had already gone on far too long and had cost far more in lives and dollars than anyone had anticipated. The new president was determined that the conflict in Vietnam, which had become "Johnson's War," and then "Nixon's War," would never become "Ford's War." Hanoi's directorate understood that the United States still possessed formidable military power and these forces were positioned to intervene in Indochina, but they made a judgment that powerful domestic and international constraints precluded Washington's reentering the Vietnam War.

ENDGAME

In mid-December, concluding that the time had come to initiate the final phase of the postwar war, General Dung ordered two divisions of VietCong and PAVN forces under the command of General Tran Van Tra to attack Phuoc Long, an isolated and poorly defended province near the Cambodian border 80 miles northwest of Saigon. Dung would use the assault on Phuoc Long as a test, to find out whether Saigon and Washington would respond to a direct attack on South Vietnamese territory that clearly violated the Paris agreements. Dung and members of his staff knew of former President Nixon's commitments to General Thieu, and they wanted to find out if his successor intended to honor them.

Within three weeks, the Communist forces had overrun the province and captured the provincial capital, Phuoc Binh. The RVNAF forces could do little to prevent the disaster. The VNAF pilots lacked the skill to fly close air support missions; in fact, they killed many of their own troops when they dropped their bombs from a high altitude to avoid enemy antiaircraft fire. The ARVN helicopter squadrons lacked the airlift capability to fly in reinforcements. The ARVN defenders took heavy casualties during the three weeks of fighting in Phuoc Long. Nearly all of the 5,400 ARVN soldiers were either killed or captured in a failed effort to prevent the loss of the province.

Phuoc Long was the first provincial capital to be lost to the Communists since Quang Tri was captured during the Nguyen Hue offensive of 1972. The Phuoc Long debacle demonstrated that Thieu's government lacked both the means and the will to defend its territory against the first major NVA offensive in three years. More important, it soon became evident to the North Vietnamese that U.S. officials responded indifferently to this latest threat to their ally. South Vietnamese leaders were stunned by the relative ease of the Communist takeover of Phuoc Long and dismayed at the U.S. indifference to the North Vietnamese offensive. But it was the signal that Dung had been looking for. Hanoi concluded that the Ford administration would not intervene militarily in South Vietnam, regardless of the provocation or threat.

When Hanoi's directorate perceived that Saigon could not defend Phuoc Long and that the Ford administration would not intervene, they ordered a second phase of the offensive to begin, a series of attacks to be launched in the central highlands.[29] The North Vietnamese army that General Dung prepared to unleash in the central highlands was much improved over that of 1972. The NVA had modernized its logistics capability, had refined its tactics, and had significantly enhanced its air defense capabilities. The army that was poised to slam into the central highlands was a powerful and mobile strike force capable of defeating the RVNAF forces and overthrowing the RVN. It might have fought effectively even if the Americans had reentered the war and thrown their air power at the NVA. South Vietnam's final agony was about to begin.

On March 10, five PAVN main force divisions, joined by regiments of tanks, artillery, antiaircraft batteries, and engineers, attacked the strategic city of Ban Me Thuot, the capital of the Darlac province. Dung concentrated his forces to mount an overwhelming attack on the city. The outgunned ARVN defenders fought bravely, but Ban Me Thout fell to the Communists within one week. The fall of Ban Me Thuot represented a strategic disaster for the GVN. With the takeover of that city, the NVA had positioned itself to achieve its long-standing strategic goal, the bisection of South Vietnam.[30] After the fall of Ban Me Thuot, no powerful ARVN forces blocked the PAVN's march to the sea. South Vietnam was about to be cut in two.

While the battle for Ban Me Thuot was being fought, General Thieu made a fateful decision that hastened the demise of his country. He suddenly abandoned his strategy of holding as much South Vietnamese territory as possible. Convinced that the outnumbered and outgunned defenders of Pleiku and Kontum could not hold off the Communist attackers, he ordered his commanders to withdraw their forces. Thieu wanted to redeploy them to try to hold all of South Vietnam south of a line running from Tuy Hoa on the coast to the Cambodian border.[31] Most of South Vietnam's strategic resources and population lay south of this line. General Thieu decided to trade territory for time and for a chance to consolidate his defenses farther to the south. He would accept the loss of the northern half of his nation in order to preserve the southern half. He would "lighten the top and keep the bottom."[32] Pleiku and Kontum fell to the Communists within a few days.

Thieu had acted without planning or any prior warning. His military commanders in the central highlands had made no plans for a tactical retreat, and they were ill prepared to carry out one of the most difficult and dangerous military operations, a controlled retreat while under heavy enemy fire. The ARVN military discipline broke down, and the retreat quickly turned into a rout. Hundreds of thousands of terrified civilians joined the demoralized and panicked soldiers as all fled the central highlands toward the coastal city of Tuy Hoa. The two-week trek of soldiers and civilians streaming for the coast turned into a Convoy of Tears. During that hideous fortnight, two-thirds of the 60,000 RVNAF soldiers were killed or captured, and thousands of civilians perished as well. Most of the civilian casualties came from NVA fire, as the Communists continually attacked the virtually defenseless columns of intermingled soldiers, dependents, and refugees. Only about 20,000 South Vietnamese soldiers and perhaps 60,000 civilians reached their destination.[33]

General Thieu's decision to abandon the central highlands was a strategic, political, and psychological disaster that cost his country ten provinces, perhaps 200,000 civilian casualties, and more than two divisions of troops. Within two months, the NVA invaders captured most of the central provinces. During those two months there occurred the most dramatic shift in the military and political balance of power since the Vietnam War began. Thieu's decision to abandon the northern half of his country also cost him the remaining confidence of the South Vietnamese people in his abilities to protect them from the enemy. Loss of the central highlands "opened the way for even greater catastrophe in the coastal cities of South Vietnam."[34]

Thieu's decision to abandon the central highlands and the rapid crumbling of his armies caught the Communists by surprise. Although they were confident of ultimate victory, the North Vietnamese had anticipated stubborn resistance and hard fighting from Thieu's forces over the next two years. They had been at war with the RVN for nearly 20 years, and never had they achieved a major military victory or scored a decisive strategic breakthrough—until now. The rapid military breakdown following Thieu's hasty decision to abandon the central highlands astonished and, of course, delighted the cautious old men of the Politburo. Perceiving that their armies could probably conquer all of South Vietnam before the rainy season struck, they ordered General Dung to move up his timetable for victory by one year, from 1976 to the spring of 1975. They sensed they were at last getting close to achieving victory in the cause to which they had devoted their lives.

As the RVN forces abandoned the central highlands, an even greater catastrophe occurred in the north. General Dung sent five NVA main force divisions, along with artillery, tank, and antiaircraft regiments, to attack key sites in the five northern provinces

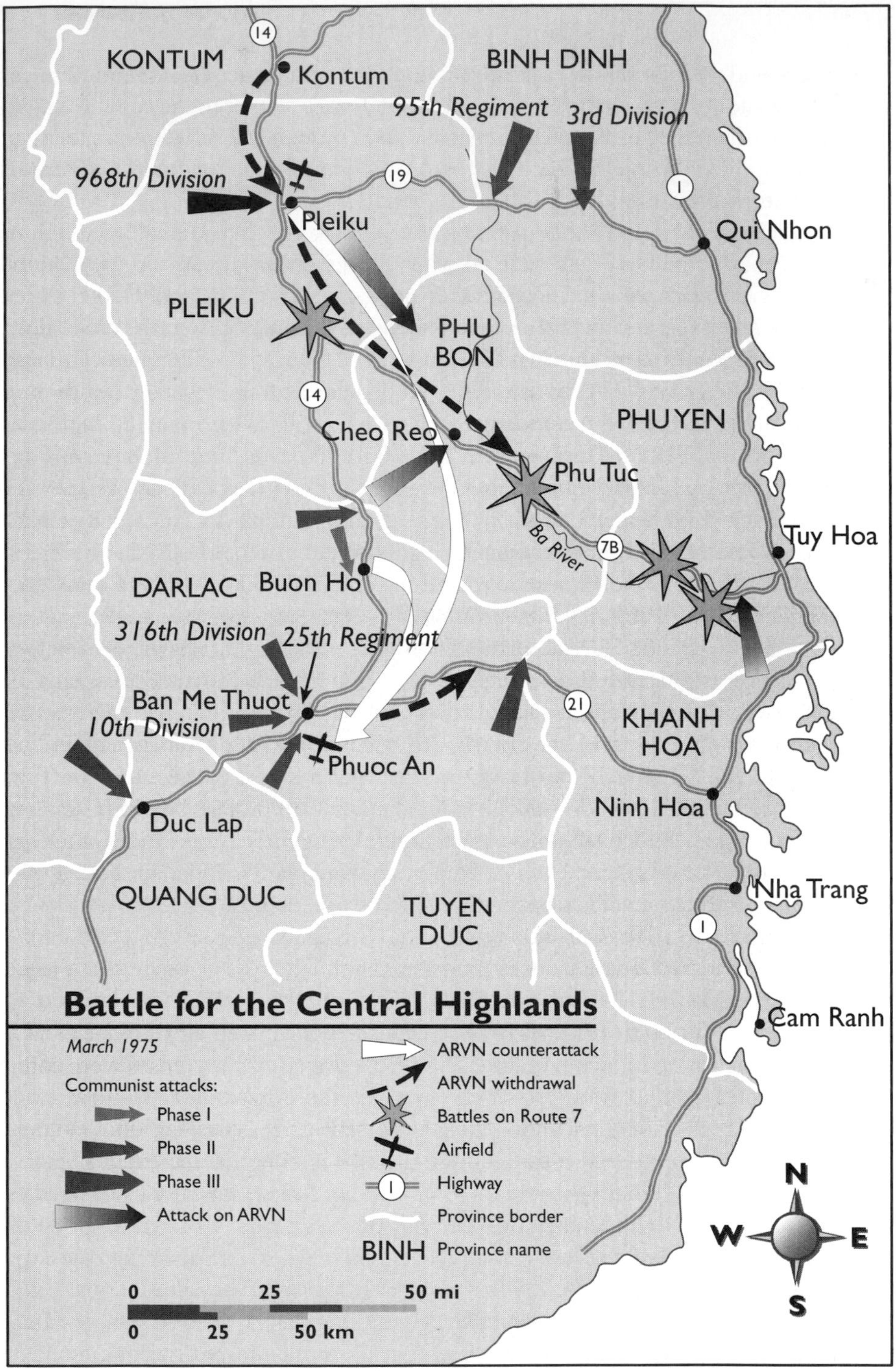
KONTUM
Kontum
BINH DINH
95th Regiment
3rd Division
968th Division
Pleiku
Qui Nhon
PLEIKU
PHU BON
PHU YEN
Cheo Reo
Phu Tuc
Ba River
Tuy Hoa
DARLAC
Buon Ho
316th Division
25th Regiment
Ban Me Thuot
10th Division
Phuoc An
KHANH HOA
Ninh Hoa
Duc Lap
Nha Trang
QUANG DUC
TUYEN DUC
Cam Ranh
14
19
1
7B
21
Battle for the Central Highlands
March 1975
Communist attacks:
Phase I
Phase II
Phase III
Attack on ARVN
ARVN counterattack
ARVN withdrawal
Battles on Route 7
Airfield
Highway
Province border
BINH Province name
0 25 50 mi
0 25 50 km
N
S
W
E

Figure 9.2 Battle for the Central Highlands. *Source:* Public Domain.

of South Vietnam that constituted Military Region I. In some of the battles, the out-numbered ARVN forces fought hard, but the Communist quickly overpowered them. Refugees poured into Hue and Danang, the two largest cities in the region. As the PAVN forces approached these cities, the South Vietnamese defenses simply melted away. The ARVN soldiers and the militia abandoned their weapons, and many of them joined the mass air, sea, and land exodus from the doomed cities to Saigon. Hue fell on March 26. Four days later, the victorious NVA forces marched into Danang without meeting any resistance. Almost 10 years to the day, after the first U.S. Marines hit the beaches near Danang to initiate the American Vietnam war, South Vietnam's second largest city fell to the advancing Communist armies.

"The evacuation of Danang capped a disaster of far greater magnitude than the flight from the central highlands."[35] Only about 16,000 South Vietnamese troops were evacuated from Danang. Four infantry divisions, additional main force units, and ter-ritorial forces were either dispersed, detained, or destroyed. Of the 2 million people densely packed into Danang at the end, over 1 million of them refugees, perhaps 50,000 got out before the Communist conquerors arrived.

The last flight out of Danang on March 29, 1975, was a World Airways 727 bound for Saigon. It was commandeered by a mob of 320 uniformed soldiers from the ARVN 1st Division who shoved aside women and children, often trampling members of their own families, in their panic-driven haste to board the plane. As pilot Ken Healy began to taxi the big plane toward the runway, crazed soldiers standing on the tarmac fired their rifles and threw grenades at the plane. If they could not leave, they were determined that no one else would either. One exploding grenade jammed the flaps on the left wing of the 727. Because a stalled VNAF A-37 jet fighter with bombs slung under its wings blocked the main runway, Healy was forced to use the short taxi strip for takeoff. As the overloaded plane struggled into the air, observers on the ground could see bodies hanging from the plane's undercarriage and wheel wells. Ninety minutes later, the plane, nearly empty of fuel, delivered its payload of "patriots" safely in Saigon. A rabble of cheering enlisted men poured out of the aircraft.[36]

During the first week of April 1975, the coastal cities of Quang Ngai, Qui Nhon, Tuy Hoa, and Nha Trang fell to the NVA attackers as they rapidly advanced down the South China seacoast toward Saigon. The South Vietnamese defenses were collapsing so fast the Communist forces could scarcely keep pace. The PAVN forces also occu-pied Cam Ranh, formerly the site of the largest U.S. logistics facility in South Viet-nam. Hanoi, sensing that final victory was near, ordered General Dung to marshal all of his forces for an immediate offensive against Saigon. The North Vietnamese had to attain final victory before the summer monsoons arrived. They also wanted to strike for the jugular while the South Vietnamese armies were in disarray. They did not want to give the Saigon government a chance to regroup and perhaps rally the people to resist the advancing NVA forces.[37] As the Communist leaders planned the final campaign designed to bring their war that they had begun 30 years ago for independence and na-tional unity to a victorious climax, they named it the Ho Chi Minh Offensive.

As Thieu's armies disintegrated and the Communists geared up for the final thrust to Saigon, U.S. efforts turned to humanitarian aid. The Ford administration developed Operation Babylift to evacuate some 1,500 children for adoption in Australia and the United States. Only orphans were eligible, but many of the children involved were not orphans. Parents who feared the worst for their children at the hands of the VietCong placed their children in the program. The first Operation Babylift aircraft, a giant Air Force C-5A transport, took off from Tan San Nhut Air Base on April 4 with 243 children on board. Scarcely a half-hour later, the plane crashed, killing 178 of the children. Americans watched the terrible scene unfold on television. For many viewers, the fiery crash and the death of so many children epitomized much of the horror and futility associated with the American involvement in Vietnam.[38]

On the same day the Operation Babylift plane crashed, Army Chief of Staff Frederick Weyand, back from a factfinding mission to South Vietnam, told President Ford that Thieu's government verged on defeat. Even if the United States significantly increased its military aid to Saigon, General Weyand thought its chances of survival were meager at best. Weyand also rejected General Westmoreland's call for renewed air strikes over North Vietnam, pointing out that Congress would never support such action. CIA director William Colby agreed with General Weyand's assessment of the military situation. Ford, understanding that the South Vietnamese had lost the war, knew that the American people would never support a U.S. military intervention to try to salvage a hopeless cause.[39]

XUAN LOC: THE LAST BATTLE OF A LONG WAR

By mid-April, advance elements of the North Vietnamese army were approaching Saigon. The last major battle of the postwar war occurred at Xuan Loc, a strategic crossroads that formed the center of Saigon's forward defenses. At Xuan Loc, about 30 miles east of the capital city astride Route 1, the main Vietnamese north-south highway, the 18th ARVN Division, under the command of General Le Minh Dao, made a gallant stand against four NVA divisions that were reinforced with tank and artillery regiments. In an epic struggle, the defenders of Xuan Loc held their positions for a week against vastly superior forces. Although the heroic defenders of Xuan Loc could delay the North Vietnamese advance, they could not stop it. Xuan Loc was the bloodiest battle of the Second Indochina War. After the fall of Xuan Loc, the road to Bien Hoa Airport and Saigon lay open. "After Xuan Loc, it was a slide into the abyss for the South Vietnamese."[40]

AMERICA ABANDONS CAMBODIA

As the end of the Republic of South Vietnam approached, the civil war in neighboring Cambodia that had destroyed much of the country and left most of its survivors impoverished played itself out. With the defensive perimeter around the besieged capital of Phnom Penh shrinking daily, the hapless leader of the Khmer Republic, Lon Nol, was forced to resign on April 1. Efforts by Secretary of State Kissinger to arrange an eleventh-hour peace settlement were spurned by Prince Sihanouk and his Chinese patrons. On April 10, Congress refused to support a bill calling for $222 million in emergency military aid for the dying Khmer Republic. Two days later, the American evacuation of Phnom Penh began. After five years, at a cost exceeding $1 billion, the U.S. effort to prevent a Communist takeover in Cambodia had failed. On April 17, abandoned by the Americans, the Cambodian Khmer republic fell. The Khmer Rouge occupied Phnom Penh. An eyewitness, *New York Times* reporter Sydney Schandberg, described Phnom Penh's conquerors as "grim, robot-like, brutal."[41] They immediately began evacuating the 2 million people crammed into the city. The Cambodian holocaust was about to begin.

America Abandons South Vietnam

Washington had known for months that the Khmer Republic was doomed, but the sudden collapse of the South Vietnamese armies in the central highlands and northern provinces in the spring of 1975 had stunned American officials. Intelligence reports had given them no indication that Hanoi had planned a major offensive for 1975. U.S. officials had assumed that South Vietnam's defenses were adequate to withstand any attacks the Communists were likely to mount that year. But it soon became clear, even in the face of mounting disaster in southern Vietnam, that the Ford administration had no plans for any further U.S. military intervention in that region. Both Ford and Kissinger understood that it would be politically impossible for the United States to send in U.S. aircraft to bomb and mine, as Nixon had done in 1972, to try to save the South Vietnamese armed forces from the latest NVA offensive.

On April 10, in a televised speech to Congress, Ford asked the lawmakers to appropriate an additional $300 million in emergency military assistance for General Thieu's imperiled government. Even though he knew that Congress was not going to provide the funding, Ford sounded all of the familiar themes to support his request. He pleaded with Congress to honor a sacred American commitment, a commitment embraced by every president from Truman to Nixon. He spoke of America's "profound moral obligation" to the South Vietnamese people. He told the legislators and the American people that the United States would dishonor the sacrifices made by the tens of thousands of American soldiers who had died in Vietnam if it failed to help the people of South Vietnam in their hour of mortal danger. He raised the specter of a bloodbath in which thousands of South Vietnamese, particularly Catholics, would be slaughtered by the victorious Communists.[42]

Few congressional leaders on either side of the aisle responded to Ford's powerful appeal with any enthusiasm. Weary of a seemingly endless war, most members of Congress were not in a generous mood. Most of them viewed the cause in Vietnam as being already lost; they were more concerned about assuring the evacuation of all

Americans from Saigon than they were about sending General Thieu's failing government any more aid. Four days after delivering his speech, Ford met with several members of the Congress. They told him there would be no additional funds for military assistance. Congress was interested only in providing humanitarian assistance, and they were concerned mainly for the safety of U.S. personnel who remained in South Vietnam. On April 17, the same day Xuan Loc fell and the Khmer Rouge entered Phnom Penh, Congress formally rejected Ford's request for military aid for South Vietnam. Kissinger observed fatalistically, "The Vietnam debate has run its course."[43]

Most Americans, facing serious domestic economic and energy problems, and concerned about important foreign policy matters elsewhere, had long since lost their crusading enthusiasm for saving South Vietnam from Communist aggression. Opinion polls taken in April 1975 showed that a large majority of Americans opposed any further U.S. military action in South Vietnam, even if the failure to take such action resulted in a Communist takeover. Most Americans were surely unhappy about the prospect of a Communist victory in Vietnam, but they were resigned to its occurrence. Most Americans also believed that they had already sacrificed far too much of their blood and treasure in Indochina, and they refused to contribute more.

Even as President Ford, Congress, and nearly all Americans clearly indicated that the United States would no longer provide military assistance to South Vietnam, Graham Martin, the last U.S. ambassador to that dying country, energetically tried to persuade someone, anyone, to come to their rescue. Martin, who remained a true believer to the bitter end, tried to get Saudi Arabia to finance South Vietnam's continuing war effort. But the Saudis, who could recognize a losing cause when they saw it, politely declined. Martin also resisted efforts at humanitarian assistance, fearing that such aid would convince the South Vietnamese that U.S. officials had concluded their cause was hopeless. Further, Martin delayed as long as possible before ordering the evacuation of all U.S. personnel, their dependents, and those South Vietnamese who had worked for the Americans.[44]

General Thieu, convinced that the Americans were not going to send South Vietnam any more military aid, nor would they attempt an eleventh-hour military intervention to save his country, resigned on April 21. That evening, Thieu spoke for the last time to his countrymen. Most of his 90-minute televised speech amounted to a tearful often hysterical defense of his leadership and a bitter attack on his long-time ally, the United States. He denounced Henry Kissinger for having forced him to sign the Paris Accords and then refusing to honor former President Nixon's pledges of support when North Vietnam renewed its aggression in violation of the Accords.

> Kissinger didn't see that the agreement led the Vietnamese people to death. . . . The United States has not respected its promises. It is unfair. It is inhumane. It is not trustworthy. It is not responsible.[45]

Four days after resigning, General Thieu fled his country.

Thieu's successor was the elderly and feeble Tran Van Huong, the RVN vice president, who, during his few days in office, tried futilely to seek a negotiated settlement of the war. The North Vietnamese, positioning their forces for a final assault on Saigon, had no time for desperate proposals for a political solution to a war that they were about to win on the battlefield. On April 22, General Dung signed the order to begin the Ho Chi Minh Campaign to conquer Saigon. At that moment, 10 NVA divisions encircled the defenseless city.

On April 23, speaking to a large audience at the Tulane University field house, President Ford made U.S. abandonment of South Vietnam official. He urged Americans to forget about the Vietnam War and avoid arguments about who was to blame for its disastrous outcome. He told the crowd:

> America can regain the sense of pride that existed before Vietnam. But it cannot be achieved by refighting a war that is finished as far as America is concerned.[46]

As Ford uttered the magic word, "finished," the predominantly student audience of 4,500 erupted with frenzied whistling, cheering, clapping, foot-stomping, and shouting that lasted for several minutes. The president had given voice to the national mood existing at the moment the PAVN forces readied themselves to win the final victory of the long Vietnam War.

The Disappearance of South Vietnam

As the Communists drove relentlessly toward their final triumph during the last days of April 1975, the contrast in the national mood with what it had been nearly 10 years earlier when President Johnson had sent U.S. armed forces off to fight a land war in Southeast Asia could not have been greater. That combination of pride, arrogance, innocence, crusading anti-Communism and expectations of a quick and easy triumph that had propelled the country into the war had long vanished. During those woeful final days, the national mood was dominated by an overwhelming desire to be rid at last of an endless war. It was a war that had already cost far more in lives and dollars than any worst-case scenarist could have imagined at the outset of the American effort to contain the spread of Communism in Southeast Asia by thwarting the Vietnamese national revolution supported by China and the Soviet Union. A nation that had been badly divided by internal divisions, and political and cultural crises, all exacerbated by the nation's longest war, wanted only for the war to cease. As the Saigon government, which the United States had helped create and sustained for over 20 years, suffered its death agonies at the end of April 1975, most Americans averted their eyes.

The North Vietnamese and VietCong had the city by the throat; their tanks and artillery were ready and their troops were positioned for attack. But for a few days they held back to allow the Americans and the Vietnamese who had worked for U.S. officials to leave. Within the doomed city, thousands of Vietnamese tried desperately to escape. Everywhere, Americans were accosted by Vietnamese brandishing letters and documents, pleading for a way out of their country. To facilitate the evacuation of South Vietnamese nationals, the U.S. Congress hastily approved legislation waiving entry restrictions for 150,000 Indochinese aliens, including 50,000 high-risk Vietnamese. Each day, thousands of Vietnamese flew out of Tan Son Nhut Airport onboard C-141s and C-130s that formed a round-the-clock airlift to freedom.

On April 27, the Communists launched their first attack on Saigon, a rocket barrage that they deliberately aimed at densely populated areas of the city: downtown Saigon and the suburb of Cholon. The rockets killed and wounded hundreds of people. On the same day, the hapless Nhu Tang Troung resigned the GVN presidency. The South Vietnamese Assembly then replaced Troung with General Doung Van Minh, the man who had briefly headed the military directorate that had replaced Ngo Dihn Diem in November 1963. The Assembly charged Minh with the task of restoring peace to South Vietnam. The Communists quickly made it unmistakably clear that the only political settlement they would consider accepting from General Minh would be unconditional surrender.[47]

On April 28, fighting erupted along the outskirts of Saigon. Late in the day, the only NVAF air strike of the entire war hit Tan Son Nhut Air Base. Five American-built A-37s, in a perfectly executed operation that fooled the defenders, destroyed or damaged several aircraft parked along the main runways and disrupted the U.S. airlift for several hours. The attack had been led by a VNAF defector, Lieutenant Nguyen Thanh Trung. Now a captain in the North Vietnamese Air Force, Trung had trained a group of MIG pilots to fly the A-37s that had been captured from the South Vietnamese earlier in the 1975 offensive.[48]

Early on the morning of April 29, the NVA launched a rocket attack on Tan Son Nhut Airport. The first rockets slammed into a Marine guard post. They killed Lance Corporal Darwin Judge and Corporal Charles McMahon Jr. Corporals Judge and McMahon were the last U.S. casualties of the Vietnam War, the last of more than 58,000 who were killed. Shortly after the first rocket barrages struck, long-range artillery shells began falling on the air base. The rocket and artillery barrages forced the fixed-wing airlift operations to shut down.

President Ford then ordered the final phase of the Saigon evacuation, code-named Operation FREQUENT WIND, to begin. It was a massive helilift designed to remove the remaining Americans and the eligible Vietnamese and third-country nationals from the surrounded city and fly them to a large fleet of U.S. naval ships stationed some forty miles out to sea. Buses navigated the crowded city streets to designated pickup sites, gathered the evacuees, and hauled them to Tan Son Nhut Airport and the waiting helicopters. At every assembly site, the number of people waiting to board the buses vastly exceeded their carrying capacities. Many eligible Vietnamese never got evacuated.[49] By afternoon, the entire city had dissolved into chaos. Frenzied mobs roamed the streets. Vandals overturned cars and set fire to buildings. Looters ransacked homes and apartments. A crowd of perhaps 10,000 Vietnamese converged on the U.S. embassy either in the hope of finding a way out or to vent their rage at the departing Americans. Marine security guards, standing atop the compound walls, used their rifle butts and boots to beat back the hordes of Vietnamese trying to get onto the embassy grounds. Nevertheless, several thousand Vietnamese managed either to climb the walls or storm the gates. Angry South Vietnamese soldiers on the streets outside of the embassy grounds fired at the departing helicopters leaving them behind.

By 8:00 P.M., the evacuation from Tan Son Nhut Airport had been completed. The last Americans to depart the airport were a detachment of Marine security guards who had been assisting the evacuees. Before the Marines boarded the last helicopter, they prepared the Defense Attache Office complex for destruction. Formerly the headquarters of MACV, the buildings had symbolized for a decade the U.S. commitment to defend South Vietnam. From their vantage point aboard the helicopter ascending into the night, the departing Marines watched the structures that had housed sophisticated communications equipment, secret documents, and a vault containing $3.5 million dollars in U.S. currency collapse into rubble.[50]

Figure 9.3 As Americans abandoned Vietnam, they took thousands of Vietnamese with them. The last-minute, chaotic helicopter flights from a rooftop somewhere in downtown Saigon represented the utter failure of the U.S. mission to build a democratic nation in southern Vietnam that would block further expansion of Communism in Southeast Asia. Photographer: UPI. *Source: CORBIS.*

During the early morning hours of April 30, helicopters flying from the American embassy made the last evacuations of the Vietnam War. Just before 5:00 A.M., a weary Ambassador Martin and his senior staff members departed the embassy. But there were not nearly enough places onboard the available helicopters to evacuate all of the remaining Vietnamese and third-country nationals. Between 400 and 500 people were left behind on embassy grounds. Looking down at the stranded people milling about helplessly as his helicopter headed for the open sea, one of the U.S. officials could think "of no word in any language adequate to describe the sense of shame that swept over me."[51] The last Americans to leave Vietnam were the Marine security forces who had barricaded themselves on the embassy rooftop to await the final helicopters that would take them to the waiting ships. As the last U.S. helicopter lifted off, Sergeant Juan Valdez observed Vietnamese evacuees trying to push their way through the still-barricaded door, waving papers at the sky to show that they too should be allowed to leave Vietnam.

At about noon, North Vietnamese tanks rumbled by the American embassy, headed for Independence Palace, the South Vietnamese capitol and official residence of President Minh. Alongside the tanks rolled trucks crammed with young PAVN sol-

Figure 9.4 Thousands of desperate Vietnamese crowded the gates of the U.S. Embassy in Saigon, hoping for a way out before the VietCong and NVA troops occupied the city. Photographer: Nik Wheeler. *Source:* CORBIS. ©Nik Wheeler/CORBIS.

diers. As it approached the palace grounds, the lead tank barreled through the steel front gate, smashing it down. The tanks gathered in a semicircle facing the entrance to the Palace, their big guns trained on the capitol. In a gesture of triumph, a lone soldier, waving a huge blue and red flag with the yellow star of the National Liberation Front, raced up the steps of the Palace. PRG officials announced over radio Saigon that the city had been liberated. In Paris, Communist envoys announced that Saigon had been re-named Ho Chi Minh City. Inside of Independence Palace, President Minh awaited the victors in his office. As they approached, he tried to surrender to the senior officer present, NVA Colonel Bui Tin, but Tin curtly informed him that all power had already passed into the hands of the revolution: "Your power has crumbled. You cannot give up what you do not have."[52] Minh and the other RVN officials who had assembled in his office were taken into custody.

Some of Saigon's inhabitants welcomed their conquerors. Most greeted them with indifference, or with uncertainty and fear. On May 8, a large crowd gathered in front of the presidential palace to hear the head of the new provisional government, General Tran Van Tra, proclaim the triumph of the Vietnamese revolution. Even before the cheering stopped, the victorious North Vietnamese began rounding up many Saigonese residents for "reeducation" at camps being set up in the countryside. The Republic of South Vietnam was quickly swept into the ashheap of history. America's limited war fought in Indochina to contain the expansion of Communism had failed. Henry Kissinger observed: "Vietnam was a great tragedy. We should never have been there at all. But it's history."[53]

WHY WE LOST AND THEY WON

The American effort at nation-building, at assisting in the creation of an independent South Vietnam, was doomed to fail from the outset. The Republic of South Vietnam could never have become a viable nation-state. It could never overcome its origins as a puppet government, an instrument of Western imperialism.[54] From Ngo Dinh Diem's to Nguyen Van Thieu's, every one of the succession of inept, weak, and corrupt governments, all strongly supported by the United States, failed to develop a popular base of support, failed to achieve political stability, and failed to unite a politically fragmented people. They all failed to enlist the loyalties of or appeal to the self-interest of most peasant villagers who made up the large majority of their citizenry. Failure to achieve local legitimacy ultimately doomed the South Vietnamese cause. American firepower killed and wounded huge numbers of VC and NVA soldiers, but it could neither eradicate the Vietnamese national revolution nor its appeal. It could never win the hearts and minds of a majority of the Vietnamese peasantry for a succession of South Vietnamese governments. Since the South Vietnamese government lacked the will to fight and Pentagon planners never devised strategies that could achieve victory, only a Communist triumph could bring peace to southern Vietnam.

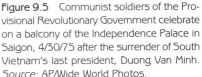

Figure 9.5 Communist soldiers of the Provisional Revolutionary Government celebrate on a balcony of the Independence Palace in Saigon, 4/30/75 after the surrender of South Vietnam's last president, Duong Van Minh. *Source:* AP/Wide World Photos.

Because they never acquired legitimacy in the eyes of the majority of their people, South Vietnam's governments never acquired the ability to defend themselves from the revolutionary war waged unrelentingly against them for nearly 20 years. With or without U.S. backing, there never was a viable political alternative to the revolutionary nationalism that swept Vietnam after 1945. The United States and its succession of client governments in South Vietnam could never solve the essential South Vietnamese conundrum: how to achieve a stable political order without supporting revolutionary changes.[55] There could be no long-term stability in southern Vietnam without revolutionary change, and neither the U.S. officials or their RVN clients could accommodate the Vietnamese nationalist revolution.

In the early 1950s, both the Truman and Eisenhower administrations openly supported the failing French effort to reimpose colonialism on the Vietnamese people with money and arms. Following the failure of the French cause in 1954, the United States intervened to try to create a new nation-state in southern Vietnam in violation of the Geneva Accords. By the early 1960s, the United States significantly increased its support of the Republic of South Vietnam, which was trying to defend itself against the resurgent revolutionaries, now committed to winning control over the entire country and reuniting it under their rule. In 1965, perceiving that the South Vietnamese government was nearing collapse, despite massive U.S. economic and military aid, Americans assumed the major burden of the fighting against the VietCong revolutionaries. After 1969, when a majority of the American people turned against the Vietnam War, America shifted the burden of the fighting back to its South Vietnamese clients. But Vietnamization never worked—never could have worked. Until the end, the South Vietnamese state remained dependent on the United States for its security and survival. When all of the U.S. soldiers went home and Congress drastically curtailed its support for the RVN, when they were on their own, their cause was hopeless. The Communists, with relative ease, swiftly administered the *coup de grâce* in the spring of 1975.

But the failure of the South Vietnamese state to establish itself and survive is not just the story of the failure of a succession of inept, corrupt, elite-based governments to develop a strong political base and the ability to defend themselves. And it is not just the story of a major U.S. foreign policy failure, the failure of a succession of American administrations, from Truman's through Ford's, to develop effective aid, counterinsurgency, and pacification programs, or effective military strategies that could neutralize the revolutionary war strategies.

To understand the outcome of the Vietnamese revolution, the focus must necessarily be on the North Vietnamese and VietCong, and on the myriad of factors that enabled them to ultimately prevail after a three-decades-long struggle. The focus must be on local, particular Vietnamese realities. It was not easy; the Communists made a lot of mistakes over the years. Victory cost them dearly. The revolutionaries paid an appalling price in blood and money, and when they finally prevailed after a long struggle, they found that they governed an impoverished nation whose physical environment, economy, and social fabric had been battered by decades of war. Most nations that have lost wars have sustained proportionately far fewer casualties and suffered much less physical, economic, and social damage than did the victorious North Vietnamese.

But they enjoyed many advantages during the long war, and they made skillful use of them all. The revolutionary cause attracted the best and the brightest of Vietnam's elite classes. They had able and determined leaders from Ho Chi Minh, Vo Nguyen Giap, and their associates, to the local cadres who organized villages, indoctrinated soldiers, and penetrated all levels of the South Vietnamese civilian and military bureaucracies. Although the revolutionary leaders were all committed Communist ideologues, they also were Vietnamese nationalists. They harnessed the powerful patriotic feelings of most Vietnamese to their cause—to reunify the fatherland under Vietnamese leadership that was independent of all foreign influences. They also appealed to the xenophobia of the Vietnamese, whose entire history had conditioned them to hate and fear foreigners, especially powerful foreigners like the Chinese, French, and now the Americans, who came to conquer and exploit them, and to impose their cultures. Their social reform agenda, particularly the promise of land to poor and landless peasants who constituted the bulk of Vietnamese rural populations, enabled them to rally the masses to their cause. For the peasant masses, the revolution had a powerful dual appeal: to their patriotic feelings—a unified, independent, and sovergin Vietnamese nation—and to their economic self-interest—land of their own.

The Vietnamese revolutionary leaders also skillfully exploited the rivalry between the major Communist powers, the Soviet Union and the Chinese, to extract the economic and military aid from both nations that the Vietnamese had to have in order to have a chance to win the war. They received the aid they required, and they played one powerful ally against the other without compromising their cause or independence.

Drawing on the rich warrior tradition of Vietnamese history, as well as on modern Chinese models of revolutionary warfare, the Vietnamese Communists fashioned a complex, sophisticated, and ultimately successful strategy of "people's warfare," a form of protracted warfare that shrewdly blended military, diplomatic, and political tactics. They heeded the lessons of their own national historical experience. They knew that if they were patient, retained the tactical initiative, avoided battles where they could suffer ruinous losses, and inflicted sizable casualties on the invaders over a lengthy time period, then Americans would tire of the war and go home. Just as the French did before them, and the Chinese before the French.

U.S. officials defended the long American involvement in Vietnam as an effort to maintain political stability in Southeast Asia. The domino correlative to America's containment ideology magnified the significance of the endeavor to create a pro-Western and non-Communist alternative to revolutionary nationalism in southern Vietnam: The larger U.S. mission in Indochina was always defined as preventing the spread of Chinese and Soviet influence throughout Southeast Asia. Successive U.S. administrations perceived Vietnam as a conduit of Communist expansionism that had to be closed to keep southern Vietnam, the rest of Indochina, and the nations of Southeast Asian within the Western orbit. For the Americans, Vietnam was always about much more than Vietnam.

At every stage of the U.S. involvement in Indochina, it was always of great importance to the U.S. officials to maintain U.S. credibility. "From the beginning, Americans fought to influence others' opinions of what the United States would do elsewhere."[56] U.S. officials backed the French effort to reimpose colonialism on the Vietnamese to maintain credibility with the French that the United States was their staunch ally who would support their efforts to resist Communist expansion whether it occurred in Southeast Asia or Western Europe.

U.S. officials embarked on a quixotic nation-building crusade in southern Vietnam to show their allies that they could protect vulnerable nations from falling like so many dominoes to Communism, and to show the Soviets and Chinese that "wars of national liberation" could not succeed. To maintain credibility with the South Vietnamese that the United States would stand by them no matter what, U.S. officials launched a devastating aerial war against North Vietnam. To demonstrate to the world that Americans had learned the hard lessons of Munich, Lyndon Johnson Americanized the Vietnam War by putting in a half million ground combat forces. And for years, to prove to the North Vietnamese that they could not achieve via negotiations what they could not win on the battlefields of Vietnam, U.S. officials backed a succession of South Vietnamese governments and refused to make the necessary concessions that could produce a political settlement.[57]

But the outcome of the American Indochina war invalidated its prime ideological justifications and suggested that the containment ideology itself had been misapplied. A policy developed to contain the spread of Soviet influence into Southern and Central Europe could not be applied effectively to the regional conflicts and civil wars of Southeast Asia. Following the triumph of Communist forces in Vietnam, Laos, and Cambodia, American security was not seriously threatened. American alliances elsewhere were not weakened, nor were American allies disheartened by the outcome. After the fall of Saigon, Vientiane, and Phnom Penh, there was no deluge of Communist takeovers in Southeast Asia. Communist influence did not reach beyond Indochina. Outside of Cambodia and Laos, countries that had become extensions of the Vietnam War, which was really the Second Indochina War, the dominoes never fell.

Within Indochina, the Communist dominoes soon crashed into one another. Military victory only accentuated the deep internal divisions within the Communist world. In Cambodia, the Khmer Rouge leadership implemented a savage reign of terror that cost between 1 and 2 million lives. The Vietnamese, nursing an imperialistic agenda of their own, invaded Cambodia in 1978 and overthrew the Khmer Rouge regime it had previously helped bring to power. Hanoi established a replacement regime, a puppet government in Phnom Penh supported by Vietnamese troops. China, which had close ties with Cambodia, then sent 220,000 ground combat soldiers into northern Vietnam in 1979 to punish Vietnam for its aggression in Cambodia. There ensued a short, bloody war between the two erstwhile allies in which the battle-hardened Vietnamese repelled the invaders, inflicting massive casualties and political humiliation on the Communist giant. The United States, which had gone to war in Vietnam in 1965 to contain Chinese expansionism in Southeast Asia, found itself quietly backing China's efforts to contain Vietnamese expansionism in 1979. In these intramural Communist power struggles for regional hegemony, the Soviets backed the Vietnamese against the Chinese and their Cambodian allies. Clashing perceptions of national interest and historic cultural and national rivalries consistently overrode ideological considerations in guiding the actions of Soviet, Chinese, and Indochinese Communist political leaders during the late 1970s. These internecine conflicts among leading members of the "international Communist conspiracy" must have given pause among hard-line American anti-Communist ideologues, prisoners of vintage reductive Cold War conceptions.

In the aftermath of the Communist takeover of Indochina, the elaborate edifice of international economic and political relations that the United States had constructed in the Far East during the 1950s and 1960s did not crumble. In the years since the end of the Indochina War, the non-Communist nations of Southeast Asia have enjoyed unprecedented stability and prosperity. The Association of Southeast Asian Nations (ASEAN), which includes Thailand, Indonesia, Malaya, Singapore, and Brunei, developed strong commercial and financial ties with the United States, Japan, and Western Europe. The energetic populations and vibrant economies of the ASEAN nations contrasted starkly with the Communist-controlled nations of Vietnam, Cambodia, and Laos, which remained grim pockets of poverty and repression amid a sea of prosperity long after the Indochina wars had played out and the physical damage done to these countries had mostly disappeared.

The Communists proved to be harsh conquerors of the South Vietnamese. Although dovish critics of the American war effort scoffed at Richard Nixon's and Gerald Ford's dire predictions of a bloodbath of nightmarish proportions following the Communist takeover, a bloodbath did nevertheless occur. Many former high-ranking officers in the South Vietnamese armed forces and many former high government officials were executed. Thousands of executions occurred between 1975 and 1983. In addition, hundreds of thousands of minor officials and supporters of the vanished RVN were put in harsh "reeducation" centers, which often resembled Soviet *Gulags.*[58]

Since the Communist victory, an estimated 1.5 million Vietnamese have fled the country. Thousands perished during the attempt; additional thousands languished in squalid refugee camps in Hong Kong, Thailand, and other nations of Southeast Asia. Approximately 300,000 of these refugees resettled in France, and another 500,000 have come to the United States. Despite the horrible circumstances that brought most of the Vietnamese to the United States in the mid- and late-1970s, the new Vietnamese American population has generally done very well in its adopted land. They have replicated the oldest success story in American history: refugees from tyranny and poverty who made a fresh start in a new land. Thousands of individual success stories abound: of people arriving knowing no English, possessing little more than the clothes on their backs acquiring good educations, becoming good citizens, and achieving successful careers in business and the professions. Many of these people received help of various kinds from government and private agencies, and from compassionate individuals. They have adapted well to America, and have made it possible for their children to enjoy productive and fulfilling lives.

For thousands more, however, America has remained an alien and unfriendly place. Many of these uprooted Vietnamese, victims of hostility, discrimination, and prejudice, have fared poorly in their adopted land. Often they have been forced to go on welfare and have been tempted by vice and crime. They are the ultimate losers, confined to bleak lives at the social margins, victims of both Vietnamese and American history.

Within Vietnam itself the costs of the 30-year war were horrendous, for much of which the Americans bear direct responsibility: catastrophic human loss and suffering, and extensive damage to a fragile preindustrial economic infrastructure struggling to escape the legacies of French colonial exploitation. Millions of acres of forest and crop lands were destroyed. Millions of South Vietnamese were turned into refugees, most of whom poured into the slums and back-alley labyrinths of southern cities. Twenty years of American aid programs had created an artificial consumer economy in South Vietnam that retarded commercial and industrial development. This ersatz economy collapsed during the 1974–1975 period, leaving southern Vietnam without a viable urban economic base.

The victors' efforts to carry out Stalinist-era reforms, including forced-draft industrialization and collectivized agricultural, only made terrible economic conditions worse for many people. The annual growth rate stagnated at 1 to 2 percent, and the per capita annual income hovered around $150, making Vietnam one of the poorest countries in the world. After endeavoring to create a socialist political economy in southern Vietnam, the Communist rulers made a pragmatic accommodation with the capitalistic traditions of the region. Some businesses were taken over by the state, and the land of some rich landowners was seized. But the government allowed many small- and medium-sized enterprises to remain in private hands. The government also redistributed land to many poor and landless peasants and set up programs to encourage urban dwellers to return to the land.

The Wounds Within

Within the United States, following the fall of Saigon, there was no bitter "who lost Vietnam?" debate or a resurgence of McCarthyite redbaiting. The fact that there was no search for scapegoats or the development of "stab-in-the-back" theories of the kind that had contributed to the destabilization of the Weimar Republic came as a pleasant surprise to Cold War intellectuals like Henry Kissinger. He had feared the worst, that America would tear itself apart in an orgy of recrimination following the U.S. failure in Vietnam. In a moment of frustration and anger during the spring of 1975, as South Vietnam disappeared from the planet, Kissinger had invoked the potent Munich analogy, the rationale used by every president involved with Indochina to justify U.S. participation in the war.[59]

Instead of recriminations, historical amnesia set in, symptomatic of moral and political exhaustion. Most Americans did not want to think or talk about Vietnam for years, much less argue about it. Amnesia persisted until the early 1980s when there was a revival of interest in the war and controversy over its lessons and legacies. Conferences and symposia of concerned scholars, journalists who had covered the Vietnam beat, and former civilian and military officials involved in the war convened to examine and explain the war from multiple perspectives. A veritable flood of scholarly and popular literature on the war suddenly issued forth. Hollywood and network television discovered Vietnam, and the war quickly became a staple topic of popular culture. A conspiracy of silence rapidly gave way to an obsessive interest in the first major foreign war the United States ever lost.

The fallacies of U.S. Cold War ideology may have been exposed by the internecine Communist wars in Indochina and the absence of a McCarthyite backlash at home. Vital American foreign policy interests in the Far East, Middle East, and Europe may have suffered no permanent setbacks following the U.S. withdrawal and subsequent defeat in Vietnam. However, the damage done to the United States by its Vietnam ordeal was nevertheless severe and lasting. George Kennan, the principal architect of America's Cold War foreign policy, based on containing Communism's expansionist tendencies, has called the Vietnam War "the most disastrous of all America's undertakings over the whole two hundred years of its history."

The fall of Saigon in April 1975 was a severe blow to the pride and self-confidence of a nation whose fondest boast had been that it had never lost a major war. The tragic outcome of the long war on the eve of the bicentennial dampened many Americans' enthusiasm for celebrating their nation's 200th birthday. The Vietnam War had consumed over 58,000 American lives and left another 300,000 soldiers wounded.

In addition to the human costs of the war, the economic and financial costs were high. Except for World War II, the Vietnam War cost more than any other war in American history—an estimated $167 billion. President Johnson's efforts to finance simultaneously a major war and Great Society reform programs without imposing major tax increases or economic controls ignited inflation. The long-term economic costs of the Vietnam War were even more serious. The U.S. economy was booming at the time the United States Americanized the war. By the early 1970s, as America gradually disengaged from the war, the U.S. economy had entered an era of relative decline. The Vietnam War was one of the major causes of American economic decline, and it accelerated that decline. The war helped launch and sustain the great inflation that ravaged that economy, weakened many important industries, eroded purchasing power, reduced living standards, and undermined citizen confidence in the American system of political economy.[60]

The Vietnam War also exacted a high political price. It undermined public faith in the competency and honesty of elected officials and helped force two strong presidents out of office prematurely. It enlarged the administrative state in a nation that lauded private initiative and private-sector solutions to problems. It weakened the value of public service and engendered fear, suspicion, and hatred of government in the hearts and minds of millions of Americans. One of the enduring legacies of the Vietnam War in this country has been the persistent distrust of governmental institutions and the officials who run them.[61]

The Vietnam experience discredited military service for years. Americans lost respect and goodwill for the nation's armed forces. With the cancellation of the draft, the military services struggled to recruit enough personnel to meet minimal staffing levels. By the mid-1970s, the reputation of the all the military services, but especially the U.S. Army, had sunk to its nadir. Much of the Vietnam-induced damage was repaired during the 1980s under the leadership of President Reagan, but it was not until the Persian Gulf War in 1991 that Americans once again could be proud of the U.S. armed forces.

The Vietnam War shattered the bipartisan consensus that had guided American foreign policy since the late 1940s, and it inaugurated an era of confusion and conflict that has never been entirely resolved. The losing war also demonstrated that America's vast wealth and powerful military technology could not defeat a poor Third World nation determined to achieve national reunification, nor could the United States support forever an ineffective regime that lacked a popular base of support and the will to fight.

Americans also discovered that there were limits to American power and limits to the burdens the American people would shoulder in pursuit of foreign policy objectives. For the first time since the Cold War began, many Americans questioned the validity of their global mission to contain Communism. Some analysts believed that the nation had overreached its capabilities and thereby had entered an era of relative economic and strategic decline. The Vietnam War represented an economic, political, and military disaster for the United States. American stature in the world declined for a time as a consequence of the U.S. defeat in Vietnam.

There were other costs of war. A bitter controversy erupted over whether hundreds of thousands of draft evaders and resisters, and deserters, should be granted amnesty or severely punished for their violations of Selective Service laws. The debate perpetuated the war-sown divisions between doves and hawks. The Vietnam War was the most controversial and least popular war in U.S. history. It divided Americans more deeply than any conflict since the Civil War, 100 years earlier. Most Americans had become disillusioned with the national crusade to save South Vietnam from Communism and had stopped supporting the U.S. war effort long before it ended. Millions of Americans opposed the Vietnam War, and hundreds of thousands of those opponents actively demonstrated their opposition.

The gravest damage done to America by the Vietnam War occurred in the realm of the spirit. It was a deep wound within the national psyche. The ultimate domino was America's mythic conception of itself. Before Vietnam, America's most cherished vision of itself was expressed in the famed metaphor of a shining "city upon a hill." America's mission in the world was to redeem history. In secular terms, America's mission was to set a democratic example to guide and inspire the rest of the world. America's post–World War II foreign policy was founded on the principle of thwarting the spread of Communism to preserve the sphere of freedom, the empire of liberty, in the world. The redeemer-nation sent its citizen-soldiers to southern Vietnam to save its inhabitants from the evil embrace of expanding Communism. But once launched upon their errand into the wilderness of Vietnam, Americans made the horrible discovery that the red-white-and-blue alternative to revolutionary nationalism was only death and destruction and, ultimately, defeat for their soldiers and for the Vietnamese people that they had tried so hard for so long to help. The lofty American conception of itself as the world's redeemer civilization perished in the jungles, swamps, and rice paddies of southern Vietnam.

Within the nation, some healing has occurred from the trauma of Vietnam with the passage of time and with much study and reflection about the war experience. In the case of Vietnam veterans, Americans gradually understood that most of them had not committed atrocities against helpless peasants, that most of them were not junkies, alcoholics, or crazies. Despite encountering some difficulties deriving from their war service, most Vietnam veterans completed school, obtained jobs, went to college, entered the professions, married, had families, and became solid and productive citizens in their communities. Per capita income of Vietnam-era veterans exceeded that of their non-veteran contemporaries. It also was gradually understood and accepted that dysfunctional veterans were not weaklings, losers, or criminals; they suffered from serious medical and psychological disorders. They needed sympathy and support, and above all they needed medical services, not rejection or condemnation.

Doves who had previously denounced Vietnam veterans as racist killers of women and children now viewed them in a different light. They saw them as 19-year-old boys drafted and sent to fight an immoral war. They realized that many veterans themselves were victims of a war policy that was misguided and wrong. Hawks belatedly acknowledged that most Vietnam veterans had fought with valor and tenacity under circumstances that precluded the possibility of victory. They had fought bravely, they had won all of the major battles, and they had always inflicted far greater casualties than they took; but politicians had denied them victory. Both hawks and doves, in simple moral terms, in time accepted the Vietnam veterans. They agreed that they had been good soldiers in a bad war, although "bad war" still meant something quite different to a dove than it did to a hawk.

The most compelling symbol of the new esteem accorded the Vietnam veterans was the Vietnam Veterans' Memorial in Washington, DC. The memorial was conceived by a small group of Vietnam veterans and built entirely with private contributions. It was dedicated in a moving ceremony on November 23, 1982. It stands in a grassy meadow near the Lincoln Memorial. It was designed by Maya Ling Lin, an undergraduate architecture student at Yale University. The memorial is stark and simple; it consists of two wings of black granite rising out of the earth and then sinking back into it. On the reflecting panels are carved the names of the 58,235 men and women who died in the Vietnam War. The memorial is a shrine to honor the war dead.

In the years since its opening, the memorial has become one of the most often visited of Washington's many monuments. The wall of names exerts enormous emotional power over all who come to see it. As one approaches the granite slabs, one has the distinct sensation of descending into a valley of death, a valley of death consecrated by the blood of heroes who died in a faraway place for a murky cause they scarcely comprehended.

On a bright summer day, a bearded man in a wheelchair, dressed in battle fatigues and carrying his two children in his burly arms, comes to find the names of fallen comrades. A mother comes to touch the name of her son, and a widow comes to touch the name of her husband. They leave mementos—flowers, combat decorations, photographs, a pair of cowboy boots, and a teddy bear. Those visitors who had known none of the dead, who had lost no one in Vietnam, even those who protested against the war, are

Figure 9.6   Vietnam War Memorial Wall. On its stark granite walls are engraved the names of the 58,235 servicemen and servicewomen who lost their lives in Vietnam. Note the items visitors have left to memorialize lost comrades, friends, spouses, and relatives. *Source:* Smithsonian Institution Office of Imaging, Printing, and Photographic Services. Smithsonian Institution Photo No. 17B.

deeply moved by the wall of names. They too are filled with grief and sadness at the loss, and perhaps rage at the waste and futility of an unnecessary and unwinnable war.

THE SPECTER OF VIETNAM

The specter of Vietnam lurked in the background of every American foreign policy debate of the 1970s, 1980s, and 1990s, and continues to haunt the nation as it wages a global war against Islamicist terrorists. In 2003, Washington's controversial war to remove the Iraqi dictator Saddam Hussein from power and replace him with a more democratic political order reignited the Vietnam syndrome with a vengeance.

After the ordeal of Vietnam, there was a manifest unwillingness to intervene militarily in any Third World countries for fear of being trapped into extended military operations. An arrogance about the uses of U.S. military power that had existed before the Vietnam War had given way to a diffident neoisolationist yearning to avoid all military involvement in the world.

The ghost of Vietnam influenced the public debate over President Reagan's interventionist policies in Nicaragua in the early 1980s. The Reagan administration vigorously waged a proxy war against the Sandinista government by arming and training a counterrevolutionary army, the *Contras,* to overthrow them. Democratic congressional opponents of the *Contra* policy cried, "No more Vietnams in Central America!" Defenders of the Reagan policy insisted that Nicaragua was different from Vietnam, and that they would not make the same mistakes that had allegedly undermined the U.S. effort in Southeast Asia. They were not sending American ground combat forces to get bogged down in a stalemated war; they were training, equipping, and supporting Nicaraguan "freedom fighters" who could defeat the Sandinista forces and liberate Nicaragua without a direct U.S. military intervention. In this debate, both critics and defenders of the American intervention in Nicaragua revealed that they drew different lessons from the Vietnam experience. The debate also suggested that its participants were more interested in using the history of Vietnam to score debaters' points in the present than they were in coming to terms with what really happened in Indochina.[62]

Memories of Vietnam dominated public debate over the Persian Gulf War and shaped the first Bush administration's war policy during the period 1990–1991. Congressional opponents of President Bush's plan to use military force to drive the Iraqi army out of Kuwait warned of the dangers of getting bogged down in a lengthy and costly war in a Third World country. These critics preferred to use economic sanctions to drive the Iraqis out. Mindful of the fears of millions of his fellow citizens, when President Bush launched the Gulf War, he pledged that "this will not be another Vietnam. Our troops will . . . not be asked to fight with one hand tied behind their back."[63] The military's handling of the media coverage of the Gulf War reflected its mistaken belief that uncensored and biased media coverage of the Vietnam War had contributed to the American defeat in Indochina. The heroes' welcome given to the returning DESERT STORM veterans was shaped, in part, by guilty memories of the shabby treatment given to returning Vietnam War veterans. In fact, many Vietnam-era veterans joined the parades honoring the returning Gulf War veterans. It was, for many of them, a long-overdue celebratory reception. After the victorious outcome of the Gulf War, President Bush proclaimed that Americans had once and for all licked the Vietnam syndrome.

The Vietnam specter surfaced once again during the 1992 presidential election. Democratic candidate William (Bill) Clinton was attacked repeatedly by George Bush for having evaded the draft while the Vietnam War was raging and for having helped to organize antiwar demonstrations in London in 1969 while he was a Rhodes Scholar at Oxford. Although less was made of it, Bush's running mate, Vice President Dan Quayle, had to rebut the charges against him that had surfaced at the time he was chosen to be Bush's running mate in 1988. Quayle allegedly used family political connections to land a prized slot in an Indiana National Guard unit in 1969 to sidestep a possible tour of duty in Vietnam. Neither Quayle nor Clinton appeared to suffer much political damage from these attacks, but the attacks against them attested to the continuing troublesome legacy of Vietnam. The charges dredged up bad memories of bad times and of a controversial war that forced many young men to make hard choices, in many instances, morally ambiguous choices about the war.

"The ghosts of Vietnam still lingered"[64] during the 1990s. President Clinton was forced to withdraw U.S. forces from Somalia in 1993 after the forces had expanded their original humanitarian mission to include efforts to shape the political destiny of that impoverished land. Eighteen American Marines got killed in the crossfire of two factions fighting for control of Somalia, and Clinton had no choice but to withdraw all U.S. forces lest Somalia would become the latest Vietnam.

Americans were divided over whether to intervene military in the brutal ethnically driven civil wars in Bosnia-Herzegovina from 1993 to 1995. Opponents of U.S. intervention once again evoked the specter of another Vietnam-like quagmire. Many of Clinton's advisers warned him of the political fate that awaited presidents who got their country bogged down in an unpopular war. Polls showed that a majority of congressional members and a large majority of the American people opposed the Clinton administration's decision in December of 1995 to send 20,000 U.S. combat soldiers as part of a 60,000-person NATO contingent assigned to keep the peace in Bosnia, who were attempting to regenerate a national rebirth in that tortured land. In March 1999, when Washington joined with NATO forces to wage an air war against the remnants of the Yugoslav Federation to protect the ethnic Albanian inhabitants of Kosovo, President Clinton felt compelled to rule out sending U.S. ground combat forces lest he once again stir the cooling embers of Vietnam-era antiwar emotions.

VIETNAM AND IRAQ: ANALOGIES AT WAR

Historians who seek to draw parallels between wars fought more than 30 years apart do so at their peril. Especially when they seek to compare a war fought when a majority of the approximately 292 million (2005 estimate) Americans alive today either were not born or were children too young to have any meaningful understanding of that war with a controversial war and occupation that is still ongoing with no decisive outcome in sight. Additionally, historical analogies are generally superficial, incomplete, and reductive. They are as likely to distort as they are to broaden and deepen our knowledge of significant historical events such as major wars that engage us emotionally and require the commitment (and often the loss) of major material and human assets. Analogies also often provide us with a spurious view of history as cyclical; they tend to reinforce Ecclesiastes' dictum that "there is nothing new under the sun," that all wars are essentially the same. They only differ in the details—as to time, place, technology, and choice of opponent.

Further, the Vietnam analogy as applied to Iraq has become a political weapon used by opponents of the war and critics of the occupation that followed. Massachusetts senator Ted Kennedy, an outspoken critic of the war, has exclaimed, "Iraq is George

W. Bush's Vietnam." Senator John McCain, a decorated Vietnam veteran who survived five and a half years as a POW, rebutted his senate colleague when he stated bluntly, "Iraq is not Vietnam," adding, "and I know something about Vietnam."

Kennedy's rhetoric played to the concerns of those who believe that the military intervention in Iraq to remove the dictator Saddam Hussein from power was ill-advised and illegitimate because it did not have strong multilateral support. Kennedy reminded them of a bad time in our national history when the United States involved itself in a long, controversial war that ended in disaster for Americans and their allies in South Vietnam that we tried so hard for so long to help. By raising the specter of Vietnam, Kennedy may have intended to diminish popular support for the Iraq war and occupation and to put pressure on the Bush administration to move up the timetable for a U.S. pullout of its forces fighting the insurgents in Iraq.

Unlike the readers of this book, most Americans do not understand how we came to be involved in the Vietnam War, why we got bogged down in a seemingly interminable war, and why we eventually suffered a catastrophic defeat at the hands of the North Vietnamese and the VietCong. But Kennedy's remark heightened a set of bad memories that have passed into history and vague contemporary fears that the Iraq enterprise will likewise play out badly for the United States, that it will become another Vietnam.

The Vietnam War and the Iraq war/occupation occurred in very different historical contexts. They took place in different worlds. The Vietnam War is best understood as a major episode of the Cold War, with two superpowers involved and the constant, if remote, threat of nuclear annihilation. Even though the two Communist powers, the Soviet Union and China, had major conflicts during the Vietnam War era, the diplomatic and strategic imperatives of the Cold War put them on the side of the North Vietnamese and VietCong revolutionaries.

Embracing the domino theory, the United States intervened in Vietnam and subsequently all of the former French colonies that had comprised French Indochina in order to contain the spread of Communism in Southeast Asia. They endeavored to plug the Vietnamese conduit before all of the governments of Southeast Asia were destabilized and perhaps overthrown. But on the whole, during the Cold War era, the world was balanced politically and militarily. Both sides kept channels of communication open and played by the rules. They often negotiated agreements that resolved serious conflicts and applied a measure of restraint to their ongoing nuclear arms race. There was conflict and competition, and incessant ideological warfare, but the world was a relatively safe and stable place for the duration of the Cold War. Further, the Cold War ended during 1989-1991, first with the collapse of the Soviet empire and then of the Soviet Union itself. The Cold War ended in victory for the United States and its allies. The United States may have lost the Vietnam War, but it prevailed in the much larger, longer, and vastly more significant Cold War.

The Iraq War, fought in March and April 2003, took place within a fundamentally different historical context. With the collapse of the Soviet Union in 1991 and the end of the Cold War, America emerged as a hegemon dominating a unipolar world. The economic, political, and strategic power of the United States was so great that no nation or concert of nations could realistically hope to counter it. But the post-Cold War world quickly proved to be a much less stable and far more dangerous place than its predecessor. The ending of the Cold War era coincided with the onset of a series of crises and disasters around the world. The decade of the nineties offered a series of brutish small-scale civil wars, ethnic cleansing, genocidal attacks, and mounting terrorist assaults by militant Islamic groups.

As they entered the new millennium, most Americans, surveying an increasingly disorderly world, believed that they were insulated from the contagion of violence sweeping the globe by their geographic location, immense military power, and unmatched wealth. The nightmare of 9/11/01 forever shattered whatever sense of security Americans had enjoyed for a decade following the end of the Cold war and the disappearance of the Soviet Union.

The U.S.–led military intervention into Afghanistan in 2002 aimed to eliminate the government that harbored the *al-Qaeda,* to hunt down and kill or capture Osama bin Laden and other *al-Qaeda* leaders. A year later, the United States went to war in Iraq to overthrow Saddam Hussein whom President Bush portrayed as an "imminent threat" to America and its people. To bolster his claim that the Iraqi dictator posed an immediate threat to U.S. security, he cited intelligence data purporting to prove that Saddam had stockpiles of WMDs (weapons of mass destruction), including chemical and biological weapons. President Bush, in his State of the Union address given January 7, 2003, cited a British intelligence source that indicated the Iraqis were reviving their efforts to build nuclear weapons. The president also linked Saddam with the *al-Qaeda* and portrayed the war in Iraq as part of a new American proactive strategy in an ongoing war against terror. In plainer language, the proactive strategy aimed "to get them before they get us."

Unlike the Vietnam War, and for that matter, unlike any of America's previous foreign wars, the main enemy in the war on terror was not a hostile government using its military forces against the United States and its allies, but rather a shadowy network of stateless terrorists who owed allegiance only to a radical Islamic ideology that demonized American foreign policy and American culture.

The Vietnam War was the longest war in American history, one of the largest and costliest, and one of the most lethal. Of the approximately 900,000 U.S. servicemen and servicewomen who served in Vietnam, over one-third were drafted. Over 58,000 American military personnel lost their lives; another 300,000 were wounded. A third of those killed or wounded were conscripts. Approximately 2 million Vietnamese, including civilians as well as military personnel, lost their lives during the long war. Abandoning its allies in South Vietnam and losing the war did immeasurable damage to American morale and the nation's idealistic self-image.

The North Vietnamese army evolved into one of the world's most effective fighting forces. The air defenses set up for the North Vietnamese by the Soviets were deadly. U.S. Air Force and Navy pilots had to fly against a layered air defense system consisting of anti-aircraft fire, SAMs (Surface-to-Air Missiles), and fighter aircraft that took a huge toll in planes and pilots.

The United States drifted incrementally into war in Southeast Asia over a period of many years. The U.S. war in Vietnam began as a secret, low-intensity, small-scale conflict in 1961–1962 during John Kennedy's presidency. U.S. troops serving in advisory and support capacities with the South Vietnamese armies would occasionally be involved in fire fights of short duration that claimed few casualties. In February 1965, Lyndon Johnson drastically escalated the U.S. involvement in the developing conflict when he began an air war against North Vietnam. A month later, the first U.S. ground combat forces hit the beaches south of Danang. By the summer of 1965, the United States was engaged in a large and growing war against both the VietCong and North Vietnamese forces. But President Johnson took the nation to war by stealth; he played down the expanding U.S. combat role and only gradually did Americans come to understand that its military forces had been committed to fighting a major war in Vietnam.

The contrast with the way George W. Bush took the nation to war in Iraq during 2002–2003 could not be more dramatic or extreme. The American-led buildup for the Iraq War was the most open and well publicized in the history of modern warfare. When the war came after months of open preparation, warnings, and ultimata from Washington and its major allies, about the only person on the planet who was surprised was Saddam himself. He remembered that President George H. W. Bush had called off the Gulf War in 1991 and permitted him to remain in power after the U.S.-led coalition had destroyed the Iraqi army. He apparently deluded himself into believing either that the Americans did not have the stomach for another war, or if they did come after him, his elite military forces could defeat them.

The United States fought the Iraq War with an all-volunteer, professional military force, supplemented by National Guard units. With unchallenged control of the seas, the U.S.-led coalition forces had the capability of putting their forces ashore whenever and wherever they wanted. Coalition aircraft obtained total air superiority. They attacked Iraqi command and control facilities with cruise missiles and laser-guided "smart bombs" in a "shock and awe" campaign. Even the Iraqi elite Republican Guard divisions were helpless. They could not defend themselves much less interdict the Coalition's onslaught of high-tech weaponry. The mobility and lethality of the Coalition ground combat forces enabled them to make one of the most remarkable advances in the history of warfare—435 miles in two weeks against a military force that outnumbered them three to one and who were defending their homeland. This rapid, efficient, and deadly campaign brought down Saddam Hussein's criminal regime in 20 days. Coalition casualties were light, 136 dead.

The U.S.-led forces failed to consolidate their rapid military victory that had so quickly destroyed the Baathist regime. Because of a new Pentagon policy of using a comparatively small number of ground forces to win the war, the Coalition simply did not have enough boots on the ground to establish a peaceful, secure environment in which reconstruction and nation-building could go forward. A Coalition decision to immediately dissolve the Iraqi army also removed a force which, purged of its Baathist elements, could have been used for maintaining order. In the wake of the war, an orgy of looting ensued as a suddenly free people went on a rampage. Because of the damage to the Iraqi infrastructure that had occurred during the execution of the war, millions of ordinary Iraqis did not have adequate supplies of food, fresh water, cooking oil, or electricity.

U.S. leaders failed to anticipate the rise of an insurgency, initially rooted in the Sunni triangle, which had comprised Saddam's political base. The insurgency grew rapidly in numbers and firepower, abetted by foreign *Jihadists,* who streamed across Iraq's porous borders with Syria, Saudi Arabia, and Iran. There were insufficient Coalition troops to seal Iraq's borders and interdict the arriving terrorists.

As spring 2005 arrived, the occupation, completing its second year, had claimed another 1,500 U.S. casualties. A recent survey indicated that as many as 100,000 Iraqi civilians, soldiers, and insurgents have died since April 2002. But the scale of casualties of the Iraq war to date do not begin to compare with the casualties of the Vietnam War. The insurgents received far less external aid than the Soviet Union, China, and Eastern Bloc countries provided the North Vietnamese and Vietcong during the Vietnam War. The Iraqi insurgents lack an overarching ideology or a charismatic leader of the stature of Ho Chi Minh. The complex ethno-religious divisions among Sunnis, Shia, and Kurds has created a balance of antagonisms rather than a unified resistance movement.

Even though the casualties of the Iraq War and occupation are small in relation to the Vietnam conflict and they are all volunteers, large numbers of Americans may eventually turn against the war in Iraq if they decide that the government was deceptive in announcing its reasons for prosecuting the war. A UN inspection team headed by Hans Blix could find no WMDs or facilities for producing them prior to the Coalition invasion in March 2003. Following the destruction of Saddam's regime, subsequent teams of U.S. inspectors likewise found no weapons of mass destruction nor operating facilities capable of producing them. Consequently, U.S. officials have adopted the position that Saddam Hussein intended sometime in the future, perhaps after the sanctions were lifted, to fire up his WMD factories and reconstitute his arsenal.

When the documents cited in the British intelligence report suggesting that Saddam Hussein might be trying to revive his nuclear weapons program proved to be crude forgeries, which any experienced intelligence analyst should have recognized, President Bush was forced to acknowledge that he was mistaken. A Senate committee, after a thorough investigation conducted during the summer 2004, could find no evidence that a "collaborative relationship" between Saddam Hussein and *al-Qaeda* ever existed. However, the Bush administration continues to insist that they have credible evidence showing that officials in Saddam Hussein's government and *al-Qaeda* operatives worked together.

Despite worldwide opposition to the U.S.-led war in Iraq, the Bush administration's failure to prove that Saddam Hussein had stockpiled WMDs or that he was working with *al-Qaeda* terrorists, and the Coalition's failure to suppress the insurgents; domestic opposition to the Iraq war has not even approached Vietnam-era proportions. In the spring of 2005, there was a small activist anti-Iraq war movement in the nation. Students enrolled at the nation's leading colleges and universities who furnished most of the shock troops of the Vietnam-era antiwar movements were nearly all preoccupied with their studies, part-time work, and social lives—that is, with business as usual.

If the insurgency continues to grow, becomes more sophisticated, that is, more deadly, if more and more ordinary Iraqi citizens become enraged at the American occupiers of their country, if the new Iraqi government fails to take hold, and Iraq dissolves into civil war, many pundits may be comparing the Iraq "quagmire" with Vietnam.

U.S. officials have also discovered that their decision to invade Iraq without the approval of the United Nations Security Council and support of their major NATO allies has alienated world opinion. Following the terrorist attacks of 9/11/01, there was nearly universal support among the world's nations for the U.S. war against the Taliban regime that harbored the *al-Qaeda* in Afghanistan. Eighteen months later, reacting to the U.S.-led war against Iraq, many of the world's national leaders and most of their citizens viewed the United States as the major threat to global security—a great power using its great power irresponsibly. The moral standing of the United States among Latin Americans, Europeans, and Moderate Muslims in the Middle East is the lowest it has ever been. As great as its power and wealth is, the United States cannot reconstruct Iraq and establish a functioning democratic government in that nation on its own.

For both the Vietnam and Iraq wars, the senior government officials who made and implemented war policies knew nothing about the history and culture of either country, nor did they consult with experts who did. For both wars U.S. intelligence was often faulty, incomplete, misleading, and sometimes just plain wrong. Further, there is evidence indicating that in both wars officials either disregarded intelligence data that did not support what they believed to be true or wanted to do, or else they tweaked the data until it did.

There is another disturbing similarity between the Vietnam and Iraq wars. The chief lesson that the American leaders supposedly learned from the Vietnam debacle was that any military intervention must have a well-defined mission, use enough force to accomplish it, and include a clear exit strategy. President George W. Bush and his senior advisers did not heed this lesson and plunged recklessly into war in Iraq without either a winning strategy or an exit plan.

These officials apparently assumed that most Iraqis would welcome the Americans as liberators. They also apparently assumed that many Iraqis would come forward, eager to create and implement a more democratic polity and that the UN and NATO nations that had opposed the war would join with the U.S.-led coalition forces to quickly restore order, assist in reconstruction efforts, and establish a functioning democratic government. These assumptions have proven to be invalid.

Finally, there is another way in which the Vietnam and Iraq wars are distressingly similar. The American mission in Vietnam was to suppress the VietCong guerrillas and to beat back the North Vietnamese forces in order to create a secure and stable environment for South Vietnam. Once the South Vietnamese people felt secure, U.S. officials assumed that they would join with the hordes of U.S. experts and technical advisers representing various government and private agencies to build a modern democratic nation. The U.S. and South Vietnamese governments never came close to achieving those goals. Once the U.S. military forces departed Vietnam, Vietnamization was exposed as the combination sham and wishful thinking that it had always been. South Vietnam quickly disappeared after a precarious 20 year existence.

The Americans and the Iraqis who are working to establish a stable democratic government, which can achieve legitimacy in the eyes of a large majority of the Iraqi people, have discovered that, while it was comparatively easy to overthrow an oppressive government defended only by a hopelessly politicized and incompetent army, building a durable nation state to replace it is immensely difficult.

The successful Iraqi election carried out under extremely difficult circumstances on January 30, 2005, which created the first democratically elected government in Iraqi history, suggests that it is at least possible for the Iraqis to one day achieve a stable popular government, which can protect its territory and suppress the insurgency. However, it is also clear that Coaltion forces, mostly U.S. troops, will have to remain in Iraq indefinitely.

Compounding the difficulty, the stated goal of the United States is to create a unified democratic Iraq as the first building block in the broader democratization of the Middle East. That vast, ambitious enterprise raises the question: Can it be done?

Some U.S. foreign policy analysts see the stirrings of popular discontent with the political status quo in Lebanon, movement toward resolving some of the interminable conflicts between Israelis and Palestinians, gestures toward democracy made by Egyptian and Saudi rulers, and the widespread popular disaffection with the ruling mullahs in Iran, especially among young Iranians, as signs that the U.S.-led intervention in Iraq is having a transformative impact on Middle Eastern political culture. Perhaps, but it will be a long-term project, which will require a careful, patient construction of a new Middle Eastern order.

Historians are instinctively cautious about predicting future trends, because they know how difficult it is to get an accurate reading of the past, even after decades of research, thinking, and writing about it. In the spring of 2005, the forces of disruption and construction coexisted in Iraq in a kind of shifting balance that cannot be precisely measured. At that particular historical moment the future of democracy in Iraq and the greater Middle East was opaque.

Vietnam remains a metaphor haunting the American imagination. It serves as a cautionary tale of the catastrophe that awaits a nation, however rich and powerful, that allows its crusading idealism to override its realistic sense of limits.

Notes

1. Quoted in Lipsman and others, *The False Peace,* 51.
2. Isaacs, *Without Honor,* 173–80; Hess, *Vietnam,* 145–47.
3. Isaacs, *Without Honor,* 217–40; Lipsman etal. *The False Peace,* 53–57, 118–22, 124–33, 171–72.
4. Kissinger linked the return of the POWs to the departure of the final contingents of U.S. ground forces to ensure that these provisions of the Paris agreements were carried out.
5. Terry, Wallace, ed., *Bloods: An Oral History of the Vietnam War by Black Veterans* (New York: Ballantine, 1984), 281–83.
6. Frey-Wouters, Ellen, and Laufer, Robert S., *Legacy of War: The American Soldier in Vietnam* (Armonk, NY: M. E. Sharpe, 1986), 39–72; Lifton, Robert J., *Home from the War: Vietnam Veterans: Neither Victims nor Executioners* (New York: Simon and Schuster, 1973).
7. During 1986–1988 the Veterans Administration funded an extensive survey of the mental health of Vietnam War veterans. Researchers found that about 15 percent of all Vietnam combat veterans still suffered from PTSD.
8. Herring, *America's Longest War,* 257; Schulzinger, *A Time for War,* 305. Although most Americans neither knew nor cared, the ARVN lost on average 1,000 troops per month fighting the VC and PAVN forces during 1973 and 1974.
9. Turley, *The Second Indochina War,* 162–65.
10. Hess, *Vietnam,* 136.
11. Operation Homecoming was originally designated Egress Recap. Denton's statement is taken from Schulzinger, *A Time for War,* 311.
12. Szulc, *The Illusion of Peace,* 672–76; Duiker, *The Communist Road,* 301–2.
13. Porter, "Statement by the Provisional Revolutionary Government Foreign Ministry," November 2, 1973, *Vietnam Documents,* vol. 2, Document 345, 642–45; Duiker, *The Communist Road,* 302–5.
14. Schulzinger, *A Time for War,* 312–13.
15. Porter, *Vietnam Documents,* vol. 2, Document 341, 639; "Fulbright-Aiken Amendment—Public Law 93–52, Section 108," July 1, 1973; Isaacs, *Without Honor,* 143, 226–28, 234–37.
16. Davidson, *Vietnam at War,* 741–42; Turley, *The Second Indochina War,* 173–74.
17. Herring, *America's Longest War,* 261–62.
18. In mid-1974 total RVNAF forces numbered about 1.1 million. The Vietcong and PAVN forces in the South totaled about 240,000.
19. Quote is from Turley, *The Second Indochina War,* 167; Hess, *Vietnam,* 136–37.
20. Lipsman et al., *The False Peace,* 138.
21. Quote is from Hess, *Vietnam,* 137.
22. Turley, *The Second Indochina War,* 173–74; Lipsman et al., *The False Peace,* 140–41.
23. Lipsman et al., *The False Peace,* 182–83.
24. Isaacs, *Without Honor,* 313–21; Lewy, *America in Vietnam,* 207–9.
25. Quote is from Hess, *Vietnam,* 138.
26. Snepp, Frank, *Decent Interval: An Insider's Account of Saigon's Indecent End Told by the CIA's Chief Strategy Analyst in Vietnam* (New York: Vintage, 1977), 116–24.
27. Porter, *Vietnam Documents,* vol. 2, Document 351, 658–59, "General Dung's Account of the October Political Bureau Conference,' (extract). Dung conceded that U.S. intervention remained a possibility, but he also stated that even if the Americans did reenter the war, they could not save Thieu's government from collapse. Duiker, *The Communist Road,* 306–8.
28. Lipsman et al., *The False Peace,* 182–83.

29. Duiker, *The Communist Road,* 308–9; Davidson, *Vietnam at War,* 762–64; Isaacs, *Without Honor,* 331–35.

30. Isaacs, *Without Honor,* 345–52; Davidson, *Vietnam at War,* 770–74; Dougan, Clark, Fulghum, David, and the editors of Boston Publishing, *The Fall of the South* (Boston: Boston Publishing Co., 1985), 48–52, a volume in the series *The Vietnam Experience.*

31. Davidson, *Vietnam at War,* 774–77; Isaacs, *Without Honor,* 353–56; Turley, *The Second Indochina War,* 179–81.

32. Quoted in Hess, *Vietnam,* 139.

33. Davidson, *Vietnam at War,* 777–79; Dougan et al., *Fall of the South,* 56–63.

34. Quote is from Herring, *America's Longest War,* 265.

35. Quote is from Dougan et al., *Fall of the South,* 83.

36. Isaacs, *Without Honor,* 366–71; Dougan et al., *Fall of the South,* 81–82; CBS television documentary, "Vietnam: A War That Is Finished," first shown in August 1975.

37. Hess, *Vietnam,* 138.

38. Schulzinger, *A Time for War,* 321–22.

39. *Ibid.,* 322–23.

40. Davidson, *Vietnam at War,* 790.

41. Quoted in Isaacs, *Without Honor,* 281–82. Isaacs has a riveting account of the final days of the Khmer Republic. See his chap. 8, "Fall of the Khmer Republic," 241–89.

42. *Ibid.,* 407–13; Dougan et al., *Fall of the South,* 107–8, 118–21, 127–29. Although it rejected Ford's request for military assistance, Congress authorized a final $300 million that the president had requested to provide humanitarian aid and to pay the costs of the evacuation from South Vietnam.

43. Quoted in Herring, *America's Longest War,* 266.

44. Schulzinger, *A Time for War,* 324.

45. Thieu's remarks quoted in Hess, *Vietnam,* 140; Snepp, *Decent Interval,* 392–97.

46. Ford's remarks were recorded on CBS video, "Vietnam: A War That Is Finished."

47. Dougan et al., *Fall of the South,* 154–55.

48. *Ibid.,* 157–58.

49. *Ibid.,* 163–64.

50. *Ibid.*

51. Quoted in Dougan et al., *Fall of the South,* 171.

52. Colonel Tin's remarks are quoted in Hess, *Vietnam,* 140; Isaacs, *Without Honor,* 447.

53. Quoted in Isaacs, *Without Honor,* 485.

54. Herring, *America's Longest War,* 3d ed., 298; Bergerud, Eric M., *The Dynamics of Defeat: The Vietnam War in Hau Nghia Province* (Boulder, CO: Westview Press, 1991). In detailing the various South Vietnamese and American pacification efforts in a specific locale, Bergerud discovered that nothing they could do could overcome the Saigon government's lack of local legitimacy. The Phoenix program badly damaged the NFL infrastructure in Hau Nghia province, but the Saigon government could never replace it. According to Bergerud "The difficulties Americans faced were virtually beyond solution."

55. Had U.S. forces really pressed the North Vietnamese, the Chinese would have intervened militarily to preserve the Hanoi regime. See Qiang Zhai, *China and the Vietnam Wars, 1950–1975.*

56. Schulzinger, *A Time for War,* 329.

57. *Ibid.*

58. Hess, *Vietnam,* 150. The source for the estimated numbers of South Vietnamese executed by the Communists is a study based on the testimony of Vietnamese immigrants to the United States.

59. Herring, *America's Longest War,* 3d ed., 303.

60. *Ibid.*

61. Galambos, Louis, "Separating the Wheat from the Chaff: Vietnam's Implications for the Future," unpublished paper delivered at the Fourteenth Military Symposium on "Vietnam, 1964–1975: An American Dilemma," held at the United States Air Force Academy October 19, 1990.

62. O'Keefe, Kevin, "The Vietnamization of Nicaragua," in Moss, George Donelson, ed., *A Vietnam Reader: Sources and Essays* (Englewood Cliffs, NJ: Prentice Hall, 1991), 301–13.

63. Quoted in Kiernan, Ben, "The Vietnam War: Alternative Endings," *American Historical Review* 97, no. 4 (October 1992): 1136.

64. Herring, *America's Longest War,* 3d ed., 312.

APPENDIX A

A Pronunciation Guide for Vietnamese Words

For this book, the Vietnamese words have been written as a system of imitated English pronunciations, so the words can be read as if they were English.

a	as in father	i	as in ing
ai	as in Thai	ny	as in canyon
ao	as in Mao	o	as in hot
ay	as in pay	oh	as in oh
aw	as in awe	oo	as in boo
e	as in bed	u	as in hut
eh	as in bed	uh	as in hut, only hold a bit longer
ew	as in few	ur	as in fur
g	as in goat	y	as in young

c	as g	ngh	same as in English
ch	as j	nh	like ny in canyon
d	like y in young	ph	like f
gh	also like g as in goat	q l	ike g in goat
gi	like y in young	t	like d in day
k	like g as in goat	th	as t
kh	like k in keep	tr	like j in jar
ng	as ng in sing	x	as s

au	as a-oo	oe	as weh
eo	as eh-ao	ua	as waw
iu	as few	uy	as wee
oa	as wa		

Note that Vietnamese is a tonal language. The pitch at which a word is pronounced determines its meaning. The same combination of sounds pronounced with different tones will produce different meanings.

Tables

TABLE A:	UNITED STATES MILITARY PERSONNEL SERVING IN SOUTH VIETNAM
December 31, 1960	900
December 31, 1961	3,205
December 31, 1962	9,000
December 31, 1963	16,500
December 31, 1964	23,300
December 31, 1965	184,300
June 30, 1966	267,500
December 31, 1966	385,300
June 30, 1967	448,800
December 31, 1967	485,600
June 30, 1968	534,700
December 31, 1968	536,100
April 30, 1969	543,400
June 30, 1969	538,700
December 31, 1969	475,200
June 30, 1970	414,900
December 31, 1970	334,600
June 30, 1971	239,200
December 31, 1971	156,800
June 30, 1972	47,000
December 31, 1972	24,200
March 30, 1973	240

Source: U.S. Department of Defense official records.

TABLE B: COMPARATIVE MILITARY CASUALTY FIGURES

Year	KIA			WIA	
	U.S.	RVNAF		U.S.	RVNAF
1960	0	2,223		0	2,788
1961	11	4,004		2	5,449
1962	31	4,457		41	7,195
1963	78	5,665		218	11,488
1964	147	7,457		522	17,017
1965	1,369	11,242		3,308	23,118
1966	5,008	11,953		16,526	20,975
1967	9,377	12,716		32,370	29,448
1968	14,589	27,915		46,797	70,696
1969	9,414	21,833		32,940	65,276
1970	4,221	23,346		15,211	71,582
1971	1,381	22,738		4,767	60,939
1972	300	39,587		587	109,960
1973	237	27,901		24	131,936
1974	207	31,219		0	155,735
Totals	46,370	254,256		153,313	783,602

Source: Jeffrey J. Clarke, *Advice and Support: The Final Years,* 275.

TABLE C: CASUALTIES, FROM JANUARY 1, 1961 TO JANUARY 28, 1973

United States	
Killed in action	45,941
Wounded	300,635
Missing	2,330
Killed or died, noncombat-related	10,420
South Vietnam	
Military: Killed in action	220,357
Military: Wounded	499,026
VietCong/North Vietnam	
Military: Killed	851,000
Civilian: North Vietnam	65,000
Third-Country Forces	
Military: Killed in action	
Korea	4,407
Australia/New Zealand	469
Thailand	351

Sources: Lewy, Gunther, *America in Vietnam;* O'Ballance, Edgar, *The Wars in Vietnam;* Thayer, Thomas C., *War without Fronts: The American Experience in Vietnam.*

TABLE D: STATISTICAL PORTRAIT OF U.S. CASUALTIES IN INDOCHINA

1. Killed in combat	45,941
2. Wounded in combat	300,635
3. Died in noncombat situations	10,420
4. 90% of combat deaths were enlisted men	41,003
5. 10% of combat deaths were officers	4,938
6. 60% of combat deaths were aged 19–21	26,931
7. 22% of combat deaths were aged 22–25	10,421
8. 18% of combat deaths were aged 26+	8,589
9. 33% of the dead had served less than 1 year	14,995
10. 33% of the dead had served between 1 and 2 years	14,853
11. Blacks accounted for 12% of the combat deaths	5,662
12. Other nonwhites accounted for 1% of the combat deaths	469
13. Whites accounted for 87% of the combat deaths	39,827
14. Draftees accounted for 33% of the combat deaths	15,404

Source: Thayer, *War without Fronts.*

TABLE E: CAUSES OF COMBAT AND NONCOMBAT DEATHS

Combat Deaths	45,941
Aircraft loss	4,178
Gunshot or small arms fire	18,385
Artillery/rocket/other explosion	12,350
Multiple fragmentation wounds	8,465
Other causes/unknown	2,563
Noncombat Deaths	10,420
Accidents	8,483
Illness	929
Murder	190
Suicide	379
Other	439

Source: Thayer, *War without Fronts.*

TABLE F: A STATISTICAL PORTRAIT OF U.S. VIETNAM VETERANS

Service during Vietnam era, 1964–1975	8,700,000
Service in South Vietnam	2,700,000
Combat in South Vietnam	870,000
Vital Statistics, (1978)	
Median age	32 years
Median education	12.9 years
Median income, ages 20–39	$12,680
Unemployment rate, ages 20–34	5.5 %
In VA hospitals	9,652

Source: Veterans Adminstration and Department of Defense official reports.

Glossary

AID: Agency for International Development (also USAID).

Airborne: People or materiel delivered by helicopters or fixed-wing aircraft.

Amtrack: An armored amphibious vehicle used by Marines.

AK-47:   A Soviet and Chinese assault rifle used extensively by the VietCong and by the PAVN forces.

APC: Armored Personnel Carrier.

ARVN: Army of the Republic of Vietnam. The regular South Vietnamese national forces.

A Teams: Twelve-man Special Forces units.

Base camp: Field headquarters for a maneuver unit, usually a battalion.

Body bags: Plastic bags used for retrieval of bodies of soldiers killed in the field.

CAP: Combined Action Program.

Charlie: GI slang for the VietCong, a short version of Victor Charlie, from the U.S. military phonetic alphabet for VC.

Chieu Hoi: Literally "Open Arms," a program set up to encourage VietCong and NVA soldiers to defect to the South Vietnamese side.

Chinook: CH-47 transport helicopter.

CIDG: Civilian Irregular Defense Groups. Teams devised by CIA operatives that combined defense functions with social and economic development programs designed to win the allegiance of the *Montagnards.*

CINCPAC: Commander-in-Chief, United States Pacific Command.

Clear and hold: U.S. military operation in which troops would hold an area permanently after killing, dispersing, or capturing all enemy soldiers in the area.

Cobra: Bell AH-1G fast attack helicopter, armed with machine guns, grenade launchers, and rockets.

COMUSMACV: Commander, United States Military Assistance Command, Vietnam.

CONUS: Military acronym for the Continental United States.

CORDS: Civil Operations and Revolutionary Development Support.

Corps: Two divisions assigned to defend a military region.

COSVN: Central Office, South Vietnam, the headquarters controlling all VietCong political and military operations in southern Vietnam.

CTZ: Corps Tactical Zone.

DAO: Defense Attache Office, an agency that was part of the U.S. mission sent to South Vietnam following the January 1973 Paris Accords that ended the American war. It was a replacement for MACV; DAO administered the U.S. military assistance program to the GVN, 1973-1975.

DEROS: Date eligible for return from overseas. The date a soldier's tour of duty in Vietnam ended, usually one year after arriving in the country.

DESOTO: U.S. Navy destroyer patrols in the South China Sea.

DMZ: Demilitarized Zone.

DOD: Department of Defense.

DRV: Democratic Republic of Vietnam (North Vietnam), created by Ho Chi Minh September 2, 1945.

EAGLE PULL: Code name of the U.S. evacuation of Phnom Penh in April 1975.

FAC: Forward Air Controller, a forward spotter who coordinated air strikes, usually airborne.

FMFPAC: Fleet Marine Force, Pacific Command.

Fragging: The murder of a commissioned or noncommissioned officer by an enlisted man of lower rank, usually with a fragmentation grenade.

Free-fire zones: Territory considered completely under enemy control. South Vietnamese officials authorized the use of unlimited firepower in such zones.

FREQUENT WIND: Code name of the U.S. evacuation of Saigon in April 1975.

FSB: Fire support base, a protected forward artillery base.

Green Berets: Famed nickname of soldiers serving in the U.S. Army Special Forces trained for counterinsurgency operations. The named derived from the green berets worn by these elite forces.

Grunt: The most frequent nickname given Army and Marine ground combat forces.

GVN: Government of Vietnam (South Vietnam).

HES: Hamlet Evaluation System. A monthly statistical report that provided CORDS with information on rural security.

Hot Pursuit: The policy, occasionally authorized, of allowing U.S. soldiers cross-border pursuit of retreating VietCong or NVA forces into Cambodia.

Huey: Nickname given the Bell HU-1 D series helicopter.

ICC: International Control Commission, created by the Geneva Accords (1954) to supervise implementation of the agreements.

ICCS: International Commission of Control and Supervision. Agency responsible for administering the January 1973 Paris Accords.

JCS: Joint Chiefs of Staff.

JGS: Joint General Staff, the South Vietnamese equivalent of the U.S. Joint Chiefs.

JMC: Joint Military Commission, consisting of members from North Vietnam, South Vietnam, the PRG, and the United States, responsible for implementing the military provisions of the Paris Accords of 1973.

JMT: Joint Military Team, consisting of members from North Vietnam, South Vietnam, the PRG, and the United States, responsible for accounting for all prisoners-of-war and MIAs.

KIA: Killed in action.

Lao Dong: The Vietnamese Worker's Party, the North Vietnamese Communist Party, founded in 1951. The ruling party of North Vietnam until 1975; thereafter it ruled the entire country.

LINEBACKER 1: Code name for U.S. bombing of North Vietnam resumed in April 1972 in response to the Nguyen Hue Offensive.

LINEBACKER II: Code name for the U.S. bombing of North Vietnam during December 1972; called the Christmas Bombings.

LST: Landing Ship Tank; a large, shallow-draft, cargo-hauling landing craft.

LZ: Landing Zone, for helicopters.

MAAG: Military Assistance Advisory Group, the forerunner of MACV, 1955 to 1964.

MACV: Military Assistance Command, Vietnam, formed in 1962, lasted until 1973.

Main Force: Regular army forces of the North Vietnamese and VietCong.

MAP: Military Assistance Program.

Medevac: Helicopters with the mission of transporting wounded soldiers quickly from the battlefield to forward hospitals.

MENU: Code name for the secret B-52 bombing missions in Cambodia.

MIA: Missing in Action.

MR: Military Region, formerly a CTZ, Corps Tactical Zone.

M-16: The standard issue U.S. automatic rifle used in the Vietnam War from 1966.

Napalm: A jellied gasoline incendiary weapon used by the French and the Americans during the Indochina wars.

NCO: Noncommissioned Officer.

Neutralize: Word used by Phoenix/Phung Hoang operatives to define putting the VCI out of action. Neutralize could mean killing, capturing, or going into the *Chieu Hoi* program.

NLF: The National Liberation Front, formed December 20, 1960.

NSAM: National Security Action Memorandum.

NSC: National Security Council.

NVA: North Vietnamese Army.

NVN: North Vietnam or North Vietnamese.

OB: Order of Battle, a comprehensive arrangement and disposition of military units deployed in battle.

OCS: Officers' Candidate School.

Operation VULTURE: A planned U.S. operation to relieve the siege at Dien Bien Phu in April 1954. It was never implemented.

OPLAN: Operations Plan.

OSS: Office of Strategic Services, a World War II intelligence organization, forerunner of the CIA.

PACAF: United States Pacific Air Force.

PACFLT: United States Pacific Fleet.

Pathet Lao: Laotian Communist insurgents who came to power in 1974–1975.

PAVN: People's Army of Vietnam; the North Viertnamese army.

PF: Popular Forces.

PHOENIX: A joint U.S./South Vietnamese program to detect and to neutralize the VietCong infrastructure.

Phung Hoang: The South Vietnamese–run program to destroy the VCI, it paralleled the PHOENIX program.

PLA: People's Liberation Army of South Vietnam, the military arm of the VietCong.

PLAF: People's Liberation Armed Forces of South Vietnam, aka the PLA.

POW: Prisoner-of-War.

PRG: Provisional Revolutionary Government, formed by NLF in 1969.

PRP: People's Revolutionary Party, the Communist Party apparatus that controlled the National Liberation Front, founded in 1962.

PSYOP: Pyschological Operations, a form of psychological warfare.

PTSD: Posttraumatic Stress Disorder.

RANCHHAND: Code name for the U.S. Air Force aerial defoliation program to deny ground cover and food crops to the VietCong.

RDC: Revolutionary Development Cadres. Teams of South Vietnamese pacification workers trained to carry out various missions.

RF: Regional Forces.

ROK: Republic of Korea (South Korea).

ROTC: Reserve Officer Training Corps.

Ruff-puffs: South Vietnamese regional and local forces used for village security.

RVN: Republic of Vietnam (South Vietnam).

RVNAF: Republic of Vietnam Armed Forces, all South Vietnamese military forces including ARVN, Regional Forces, and Popular Forces.

SAC: Strategic Air Command.

SAM: Surface-to-air missile.

SAM-2:   Medium-range surface-to-air missile. Effective up to 60,000 feet, speed about Mach 2.5.

SANE: Committee for a Sane Nuclear Policy. An organization opposed to the nuclear arms race; active in the late 1950s and early 1960s.

Sappers: VietCong commandos, used for demolition and sabotage operations.

Search-and-Destroy: Large-scale Allied offensive operations designed to find, fix, and destroy enemy forces. A form of attrition warfare.

SEATO: Southeast Asia Treaty Organization.

Seventeenth (17th) Parallel: Temporary dividing line separating northern and southern Vietnam, created by Geneva Accords (1954), pending unification elections scheduled for July 1956, which were never held.

SOG: Studies and Observation Group, MACV.

Sortie: One operational flight by one aircraft.

Special Forces: U.S. Army personnel trained to carry out counterinsurgency operations, often covert and unconventional. They also trained *Montagnards* and South Vietnamese Special Forces.

SVN: South Vietnam.

Tet: The Vietnamese lunar New Year and their most important holiday.

Third Countries: U.S. Allies that furnished military forces for the Vietnam war: South Korea, Thailand, the Philippines, Australia, and New Zealand.

USAID: United States Agency for International Development.

VC: VietCong. The word VietCong originally was a derogatory contraction of two Vietnamese words meaning a Vietnamese who is a Communist.

VCI: VietCong infrastructure; the political leaders of the VietCong, also responsible for logistic support of the military forces.

VNAF: Vietnamese Air Force (the South Vietnamese Air Force).

WIA: Wounded in Action.

Chronology
of U.S. Involvement
in Vietnam, 1942–1975

1942
U.S. pilots attached to the Flying Tigers fly combat missions in Vietnam against Japanese military installations.

1944–1945
The OSS funds Vietminh actions against the Japanese in Vietnam, and OSS operatives work with the Vietnamese to rescue downed U.S. flyers and go on espionage and sabotage missions with them.

September 1945
America supports the French efforts to reimpose colonialism in Vietnam.

May 8, 1950
The United States signs an agreement with France to provide the French Associated States of Vietnam with military assistance.

August 3, 1950
A U.S. Military Assistance Advisory Group (MAAG) of 35 men arrives in Vietnam to teach troops receiving U.S. weapons how to use them.

December 30, 1950
United States signs a Mutual Defense Assistance Agreement with France, Vietnam, Cambodia, and Laos.

September 7, 1951
The Truman administration signs an agreement with Saigon to provide direct military aid to South Vietnam.

September 30, 1953
President Eisenhower approves $785 million for military aid for South Vietnam.

April 7, 1954
At a news conference, President Eisenhower, stressing the importance of defending Dien Bien Phu, enunciates the domino theory.

July 21, 1954
The American observer at Geneva, General Walter Bedell Smith, issues a unilateral declaration stating that the United States will refrain from the threat or the use of force to prevent implementation of the Geneva Accords.

August 1, 1954
An exodus of about 900,000 refugees from northern Vietnam traveling to southern Vietnam begins.

September 8, 1954
The Manila Treaty is concluded creating SEATO. A separate protocol extends the SEATO umbrella to include Laos, Cambodia, and "the free territory under the jurisdiction of the State of Vietnam" (South Vietnam).

October 24, 1954
President Eisenhower sends a letter to the new leader in southern Vietnam, Ngo Dinh Diem, pledging U.S. support and agreeing to send $100 million to build up Diem's military forces. Eisenhower begins the U.S. commitment to maintaining a non-Communist government in South Vietnam.

April 28, 1955
Under severe pressure from a coalition of political enemies, Diem's fledgling regime almost falls. He is saved by the actions of Air Force Colonel Edwin Landsdale, who is also a CIA operative.

October 26, 1955
Diem, after defeating Bao Dai in a rigged election, declares himself to be president of the Republic of South Vietnam. His government is instantly recognized by the United States.

July 20, 1956
The deadline for holding reunification elections in accordance with the Geneva Accords passes. America supports Diem's refusal to hold elections.

May 8, 1957
Diem makes a triumphant visit to the United States. Eisenhower praises him lavishly and reaffirms American support for his government.

October 1957
Small-scale civil war begins in South Vietnam between Diem's forces and cadres of Vietminh who have remained in South Vietnam after the partition at Geneva.

April 4, 1959
Eisenhower delivers a speech in which he links American vital national interests to the survival of a non-Communist state in South Vietnam.

December 20, 1960
The National Liberation front is formed. It is the Vietminh reborn. The Communist-controlled NLF takes charge of the growing insurgency against the Diem regime. Diem derogatorily dubs the NLF the "VietCong," meaning Vietnamese who are Communists.

January 6, 1961
Soviet Premier Khrushchev announces support for all "wars of national liberation" around the world. His speech influences the incoming Kennedy administration's decision to support counterinsurgency in Vietnam.

April 1961
The Kennedy administration confronts a crisis in Laos. Kennedy considers military intervention, then decides to seek a political solution.

May 1961
Kennedy approves sending Special Forces to South Vietnam. He also authorizes clandestine warfare against North Vietnam and a secret war in Laos.

May 1961
Vice President Lyndon B. Johnson visits South Vietnam and recommends a strong commitment to South Vietnam's head of state Ngo Dinh Diem.

June 1961
Kennedy and Khrushchev, meeting in Vienna, agree to support a neutral and independent Laos. Kennedy rejects neutrality for Vietnam.

November 1961
Special Forces are deployed to the central highlands in the vicinity of Pleiku to work with *Montagnards,* and they begin developing the CIDGs.

December 1961
The *New York Times* reports that some of the 3,200 U.S. advisers are operating in battle areas and are authorized to fire back if fired on.

January 1962
The Air Force launches Operation RANCH HAND, the aerial spraying of defoliating herbicides to deny cover to the VietCong and to destroy their crops.

February 8, 1962
MACV is established in Saigon; its first commander is General Paul D. Harkins.

March 22, 1962
The Strategic Hamlet Program is launched.

July 23, 1962
Geneva Accords on Laos is signed.

December 1962
There are now about 9,000 U.S. advisory and support personnel in South Vietnam; 109 Americans were killed or wounded in 1962.

January 2, 1963
At Ap Bac in the Mekong Delta, the ARVN 7th Division, equipped with U.S. weapons and accompanied by U.S. advisers, cannot defeat a lightly armed VietCong battalion of 300 soldiers. The battle demonstrates that government troops cannot match the tactics or the fighting spirit of the insurgents.

May 8, 1963
In Hue, 20,000 Buddhists celebrating the birthday of Gautama Siddhartha Buddha are fired on by government forces. This action begins a series of events that will bring the downfall of the Diem regime.

June 11, 1963
Thich Quang Duc, an elderly Buddhist monk, immolates himself by fire at a busy Saigon intersection to protest Diem's suppression of the Buddhists.

August 21, 1963
Military forces loyal to Diem and to his brother Nhu attack Buddhist temples. President Kennedy denounces these actions. Meanwhile, a coup to overthrow Diem is being planned by dissident ARVN generals.

September 2, 1963
President Kennedy strongly reaffirms the American commitment to Vietnam. He also criticizes Diem's attacks on the Buddhists and calls for reform.

November 1, 1963
A coup, led by General Tran Van Don and General Duong Van Minh, with the fore-knowledge and encouragement of some U. S. officials, overthrows the Diem regime. A military directorate, led by General Minh, succeeds Diem.

November 2, 1963
Diem and his brother Nhu are murdered on the order of General Minh.

November 22, 1963
President John F. Kennedy is assassinated by Lee Harvey Oswald in Dallas, Texas.

November 24, 1963
President Lyndon Johnson affirms U.S. support of the new South Vietnamese government.

December 31, 1963
There are about 16,500 U.S. soldiers in South Vietnam at year's end; 489 have been killed or wounded during 1963.

January 2, 1964
President Johnson approves covert military operations against North Vietnam to be carried out by South Vietnamese and Asian mercenaries. Called OPLAN 34-A, they include espionage, sabotage, psychological warfare, and intelligence gathering.

January 30, 1964
Minh's government is overthrown in a bloodless coup by General Nguyen Khanh.

March 8–12, 1964
Secretary of Defense Robert McNamara visits South Vietnam. He affirms that America will remain in South Vietnam for as long as it takes to win the war.

April 1964
North Vietnam decides to infiltrate units of the NVA into South Vietnam.

June 20, 1964
General Harkins is succeeded by General William C. Westmoreland as COMUSMACV. Three days later, Henry Cabot Lodge resigns as the U.S. ambassador to the GVN, and is replaced by General Maxwell Taylor.

July 1964
Both sides are engaged in covert warfare in violation of the 1954 Geneva Accords. North Vietnam is using the Ho Chi Minh trail to infiltrate NVA troops south and to supply the VietCong. America implements the OPLAN 34-A operations. One OPLAN 34-A operation uses U.S. destroyers to conduct surveillance missions off the North Vietnamese coast. These operations are called DESOTO Missions.

August 2, 1964
North Vietnamese patrol boats attack the USS *Maddox,* which was on a DESOTO Mission in waters near the North Vietnamese coast.

August 3, 1964
South Vietnamese PT boats carry out OPLAN 34-A raids, attacking North Vietnamese radar installations in same area.

August 4–5, 1964
Both USS *Maddox* and another destroyer, USS *Turner Joy,* which has joined the *Maddox,* report that they are under attack at sea. Carrier-based U.S. naval aircraft fly reprisal raids ordered by President Johnson against North Vietnamese targets.

August 7, 1964
At Johnson's request, Congress enacts the Gulf of Tonkin resolution granting President Johnson the power to "to take all necessary measures to repel any armed attack against the forces of the United States and to prevent further aggression . . . including the use of armed force. . . ." Johnson will later use this resolution as a postdated declaration of war.

October 1964
General Khanh resigns and is replaced by a civilian, Tran Van Huong.

November 1, 1964
VietCong forces attack Bien Hoa Air Base. Five U.S. soldiers are killed and six B-57 bombers are destroyed. It is the first direct attack on a U.S. military installation, signaling a major shift in VietCong tactics.

December 31, 1964
About 23,000 Americans are now serving in South Vietnam. There is now a full-scale undeclared war raging in South Vietnam, and there is also fighting in Laos and Cambodia. There have been 1,278 U.S. casualties for the year 1964.

January 4, 1965
In his State of the Union address, President Johnson reaffirms the U.S. commitment to South Vietnam. He states that American security is tied to peace in Southeast Asia.

January 27–28, 1965
Tran Van Huong is ousted and General Khanh returns to power.

February 7, 1965

The VietCong attack a U.S. helicopter base and other installations near Pleiku in the central highlands. Eight Americans are killed and 126 wounded. Johnson orders retaliatory air strikes on targets in North Vietnam.

February 13, 1965

Johnson orders a sustained bombing campaign against North Vietnam that has been long-planned by his advisers. Called Operation ROLLING THUNDER, it will continue, with occasional pauses, until October 31, 1968. The American air war against North Vietnam begins on March 2.

February 25, 1965

General Khanh is forced out by Air Marshal Nguyen Cao Ky.

March 8, 1965

The first U.S. combat troops arrive in Vietnam.

April 6, 1965

President Johnson authorizes U.S. forces to take the offensive in order to support ARVN forces.

June 19, 1965

Air Marshal Ky becomes premier of the eighth South Vietnamese government since Diem was overthrown.

June 28–30, 1965

U.S. forces undertake the first major American offensive against the Vietcong in War Zone D, 20 miles northeast of Saigon.

July 21–28, 1965

President Johnson makes a series of decisions that amount to committing the United States to a major war in Vietnam. Among the decisions he makes: draft calls will be raised to 35,000 per month, 50,000 additional troops will be sent to Vietnam with additional increases as the situation demands, and the air war against North Vietnam is expanded. Johnson also makes it clear that he wants these decisions implemented in low-key fashion so as not to excite or alarm either the Congress or the American people. These decisions began the seven-and-one-half-year U.S. war in Indochina.

August 7, 1965

The Chinese government warns the United States that it will send troops to fight in Vietnam if necessary.

October 23 to November 20, 1965

In the largest battle of the war to date, the U.S. 1st Air Cavalry defeats NVA forces in the Ia Drang valley, in a remote corner of Pleiku province.

December 31, 1965

1965 was a pivotal year of the war. America began a sustained air war against North Vietnam. It also committed large numbers of forces to ground combat operations in South Vietnam. At year's end, there are 184,000 U.S. troops in South Vietnam. U.S. casualties for the year are 1,369 KIA and 5,300 WIA.

February 4, 1966
Senate Foreign Relations Committee, Chaired by Senator J. William Fulbright, holds televised hearings on the Vietnam War and allows critics of the developing war to present their views.

February 6, 1966
President Johnson convenes a conference on the Vietnam War in Honolulu.

March 9, 1966
The U.S. Department of State issues a White Paper claiming that American intervention in Vietnam is legal under international law, the UN Charter, and the U.S. Constitution.

April 7, 1966
President Johnson makes a speech at Johns Hopkins University defending his war policy against both hawkish and dovish critics.

June 29, 1966
U.S. aircraft strike North Vietnamese petroleum storage facilities near Haiphong and Hanoi.

October 15 to November 26, 1966
U.S. forces are involved in one of the biggest operations of the war in Tayninh Province near the Cambodian border, fifty miles northwest of Saigon.

December 31, 1966
The Vietnam War has become the dominant event in world affairs. During the year the United States increased its forces in Vietnam from 184,000 to 385,000. The air war against North Vietnam has been expanded significantly, 5,008 Americans were killed and 30,093 wounded during the year.

January 8–26, 1967
U. S. troops are involved in the largest offensive of the war. About 16,000 U. S. troops participate in Operation CEDAR FALLS to disrupt VietCong operations in the Iron Triangle region northeast of Saigon.

February 22–April 1, 1967
The largest Allied offensive of the war to date takes place, Operation JUNCTION CITY, involving 34 U.S. battalions. Its goal is to smash the VC stronghold in War Zone C near the Cambodian border and ease pressure on Saigon.

March 10–11, 1967
U.S. aircraft bomb the Thai Nguyen steel works near Hanoi; they are the first bombing raids on a major industrial target.

May 14–16, 1967
A U.S. newspaper reports that Chinese Premier Chou En-lai threatened to send Chinese troops into North Vietnam if the United States invaded that country.

July 30, 1967
A Gallup poll shows that 52 percent of Americans disapprove of Johnson's Vietnam war policy; 56 percent believe that America is in a stalemate.

September 29, 1967
President Johnson offers to stop the bombing of North Vietnam if they will agree to start negotiations. Offer becomes known as the "San Antonio Formula."

October 16–21, 1967
Antiwar activists hold antidraft demonstrations throughout the United States. The largest occurs at the Army Induction Center in Oakland, California.

October 21–23, 1967
Fifty thousand demonstrate against the Vietnam War in Washington, DC.

October 25–30, 1967
The air war against North Vietnam intensifies. Sustained attacks are carried out on targets near Hanoi and Haiphong.

November 2, 1967
President Johnson meets privately with a group of distinguished former leaders. Dubbed the "wise men," they generally support his war policy.

November 3–22, 1967
One of the bloodiest and fiercest battles of the war between American and North Vietnamese troops occurs at Dak To in the central highlands.

November 22, 1967
President Johnson brings General Westmoreland home to rally support for the war. Westmoreland tells his audiences that the United States is winning the war.

November 30, 1967
Senator Eugene J. McCarthy announces that he will challenge President Johnson for the Democratic presidential nomination in 1968. He will run on a platform calling for a negotiated settlement of the Vietnam War.

December 31, 1967
At year's end, there are about 500,000 U.S. troops in Vietnam. For the year, the war cost taxpayers about $21 billion; casualties are 9,353 KIA and 99,742 WIA.

January 20 to April 14, 1968
One of the most famous battles of the war takes place at Khe Sanh, a U.S. Marine base located just south of the DMZ. NVA forces besiege Khe Sanh. It is feared that Khe Sanh will become an American Dien Bien Phu. But U.S. airpower eventually breaks the siege, and the Communists are forced to withdraw.

January 30 to February 10, 1968
On the first day of the Tet truce, VietCong forces, supported by NVA troopers, launch a surprise attack and the largest offensive of the war the Tet-68 Offensive. Simultaneous attacks are mounted in South Vietnam's largest cities and many provincial capitals. The offensive is crushed by American and GVN forces. Tet is a decisive military victory for the Allies, but turns out to be a psychological and political disaster for them.

February 28, 1968
General Earle Wheeler, chairman of the Joint Chiefs, tells Johnson that General Westmoreland needs an additional 206,000 troops. A crucial point in the war has been reached. If Johnson does not send the troops, he will be conceding that the United States

cannot win a military victory. But if he sends the troops, it will require a reserve callup, and significantly raise the costs and casualties of war. Johnson delays a decision and asks his new secretary of defense, Clark Clifford, to conduct a thorough reappraisal of U.S. Vietnam policy.

March 12, 1968
Senator Eugene McCarthy, in the New Hampshire primary, makes a strong showing in a hawkish state. Four days later, Senator Robert Kennedy announces that he too will seek the Democratic nomination and run on an antiwar platform.

March 16, 1968
In what will become the most notorious atrocity committed by U.S. soldiers during the Vietnam War, a platoon of troopers slaughter hundreds of unarmed villagers in the hamlet of My Lai-4.

March 25–26, 1968
Johnson reconvenes the "wise men." Most advise against any more troop increases and recommend that the United States seek a negotiated peace in Vietnam.

March 31, 1968
Johnson announces a unilateral halt to all U.S. bombing north of the 20th Parallel and that he will seek to get negotiations started with North Vietnam. He also stuns the nation with an announcement that he will not seek reelection.

April 22, 1968
Clifford announces that GVN is going to take responsibility for more and more of the fighting. This is the first announcement of a policy that under President Nixon will later call "Vietnamization."

May 3, 1968
America and North Vietnam agree to begin formal negotiations in Paris on May 10. Peace talks begin on May 12.

June 10, 1968
General Creighton W. Abrams succeeds General Westmoreland as COMUSMACV.

August 5–8, 1968
The Republican National Convention, meeting in Miami, nominates Richard M. Nixon for president. The Republican platform calls for an honorable negotiated peace in Vietnam and for the progressive "de-Americanization" of the war.

August 26–29, 1968
The Democratic National Convention meets in Chicago. Democrats adopt a platform endorsing the administration's war policy and nominate Vice President Hubert H. Humphrey for president. On the evening of August 28, there is a riot in the streets between Chicago police and antiwar radicals.

October 31, 1968
In a televised address to the nation, President Johnson announces a complete bombing halt over North Vietnam. Operation ROLLING THUNDER ends.

November 5, 1968
Richard Nixon is elected president of the United States.

December 31, 1968
The major turning point of the American Vietnam war occurred in 1968. After Tet, Johnson had to abandon his policy of measured escalation in search of military victory and replace it with an early version of Vietnamization looking toward a negotiated settlement. Richard Nixon was elected president, and the general sense at the time was that he had a plan for bringing the war to an early end. The year 1968 is the largest and costliest of the American war in Vietnam—14,314 KIAs and 150,000 WIAs; cost, about $30 billion.

January 25, 1969
The first plenary session of the four-way Paris peace talks among the Americans, the North Vietnamese, the South Vietnamese, and the National Liberation Front occurs.

March 18, 1969
President Nixon orders the secret bombing of Communist base camps and supply depots in Cambodia to commence. Operation MENU begins.

May 10–20, 1969
The battle for Hamburger Hill takes place near the A Shau valley. In 10 days of intense fighting and heavy casualties, Allied forces take the hill. The hill is abandoned soon thereafter.

June 8, 1969
President Nixon announces that 25,000 U.S. troops will be withdrawn by the end of August and that they will be replaced by South Vietnamese forces. The gradual phaseout of the American war in Vietnam has begun.

June 10, 1969
The NLF announces the formation of a Provisional Revolutionary Government (PRG) to rule in South Vietnam. It amounts to a formal challenge to the Thieu regime for political control of South Vietnam.

August 4, 1969
Secret negotiations began in Paris between U.S. special envoy Henry Kissinger and North Vietnam's Xuan Thuy.

September 3, 1969
Ho Chi Minh dies.

September 23, 1969
Eight antiwar leaders go on trial in Chicago for their part in organizing the antiwar demonstrations occurring in Chicago at the time of the Democratic convention, August 26–29, 1968; they are known as "the Chicago Eight."

October 15, 1969
The largest antiwar demonstrations in American history take place at many sites across the country.

November 3, 1969
President Nixon makes his most successful speech in defense of his Vietnam War policies. Congress and public opinion overwhelmingly support Vietnamization as he successfully blunts the efforts of the antiwar movement.

November 15, 1969
More than 250,000 people come to Washington, DC, to protest the Vietnam War. It is the largest single antiwar demonstration to date.

November 16, 1969
First public discourse about the My Lai-4 massacre appears in the U.S. press.

December 31, 1969
At year's end, there are 479,000 U.S. troops in Vietnam. GVN forces have increased and now number over 900,000. Fighting continued during the year on a large scale. American KIAs totaled 9,414 for the year. The U.S. forces are beginning to show signs of declining morale, discipline, and fighting spirit.

February 19–20, 1970
All defendants in "the Chicago Eight" trial are convicted of conspiracy to incite rioting and receive maximum sentences of five years in prison and $5,000 fines. All will be acquitted on appeal.

March 18, 1970
In a bloodless coup in Cambodia, pro-Western General Lon Nol ousts Prince Norodom Sihanouk as head of state.

April 11, 1970
Polls show that only 48 percent of Americans support Vietnamization, down from 70 percent in November 1969.

April 20, 1970
President Nixon promises to withdraw 150,000 more U.S. troops over the next year if Vietnamization continues to make progress.

May 1, 1970
American forces totaling about 30,000 invade the Fishhook region of Cambodia. The Cambodian incursion is the last major offensive of the Indochina War involving U.S. ground combat forces.

May 4, 1970
Ohio National Guard troops fire into a crowd of student demonstrators on the campus of Kent State University, killing four and wounding eleven.

May 6, 1970
More than a hundred colleges and universities across the nation shut down because of student protests and rioting in response to the Cambodian invasion and the killings at Kent State.

May 8–20, 1970
In New York City, construction workers attack antiwar student demonstrators on Wall Street. An estimated 80,000 young people, mostly college students, demonstrate peacefully in the nation's capital. They protest the "Kent State Massacre" and call for the

immediate withdrawal of all U.S. troops from Indochina. In New York City, more than 100,000 workers march in support of Nixon's war policies.

June 24, 1970
The Senate, by a vote of 81–10, repeals the Gulf of Tonkin resolution. President Nixon states that the legal basis for the American war in Vietnam is not the Gulf of Tonkin resolution, but the constitutional authority of the president as commander-in-chief to protect the lives of U.S. military forces in Vietnam.

August 19, 1970
America signs a pact with Cambodia to provide Lon Nol's government with military aid.

November 9, 1970
The Supreme Court refuses to hear a case brought by the state of Massachusetts challenging the constitutionality of the Vietnam War.

November 11, 1970
On this day, for the first time in more than five years, no American soldier is killed in Vietnam.

December 22, 1970
Congress prohibits U.S. combat forces or advisers in Cambodia or Laos.

December 31, 1970
The U.S. war in Vietnam is winding down. At year's end there are about 335,000 U.S. troops in South Vietnam. U.S. KIAs for the year number 4,221. But the war has spread to Cambodia and no progress is reported at the Paris peace talks.

January 1, 1971
Congress forbids the use of U.S. ground troops in either Laos or Cambodia.

March 6–24, 1971
ARVN forces invade Laos to interdict enemy supply routes down the Ho Chi Minh Trail complex. Communist counterattacks drive the invaders out of Laos and inflict heavy casualties. It is a major defeat for the GVN.

March 29, 1971
Lt. William Calley is convicted of mass murder in the My Lai-4 incident.

April 19–23, 1971
Vietnam Veterans Against the War stage a demonstration in Washington, DC. It ends with veterans throwing combat ribbons and medals on the Capitol steps.

April 20, 1971
The Pentagon reports that fragging incidents are increasing. There were 96 incidents in 1969, and 209 in 1970.

June 13, 1971
The *New York Times* begins publication of the stolen portions of the 47-volume Pentagon analysis of the U.S. involvement in Vietnam through 1967; known as the "Pentagon Papers."

July 1, 1971
The 26th Amendment to the Constitution, granting the vote to 18- to 21-year-olds, is ratified.

November 12, 1971
President Nixon orders that henceforth U.S. soldiers serving in Vietnam will be assigned only to defensive roles.

December 26, 1971
President Nixon orders U.S. bombing of North Vietnam to resume.

December 31, 1971
The American war in Vietnam is ending; 156,800 U.S. troops remain. There were 1,380 KIAs that year. As the Americans withdraw, the Communists intensify their attacks in Laos, Cambodia, and parts of South Vietnam. U.S. morale continues to deteriorate. Vietnamization is not working and the Paris talks remained stalled.

February 21–27, 1972
President Nixon makes a historic visit to China. The North Vietnamese fear that China and the United States will make a deal behind their backs.

March 30 to April 8, 1972
A major NVA offensive begins as Communist forces attack South Vietnamese towns and bases just south of the DMZ. The Communists open a second front with a drive into Binh Long province about seventy miles north of Saigon. Communists forces open a third front with drives into the central highlands. The fighting in South Vietnam between GVN and Communist forces is the most intense of the entire war.

April 10, 1972
America responds with air attacks. B-52s strike targets in North Vietnam for the first time since November 1967. B-52s and tactical bombers also strike targets in South Vietnam. America is waging an air war over all of Vietnam.

May 8, 1972
Nixon announces that he has ordered the mining of all North Vietnamese ports.

May 20, 1972
The summit conference between President Nixon and Leonid Brezhnev takes place on schedule in Moscow. Both sides are unwilling to risk detente over the Vietnam war. Nixon's Soviet visit is the first ever by a U.S. president.

June 28, 1972
President Nixon announces that no more draftees will be sent to Vietnam unless they volunteer.

July 13, 1972
The Paris peace talks resume after a hiatus of about ten weeks.

August 11, 1972
The last U.S. combat unit is withdrawn from South Vietnam. There are now 44,000 American servicemen in South Vietnam.

August 16, 1972
U.S. aircraft fly a record 370 sorties against North Vietnam. Most American aircraft fly from carriers in the Gulf of Tonkin or from bases in Thailand.

September 15, 1972
ARVN forces recapture Quang Tri City. The fighting destroys most of the city, which formerly had a population of 300,000.

October 8–11, 1972
Lengthy secret meetings in Paris between Henry Kissinger and Le Duc Tho produce a tentative settlement of the war. The substance of the agreement is a cease-fire, to be followed by both sides working out a political settlement.

October 22, 1972
President Thieu rejects the proposed settlement.

November 7, 1972
Richard Nixon is reelected president by a landslide margin. He promises that he will achieve "peace with honor" in Vietnam.

November 11, 1972
The U.S. Army turns over its giant headquarters base at Long Binh to the South Vietnamese, symbolizing the end of the direct American participation in the war after more than seven years.

December 14, 1972
The U.S. breaks off peace talks with the North Vietnamese that have been going on since Nixon's reelection.

December 18–31, 1972
President Nixon announces the resumption of the bombing and mining of North Vietnam. The most concentrated air offensive of the war begins, mostly aimed at targets in the vicinity of Hanoi and Haiphong.

December 28, 1972
Hanoi announces that it is willing to resume negotiations if the United States will stop bombing above the 20th Parallel. The bombing ends on December 31.

December 31, 1972
At year's end there are about 24,000 U.S. troops remaining in South Vietnam; 312 Americans were killed in action during 1972.

January 8–18, 1973
Henry Kissinger and Le Duc Tho resume negotiations in Paris, and they reach an agreement that is similar to the one that had been rejected previously by General Thieu.

January 19–26, 1973
There is heavy fighting in South Vietnam between GVN and Communist forces as both sides try to gain as much territory as they can before the cease-fire is scheduled to take hold.

January 23, 1973
Nixon announces that the Paris Accords will go into effect at 7:00 P.M. EST, January 27, 1973. He says that "peace with honor has been achieved."

January 27, 1973
The draft ends. For the first time since 1949, America has no conscription.

February 12–27, 1973
American POWs begin to come home.

February 21, 1973
A cease-fire formally ends the 20-year war in Laos.

March 29, 1973
The last U.S. troops and POWs leave South Vietnam. Only a DAO contingent and Marine embassy guards remain. About 8,500 U.S. civilian officials stay on.

June 4 to August 15, 1973
The Senate blocks all funds for any U.S. military activities in Indochina. The House concurs. The Nixon administration works out a compromise agreement with the Congress to permit continued U.S. bombing in Cambodia until August 15. The cessation marks the end of twelve years of American military action in Indochina.

November 7, 1973
Congress enacts the War Powers Act over President Nixon's veto.

December 31, 1973
The war in Vietnam continues without U.S. involvement. Most of the provisions of the Paris agreements are not observed by either side.

August 5, 1974
Congress makes sharp cuts in the amount of military aid going to the South Vietnamese government.

August 9, 1974
Richard M. Nixon resigns the U.S. presidency. Gerald R. Ford is sworn in as president.

September 16, 1974
President Ford offers clemency to draft evaders and deserters.

December 31, 1974
During 1974, 80,000 people, both civilians and soldiers, have been killed in the war. This is the highest total for any year of the war dating back to 1945.

January 6, 1975
NVA forces overrun Phuoc Long province. When the Americans do not react, Hanoi concludes that America will not reintroduce its military forces to save the GVN.

January 28, 1975
President Ford requests an additional $722 million in military aid for South Vietnam. Congress refuses his request.

March 1975

NVA forces launch an offensive in the central highlands. In a desperate effort to save the southern half of his country, General Thieu orders his forces to abandon their central highlands positions.

March 24, 1975

Hanoi launches its Ho Chi Minh Campaign to "liberate" South Vietnam before the monsoon rains begin.

April 8–21, 1975

The last major battle of the Vietnam War is fought at Xuan Loc, about thirty miles from Saigon. After hard fighting, the Communists win.

April 12, 1975

President Nguyen Van Thieu resigns and flees South Vietnam.

April 16, 1975

The Cambodian government surrenders to the Khmer Rouge, who promptly occupy the capital city of Phnom Penh.

April 23, 1975

President Ford pronounces the Vietnam War "finished as far as America is concerned."

April 29–30, 1975

The last Americans and thousands of South Vietnamese are evacuated from Saigon.

April 30, 1975

The Communists conquer Saigon. The Vietnam War ends in victory for the VC/NVA forces. The lengthy U.S. effort to create a non-Communist state in southern Vietnam fails.

Major Sources for the Chronology

Bowman, John, General Editor. *The World Almanac of the Vietnam War.* New York: A Bison Books, 1985.

Davidson, Phillip B. *Vietnam at War: The History, 1946–1975.* Novato, CA: Presidio, 1988.

Gravel, Mike, ed. *The Pentagon Papers: The Defense Department History of U.S. Decision Making in Vietnam,* 4 vols. Boston: Beacon, 1971.

Summers, Harry G., Jr. *The Vietnam War Almanac.* New York: Facts on File, 1985.

Bibliography

Books

ACHESON, DEAN. *Present at the Creation.* New York: Norton, 1969.

AMBROSE, STEPHEN E. *Eisenhower,* vol. 2: *The President.* New York: Simon and Schuster, 1984.

———. *Nixon: The Education of a Politician.* New York: Simon and Schuster, 1987.

———. *Rise to Globalism: American Foreign Policy since 1938,* 2d rev. ed. New York: Penguin, 1985.

———. *Nixon: Ruin and Recovery.* New York: Simon and Schuster, 1991.

———. *Nixon: The Triumph of a Politician.* New York: Simon and Schuster, 1989.

ANDERSON, DAVID L. *Shadow on the White House: Presidents and the Vietnam War.* Lawrence: University of Kansas Press, 1993.

———. ED. *Trapped by Success: The Eisenhower Administration and Vietnam, 1953–1961.* New York: Columbia University Press, 1991.

ANDRADE, DALE. *Ashes to Ashes: The Phoenix Program and the Vietnam War.* Lexington, MA: Lexington Books, 1990.

ANDREWS, WILLIAM. *The Village War: Vietnamese Communist Revolutionary Activity in Dinh Truong Province, 1960–1964.* Columbia: University of Missouri Press, 1973.

APPY, CHRISTIAN G. *Patriots: The Vietnam War Remembered from All Sides.* New York: Viking, 2003.

———. *Working Class War: American Combat Soldiers and Vietnam.* Chapel Hill: University of North Carolina Press, 1993.

ARLEN, MICHAEL J. *The Living Room War.* New York: Viking, 1969.

ARNOLD, JAMES R. *The First Domino: Eisenhower, the Military, and America's Intervention in Vietnam.* New York: Morrow, 1991.

ATKINSON, RICK, *The Long Gray Line: The American Journey of West Point's Class of 1966.* Norwalk, CT: Easton Press, 1989.

BAKER, MARK, ED. *NAM: The Vietnam War in the Words of the Soldiers Who Fought There.* New York: Berkeley, 1981.

BALL, GEORGE. *Diplomacy for a Crowded World.* Boston: Little, Brown, 1976.

———. *The Past Has Another Pattern.* New York: W. W. Norton, 1982.

BARITZ, LOREN. *Backfire: A History of How American Culture Led Us into Vietnam and Made Us Fight the Way We Did.* New York: Ballantine, 1985.

BARNET, RICHARD J. *Intervention and Revolution.* New York: New American Library, 1972.

———. *The Roots of War.* New York: Atheneum, 1972.

BARRETT, DAVID M. *Uncertain Warriors: Lyndon Johnson and His Vietnam Advisers.* Lawrence: University of Kansas Press, 1993.

BASKIR, LAWRENCE M. AND STRAUSS, WILLIAM A. *Chance and Circumstance: The Draft, the War, and the Vietnam Generation.* New York: Vintage, 1978.

BECHLOSS, MICHAEL R. *The Crisis Years.* New York: Harper Collins, 1991.

BECKER, ELIZABETH. *When the War Was Over: The Voices of Cambodia's Revolution and Its People.* New York: 1986.

BECKETT, IAN F. W. AND PIMLOTT, JOHN, EDS. *Armed Forces and Modern Counterinsurgency.* New York: St. Martin's Press, 1985.

BELKNAP, MICHAL R. *The Vietnam War on Trial: The My Lai Massacre and the Court-Martial of Lieutenant Calley.* Lawrence: University Press of Kansas, 2002.

BERESFORD, MELANIE. *Vietnam: Politics, Economics, and Society.* London: Pinter Publishers, 1988.

BERGER, CARL, ED. *The United States Air Force in Southeast Asia, 1961–1973.* Washington, DC: U.S. Government Printing Office, 1977.

BERGERUD, ERIC M. *The Dynamics of Defeat: The Vietnam War in Hau Nghia Province.* Boulder, CO: Westview Press, 1991.

BERMAN, LARRY. *Lyndon Johnson's War.* New York: W. W. Norton, 1989.

———. *No Peace, No Honor: Nixon, Kissinger, and Betrayal in Vietnam.* New York: Free Press, 2001.

———. *Planning a Tragedy.* New York: W. W. Norton, 1982.

BERMAN, WILLIAM C. *William Fulbright and the Vietnam War: The Dissent of a Political Realist.* Kent, OH: Kent State University Press, 1988.

BILLINGS-YUN, MELANIE. *Decision against War: Eisenhower and Dien Bien Phu, 1954.* New York: Columbia University Press, 1988.

BILLS, SCOTT L. *Empire and Cold War: The Roots of U.S.-Third World Antagonism, 1945–1947.* New York: Oxford, 1990.

————, ED. *Kent State/May 4: Echoes through a Decade.* Kent, OH: Kent State University Press, 1982.

BILTON, MICHAEL AND SIM, KEVIN. *Four Hours in My Lai: The Soldiers of Charlie Company.* New York: Viking, 1992.

BLAUFARB, DOUGLAS S. *The Counterinsurgency Era: U.S. Doctrines and Performance.* New York: Free Press, 1977.

BLUM, ROBERT. *Drawing the Line: The Origins of the American Containment Policy in East Asia.* New York: W. W. Norton, 1982.

BODARD, LUCIEN. *The Quicksand War: Prelude to Vietnam.* Boston: Little, Brown, 1967.

BOETTCHER, THOMAS D. VIETNAM: *The Valor and the Sorrow.* Boston: Little, Brown, 1985.

BORDEN, WILLIAM S. *The Pacific Alliance: United States Foreign Economic Policy and Japanese Trade Recovery, 1947–1955.* Madison: University of Wisconsin Press, 1984.

BORNET, VAUGHN. *The Presidency of Lyndon Johnson.* Lawrence: University of Kansas Press, 1983.

BOUSCAREN, ANTHONY TRAWICK. *The Last of the Mandarins: Diem of Vietnam.* Pittsburgh: Duquesne University Press, 1965.

BOWMAN, JOHN S., General Editor with introduction by Butterfield, Fox. *The World Almanac of the Vietnam War.* New York: Bison, 1985.

BRADLEE, BENJAMIN C. *Conversations with Kennedy.* New York: W. W. Norton, 1975.

BRAESTRUP, PETER. *Big Story,* 2 vols. Boulder, CO: Westview Press, 1977.

————, ED. *Vietnam as History: Ten Years After the Paris Peace Accords.* Washington, DC: University Press of America, 1984.

BRANDON, HENRY. *The Anatomy of Error.* Boston: Bambit, 1969.

————. *The Retreat of American Power.* Garden City, NY: Doubleday, 1973.

BRIGHAM, ROBERT. *Guerrilla Diplomacy: The NLF's Foreign Relations and the Vietnam War.* Ithaca, NY: Cornell University Press, 1999.

BRINKLEY, DOUGLAS. *Tour of Duty: John Kerry and the Vietnam War.* New York: William Morrow, 2003.

BRODIE, BERNARD. *War and Politics.* New York: Macmillan, 1973.

BROWN, FREDRICK Z. *Second Chance: The United States and Indochina in the 1990s.* New York: Council on Foreign Relations, 1989.

BROWNE, MALCOLM W. *The New Face of War.* Indianapolis, IN: 1968.

BRYAN, C. D. B. *Friendly Fire.* New York: Putnam, 1976.

BUCKINGHAM, WILLIAM A., JR. *Operation Ranch Hand: The Air Force and Herbicides in Southeast Asia, 1961–1971.* Washington, DC: U.S. Government Printing Office, 1982.

BURCHETT, WILFRED G. *Vietnam: Inside Story of a Guerrilla War.* New York: International Publishers, 1965.

BURKE, JOHN P. and GREENSTEIN, FRED I., in collaboration with BERMAN, LARRY and IMMERMAN, RICHARD. *How Presidents Test Reality: Decisions on Vietnam, 1954 and 1965.* New York: Russell Sage Foundation, 1989.

BUTLER, DAVID. *The Fall of Saigon.* New York: Simon and Schuster, 1985.

BUTTINGER, JOSEPH. *A Dragon Defiant: A Short History of Vietnam.* New York: Praeger, 1972.

———. *The Smaller Dragon: A Political History of Vietnam.* New York: Praeger, 1958.

———. *Vietnam: A Dragon Embattled,* 2 vols. New York: Praeger, 1967.

———. *Vietnam: A Political History.* New York: Praeger, 1968.

———. *Vietnam: The Unforgettable Tragedy.* New York: Horizon, 1977.

BUZZANCO, ROBERT. *Masters of War: Military Dissent and Politics in the Vietnam War.* New York: Cambridge University Press, 1996.

CABLE, JAMES. *The Geneva Conference on Indochina.* New York: St. Martin's Press, 1986.

CABLE, LARRY E. *Conflict of Myths: The Development of Counterinsurgency Doctrine and the Vietnam War.* New York: New York University Press, 1988.

———. *Unholy Grail: The U.S. and the Wars in Vietnam, 1965–1968.* London: Routledge, 1991.

CADY, JOHN F. *The Roots of French Imperialism in Eastern Asia.* Ithaca, NY: Cornell University Press, 1954.

———. *Southeast Asia: Its Historical Development.* New York: McGraw-Hill, 1964.

CAMPAGNA, ANTHONY S. *The Economic Consequences of the Vietnam War.* Westport, CT: Greenwood, 1991.

CAPPS, WALTER H. *The Unfinished War: Vietnam and the American Conscience.* Boston: Beacon, 1982.

———, ED. *The Vietnam Reader.* New York: Routledge, 1991.

CAPUTO, PHILIP. *A Rumor of War.* New York: Rinehart and Winston, 1977.

CASH, JOHN A. *Seven Firefights in Vietnam.* Washington, DC: U. S. Government Printing Office, 1970.

CASTLE, TIMOTHY N. *At War in the Shadow of Vietnam: U.S. Military Aid to the Royal Lao Government, 1955–1975.* New York: Columbia University Press, 1993.

CECIL, PAUL FREDERICK. *Herbicidal Warfare: The RANCH HAND Project in Vietnam.* New York: Praeger, 1986.

CHANDA, NAYAN. *Brother Enemy: The War after the War.* New York, 1986.

CHANDLER, DAVID P. *The Tragedy of Cambodian History.* New Haven, CT: Yale University Press, 1992.

CHANDLER, ROBERT W. *War of Ideas: The U.S. Propaganda Campaign in Vietnam.* Boulder, CO: Westview Press, 1981.

CHANOFF, DAVID AND DAON VAN TOAI. *Portrait of the Enemy.* New York: Random House, 1986.

CHARLTON, MICHAEL AND MONCRIEFF, ANTHONY. *Many Reasons Why: The American Involvement in Vietnam.* New York: Hill and Wang, 1978.

CHEN, KING C. *Vietnam and China, 1938–1954.* Princeton, NJ: Princeton University Press, 1969.

CHINH, TRUONG. *The Resistance Will Win.* Hanoi: Foreign Language Publishing House, 1960.

CHOMSKI, NOAM. *American Power and the New Mandarins.* New York: Vintage Books, 1969.

CINCINNATUS. *Self-Destruction: The Disintegration and Decay of the United States Army during the Vietnam Era.* New York: W. W. Norton, 1981.

CLARKE, JEFFREY J. *United States Army in Vietnam: Advice and Support: The Final Years, 1965–1973.* Washington, DC: U.S. Government Printing Office, 1988.

CLAUSEWITZ VON, KARL. *On War,* edited by Michael Howard and Peter Paret. Princeton, NJ: Princeton University Press, 1976.

CLIFFORD, CLARK AND RICHARD HOLBROOKE. *Counsel to the President: A Memoir.* New York: Random House, 1991

CLODFELTER, MARK. *The Limits of Air Power: The American Bombing of North Vietnam.* New York: Free Press, 1989.

COHEN, STEVEN, ED. *Vietnam: Anthology and Guide to a Television History.* New York: Knopf, 1983.

COHEN, WARREN I. *Dean Rusk.* New York: Cooper Square, 1980.

COLBY, WILLIAM E., AND FORBATH, PETER. *Honorable Men: My Life in the CIA.* New York: Simon and Schuster, 1978.

———. *Lost Victory: A First Hand Account of America's Sixteen Year Involvement in Vietnam.* Chicago: Contemporary Books, 1989.

COLLINS, JAMES LAWTON, JR. *The Development and Training of the South Vietnamese Army, 1950–1972.* Washington, DC: Department of the Army, 1975.

COLLINS, JOHN M. *The Vietnam War in Perspective.* Washington, DC: Strategic Research Group, 1972.

COOPER, CHESTER L. *The Lost Crusade: America in Vietnam.* New York: Dodd, Mead, 1970.

CORNELL UNIVERSITY STUDY GROUP. *The Air War in Vietnam.* Ithaca, NY: Cornell University Press, 1972.

CORSON, WILLIAM R. *Consequences of Failure.* New York: W. W. Norton, 1974.

CURREY, CECIL B. *Edward Landsdale: The Unquiet American.* Boston: Houghton Mifflin, 1988.

DAVIDSON, PHILLIP B. *Secrets of the Vietnam War.* Novato, CA: Presidio Press, 1991.

———. *Vietnam at War: The History 1946–1975.* Novato, CA: Presidio, 1988.

DAWSON, ALAN. *55 Days: The Fall of South Vietnam.* Englewood Cliffs, NJ: Prentice-Hall, 1977.

DEBENEDETTI, CHARLES, ASSISTED BY CHATFIELD, CHARLES. *An American Ordeal: The Antiwar Movement of the Vietnam Era.* Syracuse, NY: Syracuse University Press, 1990.

DEVILLERS, PHILIPPE. *Histoire du Viet-Nam, de 1940 a 1952.* Paris: Editions du Seuil, 1952.

———, AND LACOUTURE, JEAN. *The End of A War: Indochina, 1954.* New York: Praeger, 1969.

DIEM, BUI, WITH CHANOFF, DAVID. *In the Jaws of History.* Boston: Houghton Mifflin, 1987.

DIETZ, TERRY. *Republicans and Vietnam, 1961–1968.* Westport, CT: Greenwood, 1986.

DILEO, DAVID T. *George Ball: Vietnam and the Rethinking of Containment.* Chapel Hill: University of North Carolina Press, 1991.

DOUGHAN, CLARK, FULGHUM, DAVID, AND THE EDITORS OF BOSTON PUBLISHING COMPANY. *The Fall of the South.* Boston: Boston Publishing, 1985, a volume in the series, The Vietnam Experience, a 26-volume series on the Vietnam War.

DOYLE, EDWARD, LIPSMAN, SAMUEL, AND THE EDITORS. *America Takes Over.* Boston: Boston Publishing, 1982, a volume in the series The Vietnam Experience.

———, LIPSMAN, SAMUEL, AND THE EDITORS. *Setting the Stage.* Boston: Boston Publishing, 1981, a volume in the series, The Vietnam Experience.

———, LIPSMAN, SAMUEL, MAITLAND, TERRENCE, AND THE EDITORS. *The North.* Boston: Boston Publishing, 1982, a volume in the series, The Vietnam Experience.

———, MAITLAND, TERRENCE, AND THE EDITORS. *The Aftermath, 1975–1985.* Boston: Boston Publishing, 1985, a volume in the series, The Vietnam Experience.

———, LIPSMAN, SAMUEL, WEISS, STEPHEN, AND THE EDITORS. *Passing the Torch.* Boston: Boston Publishing, 1981, a volume in the series, The Vietnam Experience.

DRACHMAN, EDWARD R. *United States Policy toward Vietnam, 1940–1945.* Rutherford, NJ: Fairleigh-Dickinson University Press, 1970.

DRENDEL, LOU. *The Air War in Vietnam.* New York: Arco, 1968.

DUIKER, WILLIAM J. *China and Vietnam: The Roots of Conflict.* Berkeley: University of California Institute of East Asian Studies, 1987.

———. *The Communist Road to Power in Vietnam.* Boulder, CO: Westview Press,1981.

———. *The Rise of Nationalism in Vietnam, 1900–1941.* Ithaca, NY: Cornell University Press, 1975.

———. *Sacred War: Nationalism and Revolution in a Divided Vietnam.* New York: McGraw Hill, 1995.

———. *U.S. Containment Policy and the Conflict in Indochina.* Stanford, CA: Stanford University Press, 1994.

———. *Vietnam: Nation in Revolution.* Boulder, CO: Westview Press, 1983.

———. *Vietnam Since the Fall of Saigon.* Athens, OH: Ohio University, Center for International Studies, 1980.

DUNN, PETER M. *The First Vietnam War.* New York: St. Martin's Press, 1985.

EDELMAN, BERNARD, ED. *Dear America: Letters Home from Vietnam.* New York: Pocket Books, 1985.

EISENHOWER, DWIGHT DAVID. *The White House Years: Mandate for Change, 1953–1956.* Garden City, NY: Doubleday, 1963.

ELLSBERG, DANIEL. *Papers on the War.* New York: Simon and Schuster, 1972.

———. *Secrets: A Memoir of Vietnam and the Pentagon Papers.* New York: Viking, 2002.

ELY, JOHN HART. *War and Responsibility: Constitutional Lessons of Vietnam and Its Aftermath.* Princeton, NJ: Princeton University Press, 1994.

EMERSON, GLORIA. *Winners and Losers: Battles, Retreats, Gains, Losses, and Ruins from a Long War.* New York: Harcourt, Brace, 1976.

ENTHOVEN, ALAIN C. AND SMITH, K. WAYNE. *How Much Is Enough: Shaping the Defense Program, 1961–1968.* New York: Harper & Row, 1971.

EPSTEIN, EDWARD JAY. *News from Nowhere: Television and the News.* New York: Vintage, 1973.

ERRINGTON, ELIZABETH J. AND MCKERCHER, B. J. C., EDS. *The Vietnam War as History.* Westport, CT: Praeger, 1990.

FAIRLIE, HENRY. *The Kennedy Promise: The Politics of Expectation.* Garden City, NY: Doubleday, 1973.

FALL, BERNARD. *The Anatomy of a Crisis: The Laotian Crisis of 1960–61.* Garden City, NY: Doubleday, 1960.

———. *Hell in a Very Small Place: The Siege of Dien Bien Phu.* New York: Lippincott, 1967.

———. *Street without Joy.* Harrisburg, PA: Stackpole, 1967.

———. *The Two Vietnams: A Political and Military Analysis.* New York: Praeger, 1964.

———. *Vietnam Witness, 1953–1966.* New York: Praeger, 1966.

———, ED. *Ho Chi Minh on Revolution: Selected Writings, 1920–1966.* New York: Harper Colophon, 1971.

FARBER, DAVID. *Chicago '68.* Chicago: University of Chicago Press, 1988.

FERBER, MICHAEL AND LYND, STAUGHTON. *The Resistance.* Boston: Beacon, 1971.

FISHEL, WESLEY R., ED. *Vietnam: Anatomy of a Conflict.* Itasca, IL: F. E. Peacock, 1968.

FITZGERALD, FRANCES. *Fire in the Lake: The Vietnamese and the Americans in Vietnam.* New York: Random House, 1972.

FOLEY, MICHAEL S., *Confronting the War Machine: Draft Resistance during the Vietnam War.* Chapel Hill: University of North Carolina Press, 2003.

FRANKLAND, NOBLE AND DOWLING, CHRISTOPHER EDS. *Decisive Battles of the Twentieth Century.* London: Sidgwick & Jackson, 1976.

FRANKLIN, H. BRUCE. *M. I. A. or Mythmaking in America.* New Brunswick, NJ: Rutgers University Press, 1992.

FREY-WOUTERS, ELLEN AND LAUFER, ROBERT S. *Legacy of a War: The American Soldier in Vietnam.* Armonk, NY: M. E. Sharpe, 1986.

FULBRIGHT, J. WILLIAM. *The Arrogance of Power.* New York: Random House, 1967.

FULGHUM, DAVID, MAITLAND, TERRENCE, and the editors, *South Vietnam on Trial.* Boston: Boston Publishing, 1984, a volume in the series The Vietnam Experience.

FULLER, TONY. *Charlie Company: What Vietnam Did to Us.* New York: Ballantine, 1983.

FURGUSON, ERNEST B. *Westmoreland: The Inevitable General.* Boston: Little, Brown, 1968.

GABRIEL, RICHARD AND SAVAGE, PAUL. *Crisis in Command.* New York: Hill and Wang, 1978.

GADDIS, JOHN LEWIS. *Now We Know: Rethinking Cold War History.* New York: Oxford University Press, 1997.

———. *Strategies of Containment: A Critical Appraisal of Postwar American Security Policy.* New York: Oxford University Press, 1982.

———. *The United States and the Origins of the Cold War.* New York: Columbia University Press, 1972.

GAIDUK, ILYA V. *The Soviet Union and the Vietnam War.* Chicago: Ivan Dee, 1996.

GALBRAITH, JOHN KENNETH. *Ambassador's Journal: A Personal Account of the Kennedy Years.* Boston: Houghton Mifflin, 1969.

GALLOWAY, JOHN. *The Gulf of Tonkin Resolution.* Rutherford, NJ: Fairleigh Dickinson University Press, 1970.

GALLUCCI, ROBERT L. *Neither Peace nor Honor: The Politics of American Military Policy in Vietnam.* Baltimore: Johns Hopkins University Press, 1975.

GARDNER, LLOYD C. *Approaching Vietnam: From World War II through Dienbienphu.* New York: W. W. Norton, 1988.

———. *Pay Any Price: Lyndon Johnson and the Wars for Vietnam.* Chicago: Ivan R. Dees, 1995.

GELB, LESLIE WITH BETTS, RICHARD. *The Irony of Vietnam: The System Worked.* Washington, DC: Brookings Institution, 1979.

GETTLEMAN, MARVIN E., ED. *Viet Nam: History, Documents, and Opinions on a Major World Crisis.* Greenwich, CT: Fawcett, 1965.

———, FRANKLIN, JANE, YOUNG, MARILYN, AND FRANKLIN, H. BRUCE, EDS. *Vietnam and America: A Documentary History.* New York: Grove Press, 1985.

GEYELIN, PHILIP. *Lyndon B. Johnson and the World.* New York: Praeger, 1966.

GIAP, VO NGUYEN. *Big Victory, Great Task.* New York: Praeger, 1967.

———. *People's War, People's Army.* Hanoi: Foreign Language Publishing House, 1961.

GIBBONS, WILLIAM CONRAD. *The U.S. Government and the Vietnam War: Executive and Legislative Roles and Relationships. Part I: 1945–1960.* Princeton, NJ: Princeton University Press, 1986.

———. *Part II: 1961–1964.*

GIBSON, JAMES WILLIAM. *The Perfect War: The War We Couldn't Lose and How We Did.* New York: Vintage, 1986.

GIGLIO, JAMES N. *The Presidency of John F. Kennedy.* Lawrence: University of Kansas Press, 1991.

GITLIN, TODD. *The Sixties: Years of Hope, Days of Rage.* New York: Bantam, 1987.

———. *The Whole World Is Watching: Mass Media in the Making and Unmaking of the New Left.* Berkeley, CA: University of California Press, 1980.

GOFF, ROBERT AND SANDER, ROBERT. *Brothers: Black Soldiers in Nam.* Novato, CA: Presidio Press, 1982.

GOLDMAN, ERIC. *The Tragedy of Lyndon Johnson.* New York: Dell, 1968.

GOLDSTEIN, JOSEPH, MARSHALL, BURKE, AND SCHWARTZ, JACK. *The My Lai Massacre and Its Cover-Up.* New York, 1976.

GOLDSTEIN, MARTIN E. *American Policy toward Laos.* Teaneck, NJ: Fairleigh Dickinson University Press, 1986.

GOODMAN, ALLEN E. *The Lost Peace: America's Search for a Negotiated Settlement of the Vietnam War.* Stanford, CA: Hoover Institution Press, 1978.

———. *Politics of War: The Basis of Political Community in South Vietnam.* Cambridge, MA: Harvard University Press, 1973.

GOULDEN, JOSEPH C. *Truth Is the First Casualty: The Gulf of Tonkin Affair—Illusion and Reality.* Chicago: Rand Mc-Nally, 1969.

GRAEBNER, NORMAN, ED. *Nationalism and Communism in Asia.* Lexington, MA: D. C. Heath, 1977.

GRAFF, HENRY. *The Tuesday Cabinet: Deliberation and Decision on Peace and War under Lyndon B. Johnson.* Englewood Cliffs, NJ: Prentice-Hall, 1970.

GRANT, ZOLIN. *Facing the Phoenix: The CIA and the Political Defeat of the United States in Vietnam.* New York, 1991.

GRINTER, LAWRENCE E., and DUNN, PETER, EDS. *The American War in Vietnam: Lessons, Legacies, and Implications for the Future.* New York: Greenwood Press, 1987.

GURTOV, MELVIN. *The First Vietnam Crisis: Chinese Communist Strategy and United States Involvement, 1953–1954.* New York: Columbia University Press, 1967.

GUTHMAN, EDWIN O. and SHULMAN, JEFFREY. *Robert Kennedy in His Own Words: The Unpublished Recollections of the Kennedy Years.* New York: Bantam Press, 1988.

HACKWORTH, DAVID H. and SHERMAN, JULIE. *About Face.* New York: Simon and Schuster, 1989.

HALBERSTAM, DAVID. *The Best and the Brightest.* New York: Random House, 1964.

———. *The Making of a Quagmire, America and Vietnam during the Kennedy Era.* New York: Random House, 1964, rev. ed. New York: Knopf, 1988.

HALDEMAN, HARRY R. *The Ends of Power.* New York: New York Times Book, 1978.

———. *The Haldeman Diaries,* with editorial assistance from Steven Ambrose. New York: Putnam, 1994.

HALEY, P. EDWARD, *Congress and the Fall of South Vietnam and Cambodia.* London: Associated University Presses, 1982.

———. *A History of Southeast Asia,* 2d ed. New York: Macmillan, 1963.

HALLIN, DANIEL C. *The Uncensored War: The Media and Vietnam.* New York: Oxford University Press, 1986.

HAMILTON-MERRITT, JANE. *Tragic Mountains: The Hmong, the Americans, and the Secret Wars for Laos, 1942–1992.* Bloomington: University of Indiana Press, 1993.

HAMMEL, ERIC. *The Battle for Hue, Tet 1968.* Chicago: Contemporary Books, 1991.

HAMMER, ELLEN J. *A Death in November: America in Vietnam, 1963.* New York: E. P. Dutton, 1987.

———. *The Struggle for Indochina, 1940–1955.* Palo Alto, CA: Stanford University Press, 1966.

———. *Vietnam, Yesterday and Today.* New York: Holt, Rinehart and Winston, 1966.

HAMMER, RICHARD J. *The Court Martial of Lt. Calley.* New York: Coward-McCann and Geoghegan, 1972.

———. *One Morning in the War: The Tragedy at Son My.* New York: Coward-McCann, 1970.

HAMMOND, WILLIAM. *Public Affairs: The Military and the Media, 1962–1968.* Washington, DC: U.S. Government Printing Office, 1989.

————. *Public Affairs: The Military and the Media, 1968–1973.* Washington, DC: U.S. Government Printing Office, 1996.

HANH, NHAT. *Vietnam: Lotus in a Sea of Fire.* New York: Hill and Wang, 1962.

HANHIMAKI, JUSSI. *The Flawed Architect: Henry Kissinger and American Foreign Policy.* New York: Oxford University Press, 2003.

HANNAH, NORMAN B. *The Key to Failure: Laos and the Vietnam War.* Washington, DC: University Press of America, 1988.

HARRIMAN, AVERELL. *America and Russia in a Changing World: A Half Century of Personal Observation.* Garden City, NY: Doubleday, 1971.

HARRISON, JAMES PINCKNEY. *The Endless War: Fifty Years of Struggle in Vietnam.* New York: The Free Press, 1982.

HASKINS, JAMES. *The War and the Protest: Vietnam.* Garden City, NY: Doubleday, 1971.

HATCHER, PATRICK LLOYD. *The Suicide of an Elite: American Internationalists and Vietnam.* Stanford, CA: Stanford University Press, 1990.

HAVENS, THOMAS R. H. *Fire Across the Sea: The Vietnam War and Japan, 1965–1975.* Princeton, NJ: Princeton University Press, 1987.

HAYDEN, TOM. *Reunion.* New York: Random House, 1989.

HEARDEN, PATRICK J. *The Tragedy of Vietnam.* New York: Harper Collins, 1991.

HELLER, CHARLES E., AND STOFFT, WILLIAM A. *America's First Battles.* Lawrence: University of Kansas Press, 1986.

HELLMAN, JOHN. *American Myth and the Legacy of Vietnam.* New York: Columbia University Press, 1986.

HELMER, JOHN. *Bringing the War Home: The American Soldier in Vietnam and After.* New York: Free Press, 1974.

HERR, MICHAEL. *Dispatches.* New York: Avon, 1978.

HERRING, GEORGE C. *America's Longest War, The United States and Vietnam, 1950–1975,* 2d ed. New York: Knopf, 1986, 3d ed. New York: McGraw Hill, 1996.

————. *LBJ and Vietnam: A Different Kind of War.* Austin: University of Texas Press, 1994.

————, ED. *The Secret Diplomacy of the Vietnam War: The Negotiating Volumes of the Pentagon Papers.* Austin: University of Texas Press, 1983.

HERRINGTON, STUART A. *Peace with Honor? An American Reports on Vietnam, 1973–1975.* Novato, CA: Presidio Press, 1983.

————. *Silence Was a Weapon: The Vietnam War in the Villages.* Novato, CA: Presidio Press, 1982.

————. *Stalking the VietCong: Inside Operation Phoenix, A Personal Account.* Novato, CA: Presidio Press, 1999.

HERSH, SEYMOUR M. *Cover-up: The Army's Secret Investigation of the Massacre at My-Lai 4.* New York: Random House, 1972.

————. *My Lai 4: A Report on the Massacre and Its Aftermath.* New York: Vintage Books, 1970.

———. *The Price of Power: Kissinger in the Nixon White House.* New York: Summit Books, 1983.

HERZ, MARTIN F. *The Prestige Press and the Christmas Bombings, 1972.* Washington, DC: Ethics and Public Policy Center, 1980.

HESS, GARY R., *The United States' Emergence as a Southeast Asian Power, 1940–1956.* New York: Columbia University Press, 1987.

———. *Vietnam and the United States.* Boston: Twayne Publishers, 1990.

HILSMAN, ROGER. *To Move a Nation: The Politics of Foreign Policy in the Administration of John F. Kennedy.* Garden City, NY: Doubleday, 1967.

HO CHI MINH. *Selected Writings, 1920–1969.* Hanoi: People's Publishing House, 1973.

HOBART, MARK AND TAYLOR, ROBERT H., EDS. *Context, Meaning, and Power in Southeast Asia.* Ithaca, NY: Cornell University Press, 1986.

HODGSON, GEOFFREY. *America in Our Time: From World War II to Nixon, What Happened and Why.* New York: Vintage Books, 1976.

HOFF, JOAN. *Nixon Reconsidered.* New York: Basic Books, 1994.

HOOPES, TOWNSEND. *The Devil and John Foster Dulles.* Boston: Little, Brown, 1973.

———. *The Limits of Intervention: An Inside Account of How the Johnson Policy of Escalation in Vietnam Was Reversed,* rev. ed. New York: McKay, 1973.

HORNE, A. D., ED. *The Wounded Generation.* Englewood Cliffs, NJ: Prentice Hall, 1986.

HOSMER, STEPHEN, ET AL. *The Fall of South Vietnam.* Santa Monica, CA: Rand Corporation, 1978.

HUMPHREY, HUBERT H. *The Education of a Public Man: My Life and Politics.* Garden City, NY: Doubleday, 1976.

HUNT, MICHAEL H. *Lyndon Johnson's War: America's Cold War Crusade in Vietnam, 1945–1968.* New York: Hill and Wang, 1996.

HUNT, RICHARD A. AND SCHULTZ, RICHARD H., EDS. *Lessons from an Unconventional War: Reassessing U.S. Strategies for Future Conflicts.* New York: Pergamon Press, 1982.

IMMERMAN, RICHARD, ED. *John Foster Dulles and the Diplomacy of the Cold War.* Princeton, NJ: Princeton University Press, 1990.

IRVING, R. E. M. *The First Indochina War: French and American Policy, 1945–1954.* London: C. Helm, 1975.

ISAACS, ARNOLD. *Without Honor: Defeat in Vietnam and Cambodia.* Baltimore, MD: Johns Hopkins University Press, 1983.

ISAACS, HAROLD. *No Peace for Asia.* New York: Macmillan, 1947.

ISAACSON, WALTER. *Kissinger: A Biography.* New York: Simon and Schuster, 1992.

ISSERMAN, MAURICE. *If I Had a Hammer: The Death of the Old Left and the Birth of the New Left.* New York, 1987.

JANIS, IRVING. *Victims of Groupthink: A Psychological Study of Foreign Policy Decisions and Fiascos.* Boston: Houghton-Mifflin, 1972.

JOHNSON, LYNDON. *The Vantage Point: Perspectives of the Presidency, 1963–1969.* New York: Holt, Rinehart and Winston, 1971.

JOINER, CHARLES A. *The Politics of Massacre: Political Processes in South Vietnam.* Philadelphia: Temple University Press, 1974.

JONES, HOWARD. *Death of a Generation: How the Assassinations of Diem and JFK Prolonged the Vietnam War.* New York: Oxford University Press, 2003.

JOYAUX, FRANCOIS. *La Chine et le reglement du premier conflit d'Indochine.* Geneve 1954. Paris: University of Sorbonne, 1954.

JUST, WARD. "Introduction" in *Reporting Vietnam: American Journalism, 1959–1975.* New York: Library of America, 1998.

KAHIN, GEORGE. *Intervention: How American Became Involved in Vietnam.* New York: Knopf, 1986.

———. AND LEWIS, JOHN. *The United States in Vietnam,* rev. ed. New York: Delta, 1967, 1969.

KAISER, DAVID. *American Tragedy: Kennedy, Johnson, and the Origins of the Vietnam War.* Cambridge, MA: Harvard University Press, 2000.

KALB, MARVIN AND ABEL, ELIE. *Roots of Involvement: The United States in Asia, 1784–1971.* New York: W. W. Norton, 1971.

KAPLAN, LAWRENCE S., ARTAUD, DENISE, AND RUBIN, MARK R., EDS. *Dien Bien Phu and the Crisis of Franco-American Relations, 1954–1955.* Wilmington: University of Delaware Press, 1990.

KARNOW, STANLEY. *Vietnam: A History.* New York: Viking, 1983.

KATTENBURG, PAUL M. *The Vietnam Trauma in American Foreign Policy, 1945–1975.* New Brunswick, NJ: Transaction, 1980.

KEARNS, DORIS. *Lyndon Johnson and the American Dream.* New York: Signet, 1976.

KEATING, SUZAN KATZ. *Prisoners of Hope: Exploiting the POW/MIA Myth in America.* New York: Random House, 1994.

KENDRICK, ALEXANDER. *The Wound Within: America in the Vietnam Years, 1954–1974.* Boston: Little, Brown, 1974.

KENNEDY, PAUL. *The Rise and Fall of the Great Powers: Economic Change and Military Conflict from 1500 to 2000.* New York: Random House, 1987.

———, ED. *To Reason Why: The Debate about the Cause of U.S. Involvement in the Vietnam War.* New York: McGraw Hill, 1990.

KHANH, HUYNH KIM. *Vietnamese Communism, 1925–1945.* Ithaca, New York: Cornell University Press, 1976.

KHOI, LE TRANH. *Le Viet-Nam: Historie et Civilisation.* Paris: Editions de Minuit, 1955.

KHONG, YUEN FOONG. *Analogies at War—Korea, Munich, Dien Bien Phu: The Vietnam Decisions of 1965.* Princeton, NJ: Princeton University Press, 1992.

KIERNAN, BEN. *How Pol Pot Came to Power: A History of Communism in Kampuchea, 1930–1975.* London: Verso, 1985.

———. *The Pol Pot Regime: Race, Power, and Genocide in Cambodia under the Khmer Rouge, 1975–1979.* New Haven, CT: Yale University Press, 1996.

KIMBALL, JEFFREY. *Nixon's Vietnam War.* Lawrence: University of Kansas Press, 1998.

KINNARD, DOUGLAS. *The Certain Trumpet: Maxwell Taylor and the American Experience in Vietnam.* Washington, DC: U.S. Government Printing Office, 1991.

———. *The War Managers.* Hanover, NH: University Press of New England, 1977.

KISSINGER, HENRY A. *Ending the Vietnam War: A History of America's Involvement in and Extrication from the Vietnam War.* New York: Simon and Schustger, 2002.

———. *Nuclear Weapons and Foreign Policy.* Garden City, NY: Doubleday, 1957.

———. *The White House Years.* Boston: Little, Brown, 1979.

———. *Years of Upheaval.* Boston: Little, Brown, 1982.

KLARE, MICHAEL. *War without End: American Planning for the Next Vietnam.* New York: Knopf, 1972.

KNIGHTLEY, PHILLIPP. *The First Casualty: From the Crimea to Vietnam: The War Correspondent as Hero, Propagandist, and Myth Maker.* New York: Harcourt, Brace, Jovanovich, 1975.

KNOLL, ERWIN AND MCFADDEN, JUDITH NIES, EDS. *War Crimes and American Conscience.* New York: Holt, Rinehart, and Winston, 1970.

KOLKO, GABRIEL. *Anatomy of a War: Vietnam, the United States, and Modern Historical Experience.* New York: Pantheon, 1985.

KOMER, ROBERT W. *Bureaucracy at War: U.S. Performance in the Vietnam Conflict.* Boulder, CO: Westview Press, 1986.

———. *Bureaucracy Does Its Thing: Institutional Constraints on U.S.-GVN Performance in Vietnam.* Santa Monica, CA: The Rand Corporation, 1973.

KRASLOW, DAVID, AND LOORY, STUART H. *The Secret Search for Peace in Vietnam.* New York: Random House, 1968.

KREPINEVICH, ANDREW F., JR. *The Army and Vietnam.* Baltimore, MD: Johns Hopkins University Press, 1986.

KUTLER, STANLEY I. *The Wars of Watergate: The Last Crisis of Richard Nixon.* New York: Knopf, 1990.

LACOUTURE, JEAN. *Ho Chi Minh: A Political Biography.* New York: Random House, 1968.

——— AND DEVILLERS, PHILIPPE. *La Fin d' une Guerre: Indochine, 1954.* Paris: Editions du Seuil, 1960. There is an English translation of this book: *End of a War: Indochina, 1954.* New York: Praeger, 1969.

LAFEBER, WALTER. *America, Russia, and the Cold War, 1945–1975,* 3d ed. New York: John Wiley, 1976.

LAKE, ANTHONY, ED. *The Vietnam Legacy.* New York: New York University Press, 1976. Oxford University Press, 1961.

LAM QUANG THI, *The Twenty-Five Year Century: A South Vietnamese General Remembers the Indochina War to the Fall of Saigon.* Denton, Texas: Univeresity of North Texas Press, 2001.

LANDSDALE, EDWARD GEARY. *In the Midst of Wars: An American's Mission to Southeast Asia.* New York: Harper & Row, 1972.

LANGGUTH, A. J. *Our Vietnam: The War 1954–1975.* New York: Simon and Schuster, 2001.

LANNING, MICHAEL LEE AND CRAGG, DAN. *Inside the VC and the NVA: The Real Story of North Vietnam's Armed Forces.* New York, 1992.

LARSEN, STANLEY R. AND JAMES L. COLLINS, JR. *Allied Participation in Vietnam.* Washington, DC: Department of the Army, 1975.

LAURENCE, JOHN. *The Cat from Hue: A Vietnam War Story.* New York: Public Affairs, 2002.

LEFFLER, MELVIN. *A Preponderance of Power: National Security, The Truman Administration, and the Cold War.* Stanford, CA: Stanford University Press, 1991.

LE GRO, WILLIAM E. *Vietnam from Cease-Fire to Capitulation.* Washington, DC: U.S. Army Center of Military History, 1981.

LEHRACH, OTTO J., ED. *No Shining Armor: The Marines at War in Vietnam.* Lawrence: University of Kansas Press, 1992.

LEVY, DAVID L. *The Debate over Vietnam.* Baltimore MD: The Johns Hopkins University Press, 1991.

LEWIS, CHESTER, HODGSON, GODFREY, AND PAGE, BRUCE. *An American Melodrama: The Presidential Campaign of 1968.* New York: Viking, 1969.

LEWY, GUENTHER. *America in Vietnam.* New York: Oxford University Press, 1978.

LIFTON, ROBERT L. *Home from the War: Vietnam Veterans: Neither Victims nor Executioners.* New York: Simon and Schuster, 1973.

LIND, MICHAEL. *Vietnam: The Necessary War: A Reinterpretation of America's most disastrous Military Conflict.* New York: The Free Press, 2000.

LIPSMAN, SAMUEL, DOYLE, EDWARD, AND THE EDITORS. *Fighting for Time.* Boston: Boston Publishing, 1983, a volume in the series The Vietnam Experience.

———, WEISS, STEPHEN, AND THE EDITORS. *The False Peace.* Boston: Boston Publishing, 1985, a volume in the series The Vietnam Experience.

LITTAUER, RAPHAEL, AND UPHOFF, NORMAN, EDS. *The Air War in Indochina,* rev. ed. Boston: Beacon, 1972.

LOCKHART, GREG. *Nation in Arms: The Origins of the People's Army of Vietnam.* Boston: Allen & Unwin, 1989.

LODGE, HENRY CABOT, JR. *As It Was.* New York: W. W. Norton, 1976.

———. *The Storm Has Many Eyes: A Personal Narrative.* New York: W. W. Norton, 1973.

LOMPERIS, TIMOTHY J. *From People's War to People's Rule: Insurgency, Intervention, and the Lessons of Vietnam.* Chapel Hill: University of North Carolina Press, 1996.

———. *Reading the Wind.* Durham, NC: Duke University Press, 1987.

———. *The War Everyone Lost–and Won: America's Intervention in Viet Nam's Twin Struggles.* Baton Rouge: Louisiana State University Press, 1984.

MACLEAR, MICHAEL. *The Ten Thousand Day War: Vietnam, 1945–1975.* New York: Avon, 1981.

MACDONALD, J. FRED. *Television and the Red Menace: The Video Road to Vietnam.* New York: Praeger, 1985.

MAITLAND, TERRENCE, WEISS, STEPHEN, AND THE EDITORS. *Raising the Stakes.* Boston: Boston Publishing, 1982 a volume in the series *The Vietnam Experience.*

MANGOLD, TOM AND PENYCATE, JOHN. *The Tunnels of Cu Chi.* New York: Berkley Books, 1985.

MARANISS, DAVID. *They Marched into the Sunlight: War and Peace Vietnam and America October 1967.* New York: Simon and Schuster, 2003.

MAROLDA, EDWARD J. AND FITZGERALD, OSCAR P. *The United States Navy and the Vietnam Conflict,* vol. 2: *From Military Assistance to Combat, 1959–1965.* Washington, DC: U.S. Government Printing Office, Naval Historical Center, 1986.

MARR, DAVID G. *Vietnamese Anti-Colonialism, 1885–1925.* Berkeley, CA: University of California Press, 1971.

———. *Vietnamese Tradition on Trial.* Berkeley: University of California Press, 1982.

MARSHALL, KATHRYN. *In the Combat Zone.* New York: Penguin, 1987.

MARSHALL, S. L. A. Vietnam: *Three Battles.* New York: Da Capo Press, 1971.

MATTHEWS, LLOYD J. AND BROWN, DALE E., EDS. *Assessing the Vietnam War.* Washington, DC: Pergamon-Brassup, 1987.

MAURER, HARRY. *Strange Ground: Americans in Vietnam, 1945–1975.* New York: Holt, 1988.

MAY, ERNEST R. AND NEUSTADT, RICHARD. *Thinking in Time: The Uses of History for Decision-Makers.* New York: Free Press, 1986.

MCALEAVY, HENRY. *Black Flags in Vietnam: The Story of Chinese Intervention.* London: Allen & Unwin, 1968.

MCALISTER, JOHN T., JR. *Vietnam: The Origins of Revolution.* New York: Knopf, 1969.

——— AND MUS, PAUL. *The Vietnamese and Their Revolution.* New York: Harper & Row, 1970.

MCCARTHY, EUGENE J. *The Year of the People.* Garden City, NY: Doubleday, 1969.

MCCORMICK, THOMAS. *America's Half Century: United States Foreign Policy in the Cold War.* Baltimore, MD: Johns Hopkins University Press, 1989.

MCCOY, ALFRED W., WITH READ, CATHLEEN B., AND ADAMS, LEONARD P., II. *The Politics of Heroin in Southeast Asia.* New York: Harper & Row, 1972.

MCDONALD, PETER. *Giap: Victor in Vietnam.* New York: W. W. Norton, 1993.

MCGLOTHEN, RONALD. *Controlling the Waves: Dean Acheson and U.S. Foreign Policy in Asia.* New York: W. W. Norton, 1993.

MCGOVERN, GEORGE. *Grassroots: The Autobiography of George McGovern.* New York: Random House, 1977.

MCMASTER, H. R. *Dereliction of Duty: Lyndon Johnson, Robert McNamara, the Joint Chiefs of Staff, and the Lies That Led to Vietnam.* New York: Harper Collins, 1997.

MCNAMARA, ROBERT S., BLIGHT, JAMES G., AND BRIGHAM, ROBERT. *Argument without End: In Search of Answers to the Vietnam Tragedy.* New York: Public Affairs Council/Persius, 2000.

———, WITH VAN DE MARK, BRIAN. *In Retrospect: The Tragedy and Lessons of Vietnam.* New York: Times Books, Random House, 1995.

MCPHERSON, HARRY. *A Political Education.* Boston: Little, Brown, 1971.

MCPHERSON, MYRA ED. *Longtime Passing: Vietnam and the Haunted Generation.* New York: Doubleday, 1984.

MEAD, WALTER RUSSELL. *Mortal Splendor: The American Empire in Transition.* Boston: Houghton Mifflin, 1987.

MERSKY, PETER B. AND POLMAR, NORMAN. *The Naval Air War in Vietnam.* New York: Kensington, 1981.

METZL, JAMES FREDERIC. *Western Responses to Human Rights Abuses in Cambodia, 1975–80.* New York: St. Martin's Press, 1996.

MEYERSON, HARVEY. *Vinh Long.* Boston: Houghton Mifflin, 1970.

MICHEL, MARSHALL L., III. *The 11 Days of Christmas: America's Last Vietnam Battle.* San Francisco: Encounter Books, 2002.

MICHENER, JAMES. *Kent State: What Happened and Why.* New York: Random House, 1971.

MIDDLETON, DREW. *Air War: Vietnam.* New York: Bobbs-Merrill, 1978.

MILLETT, ALLAN R. AND MASLOWSKI, PETER. *For the Common Defense: A Military History of the United States of America.* New York: Free Press, 1984.

MILLET, ALLAN R., ED. *A Short History of the Vietnam War.* Bloomington, IN.: Indiana University Press, 1978.

MINH, HO CHI. *Prison Diary.* Hanoi: Foreign Language Publishing House, 1966.

MIROFF, BRUCE. *Pragmatic Illusions: The Presidential Politics of John F. Kennedy.* New York: David McKay, 1976.

MOISE, EDWIN E. *Land Reform in China and North Vietnam: Consolidating the Revolution at the Village Level.* Chapel Hill: University of North Carolina Press, 1983.

———. *Tonkin Gulf and the Escalation of the Vietnam War.* Chapel Hill: University of North Carolina Press, 1996.

MOORE, HAROLD G. AND GALLOWAY, JOSEPH L. *We Were Soldiers Once–And Young.* New York: Random House, 1992.

MORGAN, JOSEPH G. *The Vietnam Lobby: The American Friends of Vietnam.* Chapel Hill: University of North Carolina Press, 1997.

MORRIS, ROGER. *An Uncertain Greatness: Henry Kissinger and American Foreign Policy.* New York: Harper & Row, 1977.

MORROCCO, JOHN, AND THE EDITORS. *Rain of Fire: Air War, 1969–1973.* Boston: Boston Publishing, 1985, a volume in the series The Vietnam Experience.

———. *Thunder from Above.* Boston: Boston Publishing, 1984, a volume in the series The Vietnam Experience.

MOSS, GEORGE DONELSON. *America in the Twentieth Century,* 5th ed. Upper Saddle River, NJ: Prentice Hall, 2004.

———. *Moving On: The American People Since 1945.* 3d. ed. Upper Saddle River, NJ: Prentice Hall, 2005.

———. *A Vietnam Reader: Sources and Essays.* Englewood Cliffs, NJ: Prentice Hall, 1991.

MROZEK, DONALD J. *Air Power and the Ground War in Vietnam: Ideas and Actions.* Washington, DC: U.S. Government Printing Office, 1989.

MUELLER, JOHN E. War, *Presidents and Public Opinion.* New York: John Wiley, 1973.

NEWMAN, JOHN M. *JFK and Vietnam: Deception, Intrigue, and the Struggle for Power.* New York: Warner Books, 1992.

NGO, VINH LONG. *Before the Revolution: The Vietnamese Peasants under the French.* New York: Columbia University Press, 1973, 1991.

NGUYEN, CAO KY. *Twenty Years and Twenty Days.* New York: Stein and Day, 1976.

NGUYEN, GREGORY TIEN HUNG. *Economic Development of Socialist Vietnam, 1955–1980.* New York: Praeger, 1977.

———— AND SCHECHTER, JERROLD L. *The Palace File.* New York: Harper & Row, 1986.

NIGHSWONGER, WILLIAM A. *Rural Pacification in Vietnam.* New York: Praeger, 1966.

NIXON, RICHARD. *RN: The Memoirs of Richard Nixon.* New York, Grosset & Dunlap, 1978.

————. *No More Vietnams.* New York: Avon, 1985.

————. *The Real War.* New York: Warner, 1980.

O'BALLANCE, EDGAR. *The Indo-China War, 1945–1954.* London: Faber and Faber, 1964.

————. *The Wars in Vietnam.* New York: Hippocrene, 1981.

OBERDORFER, DON. *Tet! The Turning Point in the Vietnam War.* Garden City, NY: Doubleday, 1971.

O'DONNELL, KENNETH P. AND POWERS, DAVID F., WITH JOE MCCARTHY. *Johnny, We Hardly Knew Ye: Memories of John Fitzgerald Kennedy.* Boston: Little, Brown, 1972.

OLSON, GREGORY A. *Mansfield and Vietnam: A Study in Rhetorical Adaptation.* East Lansing: Michigan State University Press, 1995.

OLSON, JAMES S., ED. *Dictionary of the Vietnam War.* New York: Greenwood, 1988.

———— AND ROBERTS, RANDY. *Where the Domino Fell: America and Vietnam, 1945–1990,* 1991.

O'NEILL, ROBERT J. *General Giap: Politician and Strategist.* Australia: Cassell, 1969.

O'NEILL, WILLIAM. *Coming Apart: An Informal History of America in the 1960s.* New York: Quadrangle, 1971.

OSGOOD, ROBERT E. *America and the World: From the Truman Doctrine to Vietnam.* Baltimore, MD: The Johns Hopkins University Press, 1970.

————. *Limited War Revisited.* Boulder, CO: Westview Press, 1979.

OUDES, BRUCE, ED. *From: The President: Richard Nixon's Secret Files.* New York: Harper & Row, 1989.

PALMER, BRUCE, JR. *The 25-Year War: America's Military Role in Vietnam.* New York: Simon and Schuster, 1985.

PALMER, DAVE RICHARD. *Summons of the Trumpet: A History of the Vietnam War from a Military Man's Vietpoint.* New York: Ballantine, 1978.

PALMER, GREGORY. *The McNamara Strategy and the Vietnam War: Program Budgeting in the Pentagon, 1960–1968.* Westport, CT: Greenwood, 1978.

PALMER, LAURA. *Shrapnel in the Heart: Letters and Remembrances from the Vietnam Veterans Memorial.* New York: Vintage, 1987.

PARET, PETER AND SHY, JOHN W. *Guerrillas in the 1960s,* rev. ed. New York: Praeger, 1962.

PARMET, HERBERT. *JFK: The Presidency of John F. Kennedy.* New York: Penguin, 1983.

PATERSON, THOMAS G., ET AL. *American Foreign Policy.* Lexington, MA: D. C. Heath, 1977.

———. *Kennedy's Quest for Victory: American Foreign Policy, 1961–1963.* New York: Oxford University Press, 1989.

PATTI, ARCHIMEDES L. *Why Vietnam? Prelude to America's Albatross.* Berkeley: University of California Press, 1980.

PEARSON, WILLIARD. *The War in the Northern Provinces, 1966–1968.* Washington, DC: Department of the Army, 1975.

PEERS, WILLIAM R. *My Lai Inquiry.* New York: W. W. Norton, 1979.

PETTIT, CLYDE EDWIN. *The Experts.* Secaucus, NJ: Lyle Stuart, 1975.

PIKE, DOUGLAS. *History of Vietnamese Communism, 1925–1976.* Stanford, CA: Hoover Institution Press, 1978.

———. *PAVN: People's Army of Vietnam.* Novato, CA: Presidio, 1986.

———. *Vietcong: The Organization and Technique of the National Liberation Front of South Vietnam,* rev. ed. Cambridge, MA: MIT Press, 1972.

———. *The Vietcong Strategy of Terror.* Cambridge, MA: M.I.T. Press, 1970.

———. *Vietnam and the Soviet Union: Anatomy of an Alliance.* Boulder, CO: Westview Press, 1985.

———. *War, Peace, and the Vietcong.* Cambridge, MA: The MIT Press, 1969.

PILGER, JOHN. *The Last Day: America's Final Hours in Vietnam.* New York: Vintage, 1975.

PISOR, ROBERT. *The End of the Line: The Siege of Khe Sanh,* rev. ed. New York: W. W. Norton, 2003.

PODHORETZ, NORMAN. *Why We Were in Vietnam.* New York: Simon and Schuster, 1982.

POLNER, MURRAY. *No Victory Parades: The Return of the Vietnam Veterans.* New York: Holt, Rinehart and Winston, 1971.

POPKIN, SAMUEL. *The Rational Peasant: The Political Economy of Rural Society in Vietnam.* Berkeley: University of California Press, 1979.

PORTER, GARETH. *The Myth of the Bloodbath: North Vietnam's Land Reform Program Reconsidered.* Ithaca, NY: Cornell University Press, 1972.

———. *A Peace Denied: The United States, Vietnam, and the Paris Agreements.* Bloomington, IN: Indiania University Press, 1975.

——— AND EMERSON, GLORIA, EDS. *Vietnam: A History in Documents.* New York: New American Library, 1981.

POST, KEN. *Revolution, Socialism, and Nationalism in Vietnam,* 4 vols. Belmont, CA: Wadsworth, 1989–1990.

POWERS, THOMAS. *Vietnam: The War at Home.* Boston: G. K. Hall, 1984.

PRADOS, JOHN. *The Hidden History of the Vietnam War.* Chicago: Ivan Dee, 1995.

————. *Operation Vulture.* New York: Ibooks, 2002.

————. *The Sky Would Fall: Operation Vulture: The U.S. Bombing Mission in Indochina.* New York: Dial, 1982.

———— AND STUBBE, ROY. *Valley of Decision: The Siege of Khe Sanh.* New York: Houghton Mifflin, 1991.

PRATT, JOHN CLARK, ED. *Vietnam Voices: Perspectives on the War Years, 1941–1982.* New York: Viking Press, 1984.

PRIBBENOW, MERLE L. *Victory in Vietnam.* The official Vietnamese history of the war translated by Pribbelow. Lawrence: University Press of Kansas, 2002.

RACE, JEFFREY. *War Comes to Long An: Revolutionary Conflict in a Vietnamese Province.* Berkeley, CA: University of California Press, 1972.

RANDLE, ROBERT. *Geneva 1954: The Settlement of the Indochinese War.* Princeton, NJ: Princeton University Press, 1969.

RAPPAPORT, ARMIN, ED. *Sources in American Diplomatic History.* New York: Macmillan, 1966.

RASKIN, MARCUS G. AND FALL, BERNARD B., EDS. *The Viet-nam Reader: Articles and Documents on American Foreign Policy and the Vietnam Crisis.* New York: Vintage, 1965.

RECORD, JEFFREY. *The Wrong War: Why We Lost in Vietnam.* Annapolis, MD: Naval Institute, 1999.

REEDY, GEORGE E. *Lyndon B. Johnson, A Memoir.* New York: Andrews and McMeel, 1982.

REEVES, RICHARD. *President Kennedy: A Profile of Power.* New York: Simon and Schuster, 1993.

REISCHAUER, EDWIN O. *Beyond Vietnam: The United States and Asia.* New York: Vintage, 1967.

RESTON, JAMES, JR. *Sherman's March and Vietnam.* New York: Macmillan, 1984.

RIENCOURT DE, AMAURY. *The American Empire.* New York: Dell, 1968.

ROBBINS, CHRISTOPHER. *Air America.* New York: Avon, 1979.

ROBERTS, STEPHEN H. *History of French Colonial Policy: 1870–1925,* 2 vols. London: P. S. King and Son, 1929.

ROGERS, BERNARD W. *Cedar Falls–Junction City: A Turning Point.* Washington, DC: U.S. Government Printing Office, 1974.

ROSTOW, WALT W. *The Diffusion of Power: An Essay in Recent History.* New York: Macmillan, 1972.

ROTTER, ANDREW J. *The Path to Vietnam: Origins of the American Commitment to Southeast Asia.* Ithaca, NY: Cornell University Press, 1987.

ROY, JULES. *The Battle of Dienbienphu.* New York: Harper & Row, 1965.

RUDENSTINE, DAVID. *The Day the Presses Stopped: A History of the Pentagon Papers Case.* Berkeley: University of California Press, 1996.

RUST, WILLIAM J. *Kennedy in Vietnam: American Vietnam Policy 1960–963.* New York: Da Capo, 1985.

RUTLEDGE, PAUL JAMES. *The Vietnamese Experience in America.* Bloomington: University of Indiana Press, 1992.

SAFIRE, WILLIAM. *Before the Fall: An Insider's View of the Pre-Watergate White House.* Garden City, NY: Doubleday, 1975.

SAINTENY, JEAN. *Histoire d'une paix manque.* Paris: Amoit Dumont, 1953.

SALE, KIRKPATRICK. *SDS.* New York: Vintage, 1973.

SALISBURY, HARRISON. *Behind the Lines: Hanoi, December 23, 1966–January 7, 1967.* New York: Harper & Row, 1967.

———, ED. *Vietnam Reconsidered: Lessons from a War.* New York: Harper & Row, 1983.

SANDBROOK, DOMINIC, *Eugene McCarthy: The Rise and Fall of Postwar American Liberalism.* New York: Knopf, 2003.

SANSOME, ROBERT L. *The Economics of Insurgency in the Mekong Delta of Vietnam.* Cambridge, MA: MIT Press, 1970.

SANTOLI, AL. *To Bear Any Burden.* New York: Ballantine, 1985.

———. *Everything We Had.* New York: Random House, 1981.

SCHALLER, MICHAEL. *The American Occupation of Japan: The Origins of the Cold war in Asia.* New York: Oxford University Press, 1985.

SCHANDBERG, SYDNEY H. *The Death and Life of Dith Pran.* New York: Viking, 1985.

SCHANDLER, HERBERT Y. *The Unmaking of a President: Lyndon Johnson and Vietnam.* Princeton, NJ: Princeton University Press, 1977.

SCHEER, ROBERT. *How the United States Got Involved in Vietnam.* Santa Barbara, CA: Center for the Study of Democratic Institutions, 1965.

SCHELL, JONATHAN. *The Real War: The Classic Reporting on the Vietnam War.* New York: Pantheon, 1988.

———. *The Time of Illusion.* New York: Knopf, 1976.

———. *The Village of Ben Suc.* New York: Knopf, 1967.

SCHLESINGER, ARTHUR M., JR. *The Bitter Heritage: Vietnam and American Democracy 1941–1966.* New York: Fawcett, 1966.

———. *The Imperial Presidency.* Boston: Houghton Mifflin, 1973.

———. *Robert Kennedy and His Times.* Boston: Houghton Mifflin, 1978.

———. *A Thousand Days: John F. Kennedy in the White House.* Greenwich, CT: Fawcett, 1965.

SCHLIGHT, JOHN, ED. *Second Indochina War Symposium.* Washington, DC: Department of the Army, 1986.

———. *The United States Air Force in Southeast Asia: The War in South Vietnam: The Years of the Offensive, 1965–1968.* Washington, DC: U.S. Government Printing Office, 1988.

SCHOENBAUM, THOMAS J. *Waging Peace and War: Dean Rusk in the Truman, Kennedy, and Johnson Years.* New York: Simon and Schuster, 1988.

SCHULTZ, RICHARD H., JR. *The Secret War against Hanoi.* New York: Harper Collins, 2000.

SCHULZINGER, ROBERT D. *Henry Kissinger: Doctor of Diplomacy.* New York: Columbia University Press, 1989.

————. *A Time for War: The United States and Vietnam, 1941–1975.* New York: Oxford, 1997.

SHAFER, D. MICHAEL. *Deadly Paradigms: The Failure of U.S. Counterinsurgency Policy.* Princeton, NJ: Princteon University Press, 1988.

————. *The Legacy; The Vietnam War in the American Imagination.* Boston, 1990.

SHAPLEN, ROBERT. *The Lost Revolution: The U.S. in Vietnam, 1946–1966,* rev. ed. New York: Harper & Row, 1966.

————. *Time Out of Hand: Revolution and Reaction in Southeast Asia.* New York: Harper & Row, 1969.

————, ED. *The Road from War: Vietnam, 1965–1971.* New York: Harper & Row, 1970.

SHAPLEY, DEBORAH. *Promise and Power: The Life and Times of Robert S. McNamara.* Boston: Little, Brown, 1993.

SHARP, ULYSSES S. GRANT. *Strategy for Defeat.* San Rafael, CA: Presidio, 1978.

SHAWCROSS, WILLIAM. *Sideshow: Kissinger, Nixon and the Destruction of Cambodia.* New York: Simon and Schuster, 1979.

SHEEHAN, NEIL. *A Bright Shining Lie: John Paul Vann and America in Vietnam.* New York: Random House, 1989.

————. *After the War Was Over: Hanoi and Saigon.* New York: Random House, 1991.

SHORT, ANTHONY. *The Origins of the Vietnam War.* London: Longman, 1989.

SHULIMSON, JACK. *U.S. Marines in Vietnam: 1966.* Washington, DC: U.S. Marine Corps, 1982.

SMALL, MELVIN. *Covering Dissent: The Media and the Anti-Vietnam War Movement.* New Brunswick, NJ: Rutgers University Press, 1994.

————. *Johnson, Nixon, and the Doves.* New Brunswick, NJ: Rutgers University Press, 1988.

SMITH, RALPH BERNARD. *An International History of the Vietnam War, vol. 1: Revolution versus Containment, 1955–1961.* New York: St. Martin's Press, 1983.

————, vol. 2: *The Kennedy Strategy.* New York: St. Martin's Press, 1985.

————, vol. 3: *The Making of a Limited War, 1965–1966.* New York: St. Martin's Press, 1991.

SNEPP, FRANK. *Decent Interval: An Insider's Account of the Saigon's Indecent End.* New York: Random House, 1977.

SORENSEN, THEODORE C. *Kennedy.* New York: Harper & Row, 1965.

SORLEY, LEWIS, *Thunderbolt: General Creighton Abrams and the Army of His Times.* New York: Simon and Shuster, 1992.

SPECTOR, RONALD H. *After Tet: The Bloodiest Year in Vietnam.* New York, 1993.

————. *Researching the Vietnam Experience.* Washington, DC: Analysis Branch of the U.S. Army Center for Military History, 1984.

————. *United States Army in Vietnam: Advice and Support: The Early Years, 1941–1960.* Washington, DC: U.S. Army Center for Military History, 1984.

STANTON, SHELBY L. *The Rise and Fall of an American Army: U.S. Ground Forces in Vietnam, 1965–1973.* New York: Dell, 1985.

———. *Vietnam Order of Battle.* New York: Galahad, 1987.

STEEL, RONALD. *Pax Americana: The Cold War Empire and the Politics of Counter-Revolution,* rev. ed. New York: Viking, 1970.

STEVENS, RICHARD L. *The Trail: A History of the Ho Chi Minh Trail and the Role of Nature in the War in Viet Nam.* New York: Garland, 1993.

STEVENS, ROBERT W. *Vain Hopes, Grim Realities: The Economic Consequences of the Vietnam War.* New York: New Viewpoints, 1976.

STEVENSON, CHARLES A. *The End of Nowhere: American Policy Toward Laos Since 1954.* Boston: Beacon, 1972.

STOCKDALE, JAMES B., AND SYBIL. *In Love and War.* New York: Harper & Row, 1984.

SUMMERS, HARRY G., JR. *Historical Atlas of the Vietnam War.* Boston: Houghton Mifflin, 1995.

———. *On Strategy: A Critical Analysis of the Vietnam War.* New York: Dell, 1982.

———. *Vietnam War Almanac.* New York: Facts on File, 1985.

SZULC, TAD. *The Illusion of Peace: Foreign Policy in the Nixon-Kissinger Years.* New York, Viking, 1979.

TANG, TRUONG NHU. *A Vietcong Memoir.* San Diego, CA: Harcourt Brace Jovanovich, 1983.

TAYLOR, MAXWELL D. *Swords and Ploughshares.* New York: W. W. Norton, 1972.

———. *The Uncertain Trumpet.* New York: Harper & Row, 1959.

TAYLOR, TELFORD. *Nuremberg and Vietnam: An American Tragedy.* New York: Quadrangle, 1967.

TERRY, WALLACE, ED. *Bloods: An Oral History of the War by Black Veterans.* New York: Random House, 1984.

TERZANI, TIZIANO, *Giai Phuong! The Fall and Liberation of Saigon (1976).* Milano, Italy: Tea, 2003.

THAYER, CARLYLE. *War By Other Means: National Liberation and Revolution in Vietnam.* Boston: Allen & Unwin, 1989.

THAYER, THOMAS C. *War without Fronts: The American Experience in Vietnam.* Boulder, CO: Westview Press, 1985.

THEOHARIS, ATHAN. *Spying in America: Political Surveillance from Hoover to the Huston Plan.* Philadelphia: Temple University Press, 1978.

THIES, WALLACE J. *When Governments Collide: Coercion and Diplomacy in the Vietnam Conflict, 1964–1968.* Berkeley, CA: University of California Press, 1980.

THO, TRAN DINH, *The Cambodian Incursion.* Washington, DC: U.S. Army Center for Military History, 1983.

———. *Pacification.* Washington, DC: U.S. Army Center for Military History, 1980.

THOMPSON, JAMES CLAY. *Rolling Thunder: Understanding Policy and Program Failure.* Chapel Hill: University of North Carolina Press, 1980.

THOMPSON, KENNETH W., ED. *The Kennedy Presidency: Seventeen Intimate Perspectives of John F. Kennedy.* Lanham, MD: University Press of America, 1985.

THOMPSON, ROBERT G. K. *Defeating Communist Insurgency: The Lessons of Malaya and Vietnam.* New York: Praeger, 1966.

———. *No Exit from Vietnam.* New York: David McKay, 1969.

———. *Peace Is Not at Hand.* New York: David McKay, 1974.

THOMPSON, VIRGINIA M. *French Indochina.* London: Allen & Unwin, 1937.

THOMPSON, W. SCOTT AND FRIZZELL, DONALDSON D., EDS. *The Lessons of Vietnam.* New York: Crane, Ruzzak, 1977.

THOMSON, JAMES C., JR., STANLEY, PETER W., AND PERRY, JOHN CURTIS. *Sentimental Imperialists: The American Experience in East Asia.* New York: Harper & Row, 1981.

TILFORD, EARL H., JR. *Setup—What the Air Force Did in Vietnam and Why.* Alabama: Maxwell Air Force Base, 1991.

TOLLEFSON, JAMES W., ED. *The Strength Not to Fight.* Boston: Beacon, 1993.

TONNESSON, STEIN. *The Vietnamese Revolution of 1945: Roosevelt, Ho Chi Minh, and de Gaulle in a World At War.* London: Sage, 1991.

TRA, TRAN VAN. *Vietnam: History of the Bulwark B-2 Theater,* vol. 5: *Concluding the 30-Years' War.* Ho Chi Minh City: Van Nghe Publishing Plant, 1982.

TRAN, VAN DON. *Our Endless War: Inside South Vietnam.* San Rafael, CA: Presidio Press, 1978.

TRAN, VAN TRA. *Ending the Thirty Year War.* Washington, DC: U.S. Government Printing Office, 1983.

TRAGER, FRANK N., ED. *Marxism in Southeast Asia.* Palo Alto, CA: Stanford University Press, 1959.

TREGASKIS, RICHARD B. *Vietnam Diary.* New York: Holt, Rinehart and Winston, 1963.

TREWHITT, HENRY L. *McNamara: His Ordeal in the Pentagon.* New York: Harper & Row, 1971.

TRUONG, NGO QUANG. *The Easter Offensive of 1972.* Washington, DC: U.S. Army Center of Military History, 1980.

TRUONG, NHU TANG, WITH CHANOFF, DAVID, AND DOAN, VAN TOAI. *A Vietcong Memoir.* San Diego, CA: Harcourt, Brace, 1985.

TUCHMAN, BARBARA. *The March of Folly.* New York: Ballantine, 1984.

TURLEY, WILLIAM S. *The Second Indochina War: A Short Political and Military History, 1954–1975.* New York: New American Library, 1986.

TURNER, KATHLEEN. *Lyndon Johnson's Dual War: Vietnam and the Press.* Chicago: University of Chicago Press, 1985.

UNGER, IRWIN. *The Movement: A History of the American New Left 1959–1972.* New York: Dodd, Mead, 1974.

——— AND UNGER, DEBI. *Turning Point: 1968.* New York: Charles Scribner's Sons, 1988.

VALENTINE, DOUGLAS. *The Phoenix Program.* New York: Morrow, 1990.

VAN, TIEN DUNG. *Our Great Spring Victory: An Account of the Liberation of South Vietnam.* New York: Monthly Review Press, 1977.

VAN DE MARK, BRIAN. *Into the Quagmire: Lyndon Johnson and the Escalation of the Vietnam War.* New York, 1991.

VAN DYKE, JOHN M. *North Vietnam's Strategy for Survival.* Palo Alto, CA: Stanford University Press, 1972.

VIEN, CAO VAN, *The Final Collapse.* Washington, DC: U.S. Army Center for Military History, 1982.

———— AND KHUYEN, DONG VAN. *Reflections on the Vietnam War.* Washington, DC: U.S. Army Center for Military History, 1980.

VIETNAM VETERANS AGAINST THE WAR. *The Winter Soldier Investigations.* Boston: Beacon, 1972.

VO, NGUYEN GIAP. *People's War, People's Army.* New York: Praeger, 1962.

WALT, LEWIS W. *Strange War, Strange Strategy.* New York: Funk and Wagnalls, 1969.

WALTON, RICHARD J. *Cold War and Counter-Revolution: The Foreign Policy of John F. Kennedy.* Baltimore: Penguin Books, 1972.

WARNER, DENIS. *The Last Confucian.* New York: Macmillan, 1963.

WEIGLEY, RUSSELL. *The American Way of War: A History of United States Military Strategy and Policy.* New York: Macmillan, 1973.

WELLS, TOM. *The War Within: America's Battle over Vietnam.* Berkeley, CA: University of California Press, 1994.

————. *Wild Man: The Life and Times of Daniel Ellsberg.* New York: Palgrave, 2001.

WERNER, JAYNE S. AND LUU DOAN HUYNH, EDS. *The Vietnam War: Vietnamese and American Perspectives.* New York: M. E. Sharpe, 1993.

WESTMORELAND, WILLIAM C. *A Soldier Reports.* New York: Dell, 1976.

WETTERHAHN, RALPH. *The Last Battle: The Mayaguez Incident and the End of the Vietnam War.* New York: Plume/NAL, 2002.

WHEELER, JOHN. *Touched with Fire: The Future of the Vietnam Generation.* New York: Avon, 1984.

WHITE, RALPH K. *Nobody Wanted War: Misperceptions in Vietnam and Other Wars.* Garden City, NY: Doubleday, 1968.

WHITE, THEODORE H. *Breach of Faith: The Fall of Richard Nixon.* New York: Atheneum, 1975.

————. *The Making of the President 1960.* New York: Atheneum, 1961.

————. *The Making of the President 1964.* New York: New American Library, 1965.

————. *The Making of the President 1968.* New York: Atheneum, 1969.

————. *In Search of History.* New York: Harper & Row, 1978.

WICKER, TOM. *JFK and LBJ: The Influence of Personality on Politics.* New York: William Morrow, 1968.

WILLENSON, KIM. *The Bad War: An Oral History of the Vietnam Conflict.* New York: New American Library, 1987.

WILLIAMS, WILLIAM APPLEMAN, ET AL., EDS. *America in Vietnam: A Documentary History.* Garden City, NY: Doubleday, 1985.

WILLS, GARRY. *The Kennedy Imprisonment: A Meditation on Power.* Boston: Little, Brown, 1982.

————. *Nixon Agonistes: The Crisis of the Self-Made Man.* New York: New American Library, 1970.

WILSON, JAMES C. *Vietnam in Prose and Film.* Jefferson, NC: McFarland, 1982.

WINDCHY, EUGENE. *Tonkin Gulf.* Garden City, NY: Doubleday, 1971.

WINTER SOLDIER ARCHIVE. *Soldiering in Vietnam: The Short-Timer's Journal.* Berkeley, CA: Winter Soldier Archive, 1980.

WIRTZ, JAMES J. *The Tet Offensive: Intelligence Failure in War.* Ithaca, NY: Cornell University Press, 1991.

WITCOVER, JULES. *85 Days: The Last Campaign of Robert Kennedy.* New York: Atheneum, 1969.

WOODSIDE, ALEXANDER. *Community and Revolution in Modern Vietnam.* Cambridge, MA: Houghton Mifflin, 1976.

————. *Vietnam and the Chinese Model: A Comparative Study of Vietnamese and Chinese Government in the First Half of the Nineteenth Century.* Cambridge, MA: Harvard University Press, 1971.

WYATT, CLARENCE R. *Paper Soldiers: The American Press and the Vietnam War.* New York: W. W. Norton, 1993.

YARMOLINSKI, ADAM. *The Military Establishment: Its Impact on American Society.* New York: Harper & Row, 1971.

YOUNG, MARILYN B. *The Vietnam Wars, 1945–1990.* New York: Harper Collins, 1991.

YUEN FOONG KHONG. *Analogies At War: Korea, Munich, Dien Bien Phu, and the Vietnam Decisions of 1965.* Princeton, NJ: Princeton University Press, 1992.

ZAFFIRI, SAMUEL. *Westmoreland: A Biography of General William C. Westmoreland.* New York: Morrow, 1994.

ZAGORIA, DONALD. *Vietnam Triangle: Moscow, Peking, Hanoi.* New York: Pegasus, 1967.

ZAROULIS, NANCY AND SULLIVAN, GERALD. *Who Spoke Up? American Protest Against the War in Vietnam, 1963–1975.* Garden City, NY: Doubleday, 1984.

ZASLOFF, JOSEPH J. *Origins of the Insurgency in South Vietnam, 1954–1960: The Role of the Southern Vietminh Cadres.* Santa Monica, CA: The Rand Corporation, 1968.

————. *Postwar Indochina: Old Enemies and New Allies.* Washington, DC: U.S. Government Printing Office, 1988.

———— AND BROWN, MACALISTER, EDS. *Communism in Indochina: New Perspectives.* Lexington, MA: D. C. Heath, 1975.

ARTICLES

ADAMS, SAMUEL. "Vietnam Cover-up: Playing with Numbers." *Harper's Magazine* (May 1975): 41.

BADILLO, GILBERT AND CURRY, G. DAVID. "The Social Incidence of Vietnam Casualties: Social Class or Race?" *Armed Forces and Society* 2 (spring 1976): 397–406.

BAILEY, GEORGE A. "Television War: Trends in Network Coverage of Vietnam 1965–1970." *Journal of Broadcasting* 20 (spring 1976): 147–57.

BALL, GEORGE, "The Light That Failed." *Atlantic Monthly* (July 1973): 33–49.

———. "Top Secret: The Prophecy the President Rejected." *Atlantic* 230 (July 1972): 35–49.

BASSETT, LAWRENCE J. AND PELZ, STEPHEN E. "The Failed Search for Victory: Vietnam and the Politics of War." In Paterson, Thomas G., ed. *Kennedy's Quest for Victory: American Foreign Policy, 1961–1963.* New York: Oxford University Press, 1989.

BELLHOUSE, MARY L AND LITCHFIELD, LAWRENCE. "Vietnam and the Loss of Innocence: An Analysis of the Political Implications of the Popular Literature of the Vietnam War." *Journal of Popular Culture* 16 (winter 1982): 157–74.

BOWEN, WILLIAM. "The Vietnam War: A Cost Accounting." *Fortune* (April 1966).

BRODIE, BERNARD. "The Tet Offensive." In Frankland, Noble, and Dowling, Christopher, eds. *Decisive Battles of the Twentieth Century.* London: Sidgwick & Jackson, 1976.

———. "Why We Were So (Strategically) Wrong." *Foreign Policy* (winter 1971–72): 151–62.

BRUSH, PETER. "Higher and Higher: American Drug Use in Vietnam," *Vietnam* (December 2002): 47–53.

CANNON, MICHAEL. "Raising the Stakes: The Taylor-Rostow Mission." *Journal of Strategic Studies* 12 (June 1989).

CHEN, JIAN. "China and the First Indochina War, 1950–1954." *China Quarterly* (March 1993): 85–110.

CHEN, KING C. "Hanoi's Three Decisions and the Escalation of the Vietnam War." *Political Science Quarterly* 90 (summer 1975): 239–59.

CHESNEAUX, JEAN. "The Historical Background of Vietnamese Communism." In *Government and Opposition,* vol. 4 (winter 1969): 119–35.

CLIFFORD, CLARK. "A Vietnam Reappraisal." *Foreign Affairs* 47 (July 1969): 601–22.

COLLINS, ROBERT M. "The Economic Crisis of 1968 and the Waning of the 'American Century.'" *American Historical Review* 101 no. 2 (April 1996): 396–442.

CONVERSE, PHILIP E., MILLER, WARREN E., RUSK, JEROLD G., AND WOLFE, ARTHUR C. "Continuity and Change in American Politics: Parties and Issues in the 1968 Election." *American Political Science Review* 63 (December 1969): 1083–105.

——— AND SCHUMAN, HOWARD. "'Silent Majorities' and the Vietnam War." *Scientific American* 222 (June 1970): 17–24.

CRAWFORD, HENRY B. "Operation Menu's Secret Bombing of Cambodia." *Vietnam* (December 1966): 22–28.

DEBENEDETTI, CHARLES. "A CIA Analysis of the Anti-Vietnam War Movement: October, 1967." *Peace and Change* 9 (spring 1983): 31–42.

———. "On the Significance of Citizen Peace Activism: America, 1961–1975." *Peace and Change* 9 (summer 1983): 6–20.

DUNN, PETER M. "The American Army: the Vietnam War, 1965–1973." In Beckett, F. W., and Pimlott, John, eds. *Armed Forces and Modern Counter-insurgency.* London: Croom Helm, 1985.

ELEGANT, ROBERT. "How to Lose a War: Reflections of a Foreign Correspondent." *Encounter* (August 1981).

ESZTERHOZ, JOSEPH, ET AL. "The Massacre at My Lai." *Life* (December 5, 1969).

FALL, BERNARD. "The Political-Religious Sects of Vietnam." *Pacific Affairs* 28 (September 1955): 235–49.

GELB, LESLIE. "The Essential Domino: American Politics and Vietnam." *Foreign Affairs* 50 (April 1972): 459–72.

———, "The System Worked." *Foreign Policy* 3 (summer 1971): 140–67.

GIBSON, JAMES WILLIAM. "Revising Vietnam Again." *Harper's Magazine* (April 2000): 78–84.

GREENE, DANIEL P. "John Foster Dulles and the End of the Franco-American Entente in Indochina." *Diplomatic History* 16 (fall 1992).

GREENSTEIN, FRED I. AND IMMERMAN, RICHARD H. "What Did Eisenhower Tell Kennedy about Indochina? The Politics of Misperception." *Journal of American History* 79, no. 2 (September 1992): 568–87.

HALBERSTAM, DAVID. "Getting the Story in Vietnam." *Commentary* 39 (January 1968): 30–34.

———. "Return to Vietnam." *Harper's Magazine* 235 (December 1967).

———. "The Ugliest American in Vietnam." *Esquire* 62 (November 1964): 37–40.

———. "Vietnamese Reds Gain in Key Area." *New York Times,* August 15, 1963, A1, A3.

HEINL, ROBERT. "The Collapse of the Armed Forces." *Armed Forces Journal* 19 (June 1971): 30–38.

HERRING, GEORGE C. "American Strategy in Vietnam: The Postwar Debate." *Military Affairs* 46 (April 1982): 57–63.

———. "Cold Blood: LBJ's Conduct of Limited War in Vietnam." *Harmon Memorial Lectures in Military History.* Washington DC: U.S. Government Printing Office, 1990.

———. "The 1st Cavalry and the Ia Drang Valley, 18 October–24 November 1965." In Heller, Charles E. and Stofft, William A. *America's First Battles.* Lawrence: University of Kansas Press, 1986, 300–326.

———. "The Nixon Strategy in Vietnam." In Braestrup, Peter, ed. *Vietnam as History.* Washington, DC: University Press of America, 1984, pp. 51–58.

———. "The Truman Administration and the Restoration of French Sovereignty in Indochina." *Diplomatic History* 1 (spring 1977): 97–117.

———. "Vietnam, El Salvador, and the Uses of History." In Coleman, Kenneth and Herring, George C., eds. *The Central American Crisis.* Wilmington, DE: Scholarly Resources, 1985.

————. HESS, GARY R., AND IMMERMAN, RICHARD H., "Passage of Empire: The U.S., France, and South Vietnam, 1954–1955." In Kaplan, Lawrence, Artand, Denise, and Rubin, Mark, eds. *Dien Bien Phu and the Crisis of Franco-American Relations, 1954–1955.* Wilmington, DE: SR Books, 1990.

————, AND IMMERMAN, RICHARD H. "Eisenhower, Dulles, and Dienbienphu: The Day We Didn't Go to War Revisited." *Journal of American History* 71 (September 1984): 343–63.

HESS, GARY R. "Franklin D. Roosevelt and Indochina." *Journal of American History* 59 (September 1972): 353–68.

————. "The Military Perspective on Strategy in Vietnam: Harry G. Summers's On Strategy and Bruce Palmer's The 25-Year War." *Diplomatic History* 1, no. 1 (winter 1986): 91–106.

————. "The Unending Debate: Historians and the Vietnam War." *Diplomatic History* 18, no. 2 (spring 1994): 239–64.

HOOD, JONATHAN DAVIS AND BUESSELER, JOHN AURE, COL., M.D., U. S. ARMY (RET.). "Evolution of Aeromedevac in Vietnam." *Vietnam* (August 2003), 42–43.

IMMERMAN, RICHARD, "The United States and the Geneva Conference of 1954: A New Look." *Journal of American History* (fall 1971): 818–41.

JACOBS, JAMES B. AND MCNAMARA, DENNIS "The Pentagon Papers: A Critical Evaluation." *American Political Science Review* 69 (June 1975): 675–84.

————. "Vietnam Veterans and Agent Orange." *Armed Forces and Society* 13 (fall 1986): 57–79.

KAHIN, GEORGE MCT. "Political Polarization in South Vietnam: U.S. Policy in the Post-Diem Period." *Pacific Affairs* 52 (winter 1979–80): 647–73.

KATTENBURG, PAUL M. "Vietnam and U.S. Diplomacy, 1940–1970." *Orbis* 15 (fall 1971); 818–41.

KERWIN, WALTER T. "Inside MACV Headquarters–Desperate Hours during Tet." *Vietnam* 13, no. 5 (February 2001): 27–32.

KIMBALL, JEFFREY P. "Peace with Honor: Richard Nixon and the Diplomacy of Threat and Symbolism." In Anderson, David L. ed. *Shadows on the White House.* Lawrence: University of Kansas Press, 1993, 152–83.

————. "The Stab-in-the-Back Legend and the Vietnam War." *Armed Forces and Society* 14 (spring 1988): 433–58.

KISSINGER, HENRY A. "The Viet Nam Negotiations." *Foreign Affairs* 47 (January 1969): 211–34.

KOMER, ROBERT W. "Pacification: A Look Back." *Army* (June 1970): 20–29.

LAFEBER, WALTER. "The Rise and Fall of American Power, 1963–1975." In Williams, William Appleton, McCormick, Thomas, Gardner, Lloyd, and LaFeber, Walter, eds. *America in Vietnam: A Documentary History.* Garden City, NY: Doubleday, 1985.

————. "Roosevelt, Churchill, and Indochina, 1942–1945." *American Historical Review* (December 1975): 1277–89.

LICHTY, LAWRENCE W. AND BAILEY, GEORGE A. "Violence in Television News: A Case Study of Audience Response." *Central States Speech Journal* 23 (winter 1972): 225–29.

LINDEN, EUGENE. "The Demoralization of an Army: Fragging and Other Withdrawal Symptoms." *Saturday Review* (January 8, 1972): 12–17, 55.

McLAUGHLIN, MIKE. "Anatomy of a Crisis." *American Heritage* (February/March 2004).

McMANUS, JOHN C. "Battleground Saigon." *Vietnam* (February 2004): 27–33.

MILTON, T. R. "The Lessons of Vietnam." *Air Force Magazine* no. 66 (March 1983).

———. "USAF and the Vietnam Experience." *Air Force Magazine* no. 58 (June 1975).

MIRSKY, JONATHAN. "The Never Ending War." *New York Review of Books,* May 25, 2000.

MOISE, EDWIN E. "Land Reform and Land Reform Errors in North Vietnam." *Pacific Affairs,* 49 (spring 1976): 70–92.

MOSKOS, CHARLES C. "Success Story: Blacks in the Military." *Atlantic Monthly* 257 (May 1986): 64–72.

MUELLER, JOHN E. "Reflections on the Vietnam Antiwar Movement and the Curious Calm at War's End." In Braestrup, Peter ed. *Vietnam as History.* Washington, DC: University Press of America, 1984, 151–57.

———. "The Search for the 'Breaking Point' in Vietnam: The Statistics of a Deadly Quarrel." *International Studies Quarterly* 4 (December 1980): 497–519.

———. "A Summary of Public Opinion and the Vietnam War." In Braestrup, Peter, ed. *Vietnam as History.* Washington, DC: University Press of America, 1984.

———. "Trends in Popular Support for the Wars in Korea and Vietnam." *American Political Science Quarterly* 65 (June 1971): 358–75.

NIXON, RICHARD M. "Asia after Vietnam," *Foreign Affairs* 46 (October 1967): 111–25.

NOSTRAND, MICHAEL, LT. COL., U.S. AIR FORCE ET AL. "Lessons Learned from LINEBACKER II." *Vietnam* (October 2000): 38–4 5, 72.

PARKER, MAYNARD. "Vietnam: The War That Won't End." *Foreign Affairs* 53 (January 1975): 352–74.

PATERSON, THOMAS G. "Bearing the Burden: A Critical Look at JFK's Foreign Policy." *Virginia Quarterly Review* 54 (spring 1978): 193–1212.

PATTERSON, OSCAR, III. "An Analysis of Television Coverage of the Vietnam War." *Journal of Broadcasting* 28 (fall 1984): 397–404.

PELZ, STEPHEN. "John F. Kennedy's 1961 Vietnam War Decisions." *Journal of Strategic Studies* 4 (December 1981): 356–85.

PIERRE, ANDREW. "Vietnam's Contradictions." *Foreign Affairs* (November/December 2000): 69–86.

POPKIN, SAMUEL. "Pacification: Politics and the Village." *Asian Survey* 10 (August 1970): 662–71.

PORTER, GARETH. "The 1968 Hue Massacre." *Indochina Chronicle* 33 (June 24, 1974).

PROSTERMAN, ROY L. "Land-to-the-Tiller in South Vietnam: The Tables Turn." *Asian Survey* 10 (August 1970): 751–64.

QIANG ZHAI. "Transplanting the Chinese Model: Chinese Military Advisers and the First Vietnam War, 1950–1954." *Journal of Military History* (October 1993): 689–715.

RACE, JEFFREY. "How They Won." *Asian Survey* 10 (August 1970): 628–50.

———. "The Origins of the Second Indochina War." *Asian Survey* 10 (May 1960): 359–82.

RIDDLE, TOM. "Inflationary Impact of the Vietnam War." *Vietnam Generation* (winter 1989).

ROBERTS, CHALMERS. "Foreign Policy and a Paralyzed Presidency." *Foreign Affairs* 52 (July 1974).

SALTER, MACDONALD. "The Broadening Base of Land Reform in South Vietnam." *Asian Survey* 10 (August 1970): 724–37.

SASAKI, DR. CLARENCE T. "Holding Death at Bay." *Vietnam* 5 no. 2 (August 1992): 35–40.

SAVAGE, PAUL AND GABRIEL, RICHARD A. "Cohesion and Disintegration in the American Army." *Armed Forces and Society* 2 (spring 1976): 340–76.

SCHALLER, MICHAEL. "Securing the Great Crescent: Occupied Japan and the Origins of Containment in Southeast Asia." *Journal of American History* 69 (September 1982): 392–413.

SCHANDLER, HERBERT Y. "America and Vietnam: The Failure of Strategy, 1964–1967." In Braestrup, Peter, ed. *Vietnam as History.* Washington, DC: University Press of America, 1984.

SCHECK, WILLIAM, LT. COL. "During the Struggle between $6 Million Aircraft and $15 Bicycles Along the Ho Chi Minh Trail, the Bicycles Won." *Vietnam* 13, no. 5 (February 2001): 14, 60–61.

SCHUMAN, HOWARD. "Two Sources of Antiwar Sentiment in America." *American Journal of Sociology* 78 (November 1972): 519–35.

SHEEHAN, NEIL. "In Vietnam, the Birth of the Credibility Gap." *New York Times,* October 1, 1988, A15.

———. Four articles about the life, military career, and Vietnam service of John Paul Vann appeared in consecutive issues of the *New Yorker* under the general title of "Annals of War: An American Soldier in Vietnam," vol. 44, nos. 19–22 (June 20, June 27, July 4, and July 11, 1988).

SMALL, MELVIN. "The Impact of the Antiwar Movement on Lyndon Johnson, 1965–1968." *Peace and Change* 10 (spring 1984): 1–22.

SPERLICH, PETER W. AND LUNCH, WILLIAM L. "American Public Opinion and the War in Vietnam." *Western Political Quarterly* 32 (March 1979): 21–44.

SUMMERS, HARRY G., JR. "The Bitter Triumph of Ia Drang." *American Heritage* (January–February 1984): 51–58.

SZULC, TAD. "Behind the Vietnam Cease Fire Agreement." *Foreign Policy* 15 (summer 1974): 21–69.

THOMSON, JAMES C. "Getting Out and Speaking Out." *Foreign Policy* 13 (winter 1973–1974).

———. "How Could Vietnam Happen?" *Atlantic Monthly* 22 (April 1968): 47–53.

U.S. News and World Report. "The Phantom Battle that Led to War." (July 23, 1984): 56–67.

VERBA, SIDNEY ET AL. "Public Opinion and the War in Vietnam." *American Political Science Review* 61 (June 1967): 317–33.

WARD, RICHARD. "The Origins of United States Interest in Vietnam." *Vietnam Quarterly* no. 1 (winter 1976).

WARNER, GEOFFREY. "The United States and the Fall of Diem: The Coup That Never Was." *Australian Outlook* 28 (December 1974): 245–258; "The Death of Diem," *Australian Outlook* 29 (March 1975): 3–17.

WOODSIDE, ALEXANDER. "Decolonization and Agricultural Reform in Northern Vietnam." *Asian Survey* 10 (August 1970): 705–23.

———. "Some Southern Vietnamese Writers Look at the War." *Bulletin of Concerned Asian Scholars* 2 (October 1969): 53–58.

WYATT, CLARENCE R. "At the Cannon's Mouth: The American Press and the Vietnam War." *Journalism History* 13 (autumn–winter 1986): 104–13.

DOCUMENTS

CITIZEN'S COMMISSION OF INQUIRY, EDS. *The Dellums Committee Hearings on War Crimes in Vietnam.* New York: Vintage, 1972.

Congressional Record, 88th Congress, Second Session, 1964.

GRAVEL, MIKE, ED. *The Pentagon Papers: The Defense Department History of U.S. Decisionmaking in Vietnam.* Boston: Beacon, 1971.

EISENHOWER, DWIGHT D. *Public Papers of the President, Dwight D. Eisenhower, 1953–1961.* Washington, DC: U.S. Government Printing Office, 1962.

JOHNSON, LYNDON B. *Public Papers of Lyndon B. Johnson, 1968–1969.* Washington, DC: U.S. Government Printing Office, 1970.

KENNEDY, JOHN F. *John F. Kennedy: Public Papers.* Washington, DC: U.S. Government Printing Office, 1963.

MINH, HO CHI. *Selected Writings, 1920–1969.* Hanoi: People's Publishing House, 1973.

NIXON, RICHARD M. *Public Papers, Richard M. Nixon, 1969 and 1970.* Washington, DC: U.S. Government Printing Office, 1971.

PORTER, GARETH. *Vietnam: The Definitive Documentation of Human Decisions.* Stanfordville, NY: Earl M. Coleman, 1979.

Report of the Department of Army Review of Preliminary Investigations into My Lai Incident (Peers Report). Washington, DC: U.S. Government Printing Office, 1976.

SHEEHAN, NEIL; SMITH, HEDRICK; KENWORTHY, E. W.; AND BUTTERFIELD, FOX. *The Pentagon Papers: The Secret History of the Vietnam War.* New York: Bantam, 1971.

UNITED STATES CONGRESS, HOUSE, COMMITTEE ON ARMED SERVICES. *United States—Vietnam Relations, 1945–1967: A Study Prepared by the Department of Defense.* Washington, DC: U.S. Government Printing Office, 1971.

UNITED STATES, DEPARTMENT OF STATE. *American Foreign Policy, 1950–1955: Basic Documents,* vol 1. Washington, DC: U.S. Government Printing Office, 1957.

UNITED STATES, DEPARTMENT OF STATE. Several volumes in the *Foreign Relations of the United States* series, including *Foreign Relations of the United States 1946, vol. 8: The Far East.* Washington, DC: U.S. Government Printing Office, 1971. *Foreign Relations of the United States 1947, vol. 6: The Far East.* Washington, DC: U.S. Government

Printing Office, 1972. *Foreign Relations of the United States, 1952–1954, vol. 13: Indochina.* Washington, DC: U.S. Government Printing Office, 1982. *Foreign Relations of the United States, 1955–1957, vol. 3.* Glennon, John P. (general ed.). Washington, DC: U.S. Government Printing Office, 1971.

UNITED STATES, DEPARTMENT OF STATE. *White Paper: A Threat to Peace: North Viet Nam's Effort to Conquer South Viet Nam.* Washington, DC: U.S. Government Printing Office, 1961.

ARCHIVAL AND UNPUBLISHED SOURCES

HARKINS, PAUL D. "Oral History," 1974, U.S. Army Military History Institute Archives, Carlisle Barracks, PA.

HUNT, DAVID. "U.S. Scholarship and the National Liberation Front." Unpublished paper, April 1992.

MOSS, GEORGE DONELSON. "The Vietnam Generation: The Impact of the War and the Draft on the Generation Called to Fight in Southeast Asia." Unpublished. essay, 1984.

NGUYEN, CUE HUN. "They Destroy My City." Unpublished essay by a young Vietnamese man living in Hue at the time of its destruction.

OFFNER, ARNOLD A. "The Truman Myth Revealed: From Parochial Nationalist to Cold Warrior." Unpublished essay, 1988.

O'KEEFE, KEVIN. "Media Coverage of Gulf of Tonkin." Unpublished essay, 1988.

PEERS, WILLIAM R. "Oral History." U.S. Army Military History Institute Archives, Carlisle Barracks, PA.

VANN, JOHN PAUL. "Miscellaneous Papers." Archives of the U.S. Army Military Institute, Carlisle Barracks, PA.

ZAIS, MELVIN. "Oral History Interview," 575–83. Archives of the U.S. Army Military History Institute, Carlisle Barracks, PA.

LITERATURE: POETRY, NOVELS, NOVELISTIC MEMOIRS, NOVELISTIC JOURNALISM

BUTLER, ROBERT OLEN. *A Good Scent from a Strange Mountain.* New York: Henry Holt, 1992.

CAPUTO, PHILLIP. *A Rumor of War.* New York: Ballantine, 1977.

DEL VECCHIO, JOHN M. *The 13th Valley.* New York: Bantam, 1982.

DONOVAN, DAVID. *Once a Warrior King: Memories of an Officer in Vietnam.* New York: McGraw-Hill, 1985.

EHRHART, W. D., ED. *Carrying the Darkness: American Indochina–The Poetry of the Vietnam War.* New York: Avon Books, 1985.

GREENE, GRAHAM. *The Quiet American.* New York: Penguin, 1977.

HEINEMAN, LARRY. *Close Quarters.* New York, 1977.

HERR, MICHAEL. *Dispatches.* New York, 1977.

KAIKO, TAKESHI. *Into a Black Sun.* Translated by Seigle, Cecilia Segawa. Tokyo: Kadansha, 1980. Distributed in the United States by Kadansha through Harper & Row, 1980.

KOVIC, RON. *Born on the Fourth of July.* New York: McGraw-Hill, 1976.

LE, LY HAYSLIP. *When Heaven and Earth Changed Places.* New York: Doubleday, 1989.

LEDERER, WILLIAM, J. AND BURDICK, EUGENE. *The Ugly American.* New York: W. W. Norton, 1958.

MAILER, NORMAN. *Armies of the Night.* Cleveland: World, 1968.

MASON, BOBBIE ANN. *In Country.* New York: Harper & Row, 1985.

MASON, ROBERT. *Chickenhawk.* New York: Penguin, 1983.

O'BRIEN, TIM. *Going after Cacciato.* New York: Delacorte, 1978.

————. *If I Die in a Combat Zone.* New York: Dell, 1969.

————. *The Things They Carried.* New York: Penguin Books, 1990.

SMITH, STEVEN PHILLIP. *American Boys.* New York: Avon, 1978.

STONE, ROBERT. *Dog Soldiers.* Boston: Houghton Mifflin, 1974.

WEBB, JAMES. *Fields of Fire.* Englewood Cliffs, NJ: Prentice Hall, 1978.

WILLSON, DAVID A. *REMF Diary.* Seattle: Block Heron Press, 1988.

TELEVISION DOCUMENTARIES AND TELEVISION PROGRAMS

ACCURACY IN MEDIA (AIM). "Television's Vietnam. Part 1: The Real Story; Part 2: The Impact of Media," 1984 and 1985, television documentary transcripts.

CBS NEWS. "The Uncounted Enemy: A Vietnam Deception," January 23, 1982, television documentary transcript.

CBS NEWS. "Vietnam: A War That Is Finished," July 1975, television documentary transcript.

CBS NEWS. "Vietnam: the Deadly Decision," CBS televsion documentary shown April 1, 1964.

CBS NEWS. "The World of Charlie Company." Television documentary transcript.

"Vietnam: A Television History." Thirteen-part video documentary series first shown on PBS (October 1983–March 1984).

FILMS

Apocalypse Now, fiction film.

Coming Home, fiction film.

The Deer Hunter, fiction film.

Full Metal Jacket, fiction film.

Hamburger Hill, fiction film based on the Battle of Dong Ap Bia, fought along the rim of the A Shau valley, May 11–20, 1969.

Hearts and Minds, a documentary film

JFK, a fiction film released in 1991. Written and directed by Oliver Stone. Suggests that Kennedy was assassinated by a conspiracy of government officials because he was going to phase out the American participation in Vietnam War.

The Killing Fields, fiction film based on the experiences of Sydney Schrandberg and Dith Pran.

Platoon, fiction film based on the Vietnam experiences of Oliver Stone.

VIETNAM WEBSITES

"The Wars of Vietnam: An Overview"

http://students.vassar.edu/~vietnam/overview.html

Offering an extensive overview of military conflicts in Vietnam from 1945 through the U.S. engagement, this site offers full text of historical documents including the Tonkin Gulf resolution and excerpts from U. S. presidential speeches.

"Vietnam Online"

http://www.pbs.org/wgbh/amex/vietnam/index.html

From PBS and the American Experience, this site contains a detailed, interactive timeline of the war, interpretive essays, and autobiographical reflections.

"Investigating the Vietnam War"

http://www.spartacus.schoolnet.co.uk.vietintro.htm

This site contains narratives, personal accounts, and an excellent list of annotated links to the best Vietnam sites.

"The My Lai Courts Martial"

http://www.law.umke.edu/faculty/projects/ftrials/mylai/mylai.htm

This site contains chronology, images, and court documents describing the massacre of Vietnamese civilians at My Lai

"The Psychedelic '60s: Literary Tradition and Social Change"

http://www.lib.virginia.edu/exhibits/sixties/index.html

An online exhibit, this site explores the counterculture of the America of the 1960s, addressing issues such as the war in Vietnam and the Civil Rights Movement through the poetry, literature, and pop art of the day.

"May 4" Kent State

http://www.library.kent.edu/exhibits/4may95/index.html

Through their "May 4" collection, learn more about the Kent State student shootings. The site includes photos, links to various other sites, chronologies, and information on the aftermath of the incident.

Vietnam War Bibliography

http:// tigger.vic.edu/~rjensen/vietnam.html

Prepared by Richard Jensen, Professor Emeritus, University of Illinois. Up to date and comprehensive, this site has many hot links to online sources.

Index